Liverpool Conference on Christian Missions

Conference on Missions held in 1860 at Liverpool

including the papers read, the deliberations, and the conclusions reached with a

comprehensive index shewing the various matters brought under review

Liverpool Conference on Christian Missions

Conference on Missions held in 1860 at Liverpool
including the papers read, the deliberations, and the conclusions reached with a comprehensive index shewing the various matters brought under review

ISBN/EAN: 9783743355248

Manufactured in Europe, USA, Canada, Australia, Japa

Cover: Foto ©ninafisch / pixelio.de

Manufactured and distributed by brebook publishing software (www.brebook.com)

Liverpool Conference on Christian Missions

Conference on Missions held in 1860 at Liverpool

LONDON:
STRANGEWAYS and WALDEN (late G. Barclay), Printers,
28 Castle St. Leicester Sq.

Texts

SELECTED FOR THE

OPENING MEETING OF CONFERENCE.

"This gospel of the kingdom shall be preached in all the world."—*Matt.* xxiv. 14.

"All power is given unto me in heaven and in earth. Go ye, therefore, and teach all nations. . . . . And, lo, I am with you alway, even unto the end of the world."—*Matt.* xxviii. 18–20.

"It behoved Christ to suffer. . . . . And that repentance and remission of sins should be preached in His name among all nations, beginning at Jerusalem."—*Luke*, xxiv. 46, 47.

"They that were scattered abroad went . . . . . preaching the word."—*Acts*, viii. 4.

"How shall they believe in Him of whom they have not heard? And how shall they hear without a preacher? And how shall they preach, except they be sent? As it is written, How beautiful are the feet of them that preach the gospel of peace, and bring glad tidings of good things!"—*Rom.* x. 14, 15.

" According to the commandment of the everlasting God, made known to all nations for the obedience of faith."—*Rom.* xvi. 26.

" Having hope, when your faith is increased, that we shall be enlarged by you according to our rule abundantly, to preach the gospel in the regions beyond you, and not to boast in another man's line of things made ready to our hand."—2 *Cor.* x. 15, 16.

" Thanks be to God, which giveth us the victory through our Lord Jesus Christ. Therefore, my beloved brethren, be ye stedfast, unmoveable, always abounding in the work of the Lord, forasmuch as ye know that your labour is not in vain in the Lord."—1 *Cor.* xv. 57, 58.

CONTENTS.

	PAGE
Introduction	1
List of Members	4
Preliminary Meeting of Conference	10
FIRST GENERAL PRAYER-MEETING	11

FIRST SESSION.

Resolution of Mutual Welcome	12
Moved by the Rev. Dr. TIDMAN	13
Seconded by the Rev. T. GREEN	14
Address by the CHAIRMAN	15
Paper on *European Missionaries Abroad:* by the Rev. J. MULLENS	17

Address by Rev. R. S. HARDY	25	Address by Colonel LAVIE	36
,, Rev. J. M'KEE	ib.	,, Rev. W. SWAN	37
,, Rev. B. LAL SINGH	26	,, Rev. P. LATROBE	ib.
,, Rev. T. SMITH	27	,, Rev. T. GARDINER	38
,, Rev. Dr. SOMERVILLE	28	,, Dr. LOCKHART	ib.
,, Rev. T. GREEN	29	,, Rev. H. M. WADDELL	39
,, Rev. W. SHAW	ib.	,, Rev. W. H. STIRLING	40
,, Rev. C. B. LEUPOLT	31	,, Rev. C. HEBERT	41
,, Rev. Dr. O'MEARA	33	,, Rev. R. S. HARDY	42
,, Rev. S. HISLOP	34	,, Rev. P. H. CORNFORD	43
,, Rev. J. WALTON	35	,, Rev. G. CANDY	44

CONTENTS.

	PAGE		PAGE
Address by Lieut.-Col. HUGHES	45	Address by Rev. J. B. WHITING	50
,, Major DAVIDSON	47	,, Rev. Dr. SOMERVILLE	52
,, Rev. J. H. TITCOMB	48	,, Rev. Dr. TIDMAN	53
,, Rev. Dr. O'MEARA	49		

MINUTE on Missionaries and their Plans . . 56

SECOND SESSION.

Paper: by the Rev. J. B. WHITING: on *the best Means of exciting and maintaining a Missionary Spirit* . . . 58

Address by Rev. J. GABB	64	Address by Rev. P. LATROBE	82
,, Rev. H. M. WADDELL	65	,, Rev. J. ANDERSON	83
,, Rev. Dr. BAYLEE	66	,, Rev. J. TOWERS	ib.
,, Rev. J. WALLACE	67	,, Rev. J. FORDYCE	84
,, Rev. T. SMITH	69	,, Rev. J. MULLENS	85
,, Rev. Dr. SOMERVILLE	71	,, W. LEACH, Esq.	87
,, Rev. Dr. TIDMAN	72	,, Rev. W. CAMPBELL	88
,, Rev. F. TRESTRAIL	73	,, Lieut.-Col. HUGHES	ib.
,, R. A. MACFIE, Esq.	74	,, The CHAIRMAN	ib.
,, Rev. Dr. TWEEDIE	75	,, Rev. Dr. STEANE	89
,, Rev. T. GREEN	76	,, Rev. R. S. HARDY	90
,, Rev. C. HEBERT	78	,, Rev. Dr. TWEEDIE	ib.
,, Rev. Can. WOODROOFFE	ib.	,, Rev. Dr. SOMERVILLE	91
,, Rev. S. HISLOP	79	,, Rev. G. D. CULLEN	92
,, Colonel LAVIE	ib.	,, Rev. Dr. BAYLEE	ib.
,, Lieut.-Col. HUGHES	ib.	,, Rev. J. H. TITCOMB	93
,, Rev. H. M. MACGILL	80		

MINUTE on the Means of exciting and maintaining the Missionary Feeling at Home 95

The Missionary Lectureship: Report: its Plan: and the Committee appointed 97

FIRST MISSIONARY SOIRÉE.

Address by G. F. BARBOUR, Esq., Chairman . . . 99
,, Dr. LOCKHART, on *Medical Missions in China* . 100

SECOND GENERAL PRAYER-MEETING 109

THIRD SESSION.

	PAGE
Paper on *Missionary Education:* by the Rev. C. B. LEUPOLT	111
Address by the Rev. C. T. HŒRNLÉ	116
Paper on *Missionary Education:* by the Rev. T. SMITH .	118
" " " by the Rev. J. H. TITCOMB .	123

Address by Dr. G. H. DAVIS . . 127	Address by Rev. J. L. PORTER . . 140
" Rev. B. L. SINGH . . 129	" Col. LAVIE 142
" Rev. J. M'KEE . . . 130	" Rev. Dr. O'MEARA . . 144
" Rev. G. CANDY . . . 131	" Rev. T. GARDINER . . ib.
" Rev. Dr. BAYLEE . . 132	" J. CUNNINGHAM, Esq. . 146
" Rev. S. HISLOP . . . 134	" Rev. J. SUGDEN . . ib.
" Rev. W. CAMPBELL . 135	" Rev. H. GUNDERT . . 148
" Rev. J. WALTON . . 137	" Rev. J. FORDYCE . . ib.
" H. C. TUCKER, Esq. . 139	" Rev. T. L. BADHAM . 149

MINUTE on Missionary Education 150

FOURTH SESSION.

Paper on *the best Means of calling forth Home Liberality:* by the Rev. JAMES LEWIS 153

Address by Capt. LAYARD . . . 164	Address by Rev. J. L. PORTER . . 172
" Rev. Can. WOODROOFFE 165	" Rev. J. B. WHITING . ib.
" Dr. DAVIS 166	" Rev. H. M. MACGILL . 174
" Rev. Dr. CATHER . . 167	" Rev. P. H. CORNFORD . 175
" Rev. T. L. BADHAM . 168	" JOHN CROPPER, Esq. . 176
" Rev. Dr. TIDMAN . . 169	" Rev. J. MAKEPEACE . ib.
" Rev. Dr. TWEEDIE . . 170	" Rev. D. THORBURN . ib.
" Rev. C. RATTRAY . . 171	" Rev. H. M. WADDELL . 177
" Rev. G. SCOTT . . . 172	" Lieut.-Col. EDWARDES 178

MINUTE on the Means of securing increased Liberality to Missionary Work 178

SECOND MISSIONARY SOIRÉE.

		PAGE
Address by the Rev. B. L. Singh	. . . . .	180
„ on *the Peshawur Mission*: by Lieut.-Col. Edwardes		185
„ on *Missions in South Africa*: by the Rev. W. Shaw		189
Third General Prayer-meeting	. . . .	191

FIFTH SESSION.

Communication from Rotterdam 192
Address of the CHAIRMAN on Native Agency 192
Paper on *Native Agency in Foreign Missions*: by the Rev. R. S. Hardy 194

Questions by Rev. J. Mullens	. 199	Address by Rev. Dr. O'Meara .	. 212
Reply by Rev. R. S. Hardy .	. 200	„ Rev. H. M. Waddell .	213
Address by Col. Dawes . . .	. 201	„ Rev. G. R. Birch . .	. 215
„ Rev. I. Stubbins . .	. 202	„ Rev. B. L. Singh . .	. 216
„ Dr. Lockhart . . .	. 204	„ Rev. F. Trestrail. .	. 219
„ Rev. W. Fairbrother	206	„ G. F. Barbour, Esq. .	. 220
„ C. Swallow, Esq. .	*ib.*	„ Rev. G. Pritchard	. 221
„ Major Davidson . .	*ib.*	„ Rev. C. B. Leupolt	. 222
„ Dr. Macgowan . .	. 208	„ Rev. J. Walton . .	. 224
„ Rev. T. Gardiner .	. 209	„ Col. Lavie	. 225
„ Rev. P. Latrobe . .	. 210	„ Rev. Dr. Tidman . .	. *ib.*

Minute on Native Agents 227

SIXTH SESSION.

Committee on Income of Religious Societies 232
Paper on *Candidates for Missionary Work*: by the Rev. T. Green . . . 233

CONTENTS.

	PAGE		PAGE
Address by Rev. Dr. BAYLEE	240	Address by Rev. W. SWAN	252
,, Dr. LOCKHART	244	,, Capt. LAYARD	253
,, Rev. G. D. CULLEN	ib.	,, Rev. J. H. TITCOMB	254
,, Rev. Dr. O'MEARA	245	,, Rev. W. HARCUS	255
,, Rev. R. C. KING	ib.	,, Rev. Can. WOODROOFFE	256
,, Rev. W. FAIRBROTHER	246	,, Rev. H. M. WADDELL	ib.
,, Rev. J. B. WHITING	ib.	,, Rev. T. SMITH	257
,, Rev. Dr. SOMERVILLE	247	,, Rev. J. SUGDEN	259
,, Rev. G. SCOTT	248	,, Rev. D. THORBURN	261
,, Rev. F. TRESTRAIL	250	,, Rev. Dr. CATHER	262
,, Dr. MACGOWAN	252	,, The CHAIRMAN	263

Resolution on Mr. BICKERSTETH's Letter: on the Special Week of Prayer in January, 1861, and simultaneous Sermons on Missions 260

MINUTE on the best Means of obtaining well-qualified Missionaries 264

THIRD MISSIONARY SOIRÉE.

Address on *Indian Converts in the Mutiny:* by the Rev. C. B. LEUPOLT 266
Address on *Missions in Turkey:* by the Rev. J. R. TUCKER . 270
,, on *Female Education in the East:* by Rev. J. FORDYCE 273
,, on *Medical Missions in China and Japan:* by Dr. MACGOWAN . . 275

FOURTH GENERAL PRAYER-MEETING 277

SEVENTH SESSION.

Address of the CHAIRMAN 278
Paper on *Native Churches:* by the Rev. F. TRESTRAIL . 279

CONTENTS.

	PAGE		PAGE
Address by Rev. J. Mullens	283	Address by Rev. C. B. Leupolt	296
,, Rev. G. F. Fox	287	,, Rev. R. S. Hardy	298
,, Rev. J. Wallace	ib.	,, Rev. J. H. Titcomb	299
,, Rev. P. Latrobe	288	,, Colonel Lavie	300
,, Rev. W. Shaw	289	,, Rev. J. Mullens	301
,, Dr. Davis	290	,, Rev. J. Sugden	303
,, Rev. Dr. Tweedie	291	,, D. F. Macleod, Esq.	ib.
,, Rev. T. Gardiner	ib.	,, Rev. H. M. Waddell	306
,, Rev. B. L. Singh	292	,, Rev. S. Hislop	ib.
,, R. A. Macfie, Esq.	295	,, Lieut. S. F. Page	307
,, Capt. Layard	ib.		

	PAGE
Minute on Native Churches	309
Resolutions of Thanks	313, 314
Resolution on Parting	314
Address by the Rev. Dr. Somerville	315
,, Rev. G. Osborn	317

GENERAL PUBLIC MEETING.

	PAGE
Speech of Major-General Alexander	318
,, Earl of Shaftesbury	320
,, Major Davidson	326
,, Rev. Joseph Mullens	329
,, Lieut.-Colonel Sir Herbert Edwardes, K.C.B.	337
,, Rev. Canon Stowell	355
,, Rev. G. D. Cullen	360
,, Rev. Dr. J. B. Lowe	361
,, Mayor of Liverpool	361
,, R. A. Macfie, Esq.	362
,, Earl of Shaftesbury	362

APPENDIX.

		PAGE
I. *Previous Conferences on Missions:* by the Rev. J. MULLENS		365
II. *Suggestions:* by JAMES DOUGLAS, Esq. of Cavers	. .	375
III. On the *Training of Native Agents:* by the Rev. B. LYTH of Fiji	. . . .	377
IV. Modern Works on Christian Missions	. . . .	381
INDEX		391

SUBJECTS TREATED SPECIALLY.

European Missionaries Abroad: Paper		17
Missionaries and their Plans	*MINUTE*	56
On the best Means of exciting and maintaining a Missionary Spirit: Paper, 58	*MINUTE*	95
Medical Missions in CHINA: Address		100
Missionary Education: Papers, 111, 118, 123 . .	*MINUTE*	150
Means of calling forth Home Liberality: Paper, 153	*MINUTE*	178
PESHAWUR Mission: Address		185
Missions in SOUTH AFRICA: Address		189
Native Agency: Address, 192; Paper, 194	*MINUTE*	227
Candidates for Missionary Work: Paper . .		233
Means of obtaining well-qualified Missionaries	*MINUTE*	264
INDIAN CONVERTS in the Mutiny: Address . . .		266
Missions in TURKEY: Address		270
Female Education in the EAST: Address .		273
Medical Missions in CHINA and JAPAN: Address . .		275
Native Churches: Paper, 279	*MINUTE*	309
The Mutiny in INDIA: Address		337
Results of Modern Missions: Addresses . .	. 50, 53,	329
Conferences on Missions: Paper . . .		365
Training of Native Agents: Paper		377

CONFERENCE ON MISSIONS.

INTRODUCTION.

THE Conference on Christian Missions, the proceedings of which are described in the following pages, originated in a desire to have brethren brought together, who had reflected on the duty and the lukewarmness of the churches in respect of Our Grand Commission; or who could contribute actual experiences; in order that, by their mutual consultations, all Christians of the United Kingdom might be stirred up to greater zeal, and to a more complete consecration of time, of effort, and of substance, in this work of the Lord. In God's good providence facilities were presented, and readily embraced by a number of the officers and members of Missionary Committees in London and Edinburgh; who felt that after the many years of continuous missionary labour carried on in heathen lands; after the solid advance attained in some fields, and the great experience acquired in all, it would be well for the Directors, Secretaries, and Missionaries of all Societies and Churches, to obtain an opportunity of meeting together and conferring together about their common work. It was felt that it must prove a lasting benefit for them to examine in detail the working of their various missionary agencies, to compare their different plans, and to throw into a common stock the results of that valuable experience which they have earned hardly upon the very fields of heathenism. It was felt, that while all must find abundant means of adding to their own knowledge, through the information given by brethren, all must be cheered by the tokens of missionary success; all must be stimulated to greater zeal in the service of Christ, the common Lord; and all must be bound in closer and more loving sympathy with brethren toiling for the same grand end.

Origin of the Conference.

Its proposed Objects.

With these views the invitations were issued, and means were adopted for securing as complete an attendance as possible

Measures taken.

of all who could contribute to the full discussion of the topics to be laid before them; while care was taken that the numbers should not be so great as to prevent the deliberations from being free and almost conversational in their general tone. At the request of the Mission Secretaries in London, unanimously made to him at one of their united monthly meetings, HENRY CARRE TUCKER, Esq., late Commissioner at Benares, undertook to conduct the general preparatory arrangements; in which he received assistance from the Rev. G. D. CULLEN, of Edinburgh, and other friends. The

Invitations. invitations met with a hearty response from leading members of almost all the Missionary Societies and Committees; officers of twenty-five or more taking part on the occasion: the most cordial hospitality was offered by Christian friends in Liverpool; and at the appointed time, March 19th to 23rd, a hundred and twenty members of Conference met together to carry out the work which had been planned. Some doubts and misgivings had been felt by a few, but they were soon dispelled by the free and brotherly tone of intercourse which prevailed, as well as by the frankness of those who shared in the discussions; and in the end it was acknowledged, with devout thankfulness, that the Conference had surpassed the most sanguine expectations of its warmest friends.

Its Plan. It was arranged by the promoters of the scheme, that four days should be spent in discussing the various plans of missionary labour at home and abroad; that two sittings should be held each day, morning and afternoon, of about three hours and a half each: that they should be preceded by a morning prayer-meeting, and followed by a missionary soirée at night: and that while the official deliberations should be confined to the members of the Conference, all friends should be invited to attend the devotional

Success. services. The plan was carried out with great success; the general attendance at the opening and closing services increased day by day; a happy variety was observed in the addresses delivered, and the fields of labour described; a most delightful spirit of Christian union, devotion, and prayer prevailed; and the presence of the Lord, in whose name the work was done, was largely realised.

Public Meeting. The more general services were brought to a conclusion by a Public Meeting held in the Philharmonic Hall. It proved to be the noblest meeting ever held in Liverpool in connexion with Christian missions, and was most appropriately presided over by the distinguished Earl who stands at the head of so many agencies consecrated to the salvation of men, both at home and abroad.

Of the valuable character of the Conference discussions a high estimate must be formed. They were eminently practical and searching; the addresses delivered were brief and pointed; and a large amount of earnest work was accomplished during the brief sittings. Two short-hand writers, Messrs. LEE and NIGHTINGALE, of Liverpool, were present to record these discussions as carefully as possible, in order that they might obtain permanent record, and secure a wide circulation among the agents of missionary institutions. From their admirable report, revised by the speakers themselves, they are now published; with the earnest desire that many who were not present at these hallowed meetings may catch something of the spirit which prevailed, and derive benefit from the information that was offered. The Editors have endeavoured to secure for this record as much correctness as possible; and trust that all mistakes and imperfections may be forgiven. They acknowledge with pleasure the assistance rendered them by the prompt revision of their addresses and papers by the various speakers, which will, they hope, render the work not merely a trustworthy, but a permanently valuable work of reference. *[margin: Value of the Discussions. Report.]*

They would invite special attention to the various MINUTES, in which the conclusions arrived at by the Conference, respecting the principal plans of missionary labour and economy, are embodied; inasmuch as they express, in a few brief paragraphs, the results of that valuable experience, which it has taken years to acquire in many parts of the world. *[margin: Minutes]*

May the Spirit of God bless these efforts made to secure greater support and efficiency for our missionary operations. Would that the whole Church of Christ on earth thoroughly realised its responsibility and privilege as His appointed instrument for making the truth known to Jew and Gentile throughout the world; and that in obedience, faith, and love, there were conveyed and preached, unto all nations, the message of peace and good-will, this Gospel of the kingdom.

LIST OF MEMBERS.

Members.
AIKMAN, Rev. J. Logan, Anderston United Presbyterian Church, Glasgow.

ALEXANDER, Major-General, Her Majesty's Indian Army; Chairman of the Conference.

ANDERSON, Rev. John, formerly Missionary of the Church of Scotland in India, now Minister of the West Parish Church, Dalkeith.

ANDERSON, T. D., Esq., Mayor of Liverpool; Treasurer of the Liverpool and West Lancashire Church Missionary Association.

BADHAM, Rev. T. L., London, Joint Secretary of the Moravian Missions, and formerly Missionary in the West Indies.

BALLANTYNE, Rev. William, London; Secretary of the Foreign Mission Committee of the Presbyterian Church in England.

BARBOUR, George F., Esq., Edinburgh; Hon. Sec. to the Amoy Mission in China; Mem. F. C. Colonial and Jews' Committees.

BARBOUR, Robert, Esq., Manchester; Treasurer to the Home Missions of the Presbyterian Church in England.

BARRY, Rev. D. T., Southport, Association Secretary C. M. Society.

BAYLEE, Rev. Joseph, D.D., Principal of St. Aidan's Theological College, Birkenhead.

BIRCH, Rev. George R., Secretary Turkish Missions' Aid Society, London.

BIRKS, Rev. T. R., Rector of Kelsall.

BUDDEN, Rev. J. H., Belvedere, Kent, Missionary of the London Missionary Society at Almora, India.

CAMPBELL, Rev. William, Barnsbury, Islington, formerly Missionary of the L. M. S. at Bangalore.

CANDY, Rev. George, Missionary at Bombay from C. M. Society.

CARLILE, Rev. Gavin, Glasgow, Editor of "News of the Churches."

CARPENTER, Rev. Henry, St. Michael's, Liverpool, Hon. Sec. Liverpool C. M. Association.

CATHER, Rev. Robert G., L.L.D., Wesleyan Minister, Londonderry; Members. Secretary of the Systematic Beneficence Society.

CLEGHORN, Thomas, Esq., Edinburgh, Sheriff of Argyleshire; Free Church of Scotland's Foreign Mission, Jews, and Colonial Committees.

CORNFORD, Rev. Philip H., Baptist Chapel, Luton, Bedfordshire; formerly Baptist Missionary in Jamaica.

CRICHTON, Rev. Hugh, D.D., United Presb. Church, Liverpool.

CROPPER, John, Esq., Dingle Bank, Liverpool.

CULLEN, Rev. George D., Edinburgh, one of the Secretaries of the Conference.

CUNNINGHAM, James, Esq., Queen Street, Edinburgh; Member of Free Church Foreign Mission Committee.

DAVIDSON, Major D., late Bombay Army, Woodcroft, Edinburgh; Member of Free Church Foreign Mission Committee.

DAVIS, Dr. George Henry, Secretary of the Religious Tract Society, London.

DAWES, Col. M., late Indian Army, Lay Secretary C. M. Society.

DAWSON, Edward, Esq., Aldcliffe Hall, Lancaster.

EDWARDES, Lieut.-Col. Sir Herbert, K.C.B., H.M. Indian Army.

FAIRBROTHER, Rev. William, London, Secretary for Funds, London Missionary Society; formerly Missionary at Shanghai.

FEARNLEY, Rev. Matthew, Miss. in China from C. M. Society.

FFOLLIOTT, Rev. William; Secretary to the Moravian Missionary Society, Liverpool.

FORDYCE, Rev. John, late of Calcutta, now Minister of Boston Free Church, Dunse, Berwickshire; Member of Free Church Foreign Mission Committee.

FORFAR, Rev. Patrick T., Scotch Church, Oldham St. Liverpool.

FOX, Rev. G. F., Durham, Hon. Secretary of the C. M. Society.

GABB, Rev. James, Castle Howard, Yorkshire, Domestic Chaplain to the Earl of Carlisle, &c.; one of the Adjudicators of the proposed Prize Essays on Missions.

GARDINER, Rev. Thomas, Missionary of the Free Church of Scotland, Calcutta.

GEE, Dr. Robert, Liverpool, Director of the Welsh Calvinistic Missionary Society.

GRAHAM, Rev. John, D.D., Reformed Presbyterian Church, Liverpool.

Members.
GRAHAM, Rev. William, United Presbyterian Church, Mount Pleasant, Liverpool.
GREEN, Rev. Thomas, Principal of the C.M. Society's Institution, Islington, London.
GUNDERT, Rev. H., Ph.D., Basle Mission, Malabar Coast, India.
HALKET, Rev. Alexander M'Donald, Presbyterian Minister, Parkgate.
HARCUS, Rev. William, Toxteth Chapel, Liverpool; London Missionary Society Committee.
HARDY, Rev. R. Spence, formerly Wesleyan Missionary in Ceylon.
HEBERT, Rev. Charles, Brunswick Chapel, Portman Square, London; Secretary of the Colonial Church and School Society.
HENDERSON, John, Esq., of Park, Glasgow; Member of Foreign Mission Committee of the U. P. Church of Scotland.
HISLOP, Rev. Stephen, Missionary of the Free Church of Scotland, Nagpore, India.
HODGSON, Rev. T. E., Church of England, Liverpool.
HODGSON, Adam, Esq., Liverpool; Liverpool C. M. Association.
HŒRNLÉ, Rev. C. T., Missionary at Agra, from C. M. Society.
HOWELL, James, Esq., Liverpool; a Steward of the Conference.
HUGHES, Lieut.-Colonel R. Marsh, late Bombay Army, Hon. Sec. Strangers' Home for Asiatics, and Member C. M. Society.
KELLY, Rev. John, Crescent Chapel, Liverpool.
KING, Rev. Robert C., Association Secretary of Colonial Church and School Society, Everton, Liverpool.
KNOX, Rev. A., Incumbent of Birkenhead; President of the C. M. Society Auxiliary.
LATROBE, Rev. Peter, London, Secretary of the Moravian Missions.
LAVIE, Colonel Tudor, late Indian Artillery, Member C. M. Committee.
LAYARD, Captain H. L., Secretary of the London Society for Promoting Christianity among the Jews.
LEACH, Wm., Esq., Marlborough Road, St. John's Wood, Treasurer of the London Association in aid of the Moravian Missionary Society.
LEE, Henry, Esq., Broughton, Manchester.
LEUPOLT, Rev. C. B., Missionary at Benares, from C. M. Society.
LEWIS, Rev. James, Free St. John's Church, Leith; Mem. Com. Medical Missionary Society.

LOCKHART, Wm., Esq., F.R.C.S., Medical Missionary of the London Missionary Society at Shanghai, China.

LOGIN, Sir John S., Kew, late H.E.I.C. Service.

LOWE, Rev. J. B., D.D., St. Jude's, Liverpool.

LUNDIE, Rev. R. H., English Presbyterian Church, Birkenhead.

MANN, Rev. James, Congregational Chapel, Birkenhead.

MACLEOD, Donald F., Esq., C.B., Judicial Commissioner in the Punjaub.

M'CLURE, Rev. Wm., Londonderry, Secretary of the Colonial Mission of the General Assembly of the Irish Presb. Church.

M'CLURE, Thomas, Esq., Belfast.

MACFIE, Robert A., Esq., Ashfield Hall, Neston, Cheshire; Member of Foreign Mission Committee of the Presbyterian Church in England, and one of the Stewards of Conference.

MACGILL, Rev. Hamilton M., Home Mission Sec. to the U. P. Church, Glasgow.

MACGOWAN, Dr. D. J., of New York, Medical Missionary of the American Baptist Union, from China and Japan.

MAKEPEACE, Rev. Jonathan, Union Chapel, Luton, Bedfordshire, and formerly Missionary of the Baptist Missionary Society at Agra.

M'KEE, Rev. J., Missionary to Guzerat, from the General Assembly of the Irish Presbyterian Church.

MATHESON, Thomas, Esq., Liverpool; Hon. Sec. Liverpool Town Mission, and one of the Stewards of Conference.

MILWARD, Rev. H. C., B.A., C. M. Society, Calcutta.

MULLENS, Rev. Joseph, Missionary of the London Missionary Society, Calcutta; one of the Secretaries of the Conference.

O'MEARA, Rev. Fred. A., LL.D., Missionary Chaplain to the Red Indians on Lake Huron, and Superintendent of Indian Missions for the Church of England there.

OSBORN, Rev. George, Secretary, Wesleyan Mission House, London.

PATERSON, Rev. John C., Presbyterian Minister, Manchester.

PIKE, Rev. James Carey, Secretary of the General Baptist Missionary Society, Quorndon, near Loughborough.

PORTER, Rev. J. Leslie, A.M., Missionary at Damascus from the Irish Presbyterian Church.

PRITCHARD, Rev. George, late Missionary of the L.M.S. at Tahiti.

Members.
PRUST, Rev. Edmund T., Commercial Street Chapel, Northampton.
RAFFLES, Rev. Thos., D.D., LL.D., Liverpool.
RATTRAY, Rev. Charles, Missionary of the L.M.S. in Demerara.
ROBERTS, John, Esq., Secretary of the Welsh Calvinistic Methodists' Foreign Missionary Society.
SCOTT, Rev. George, Liverpool, formerly Wesleyan Missionary in Sweden.
SHAW, Rev. William, General Superintendent of the Wesleyan Missions in South-eastern Africa.
SMITH, Rev. Thomas, M.A., formerly Missionary in Calcutta, now Minister of the Free Church, Cowgate-head, Edinburgh; Member of Free Church Foreign Mission Committee.
SMITH, Rev. Thornley, Bolton, formerly Wesleyan Missionary to South Africa.
SINGH, Rev. Behari Lal, Licensed Preacher, Free Church of Scotland, Calcutta.
SOMERVILLE, Rev. Andrew, D.D., Edinburgh; Foreign Mission Secretary of the United Presbyterian Church in Scotland.
STEANE, Rev. Edward, D.D., Camberwell; Hon. Sec. of the Evangelical Alliance, and one of the Secretaries of the Conference.
STEPHENS, Rev. Wm. Robert, Curate of Seaforth, Liverpool.
STIRLING, Rev. W. H., B.A., Bristol, Secretary to the Patagonian, or South American, Missionary Society.
STOKES, Hudleston, Esq., late Madras Civil Service.
STOWELL, Rev. Canon, Manchester.
STUBBINS, Rev. Isaac, General Baptist Missionary from Cuttack, Orissa, India.
SUGDEN, Rev. John, Lancaster, late Missionary of the London Missionary Society at Bangalore.
SWAN, Rev. William, Edinburgh, formerly Missionary of the London Missionary Society in Siberia.
SWALLOW, Charles, Esq., Domestic Agent of the British and Foreign Bible Society.
TAYLOR, Rev. W. F., LL.D., Incumbent of St. John's Church, Liverpool; Hon. Sec. C. M. Society.
THORBURN, Rev. David, M.A., Free South Church, Leith; Member of the Committee of the Edinburgh Medical Missionary Society, and of F. C. Colonial and Continental Committee.

TIDMAN, Rev. Arthur, D.D., Foreign Secretary of the London Missionary Society.

TITCOMB, Rev. J. H., Secretary of the Christian Vernacular Education Society for India.

TOWERS, Rev. J., United Presbyterian Church, Birkenhead.

TRESIDDER, John Edward, Esq., Member of Committee of the Young Men's Missionary Association, in aid of the Baptist Missionary Society, London.

TRESTRAIL, Rev. Frederick, Sec. of Baptist Missionary Society.

TUCKER, Henry Carre, Esq., C.B., Bengal Civil Service, London, one of the Secretaries of the Conference.

TUCKER, Rev. Joseph Kidger, Incumbent of Trinity Church, Northwich; Clerical Secretary Turkish Missions' Aid Society.

TWEEDIE, Rev. Wm. K., D.D., Edinburgh, Convener of Committee of General Assembly of Free Church of Scotland on Foreign Missions.

WADDELL, Rev. Hope M., United Presbyterian Church Missionary from Old Calabar, Western Africa.

WALKER, Rev. Norman L., Free Church, Dysart, Fifeshire; Member of Free Church Foreign Mission Committee.

WALLACE, Rev. James, Missionary to Guzerat from the Irish Presbyterian Church.

WALTON, Rev. John, Wesleyan Missionary, North Ceylon.

WELSH, Rev. Joseph R., Canning Street Presbyterian Church, Liverpool.

WHITE, Rev. Verner M., LL.D., Islington Presbyterian Church, Liverpool.

WHITING, Rev. J. B., Central Association Secretary C. M. Society.

WHITTEMORE, Rev. W. M., Rector of St. James', London, Representative of the Society for Female Education in the East.

WILKINSON, Rev. Henry, Norwich, late General Baptist Missionary at Berhampore, near Ganjam, India.

WOODFALL, Henry, Esq., Bebington, near Liverpool; a Steward of the Conference.

WOODROOFFE, Rev. Canon, Alton, Hants.

YOUNG, Robert, Esq., Free Church Foreign Missions Office, Edinburgh.

Total Members, 126.

PROCEEDINGS OF THE CONFERENCE.

PRELIMINARY MEETING.

Monday Evening, March 19th, 1860.

<small>Preliminary Meeting.</small> The Members of the Conference met at half-past six P.M., in the lower room of Hope Hall, for a devotional service, over which the Rev. Andrew Knox, Incumbent of Birkenhead, presided. The devotions of the meeting were led by the Rev. R. S. Hardy, Wesleyan missionary from Ceylon; the Rev. Dr. Tweedie, of the Free Church of Scotland; and the Rev. Dr. Steane.

After tea, a preliminary meeting was held to arrange the business of the Conference; when it was proposed, and carried unanimously, that John Cropper, Esq., be requested to take the Chair.

The roll having been called, in order that the members might be introduced to each other, the Chairman desired H. Carre Tucker, Esq. to state the proposed order of business.

This having been done,—

<small>Chairman.</small> It was moved by John Henderson, Esq., of Park, seconded by E. Dawson, Esq., of Aldcliffe Hall, and carried unanimously, that Major-General Alexander be requested to preside as Chairman over the deliberations of the Conference.

<small>Executive Committee.</small> It was then resolved, on the proposal of the Rev. A. Knox and the Rev. Dr. Tweedie, That the following gentlemen be appointed an Executive Committee, to arrange the business of the Conference:—

Rev. George D. Cullen,	James Howell, Esq.
Rev. Joseph Mullens,	Henry Woodfall, Esq.
Rev. Dr. Steane,	Robert A. Macfie, Esq., and
Rev. C. B. Leupolt,	H. Carre Tucker, Esq.
John Cropper, Esq.	

It was moved by the Rev. P. LATROBE, seconded by Canon WOODROOFFE, and resolved, that the

| Rev. G. D. CULLEN, | Rev. J. MULLENS, and | Secretaries |
| Rev. Dr. STEANE, | H. CARRE TUCKER, Esq. | |

be appointed SECRETARIES to the Conference, and EDITORS of the Proceedings.

With a view to economise time, it was earnestly requested that, in the important discussions coming on, all speeches should be brief, and to the point; and, if possible, should not exceed ten minutes. Full authority was given to the Chairman of the Conference to interfere, if necessary, in this matter. Short Speeches.

After some conversation, it was agreed that the brief papers, kindly forwarded by friends at a distance, should be referred to the Secretaries, with a request that they should look over them, and bring forward such hints and suggestions as they might contain in reference to the topics which may come under discussion. Hints.

It was also resolved, That, while no intention exists of adopting in the Conference formal resolutions that may be supposed binding upon its various members, it is most desirable that the Secretaries should prepare, and, if possible, lay before the Conference, Minutes embodying the general opinion of the Conference upon the various subjects examined and discussed. Minutes to be framed.

After presenting their thanks to the Chairman, prayer was offered by the Rev. Dr. SOMERVILLE, and the meeting closed.

FIRST GENERAL PRAYER-MEETING.

TUESDAY MORNING, March 20th.

At 9.30 A.M. the first General Prayer-Meeting was held in HOPE HALL, at which a large number of friends were present, besides the members of Conference. First General Prayer Meeting.

The Rev. G. SCOTT of Liverpool, formerly Wesleyan Missionary in Sweden, presided.

The devotions were led by the Rev. C. B. LEUPOLT of Benares; the Rev. P. LATROBE, London Secretary of the Moravian Missionary Society; Dr. MACGOWAN, Medical Missionary at Ningpo; and Major DAVIDSON.

FIRST SESSION.

First Session. The first session of Conference took place in the Hall at 10.30 A.M., when there was a large gathering of members.

MAJOR-GENERAL ALEXANDER in the Chair.

The Chairman announced that, as an appropriate introduction to the proceedings of a Conference composed of members of a great variety of churches and denominations, there would be presented a Resolution, expressive of the pleasure felt by all in meeting together under such circumstances, to consider the best interests of the Missionary cause; and called upon the Rev. Dr. TIDMAN, who presented the Resolution as follows:—

RESOLUTION OF MUTUAL WELCOME.

Resolution of Welcome. That the members of this Conference, in commencing their deliberations respecting the work of their common Lord in the heathen world, desire to express their great pleasure at meeting each other upon the present interesting occasion, and to offer to each other a hearty fraternal welcome. Though belonging to different sections of the Church of Christ, they rejoice in that close union to each other and that practical co-operation, which have so largely prevailed among the agents of Missionary Societies, both at home and abroad. They desire that that union should grow closer day by day, and their mutual affection increase and abound. Well aware that they hold various opinions on important ecclesiastical questions, they disavow all wish to interfere with each other's conscientious convictions; while at the same time they cling with one heart to the truth as it is in Jesus, and desire to unite their most earnest efforts in spreading among the heathen the knowledge of that divinely revealed Gospel, which is the appointed means of their redemption. They pray that in their present meetings the Spirit of power, of love, and of a sound mind, may rest upon them; that they may all be instructed, cheered, and strengthened in their work by their mutual consultations; that they may be led to renewed consecration to that Divine Redeemer who has condescended to accept their imperfect service in this great cause; and that He will so graciously bless their work in His name, as to render it more efficient than ever in the conversion of immortal souls.

After apologising for speaking on this subject at very brief notice,

Dr. TIDMAN continued:—Sir, I most heartily agree with the spirit of this resolution; that we come together with great pleasure; and that that pleasure is founded on our mutual fraternal love, and still more on our deep interest in the honour and glory of our common Redeemer. The resolution recognises the fact, which we, who look upon each other's faces, could not fail to feel, that we belong to different sections of the Christian Church; but, Sir, we do not regret that these different sections of the redeemed Church are engaged after their own manner, and their own deep and conscientious convictions, in the advancement of the common interests of his kingdom. I believe that, by this division of labour, much strength is gained, much useful example supplied, many errors probably prevented; and if we can but carry on our distinct agencies in this work in the spirit of mutual goodwill and of constant prayer, then I think, Sir, this variety, like the varieties displayed in all the works of God, will contribute to strength, beauty, and efficiency. I hope that our meetings on this occasion will greatly tend to strengthen that feeling which, I am sure, we all honestly and earnestly wish to cherish and promote; and especially that we shall meet on all these several occasions in the spirit of those prayers which our brethren have presented on our behalf this morning; with a feeling of deep humiliation that we have done so little in a cause that demands so much; with the conviction that all that has been done is not by man's wisdom or by man's power; and that "neither is it he that planteth anything or he that watereth, but God that giveth the increase." In looking forward to those greater labours and those more extended glories which we anticipate in the future, our trust will still be in God, in the faithfulness of His promises, in the infinite value of the one great sacrifice offered by the Lord Jesus for the world's transgressions, and in the life-giving and transforming energy of his good Spirit. With these few remarks, Sir, I cordially offer the resolution to the meeting. (Applause.)

Rev. Dr. TIDMAN.

Christian Union.

Advantage of variety in missionary labour.

Effect of our meetings.

The Rev. THOMAS GREEN, Principal of the Church Missionary College, Islington, London, rose with great pleasure to second it. He felt, they were met together for a great and glorious object, and that it was the constraining love of Christ which animated every heart present. They were met as brethren. It had been justly remarked that they belonged to different denominations; but they were all fighting under one banner, the banner of the cross of Christ. They were all moved by one spirit, animated by one hope, influenced by one great and glorious object; that object being, the Redeemer's glory in the extension of his kingdom, the gathering in of his people, and the bringing on of that glorious day when Jew and Gentile should be one fold under one Shepherd— Jesus Christ the Righteous. However important the objects which engaged the attention of other bodies; however important the objects which engaged the attention of statesmen, politicians, philosophers, and merchants; he felt, and doubtless they would feel also, that the objects which engaged their attention at the present time infinitely transcended in importance all others. If one soul was of more value than a whole world, and that was the arithmetic which their blessed Lord and Master had taught them, then, surely, the object which they had before them was of infinite and transcendent importance. God had already greatly blessed their work, and in blessing them he had been pouring out his Spirit of light in a large measure. They had heard of those blessed outpourings in America, in Sweden, in Ireland, in Scotland, in various parts of the metropolis, and other places; and animated as they were by the ardent hope, nay, the assurance which God himself had given them, that this Spirit would be poured out upon them on this occasion, they had come together, knowing that he would bless them, and be with them from day to day; sure that he would answer the prayers which had been offered on their behalf, and that a spirit of unity, love, forbearance, gentleness, and deep humility, would pervade their meetings.

If permitted to add another remark, he would simply say: Let all differences be forgotten; let them not remember that they were Churchmen or Dissenters, Baptists or Wesleyans, Presbyterians or Episcopalians; let such thoughts be entirely swept away from their memory: let them only think that they were Christ's; that Christ was all in all; that he was verily in the midst of them; and that now, in an especial manner, he would fulfil his own promise, "Lo! I am with you alway, even to the end of the world." With very great pleasure he seconded the resolution, heartily concurring in every sentiment spoken by their dear and eminent brother, Dr. Tidman, whom for the first time he was glad to meet, and of whose valuable labours in connexion with the missionary field he trusted they would long continue to hear. (Applause.)

The RESOLUTION was then put, and unanimously adopted.

The CHAIRMAN next delivered a brief address on introducing the programme of the morning's discussion. He said: This resolution forms a happy introduction to the proceedings of the Conference. I am certain that it is accepted by us all as a Christian welcome from one heart to another. (Applause.) In this unity, then, and catching up the words of wisdom which God the Holy Spirit has put into the mouths of those who have addressed you, let us now commence these most solemn, most sublime, most awful deliberations; each relying upon the promises of our God and the gift of the Holy Spirit, that they will result in what will be for the glory of His most holy name, and for the good of millions around us who are lying in darkness and in the shadow of eternal death. Let us now go forward in dependence upon our God, and his Holy Spirit will undoubtedly be with us. Having welcomed each other, and given heart to heart in fellowship, let us, as Mr. Green has suggested, know no church but that one great Catholic Church, of which Christ is both the Head and the Foundation, and for the completion of which we wait when the corner-stone shall be brought forth with shoutings of "Grace, grace unto it!" May God in his infinite mercy guide us, guard us, keep us; and so encourage and restrain us, that every word spoken may be simply and solely for the glory of His own most holy Name.

<small>CHAIRMAN.</small>

<small>Spirit of these Meetings.</small>

The Chairman then referred to the programme which had been drawn up and printed, containing the subjects suggested for discussion. The programme for the morning session was as follows:—

<small>Programme of the day.</small>

Subject: EUROPEAN MISSIONARIES ABROAD.

    A Paper, or Address, of ten minutes, by the Rev. JOSEPH MULLENS, London Missionary Society, Calcutta.

    Necessity for a missionary at once mixing intimately with the natives, and obtaining a thorough mastery of their language.

    The use of the common Colloquial, as compared with the so-called Sacred Languages.

    Vernacular Preaching. Itinerancies.

    Visiting from house to house.

Local Pastoral Work.
Medical Missionaries.
Translation of the Bible and Christian Books.
Causes of Missionary *Success.*
Causes of *Failure.*
Should Missionary Effort be concentrated in limited localities, or diffused over a large surface?
Reflex influence of a greater degree of vital religion among our European Soldiery and Countrymen abroad.

He advised all present to adhere as closely as possible to the subjects mentioned in the list, and particularly drew attention to the importance of the point mentioned in italics, *the cause of the failure of missions.* In examining the causes which had hindered in any way the progress of Christian missions, he entreated them carefully to consider whether, in the very systems of agency that had been adopted for the spread of the gospel, they could not detect some of the clogs to their chariot-wheels, and find out why they had hitherto driven so slowly. In mission fields they had to deal with men of different minds. Take, for instance, the subtle and intellectual Asiatic in contrast with the Esquimaux, or tribes that in other lands had sunk to the lowest grades in the scale of reason and humanity. He would ask, whether it was a necessary thing that the very systems amidst which we had grown up; systems that came out of the struggles, contentions, and controversies of the Reformation; systems that had arisen in the days of Queen Elizabeth, and during the distracting times of the reigns of the Stuarts, which were manifestly imperfect in themselves, though perhaps the best that could be adapted to the states of mind and difficult circumstances, in which men were then placed,—whether such systems are what we should take and fix, like cast-iron matrices, in which to mould without necessary adaptations, the varying minds and circumstances of American Indians, Africans, Asiatics, and the inhabitants of the numerous islands of the Pacific? It was important to see whether we could not detect in these very systems causes of hindrance. From his own experience he was sure we could; and, therefore, on this subject there ought to be the freest and boldest expression of opinion, founded upon experience, and guided by the word of God. (Hear, hear.)

At the invitation of the Chairman, the following paper was then read to the Conference by Mr. Mullens:—

[margin notes: Causes of hindrance in missions. The ecclesiastical systems of Europe. Are they suited to the habits and views of other nations.]

EUROPEAN MISSIONARIES ABROAD.

BY THE REV. JOSEPH MULLENS, CALCUTTA.

1. The European missionary is the most important element in a system of missionary operations. He commences, maintains, and supervises that system. He preaches the divine message, and teaches others to proclaim it. He is the connecting link between old Churches and new ones; between the long-settled Christian Societies of one country and the new plantations founded in lands hitherto heathen. His position is full of importance in respect to his office, in respect to the Churches who send him, and to the people whom he first instructs. As missionaries flourish, are faithful in character, work, and purposes, so will missions flourish: as they go wrong, are weak, worldly, secular, or selfish, so will those missions decay. The fidelity of a missionary may tell upon many generations: the fall of a missionary may be a stumbling-block to hundreds of souls. Not only, therefore, should missionaries be well chosen, but be well sustained, and should be followed by the confidence, the affections, and fervent prayers of the brethren who send them forth. *{Importance of the missionary.}*

2. The position and office of a missionary are peculiar. A minister of Christ in any country is a Christian and something more. He is a teacher, guide, and ruler in the household of faith. A missionary again occupies a post beyond this. He is a minister, and something more. He is that minister holding a special relation to the Saviour; a special relation to the Churches; a special relation to those whom he has come to enlighten. Missionaries are eminently representative men. They are the messengers of the Churches, examples of what those Churches are and do. They are ambassadors for Christ, holding his treasure in earthen vessels, yet counted "the Glory of Christ." To the heathen they bear a new religion; they expound it, explain, and defend it. They enforce it in every way they can; by head, by heart; by tongue, by life; by love, by suffering, by patience, and by toil. In these things the New Testament teachings are their best guide; they were in many cases addressed to missionaries and mission churches by an Apostle who was himself a model missionary. *{Peculiarity of his position.}*

3. Apart from every peculiarity in his sphere of labour, and in his plans of usefulness, the *personal character* of the missionary *{His personal character.}*

should be his prime object of concern. He must be "blameless, as the steward of God;" "giving no offence in anything, that the ministry be not blamed ; but in all things approving himself as a minister of Christ." All secularity must be avoided. "No man that warreth entangleth himself in the affairs of this life ; that he may please him who hath chosen him to be a soldier." Everything unchristian in his character and plans must be removed, for "if a man strive for masteries (even over heathenism), yet is he not crowned except he strive lawfully." Opposers he will have many, still "the servant of the Lord must not strive, but be patient unto all men ;" that he may be able "by sound teaching to exhort and to convince gainsayers ;" pure, sober, hospitable, kind unto all men, he who is of the contrary part will be ashamed, having no evil thing to say of him. Thus watching like a faithful servant ; in doctrine sound, decided, and sincere ; in temper gentle, self-restrained, and patient; in conduct holy and approved unto God; pressed by the Apostle's burden, "Woe is unto me, if I preach not the Gospel," he will be earnest, in season and out of season, in preaching the divine word of grace ; making full proof of his ministry; and purifying himself from all evil, will strive to become a vessel unto honour, sanctified to the Master's use, filled with the Spirit, and even upon earth made meet for heaven.

Questions respecting his qualifications. 4. Securing, however, missionaries of sound religious character, many questions arise respecting plans, and prominent before some minds come inquiries like these :—

   1. Are piety, good religious character, and zeal, sufficient in the missionary ; or,
   2. Do we require very intellectual and able men ?
   3. Should all study the vernacular ; should they confine themselves to it ; or,
   4. Should they study, besides, the learned languages ?
   5. Should these studies be carried on to any extent in England ?
   6. Should missionaries deal chiefly with the common people or with the learned ?
   7. Should they fix themselves in one locality or be on the move ?

A careful survey of our wide fields of labour, and of the experience acquired during many years, will show that truth does not lie exclusively on the side of any single answer to these questions. Many answers are possible, each of which shall be correct in its own sphere: a careful discrimination will, however, without fail, enable us to distinguish where to apply them.

5. Several of these questions will find their answer in considering another: *What is the purpose which the missionary has in view?* Leaving out of our calculations the ministers who go forth to instruct our countrymen in the colonies, let us consider, that the missionary who goes among the heathen aims to convert souls, to found churches, to set over them native pastors, and so to build them up and bring them forward to manhood in the Gospel, that they shall both sustain it among themselves and carry forward missionary work amongst others. To accomplish all this, he has to employ one divine instrumentality, the Gospel; and this Gospel he must convey into the minds and hearts of the people to whom he is sent. He must therefore consider his own agency, as well as the circumstances of the people. His purpose.

a. In regard to himself, he must study the conditions of sound health in the country of his sojourn, and the arrangements for his own comfort necessitated by its climate. Here he will find no rules of universal application, but should seek for the advice of experienced men who know his sphere of labour. His own health.

6. *b.* As to the people, he must seek also thoroughly to know *them*. He must know their language, their customs, their notions, their habits, their religious ceremonies, the motives by which they are most powerfully swayed. He should understand all the accompaniments and agencies of that training which has made them what they are. His own training, knowledge, and habits are usually so different from theirs, that, quite apart from the difficulty of getting Christian doctrine into their minds, in ordinary intercourse with them he may make such mistakes, and so offend their prejudices, as quite to set them against him and his plans. By carefulness in these things, by correct information, and by that consideration which wins confidence all the world over, he may break down the barrier which divides him from them, and secure an open door for the word which he bears to them from heaven. He ought, therefore, to know them, that they may know him. He acts in this matter under a general law, which rules every minister of Christ in the world, that he must adapt himself to those whom he is going to instruct. Necessity of knowing the people well.

He must know the current notions, customs, ceremonies, practices, ruling motives, superstitions, hopes and fears, of the people around him. He must know not merely ancient China, ancient India, ancient Africa; he must know living China, living India. And He should learn their language.

to know them intimately, he must be able to communicate with them. Hence it would seem to be a *good rule*, right and wise, that every missionary going to a heathen land should thoroughly master the current vernacular, and be able to address the people in their own tongue. It was partly for this great end, as well as a divine seal of their commission, that at the outset of missionary labour the gift of tongues was bestowed upon the apostles and their brethren. There may be exceptions to the rule in cases where the heathen understand the language of the missionary, as in a few great cities in India. We know many honoured and useful missionaries so situated; but I do not know one missionary who does not consider that, to have learned the language when commencing missionary life, would have added greatly to his usefulness. To be able fluently to preach in the language of a heathen people is a great talent, most powerful for their evangelisation.

Beginning at home.

7. Where should a missionary learn the language and manners of a foreign people? He will learn the greater portion best upon the spot, among the people themselves, and from constant conversation with them. But the human mind moves slowly, takes in slowly, especially the beginnings of what is new. There are certain points in grammar, language and ideas, which are almost entirely matters of memory. Hence I draw the inference, confirmed by experience, that the *beginnings of his knowledge* a missionary may well secure at home. While continuing other studies, he may for twelve months give attention to his new language; to the verbs, nouns, and common terms; and endeavour to secure the thorough acquisition of a small vocabulary. The pronunciation he should learn under a competent teacher.

With a view to secure this desirable end, might I suggest that every Missionary Society should have prepared, and be able to put into the hand of every new missionary, when his sphere of labour

Manual.

is fixed, a BRIEF MANUAL of the language, customs, notions, and religious ideas of the province or country to which he is going: including a few rules, or hints respecting climate, dress, health, food, and the like; a statement of the labours carried on by the brethren whom he will join, and the like. Such a manual need not exceed 120 pages, and would not be expensive to prepare. This he should learn by heart, and know thoroughly by the time he reaches his station. His progress then will be rapid, and his course of usefulness sure.

The language to be learned at once:

8. With such an efficient preparation, let every missionary, on his arrival at his sphere of labour, strive to enter as much as

possible among the people. That he may learn the language thoroughly, let him devote a considerable time each day to its acquisition. Let him walk abroad, and though he cannot speak much, let him see much, and familiarise himself with all the outer manifestations of native life. For the first year or two, his principal attention should be given to the language and to books about the natives. He need not, however, be inactive in his direct work. Where opportunity is given, to teach young people for a short time each day will both add to his knowledge and stir up his zeal. It is an excellent plan at the outset for a missionary to reside at a country station. Even with the best advantages, however, the work is hard. I never learned to speak a thing rightly, without having first said it wrong. Still, let every missionary persevere; he will learn much from his mistakes. A native preacher may speak more correctly than he, but he will speak with most authority. *among the people themselves.*

9. When settled in work, vernacular preaching will generally occupy the most conspicuous place in his plans, as the most direct method of reaching the souls of the heathen. But it is not a common work. It is not anything that will do here. He needs well-prepared discourses, that clearly expound the gospel, show where it opposes idolatrous views and practices, anticipate objections, fall in with native modes of thinking, and, starting from their own platform, convey knowledge which they never had before. Extensive study will be required, and great material, before any one becomes very competent and distinguished in so wide and valuable a field of labour. *Vernacular preaching most important.*

The time seems now to be come for employing this agency to the largest extent. Books, tracts, and portions of Scripture have long been available as its auxiliaries. Much knowledge of gospel truth has been spread, and efforts already made should be closely followed up. Where a large population exists, it is well to maintain settled stations, that the missionary may repeat his instructions again and again until the gospel is thoroughly understood, believed, and accepted.

10. But with this settled plan, itinerancies in ill-instructed parts of a country well agree. These itinerancies should if possible be made systematic, be repeated, be limited to comparatively small districts each time, and each time be carefully carried out in detail. *Itinerancies also.*

Vernacular preaching is a work of such great importance, and the power to carry it on is so valuable, that missionary societies should give it their best attention. Wherever they secure men thoroughly competent to carry it on, whether native or European, they should secure them for that work alone, and set them free from all other pressing toil.

<small>Schools.</small>

11. Many other agencies may also be legitimately employed in carrying out the great purpose of evangelising a people. The position occupied in the system by *mission-schools* will be specially discussed hereafter.

Sometimes a mission is not able at once to reach the heart of a people: there are barriers in the way, arising from their ignorance, prejudices, customs, and other causes, which it is desirable to remove; and all agencies that are efficient for this end may be legitimately employed in the cause of the gospel.

<small>Medical missions.</small>

Medical missions have proved especially valuable in this way. Like the miracles of healing in the first days of the church, they exhibit, in a most prominent manner, the humanity and benevolence of the gospel and its professors: and by their works of disinterested kindness, conciliate those who would otherwise be prejudiced against missionaries as foreigners and people of a strange faith. In China and other countries, where real medical skill is unknown, they are specially useful. India has been largely supplied with dispensaries and surgeons by the Government, and to a considerable degree they are not so necessary. But there are many cities, towns, and retired districts, in which they might be employed with great benefit to the mission cause.

<small>Varieties of acquirements.</small>

12. We advance to another question. Will piety, with ordinary capacity, suffice; or do we require men of great mental ability and acquirements in the missionary work? This question is answered by another. Abroad, as at home, all spheres of labour are not alike. There are many kinds of labour now, as in apostolic days. "When he led captivity captive, he gave gifts unto men." Look at the case in England. We do not ask Dean Alford to go into St. Giles's. We do not expect the Marian of St. Giles's to preach in the Britannia Theatre, or sit in the Professor's chair.

<small>Varieties in the spheres of labour.</small>

13. Apart from *theory* (though that is in favour of men of all grades of ability,) a due regard to the varying condition of the spheres of missionary labour will indicate the kind of men required for missionaries. Look at the different countries of the world: the Negro population of the West Indies and West Africa; the Hottentots, Caffres, and Bechuanas of South Africa; at pastoral work in the South Sea Islands, literary work in China, varieties of work in Burmah and in India. There is simple work among people of

simple notions and habits of life; work of wisdom in guiding growing communities; careful scholarship in providing Christian and general literature; grasp of mind in dealing with great systems, lordly, clever priesthoods, and dangerous, deep-seated errors. It is a matter of plain common sense that, according to the sphere and its demands, so should be the man who is to occupy it. *Missionaries should be adapted to the places they occupy, and the labours they are to carry on.*

14. *Spheres, too, may change their character:* the same place does not always demand the same work. I would point out a peculiar tendency now visible in all our older missions, even in India, which has a most important bearing on missionary character and labours. When missionaries began their labours abroad, everything was heathen. They had to begin everything; grammars, dictionaries, translations, first studies of heathen customs, ceremonies, and religions. Naturally, the missionary became the first pastor of the native church, when it was gathered. Now, in almost every land, progress has been made. And there is a strong tendency in the very circumstances of their work, to throw missionaries back into their true position, not of pastors of single churches, but superintendents of many: not teachers of one congregation, but advisers and helpers of the native teachers. Look at Mr. Vinton, superintendent of forty-two Karen churches; at Mr. Thomas, in Tinnevelly, at one time superintendent of 5000 Christians; and so with many others. Missionaries in the South Sea Islands have been superintendents of whole islands, and presided over theological seminaries. Who is not glad and thankful to see it so? Here is a practical New Testament Episcopate, sprung not from theory, but from circumstances; an episcopate forced on men of all churches,—Episcopalians, Presbyterians, Independents, Wesleyans, and Lutherans: an episcopate, however, more flexible than any one of our many systems, and specially adapted to the case of young Christians, who are dependent upon the advice and experience of Christians in churches established for many years; a missionary episcopate which entirely disappears when the churches grow out of their tutelage, attain full growth, and need the foreign missionary no longer.

_{Tendency in modern missions to make missionaries superintendents and advisers.}

_{Instances.}

If such be the tendency of modern missions, a tendency increasing year by year, it seems to furnish an argument stronger than any other I have heard for great carefulness in the selection of missionaries. Such superintendents ought to be wise men; men of large hearts, of comprehensive views; men not wedded to

_{Kind of men now needed.}

English ecclesiastical systems, but willing to suit their measures to the circumstances of their flocks and of the idolaters around them.

Dealings with native scholars.

15. In respect to idolatry, too, a higher position has been taken. We have dealt in controversy with common notions, traditions, ceremonies; and an immense deal remains to be done. Good plain men, who can speak the language fluently, and argue with common people clearly and cogently, are still needed, and will be needed for long years to come. But we do need also the few who can study the notions and deep theories on which Hinduism and Chinese Buddhism are based, and deal boldly and successfully with the ultimate points of controversy, on which learned scholars rest. For them we must look not to young men newly arrived, but to men of experience, who have been training themselves by long studies for such things.

The learned languages.

16. The same great rule brings us forward to another point. As a missionary acquires experience, comprehends the current life around him well, and speaks the vernacular well, in a few years he will perceive that many of the notions most tenaciously held by the people are traceable to old times, and are defended by ancient authorities. Let such a one, if he possesses the faculty, study Sanskrit, learn Arabic and Persian, like Dr. Pfander; go deep into Chinese lore; master the controversies, and provide books not only suitable for the heathen, but for his brethren. That is one sphere of missionary labour, and all must feel that it is but right to have it supplied.

Wise to win souls.

17. Be this as it may; though differing in judgment as to the details of their work; though endowed with various gifts, and feeling predilection for peculiar spheres of labour; though occupying various positions of usefulness, all bearing upon the progress of the kingdom; let every missionary, consecrating all his powers to the Redeemer with a single eye, daily make it his prayerful study that he be "WISE TO WIN SOULS."

Rev. W. M. Whittemore.

The Rev. W. M. WHITTEMORE wished to ask two questions: First, did he clearly understand Mr. Mullens to say, that the missionary should be altogether disconnected from secular engagements: for it was a very interesting point to decide whether the missionary should be altogether given up to the work, or whether he might usefully connect with the missionary work anything like a secular occupation by which a man got his living. The second point was, whether the superiority which Mr. Mullens ascribed to the European preacher over the native arose, in his judgment,

Secularities in missions.

Are Europeans superior to

from the fact of his being a European, or from the superiority of his previous theological training over that of the native preacher? *Natives as preachers?*

Mr. MULLENS replied, that his own conviction was, decidedly, that the less a missionary has to do with secular employment the better; it is one of the great benefits of missionary societies that they enable a man to devote himself entirely to the work of God. The superiority of the European over the native arises from many considerations. It arises partly from his being a European; also from his energy of character, his superior knowledge; and especially from his being, as a missionary, the source whence knowledge of the doctrine and life of Christianity, the new religion which has displaced the old, is to be first derived. *Rev. J. MULLENS. Answer.*

The Rev. R. S. HARDY, formerly Wesleyan missionary in Ceylon, said, he must be allowed to answer the second question, having been a missionary in Ceylon for upwards of twenty years, and having had very considerable intercourse with the natives. It was frequently his duty to catechise the children on the Monday, after he and others had been preaching to them on the Sabbath-day. He invariably found, when he asked them about the sermons preached by the European and the native, that relatively they could always give better answers as to the sermons of the European, than they could with respect to those of the natives. Of course, the idiom spoken by the natives was much better than what the Europeans could possibly acquire; but with the discipline which European missionaries had to go through, the comparative clearness of their ideas, and the readiness with which they threw them before the people, without that circumlocution which an uneducated native must almost necessarily exercise, he invariably found that they could tell much more about the sermon of the European than about that of the native; and he accounted for it in that way. Not that the native children, as some might suppose, had much greater respect for the European than for the native minister; but the clearness and precision of the ideas of the former had made a deeper impression, and his teaching was more easily recalled. *Rev. R. S. HARDY. English-man's sermon best remembered. Why?*

The Rev. J. M'KEE, missionary to Guzerat, said:—With regard to the secular employment of the missionaries, we, in India, find that it is almost impossible for a missionary to keep himself altogether free from secular employment of a special kind, though *Rev. J. M'KEE.*

Industrial schools where useful.

not needed for his own support; that is, he must have an industrial establishment of some kind, less or greater, according to circumstances. The circumstances of some missionaries are such that they cannot altogether avoid it. An inquirer comes to us—he embraces the truth—he has, probably, been driven from his home and obliged to give up everything. The missionary must, therefore, in some way or other, find employment for him. Hence we find, for example, our missionary presses and our farming establishments are required. I think that if inquiry be directed to the subject, it will be found that wherever we have had industrial establishments to any extent they have been perfectly successful.

Rev. B. L. Singh.

The Rev. BEHARI LAL SINGH, licensed preacher of the Free Church of Scotland in Calcutta, though he regarded with very great respect the remarks of those fathers and brethren who had spoken on the subject of native agency, believed they had not yet fully appreciated the value of that native agency. The history of all Christian nations, for example, proclaimed the fact, that Christians who were natives of the soil were the most successful translators of the Bible into their own language. Hitherto the plan of translating the Bible had been conducted as though foreign missionaries were the only successful or competent translators. There was a considerable difference of opinion amongst the translators themselves, and the friends of the Bible Society, as to the faithfulness, intelligibility, and acceptableness of the present versions; and he asked, whether the present versions of the Bible in the various dialects of India would ever become the standard versions of the native church? Though he made these remarks, he must also say that he honoured the memory of those venerable men who had expended their time, strength, talents, and accomplishments, in the work of translation. Was it not, then, he asked, now desirable that they should spend their time and strength in raising an effective native agency to translate the Bible with far greater purity and precision than it had ever been done before? So also with regard to the preaching of the gospel, and teaching in the schools and colleges, he believed that the same principles should be adopted, and that the same results would follow. The European missionaries sent to India should, of course, endeavour by all means to do all they could in the native language; but it would be a greater thing if these missionaries raised up a really superior native agency to teach and preach the gospel, and translate in the vernacular. The sub-

Native agents the best translators.

A native agency to be raised up.

jects for that day's discussion included all the legitimate methods employed in bringing the truths of the gospel to bear upon the native mind. They were sanctioned alike by the direction of Scripture and by the examples of the Apostles. It was quite true that the Apostles did not translate the Scriptures; but if the Jewish Scriptures and the Septuagint had not existed and been extensively circulated, there could be no doubt that the translation of the Bible would have occupied the Apostles' attention. In order to fulfil the duty and command delivered by our Lord, we must take two things into consideration. We must consider the peculiar sections of the Hindoo and Mahomedan community, and the particular qualifications and departments of the missionary work for which the missionary was qualified, by his previous training, habits, tastes, and inclinations. The missionary who by his previous training was qualified for one department of missionary labour, did not necessarily shine in others. The missionary who was qualified by his knowledge of the Oriental languages, literature, and philosophy, successfully to encounter the arguments of learned Hindoos and Mahomedans, would not equally shine in the work of translation and in general teaching. So, therefore, the missionary should confine his time and strength to that department of missionary labour for which Providence had qualified him. *Various departments for mission work.*

The Rev. THOMAS SMITH, formerly missionary of the Free Church at Calcutta, expressed his belief that native preaching, when it was of the right kind, would be found better than any European preaching. Mr. Smith went on to say that he did not agree with Mr. Mullens as to the somewhat low place which he had assigned to Medical Missions; as, for instance, in India. Perhaps there it might not be so high as in China; but from what he saw in Bengal, and in South Africa nearly twenty years ago, he was persuaded that in these countries there was a very large and important field for medical missions. Although there was something like truth in what Mr. Mullens had said respecting the provision made by Government for supplying the medical wants of the native community, it seemed to him that these were just like a drop in the bucket in comparison with what was really needed. It was quite true that there were dispensaries in the large towns; but, as far as he had seen, they did not extend in any degree whatever into the country. He did not think the medical missions in India had had anything like fair play, or done *Rev. T. SMITH. Value of medical missions in India. What Government has done.*

the good which they otherwise might have done. They had generally been placed in large towns and cities, in the very places where the wants of the people in that department were supplied: whereas medical missionaries should be sent to villages or clusters of villages, and go from house to house, very much as country practitioners do at home, carrying with them their medical skill and the love of God in their hearts, resolved to do good to all as they had the opportunity. From his own observations he should say, that there were openings for such men that no other kind of missionaries whatever could obtain. They were aware that in India it was taken as a matter of course that every European was skilled in medicine: they all got the credit of being physicians, and lawyers, and everything. No doubt, many of his missionary brethren present had often been applied to, as he had been, to prescribe for cases which they knew just as little about as any man living. He had often, from this false impression in regard to his medical skill, had opportunities, on the faith of being a medical man, which he could not have had otherwise, of doing good spiritually to the people; and he had no doubt that the medical men in the Bengal villages could have access to the people, both males and females, in a way which no other missionary could.

Where to place them.

Their great influence.

The Rev. DR. SOMERVILLE, Secretary of the Foreign Missions of the United Presbyterian Church, had listened to Mr. Mullens's very able paper with great interest, and thought the Conference were exceedingly indebted to him for its production. If published, it would, no doubt, be found of extreme value to those who had the conduct of missionary operations. With respect to the order of discussions, the Chairman had suggested that the two central points should be "the causes of missionary success and failure." If this met the mind of the Conference he had no objection, but there were other points which might also be suggested, and other topics which might be advantageously dwelt upon; such as "the object the missionary was sent to accomplish," "the best way of accomplishing the missionary work," and "the best mode of training missionary converts." Now he apprehended, that if such general topics as these were submitted, they would embody everything.

Rev. Dr. SOMERVILLE.

Order of topics to be discussed.

The CHAIRMAN reminded Dr. Somerville, that what he had suggested actually comprehended the whole programme, and that

CHAIRMAN.

it would be much better to adhere to central points during each particular discussion.

The Rev. THOMAS GREEN, Principal of the Church Missionary Institution, London, said that he had a missionary friend in North India, the Rev. Mr. Bruce, whose observations upon the subject under discussion were so pertinent that, though the remarks were made at a distance of some ten or fifteen thousand miles, they might possibly give a practical turn to the present conversation. Mr. Green then read these remarks, which were to the effect, that in learning the native language the first year was everything. If the missionary made the language his sole work, in six months the difficulty of acquiring it would be broken. Mr. Bruce had now given up the English Bible. "Take up," said he, "the language in a half spirit, and years will pass away ere you can speak properly in it; or rather you never will. Give yourself wholly to it, mix but sparingly in English society, and my opinion is, that the most ordinary intellect will be sure to acquire the language after a short time. With all humility I would say to a missionary: If he cannot give himself wholly to the work in this way, he had better stay at home." Mr. Green concluded by saying that it was only fifteen months since Mr. Bruce had gone out to India, and he was now going about preaching to the people in their own tongue. (Applause.)

Rev. T. GREEN.
Note from Rev. T. BRUCE.
Languages should be learned at once.

The Rev. WILLIAM SHAW, Wesleyan Missionary from South Africa:—I am quite aware, Sir, that I can have no claim to address an assembly of this kind, except that which arises from the mere fact of my having been a missionary, labouring in a very extensive region of Southern Africa, for more than thirty-three years. (Applause.) I have listened to the admirable paper read by Mr. Mullens with the deepest interest, and, I trust, with much instruction; and I entirely concur (speaking from African experience) in the conclusions to which my esteemed friend seems to have been brought by his Indian experience. If I failed to hear anything in that paper which seemed particularly new to myself, it was not the less interesting to me; but it afforded rather a confirmation of the feelings and interest raised in my mind by the important topics introduced, to find that men in such different spheres of action had been brought, in the prosecution of their missionary labours, to very much the same conclusions. (Hear, hear.) It is of the utmost importance that a missionary should

Rev. W. SHAW.
Similarity of missionary experience.

very early acquire the vernacular of the country to which he is sent. There are, however, in some instances, serious difficulties in the way. There is a class of pioneer missionaries, who have had to go into new countries, where languages have not been formed or written. Of course their difficulties are of a very peculiar character, inasmuch as they can have no previous acquaintance with the language they are required to learn; and usually in countries of that kind, there are many extraneous difficulties not found in more civilized regions. But I would humbly express it as my opinion, that, even under these very unfavourable and trying circumstances, it is the first duty of the missionary to endeavour to acquire the language of the people amongst whom he is sent to labour. I shall not speak of the peculiar difficulties of attempting to reduce an unwritten language to writing, and then proceeding afterwards to the translation of the Holy Scriptures; but I conceive the missionaries, under these circumstances, are shut up to only one possible method of acquiring the language; and if I may judge from the experience of several honoured brethren of various missionary societies, I believe intercourse with the people is the best practicable way of acquiring their language. Of course I don't mean to say that there are not instances where a judicious and sensible man may avail himself of every benefit and advantage, which he can derive from the written labours of predecessors or other gentlemen, who are able to assist him in so important an inquiry as learning the language which he is to speak. But, even if all these advantages are afforded, he must endeavour to acquire it from actual conversation with the people; and I would venture to express an opinion, that though grammars and dictionaries may afford help at first, they will be a very imperfect means of learning a language, unless followed up by direct personal intercourse with the people. (Hear, hear.) It will require that the missionary should indulge a little feeling of self-sacrifice; indeed, a man must be first willing to become "a fool for Christ's sake," in this respect. I have known some of the most able men spend a long time before they became perfect in the language; and I strongly suspect that this was because they were unwilling to make blunders in their first attempts. (Laughter.) This is a lesson which all missionaries, and especially young ones, should bear in mind, — that it is no matter if, in the first instance, they should make a few blunders; for there is even amongst the most barbarous tribes all the world over, and particularly those of Africa, such a natural

Marginal notes: Difficulties in learning native languages. Intercourse with the people essential. Don't be afraid of mistakes.

politeness, that when they see a man really striving to convey some information, they feel that some indulgence ought to be exercised towards him in his mode of conveying the truth. (Hear, hear.) I am not so sure that even the Apostles themselves, when they went forth with the gift of tongues, were in every instance able to speak with the correct pronunciation and exact style of the people among whom they were sent to labour. I very much doubt whether that noble protest, which St. Paul made upon Mars' Hill at Athens, against the polytheism of that period, and in which the assertion was made of the power and goodness of the one great God— I very much doubt whether that protest was uttered in language exactly such as would have been used by the celebrated orators of that famous city. (Cheers.) I suspect that there would be something of an uncouthness, and of a foreign accent, even in St. Paul's utterance (laughter); for it is in that way that I understand the remarks made by the Corinthians who were opposed to him, when they said that his "speech was contemptible." There may have been these peculiarities in his speech, and some verbal peculiarity in his mode of uttering the truth; but of this much I am quite sure, that if we go forth, beginning with the few words we have, giving a few simple lessons, and learning as we go on, even our blunders will become instructive to us, and by and by we shall preach, with fluency and freedom, the glorious gospel of the blessed God. (Applause.) *Was Paul's Greek perfect?*

I will conclude with one or two practical suggestions. The Societies should endeavour to send out their men *not too old*. I don't mean to say that God has no use for elder men, or that he has not done much by many men who are beyond the age at which it is possible to learn a language so as to speak it fluently; but, as a rule, it is most desirable that your missionaries should, if possible, get into their work before they are twenty-five years of age. The other suggestion I have already anticipated, that the missionary, as soon as he arrives in the country, should endeavour to learn the language by constant personal intercourse with the people. *New missionaries not to be too old: under twenty-five.*

The Rev. C. B. LEUPOLT, of Benares, said,—Every missionary committee should make a law, as inflexible as the laws of the Medes and Persians ever were, that no missionary going to a new sphere of labour should have anything to do with English for a year and a half, even though he be appointed a teacher to one of the English colleges. He should be requested to spend his first *Rev. C. B. LEUPOLT.*

At first every missionary should study the vernacular exclusively.	year and a half entirely in studying the language of the new scene of his efforts; and if he does not acquire the language in that year and a half, he will never learn it at all. (Hear, hear.) This is what I have seen during the twenty-six years I have been in India. (Hear, hear.) Clearly no missionary will be able to preach in a bazaar, or other place where he may meet with natives, who has not mixed extensively with the people. If what he knows is only the result of studying the learned books of the Hindus, the people will not know, on his addressing them, whether he speaks
That is, the current vernacular.	in Greek or any other language. He must learn the language current amongst the people; he must study chiefly the dialect which they speak in their daily life; and then he will be able to come home to the hearts and minds of the people. I would likewise recommend to the missionary committees that they request their missionaries, after they have spent six months in studying the lan-
He should also learn from experienced missionaries.	guage, to commence work, if possible, under some experienced missionaries; or, at all events, to go regularly with the elder missionaries of the city to hear them preach, and to see with their own eyes what is going on there. If they do this, I am perfectly sure that they will soon acquire the language, and prove themselves efficient missionaries. But I will repeat again, that if a young man have not learned a good deal of the language in the first eighteen months, he never will be hereafter an efficient missionary.
Age on going out, twenty-five.	Age, also, is a most important consideration. I myself was two years too old when I took to the acquisition of language. If I were to remain fifty years in England, I should never be able to speak clearly the idiom and style of the English language. A missionary applying himself when twenty-seven years of age may, however, still learn a language, but not so easily as he might have done at an earlier age. If practicable, a missionary should reach
Itinerancies to be made very carefully.	his station before he is twenty-five. With regard to itinerating; in North India it can only be done during five months in the year. I do not think any missionary is able in the Upper Provinces to itinerate any longer; at any rate, he should never take too large a circle during the five months, but rather go slowly over the ground, preaching for some time in each place: for if he make a long tour of some three or four hundred miles, he will be like a man who goes into the jungle, and sows here and there, and leaves the seed alone. It may spring up, or it may not. I have a theory of my own, which I should like to see adopted with regard to itinerating. I would divide certain

districts into parishes, if you like to call them so, and place in every large central village a catechist and reader. Each missionary might have from ten to fifteen readers, and these he should visit constantly; praying with them, preaching, assisting, and helping them upon every hand. By these means he would always find a large congregation in these villages. I have experienced, when I have come a third time to a heathen village, that a great deal of enmity had arisen meanwhile. I have not known why, but it was so. I have been opposed, and could scarcely get a congregation together. But where Christian catechists are stationed in villages, the feeling of the people has changed within the last nine or ten years. At first when we came to the district we were hated, and could not get a bit of straw for our people to sleep upon. But now I can go from zemindar's house to zemindar's house, and get my breakfast; and the people assemble around me, to whom I can speak fully the word of God. (Applause.)

<small>A good mode of preparing the way for them.</small>

<small>Progress.</small>

The Rev. Dr. O'MEARA, of the North American Indian Mission, said,—As I am the only missionary present connected with the Red Indians, it may not be out of place to give my experience in connexion with the subject of languages. The language which I have been enabled to acquire, and into which I have had the privilege of translating a great portion of the Scriptures, is one of those which have been mentioned as not previously written. When the application was first made to me to go amongst the Red Indians of North America, I was told that I should find no difficulty with regard to the language, and that all missionaries before me, and those then engaged in the work, had preached and were preaching through interpreters. I believe this is a practice, in a great measure, confined to North America, and that it does not exist in Africa or in Asia. I think myself, it is an unfortunate mode of impressing religious truth upon the mind; and when I said that I thought I should be able to learn the language of the people, and speak to them myself in their own tongue, a smile passed over the countenance of the missionary who was speaking to me. "No white man," he said, "could ever get his tongue round the long Indian words which seemed to have been growing since the deluge itself, so long and so immense are they in size." I remember answering him, that I was quite convinced that God was the author of language, and also the author of revelation; and that I did not believe that God was the author of any language into which the method of salvation was not communicable and translateable. I

<small>Rev. Dr. O'MEARA.</small>

<small>Red Indian tongue unwritten.</small>

<small>Interpreters employed.</small>

<small>Objections to the plan.</small>

<small>Difficulties of the Indian tongues.</small>

D

said; I was quite convinced that it was my duty to endeavour to acquire the language, and if I did not succeed, it would be a proof to me that my mission was not to labour amongst the Indians of North America. I went forth under this impression, and declined altogether the assistance of an interpreter during the first year of my labours. I went away sometimes forty or fifty miles from where any person could speak a word of English, and where the only white face was my own. I placed myself amongst the Indians, and listened to their language. At first it appeared a very strange language; the words were so long; even the sentences appeared to consist of but one long word. My first step, no unimportant one, was to ascertain where one word began and another ended; but under the blessing of God I attained that step, and then proceeded by signs and otherwise to find out the nouns of the language; then the verbs; and then to put verbs and nouns in a very summary way together. I then endeavoured to form sentences. One of our brethren to-day has spoken of blunders: those "blunders" were my only teachers; and a smile upon the countenances of the poor Indians sufficiently indicated when I had made a "blunder." I always took care, however, that these blunders were in common things, and not in matters of consequence, which might leave an impression on their minds not easily removed. I rejoiced when their smiles indicated my blunders, and I rejoiced also when their looks of intelligence showed me that they understood what I said. The first year was spent in this way. I afterwards obtained the assistance of an interpreter; but his principal work was to aid me in getting a more extensive vocabulary of the language. By the blessing of God, at the end of about three years, without any assistance from teachers or books, I felt myself able to minister to the people in their own language, and I have now been more than twenty years engaged in that happy work. (Cheers.) I look upon it as of paramount importance, that every people on the face of the earth should have the gospel preached to them; not through a language they do not understand, or through the imperfect medium of an interpreter, but in their own language, and from the mouth of the messenger of God. (Applause.)

The Rev. S. HISLOP, Free Church missionary at Nagpore, said:—Mr. Mullens had covered the exception he was about to take to the discussion; namely, that every missionary shall be required to learn the language in his first year. He appealed to the Chairman's own experience, and his knowledge of their mutual friend, JOHN ANDERSON, of the Free Church in Madras, who had laboured quite as successfully as most missionaries in India, though even at the end of his life he was not familiar with the native language. He should regret if it were to be understood as an essential qualification for every man, without exception, and whatever the circumstances in which he were placed, that he should learn the language of the natives, and could not be useful without it. *to the rule now advocated.*

The CHAIRMAN:—I think you will remember that, in the opening of his paper, Mr. Mullens brought before us very beautifully the entireness of the missionary field, and showed how every labourer has his particular sphere of operations. Most assuredly there is a wide scope for our Free Church brethren; and if John Anderson, whose memory I love, as I loved him in person, were here, he would, I believe, coincide in what Mr. Mullens has said. *CHAIRMAN. Spheres for all.*

Mr. HISLOP remarked, that he agreed with Mr. Mullens, though he dissented from the opinions of some of the subsequent speakers on this point. *Rev. S. HISLOP.*

The Rev. JOHN WALTON, Wesleyan missionary from Jaffna, in Ceylon:—With regard to interpreters, I can say of India, that there is no such practice amongst the missionaries in any of the churches with which I am acquainted. Many of the remarks made this morning have touched my early experiences. In the study of the Tamil language I lost a great deal of precious time. I had been six months engaged in this study at the mission-house before I discovered that there are in Tamil a *written* language and a *spoken* language; and when I had made considerable progress, as I thought, in the knowledge of the written language, I found myself incapable of holding a common conversation with the people in whose midst I lived. I found that, in attending the ministrations of some of our European missionaries, I could understand them much better than I could the natives; and that when I began to preach, the natives could not understand *me*. There was some point of communication between myself and my European brethren, not arising merely from the fact of their being Europeans, but from another cause: they had devoted themselves chiefly to the study of the *written* language of the people. Now, it seems to me, one of the best tests of a man's *Rev. J. WALTON. Difference between the written and the spoken languages of India.*

progress in Tamil or any other Indian language, is his ability to hold a discussion with a Hindoo of ordinary intelligence. I shall never forget such a discussion which I myself held, after I had been in the country about eighteen months. A native member of the congregation objected to something I had said, and challenged me to discussion. I shall never forget my feelings when, warmed with discussion, that native began to talk; for I have met nowhere with eloquence like Indian eloquence. When the man answered my questions, and addressed himself in reply to me, I did not know what he said, and I felt myself confounded in his presence. (Laughter.) The learned Beschi, in his Grammar, tells an anecdote of this kind:—A missionary had been preaching in Tamil (as he thought) to a large audience. I strongly suspect Beschi meant a Protestant missionary. After speaking to them for about half an hour with great earnestness, an old woman in the congregation rose and begged that he would tell them in *their* language what he had been so eloquently describing in *his own*. Beschi adds: "The man was ashamed, for he thought he had been speaking Tamil."

Colonel LAVIE, late in the Indian Artillery, said:—He had known very few officers who spoke the native language with fluency, who had not been able to pick it up during the first two or three years of their residence in the country. If they did not attend to this on first arriving in India, they seldom proved good linguists. If we were to have itinerating missionaries and evangelists, one of their first considerations should be, to learn the language as speedily as possible. The next question was, How was this to be done? Whether was it best for missionaries to acquire the language in the Presidency towns, and among European societies, or to go into the country districts to acquire it by intercourse with the natives? His opinion was, from long experience in the Presidency of Madras, that those who remained for any lengthened period at Madras itself had not picked up the language as rapidly as others who had gone into the interior; and, in fact, that until they had gone into the interior they possessed a comparatively imperfect knowledge of the language, and were not able to communicate freely with the multitude. He repeated, therefore, his firm belief, that if they wanted evangelists or itinerating missionaries, the more closely they were kept during their first twelve months in India to the study of the language, the better.

The Rev. WILLIAM SWAN, formerly missionary of the London Missionary Society in Siberia, concurred, to a great degree, with what had been said regarding the initiatory processes of missionary work, and the necessity of moving about among the people, in order to acquire, as early as possible, the native language. The first thing should be to acquire the language. Another point, however, should be borne in mind. They had been contemplating the missionary very much as an isolated individual, labouring in a field by himself. This must necessarily be the idea of the minds of some who themselves have been solitary in the field; but they must bear in mind, that if missions were to be conducted wisely, and with a view to great success, every mission should have a full staff of missionaries, and these men would gradually find out the department of work for which each was best fitted. The man who had the greatest fluency in the use of the language would be the best suited for the itinerating work; and he of great research, study, and learning, would be the most fitted for translating and other literary duties. In the course of years there would, in every mission thus organised, be found a sufficient number of men to engage in the various departments, and each would find his proper place and work. As to the importance of itinerating, and whether large or small districts should be occupied by those who went out, such questions would very much depend upon the varieties of place and district; and no general rule could be laid down applicable to all cases.

Rev. W. Swan.
Language the first work.
Each mission should have several men.
Variety of spheres for them all.

The Rev. P. LA TROBE, Secretary of the Moravian Missionary Society, said:—My colleague and myself being the only representatives of the Arctic missions, I beg to observe that the experience of our missionaries in Greenland and Labrador fully bears out the truth of the remarks made by the majority of the brethren here, upon the importance of missionaries going early to their work, and of giving all possible pains to acquire the language; mixing with the people, and getting acquainted with their modes of expression, so as to learn the best mode of reaching their hearts. Many of our missionaries in Labrador and Greenland have manifested very extraordinary talent in acquiring languages. Some of them have really done wonders in the translation of Scripture; but these are not always the most successful spiritual labourers. (Hear, hear.) That is a very important distinction to draw.

Rev. P. La Trobe.
Experience in Greenland.
Good linguists there.

Rev. T. Gardiner.

Itinerancies should be limited, and be repeated.

Novelty.

Patience needed.

The Rev. THOMAS GARDINER, Free Church Missionary in Calcutta, said:—I entirely agree with Mr. Leupolt, that in the work of itinerating it is desirable that missionaries should confine themselves to districts of limited extent. This plan would not, perhaps, be found the most pleasant for missionaries themselves. A missionary goes to a village for the first time, and gathers the whole people around him without difficulty; they listen; he is a stranger, or a European, and they manifest the utmost interest. "The people were very attentive," may form an entry in his journal: he sends it home, and it will probably be quoted as an illustration of success in the simple preaching of the gospel. But let that missionary go a tenth time, or a twelfth time, and I will venture to say that his visit will have lost its interest—the novelty will be worn off; and instead of their coming in crowds to him, he has to go to seek them. This is, no doubt, very trying: it is very much more pleasant to gather a crowd in a village than to go into a verandah, or into a shop, to speak to single persons. But still, in order to speak successfully to people living in a world of thought, and feeling, and sympathy, different from ours, and going there to tell them a strange story, requiring the importing of new terms, paraphrases, and words to be coined for the occasion, to get them to understand our message, it is perfectly clear that we must go to them again and again; nor must we be discouraged, though the interest they have at first, through politeness or from a sense of novelty, shown, have given way; and to carry on the work will require the true evangelizing spirit of which we speak. Therefore, I agree that if a missionary wishes to evangelize thoroughly a district by itinerating alone, he must confine himself to one of limited extent, returning thither from time to time; and go forward in the strength and grace of God, believing that he is doing God's work, and preaching his free Gospel. Leaning not upon any human instrumentality, but simply on the might of God's Spirit, I believe he will do the work of itinerating most efficiently, and, by God's blessing, with great success.

Dr. Lockhart.

Every China

Dr. LOCKHART, Medical Missionary of the L.M.S., at Shanghai, observed that he had seen a great deal of the itinerating work in China. With regard to the question of language, he believed that no missionary would be worth retaining in China who did not thoroughly learn the language. Although there might be exceptional cases, he thought that the rule ought to be strictly laid down by all Societies, that the acquisition of the language was essential; for if a missionary learned not the language, the sooner he returned home the better. *[missionary should learn Chinese.]*

With regard to itinerating, it was one of those plans which had been most blest of God in China, and had been productive of greatest success. *[Itinerancies there very successful.]* In the station where he was employed they had carried out a succession of itinerancies, which had been commenced in the first instance by Dr. Medhurst and himself in 1843, and had been continued to the present time. They had adopted the plan spoken of by Mr. Leupolt, in having one large station where there were several missionaries; *[Value of principal stations.]* and he pressed upon the secretaries and officers of Missionary Societies the great advantage of having large and efficient establishments in certain localities, with a sufficient force of itinerants to go into the surrounding districts. It was essential to observe, in regard to itinerating, that single visits were almost useless. *[Itinerancies to be repeated.]* It was by keeping up a steady succession of efforts through a district of country that the real good was done. At Shanghai they had repeated instances of the good effects which followed these itinerating labours. The missionary remained a week in one place; then went to another and another, and returned to Shanghai in the course of a few weeks; from whence he began the same circuit again. The impression was thus kept up, and at all the missionary stations of the London Missionary Society near Shanghai little churches were springing up. *[Good result.]* He had been informed by recent letters from his colleagues, that many little places and villages, with which he was well acquainted, were being brought to a knowledge of the truth; and that within a circuit of fifty to eighty miles round Shanghai little churches had been formed, which had been in the first instance gathered together by this practice of itinerating, and which were now under the care of the various native agencies. In conclusion, Dr. Lockhart observed, that at a subsequent period of their deliberations he should like to make some remarks upon the work of the medical missionary, being a medical missionary himself.

The Rev. HOPE M. WADDELL, Missionary of the United Presbyterian Church from Calabar, West Africa, said:—The circumstances of different countries and of their inhabitants are so various, that I apprehend no general rule, either as to itinerating or language, will apply to all. (Hear, hear.) With regard to *[Rev. Hope Waddell.]*

Value of central stations. itinerating, my own experience of twenty-nine years in the West Indies and in Western Africa warrants me to say, that the best plan I have found is to have a fixed centre, and make that the principal scene of labour, radiating thence in itinerancies, but consolidating our labours there. As far as we can, the visits should be regularly repeated; for with a people very low and degraded, *Visits to be repeated.* it is quite obvious that a single visit must be all but lost. They scarcely know the sound of your voice and the meaning of your words; and "line upon line, and precept upon precept," are necessary for them to know what you are about. True, they may at first appear interested, from the novelty of the circumstances, or out of the respect due to a stranger; and it may be from the hope of benefiting in some way, though perhaps not in the way you anticipate. But if you establish a central point, bring all your labours to bear upon that point, and make frequent visits to surrounding places, the work will be best accomplished. Certainly it is of the first importance that a missionary should acquire the native language as soon as possible. There are circumstances, however, in which he cannot give himself entirely to this work, and in which *Interpreters sometimes useful:* he may find it of great importance for a time to use an interpreter. I have been in such circumstances, where God has blest the labours of preaching even through an interpreter. Again, the missionary may be in circumstances where he cannot give up his own language; where, for instance, the people wish to learn his *English also.* language, and open their towns to him, and go to his school on this condition. In these cases, we go to them on certain terms, and promise to teach them English if they will learn other and better things; and in teaching them our language and our Bible, we open to them the treasures of all languages, and give them access to the literature of the world. (Applause.)

Rev. W. H. Stirling. The Rev. W. H. STIRLING, Secretary of the Patagonian or South American Mission, remarked, that what they had to consider was, not the best means in the abstract of making known the Gospel *Abstract rules not admissible; force of circumstances.* of Christ, but the best means under the circumstances. These circumstances were of a most varied character; and, therefore, although they might agree that the acquisition of a language was of primary importance, and that mingling with the natives was a work of scarcely secondary importance to the acquisition of language—and, indeed, a most essential means of acquiring the language—yet the modes of approaching the people, and communicating to them the Gospel, were subjects for very fair discussion, and involved wide differences of opinion. He was connected with a Society, the aim of which was to introduce Christianity to the aboriginal races of South America generally, but some of whose immediate objects of attention were usually considered amongst the most degraded of the human race. Their missionaries were brought into contact not only with Indians dwelling in the forest, or the plain, but with tribes who lived almost entirely in their canoes, and upon fish. Their subsistence was of the most precarious kind, and they were destitute of all the resources of civilized life. Yet, under these circumstances, the missionaries had to approach them, and, as they were destitute of written forms of language, to provide them with those forms. The present was the third attempt made to approach these people; two former attempts having been unsuccessful. The circumstances, therefore, attending these labours and modes of operation, were of a remarkable kind. Their station, and basis of operations, was in the Falkland Islands, and they approached the natives by "itinerating" in a mission vessel. They went up and down amongst the channels of Tierra del Fuego, in a vessel bearing the honoured name of ALLEN GARDINER. (Hear, hear.) In order that their efforts might be attended with more permanent advantages, they had succeeded, under God's providence, in bringing over to their station natives from those parts, who were submitting to instruction; and from whom they had acquired, to a considerable extent, an insight into the language they used. By these means the way was being prepared for future settlements amongst these people. Therefore, if any one were to apply the principles of Indian missions to the missions in these Antarctic seas, they would come, perhaps, to unfavourable conclusions. He rose, therefore, at that moment, to prevent the conclusion being come to, that no means were to be adopted under peculiar circumstances like these, except such as were successful in India, China, or Africa. It was not that he had anything specially new or important to communicate; he merely wished to point out the peculiar features of a special mission, lest principles not applicable to that mission should be adopted exclusively, and sanctioned by the Conference.

<small>Character and plans of the Patagonian Mission.</small>

<small>A fixed settlement begun.</small>

The Rev. CHARLES HEBERT, of the Colonial Church and School Society, was desirous of drawing the attention of the Conference to the immense importance of what he might call the "border-land" of missionary work, and the very great necessity which exists for remembering that every European who went to foreign countries

<small>Rev. C. HEBERT.</small>

Missions necessary among Europeans abroad.	was a missionary either for good or evil; and that, therefore, those Societies which endeavoured to promote religion among the English who went abroad, required very much of the support of the Christian community at home. He had heard, and those who had been in India would say whether it was true or not, that the success of missions in India, where numerous Europeans resided, was but small; and that the success was chiefly in the country places, where the European population were found but in a small degree.* If this were a fact, it was evident, that a Society which endeavoured to promote religion among our countrymen abroad must be of the very greatest value. He was happy, however, to be able to say, that the Government of India gave a hundred rupees monthly to every person sent out by the Society with which he was connected, who could occupy the post once occupied by a chaplain in India.
Rev. R. S. HARDY.	The Rev. R. S. HARDY said:—I resided for a number of years at the station of Negombo, in the island of Ceylon, and the way in which the station was worked was this:—We had what we called a plan, upon which there were the names of twenty-seven different
Instruction given in detail:	villages, to each of which villages we gave religious instruction every Sabbath. Sometimes a schoolmaster would read the sermon, which had been translated or written by a native assistant
in villages;	for that purpose; sometimes the village was visited by a catechist; and sometimes by what what we call a local preacher; that is, a person, permitted to preach, but engaged in secular matters during
by the missionary;	the week, and receiving no pay from the mission. Each place was also regularly visited by a missionary, so that, though the missionary could not often visit these places on the Sabbath, still he had each place in some measure under his eye, and knew what was going forward in each. By these means, each place had every Sabbath the preaching of the gospel, and the people were ac-
by native preachers;	customed to assemble in these villages in the same way, and with the same regularity, as they do in England. Those preachers who were more particularly under the care of the missionaries assembled on Fridays, and generally told us what subject they were going to talk about on the following Sabbath, and the manner in which they were going to treat it; or if such an opportunity was not presented, they told us on the Friday afterwards, so that we knew the
and by pastoral visits.	manner in which they taught the people. Then, as to pastoral visitation, the missionary visited each village in the week-day,

* Other causes, however, besides the absence of Europeans, contribute to the greater numerical success of the country missions.

taking them in as great numbers as he could, and visiting from house to house. There is not that objection among the Buddhists of Ceylon to family visitation, which there would be among the Brahmins of India and other places; during one year I have visited no less than 1700 houses belonging to the natives, and had an opportunity in each of saying something relative to the work of God, and in almost every house was permitted to pray with the people. In addition to this we occasionally itinerated in the manner adopted upon the Continent of India; but taking tours of one to two hundred miles simply for the purpose of scattering tracts and copies of the Scriptures, in places where we thought they would be appreciated and read. In some instances there are as many perhaps attendant upon the services of that neighbourhood, in proportion to the population, as in any part of England.

Visitation in Ceylon.

Itinerancies.

Again, we not only visit the people in the way we have represented, but we also meet them afterwards in what are called Classes:—that is, every quarter or so, all the communicants are privately spoken to, relative to the progress of the work of God in their souls. This is the course we Wesleyans generally pursue, and we have found that it has generally been attended by the blessing of God.

Classes.

The Rev. P. H. CORNFORD, formerly Baptist missionary in Jamaica, observed, that Missionary Societies were generally poor, and the great question was, How should the work be done with the greatest measure of success? If with small means they attempted the accomplishing of everything at once, it was evident they must fail to a very considerable extent. He was impressed forcibly with the idea that missions had been attended with the greatest success where the missionaries had gone to the very poorest and lowest of the people; made common cause with them; shown themselves to be their friends in every possible way; and thus endeavoured, as far as possible, by evangelistic labour, to spread the cause of God. The higher branches of missionary work would grow out of this. Missionaries must identify themselves with the temporal condition of the people, and the failure of missions arose, in some instances, from the missionaries themselves not going low enough, nor humbling themselves sufficiently. The missionaries in the West Indies, in the South Seas, and among the Karens, had enjoyed the greatest measure of success, but they had addressed themselves to the poorest of the people, and made common cause with them. Sometimes missionaries had been

Rev. P. H. CORNFORD.

Missionaries to work also among the lowest,

and help them in every way.

denounced for being too political; but circumstances frequently required missionaries to take a political interest in the people. This was not always necessary; but there might be occasions when it was desirable. The medical knowledge, also, with which every missionary should be invested, was one great aid to influencing the natives. The vernacular of the heart was understood in all countries. Missionaries should not regard too much their own dignity, nor endeavour to fix themselves among the people as pastors, but should divest themselves of anything likely to elevate them too far above the level of the people, and by visiting them from house to house and cot to cot, they should take every means to gather the hearts of the people, and prepare them to receive the word of God. He was desirous of impressing such considerations upon the attention of every missionary meeting and missionary secretary throughout the world.

Rev. G. Candy.

The Rev. GEORGE CANDY, of the Church Missionary Society, Bombay, was afraid that the "causes of success and failure" would not come before the Conference, unless they kept these important points more closely in view during the discussion. A residence of nearly thirty-six years in India would enable him to say something upon nearly every point brought forward, but he did not know that he could throw any new light upon the valuable suggestions already made. Certainly the impression produced on his mind had confirmed the conviction, which he before held, that, if it were possible for them to arrive at the best modes respectively of conducting the missionary work, they would be no gainers thereby. If they set themselves to make laws like those of the Medes and Persians, he was quite sure they should go contrary to the mind of God. The principal thing was for each labourer to live in daily and hourly communion with God, to be able to apprehend the will of God, and to follow that will. Alluding to the point of the reflex influence of a greater degree of vital religion among our European soldiers and countrymen abroad, Mr. Candy said that the consideration of this point would help them in a great measure to discover the causes of failure and success. It was thirty-nine years ago since he went out to India; on his arrival in the country the state of religion among his own countrymen was exceedingly low, and the success of the few missions which were established, at the lowest point: but, no sooner did it please God to begin a good work amongst the Europeans there, than it told immediately upon the minds of the people. When the

Fixed rules inadmissible.

Influence of missions on Europeans abroad.

natives had an opportunity of seeing Christianity embodied in the conversation, temper, and conduct of those who called themselves Christians, they perceived a power in Christianity which they had failed to see before. Previously they had looked upon the exhortation of the missionary, merely as the setting forth of some theory or system similar in its character to their own. The views and opinions of a native did not influence his conduct: his religion consisted in his observances, and not in his theories; and so our missionaries failed to produce much effect upon the minds of the natives, until the latter had an opportunity of seeing Christianity as exemplified in the lives of our fellow-countrymen. When first he arrived in India he was struck with the low state of religion among the English officers and gentlemen residing there. Being himself at that time in the army, he had an opportunity of observing this very closely, and of noticing the change which took place when the Gospel spread amongst his fellow-countrymen. With respect to India, he considered that the causes of failure had been very much owing to the slackness of their countrymen at home. There had not been that unremitting zeal and devotedness for the good cause which ought to have been manifested. The conduct of the British Government also had had a most important bearing upon missionary operations in that country. *Good effect of their piety on the natives.* *Other causes of hindrance.*

The CHAIRMAN observed, that they would all sympathise with and appreciate the remarks of Mr. Candy as to the conduct of professors of religion abroad being one of the causes of the failure of missions. The conduct of professing Christians had been the reproach of our religion in India. He requested that some of their experienced brethren, who had been working at home in sending out missionaries and watching their progress abroad, would bring this subject before the Conference clearly and concisely. He urged also that, in considering the hindrances to the progress of missions, we should examine whether in our own ecclesiastical systems there were any impediments to prevent the free course of the gospel among peoples who had not grown up in habitual conformity to them. *CHAIRMAN.* *Confirms Mr. CANDY's views.*

Lieut.-Col. HUGHES, Secretary of the Asiatic Strangers' Home, said:— It is a lamentable and yet an acknowledged fact, that the ungodly walk and conversation of professed Christians at home and abroad has been, and continues to be, one of the great hindrances to the spread of the gospel. From the experience I have *Lieut.-Col. HUGHES.*

had during the past five years amongst the natives of the East who have visited this country, I can bear my testimony to the fact that many of these natives have visited Christian England no less than on seven or eight occasions, and that during the time they were in this Christian land they never had a word regarding Christ or his gospel set before them. On one occasion I was making some visits in the East of London, and met several natives of India, one of whom told me that he had on seven different occasions within the last fifteen years been in England, and that he had never heard a word about Christ. On another occasion, when speaking to a native of India, I asked him if he had heard of the Gospel. He said,—Often. I said,—Where? He replied,—I heard it in Calcutta. I put Henry Martyn's Testament into his hand and asked him if he had seen it before. He said,—Yes, I have seen it and heard it read at Calcutta; but he told me that he never heard a word regarding Christ or the Gospel in Christian England. I was walking in the East of London on another occasion with a few friends, when a native of India passed us. We stopped him and asked him who he was. He told us that he belonged to the 34th Bengal Native Infantry, and having heard much of England, he had come over on leave of absence to see what it was like. He had heard great things of Christianity in England, and yet, though that man had been six weeks in London, he had never heard a word about Christ or his Gospel! He said he was acquainted with several missionaries, and with the excellent Colonel Wheeler; that he knew several chaplains and pious officers in India, who had repeatedly spoken to him of the word of God and set before him the gospel; but that he had never heard a word on these subjects in Christian England during the six weeks he had lived there. That man was a member of the Baptist communion, and a few days afterwards returned to India. What an account must he have taken back of what he had heard and seen in England! In this matter we have not been faithful to our God. We have neglected these poor men and foreigners who have come to our shores; and shame to us that we have not set before them the gospel!

I will give you another instance. In the year 1854 there were twenty-eight Tahitians cast adrift on the streets of London from two American vessels. They were found sleeping under some carts in Whitechapel by a City missionary, and a few of them were taken by a friend of my own to the neighbouring workhouse, whence they were driven away by the porter with curses. And who were these men? Why, these were the converts of the beloved and esteemed Williams. The greater portion of them had been members of a Christian church for many years. They had heard of Christian England, and had taken service in the American vessels, knowing they were coming to Christian England, and expecting to meet with Christian liberality and Christian communion. What a reproof is this to us! I trust, that what I have spoken in so imperfect a way will lead to greater efforts being made to set the truth before those who come amongst us; so that when they return to their native land they may take back with them a good report of what they hear and see in this professedly Christian country.

What we ought to do.

Major DAVIDSON, lately in the Bombay army, said:—I have very great pleasure, Mr. Chairman, in adding my testimony to that of Colonel Hughes as to the advantages which we owe to missionaries in India; at least, those of us who are soldiers. I have great satisfaction in following Colonel Hughes, for it brings back to my recollection the circumstances of my early life, when, as a very young Ensign, I commenced my career in India; and when, as perhaps Colonel Hughes himself may not remember, I was put under his immediate care as the adjutant of the first regiment in which I did duty. We have not met since then; and it affords me very great pleasure that we should meet now under circumstances like these. (Cheers.) After doing duty for a short time with that regiment, the first ten years of my career were spent in places where we had no regular chaplain. At one station there was nothing to distinguish the Sabbath from the week-day, but the flag flying from the citadel of the fortress. Now, considering that the only ministerial advantages we could enjoy were those that we received at the hands of the missionaries, I am sure it would be unbecoming in us not to testify to the great advantages which Europeans in India derive from the missionaries. (Hear, hear.) I have been at a good many stations where there have been missionaries, and have observed that some missionaries felt it their duty to act differently from others with respect to labours amongst Europeans. At one station they went professedly very little amongst the Europeans, but gave themselves to the work of the mission to the heathen. At that station there was a chaplain, whose duty it was to labour amongst the Europeans. The missionaries, therefore, confined themselves to having a weekly prayer-meeting for Europeans, and, under the circumstances in

Major DAVIDSON.

Good done by missionaries in India among Europeans.

which they were placed, I conceive they acted rightly. But it is well for Europeans in India that all missionaries do not find it necessary to confine themselves to one rule in this respect. I was at another station where there was for years only one poor feeble witness for Christ. It was visited by a missionary who made it his business to go about from house to house, and to speak to every European at the station about his or her soul. He was only three days at the station; yet the result of that visit was such, that for months afterwards there was a remarkable revival amongst the Europeans there. There were meetings at each other's houses for prayer and reading the word; grace was said at the mess-table; and after the mess a few of the officers would retire to each other's houses, to unite in the reading of the word of God and in prayer. These same officers were wont to meet every morning also at eight o'clock, for the same purpose. This all resulted from the visit of a missionary which extended over only three days. He certainly had his heart in his Master's work, and he made us feel so; for he left the most precious savour of his presence behind him. (Cheers.)

Example.

The Rev. J. H. TITCOMB, Secretary of the Christian Vernacular Education Society for India, said he was perfectly satisfied that the remarks of Colonel Hughes with regard to the reflex influence of the conduct of our countrymen in India upon the natives, formed a painful, but most true and melancholy commentary upon the *apparent* inefficiency of our own mission work. What struck him, however, as the most important of all was, that they had not in their various Missionary Societies depended sufficiently upon native agency. The subject of vernacular preaching was fundamentally important; and in connexion with it he would, therefore, beg to refer the Conference to a report of the South Indian Missionary Conference, where a paper was read by the Rev. J. Scudder of the Reformed Protestant Dutch Church of America, who in his remarks on vernacular preaching endeavoured to show in strong terms, that one great advantage of that system of missionary labour was the indirect manner in which it tended to foster a native pastorate. It appeared to him that, if in the itinerating preaching of their missionaries they were to gather together their most useful converts, take them with them, and use them as adjuncts for their own work for the sake of preparing them for, and instructing them in, the duties of the pastorate, they would not only do a good work in this way by their own labour,

Rev. J. H. TITCOMB.

Importance of training a native pastorate.

but they would be preparing indirectly, and building up the foundations of a native church, which might afterwards be successfully carried on by the labours of those native pastors. By means like these, he believed that missions would be endowed with much greater success, and under God's blessing they would be enabled to leave the work to others, and plant in India, America, and Africa an indigenous church, which would be the only permanent hope of Christianity in those lands. (Applause.)

The Rev. Dr. O'MEARA said:—I rise to mention a circumstance bearing on this most important subject. We have all heard of the visit of the Ojibbeway Indians to this country, thirteen years ago. Some two years ago, in the performance of my duty as superintendent of Indian missions on Lake Huron, I visited a very flourishing mission on the banks of the St. Clair river. The missionary there, who has been most successful and laborious, told me, that there was one Chief over whom he had no influence whatever, and he said, "I think that you, from your greater acquaintance with the language, and much longer experience amongst the natives, will have some influence with him; and I beg, therefore, that you will go and see him." I went to see him, and entered into conversation with him, talking to him about his opposition to Christianity, and asking his reason. It turned out that this was the very Chief who had been in this country at the head of the body of Indians who were brought over by a white man, an adventurer, for his own purposes, and that he might make a show of them. He said to me, "Your missionaries are always telling us that there is no way like your own way. You tell us that the people across the Great Salt Lake, where the sun rises, hate our ways and dislike them. I went over there with my people, and we were very well received and treated; but we never heard of those things of which the missionaries are always telling us." He said, very shrewdly, "People don't usually pay for what they dislike. You tell us that we are superstitious; that our war and medicine-dances, and so on, are bad things; that they are from the Evil Spirit, instead of from the Good Spirit; but the people of England don't seem to think so, for they were very glad to see us dance our scalp and war-dances, and see us do all the things you spoke so much against. I cannot, therefore, put any confidence in what you say, having seen such a different state of things from what you describe." Thus much, Sir, for a visit to Europe on the minds of those Indians! I will mention another fact, in *and in their own country.* reference to the effect of the character of Europeans on the natives in their own country. I remember an Indian chief on Lake Huron who had given special opposition to the Christian work amongst his people. I visited him, and I spoke my mind to him very freely, telling him that it was not so much a love of his own superstitions, as a love of the fire-water, that made him dislike the mission; that he wished to have his young men join him in his drunken frolics; and did not wish them to become Christians, for he knew that if they became Christians they would cease from such doings. I shall never forget the way in which that Indian chief drew himself up to his full height, and the look of scorn with which he regarded me when he said, "Is it you, a white man, who address me in that style? Who brought the fire-water to us? We knew nothing of it till you came amongst us; we ate the flesh of the deer; and when we had got enough of that, we went to the edge of the lakes and rivers and drank our fill, and it did us no harm: but you white men came with this fire-water in your hands. We thought it strange, bad medicine, at first; but you told us that it would do us good, make us happy and joyful, and we took it and drank it. It did make us very happy and joyful; and since then we have liked it, and we will have it whenever we can get it. If you want us not to take the fire-water, go and tell your own people so. We cannot make the fire-water; if they don't make it, we cannot get it; and if they don't bring it amongst us, your work is done: but teach your own people about it first." (Applause.) There is another matter also I would wish to mention. It has often been said that commerce is the handmaid of religion; but I am sorry to say, that amongst the North American Indians commerce has proved the enemy of *Opposition from traders.* religion, and the missionary has often to become the enemy of the trader. The trader finds, that when the Indians are Christianised they become civilised; that their minds are improved; that they begin to know the value of their own wares; that he cannot carry on so profitable a trade; and, therefore, he hates and abhors the progress of Christianity, because he cannot put so much of this world's pelf into his own pocket. The missionary, therefore, has often to stand in opposition to the trader, in the defence of those whom the trader injures in their temporal prosperity.

Rev. J. B. Whiting. The Rev. J. B. WHITING, Central Association Secretary of the Church Missionary Society, remarked, that he did not quite like the word "failure" in the programme. (Hear, hear.) It had been his duty, as an advocate of the Church Missionary Society, to plead the cause of missions in various parts of England, and he had endeavoured to acquire some information as to the amount of success with which God had blest missionary efforts. He found that the Bible had been translated during the last sixty years into upwards of 100 languages. There were 100,000 professing Christians in New Zealand; 100,000 in Burmah and Pegu; 112,000 Protestant Christians in India; 5000 or 6000 in Mesopotamia; 250,000 in Africa; 40,000 in America; and 250,000 in the islands of the Pacific. There were Christians in China, Madagascar, Mauritius, and many other parts of the world. There were 200,000 or 300,000 Negroes under the care of Christian pastors in the West Indies. There are more than a million and a quarter of living Christians who, but for the labours of the missionaries, would all have remained idolaters. We were apt to compare the missionary successes of the present time, in disparaging terms, with the successes which attended apostolic labour. He had inquired, however, from the most competent authorities, as to how many individuals, in their opinion, were gathered out of heathendom by the labours of the inspired apostles during the first sixty years of mission work, after the Ascension of the Saviour; and he had been assured that, as far as they could judge, not more than one million of living Christians were found after those first sixty years. They must remember also the hundreds of thousands who were now sleeping in their graves round the mission churches; and how many had gone to their heavenly home from far-distant recesses of heathendom, who were never known to the missionaries, but who had learnt from tracts, Bibles, and other means, of the salvation which is in Christ. (Applause.) Then, again, the 1600 missionaries, who had gone forth from Europe and America, were now accompanied by more than 16,000 native ministers, religious catechists, Scripture-readers, and schoolmasters, who were evangelising their own fatherlands. The native ministry, moreover, had passed into the second generation; and from our schools and orphan-asylums the native apostles would arise, whose crown of rejoicing would be multitudes of Christian converts. They ought not, therefore, to indulge in a spirit of despondency, but rather lift up their hearts in devout gratitude to Almighty God, for the great success with which he had so far blest missionary labours; and indulge in the joyful hope of still greater blessings in days to come. (Applause.)

Marginalia:
- Has there been failure at all?
- Great number of converts in modern missions.
- Our success equal to that of the Apostles.
- Number of Native Agents.

The Rev. Dr. Somerville trusted that one effect of their proceedings would be to encourage their esteemed brethren labouring in the mission field; and though they produced no other effect than this, they would have to thank God and be grateful that they had come together. It was most desirable also, that the results of their proceedings should be of a practical character, and influence the whole church. There were various reasons for missionary success as well as for failure, arising from the peculiar habits of the people amongst whom the missions were planted. To these he would not advert. They must all recognise, however, this most important principle, that "it was not by might nor by power, but by the Spirit of the Lord of Hosts," that the work was to be done. It was the province of God to make a new creation as he made the first; and whatever causes they might assign for success, they were all secondary to the work of the divine and gracious influence. He was forcibly impressed with the thought that there was a most intimate connexion between missionary success and the state of the home church. Missionaries were messengers of the churches: they went to do the work of the home church. Now he was afraid that the home church had satisfied itself too much with the position of merely sending forth the men and giving them support. He had been looking into the Scriptures closely of late, and he was prepared to make this statement—and if his brethren should hesitate about it, he asked them to consider the matter and examine it for themselves. The statement was this, that there is not, in the word of God, an intimation of very rapid success in the extension of the Gospel, that is not preceded by an account of the revival of religion in the home church; and that, on the other hand, there is not, as far as he had been able to ascertain, a statement of the revival of the Church of God, of the manifestation of his gracious presence and of the outpouring of his Spirit, that is not succeeded by an account of the rapid extension of the Gospel. Now, if this be true, how were they to get success abroad? They must begin at home. They must get their own hearts warmed. They must plead with God with the urgency of Jacob for the conversion of the heathen. He was satisfied, that if the home churches were to realise their responsibility, were to plead with God and to give him no rest upon this point, they would hear of the most glorious results in all parts of the earth. Having alluded to the recent revivals, Dr. Somerville said he rejoiced in the movement which had thus spread, believing that from it would go forth an influence which would animate and make more productive all other religious movements. Since this revival movement had taken place, he had not had a letter from a foreign missionary in which joyful reference was not made to the fact, and in which thanks were not given that the home church was holding up the hands of the missionaries and helping them in their work; and in which anticipations were not expressed that the blessings which God was pouring out over this country would soon reach the most distant lands. Let us impress upon the home church that the salvation of the world is within their reach. There were persons who said that the success of missions had been very limited and very small. Let those persons be told that they were themselves responsible for such comparatively small results; that the fault was their own, and not that of the missionaries; that the missionaries were labouring nobly, zealously, and with great self-denial. Let the home church be told that, if they wanted to see a harvest waving with holy grain, this would only be the result of an increased spirit of prayer and vital godliness manifested by the whole church. *Revivals at home bring revival abroad.*

The Rev. Dr. TIDMAN.—We have heard a great deal about the failure of missions, but I have yet to learn, Sir, where missions have failed. I have yet to learn, that in any region where the great command of Christ to preach the Gospel has been carried out, and where this has been accompanied by humble dependence and earnest prayer, there has been failure. I assent, of course, to all that our friends have said, that there are grievous impediments to success. That is one thing; but, when we saw evil and only evil sown, no wonder that the fruit was bitter and deadly. No wonder that, when our countrymen, calling themselves Christians, went to India, and lived as heathen, they confirmed the heathens in their heathenism, and impeded the progress of better men. But nevertheless, Sir, have we not proved to-day that the carrying of the Gospel to India by our missionaries has done much for our own countrymen? (Hear, hear.) Do we not know that there was a period within the lives of some present, when an eccentric, but good man, advertised for a Christian in Calcutta; and do we not know now, have we not heard to-day, that our excellent friends, both military men and civilians in India, are some of the most valuable auxiliaries the missionaries now have? (Cheers.) People from India, no doubt, come to the east of London and see *Rev. Dr. TIDMAN. Has there been failure? Success among our own countrymen.*

much vice and very little good; but that is not sufficient to prove the failure in missions. Considering the amount of work we have abroad, the limited agency we have employed, and the comparatively recent period in which this great work has been accomplished, we have had a measure of success, that has far exceeded the sanguine expectations of the fathers and founders of modern Protestant missions; and that should make all our hearts rejoice and give thanks to God. (Applause.) If we want more success, our first duty is with ourselves, for we lie under serious responsibility. I agree with Dr. Somerville, that the Church at home has not done its duty to our missionary brethren abroad; that we have not sufficiently considered their difficulties and discouragements; not sufficiently prayed for their prosperity and success; and therefore, Sir, sin lies at our door, which no parade about our liberality and zeal will by any means counterbalance. But as regards the general view of the mission-field, let me remind you that within the last fifty years the Gospel has been carried from England and America, and from a few Protestant Churches of Europe, to almost every region of heathenism. And tell me where it has failed. Why, we heard just now from Mr. Whiting, that in the islands of Polynesia more than a quarter of a million of human beings — if they could be regarded as such before the Gospel reached them—cannibals and murderers, have been brought under its influence, and elevated not only to civilisation, but in some instances to the highest forms of Christian excellence. A Christian friend once told me that, when he first went to Polynesia, a man lived near him, who in the days of his heathenism was often seen with a piece of human flesh attached to a hook, and thrown over his shoulder; he knew not how many he had slain; and all, or nearly all, he had destroyed, not from a spirit of revenge, but from a love of human blood. That man lived to be a teacher of the Gospel, and to exhibit it in some of its most refined amenities. (Cheers.) In all the missions of Polynesia— and you will remember, almost every missionary institution has its missionaries there — there has been a greater amount of success than has attended the labours of our brethren elsewhere. (Applause.)

When we look to India, that most difficult of all missionary fields, especially remembering what it was half a century ago, has there been failure in India? (No, no.) I won't talk about the number of professing Christians,—from 120,000 to 130,000,—but we have had specimens of Christianity among the natives lately that may well make us ashamed. Don't we know that during the mutiny, whilst some nominal Christians denied their faith rather than submit to the fearful consequences which a confession involved, there were Christian natives, men of yesterday, mere babes in knowledge and faith, who laid down their lives gladly for the sake of the Lord Jesus Christ? (Applause.) Sir, I admit, many of these heathen converts are very deficient in knowledge and defective in character; but don't I learn from the Epistles of the New Testament that that is one of the inseparable adjuncts of a recent redemption from heathenism? Do our missionaries find in their churches at this day any crimes and weaknesses which are not marked in those inspired letters? But although in some respects they bring with them these early disadvantages, they bring with them also the freshness of that new nature and the vigour of that Divine life which God has imparted to them. Let us not talk about failure, when we have such instances of primitive power and Christian dignity as we have lately seen upon the plains of India. *The recent martyrs.*

Look to Africa, and thank God the different parts of Africa are dotted almost everywhere with the results of missionary efforts, and look at those churches which have been under cultivation more than twenty or thirty years. Has there been any failure there? Is it not true that one of our honoured brethren —the friend of my early age and still my friend, now I am no longer young—Robert Moffatt, when he plunged into the deserts of Africa, did he not find a race of the most degraded and savage creatures which could possibly be pictured to the imagination? He went amongst them as their friend; lived with them as one of themselves; learned their language from their own lips; then gave it back to them in a written form; and now he has lived to present to them the Word of God, translated, and printed, and published in South Africa, by his own immediate influence. Now, there are hundreds and thousands of those people who were at first astonished at a letter, and thought it a spirit, who can read intelligently — more so, perhaps, than many around us — the Word of God, which they love and which they honour. (Applause.) I want to know what we ought to have expected, Sir, beyond the success which we have had? Had we done more we should have had a larger reward. If we send more men, the harvest will be greater. I thank God, too, that we have had such agents as He has given to us; that we can point to men of our own country and time with delight and thankfulness, whom God has made not only faithful, but learned, and great; and *Success in Africa.* *Moffatt's work.* *Character of missionaries who have laboured.*

<small>Hard work remains.</small> that he has given us men for every kind of work which the circumstances of the Church demand. Let us persevere in the spirit of cheerfulness, confidence, and gratitude. Don't let us mourn over obstacles and temporary obstructions. These are what we must expect to meet. If this world is to be evangelised, it must be by hard struggling and long-continued toil. But let us toil on, and in twenty years to come we shall find,—at least, those of my young friends who may see twenty years hence, will find— that the seed which is now sowing for the second or third time will bring forth corresponding results; and it may be our happiness to look down from a brighter and better world, and find our joy even there augmented as we witness the growing splendours of the Saviour's kingdom in this lower sphere. (Loud applause.)

The following Minute on this discussion was unanimously adopted:—

MINUTE ON MISSIONARIES AND THEIR PLANS.

<small>The missionary's character.</small> The members of this Conference consider that in all systems of missionary labour, the gravest importance should be attached to the position and the personal character of the European missionary himself. It appears to them a wise general rule, that every missionary on going abroad should at once endeavour to attain a thorough knowledge of the language, manners, customs, and religious views of the people to whom he is sent; and that he will best do so by entering into close, constant, and personal intercourse with them. They consider that he should strive to adapt all his plans to the circumstances and condition of his sphere of labour; but that whatever forms his plans may assume, his aim should ever be, as directly as possible, to convey the Gospel of divine grace into the minds and hearts of those whom he instructs. Amongst those plans they regard the work of preaching the Gospel to the people in their own tongue as one of primary importance, whether carried on by European or native agents. While recognising the necessity of maintaining fixed stations in important localities, they consider that a missionary should not tie himself down to pastoral work, except in the infancy of a mission; and that he should always aim to make his labours tell upon the

<small>Language, &c.;

how learned.

Adaptation of his plans.

Aim one.

Preaching.

Stations.</small>

heathenism of the country. While he preaches constantly in a *Itinerancies:* fixed station, they think it well that at favourable seasons he should itinerate in the more retired and ill-instructed districts. Such itinerancies they reckon as of high value in spreading sound *their character.* scriptural knowledge, and preparing the way for a future extension of the mission by the establishment of new stations. But to be effective, they should be systematic, limited to a comparatively small district, carefully carried out, and repeated again and again.

Medical missions they consider a valuable auxiliary to the direct *Medical missions.* work of the gospel, in densely peopled countries, as China and India, where deep prejudices against its teachers may be removed by their means, and where medical aid is largely needed. But every medical mission should be a Christian mission, and faithful instruction should ever accompany the humane work of the physician.

They learn with pleasure that, though not primarily sent to *Efforts among Englishmen.* their countrymen abroad, the occasional labours of missionaries in English congregations have been blessed to their spiritual good; and have in many countries tended to diminish the hindrances to the gospel found in the lives of ungodly Europeans.

In looking at the results of the Christian missions carried on *Results of modern missions.* during the last sixty years, and to the high position which they have now attained, they record with adoring gratitude that, notwithstanding their own imperfections and shortcomings, the Lord has blessed them with great success. They pray that all impediments existing to the progress of the gospel abroad may be entirely removed; and that the Church at home may be largely revived; while the glory of all that has been accomplished they humbly ascribe to the Spirit of grace, under whose ministration this work of mercy is carried on.

The Conference concluded the morning session with prayer.

SECOND SESSION.

TUESDAY AFTERNOON, March 20th.

AFTER dining together at the *London* Hotel, the Members of Conference re-assembled at Hope Hall, at four o'clock;

MAJOR-GENERAL ALEXANDER in the Chair.

After prayer had been offered by the Rev. W. SWAN, the following Programme of discussion was taken up:—

Programme. *Subject:* HOW BEST TO STIR UP, DIRECT, AND WORK, THE MISSIONARY FEELING AT HOME.
A Missionary Intelligencer. Missionary Periodicals.
Correspondence of Missionaries with University Prayer-Unions, and Missionary Associations in their Native Towns.
Deputations.
Juvenile Associations, and Missionary Effort on the part of the Young.
A Professorship of Missionary History at the Universities.

At the call of the Chairman, the following paper was then read by its Author:—

ON THE BEST MEANS OF EXCITING AND MAINTAINING A MISSIONARY SPIRIT.

BY THE REV. T. B. WHITING, C.M.S.

Missionary spirit defined. By a missionary spirit is to be understood, not that cold acknowledgment of the duty which unlocks the purse at stated intervals; but such an interest in the cause as will ensure self-denial in its behalf; make it an object of frequent thought and deep affection, and a principal topic in prayers and thanksgivings. The question before us is: How can we most effectually increase the number of individuals animated by such a spirit, and the number of churches thoroughly identified with the work?

The object of our missionary enterprise is the ultimate ruin of the empire of Satan by the establishment in every heart of the throne of the Lord Jesus. The human means for accomplishing this object is the proclamation, in all its simplicity, of that gospel which is "the power of God unto salvation to every one that believeth;" and which we are bound by the command of the everlasting God to proclaim "for a witness to His Name," and "for the obedience of faith." It follows, that none but the subjects of divine grace can be animated by a true missionary spirit. The increase of the missionary spirit, therefore, depends upon the number of *truly converted* hearts. Therefore every labour for the advancement of true religion, and all that tends to excite and maintain a spirit of vital godliness and living faith, will tend to excite and maintain a missionary spirit; and although a revival may not be attended by an immediate increase in the aid afforded to Christian missions, yet such revival will speedily multiply the zeal, the self-denial, the money, the men, the missionary prayers and thanksgivings, which indicate the existence of a spirit of aggressive Christianity in a church, and in individual disciples of the Redeemer. *Its subjects.*

Its manifestations.

But, like every other Christian grace, the missionary spirit needs to be fostered in the hearts of God's people. It is only too sadly true, that the intensity of the *existing* missionary spirit is utterly disproportionate to the number of true believers. Thank God, there are Christians fully alive to the missionary obligation! Thank God, the number has largely increased of late years; but where are the churches filled with burning zeal and unceasing prayers? *To be fostered.*

Some of the following suggestions may commend themselves to the minds of one and another of those who desire to foster the missionary spirit:—

1. We must exalt the missionary spirit to its proper position, on an equality with other Christian duties; as, for instance, with prayer. Active hatred to the reign of sin is a part of holiness. Self-denying effort to win sinners from sin and eternal death, is an important element of charity. It is not something which we may or may not do, but which we must do. It is a means *Exalt missionary duty.*

of grace to ourselves, and essential to the fulness of spiritual life.

Foster it in pastors;

2. We must fan the flame of missionary zeal in the pastor. Can an icicle light a fire? If the pastor feels no warmth of missionary zeal, his attempts to arouse the hearts of his people will fail. If he knows and cares little about the work, his people will be in like case. (May I not add, that much the same may be said regarding the influence of the pastor's family?) "People will always give to the missionary if the parson do uphold them." It is of great importance, then, to omit no exertion to influence the minds of the students in our theological colleges, that the future pastors may have a lively interest in the cause.

in laymen.

3. We should neglect no opportunity of winning the interest of influential laymen. Each Christian should strive to impress his or her own family. The best means of doing this will be, not to weary unwilling listeners with the whole of a periodical, but to read privately the Records, &c., to mark the most interesting facts, and to bring these *regularly every month* before the family. If this can be done on a stated evening, so much the better.

Information to be sought by all.

4. Whoever, pastor or layman, desires to excite, and especially to maintain, a missionary spirit in others, must strive that his own love for the cause should increase, and seek to have an intelligent knowledge of the mission-field, both as it *has been and as it is*, so as to be ready to impart information and meet objections. It is mournful at a missionary meeting to hear a pastor or Christian say,—"I really can give you no information. I will, therefore, make a few general remarks." Every heart animated by a thorough missionary spirit will bring especial details from the mission-field before the throne of grace. We should earnestly recommend the practice to our friends; it will deepen their love for the work, maintain their missionary zeal, and greatly tend to spread the missionary spirit.

A catholic spirit.

5. We must be careful lest we seem to work for a system, a particular Society, or a party, rather than for the advancement of the Redeemer's kingdom. We ought to have a *reasonable* preference for the Society we support; but nothing will more certainly damp a rising feeling of missionary interest than an unkind display of feeling against, or even a forgetfulness of, every other institution except our own. While nothing elicits a more cordial response than an appeal which manifests a catholic spirit.

By prayer.

6. Private prayer. The Christian grace of a missionary spirit is eminently a work of the Holy Spirit upon the heart; and then

shall we most effectually labour to inspire missionary ardour, when we labour upon our knees in our closets, praying that our God would reveal even this unto those who do not adequately feel the obligation.

7. The pulpit affords the opportunity of making the subject familiar to the people by frequent allusions. For instance, by illustrating our subject by incidents from the mission-field. Many a sermon might thus be enriched, and afford interest, and arouse the attention of fatigued listeners. These allusions should be very frequent. It is not enough to have an annual sermon to excite a transient enthusiasm. The missionary idea should be a ruling principle in the mind of a preacher. *In the pulpit.*

8. The friendly and social intercourse we have with our neighbours affords many opportunities of introducing the subject, and supplying the lack of information which exists so widely. Missionary evening parties might be gathered, and thus throw a fresh interest into the communion of saints. *In society.*

9. Newspapers afford a very powerful means of spreading widely missionary information. Incidents and facts introduced into newspapers, would catch many an eye which would never look upon a missionary periodical. *The press*

10. Missionary periodicals should be circulated in book-clubs, and in every possible way. They should be written in a thoroughly interesting and clear manner, and contain not merely dissertations, but histories, memoirs, and facts. Letters from the mission-field should contain incidents and descriptions. We cannot, of course, expect that incidents of an interesting character will always be at hand; but our dear brethren will, I trust, pardon my mentioning the matter. The nature of the communications required is well described in a few admirable lines in Mr. Mullens's *South Indian Missions,* a book worthy of wide circulation. "To understand a mission thoroughly, we should know something of its locality; the people among whom it is carried on; their former condition and history; their habits of life; the history of missionary effort among them; its discouragements and pleasing features; its present character and fruits." P. 91. *Missionary periodicals.*

11. Reading-books, &c., used in schools of all classes, have been almost entirely overlooked as a means for carrying out our object, but they might become a most abundant and powerful channel of information. Introduce missionary scenes into the reading lessons; circulate quarterly tokens, instructors, and picture-cards. *Readers in schools.*

Prints.

12. Larger coloured missionary prints might also supplant "the unseemly relics of depraved and immoral art" upon our cottage walls, and finely-drawn pictures might lie upon drawing-room tables. The pictures should always be true scenes, and not creations of the fancy. For the originals of these we must look to our friends abroad.

Missionary meetings.

13. Missionary meetings were held in apostolic times, and the missionary speeches of Paul and Barnabas caused "great joy to all the brethren." Some have called missionary meetings necessary evils. They are evil, if badly conducted. But when a holy spirituality pervades the speeches, and when facts of an interesting character are related and recent information given, they have continually proved to be blessed means of grace, and powerful agencies for exciting and maintaining a missionary spirit. This result is in accordance with the constitution of the human mind, which God has made very sensible to the sympathy of numbers, and peculiarly apt to be influenced by the living voice. Thus information is largely imparted, and burning zeal enkindled, which will afterwards seek to interest others.

Information to be given.

What is wanted on these occasions is—not orations—nor portions of sermons—but short affectionate appeals, clear statements of missionary principles, and, above all, a simple answer to the question, "What are you doing? What is going on now in the mission-field?" The living missionary can best give this answer with reference to his particular field. Those who have studied missionary records can do it in a more comprehensive manner. We have much *accessible* information from missionaries.

Facts, facts.

If the advocates of missions would study, dig out, condense, arrange, and relate the facts and incidents within their reach in the various periodicals, missionary meetings would exercise a more pervasive influence upon society at large; and it ought to be impressed upon Christian laymen, and especially upon ministers of religion, that it is a duty to spend a few hours every month in the acquisition of this information, that they may always have "something to say."

Dull speakers not allowable.

Let no consideration permit a defective speaker to weary an assembly; and I venture to think that we ought never to ask any one to preside, however influential in other respects, who is not himself truly a Christian. I will also add, that it appears to me that a very sad tendency exists to make the cause depend upon the presence and advocacy of great and popular men, rather than upon its own merits. There is too great an eagerness to have a "well-known

Are "great men" needed?

man," or a person of distinction. *This may create a transient excitement,* but the cause of missions must depend upon its own greatness, and its own sacred and intrinsic interest.

Will it not be well to introduce a larger element of prayer and praise into our meetings?

14. The last remark is especially applicable to the quarterly, or more frequent meetings. It might be well to bring the cause of missions monthly before a congregation: such a meeting might last an hour, or an hour and a half—a hymn, a prayer, a portion of Scripture, a short comment, an address of twenty minutes, a hymn, and a prayer embracing the topics alluded to, with a collection, would form the programme of such a meeting. The address might relate in successive months the missionary work in Benares, Liverpool, Sierra Leone, Madras, London, Tahiti, &c. These more frequent meetings are necessary. It is not enough to stir the flame of missionary zeal once a-year. Dissolving views of missionary scenes might be *occasionally* introduced. *[Meetings more devotional. Information to be given on system. Dissolving views.]*

15. Lecturers before literary societies have abundant opportunities of alluding to the missionary work.

16. Ladies' missionary-working parties are an important means of enlisting sympathy in the cause. They should always begin with prayer and a portion of Scripture, and the passages read should be well selected and interesting. *[Working-parties.]*

17. Juvenile Associations are especially important, not only on account of the large sums they produce, but also because they early enlist the sympathies of the heart. *[Juvenile societies.]*

18. Every Association should be, if possible, thoroughly organised. It should have a president, secretary, treasurer, and committee; and the members of such committees should be regularly supplied with all the important recent information, even when it is not possible to obtain frequent meetings of committee. *[Organisation.]*

19. Increase the number of families and parishes represented in the mission-field. A representative returning home and telling his fellow-parishioners and companions, what "Christ hath done by him, to make the gentiles obedient by word and deed," will wonderfully excite and cherish the missionary spirit. The friends of missions should bear this always in mind, and keep their eye upon promising youths, aiding them by counsel and instruction to prepare to offer themselves for the work. *[Youths suitable for mission-work.]*

20. A great impediment to the diffusion of a missionary spirit is to be found in the irreligious conceptions which so lamentably prevail, as to the proportion of money to be devoted to the service *[Christian liberality.]*

of the Lord. This is a large subject and cannot be more than touched. But we should labour to inspire the Christian Churches with the glowing ardour of devoted affection, which will impel them, "whether they eat or drink, or whatsoever they do, to do all to the glory of God." It is the duty of every pastor to give his flock frequent opportunities of contributing to the great cause, and to leave to the people the responsibility of not giving.

But, after all, we return to the statement already made,—that it is to the increase of the converted people of God, and to this alone, that we must look for an enlarged missionary spirit. It is the humble believer who exclaims from his heart,—

> "Jesus, I love thy charming name,
> 'Tis music to mine ear;
> Fain would I sound it out so loud
> That earth and heaven might hear."

May God, for the sake of our Lord Jesus Christ, be pleased to pour out his Holy Spirit, and cause a great revival of true godliness throughout all Christian Churches. Amen.

Rev. J. Gabb.

The Rev. JAMES GABB, Domestic Chaplain to the Earl of Carlisle, was desirous of bringing before the Conference two suggestions, and of ascertaining the general feeling with regard to them. The first he made at the request of the Rev. C. Hodgson, Rector of Barton-le-Street, who had for twenty-five years been a diligent and successful advocate of the interests of the Church Missionary Society in the north of England. He believed the period had arrived when a weekly penny missionary newspaper, containing selections from all the Protestant missionary publications of this country and America might be published with advantage and success. It would be Catholic in spirit, and greatly conduce to Christian union; and there was sufficient room for the dissemination of such a periodical, without interfering with existing denominational publications. The periodicals at present circulated were thought to be imperfectly read by many; perhaps because the details they contained were too diffuse, and required a more minute acquaintance with foreign countries, their geography, politics, &c., than most readers possessed. The newspaper, however, which he proposed, would contain the cream of such publications; and if published at a low price, and perhaps illustrated, would be acceptable to a large body of poor people in the country and elsewhere, who did not read the publications themselves. Such people, for the most part, took in their Saturday

A penny missionary newspaper.

penny newspaper, containing the news of the district in which they lived, and would be glad to read an intelligible periodical giving the missionary news from abroad.

The other suggestion he had to make was, that the missionary work might be greatly advanced amongst the higher and more intelligent of the middle classes by the publication of a first-class *Quarterly Review of Missions*, devoted to the discussion of all those subjects which had brought this Conference together; and in which men of ability, experience and piety, might advocate their views in regard to the home and foreign operations of Missionary Societies. Christian missions in all ages; the condition and relations of ancient and modern churches; missionary biographies in connexion with the work; special features of particular missionary fields; heathen systems of religion and philosophy; books of travel, and the like,—so far as these cross the path, or affect the proceedings of the missionary—might be discussed with great advantage to the Committees of the various Societies, to missionary students, and to the missionaries themselves. Such a Review would afford the means of discussing critically, comprehensively, and philosophically, all the secondary influences which affect and determine the religious faith of men, and would be read by a numerous class of persons well disposed to the mission cause, who would be more interested in that cause, if they had its principles and proceedings brought before them in a higher form than is done in the monthly publications and occasional meetings of the year.

Missionary Review.

Its topics.

The Rev. H. M. WADDELL observed, that some of the missionary periodicals were very admirably conducted, while in some, perhaps, there was room for improvement. They had, in the North at least, a monthly missionary newspaper, called the *News of the Churches and Journal of Missions*, very much like what had been suggested. A quarterly missionary review, however, was still very much wanted, and had been long, in his opinion, the desideratum of missions. Our literary men would not read the *Missionary Monthly Intelligence;* they were ignorant of the facts contained therein, and yet they expressed low opinions of the work which influenced multitudes of minds. They themselves required to be enlightened; and if they could get the facts, and arguments, and philosophy of missions, set forth in a first-class literary style, in a Review which would command its position in the country, no doubt these men would read it. This was so

Rev. H. M. Waddell.

A good Quarterly wanted.

important a subject that he hoped a Conference like this, comprising the representatives of all Societies, would not break up without resolving to have a first-class missionary publication for the review of all topics bearing upon missionary operations, which were now a power in the world, and should be worthily exhibited.

<small>Rev. Dr. BAYLEE.</small>

<small>The same.</small>

<small>Our human systems:</small>

<small>shaped by controversies.</small>

<small>Human nature to be studied.</small>

The Rev. Dr. BAYLEE had a very strong opinion as to the want of a first-class missionary publication. He had now under his training fifteen missionary candidates, and the number was steadily increasing; and he felt very greatly the want of some assistance, such as a first-class periodical of this kind would afford. He cordially agreed with the observations which had fallen from the Chairman as to the defects of our human systems of theology. The attention both of Christians at home and missionaries abroad had not been sufficiently directed to this point. He deeply felt that our theological systems—and he did not except the Church of England—were the products of controversy; and had, in consequence, departed from the simplicity and fulness of the teaching of the Bible. A large proportion of the Thirty-Nine Articles were chiefly anti-Romish, and bore the impress of a controversial age. The *Westminster Confession of Faith* and the *Assembly's Catechism* partook too largely of scholastic and controversial features to be fit instruments for presenting Christianity to the heathen world. He would go farther, and venture to say of that magnificent confession of our faith, the Athanasian Creed, that even it, gloriously true as it was, wanted that scriptural simplicity in which the Apostles presented Christianity to its first converts. It was not that he doubted the truth of any of these documents; he was prepared to defend every statement in the Thirty-Nine Articles and in the Athanasian Creed; but they presented Christianity from the view of its historical and controversial development; and if we were to win the world over to the faith of Christ, we must go amongst the heathen with the simplicity and fulness of the Word of God itself. All human systems of theology presented not Divine truth, but human views of Divine truth, and therefore partook of human infirmity. God would bless His own word as our simple and all-sufficient standard. Another great want with regard to the missionary work, was the want of a scriptural study of human nature. We sent out men primed with texts of Scripture, and well primed also with the ecclesiastical systems of the different schools, but knowing very little indeed of human nature as the Bible presented it to us. Having expressed the pleasure which he felt at meeting with the Rev. Mr. Hardy, whose works he had read with so much profit and satisfaction, Dr. Baylee alluded to Mr. Hardy's able work on Buddhism; and related an anecdote of a discussion between a Buddhist priest and a Christian missionary, in which it was doubtful which had the best of the argument. The missionary was thrown away from his texts of scripture and his theological systems, to discuss the best condition of human nature with regard to God, to eternity, and to the subjugation of the human will. He was not prepared to meet his opponent. In conclusion, Dr. Baylee observed, that a periodical which would deal with subjects of this kind, in a large and not a textual sense, but in the true spirit of the Bible, would be of great use in preparing an elevated class of Christian missionaries. (Applause.) *[Instance.]*

The Rev. J. WALLACE, missionary of the Irish Presbyterian Church in Guzerat, said;—I think it is exceedingly important in directing public feeling at home upon the subject of missions, that the public should be enlightened as to the nature of the mission field. A great many people in thinking of heathenism, and, I fear, sometimes even the advocates of missions themselves, just think of it in the mass, without drawing a distinction between one mission field and another. Now, in foreign missions there are two great fields; one where there are people of organised systems, based upon pretended revelations, and the other where they are in a state of comparative barbarism, and in a great measure unsophisticated. It will be found, I think, that hitherto the great success has been amongst the comparatively barbarous people; and, therefore, it is of great importance that the public at home should be thoroughly enlightened upon this point. Dr. Tidman has well said that India is probably one of the most difficult mission fields in the world, just because there we have a regularly organised system: the people feel that they have something to defend, and that they must give up something if they accept the Gospel. We find the same in Buddhist countries. I was much struck with an observation in the life of Dr. Judson, bearing upon this point. In tracing the great success of missions among the Karens, as compared with their success among the Buddhists, he said that the Karens were like men with empty vessels, that only wanted filling; while the Buddhists had vessels to empty, and they were most unwilling to do so. (Hear, hear.) It has been mentioned that a missionary in Ceylon, in disputing with a Buddhist, had really the worst of the argument. I think, therefore, that in missionary periodicals, special attention should be drawn to the character of the subjects in the different fields, and the character of the qualifications which those who work in those fields should possess: and, in the same way, that the public generally should be enlightened on these points. If this were the case, we should not find parties, as I believe is sometimes the case now, speaking of the want of success in India. We should remember that in India we had a citadel of sin, and that in the South Sea Islands there existed only some of Satan's outposts. (Hear, hear.) The Church at home should feel this, and, when they go to take the citadel, it should be with determination. They should endeavour to increase the number of agents, and, in particular, should feel the necessity of special prayer in behalf of such places. When they speak of the difficulties connected with the spread of the gospel in India, in Buddhist countries, and where the Mohammedan delusion prevails, they should bring this difficulty to the throne of grace, praying for a special outpouring of the Spirit of God. (Hear, hear.) I would also suggest that those who labour among the Buddhists, or Mohammedans, or Hindoos, should feel the necessity of specially qualifying themselves for the work, by learning the nature of the system with which they have to contend. We are not to suppose that the Spirit of God will supply those defects in our labours which arise from our own indolence and want of preparation for the work. I throw out these hints, rather for the guidance of other speakers; and, in conclusion, I will observe that, in the conversion of foreigners generally, the great distinction between the mission fields themselves has been very much overlooked, in speaking of the success in some, and of the want of success in others.

The Rev. G. D. CULLEN here read a brief paper forwarded by Mr. Douglas of Cavers, observing that Mr. Douglas was a munificent supporter of missions; that he had published on the subject long ago; and had furnished the article on "Missions," to the *Encyclopædia Britannica*. (For the paper read see Appendix.)

Mr. CULLEN said:—The hints which their esteemed friend had thrown out in his paper illustrated the advantage of a well-conducted and well-supported Quarterly Review. Objections to multiplying periodicals had often been made, and the opinion had been expressed—an opinion with which he sympathized— that it would be much better to get missionary intelligence diffused through existing periodicals than to institute a new one; but the idea, which had been so well suggested, was to bring out something like the *Calcutta Review*, in which might be published well-prepared articles on the philosophy of missions.

Existing periodicals may be used.

The Rev. Mr. WHITING, referring to Mr. Douglas' desideratum, said the Church Missionary Society were about to publish the contents of the works of Dr. Pfander.

The Rev. THOMAS SMITH:—My attention has been much turned to the subjects introduced into this paper—namely, the pulpit, the press, and the platform. I shall confine myself now, however, to the subject of the press. I think the tone of the discussion indicates that there is a felt want in regard to this matter. There are various classes of existing periodicals, general and denominational. I have not seen them all; but of those I have seen, I should—being about to pronounce a pretty sweeping sentence of condemnation—except one—the *Church Missionary Intelligencer* —which is, I think, a really good publication. Be it understood, I have not seen all; but, with that exception, I think they will be found to fall very far short of what such publications ought to be. The information they contain may be, on the whole, correct. They give statements, but they give no idea whatever of what is going on in the mission field as a whole; and it is sometimes impossible to make out anything intelligible by putting their statements together. You read in some of them, that at some place with an unpronounceable name Mr. So-and-so had baptized ten converts; and that, perhaps at some other place ten thousand miles off, some other person had baptized three other converts. Now, I beg to suggest that that is not missionary intelligence to any practical or useful purpose. And this is very much the character of most of the denominational periodicals of this kind. Mr. Whiting, in his paper, threw some of the blame on the missionaries for not sending more information; but the greatest share of the blame is not due to them, but to the fault, or rather the misfortune, of the editors to whom that information is sent, and who do not know in what way to make a good use of it. (Laughter.) The result is, in point of fact, that our denominational missionary periodicals are not read to any great extent, and I believe the reason is, that they do not deserve to be read, and ought not to be read. This may

Rev. T. SMITH.

Missionary periodicals generally very poor.

Often not intelligible.

seem strong language, but it is a subject on which I feel very deeply: I think it is one which lies at the root of the whole matter with respect to the future prospects of Christian missions.

The press moves public Christian opinion. The press is a most powerful agency in bearing upon public opinion; and Christian opinion is public opinion; and it is upon Christian opinion, feeling, and sentiment, that the success of missions depends. (Hear, hear.) It is in direct proportion to Christian sentiment and Christian feeling with regard to missions at home, that there will be success with regard to missions abroad. I do hope, therefore, that this subject will occupy a very full share of attention not only here, but when the members of the Conference return to their own homes, and that they will bring their influence to bear on our denominational bodies with respect to it. This kind of publication, after all, in the special circumstances of the Church, is fitted to be most effective. There is something in the denominational feeling which we may regret or approve. There are differences between us, and they do affect us so that people will, whether they wish it or not, take more interest in the missions to which they themselves subscribe, and which are con-

Our periodicals should be improved. ducted according to their own views, than in others. Therefore, I think the time has not yet come to give less importance to the denominational publications, or to abolish them; and that being so, I do hope that a vigorous effort will be made by the various Churches for elevating, and for improving their various denominational periodicals. The only really good one I am acquainted with is, as I have said before, the *Church Missionary Intelligencer.* I do not mean to say that it cannot be made better; but it may be taken as a sample, and the others have a very great stride to make before they come to its level. Perhaps by that time, it will also have taken another stride in advance, and I hope it may. (Hear, hear.) When all this, however, has been done, there remains the other question of a more important kind of

Former proposed Quarterly. periodical, which should discuss principles, and contain articles of length on subjects bearing on missions. I recollect a very distinguished man in the literature of our country,—Mr. Isaac Taylor —sent a detailed prospectus to India, about 1844 or 1845, proposing to establish a Missionary Quarterly, and requesting contributions. Not being in this country at that time, I do not know why it was not set a-going; but I suppose there was not found sufficient pabulum, either in the way of contributions of literary matter, or sufficient support of a pecuniary kind. But, if this were the case then, I hope it need not be the case now, because it was stated this morning that the number of missionaries during the last fourteen years has been about doubled. I am sure the interest at home has also been doubled during that time. And the time must have come now, if not then, when a man like Mr. Isaac Taylor, or some other giant of our literature, might consecrate his strength to the diffusion of information, and the elucidation of sound principles through the medium of such a publication. For practical and immediate purposes, the daily press is the most powerful engine; next, the weekly; and then the monthly; and I suppose it is to these we must look, at present, as a kind of smaller musketry: but still we should bring the heavy cannon of the quarterly press to bear, in order to demolish the strongholds of prejudice and ignorance at home. I never thought before of the points mentioned by Mr. Waddell, in regard to the training of missionaries by the press, but it seems to be a very important question. At a meeting, in Edinburgh, some months ago, I expressed a hope that one result of this Conference would be the establishment of such a periodical as that which has been now suggested. If such a periodical is to originate in the Conference, as I certainly hope it will, I beg to say to all our Liverpool capitalist friends, that we want no help from them. (Laughter.) If it succeeds, it must succeed simply and entirely by its own merits, and not by being propped up with contributions. No publication can do good, unless it pays itself by circulation. Recollect, we are not begging for such a publication. If it cannot help itself, let it fare as it deserves. *Why not establish one now.*

The Rev. Dr. SOMERVILLE submitted that it was scarcely fair in Mr. Smith to condemn a class of publications *en masse*, without giving their names or stating how many he had read. He had excepted one for commendation; and he thought that, as Mr. Smith had stated that he had not read all, he was bound in equity to specify those which he considered unworthy of being read. He felt personally interested in this matter, being himself an editor (laughter); though he felt satisfied that Mr. Smith's statement could not apply to his publication, which had a circulation of upwards of 40,000 copies, and which he had reason to know, was generally read. If such sweeping condemnations as Mr. Smith's went abroad, they could not fail to injure the various missionary publications. *Rev. Dr. SOMERVILLE objects to Mr. Smith's censures.*

The CHAIRMAN reminded Dr. Somerville that Mr. Smith had *CHAIRMAN.*

been speaking in all the freedom and confidence which was particularly desired. He had spoken, not of persons, but of things. Of course Mr. Smith had spoken generally. (Laughter.) A publication, like Dr. Somerville's, with a circulation of 40,000, was excepted.

Rev. Dr. TIDMAN.

The Rev. Dr. TIDMAN,—Sir, it falls to my lot to conduct one of these publications; and my great relief is, that our good friend, who is the censor, does not take the trouble to read what he condemns. That goes a great way to neutralise the force of his censure. (Hear, hear, and laughter.) There are more than 200,000 of these monthly missionary periodicals circulated by the different societies; and it is worthy of grave thought whether anything should be said in this Conference tending to depreciate that means of extensive good. It may be all very true that there are many gentlemen like the speaker, who look upon these *penny* publications not with favour; but there are hundreds of thousands of our cottagers and villagers, and others, who look upon these penny publications with great interest, and whose missionary life depends upon their contents. Now, as we depend for our funds upon the many, and not upon the few, I submit it would be an injurious influence, which I should be sorry to see go forth from this Conference, if anything should tend to depreciate the value of that, which in its place is truly good and essentially needful. With regard to that higher class of periodicals, it is nothing new to many in this Conference. My friend opposite (Dr. Steane), and other gentlemen now present, were engaged fifteen years ago in securing the services of Mr. Isaac Taylor for this quarterly periodical; and it was no fault, either of those who planned, or of Mr. Taylor, who was ready to undertake it, that it was not carried into effect. Much as our friend, Mr. Smith, despises money, the fact is, that want of funds was the cause of that failure (laughter); and if you are to depend, at the outset, upon the merits of that kind of work, you will never secure it from one year to another. There is a great difficulty in getting these periodicals up the hill; though, when they attain the acclivity, they may go on pretty well; still, it must tax the pockets of our Liverpool friends, and other friends, too, to raise the sum of 5000*l.* as a minimum to establish a quarterly publication of this sort. And when you have got the money, where are the men to conduct it with efficiency? Nothing is more difficult than to conduct our Quarterlies; and were it not

Value of the regular missionary periodicals.

Difficulty in the way of the Quarterly.

Money required, and men.

for the great interest put forward to support them, who knows which would fall first?

The Rev. F. TRESTRAIL, Secretary of the Baptist Missionary Society, observed, that he had taken a lively interest in periodicals connected with the religious body to which he belonged. Take, for instance, the *Baptist Magazine*. He invariably found amongst his brethren a class of gentlemen who were extremely literary, and loved everything that was highly intellectual, polished, and refined. This class did not like the *Baptist Magazine*; they always condemned it; but they never read it. This was true also with periodicals, which represented their missions. Their friends of this class did not read them; that was the fact. The great bulk of the support of all Societies came from the mass of the people; the Bible Society not excepted. It was the mass of the people who read these things. Some years ago, in consequence of the great difficulty experienced in getting the publication into the hands of their friends, their quarterly paper was put an end to; but a year and a half ago, they got the consent of their committee to re-establish it; and now, through the medium of the book-post, they could send considerable quantities for a penny. They announced through their magazine, and through their secretaries and collectors, that these publications would be given away to every subscriber of one penny a-week. During the first quarter they had only applications for 3000, but now the demand had gone up to something like 12,000 or 13,000. It was increasing every quarter; and he had no doubt that in a short time it would reach 25,000. They knew that it went into the hands of the people; for, unless they wanted it, and felt an interest in it, they would not have it.

The editors were charged with not knowing how to use the information communicated to them; but they did use what they got. They did not manufacture the facts, nor trust to their imagination for the things recorded. They certainly exercised their discretion as to what proportions of the communications they used; and sometimes it required a glossary to unravel the difficulties and changes in the technical terms employed. To his knowledge, the spelling of the word "Koran" had altered half-a-dozen times within eighteen months, and they were obliged constantly to send out to the missionaries to request them to use those terms with which people were now familiar at home.

With respect to the order in which the information was generally placed in the periodicals, he could state that it was placed in a definite order; that India, Africa, and the West Indies, had their respective positions; and that there was never a jump of ten thousand miles from one sentence to another. He thought that Mr. Smith's condemnation was much too sweeping. He thought that this great publication—the proposed Quarterly Review— could only be for the few. A large number of persons could not be influenced by it. Even if launched, and supported by all the talent that the Church could afford, it would not reach the great mass of the people, in whose hearts they wanted to keep alive the love of God and pity for dying men. The editors would be glad to receive suggestions; and he begged to assure Mr. Smith that, if the missionary papers were not interesting, it mainly arose from the fact that their missionary brethren abroad did not take sufficient pains with their communications; while their friends at home were too apt to expect that their missionary intelligence was to be filled every month with something marvellous and extraordinary. It was unwarrantable, however, to suppose, that they should have to detail more marvellous results than occurred at home, unless, indeed, they wished to put their missionaries to fighting tigers and rhinoceroses. With regard to the pictorial illustrations, he believed that, for the most, they had been faithful and authentic.

R. A. MACFIE, Esq. said,—They had been told that missionary publications are not read by certain classes in society, and it was important to reach them. He did not think the want was so much in the quality of the publications as in the way in which they were made use of. He thought the primitive system, oral communication of intelligence, was the Christian system and the prudent system. The principal place which these periodicals ought to occupy, was, in his opinion, that of providing ministers with information, which they in their turn might communicate from the pulpit on the Lord's-day forenoon. The true use of missionary periodicals was to supply the means of giving to the people, in this way, information of what the missionaries were doing. He himself subscribed to a considerable number of periodicals, whose excellence he did not doubt: but he knew little or nothing of their contents, for he did not read them; and busy people could not be got to read them, as they might not find time to look at them on week-days, and on Sundays they were occupied with Sabbath-schools, their families, and other duties. The only way to reach the hearts and minds of the people was by the minister of each church reading information to his congregation. These sentiments were not entertained by himself alone. They had been brought before the Missionary Committee of the church to which he himself belonged, and they received such favourable consideration that it was proposed to ask the Synod to sanction a publication of a character somewhat different from those which now existed. It was suggested not to issue this periodical in any bulky form or at any regular interval, but as an "occasional paper:" if there was only little to say, to say that little, issuing for instance only half a sheet, and even that, only when there was matter to communicate: this publication would be sent to the ministers of the several congregations, to be read publicly at ordinary diets by authority of the Synod and its Mission Committee. There could be no objection to a paper of this kind being read from the pulpit on Sunday forenoons.*

marginal notes: Printed papers should be statedly read on the Sabbath. Periodicals proposed for the purpose.

The Rev. Dr. TWEEDIE, although belonging to the same church as Mr. Smith, differed from his brother upon the present occasion, and that very widely. He saw, moreover, one or two editors present, modest men, who were in the habit of hiding behind the majestic monosyllable WE, and who might be shy of speaking for themselves. (Laughter.) He might be allowed to mention, therefore, what took place with reference to periodicals in the section of the church to which he belonged. They had a *monthly*, with a circulation ranging from 20,000 to 23,000 copies,—not a very large circulation, but still leavening a goodly number of thousands with the truths which the missionaries conveyed. They had also a quarterly publication. Mr. Smith might undervalue it in a literary point of view; but the matter which it contained was just such as that esteemed brother himself was accustomed to send home when he was a missionary far away in India. (Laughter.) Of this about 95,000 copies were circulated every quarter, and if they thus reached 95,000 persons with only one sound idea, they would do some good. (Hear, hear.) He quite agreed with Dr. Tidman with regard to the larger periodical, and had done what he could to promote its establishment many years ago. Could it be revived he had no doubt it would be productive of great benefit to the missionary cause; and for this reason, that the ideas which came to govern the public mind were first planted in one mind, or two, or twenty, and were thence conveyed to the minds of the masses; and could they work out strong and

marginal notes: Rev. Dr. TWEEDIE. Defends the Free Church periodicals. The quarterly advisable, if practicable.

* Sanction has since been given.

powerful thoughts about the missionary cause through some high-class periodical, and get it to bear with all its weight in high quarters, he had no doubt that, beginning with the higher minds, they would work downwards, and so influence myriads of the minds of the country. Mr. Smith had discountenanced pecuniary contributions for such a work, but he (Dr. Tweedie) had no doubt that contributions for it could be got up before the Conference closed, if it were thought desirable. He was quite sure that if such a periodical could be started, of which he was far from sanguine, it would do good in the sphere to which it would be limited, perhaps five or six hundred being, he feared, its maximum circulation. He would not, however, have it for a moment supersede the smaller and simpler class of publications.

Rev. T. Smith.

The Rev. THOMAS SMITH explained that he had distinctly stated that the smaller periodicals must be the great means of influencing the people. It was to the improvement of these publications that he was directing his attention, and the establishment of the other literary undertaking he regarded as a secondary, though still a very important matter.

Rev. T. Green.

The Rev. T. GREEN would follow up the remarks of Mr. Macfie, which he deemed exceedingly important. He believed that if they wished to influence and direct aright the public feeling with regard to the missionary work they must adopt the suggestion which Mr. Macfie had made, particularly in the use of the pulpit; for it was marvellous how little the pulpit was used in reference to that great object. If they looked at the New Testament, they would be surprised at the amount of missionary intelligence which that portion of the word of God contained, when contrasted with the very slight references to missionary matters which the pulpit, in the present day, generally gave forth. He would not allude to the missionary journeys of our Lord, narrated in the four Gospels, nor to the details of missionary journeys in the Epistles; but looking at the Acts of the Apostles, which was from the beginning to the end a missionary record, he asked if they had ever considered how large a proportion the Acts of the Apostles bore to the whole of the New Testament? They would find that it was one-eighth part of the entire book which was thus taken up by a missionary record; what proportion then did the missionary work bear in their own pulpit discourses to this New Testament proportion? Mr. Macfie had stated that persons like himself rarely perused the monthly, or even the quarterly, missionary

The pulpit ought to be used more largely.

The "Acts" one-eighth of the N. T.

publications, and that if they were to be made acquainted with them at all it must be from the lips of their pastors. When he (Mr. Green) had charge of a parish, some time ago, he was in the habit of directing the thoughts of his people to missionary subjects on the Sabbath-day, at stated intervals, exactly in the way described: sometimes speaking of one mission and sometimes of another, and he could truly say that much more interest was excited whenever that Sabbath came round than by the ordinary ministrations of his Church: for thus a pleasing variety was imparted to those ministrations, at the same time that he was carrying the introduction of the missionary element prominently into the pulpit. The effect of this and of other measures which he adopted with the same object in view was the formation of a missionary association, and from 30*l*. which they raised in the first year they went on increasing, from time to time, until in the last year that he was there (ten years altogether) they were able to send up to the funds of the Parent Society a sum of 200*l*. He thought that this was mainly due to the giving of information from the pulpit in the way already referred to. He should state further, that the congregation consisted almost entirely of operatives, and contained only some half-dozen persons of moderate or affluent means.

His own efforts in this way.

Their result.

Adverting for a moment to the subject of periodicals, he might remark that members of the Church of England had no reason to complain with respect to their treatment at the hands of Mr. Smith, for he had spoken very kindly of their *Missionary Intelligencer;* but, much as he (Mr. Green) valued that periodical, he felt that it operated on a very small portion only of their contributors, some 3000 copies being sent out every month, while they had 60,000 contributors, whose names appeared in their Annual Report, and probably 600,000 contributors, whose names never appeared in any Report, contributors of their pence, their halfpence, and their farthings, weekly, to their missionary work. (Hear.) They wanted to influence these 600,000 minds, and the only way of doing this was by giving them something in the shape of a halfpenny or a penny periodical. He knew that the little *Juvenile Instructor*, unpretending as it was, had been the means of sending many a missionary student to the College at Islington, where he had become fitted for the labours of the missionary field. Other missionary publications were filled almost entirely with communications from their missionaries abroad. Until he read these publications, he (Mr. Green) had regarded them as unin-

Need of good and cheap periodicals for the many.

teresting. (Laughter.) He would recommend Mr. Smith to read the two last Numbers of the *Church Missionary Record*, the numbers for February and March, and he had no doubt that he would then admit that he had had a rich spiritual treat. They contained a most interesting communication from the Bishop of Rupert's Land, as well as other communications of great interest, from Africa and elsewhere.

<small>Rev. C. Hebert.</small>

The Rev. C. HEBERT, in reference to the best means of stirring up the missionary feeling at home, observed that nothing had been said about missionary prayer-meetings. (Hear, hear.) He was inclined to believe that they had come to a time in the history of the Church when prayer would exercise a greater influence than it had yet done; it was one of the peculiar features of the present time that people came together gladly and regularly for prayer alone. This was a most mighty engine that ought to be enlisted in the missionary cause to a much greater extent than it had been hitherto. One of our great Missionary Societies, during the past year, had determined to call special attention to this subject; and its rolls, which before, were almost destitute of candidates for the missionary work, were suddenly replenished; so that when its friends met together to consider what they should do, their minds were filled with gratitude, and the language of scripture was put into their mouths: "Before they call I will answer; and whilst they are yet speaking I will hear." (Hear.) He believed that if the authority of this Conference were given to the establishment of missionary periodicals, either monthly or quarterly, and of missionary prayer-meetings, they would gain a new fund of strength, and secure a blessing from God, which would tend more than anything else to the increase of the missionary spirit.

<small>Prayer to be employed.</small>

<small>Example of its results.</small>

<small>Rev. Canon Woodrooffe.</small>

The Rev. Canon WOODROOFFE, of Alton, Hants, wished to say a word by way of supplementing Mr. Green's remarks. He regarded it as one of the best means of gaining support among the working classes, to have periodical meetings of a devotional character, and to make those meetings the means of disseminating missionary information. It had been his practice for years to assemble his people thus once a-month, for prayer and reading the scriptures, and for communicating missionary intelligence upon scriptural principles. He had found no lack of heart or interest among his congregation with reference to the smaller missionary

<small>Periodical meetings.</small>

publications. The little children came eagerly for their *Juvenile Instructors*, and the working men for their quarterly papers, and they might depend upon it that whenever the work was taken up in earnest in centres of this kind, a blessing would be sure to follow.

The Rev. S. HISLOP advocated the formation of Missionary Associations, which should meet quarterly, for the reception of missionary intelligence, for the giving of contributions, and for engaging in united prayer. He had enjoyed the privilege of forming such a Missionary Association in a locality recently blessed by a remarkable outpouring of God's Spirit; and he had had the happiness of witnessing the lively and earnest interest with which poor fishermen, who had only recently themselves tasted of the grace of God, had entered into this grand work of diffusing that salvation, which they had thus experienced, over the whole world. He (Mr. Hislop) gathered fresh encouragement to go forward in his work, from the knowledge that these men, who knew what prayer was, were meeting together for the promotion of this great missionary work.

<small>Rev. S. HISLOP.</small>

<small>Interest in missions among the pious poor.</small>

Colonel LAVIE observed, with reference to the circulation of periodicals, that in the neighbourhood in which he himself resided, —Blackheath, Greenwich, and Deptford— there was a good work going on in this respect. Last month he had been asked to preside at a missionary meeting of the children composing a Sunday-school, gathered in from the Ragged Schools of the neighbourhood. The missionary boxes, with the contributions of these children for the three previous months, were opened at this meeting; and, to his astonishment, in farthings, half-pence, and pence, the collection amounted to no less a sum than 4*l*. 1*s*. 1½*d*.; and on inquiry he found, that the interest of these children had been brought about to a very great extent through the reading amongst them of this *Church Missionary Juvenile Instructor*, known by them as the "good green book," and by other similar simple publications.

<small>Col. LAVIE.</small>

<small>Periodicals. Instances.</small>

Lieut.-Col. HUGHES observed, that he had been permitted some six years ago, to establish a Juvenile Association in St. John's Wood, which now numbered upwards of 2000 members, and which had contributed altogether during the last six years a sum of 1200*l*. In order to show the remarkable interest taken by Sunday-school children, — the children of the poor, in the work of Christian

<small>Lieut.-Col. HUGHES.</small>

<small>Juvenile associations, their extent and usefulness.</small>

missions, he would mention the fact, that in no single instance, during the six years, had he received less than 40*l*., and, in two instances, he had received upwards of 50*l*. in pence, halfpence, and farthings, from Sunday-school children. He had circulated monthly, during the six years, at the rate of never less than 500, but usually from 600 to 700 copies of the *Church Missionary Juvenile Instructor* and the *Gleaner*. He had received on an average 3*l*. quarterly, or thereabouts, for these publications; for they held their regular quarterly meetings, and this money came, not from the rich, but from the poor Sunday-school children. When he told them that 63,000 copies of the *Church Missionary Juvenile Instructor* were circulated monthly, chiefly among the poorer classes of society, and that contributions were received by the Church Missionary Society in small sums from the poor amounting to 20,000*l*. annually, he was sure they would say that a great evil would be done if the circulation of these admirable publications was in any way curtailed. Although a publication of a higher order might be required by persons in the higher ranks of society, yet it would be doing a great injury to the missionary cause if these little penny publications were to be put a stop to. (Hear, hear.)

_{Great value of the missionary periodicals.}

The Rev. HAMILTON M. MACGILL entirely agreed with those who thought that a periodical of a higher class would be of immense service: and with respect to the inferior class of publications being more widely circulated, he believed it was quite possible to show, that contributions to missions had increased in proportion to the circulation of those periodicals; the diffusion of missionary sentiment creating a demand for missionary publications, and the publications, in their turn, ministering to that sentiment, and leading to larger and more liberal contributions. He could name a church—the United Presbyterian Church—consisting of 157,000 communicants, in which 74,000 copies of periodicals are circulated and paid for by the readers, monthly. When the circulation of these periodicals began, the missionary contributions of that church amounted to about 5000*l*., whereas now they had reached 25,000*l*. a-year. Facts like these threw some light upon the usefulness of this minor class of publications in the advancement of the cause of missions; for in that cause the contributions had increased *pari passu* with the increase in the circulation of the periodicals. There were one or two other matters bearing upon the missionary spirit in the Church at home to which it was

_{Rev. H. MACGILL.}

_{Liberality grows with information.}

_{Example.}

desirable to look. He believed that in proportion as men worked out the missionary principle in their own lives, in that same proportion would they be able to induce others to go along with them, either in the way of personal exertions, or of contributions to the cause of Christ. He believed, however, that the work must begin with the pastors. Those most emphatic words, which formed the very jet and essence of their commission, "Go ye into all the world, and preach the Gospel unto every creature," must be better understood. The pastor must "go" himself, and work the work of a missionary, as he had opportunity; and acting thus himself, he would be led to employ his people in the same way, giving them all an inducement to work for the cause of Christ. The great missionary lesson must be learnt by personal work. "If any man will *do* the will of the Lord, he will *know* of the doctrine:" and in proportion as he carried out into his personal life and labours the true missionary spirit, in that same proportion would he be blessed, in inducing others to go along with him, and to join with him, both in prayer and in Christian contributions, for carrying on this great work. Christian contributions must be regarded as being as certainly Christian, and as certainly devotional, as any other act of the Christian life. And until their people thoroughly understood this, their efforts to enforce the habit, and the duty, of Christian contribution on their respective congregations, would never be attended with full or perfect success. Both in the Old and in the New Testament this duty of Christian contribution was presented as matter of worship. In the 72d Psalm, they were told, "And he shall live, and to him shall be given of the gold of Sheba. Prayer also shall be made for him continually, and daily shall he be praised." Thus the giving of gold and prayer were spoken of in the same breath by God himself. In this matter of giving, much depended on the circulation of ideas, the old idea being, that a man might give a gift to the cause of Christ, provided he happened to be in particularly good circumstances. A friend of his had recently waited on him, and made an offer of 1000*l*. for missionary objects upon certain conditions. A relative of this kind donor, shortly afterwards, waited on him, and cordially agreed with him in saying, that the very *idea* of giving a a thousand pounds to the missionary cause was worth *ten* thousand. He was persuaded that they were ruled very much by the ideas that were abroad; and it was important to recollect that these missionary publications had, during the last twenty years, been circulating the thoughts which had resulted in these large gifts. He found, from an article in the *Encyclopædia Britannica*, that the missionary contributions of all Christendom, in behalf of heathendom, amounted to about 600,000*l.* a-year, excluding contributions made to Bible Societies. He believed this was an under statement. But, even supposing that the real amount was 1,000,000*l.* there were a hundred men in Christendom who ought to give every farthing of that amount, leaving the missionary contributions of all the rest of Christendom entirely out of the account. (Hear, hear.) We were now only at the beginning of the work. When God saw the Church to be prepared for it, he would put more substance into her hands; and when she had more life, she would obtain more means in the shape of Christian contributions for carrying on this great work. The great want of the Church, indeed, was more life. And when she had more life she would have more prayer and larger contributions. They had special reason to thank God for the revival with which he had visited many parts of their country. That very morning he had opened a letter in the Conference, telling him of a most striking revival of religion which, during the past week, had taken place in one of the towns of the North, and which was deeply impressing the people there. If this movement were to extend over the country; if there were more life and Christian exertion in the Church at home; they would very soon find that God would pour a larger blessing on the heathen world; and the type of Christianity, which existed at home, would, if they thus laboured, be reproduced abroad. (Hear, hear.)

The Rev. P. LA TROBE thought that all the three methods of circulating missionary information, which had been recommended, were very desirable and could not be dispensed with; yet a quarterly journal of a higher character would be a great addition to missionary literature. He (Mr. La Trobe) was one who assisted at the consultation with Mr. Isaac Taylor, fifteen years ago, and could confirm Dr. Tidman's statement as to the causes of its failure. He, however, quite agreed with those who thought that only a small portion of those interested in missions would be benefited by such a periodical. They could not altogether dispense with their present quarterly and monthly missionary journals, though such publications might doubtless be improved, and greater discrimination exercised in selecting the matter. He felt, however, especially as regarded ordinary and juvenile readers, that they would sustain a very great loss—a loss, of which they would feel the consequences—were they to put a stop to these periodicals. Their missionary brethren and sisters abroad, to whom these publications were fraught with instruction and interest, would sustain a serious privation, and have just ground of complaint, were they withdrawn. It was most important also, to bring missionary information more frequently forward from the pulpit, and that periodical meetings of Associations should be held; advantage being always taken, when possible, of the presence of missionaries visiting Europe, and of such as had retired from active service. They would all agree as to the necessity of more fervent, united, and continuous supplications at the throne of grace. Periodical prayer-meetings on behalf of the missionary work would do much to increase the zeal and interest of congregations at home, and to edify the hearts, and support the efforts, of missionaries abroad. *The pulpit. Meetings. Prayer.*

The Rev. J. ANDERSON, formerly of Calcutta, said, that since his return to England, he had felt very deeply how necessary it was for ministers in this country to hold up distinctly, prominently, and constantly, the idea that every member of the Christian Church, be he great or small, had a work to do with regard to the conversion of souls. First, with regard to his own household; secondly, amongst his companions and fellow-countrymen; and thirdly, amongst the heathen. It was preposterous for the treasury of the Lord to be filled with contributions for carrying the gospel to distant parts of the earth, from individuals who were not known in any way to manifest a warm love for Christ and his gospel in their hearts and lives. He wished therefore to know the mind of the Conference upon this point. If the treasury of the Lord was to be filled, in order to carry on his work, should it not be by the Lord's people offering spontaneously and entirely from their own hearts that which their love of Christ and their appreciation of the glorious gospel led them to give. *Rev. J. ANDERSON. All gifts should come from spiritual men.*

The Rev. J. TOWERS, of Birkenhead, approved very much of the suggestion of a weekly newspaper or periodical, which should bring before the churches the great mission work which was going on in all denominations. It was hard for a minister to make bricks without straw, and in giving information once a-month on missionary subjects, he had often felt this difficulty; whereas if *Rev. J. TOWERS. A weekly newspaper very desirable.*

ministers were supplied on Saturday morning with a missionary newspaper, giving an account of what was going on in various parts of the world, they would be able to warm and interest the hearts of their people in the missionary cause, and a prayerful and liberal feeling would be established. He greatly preferred this proposal to that of the magnificent quarterly. (Laughter.) Working men with their wives and families would value such a newspaper, and soon consider it a necessity; while the acquaintance which it would bring about, amongst Churchmen and Dissenters, would be in itself a happy and important feature of its position. By being thus mutually informed as to what was going on in their respective churches in the department of missionary operations, much of denominational exclusiveness and ignorance would be dissipated.

<small>Rev J. FORDYCE.</small>

<small>Good to get missionary information into existing papers.</small>

The Rev. J. FORDYCE, late of Calcutta, thought it very desirable to have a quarterly review of missions, but did not approve of the proposal for starting a missionary newspaper. The *News of the Churches and Journal of Missions*, which was already established, and was not denominational, answered very much the purpose which had been suggested by Mr. Towers. It would be better he (Mr. Fordyce) thought, though perhaps more expensive, to infuse more of a Christian spirit into the cheap newspapers already existing, than to establish a cheap missionary newspaper. They might have a quarterly for a higher style of missionary periodical. He thought it would be well also if the editors of their denominational publications could keep in view the remarks and criticisms which had been made, as much good might be done in this direction. When he himself was in India, he had little cause to complain of with reference to his communications not being published; though he did hear those who had been longer in the country, and who were more experienced, complain of the treatment which many of their letters had received at the hands of editors. A complaint he heard more than once, was this:— That there was too much culling of the bright paragraphs from the missionaries' letters, and too much repressing of those things which they wrote in the agony of their hearts. (Hear, hear). He wished particularly to draw attention to this, because when travelling at home in support of missions, he had found good reason to believe, that those passages which indicated the trials of missionaries were just the passages to quicken the missionary spirit and to draw forth missionary prayers. With regard to

<small>Bright paragraphs in missionary letters.</small>

<small>Trials of missions stir up prayer.</small>

deputations, though large deputations no doubt did a great deal of good, he wished to call attention to a humbler class of deputies and localities. He had often found after his return home, that in large towns a missionary from India was a very frequent visitor; but, that in going to remote and country places, crowds were collected by the visit of an Indian missionary, who had perhaps never been seen before, and enthusiastic and successful meetings were held. He believed if some of their friends from abroad or missionaries at home, who had strength for it, would go round in this way to some of those country towns, many fresh springs would be opened up, which, although not very productive in money, would be fruitful in prayerful interest, and perhaps result in more real benefit than did the great public meetings in some of our provincial towns. It was most important that the interest amongst the juvenile portion of the church should be thoroughly maintained and encouraged; not only from the value of the juvenile offerings themselves, but from the fact that these children would be amongst the chief supporters of missions some ten or fifteen years hence, and that many from amongst them might yet go forth as the messengers of the churches in heathen lands.

Missionaries should visit villages as well as towns.

Importance of juvenile societies.

The Rev. J. MULLENS, alluding to the remark made by Mr. Whiting as to the character of the communications sent home by missionaries, said that he and his missionary brethren present would be glad to receive any hints that their experienced brethren at home might give them, as to the kind of letters they should write and the topics which they should discuss. The fact was, that all the details of missionary life became so familiar to them, that things which a stranger would regard as of great interest, they were apt to pass over as an ordinary matter not worth describing. He had been quite astonished to find how references to Indian customs, and to the details of Indian life, which they in India passed over as ordinary, attracted considerable attention among friends at home. With regard to Deputations, he thought that it was well for missionaries, when they came home, to receive a few hints upon this subject. Many missionaries had made the mistake of confining themselves, in their sabbath services and even on the platform, to addresses enforcing the duty of carrying on missions, and the like. These general topics the people say they can hear discussed by their own ministers at any time; but from a missionary, whether on the sabbath or on other days, they like

Rev. J. MULLENS.

What point should missionary letters dwell upon.

Missionary deputations should give facts.

to hear everything he can tell them of what his eyes have seen in the work of the Redeemer abroad. He thought it both right and wise for all missionaries, when going through the country as deputations, to keep this desire in mind. He had himself made mistakes in the matter at first, but latterly had made it a rule to bring before his audiences the facts of Indian missionary life, the history and prospects of various fields, and striking incidents that had occurred. He had found that their friends felt a deep interest, not only in the successes, but also in the discouragements, of missionaries. He never found that the relation of cases, where the hearts of missionaries had been grieved by the open and avowed apostasy of some of their converts, did the slightest injury to their interest in the mission cause; for they showed to their friends the true character and difficulties of the mission work; they showed how it was carried on now under the same conditions, as was the work of our blessed Lord himself, and of his Apostles, who met with the same discouragements. Some persons have, indeed, spoken in disparaging terms about the relation of stories at missionary meetings; but while they would all object to pander to a morbid appetite for stories about alligators, monkeys, and tigers, stories about converts were only instances of Christianity individualised. Such were the stories of Cornelius, of Lydia, and of the Gaoler. The way in which the truth worked and brought forth its fruit was illustrated by these details of individual life in the New Testament; and what could the missionaries do better than adopt the same course? It was the glory of Christianity, as propagated in a true Christian spirit and method, that it took hold of individuals. The whole world was to be Christianised by the Christianising of individuals; and the gospel went from individuals to their connexions, their families, and the nations to which they belong. The progress of the gospel among the devil-worshippers of South India was most interesting; the story of the progress of the gospel among the Karens was more interesting still; and he thought that his missionary brethren could not do better than give all the information they possess about the facts of their missionary life, and the progress of the gospel in heathen lands.

The Rev. Dr. O'MEARA thoroughly coincided with Mr. Mullens' observations, that it was by facts, and facts alone, that the individual interest in missionary work was to be kept up.

WILLIAM LEACH, Esq. of London, referring to the proposed aid from Juvenile Societies, expressed his regret that active effort to obtain support for missions was comparatively little used by *lay gentlemen*—persons who were impressed with the importance of the object, but who rendered comparatively little help in the great work. The amount of assistance which might be rendered by laymen was inconceivably great. If all did their duty in this respect, missionary operations, so far as resources were concerned, might be increased a hundred-fold or more. If gentlemen would give their energies to the subject—as Colonel Hughes, for instance, had done—there would soon be a wonderful spread of missionary supply. They all knew, who attended committees in London, how difficult it was in many Societies even to get a quorum, and how little was done out of the Committee—the work most needed. Unwilling as he was to refer to his own case, might he be permitted thus to encourage others to "provoke to love and to good works?" He was himself induced to take up a work of this kind, in connexion with a particular Society; and he well recollected the remarks made to him by a much-respected clergyman who consigned that Society to his care: he said, "Do all you can to call forth the help of brethren, the Lord will bless you in it, but don't expect it to be an easy work, for it will be a cross as long as you live." This was more than fifty years ago, and he (Mr. Leach) could truly say that, though these works had been acts of self-denial, the blessing of God had largely attended his efforts,—to Him alone be the praise.—He recollected very well an observation made not long ago by Lord Shaftesbury: "I have learnt that if we want money, we must ask for it." This, he was sure, would be the experience of the Church, and they must not be above asking; for it was an occupation which Apostles did not disdain to follow. They sought the contributions of those who were under their influence, and were not ashamed in person to convey those contributions to the relief of the poor saints at Jerusalem. He hoped that this discussion would have much effect in calling forth the missionary spirit, and a determined feeling to help forward the work of God in any way that they could. He could fully testify to the fact that, whilst engaged in very laborious occupations he could always find some time for helping such objects; and he recommended his brethren to consider engagements of this sort as primary obligations—and as work to be done for God, which must always take the precedence of all minor engagements.

Rev. W. Campbell.

Value of deputations.

The Rev. W. CAMPBELL wished to offer one or two remarks about Deputations. A very excellent man in Bristol said to him, not long ago, "Your deputations are the life-blood of your societies." With this sentiment he fully agreed; but he could not, also, help mentioning as a fact, that he had heard of gentlemen preaching for Missionary Societies and not once mentioning the name or work of the Society whose cause they professed to be advocating. Was this pleading the missionary cause? It was a mistake, in his opinion, to reserve all the facts for the missionary meetings; for missionary meetings, as a rule, were generally but poorly attended: people were not sufficiently interested in the subject, and would not come out to attend them. To meet this difficulty, it was necessary that deputations should fill their sermons with great facts respecting the missionary work. He fully agreed with Mr. Macfie with respect to the importance of pastors being well posted in regard to missionary information, in order that they might diffuse it among their people on the sabbath-day. Until the seed was sown among the people, they could not expect the results.

They should give information in the pulpit as well as on the platform.

Lieut.-Col. Hughes.

Lieut.-Col. HUGHES observed that his experience during the last eight or ten years had convinced him that the great opposition and difficulties with which he had to contend, had arisen from the little interest taken by the clergy and ministers of the gospel in missionary efforts. Unless ministers of the gospel, to whatever denomination they belonged, took an interest in the question, and brought it fully and regularly before their congregations, it was impossible for any layman to do what Mr. Leach recommended.

Work for the clergy.

Chairman.

The CHAIRMAN, touching the point mentioned by one of the preceding speakers, as to the spirituality of giving, said that one of the first lessons which he had learned when it pleased God to draw his heart towards Himself, had reference to this subject. He thought he was doing a very meritorious thing in contributing a liberal sum for some missionary purpose. He took it to a brother officer, who knew very well what his life had been, and who, looking him earnestly in the face, said, "I don't think I ought to take this from you at all." "Why not? it is for the missionary work." The officer questioned him closely as to his motives; and this lesson had never been lost upon him. Remembering this incident, he felt quickened by the address of his friend on the left, Mr. Anderson; and he urged them all to remember that it

Spirituality in giving.

was "not by might nor by power, but by my spirit, saith the Lord." However empty the treasury might be, let them go forward in faith, and be sure the Lord could do his own work with a little money, by means of his ministering servants, as well as by much. He trusted that in future they would look more to the gift being sanctified by the spirit which presented it.

Adverting next to the subject of deputations, the Chairman asked if they had never seen men who, for their intellectual powers and eloquence, were brought to meetings, such, for example, as those which would shortly take place in the metropolis, go back from those scenes, and in other parts and spheres take a more active part against the pure gospel of Christ than they had appeared to give assistance to it by their eloquence on the platform. These were important considerations for the Church; and here he thought, in connexion with other inconsistencies, might be found one of the causes of that want of success in missions which, under the name of "failure," had been inserted in the programme. With regard to the influence of publications in exciting sympathy and gaining means of support for missions, the Chairman said that he believed it was to Scotland we were indebted for the first movement in a most beautiful characteristic of missionary work—namely, Sunday-school children supporting converts in far distant lands, and thus establishing a bond of Christian love that spanned the hemispheres, and united in one spirit now those who shall hereafter be worshipping spirits around the throne of Christ in heaven. *Eloquent speakers not always the best friends of missions.*

Schools supporting converts.

The Rev. Dr. STEANE remarked that there was another aspect of the subject. We expected our missionary brethren to send us information: had we ever thought of what was due from us in sending information to them of what was going on in our own churches? He had been the editor, for fourteen years, of a periodical (*Evangelical Christendom*) which interested itself more particularly with the Continental and other Churches, the Churches of the Reformation and the Oriental Churches. He might mention a fact which he felt assured would gratify the meeting, that the proprietors of that journal had come to the resolution of sending it monthly, free of all cost, to every Protestant missionary throughout the world. (Applause.) It had been sent already in considerable numbers to missionaries belonging to different Societies; and the letters received from their dear brethren, especially those at the outside stations, and far from *Rev. Dr. STEANE.*

Information should be sent to missionaries.

"Evangelical Christendom" sent to them all.

the centres of information, showed how highly they had been gratified, how their hearts had been cheered and encouraged, and how much they prized the information which such a periodical afforded them.

Rev. R. S. Hardy.

Improved tone of the modern press.

The Rev. R. S. HARDY would merely observe, as a missionary, that they would omit a great duty if they did not express the deep gratitude which they owed to the editors of *Evangelical Christendom*. He also wished to express his own sense of gratitude at the change which had taken place in the principles of our chief Quarterlies, such as the *Edinburgh* and *Quarterly Reviews*. They were not yet all that they could wish them to be, but certainly their tone had very much changed from what it was a few years ago. With reference, also, to the daily press, *The Times* especially, he felt he could make the same remark: though the public newspapers were not what they should like them to be in all particulars, yet they had very much changed in their tone and tendency for the better within the last few years. As to the *News of the Churches*, he read it regularly, and was much interested by its varied and valuable contents.

Captain Layard.

Captain LAYARD, as the representative of the Jews' Society, begged to thank Dr. Steane and the supporters of the publication in question, for the valuable information it contained, and for the liberal manner in which it had been distributed.

Rev. Dr. Steane.

Quarterlies losing influence.

Weeklies have more influence.

Dr. STEANE, having had some practical experience of periodicals, would like to add a remark in reference to the proposed Quarterly. The Quarterlies, and the larger publications of that kind, were now obtaining less and less circulation; and it was with extreme difficulty that some of the most intellectually valuable ones maintained their ground. He thought if they could bring the sanctified intellect of the Church into a periodical such as the *Saturday Review*, it would obtain a far wider circulation and greater influence than any which could be hoped for from a Quarterly.

Rev. Dr. Tweedie.

Missionary professorship.

The Rev. Dr. TWEEDIE rose solely to express his regret that they could not go, even at some length, into the last subject mentioned in the Programme; the subject of a Professorship of missionary history and duties at the Universities and Colleges. There was a difference of opinion as to whether it would be better to have a separate professor for that department, or whether more of the missionary spirit should be infused into the work of all the professors? It was an open question; but he thought it was the duty of the Conference not to omit all reference to the subject. And he was sure it must be the feeling of all who were interested in the training of the future labourers of the Churches at home or abroad, that as certain a sound as possible should be given with respect to the importance of thoroughly training students for the missionary work. As a student of theology himself, he did not recollect having heard a single missionary lecture while attending the Hall. They had, of course, information out-of-doors, through Societies and various other agencies; but professionally they were not trained in any right views of the work: and although, of course, there was a great improvement in the course of a quarter of a century, since he studied, he did not know whether even now, in the theological institutions of any section of the Christian Church, missionary principles and missionary views received the prominence which they deserved, or which the New Testament gave them. He thought the subject should have more attention bestowed upon it than could be given in a course of half-a-dozen lectures. He knew a devoted missionary who was offered the opportunity of delivering six lectures in the course of the winter, to the students attending a Hall; but he declined the offer on principle, although he could have done it easily, and would doubtless have done it admirably; because he would not, he said, accept a composition, when he wished for full payment, with reference to this great subject. If something of this kind were well impressed upon the minds of all, it would be of great service to our future ministers and missionaries and be blessed, he was sure, to revive and invigorate all the Churches. (Hear, hear.)

<small>All students of theology ought to be instructed in missions;</small>

<small>as an essential part of their studies.</small>

The Rev. Dr. SOMERVILLE said,—He had felt this subject to be one of great importance; and he might state, that the Church to which he belonged had Synodically enacted, that it was a part of theological teaching, incumbent on the theological professor, to bring missionary subjects before his students; touching on the claims of the mission-field, the qualifications necessary for the work of a missionary, and the best methods of performing that work. They could not look into the New Testament without seeing, that the missionary enterprise was the outstanding and prominent part of theology. The commission given by our Lord immediately before his ascension was, "Go ye into all the world

<small>Rev. Dr. SOMERVILLE</small>

<small>The same.</small>

<small>Synod of the U. P. Church have so ordered.</small>

and preach the Gospel unto every creature;" and no professor could teach the Bible without teaching missions. He would mention a fact, which many of them, perhaps, were aware of; that at the New York Missionary Conference, held in May 1854, the following recommendation on this very point was agreed to:—" Moreover, that, for the due preparation of candidates for the foreign field, it were very desirable that provision were made, in our theological seminaries generally, for bringing the entire history and obligations of the missionary enterprise before the students, in what may be briefly designated as a course of evangelistic theology." He (Dr. Somerville) was not prepared to say that we had reached the period when a professorship of missionary history would be an advantage; but, certainly, every theological professor should make it a matter of duty to inculcate missionary principles, and to enforce missionary obligations. Much had been said about a higher class of missionary periodicals, but he believed that if they could get missionary principles introduced into the Universities, and into the prælections of the Professors, they would thus influence the educated minds of the country, and, through them, would influence the literature of the country also.

The Rev. Mr. CULLEN observed, that Dr. Coldstream, of Edinburgh, a very enlightened friend of missions, had, during the last session, delivered a course of lectures on ethnology and ethnography, which had proved exceedingly useful to the missionary cause. Medical missionary students and other friends had been invited to attend these lectures, which were prepared with very great care, and contained much valuable information such as the missionary required. He (Mr. Cullen) knew of nothing more calculated to diffuse through the University, and, by means of the Universities, throughout the church at home, a love of missionary enterprises, than lectures of this kind.

The Rev. Dr. BAYLEE observed, that the subject was one of the deepest importance. Some years since he had brought before the Jewish Missionary Society a plan of Christian Advocacy in Liverpool, in which he proposed that some man who had studied the subject should give four or six lectures annually in Liverpool, treating the Jewish subject in its higher and more philosophical aspects.

If all our large towns had an annual course of lectures of this kind, he believed they would be looked forward to with as much interest, as in Oxford, people looked forward to the Bampton Lectures. The subjects should be varied from year to year. He believed that the adoption of this course would be much more advantageous than the institution of Professorships in the Universities. The number of persons in the Universities was necessarily limited. *Recommends an annual missionary lecture.*

He could speak with great feeling on this subject, having nearly sixty theological students entrusted to his care; and if his friend Mr. Hardy, for instance, were to deliver in Liverpool a series of lectures on Buddhism, he could promise him, as often as he chose to lecture, an audience of at least fifty. Such lectures would be a most important aid to professors in his own position. A Professor of Theology had too many things to attend to to make himself master of all. It was quite impossible, for instance, for him to be a Professor of Buddhism, or a Professor of Brahminism; although, of course, he ought to know a little of everything; but, really, to know subjects like these, as a Professor should know them, required a man to give his whole study to them. He believed that the adoption of some such plan as that which he had ventured to suggest would lead to the development of a higher class of talent among missionaries. The men who delivered these lectures should be those who had distinguished themselves in their own particular departments. The lectures themselves might be delivered in London, and repeated in the leading provincial towns: as, for instance, in Liverpool, Bristol, and Leeds; and afterwards published. He was convinced that the lectures would be advantageous, not only to theological students, but to large numbers of intelligent persons, who would listen to them with interest and profit. *What it might do. Professors can't teach everything. How the plan may be carried out.*

The Rev. J. H. TITCOMB, — I have resided for fourteen years in the University of Cambridge, and I may, therefore, state what is doing there in connexion with missions. There are one or two annual University sermons preached by request for the express purpose of setting forth before students the missionary work. There is an officer who holds the appointment of Christian Advocate, whose duty it is to publish a work each year bearing upon the subject of Christianity in relation to various forms of idolatry and false philosophy throughout the world. In addition to that, we have three divinity professors, one of whom, by his office, is obliged to deliver periodically a series of lectures upon pastoral *Rev. J. H. TITCOMB. Missionary teaching in Cambridge. The "Christian Advocate."*

theology. The subject of missions, of course, comes within these lectures as a particular department. With regard to the students, although there is no professed or formal and stated examination in connexion with missions, there is a very large amount of exertion every term going forward among the young men on their behalf; and thus without any formal training, they are being practically trained for their future work. Year after year numbers of young men come up from the very first term of their residence, determined to devote themselves to the missionary work. They meet with every favour that the parochial ministers can give them in order to foster and encourage these principles. Beside which, there are Terminal meetings, at which one of the Secretaries of the Church Missionary Society usually attends. In connexion with this body of young men there is also a missionary reading-room, to which the publications of all Societies are sent. In addition to these, there is a large number of young men not merely interested in reading, but who deny themselves so far as to go, through evil report and good report, collecting in their various colleges contributions for the missionary cause. Then there is the Missionary University Prayer Union. Some years ago a number of good and earnest young men in Cambridge started that union, the object being to pray for the outpouring of a greater missionary spirit in the University itself and the world at large; and it has now extended to Oxford and Dublin, and I believe it has ramifications in the Law and other departments of the professions in London. Taking, therefore, all things into consideration, I think the missionary spirit in the University of Cambridge is by no means lacking. Perhaps a professorship of missionary history in the University is scarcely possible or desirable; nor do I think it at all necessary. I think the free and unreserved labour of love which I have described is amply sufficient to carry on that work, if it is carried on only with the same faith and earnestness.

The following MINUTE, embodying the view of the Conference on the important subject of this discussion, was, after careful consideration, unanimously adopted:—

MINUTE ON THE MEANS OF EXCITING AND MAINTAINING THE MISSIONARY FEELING AT HOME.

The members of this Conference consider, that a variety of agencies may with great propriety be employed to stir up the hearts of the several classes of contributors by whom Christian missions are supported. They consider, that while the work of missions should be enforced as an appointed Christian duty, nothing will tend to increase and sustain an interest in this work so much as the widest diffusion of correct information respecting all its departments. That information, in their opinion, should be as full and as clear as it is possible to make it. It should embrace not only the facts of missionary life and labour, but the explanations needed to put them in a proper light; not only the favourable elements of the picture, but the difficulties and disappointments with which missionaries meet. *Minute. Information essential. Of what kind.*

For the spread of such information they think that the pulpit, on the Sabbath-day, ought to be much more extensively employed than it has been; and they would rejoice to see all the pastors and ministers of our churches so endeavouring, systematically, to inform and stir up the hearts of their people in the work of the Lord. For the stated missionary prayer-meetings, so long maintained by all branches of the Church of Christ, they express their heartfelt gratitude; but they desire to see them more numerously attended, sustained with deeper interest, and more completely employed both for directing to mission fields the minds of Christ's servants, and drawing down upon them the blessing of the Most High. *The pulpit. The pastor. Prayer-meetings.*

Under the same conviction they think that in public meetings, held for missionary purposes, the diffusion of information should be kept very prominently in view; and that Deputations, especially missionaries, both in their sermons and addresses, should do their best to convey it as fully and clearly as they can. *Deputations*

In the same cause they reckon as of high importance the influence and the employment of the Press. They rejoice to find, that the cheaper periodicals of the various Missionary Societies *The press.*

Missionary periodicals. have secured so large a circulation, and have proved so extensively useful, in increasing the knowledge and deepening the interest in missions, of the great mass of their supporters. They are thankful also that several other missionary publications, of a more general character, ably sustain the mission cause.

A high-class ditto. They deeply feel, however, that it would be exceedingly desirable to secure the establishment of a periodical of a higher class, that shall treat of Christian missions at large; so that while the friends of missions naturally support the periodicals of their own Societies, they may, through such a general periodical, also secure regular and full information respecting the numerous missions of their brethren. Till its establishment, however, they suggest that attempts should be made to employ in the cause of missions the service of existing periodicals.

Efforts to enlist the young. The careful maintenance of Juvenile Associations, and other efforts to infuse a missionary spirit into the hearts of the young of all classes and ranks in the Church of Christ, they deem to be an object of immense importance, and worthy of the most able and systematic attention. They feel that all Christian children should be trained to take an interest in the mission cause; they may then, under God's blessing, rise up in large numbers to be the future supporters of missions, and many will probably become missionaries themselves.

Missions to be introduced into the theological course. They further consider that the subject of Christian missions, in all their bearings, their history, difficulties, successes, and obligations, should be brought systematically before theological students, as a part of their college course: that they may thus be trained in the practical conviction that missionary work is the regular work of the Church of Christ; acquire information respecting its position; and themselves go forth to share its toils.

A COMMITTEE was appointed to consider Dr. Baylee's suggestion of a Missionary Lectureship; and the Conference, after singing the Doxology, adjourned.

MISSIONARY LECTURESHIP.

At a subsequent sitting, the following Report was brought up by the Committee, and unanimously adopted.

The Committee appointed to "consider and report on the desirableness and practicability of instituting a permanent Lecture on Christian Missions," in presenting a Report on the important subject committed to their consideration, must throw themselves on the kindness of their brethren, to make allowance for any imperfections in the form in which their conclusions are presented, attributable to the circumstance that they have had so short a period in which to prepare them. On the other hand, the subject had so long individually occupied their thoughts that, when they met together, they were greatly strengthened in their views by the unanimity of judgment which they found to obtain among them. *[margin: Missionary Lectureship to be established.]*

They are induced, therefore, to present the following propositions to the Conference for their consideration, and, if they deem them of sufficient practical value, for their adoption:—

1. That a LECTURESHIP be instituted, for the discussion of the principles involved in those higher relations, under which the great subject of Christian Missions may present itself to those who have hitherto given little or no consideration to it; but who, from their intellectual superiority, literary attainments, or commanding position, exert a powerful influence in forming and directing the public mind. *[margin: Its object.]*

2. That, in order to the attainment of this object, a FUND be immediately raised, sufficient to defray the expense of the proposed Lectureship for Five or Seven Years, at an estimated cost of 300*l.* per annum. *[margin: Funds.]*

3. That a COMMITTEE be appointed by the Conference, to whom the necessary arrangements for carrying this scheme into effect shall be confided; and that this Committee con- *[margin: Committee.]*

H

sist of a selection of brethren from the different bodies of Christians engaged in missionary work, as represented at this Conference, with power to add to their number.

Lecturer.

4. That the Committee be instructed to appoint a LECTURER, if practicable, annually, who shall deliver his Lectures in one or more of the principal centres of population or of learning, as the Committee may direct; and that his Lectures be afterwards published in a Volume. The Lecturer in each case should have the selection of his own subject, but the choice should be sanctioned by the Committee.

Permanency of the plan.

5. That in the event of this experimental measure proving, under the Divine blessing, successful, the Committee be instructed to adopt such plans as may seem to them proper for making the Lecture a permanent institution, and raising funds for that purpose.

Committee appointed.

6. That the Conference will be gratified if the following brethren will act on the proposed Committee, and they are hereby, on acceding to the request, appointed:—

Rev. H. VENN.	Rev. M. THOMAS.
Rev. G. OSBORN.	Hon. A. KINNAIRD.
Rev. Dr. TIDMAN.	H. CARRE TUCKER, Esq.
Rev. Dr. STEANE.	THOMAS FARMER, Esq.
Rev. P. LA TROBE.	T. M. COOMBS, Esq.
Rev. Dr. NORMAN M'LEOD.	Sir S. M. PETO, Bart.
Rev. Dr. TWEEDIE.	W. LEACH, Esq.
Rev. H. MACGILL.	Sir J. CAMPBELL.
Rev. Dr. GUTHRIE.	JAMES CUNNINGHAM, Esq.
Rev. Dr. HAMILTON.	J. HENDERSON, Esq.
Rev. Dr. MORGAN.	R. A. MACFIE, Esq.
Rev. C. J. GOODHART.	

Secretaries, { Rev. EDWARD STEANE, D.D.
{ Rev. H. M. MACGILL.

FIRST MISSIONARY SOIRÉE.

Tuesday Evening.

AFTER tea and social intercourse in the rooms beneath Hope Hall. a Public Meeting was held at eight o'clock, at which a large number of ladies and gentlemen, with most of the members of Conference, were present. *Soirée.*

GEORGE F. BARBOUR, Esq., of Edinburgh, having taken the Chair, a hymn was sung, and the Rev. J. B. LOWE, of Liverpool, offered prayer.

The CHAIRMAN, in opening the proceedings observed, that we lived in a very remarkable age; that we were entering into a new era of the Christian Church; and that we had reason to expect the fruit of the Divine blessing in a new impulse being given to missionary exertions, and in the opening of the hearts of the Christian people of this country in a way never previously known. Having reviewed the leading topics which had occupied the attention of the Conference during the day, the Chairman touched upon the question of contributions, and observed that the Christian Church was much to blame, not only for its small and niggardly contributions, but also for the mixed and doubtful motives which had often influenced those contributions, and which had, to a great extent, prevented a blessing upon their missionary work. Their hearts, also, should condemn them for the very little prayerful energy which they had put forth. Perhaps they had too much looked at missions in the light of a question of arithmetical calculation: Given a certain amount of labour,—so much money and machinery,—that the result would be a relative amount of blessing. But the whole history of Christian missions showed the falsity of such calculations. God, in his own sovereign grace, worked in his own blessed way; and it was our duty, whatever our engagements or fields of labour, to sow the seed in faith, working earnestly and perseveringly in the path allotted *CHAIRMAN.* *The Church backward in gifts, prayer, and faith.*

to us, and believingly looking to him for that blessing without which our work would be useless. (Applause.)

He rejoiced that there were present that evening two successful labourers in one special department of the missionary field, that of Medical Missions; who had been invited to detail the results of their experience in this difficult but most interesting sphere of mission work.

ON MEDICAL MISSIONS IN CHINA.

By Dr. Lockhart of Shanghai.

Dr. Lockhart. Dr. LOCKHART, of Shanghai, who was received with hearty cheering, then rose and said;—I am glad to have the opportunity of advocating the cause of MEDICAL MISSIONS in this, my native town, which I left more than twenty years ago, to proceed to China under the auspices of the London Missionary Society. *Their object.* Probably you all know the object and scope of Medical Missions. They were commenced by the various Missionary Societies in England and America, in imitation of the example of Him "who went about doing good," and "healing all manner of sickness and disease among the people." The experiment thus made was to *Their plan.* send out surgeons to various heathen lands, to endeavour to win the affections and confidence of the people, by healing their infirmities; while at the same time their minds were directed to Him who is the "Great Physician," and who can cure them of the deeper malady of sin. In 1838, I was sent out by the London Missionary Society as their first medical missionary to China. *Suitable in India and China.* The experiment has been tried in India to some extent; and it is said, though I think erroneously, that the operation of medical missions in India is not so much required as in other lands. I believe that, if fairly tried in that country, they would be found quite as useful as in China. In China, by this means, we have met with great success. We have won the confidence and respect of the people; and I think the same results would take place in India were the agency employed to the same extent.

Dr. Lockhart's personal labours, In 1838, I began my medical labours in China, in the city of Macao; where I remained for some time, and until I was expelled that city with other English residents. After a short sojourn in Batavia and other places, in 1840 I went north to the island of *in Chusan:* Chusan, which had been shortly before occupied by our troops, and placed under the British Government. I was the first Protestant missionary who went to reside in the north of China. My work was new amongst the people, and they neither comprehended my object nor my errand. I went alone, and began my hospital immediately on landing at Chusan. In the first place I opened my house, prepared it for the reception of patients; and then went into the various towns and villages about Ting-Hai, telling the people, if they came to my house, they would be received and have their maladies attended to. During the first few days only some three or four came; shortly afterwards about twenty; and after the lapse of a week, some hundreds arrived, so that my hands were soon filled with work. After some six months' residence at Chusan, when that island was restored to the Chinese, I returned to the south of China; and subsequently, when the Treaty of 1842 had been made, I again went north, and settled in Shanghai; there I continued to labour until I was compelled, about two years ago, by domestic circumstances, to retire from China for a time. *In Shanghai.*

The nature of the work performed in the medical part of the mission was something of this kind. A house was taken for a dispensary and hospital; and the people round about were informed, that at that place they would receive gratuitous medical attendance. At Shanghai, Dr. Medhurst and I were alone; Dr. Medhurst preaching to the people in their own tongue. This, in a great degree, won their confidence; and when I opened the dispensary, and the people discovered its object, they came to me in great numbers; so that in the course of a few weeks our house was quite full, and the street was crowded every morning with patients flocking to us for aid. In China, although they have physicians, who learn the art of healing internal diseases, their surgery is of the crudest and most barbarous kind. They know nothing of it in its scientific character; and consequently, persons who are exposed to various external accidents, diseases of the eye, and so on, are in a hopeless condition in the hands of the native practitioners. We found large numbers, quite prostrated by these diseases; but when they found that the foreign surgeon could relieve them from their various infirmities, they came readily, and placed themselves in his hands. This was at a time, not as now, when there are several surgeons and medical missionaries at Shanghai; but when, in that city, they had hardly seen the face of a European before. They were at first afraid to come near our houses; and still more terrified, when *Nature of the work: its popularity. No native surgery in China. Fears overcome.*

we approached to speak to them; but when they found themselves relieved of their diseases, their confidence and esteem were won. They came in great numbers, day by day; and it was pleasant to see how soon, by this work of humanity, we could find a way to their affections and their hearts. I was glad we could employ this means of commencing our European intercourse with the people of northern China: for, while I was engaged at the hospital and dispensary in relieving their maladies, Dr. Medhurst, at that time, and afterwards other colleagues who joined the mission, would preach to them of " Christ and his salvation." It was most gratifying to see how the people who had been thus relieved would dwell upon the words of the preacher. I believe the truth thus found its way to the hearts of many, who without the hospital would never have known the " glad tidings of the gospel." (Applause.) Many persons came from the northern and western provinces of the empire to the hospital at Shanghai. When, under treatment there, they heard the preaching of the gospel. Returning to their distant homes, they took with them portions of the word of God, and various religious tracts; and thus the message of salvation found its way into large districts of country, which, without this agency, we had no means of reaching. This is the great object of Medical Missions. We strive to win the confidence of the people; to get them around us; to open their hearts by kindness to receive the Divine word; and sowing the seed at a favourable time, bring many to know Christ, whose hearts might otherwise have been prejudiced against his truth. We repeatedly heard of patients who, having been to the hospital and attended the preaching of the gospel, carried with them portions of the word of God to their native villages, and induced others of their friends to come down, in order to participate in the same benefits. So the work went on; and I say it with confidence, that Medical Missions in China have been successful in winning an entrance to the hearts and consciences of the people, which no other agency could have so well effected. (Cheers.) I believe the experiment has been carried out fully and efficiently; and therefore I come back to tell the churches in England of my labours there with much satisfaction, confidence, and joy. Glad I am that I ever left my native town to spend my days in China; and were I a young man, about to commence life again, I would go out more earnestly, hopefully, and trustfully, to those far-distant regions. (Renewed cheers.) Permit me now to state a few particulars as to the character of the cases which came under my observation. And first, with regard to the practice of vaccination. You probably know that in Eastern countries smallpox commits great ravages amongst the people; spreading from village to village, from city to city, and devastating large populations. They have no means of effectively checking or removing it. They certainly do inoculate their children in early life, and that is a little protection; but inoculation is only a doubtful benefit. Many children take the disease in this manner to a very severe extent, and occasionally lose their lives or their sight. Inoculation of the smallpox perpetuates the disease in the country, and keeps it ever present among the people; whereas vaccination in most cases prevents, and in all cases mitigates, the disease of smallpox, and does not tend to perpetuate that fearful malady. The Chinese in the south of the country had been made acquainted with the principle of vaccination; but in the north of China it was wholly unknown till I introduced it, shortly after my arrival. When I went to Shanghai, I was enabled, through the kindness of friends in Calcutta and London, to procure some vaccine lymph; and I immediately began the practice of vaccination with a few children. The people were at first astonished and amused; and for some time they could not be persuaded that this was a beneficial process, and would relieve the children from dangerous disease. When they found, however, that it was really a preventive, more children were submitted to the treatment; and by and by crowds were brought every day. Soon the officers of the Government heard of the foreign system, and brought their children; and their servants also brought their children. The colonel of the garrison at Shanghai sent all his children; and having sent word to his relatives in Soochow, a crowd of children were brought from that place also. I was sent for by many of the respectable families in Shanghai to operate on their children: so that, by means of this process of vaccination, I obtained, together with my wife and the other ladies in the mission, more access to the families of the respectable Chinese, and especially to those of the officers of the Government, than by any other agency which I could have adopted. We thus saw more of domestic Chinese life than we could otherwise have done. (Hear, hear, and cheers.)

Vaccination:

it becomes popular:

in official and respectable families.

Then with regard to diseases of the eye. There are epidemics of purulent ophthalmia in China. It is a fearful malady, which particularly affects the Chinese and other Eastern nations, and though very readily cured by our modes of treatment, is utterly incurable by theirs. When an epidemic of the kind seizes a

Ophthalmia common.

village large numbers become blind. Such an epidemic once raged in Shanghai and the district round it, while I resided there.

Benefits of the Mission hospital.

A few people came to the hospital, and after two or three days' treatment, though they were almost blind when they came, the pain was removed, the disease was checked, and they returned to their families in perfect health, with their sight restored. The news soon spread throughout the district; and day after day I was besieged by large crowds of these people, who were suffering from pain and disease to such an extent that they were led in a helpless and miserable condition to the hospital. These in their turn, however, being relieved and restored to sight, returned home and spread further still the fame of our doings.

Surgery:

With regard now to operative surgery. At one time the city of Shanghai was taken by a number of pirates, the members of one of the Triad Societies, called, by way of distinction, the Dagger Society, or Small-knife Society, and held by them for some time; these were in their turn besieged by the troops of the Imperial Government.

after several battles.

There were constant battles; and great numbers of gunshot wounds were inflicted. The wounded were immediately brought to the hospital, which sometimes almost presented the appearance of a field of battle, the large hall being covered with blood. Hard work it was for me to attend to all the wounded; yet such was the confidence in the relief afforded at the hospital, that in its wards were to be found at the same time the wounded pirates, the imperialists, and the poor unfortunate natives who had been wounded by both parties, all receiving equal attention, and the best aid we could afford. (Loud cheers.)

Work done by others.

I have thus endeavoured to give a brief account of the mission in which I have spent many years of my life, and have spoken in the first place of my own work, as being that in which I could address you from personal experience; but I think it desirable that some account should be given of others who have been engaged in introducing the principles of medical missions, and in affording medical relief to the Chinese suffering from disease and pain.

First efforts in Canton and Macao.

The first English surgeon who attended to the wants of the Chinese, was Mr. Alexander Pearson, one of the surgeons of the East India Company's civil service in Canton. In 1805 he vaccinated great numbers of the Chinese, and was enabled to establish a vaccine institution in the city of Canton, where multitudes of the people were vaccinated: this was placed under the care of an intelligent native who was taught the art of vaccination, and this establishment is still carried on efficiently. In 1820 Mr. Livingston, another surgeon of the Company, in connexion with the Rev. Dr. Morrison, established a dispensary for the relief of sick Chinese. Subsequently in 1828, Mr. Colledge, also surgeon to the British factory, opened a dispensary in Macao for the relief of diseases of the eye, which was conducted by him with encouraging success for several years.

The idea of using the practice of medicine as a means of affording opportunities to introduce Christianity among the Chinese, was first practically adopted by the American Board of Commissioners for Foreign Missions: and Dr. Peter Parker proceeded to China with that view. He opened an ophthalmic hospital in Canton in 1835; and his labours were attended with a success that his most sanguine hopes could hardly have anticipated. His work was long continued; and he won the confidence of the Chinese in a remarkable degree. Since that time various other medical missionaries, with myself, have occupied important spheres of labour in the country. Dr. Hobson was sent out by the London Missionary Society in 1839, and conducted a large hospital at Hong Kong, afterwards at Canton; where much good was done, and several of the Chinese were brought to a knowledge of the truth. Dr. Hobson also published an extensive series of translations into the Chinese language of English works on Medicine and Surgery. One was a treatise on Anatomy; one on general Surgery and on Diseases of the Eye; one on Midwifery; one on the Practice of Medicine; and also a treatise on Natural Philosophy. These works have had a wide circulation, and have been reprinted by native gentlemen both in China and Japan. Dr. Wong-fun, a Chinese educated in Edinburgh, has had charge of the hospital at Canton belonging to the London Mission; and Dr. Kerr, an American medical missionary, also labours at Canton.

At Amoy, Dr. Cumming and Dr. Hepburn, from the American Churches, and Dr. Hirschberg of the London Mission, have had hospitals for several years; and Dr. Carnegie of the English Presbyterian Church Mission has an hospital there at present.

At Foochow, the late Dr. Welton of the Church Missionary Society, conducted an hospital with great efficiency for several years; till failing health compelled him to return home to England, where he died.

Ningpo.

At Ningpo, Dr. Macgowan and Dr. McCartee, from the American churches, have each conducted hospitals for many years with a very large measure of success; and Dr. Macgowan edited a Chinese magazine which had a large circulation. Dr. W. Parker, from England, has also within the last few years been a medical missionary at the same place.

Shanghai.

At Shanghai the Chinese hospital, that I was enabled by the liberality of foreign merchants residing there to establish, is now intrusted to the care of Dr. Henderson, who lately went out on account of the London Missionary Society. Dr. Burton, from the American Baptist Society, has also been a medical missionary at Shanghai for some years past; and Mr. Collins, of the Church Missionary Society, has commenced his labours there, having a dispensary attached to that mission.

Appeal for more men.

Such is the work in which we have been engaged. Are there any surgeons in Liverpool who will go out to carry on this undertaking? There is a wide field of effort, not only in the stations of the London Missionary Society, but in those also of the Church and Wesleyan Missionary Societies; and also, Sir, in the stations of your own Mission of the English Presbyterian Church; for your missionaries have laboured long and most assiduously in the island of Amoy. I hope some will be found in this town to consecrate themselves to this work. Though at present there are obstacles which prevent our entrance into the heart of China, the day, I believe, is not far distant when we shall have free access to the cities, towns, and villages, of that mighty empire; and beginning the work through our medical missionaries, winning the esteem and confidence of the people by relieving their bodily infirmities, we may lead them to the "balm of Gilead," and to Christ the Physician of their souls. (Cheers.)

Great obstacle to the gospel in China:

Before I close, I would allude for a moment to one thing, which has been found a great obstacle to the success of missions in all Eastern and heathen countries; and, in a sea-port like this, I would speak of it with all the power and emphasis that I can employ. I refer to the debauchery, licentiousness, and wicked-

the vices of our sailors.

ness of our sailors, who go forth and sow the seeds of wickedness and sin in all heathen lands, and in none more than in China. It makes the heart of the missionary sad indeed, to see his work day by day undone by the wickedness and debauchery of these sailors. It is the same in the ports of India, in the South Seas, in Africa, and in the West Indies. When the Chinese see, for instance,

our sailors on leave ashore on the Sabbath-day getting drunk, How they affect the Chinese.
going into the various villages, and by their violence and wickedness setting the minds of the people against them, they naturally say to us—"You teachers come and preach the Gospel of Jesus Christ; do you call these men Christians? Is it to make us men like these that you preach to us the Gospel of Christ?" And what can we say in reply? (Hear, hear.) Here are men from Christian England exhibiting not the fruits of holiness, but of wickedness and sin. I call your attention to this great obstacle to the success of missions; because much can be done by getting the fact thoroughly known in England, that this, more than anything else I know of, interferes with our success. (Cheers.) Look In Japan. at late events in Japan. That empire is now almost shut against us a second time, solely and absolutely from the depravity and viciousness of our fellow-countrymen. (Renewed cheers.) I hope that by your personal influence, and in various other ways, you will endeavour, as far as in you lies, to get this well known in your own town and throughout the country; in order that we may have public opinion brought to bear upon it, and get it removed out of our way. Labouring zealously in Christ's name, and for Prospects. his service, we may look forward to that glorious time when China and all other heathen lands shall be won to Him; and the people thereof shall sing to the "praise, and honour, and glory of Him that sitteth upon the throne, and to the Lamb for ever." (Loud applause.)

Dr. MACGOWAN, Baptist Medical Missionary from Ningpo, Dr. Macgowan. was then introduced and loudly cheered. He said; that as the hour was late, he would reserve his address for one of their meetings on a future evening.

The Rev. Dr. CRICHTON, of Liverpool, in the name of the Rev. Dr. Crichton. Committee appointed to manage the affairs of the Conference, expressed their pleasure at meeting so large an audience.

Capt. LAYARD briefly alluded to the intelligence just received, Capt. Layard. of the death of their valued missionary brother Dr. MACGOWAN, of Jerusalem, after a lengthened service of eighteen years. He died triumphing in the knowledge and love of Jesus.

The Rev. W. H. WRIGHT, of Christ-Church, Liverpool, addressed a few words of welcome to the strangers present, and Rev. W. H. Wright.

more especially to the missionaries who had come down to attend the Conference. He trusted that the proceedings of the Conference would result in a measure of blessing which should be felt to the ends of the earth.

<small>Rev. J. Mann.</small>

The Rev. JAMES MANN, of the Congregational Chapel, Birkenhead, having made some observations on the same subject, the proceedings were closed with prayer and the Benediction, by the Rev. WILLIAM BALLANTYNE, of the Islington Presbyterian Church, London.

PROCEEDINGS OF THE CONFERENCE.

WEDNESDAY, March 21st.

SECOND GENERAL PRAYER-MEETING.

WEDNESDAY MORNING.

The second general Prayer-meeting was held at Hope Hall, at 9·30 A.M., when as on the previous days a large number of ladies and gentlemen joined the members of Conference in supplicating the Throne of Grace.

<small>Second Prayer-meeting.</small>

The Rev. CANON WOODROOFFE presided.

The devotions of the meeting were led by the Rev. GEO. CANDY, of the Church Missionary Society in Bombay; the Rev. HAMILTON M'GILL, one of the mission secretaries of the United Presbyterian Church in Scotland; Lieut.-Col. HUGHES, Secretary to the Asiatic Strangers' Home in London; and the Rev. G. R. BIRCH, Secretary of the Turkish Missions Aid Society.

THIRD SESSION OF THE CONFERENCE.

WEDNESDAY MORNING.

Major-Gen. ALEXANDER in the chair.

The following are the topics contained in the Programme proposed for the present sitting :—

<small>Programme of the session.</small>

Subject: MISSIONARY EDUCATION.

Paper, or Address, of ten minutes, by Rev. C. B. LEUPOLT, C.M.S., Benares; also Papers by Rev. T. SMITH,

Free Church Mission, Calcutta; and Rev. J. H. TITCOMB, Secretary of the Christian Vernacular Education Society.

Education.

English Schools and Institutions.
Village Schools.
Orphan and Boarding Schools.
Industrial Institutions.
Female Education.
Vernacular Training Institutions, as Nurseries of Teachers and Evangelists.
Government System of Education in India, its effects. Necessity for basing it upon the Bible.
Should Missionary Schools be open to all Classes?
Should non-Christian teachers be employed?
Results of the different kinds of Schools, as regards,
   a. Direct conversion.
   b. The formation of efficient mission agents.
   c. The general enlightenment of the country.
Should Education, so far as it is supported by Mission Funds, have a direct reference to the training up of Native Mission Agents?

Literature.

VERNACULAR LITERATURE, PERIODICALS, TRACTS, AND SCHOOL BOOKS.

Style of such works.
How they can best be circulated, so as to permeate the country.

The Conference having been again formally opened, the first of the appointed Papers was read, as follows:—

ON MISSIONARY EDUCATION.

By the Rev. C. B. Leupolt,

MISSIONARY OF THE CHURCH MISSIONARY SOCIETY IN BENARES.

Education being made the subject of our second day's Conference, it is evident that we consider *the direct preaching of the Gospel* the *primary instrumentality* of making known the glorious Gospel of our Lord. A *second instrumentality* for carrying out our Lord's command is *education by means of schools*. <small>Education a missionary instrumentality.</small>

The kinds of educational institutions which we require for this great end are those in which the primary object is the conversion of the children to God. With this object a second should be combined, that of imparting to children such an amount of secular knowledge as will qualify them to become useful members of society.

These institutions require to be of two kinds; for they have to aid in accomplishing a double end; that of promulgating the truths of the Gospel among those who are not Christians, and that of consolidating the Church of Christ where it is already planted. <small>Two ends.</small>

Although missionaries daily preach the gospel, there still remain two classes of human beings in India whom the missionary in his preaching cannot reach at all, or but partially; these are *the young* and the *female population*. <small>Classes not reached by preaching:</small>

Our bazar preaching is but partially adapted to the young; the juvenile and immature mind requiring teaching in a manner peculiar to itself. As regards the female population, they are prevented from attending our preaching by the customs and usages of the country; and as neither missionaries nor their wives have, as yet, with few exceptions, access to the zenanas, females can only be reached by the gospel in schools. <small>the young: and women.</small>

In order, therefore, to make known the gospel to these two classes we require *English, village,* and *girls' schools*. No missionary establishment in a great city is complete without an English school. At the present time English schools have some advantages over vernacular schools. There is a certain class of young men whom the missionary cannot reach by vernacular schools; for they are able to obtain a knowledge of their own language at home; but they cannot obtain English, and will <small>Advantages of English schools.</small>

therefore, for the sake of acquiring English, gather around the missionary, and thus come under the sound of the gospel.

Again, lads attending English schools usually remain much longer under instruction than those attending vernacular schools; and the missionary is thereby enabled to impart to his scholars a more complete knowledge of Christianity, than he is able to do in any other way, preaching included.

Their plan. Of the plan of instruction for these schools, nothing definite can be laid down. Each school will require a plan adapted to the scholars. One error, however, should be avoided, which is, that of aiming at subjects too high for the scholars. Solidity in all our instructions should be preferred to high-sounding names.

The vernacular should be thoroughly cultivated and be made the medium of all scriptural instruction.

If vernacular education is to be connected with English schools, two Europeans will be required for the establishment; one to devote to himself to the English, the other to the vernacular department. If one man is to attend to both, the vernacular education will be but a nominal one; as it is in many schools. The scholars should also be made to pay.

English schools, however, are insufficient for the country at large. In these we can only teach a limited class of youths residing in towns; but the children in the villages, and of the poor, have also souls to be saved. We require, therefore,—

Vernacular schools. 2. *Village or Vernacular Schools,* for the millions of India.

I fully agree with Mr. Josenhans, the Principal of the Basle Mission College, that the newly-formed Vernacular Education Society has fixed upon the right plan to benefit India at large; and I hope that, when they commence active operations in India, the missionaries will offer to take the superintendence of their schools, and connect with them their missionary operations in the villages. We require further;—

Girls' schools. 3. *Female Schools.*—The necessity of girls' school is now thank God! felt by all; and I hope increased efforts will be made to bring a large portion of females under scriptural instructions. If all the mothers of India were imbued with gospel truth, what a different aspect India would exhibit as to the moral character of her sons! We can, therefore, never overrate female education.

Female missionaries. But I would go a step further, and advocate the agency of female missionaries in India. It would not be their duty to preach in the bazar; but to go from house to house, and speak to the native women of the love of Jesus, wherever they find access.

The *second* great object of our educational institutions must be *to aid in the consolidation of* Christianity where it is established. If we desire to perpetuate, under God's blessing, a pure, scriptural profession of Christianity in our missions, we must impart to our young people, from their infancy, sound biblical knowledge. For this purpose we require,— *Consolidation of Christian communities*

1. *Infant-Schools, Schools for Christian Children, and Orphan Schools.*—Rightly conducted *infant-schools* exercise an immense influence in a native Christian congregation. We have experienced this in Benares; and I cannot too strongly recommend the establishment of such a school in every mission settlement where there is none. Whilst they elevate the minds of the children and raise the moral tone from childhood, they affect the mothers at home, and prove a source of blessing to the congregation at large. *Infant-schools.*

Infant-schools should be *conducted in the vernacular*, though each of them might have an English class to which the most talented children might be admitted.

2. *Schools for Christian Children* must follow. They will build upon the foundation already laid in the infant-school. They should be *separate* establishments from the schools attended by heathen boys, but in every respect equal to them; so that Christian parents may not be obliged to send their children to an English school, consisting of heathen boys, in order to insure for them a superior education. English classes, therefore, should be formed in each of them; but English should be taught only as a language; Scripture, and all secular knowledge, should be communicated in the vernacular. Fees should be required for English; additional fees. *Schools for Christian boys.*

3. *Orphan Schools.*—No mission should be without an orphan establishment for boys and girls, where such children are to be had. These institutions have advantages which no other school possesses. The children are usually received when very young, and thereby escape contamination from their heathen countrymen. They are entirely in the charge of the missionary. He can operate on their minds at prayer, in and out of school; for they form, as it were, one great family with the missionary, and he has full opportunity of impressing his own mind upon them. *Orphan schools.*

Orphans should likewise have separate schools; for the experience of many years has convinced me that our orphans are injured by attending the same institution with heathen lads; because the number of orphans is usually too small to affect a large school of heathen boys; and, consequently, if they are not *separate.*

decidedly pious, they lose ground themselves. Orphans and the children of Christians might be instructed in the same institution.

Industrial element.

As not all the orphans sent to our institutions are possessed of great abilities, manual labour should, from the first, be introduced into the plan of their education; for if they have been occupied in mental pursuits, unaccustomed to any kind of manual labour until the fifteenth or sixteenth year, yet have no hope of ever being able to earn their bread by mental labour, they find it then most difficult to apply themselves to manual labour; they become therefore unsettled, idle, find it almost impossible to earn a livelihood, and are for years a trial to the mission.

Training-schools.

4. But, to carry out these missionary efforts, we require a fourth kind of schools; namely, *Training Institutions for Teachers and Evangelists.*

As the number of teachers required for English schools will ever be but small, they can easily be trained, as regards a knowledge of English, in the English Institution; but for our preaching department and vernacular schools we require special institutions for training native teachers and evangelists. We need able native assistants; for European missionaries alone will never be able to convert India, nor fill it with the sound of the gospel from one end to the other. We must have able male and female native teachers throughout the land, and until we have such, our efforts will be limited, and our success small. There are several such establishments now maintained in India; and they are, no doubt, sources of great good to the districts in which they are established. We have one at Benares on a small scale, called our Head Seminary; and although we have never had a missionary able to give his whole time to it, we have, nevertheless, raised a number of valuable assistants for the great work, two of whom were last year ordained, and three more are qualified for ordination. We hope in future to be able to establish such institutions for both sexes on a large scale; the Lord having already given us an earnest towards it.

Native agents essential.

Under present circumstances I would not confine these training institutions to Christians, though they should, at all times, form the majority; but I would admit well-disposed young men and women of any creed; for whilst the Scriptures should be taught only by Christians, there are many branches taught in every school which others can teach. I would, however, make it a point of never admitting any Hindoo or Mahommedan opposed to Christianity, nor employ such in our schools. The training of teachers for our vernacular schools should be confined to the vernacular.

As regards the admission of boys into our schools, established in towns and villages, for other than Christian children, I would admit *every boy that came* and paid his entrance-fee, irrespective of his caste: yea, I would not even enter his caste into the school-register, nor ask of what caste he is. This can be done without upsetting our schools, because we have admitted low-caste boys; the London Society in Benares has done the same; and indeed the rule is universal in missionary schools. Caste ignored.

The results arising from these schools will not be everywhere the same. Speaking from my own experience and conviction, I should say that from the nature of the institutions, direct conversions will proceed more from orphan and Christian schools. Before leaving India I wrote down the names of all our converts, and classified them, as far as we can judge: and I found that we had more real conversions from among our orphans than from our united efforts in preaching and in schools. This will also hold good as regards the formation of missionary agents. In our missions at Benares the number of agents in the field are three to one from the orphan institution. But with regard to the spread of a general knowledge of Christianity, preaching stands foremost; and next to preaching, schools. Schools based on the Bible are mighty engines in undermining the whole fabric of Hindoo and Mohammedan superstition, and for diffusing light in religion throughout the land. The knowledge of the gospel imperceptibly influences the hearts of the pupils, and raises the tone of their morals. And the simple fact that throughout the late mutiny, among the thousands of rebels who joined the mutineers, not a single man was found who had been educated in a mission-school, declares loud enough that the word of God taught in these schools affects the heart and morals of the pupils in after-life. The general effect of our schools upon the population is, therefore, great; and if our gracious Queen really wishes to benefit her subjects in India, and make them good and loyal subjects, let her follow our plan, and base the instruction in all her educational institutions on the word of God. Results of schools. Effect on the native religions.

But what kind of Europeans are required for carrying out this great object of educating the young for time and eternity? Should they be missionaries or laymen, or what? My conviction is that training the young is such an important branch of missionary labour, that those engaged in it should be in nowise inferior to those engaged in preaching. We require men for this second branch of missionary labour, with minds well trained for school-work; Missionaries and laymen both suitable.

devoted in heart and soul to their Master's cause, apt to teach the young; *otherwise let them not engage in this branch of missionary labour;* patient, persevering, never weary in well-doing; for in India their patience and perseverance will be tested to the utmost.

Ordained men suitable.

But are ordained missionaries justified in devoting a part of their time and strength to secular instruction? Some think they are not; but I would say, yes! Let those who engage in training the young devote all their energies to them; let their prayers, their labour, their influence in and out of school, centre in the training and welfare of the young. Let the missionary operate upon his pupils in school hours, and draw them around him out of school hours; so as to prevent them from losing at home what they have learnt in school, and to enable *him* to impress his own mind, as much as possible, upon his pupils. A right-minded missionary can make every branch of instruction subservient to the gospel.

Laymen also.

But if it be thought preferable to have laymen for schools, have them; only let them be missionaries in heart and soul and qualifications; no inferior Europeans should be employed in our schools. These laymen should be placed on a level with ordained missionaries; and, after a few years' faithful labour, be eligible for filling the posts of principals. If this position be not granted them, they will strive for ordination in order to obtain it. Every European engaged in our schools should possess a good knowledge of the vernacular, so as to be able to impart instruction in the vernacular in every branch taught in his school. As regards the external arrangements of our educational institutions for both sexes,

Circles of schools.

I would propose to form circles of schools; in one Society, each missionary district to form one circle. I would then introduce into all the schools the same course of instruction; and appoint a general inspector, either an ordained or lay missionary, for visiting these schools, to strengthen the hands of and to advise and help those engaged in their most arduous, difficult, but blessed task of training the young. Thereby unity would be obtained in our system of education; a host of difficulties removed as regards plans to be pursued and books to be used; and the great end of our schools — that of aiding in making known the gospel to the young, and of building up infant churches already established — would be best secured.

Rev. C. T. Hœrnle.

The Rev. C. T. HŒRNLÉ, of the Church Missionary Society in Agra, said:—He had witnessed the influence which these schools had exercised; he was convinced that, as far as the native Christians were concerned, it was necessary to give them a good education, and, to some extent, he thought they had been successful. He would strongly recommend that, with regard to caste no distinction should be made; and with regard to the Bible, it had all along been the conviction of missionaries that education should be based upon the Word of God. Whatever objections had been made to it had, he thought, been disproved by the actual experience of their missionary schools. In the schools at their station of Secundra, in Agra, half the number of boys were Hindoo and Mahommedan, and the other half Christians. The school was open to all; but those who wished to attend must conform to the rules laid down, having the option to come or not to come. He did not know a single instance of any boy ever having made an objection to the rules laid down; he did not recollect a single instance in which an objection had been made to reading the Bible, learning the catechism, or attending the Scripture instructions in the school; but he knew that in the morning, when the school was opened with prayer, the heathen boys and the Christian boys were kneeling down together, and uttering the same prayer in the name of Jesus Christ. (Hear, hear.) He knew that all were glad to read the New Testament; and as he was frequently in the school himself giving instruction in the Scriptures, he knew many instances where heathen boys gave replies which were by no means inferior to what he would have received from Christians; and he knew instances of gospel truth having been carried home by them. He would refer only to one. One of the boys left the school, and he (Mr. Hœrnlé) expressed a regret to his mother that she should have taken him away so early. She replied,— "Never mind, he has brought his books, and he reads out of those books to me in the evening when he is at home." As to the infant-schools, he could only say, that it was a pleasure to see the little children brought under their instruction; and he would strongly recommend that every mission should have an infant-school attached to it. The great difficulty, however, was to get suitable teachers.

Caste to be ignored.

Heathen boys willing to enter Christian schools.

Infant-schools.

The second paper appointed was then read, as follows:—

ON MISSIONARY EDUCATION.

By the Rev. Thomas Smith,

LATE MISSIONARY OF THE FREE CHURCH OF SCOTLAND IN CALCUTTA.

Controversies on this subject have been numerous.

There is, perhaps, no branch of missionary work that has been the subject of more or keener discussion than Education. In venturing to bring this important subject before the Conference, I might, perhaps, be disposed to claim for my sentiments a certain amount of respect, on the ground of their being the result of twenty years' laborious experience; but I am quite aware that another reading of that phrase would be twenty years' accumulated prejudice. I shall, therefore, beg that all reference to the author be waved; and shall, with much deference, submit a few arguments, which, I trust, will be received and considered without regard to aught but their intrinsic soundness or unsoundness,—a few facts, for whose accuracy alone I vouch, leaving to the judgment of the Conference to determine whether they are pertinent or otherwise.

Education a legitimate sphere of labour.

1. My first proposition is, that *Education is a legitimate branch of Missionary operation.* In defending this position, I will not make use of an argument that has sometimes been used in discussions on this subject, to the effect that *teaching* is either put on the same footing with *preaching* in the commission given by our blessed Lord, or else that the two terms are convertible. This statement is quite true; but I am quite willing to admit that,

The point at issue.

as an argument with respect to the only point really at issue, it is of no value whatever. For that point is not whether the Gospel is to be made known in one way or another; whether in the way which is now technically called preaching, or in that which is technically called teaching; but in reality, whether it is right for

May we teach other things than the gospel.

the missionary to teach *other things* than the Gospel, with the view to the introduction of Christianity into a country, and the establishment of it there. Now I maintain that education, in its proper sense, of at once storing the mind with instruction, and cultivating all its faculties and powers, is a legitimate method of fulfilling the great object of Christian missions. In this respect, I would put it on precisely the same footing with that method which

Such is done in the Moravian system:

is so nobly connected with the name of the venerable fathers of modern missions, of whom it is our privilege to have at least one honoured and worthy representative amongst us. Our educational missions in India are just a carrying out of the *Moravian* system; which again is substantially that adopted by the most successful missionaries of our times, those in the South Seas, and that adopted by the missionaries of all denominations in South Africa. It is substantially the same also with that system which last night received so hearty a recognition from this Conference and the Christian people of this city, who so cordially united with us in giving glory to God for the success that has attended Medical Missions. <small>in Medical Missions:</small>

I would call attention also to the fact, that even the most violent opponents of educational missions that I have ever met with, virtually admit the principle for which we contend in their advocacy of Female Education in India. I have never met one who has not admitted that, if the millions of Indian females are to be Christianised at all, it must be to a great extent by means of educational operations. But if this be admitted, then I submit that the whole principle is conceded. The only question that then remains is as to the existence or non-existence, in particular cases, of the circumstances which may render the application of the principle expedient. <small>and in Female education.</small>

I would now very briefly point out what I conceive to be a mistake that lies at the root of a considerable portion of the opposition that has been offered in this country to Educational Missionary operations. I wish I could be as sure of finding terms in which to describe it, which may not give offence to any of my hearers, as I am sure that I do not wish to give offence to any of them. I refer to the fallacy, unintentional no doubt, of confounding things that are essentially different, because they happen to be called by the same name. In this country there is not, and probably there never was, any such thing as a Missionary-school. I send my sons to school, not with a view of their conversion to God, although with a humble and earnest desire that all their acquisitions made there may be sanctified, so as to make them better men and better Christians. Still my object in sending them to school is not their conversion, and the object of their teachers in meeting them there is as little their conversion. Now in this respect there is, indeed, no essential difference (I mean essential to the argument) between the ends and aims of the English parent, and the ends and aims of the Hindoo parent. But there is all the difference in the world between the ends and views,— the perfectly legitimate ends and views—of the English teacher, and those of the Missionary teacher. Now no one who thinks of the <small>Mistakes in opposing missionary education.</small> <small>Aim of education in England.</small> <small>Aim of the missionary in India.</small>

Effect of the difference. — matter can fail to perceive that this difference will entirely modify the whole course of the education; and it will be evident that any argument which concludes that missionary schools are not legitimate instruments of carrying on missionary work, on the ground that such schools as alone we have in England would not be such, is altogether faulty and utterly valueless as an argument. To say that the conductors of Missionary Institutions do not always keep this distinctive end in view, is simply to say that they are imperfect and weak men. I am myself conscious of an almost overwhelming amount of imperfection in this respect; but I have sometimes realised the great object to such an extent as to convince me that it was possible to realise it habitually; and I have seen it realised by my colleagues to a far greater degree.

Educational work not suitable to all localities. — 2. My second proposition is, that *while Educational operations are not suitable to some localities and circumstances, they are peculiarly suitable to others.* The former branch of this statement needs no enlargement or enforcement, as I presume that no man ever did or ever will controvert it. The latter branch of it I cannot do aught like justice to within the limits prescribed to me. I can only indicate a few of the circumstances which in my mind seem to point out a locality as a suitable one for educational operations as a branch of Missionary work. If I find, then, that there is in a land a system of heathenism mainly supported by a system of *Where suitable.* — education pervaded, both as to the matter taught and the manner of teaching it, by that heathenism;—if I find that the effect of that heathenism is utterly to pervert the understanding and to sear the conscience, so as to make it to the whole body of a people a matter of most earnest, and, in one sense, most honest, belief that there is and can be no distinction between moral good and evil, no difference between God and the creature, and, consequently, no responsibility; and that the great body of the people not only, like unregenerate men everywhere, do not feel the guilt of sin upon their consciences, but constantly believe and feel that sin is an impos- *Where it is needed:* — sibility and a contradiction in terms;—I think myself as much entitled to try to teach the people of that land that there is a real and actual difference between moral good and evil, and between truth and falsehood, as I should feel entitled in a land of cannibalism to strive to put a stop to the horrid practice. And *and where a desire for it exists.* — if I find that in that land, or in certain places of that land, there is excited, by providential circumstances, an earnest desire for that sound training of the mental and moral faculties, which is the legitimate and heaven-appointed instrumentality for eradicating such notions, subversive of all morality and all religion, I dare not turn a deaf ear to the call that seems addressed to me by God in his providence, to make use of the means wherewithal he has furnished me to do what is unquestionably a work well-pleasing to him. And the call, perhaps, comes with redoubled force, if I find that there are other means and agencies ready to supply the *felt* want, and yet to leave the *real* want utterly unsupplied. To no one even slightly acquainted with the state of things in India, and certainly to no member of this Conference, need I point out that I have been describing the actual condition of many parts of it; and I humbly submit that those who in those localities have regarded Educational operations as a legitimate means of introducing the Gospel, merit no condemnation at your hands, but rather a frank and hearty and brotherly God-speed.

3. My third statement is, that even in the localities the best suited to educational operations, *these ought not to engross too large a proportion of Missionary strength and means.* What is the due proportion it is impossible to determine abstractly. I am free to admit that I think this proportion has probably been exceeded in Calcutta; not because there is too much labour or means expended on Educational operations, for I think there is still too little, but because there is far too little expended on other departments. When I joined the Church of Scotland's Institution in 1839, the whole amount of missionary strength given to education was the labour of myself and one colleague, and a very limited portion of that of another. At that time there were ten or twelve men whose whole time was devoted to vernacular preaching. Now the amount of vernacular preaching by Europeans is certainly not greater than it was then, while the amount of labour devoted to Educational Institutions has been increased, I suppose, not less than sixfold. Very glad were we to welcome our brethren of the London and the Church Missionary Societies as fellow-labourers in the Educational field, which we had begun to think peculiarly our own; and we know that it is only by the hand of God sending sickness and death, that the number of vernacular preachers has been sunk below its proper proportion. But while we should greatly grieve to see the Educational resources of Calcutta diminished, we earnestly hope that the proportion may be restored by a large increase of the number of vernacular preachers.

<small>Education not to engross too much labour.</small>

<small>In Calcutta, too little attention given to preaching.</small>

4. Did my limits permit, I should now enter upon a consideration of the *success* that has attended Educational operations in India, and especially in that part of it with which I am most <small>Success.</small>

acquainted. This I cannot do, but shall merely indicate the points on which I should have dwelt had there been time. I should have spoken of the elevation and social changes that have been produced, and the general elevation of public sentiment, which every one who knows India will testify to be very great, and which few will deny to be mainly the result of Education. Then I should have spoken of the number of conversions, which, although not many, have yet been far more numerous in proportion to the missionaries employed than those effected in the same place by other means. Then I should have spoken of the influence exerted and likely to be exerted by the converts, in consequence of their education, and the position that many of them are occupying, and are destined to occupy, in society. Then I should have said something as to their qualifications for evangelistic work among their countrymen. This last is the only point on which I shall venture to ask the indulgence of the Conference for a single remark. There are many classes of native labourers required for India; and for some departments of work the converts, who are the results of Missionary Institutions, and who have continued their studies in these Institutions after their conversion, with a view to missionary employment, are undoubtedly well, and, I may say, peculiarly fitted. But for others, and those important ones, it must be admitted that the system adopted in these institutions has not specially qualified them. My ideal of an evangelist for the village population of Bengal would be realized provided we could combine two terms that have hitherto, in general, been almost antagonistic, and raise up a body of *Christian Pundits;* that is to say, if we could give sound Christian principles and sound Christian learning, and retain the simple habits and the national feelings and sympathies which give the Pundits so strong an influence over the people. But it must be admitted that it is difficult to educate, without, to a certain extent, denationalising. It is true that the denationalising effects and the educating effects of the process will not be proportional; that is to say, that the best and strongest minds will get the maximum of good and the minimum of evil from their education, just as amongst ourselves, we have men of mighty intellect who equally excel in handling the deepest themes, and in preaching the simple Gospel in its simplest form to the simple poor; while minds of inferior order are often unfitted for the simple duties of their calling, until they unlearn a considerable portion of their little learning. I have stated this with all frankness as a weak point of the system that I have taken upon myself to defend. But I believe the evil is capable of a cure, and that cure is already at work. It is by improving and giving a proportionally larger share of atten- tion to the Vernacular department of the educational course, that the denationalising tendency is to be counteracted. It has always been a difficulty to get those who were acquiring an English education to pay sufficient attention to their own language. I believe I may say, that the superintendents of our Missionary Institutions in Bengal have, ere now, come to the conclusion that the difficulty must and shall be overcome; and that they are bringing to bear upon it an energy which has, by the blessing of God, overcome greater difficulties, and will, by the same blessing, overcome this also. I ask for them the hearty sympathy, in their most laborious and difficult work, and the frank, brotherly recognition, and the fervent, effectual prayers of all the members of this Conference, and of all who long for the overthrow of Satan's kingdom, and the establishment in righteousness of His throne whose right it is to reign.

More vernacular needed.

The Rev. J. H. TITCOMB, having also prepared a paper on the same subject, was requested to read it, which he did as follows:—

ON MISSIONARY EDUCATION.

By the Rev. J. H. Titcomb,

SECRETARY TO THE VERNACULAR EDUCATION SOCIETY FOR INDIA.

What is a mission school? What is its proper place in the field of missions? How should it vary in different places, and in different stages of a mission's growth? More important questions can scarcely be asked; nor can any be considered with greater advantage to the progress of the Gospel in heathen lands.

Questions on this subject.

In making the following remarks as a contribution toward their settlement, I observe that education, to be really effective, ought always to be developed according to the progressive advancement of the mission for which it is intended. There appear to be three stages in this development; which I venture to call the *introductory*, the *permanent*, and the *reproductive*.

Three stages.

I. *The Introductory stage of Missionary Education.* When a mission is opened in a new country, it must be necessarily started by providing schools for the heathen. In doing which it

1. Introductory.

naturally commences by teaching the English language: because (1) the missionaries are most familiar with it themselves; (2) they have no printed books in the vernacular; (3) it is sure to attract the natives; (4) it opens to them all our own stores of sacred literature.

When a mission grows, however, and converts have been made in the surrounding villages, then the school which was formerly used for heathen, becomes occupied by the children of native Christians. Meanwhile, a few native teachers having been educated, facilities for vernacular education spring up. Until, at length, the mission, having extended itself far beyond its original centre, English becomes gradually of less importance in a missionary point of view, and the vernacular proportionately imperative.

<small>2. Permanent stage.</small>

Under these circumstances we are led to consider

II. *The Permanent state of Missionary Education.*—I believe it is now universally allowed that, to evangelise a large heathen population, we must create a native agency which shall be capable of enlightening the masses through the medium of their mother tongue. It is, therefore, obvious, that the form of education most permanently required will be vernacular.

The question is,—how shall we best adapt our missionary arrangements to promote it? And here, let me add, that in all my following remarks I shall refer more especially to British India.

<small>English schools useful:</small>

There is no doubt that, in order to qualify our superior converts for important positions in the native church, good English schools will always be wanted. At the same time, if care be not taken, they may exhaust too much of our missionary strength, and impede the progress of a native pastorate. For, (1) they have a

<small>their dangers:</small>

tendency to hinder missionaries in their acquisition of the vernacular. (2) The education they give the students unfits them for the humble and unremunerative labour of village-teaching. (3) They are not wanted now as formerly. At first they were necessary starting-points for mission work. But now the case is altered. We have advanced to higher ground; and are not so much called upon to educate the general community as to develope the resources of native agency.

<small>The vernacular now greatly needed.</small>

Let us remind our missionaries, therefore, that they have passed the introductory stage of education; that they are now beyond the need of mere pioneering and civilising processes, and should take advantage of their position to make all their educational institutions bear more directly on vernacular instruction.

Are these views peculiar? They were felt so strongly by the American missionaries five years since, that, after conference with a deputation sent to India by the American Board of Commissioners for Foreign Missions, they resolved on introducing extensive changes into their Anglo-vernacular seminaries. At Batticotta they reduced the number of its students, and restricted their studies solely to preparation for village mission work. In the Mahratta mission they reported,—"There is no reason for the study of English in schools for catechists and teachers, at least in the Deccan." In the same spirit the Madura mission decided that young men preparing for schoolmasters, catechists, and pastors, "should be restricted purely to Tamil studies." Even Dr. Duff has lately expressed his opinion, that if we are ever to evangelise the ignorant masses, it must be simply and entirely through the vernacular.

Granting, then, that vernacular village schools must form the permanent stage of missionary education, it is obvious that we want greater facilities in preparing suitably qualified agents for conducting them. I therefore pass to the third point of inquiry,—

III. *The Reproductive Stage of Missionary Education.* 3. Reproductive stage.
Nothing can be really permanent unless it contain within itself the germs of reproduction. Indifference to this truth has been one of the greatest weaknesses of our whole missionary system, which has hitherto depended too much on the constant supply of new missionaries, and relied too little on the capabilities of its own converts. It is, however, one advantage of these schools, that they develope the internal resources of a mission, and become nurseries for native teachers and pastors.

But for these offices further training is needed. How can it be effected?

It will often happen that the parents of the most promising pupils are too poor to support them after they can earn their own living; in which case we see the great use of *boarding-schools*, where such lads may be received at the expense of the mission, and be properly superintended while studying for future service; and, similarly of *industrial schools*, where, though learning some trade, in order to be less burdensome to the mission, they may, nevertheless, join the other students in their classes, and become prepared for some higher employment. Boarding-schools.

In regard to the method of training, the example of our American brethren is worthy of all imitation. English and Angli-

Village-schools.

cising influences must be abandoned. Proper institutions must be formed in the midst of village districts; by means of which the native church may not only ultimately become self-sustaining, but at no very distant day aggressive. Let it not be said that this will involve our Missionary Societies in too great an expense. It is a vital question; especially in reference to schoolmasters. The school of the village is the corner-stone of the native church; for while the master produces the pupil, it is from the pupil we must draw the catechist and pastor. Thus any radical inefficiency in the first will necessarily injure the whole. It therefore appears idle to rest satisfied with the employment of heathen or half-trained Christians on the ground that separate institutions are expensive. Shall we be slower in learning our duty than the Government? The State has long since perceived that to reach the masses of India it must train its own schoolmasters; and it has already instituted sixteen normal vernacular colleges for that purpose. Why should it be otherwise with Missionary Societies? Will they be content to yield the race to their non-Christian rivals? Shall labour or expense prove a hindrance, when it can clearly be shown that without such means the native churches of India can never flourish?

Training-schools.

But here another difficulty opens:—Who is to train these native masters? The technical routine which is necessary for this work can never be effectually accomplished by ordinary missionaries. In an early stage of missions the attempt is necessary; but as schools multiply and education improves, a division of labour comes into play, and men are required to train teachers, who have been themselves trained for the work, and who can devote their whole time to it. Where, then, are our Missionary Societies to obtain native masters who shall be capable of conducting training-classes?

The Vernacular Education Society.

Happily, the solution of this difficulty may be found in a society which has been lately formed for promoting Christian Vernacular Education in India, and which is about to commence its operations by opening an institution in Madras for training native training-masters. Its object will be to gather from the various missions a number of well-selected converts; and, having qualified them for the work of training others, return them for employment in their mission service. Thus each Society may soon have its vernacular institutions in good working order, and from thence supply all its village-schools with Christian teachers. A central agency of this kind will prove a great economy of labour.

It appears to me that, in regard to the reproductive stage of missionary education, this lies at the root of the whole matter, and will ultimately have a most important bearing on the prosperity of the native churches of India.

I may add, that all which has been here said regarding boys' schools will apply with even greater force to girls'. If a native church is to become strong and healthy, *female education* must be recognised as a social institution. To this end boarding-schools and Zenána tuition are, no doubt, extremely valuable; but eventually we must look forward to a much more general and systematic method of instruction. We must have girls' day-schools, for which mistresses shall be as carefully trained as we propose to train the masters. The difficulties attending such an effort will be gigantic; yet, I fear, we shall be only trifling with our responsibilities till we set ourselves more seriously to accomplish it. *Girls' schools.*

Another work which needs to be taken up with equal energy, if ever we are to utilise the reproductive powers of missionary education, is the promotion of Christian vernacular literature, especially for the young. As village-schools grow, and a thirst for reading is excited, we shall want an increasing number of simple, lively, educational works, adapted to the Oriental mind,—some for the school, and others for the home; we shall want a serial literature adapted for all classes, books on experimental religion, commentaries on Scripture, &c. In prosecuting this purpose we shall do well to lose no time. The native presses of Delhi and Calcutta are annually producing large editions of secularising literature. Let us hasten to cast salt into the waters. Let the various Tract and School-book Societies, aided by that valuable auxiliary to Christian vernacular education before alluded to, enter with greater and more concentrated efforts into this great work. They will in that way consolidate and crown our missionary education, and become largely instrumental in bestowing upon British India the inestimable blessings of an indigenous Christian Church. *Vernacular literature.*

Dr. G. H. DAVIS, Secretary of the Religious Tract Society, said:—The latter part of the paper just read introduced a subject which he found on the list for that day, but to which the other papers did not appear to have drawn attention, namely, "Vernacular Literature; how it may best be circulated." A document had come into his possession on the previous day, *Dr. G. H. DAVIS.* *Vernacular literature.*

which showed how vernacular literature might be circulated by native colportage; and when good Christian books were put into circulation in that way, he thought it would be much for the benefit of India. But Christian vernacular books ought, if possible, to be originals rather than translations. Those acquainted with the language of France and Italy said:—
"Your English translations don't suit our mind: English translations don't reach the hearts of the people;" and the same must be true in the East. While an English book may furnish the skeleton, we must clothe it in the vernacular idiom if it was desired to reach the hearts of the people. (Hear, hear.) From the native presses of Madras a large number of vernacular works issued of a very deleterious character. Dr. Murray Mitchell has pointed out the extent to which the native presses in Bombay poured out vernacular literature, and the necessity for meeting them with a Christian literature. In the year 1857, 571,670* books had been issued for sale from the vernacular presses of Calcutta; and he (Dr. Davis) was grieved to say, that of the whole of these not more than 9550 were distinctly Christian, published for sale by the Bible and Tract Societies. Nearly 80,000 had been circulated by those two bodies, but the number printed for sale was only 9550. As to the character of these native works, he would say a word. The Almanacs printed for sale — and he had no doubt sold — numbered 135,000. What did these Almanacs teach? "They were as necessary for the Bengalee as his *hookah* or his *pan*. Without it he could not determine the auspicious days for marrying (twenty-two in the year); for first feeding an infant with rice (twenty-seven days in the year); or for feeding a mother with rice in the fifth month of gestation (twelve days in the year); or for commencing to build a house; and the like." Then they came to educational works, relating to agriculture, algebra, arithmetic, &c., of which 145,300 were issued, and from them religion was systematically excluded. He who read them learned nothing of God, or of Christianity, or of moral and spiritual truth. There were printed also 14,250 books of an "erotic" character, books abounding in obscene passages; 33,050 copies of works of fiction, amongst which the cleverly-written but indecent tale of *Vidyà Sundar*, composed last century, with all the ability and licentiousness of a Fielding,

---

* Dr. Davis quoted these statistical details from a Report, in his hand, on the Vernacular Press of Calcutta in 1858, prepared by the Rev. JAMES LONG, C. M. S., and published by the Government of Bengal.

holds a prominent place, and is sold sixty pages to the anna. Besides these, there were 96,150 copies of works printed to sustain the systems of Mythology and Hindooism. The Bible Society and Tract Society distributed only about 80,000 Christian books, which were met by 96,150 on Mythology and Hindooism. Christians must awaken to these facts, and endeavour to produce something at least equal to the native issues. It was quite clear that if it were only to meet the issues of the native presses something must be done; done on a large scale; and done right speedily. (Applause.) Missionaries had done much to meet the want;—much more than was generally supposed, and they deserved all credit for their labours. In Bengalee, during the last ten years, there had been published thirty-nine tracts and fifty-eight books, including Wayland's *Moral Science*; in Canarese, seventeen tracts and nineteen books, including the Tract Society's editions of Paley's *Horæ Paulinæ*; in Gujerati, seven books, three of elementary instruction and four for adults, amongst which was the life of the Rev. S. Flavel; in Hindi, nineteen tracts and sixteen books; in Hindustani, fifty tracts and thirty-three books; in Malayalam, eleven tracts; in Marathi, nineteen tracts and thirty-six books; in Uriya, twenty-eight tracts and ten books; and in Tamil, eighty-six tracts and fifty-five books. The Christians of Ceylon acted with extraordinary power and vigour under the guidance of Mr. Murdoch, who in India was almost ubiquitous and universal; for he (Dr. Davis) found his name as Secretary of the Singhalese Vernacular Society, of the Madras Society, and also Secretary of the Calcutta Society. (Applause.) He would just leave these facts before the Conference; and hoped, that from them some impetus would go forth throughout the whole of India, to urge their brethren to engage more energetically in the production of a vernacular Christian literature. (Applause.)

The Rev. BEHARI LAL SINGH said,—He was most desirous to impress upon the fathers and brethren of the Conference, that the natives would be found the most successful translators of the Bible into the vernacular, if they were properly trained for the work. With regard to the results of missionary institutions in the form of native agencies, it was most desirable, in order to be able to judge of them properly, to inquire how many of these young men, who had been fed, clothed, and educated, at the expense of Missionary Societies, were now in the ministry and how many had left for other pursuits? (Hear, hear.) Next, how many of those who had been ordained were satisfied with their present position, or with a moderate salary? If any of the principals and professors of our missionary colleges could enlighten us on this point, the church would then be in a position to improve our great educational system, which has produced in other respects such unparalleled results. He made this remark without in any degree wishing to disparage missionary institutions; in one of which he had been brought up, and to which he owed all his religious and educational training; but it was necessary, in his opinion, while the virtues and great doings of our agents were extolled in the missionary magazines, that their weaknesses and imperfections should be brought forward, in order that prayer and sympathy might be exercised on their behalf in these matters.

Character of vernacular books. With regard to our vernacular literature and periodicals, it depends a great deal upon the various sections of the native community for whom these vernacular books and papers are intended. Many of the books in the vernacular have been written in a very simple style, suited for the mass of the people; but he did not think our learned pundits and moulvies would take much interest in these books; and that they would require a higher style of literature and class of thought. He believed, with great deference to all his European fathers and brethren, that it would be well if much of the production of vernacular literature were left to able and pious natives.

Rev. T. Smith. The Rev. Mr. SMITH suggested, that the only two books that should be translated should be *Robinson Crusoe* and *Pilgrim's Progress*.

Rev. J. M'Kee. The Rev. J. M'KEE, missionary to Guzerat, wished to make a few remarks on the Government system of education. He hoped that the Conference and people generally at home would fully understand the action of the Government of India in this respect. *Government education.* Government said to the natives, "We wish you to understand that we have no religion at all;" and this was just what the natives would not understand. They understood that every man had his religion; and, therefore, they did not understand our Government when they said they were of no religion at all; hence the mistrust *Government not neutral.* of Government on the part of the natives. Another point, also, was, that Government had not been neutral, but had closely connected themselves with the idolatry of the country up to the present time. He was rejoiced to say that with regard to the temples in India, a very great change for the better had taken place; but there was still a close connexion between the Government and the heathen festivals of the country. In illustration of this he would instance one fact, because it affected the neighbourhood where he resided. In the native principality of Baroda there was a great heathen festival every year; it was observed over the whole of India, but principally in Baroda. On this occasion the priest of Baroda collected a great many Brahmins, and multitudes of natives, and the image of Gunputti having been prepared, they marched forth to celebrate the honours of Gunputti. He had not time to give the whole details with reference to this festival; but it was the law of the Government that the Resident Officers and sepoys must go out and meet the ruler, the Guicowar, and present the salaam of Her Majesty Queen Victoria, while he and his people were engaged in this procession. He would also mention one other fact with reference to the discouragement which our Government gave to Christianity. He could give a great many facts illustrative of this; but this one recently occurred in the Punjab:—The 24th Punjaubee Native Regiment had got a few native tracts, and having been impressed with them, and there being no missionary at hand, they applied to some officers for further information regarding particular statements. Our officers, as free men, and enjoying liberty of conscience, expounded to them the nature of Christianity; and in the absence of a missionary, a few meetings were held. Immediately, however, or shortly after it became known, a positive command arrived from the Viceroy that no such information should be given, that no such meetings should be held, and that our officers should never converse with sepoys respecting Christianity. Mr. M'Kee further observed that he believed as long as we withheld the truth from the sepoys and the native soldiery, India would not be safe.

<small>Baroda festival.</small>

<small>The 24th Punjaubee Regiment.</small>

The Rev. GEO. CANDY, of Bombay, said he wished to make two remarks. Though English people at home are entirely unfit to prepare works for India, yet English people who have spent a long time abroad are perfectly competent, and in some respects more so than the natives. He would stimulate native brethren to try to excel, or to do better, yet he could not agree to leave the work to them. The other point is with regard to the dissemination of vernacular literature. Some seven or eight years ago

<small>Rev. G. CANDY.</small>

<small>Englishmen fit to write native books.</small>

Sale of tracts in Bombay.

the Bombay Tract Society came to the resolution not to give any more tracts away, but to put a merely nominal price upon them. There were some at that time who anticipated an injurious result from this resolution, but there were others who as confidently anticipated success. It was a matter for thankfulness that they were borne out by the result. The circulation after this resolution increased, in four or five years, five-fold. (Hear, hear.)

Rev. Dr. BAYLEE.

The Rev. Dr. BAYLEE said he had not had much practice in translation, but he had been at various times engaged in religious controversy and teaching with the natives of different countries.

Principles for translating the Bible.

He had for three years conducted the services of the Church of England in the Irish language on the west coast of Ireland; and as the principle of translation was the same, whether in Ireland or in India, the experience which he had gained there would apply to India.

In reading the Church Service in the Irish language, they had been obliged to alter some of the expressions to come nearer to the popular idiom.

His own experience.

The feeling of this want had induced Mr. Nangle and himself to attempt a revision of the Bible in Irish. They had a schoolmaster, who was what he might call an Irish pundit. He was a man well acquainted with the oral literature of his native land. He could recite, for example, 1200 lines of Ossian in the original Irish without hesitation.

A triad:

they combine their knowledge.

That man knew nothing but Irish, and what English he had learned colloquially.

He (Dr. Baylee) knew very little of Irish; only what he had acquired by book study: but he had given years of attentive study to Hebrew and Greek, as well as to the general philosophy of language.

Mr. Nangle knew nothing of Hebrew, and was not a scholar or a linguist; but he had a thorough familiarity with Irish, and had had the ordinary University education.

The result.

Each one was, therefore, very imperfect; but he would venture to say that the three combined constituted very nearly perfection, for the particular task which they undertook. (Laughter.)

Dr. Baylee could tell Mr. Nangle the exact meaning of the Hebrew word; and knew enough of Irish to judge whether the Irish sentence, as composed by Mr. Nangle, and explained by the Irish pundit, corresponded with the Hebrew.

It was on some such plan as this that our present Indian versions may be thoroughly adapted to the wants of the natives.

It will take generations before the natives themselves will be able to execute the task of a native version.

On this subject, we must not confound two very distinct questions; original treatises on religious subjects, and the translation of the Bible. _{Two things.}

Educated Christian natives may write better books for their countrymen than Europeans could do; but our University training, our philological studies, our centuries of experience in biblical versions, have given us a discipline for which the native mind is at present unfit. _{University training.}

The knowledge of a language vernacularly, and even the knowledge of it extensively, in its literature, is a far different thing from a philosophical and critical knowledge of the same language. For example, in English, take the word *Religion*. He would venture to say that nineteen out of twenty of any cultivated audience in England would be unaware of the meaning of that word. Let him ask them individually the meaning of Jas. i. 27, " Pure religion and undefiled," they would almost universally say that it meant "godly piety." They would be startled at being told that it meant no more than a true attention to the outward services of religion. Yet every competent Greek scholar would agree with him. _{What is knowing language.}

In the Bible the word religion is never once used for godliness or piety. Some time since he (Dr. Baylee) was much struck with a passage in Philo Judæus, who says of the ignorance of the heathen; "They have a religion (θρησκεια), and they call it godliness (ευσεβεια)."

It may seem paradoxical; but he (Dr. Baylee) would venture to say, that a first-rate Greek scholar from Oxford or Cambridge was more critically acquainted with the Greek language than was Chrysostom, or Basil, or even Plato.

In the present day we have a remarkable proof of this amongst the Jews. Every body knows the wonderful amount of knowledge which a learned Jew has of the literature of his own language. Dr. Baylee has had much controversy with men of that class. He had had the happiness of baptizing in his own church nearly twenty Jews. _{The Jews.}

In controversy with them, he found his critical knowledge of the Hebrew was far greater than theirs, although they had read a hundred times as much as he. This was to be attributed, not to any superior talents, but to the inestimable advantage of our University training.

The English and German versions.

It would also interest English readers to know how incomparably superior our English version is to all others. In dealing with German Jews, Dr. Baylee constantly found Luther's German version fail him. He never found this with the English. To give one example. That important passage, "Let thy hand be upon the man of thy right hand, upon the Son of man whom thou madest strong for thyself:" (Ps. lxxx. 17) Luther renders "man," *das Volk,* "the *people* of thy right hand;" thus destroying the sense of the passage. His version is a noble one; but he constantly sacrificed critical accuracy to the beauty of poetic feeling.

On these grounds, therefore, he would earnestly press on the Conference the great difference between original compositions by natives of India and the translation of the Bible.

Rev. S. Hislop.

The Rev. S. HISLOP, of Nagpore, stated, that the countenance given by Government to the religion of the natives was not confined to Baroda, but extended to Cutch, Indore, and Gwalior, at all of which courts the Rajas continued to receive honours that were necessarily associated in the minds of their subjects with the festivals, on which they were paid. The same practice had prevailed at Nagpore till the period of its annexation, since which the encouragement given to Hindooism had not ceased, but only changed its form. He wished to make a remark suggested by what had fallen from the respected Secretary of the Tract Society, and his friend, Mr. Tucker. In Bombay they had adopted the plan of selling all their tracts. From the experience he had had during the first year and a half of their mission of the Madras system of free giving, and the experience he had had since of the Bombay system of sale, he greatly preferred that all the missionaries of India should adopt the latter practice; and in order to render it more efficient, it was desirable that they should employ the services of colporteurs. They had followed it up for about thirteen years, and found it attended with the best results. They now sold as many tracts as ever they could have given away gratuitously, and they had always the gratification of knowing that the tracts were prized, and preserved, and read, with an interest that could not be inspired in any other way. (Hear.) He would like, also, to refer to the Christian Vernacular Education Society, which he thought was likely to be a blessing to the people. At Nagpore they could not

System of selling tracts.

Need of vernacular schools.

complain of the Government education, for there was none to complain of. There had not been an attempt of the smallest kind made by the Government to enlighten the natives. This, perhaps, some may think better than if the Government were to interfere at all—at least, to introduce the system established in other parts. Still, it is sad to think that the paucity of readers is so very great. There are five districts into which the province is divided; and in the most cultivated of these perhaps the proportion of readers to non-readers is about one to two hundred; but in other districts, where the hill tribes reside, the proportion is far less. It may be one to six or eight hundred. Only one reader to eight hundred people! Now I think it is the plan of the Vernacular Education Society that, when a native teacher is trained, he is sent forth to establish a school, which shall be supported by the fees of the pupils. Here, however, arises a serious practical difficulty; for it is exactly where the educational destitution is greatest, that the demand for learning, and, consequently, the willingness to support a teacher, is least. I should rejoice, if our church could increase her agency, and do more to supply the distressing want of Christian instruction that exists at Nagpore; but meanwhile that want continues, as I have represented it. (Applause.) *Gross ignorance in Nagpore.*

The Rev. WILLIAM CAMPBELL, formerly of Bangalore, rose and said,—I am an old missionary, and belong to the old school, and was in India at a time when there was little English taught. *Rev. W. CAMPBELL.*

On my arrival at Madras, a missionary said to me, "Now, Mr. Campbell, it has almost become an axiom in India, that if a missionary does not get over the difficulties of the language within the year, there is little likelihood of his getting over them at all." Of course this spurred me on amazingly; and, by the blessing of God, I soon acquired the language, and the ability to circulate the truth among the natives. *Need of learning the native tongue.*

In the Telloogoo Hitopadeesa there is a story to the following effect. In the city of Madras, there lived a certain major who did not learn the languages of the natives, and who was, consequently, dependent on his butler as his interpreter. As he was very fond of seeing jugglers exhibit, a company came to his residence one day and erected their pole, and went through their performances, much to the amusement of the major, who sat in his verandah to watch them, and give them his sanction. *Anecdote.*

They expected a very large fee, and at length the major called his butler, "Ramaswami, there are ten pagodas for these men."

Ramaswami, thinking that this reward was far too high for such exhibitions, what did he do? He put nine of the pagodas into his own pocket, and gave the jugglers *one*, telling them to go about their business. The jugglers were very much dissatisfied with the conduct of the butler, and came to make their complaints to his master, giving utterance to their disappointment, and showing the *one* pagoda in their hand. But they could not make the major apprehend their meaning, so he appealed again to the butler, "Ramaswami! what do these men want?" "Why, sir," said Ramaswami, "they say that among the ten pagodas, which your honour has given them, there is *a bad one*, and they wish you to give them another in exchange for it." "Ramaswami," cried the major, "bring me the horsewhip!" and the poor jugglers were obliged to flee before the violence of the storm. But the moral of the story is this: *that those who will not learn the language of the natives, do a great injustice to the people.*

The dreadful mutiny has just passed over us,—a mutiny that will be held by the British in everlasting remembrance. What have been the causes that produced it? Sir Thomas Munroe—one of the first advocates of the vernaculars—the man who, in the midst of anarchy and confusion, restored peace and order to the Ceded Districts, by his thorough use of the Canarese, was afterwards embraced as the father of the people, and why? Because he insisted that every officer, civil and military, should learn the language; that he should be clever in discharging his duties among the people; that he should administer law and justice and every good in their own mother tongue; thus creating love and sympathy between the governors and the governed, and securing liberty, and right, and order, to every department.

Example of Sir T. Munroe;

also of Mr. Elphinstone.

Mr. Elphinstone, on the side of Bombay, followed in the same line, and rendered his government popular and respected. What, I ask, has been the state of the Madras and the Bombay Presidencies during this mutiny? Their people have been strong in their order, and affection, and loyalty, and their armies have been the strength of England in this terrible disaster.

But let us turn for a moment to Bengal. Has not her Government pursued a system the very reverse, and given education to her subordinates in a strange and foreign language? Yes; English has long been paramount; and thousands of young men from English schools and English colleges have been scattered over the Provinces to dispense law, and justice, and order, in the name of the Government, and according to their own authority:

What has young Bengal become? They have become the middlemen of India—they have become the stewards of the estate—they have become an immense wall to separate the governors from the subjects—to bury love, and sympathy, and hope, in the dust, and *to do great injustice to the people.* If Bengal had continued to follow the system of Madras and Bombay—if the Government there had given to the people the Bible and the worship of the living God, they would have counteracted these evils, which created this rebellion, and which have rendered Bengal the Ireland of India.

The Rev. JOHN WALTON, Wesleyan missionary from Jaffna in North Ceylon, having observed that he wished to give some information respecting the island of Ceylon, and that he substantially, though not entirely, agreed with Mr. Leupolt's paper, proceeded;—I have been connected with vernacular and English schools of a superior class in Ceylon for thirteen years. When I first went there, there were four first-class English seminaries maintained in the island; one maintained by the American Missionary Board, another by the Wesleyan, and two by the Church Missionary Society. There were three first-class English seminaries in the province of Jaffna, amongst the Tamil people; and in the south there was a first-class seminary amongst the Singhalese people, maintained by the Church Missionary Society. Some years ago the Americans in the Jaffna district abolished their seminary; but the Church and the Wesleyans continue to maintain theirs. From these seminaries we have gained the majority of our converts, catechists, and native preachers, and, though we think them improvable, we have no idea of giving them up. You must not, however, suppose that English education has ceased where the American missions lay; for I may mention a very interesting incident which will be most gratifying to the gentleman who last read his paper, and which followed immediately upon the abolition of the American seminary at Batticotta. A private English school of a first-class character was forthwith commenced by a native Christian. This, I think, is the reproductive stage, and is a matter of special interest. This man, a thorough Christian, had been employed as a tutor in the old Batticotta seminary. He commenced his school without pecuniary assistance from the missionaries or from Government, and associated with him half-a-dozen converted educated natives as a teaching staff. He collected about 150 boys, and for nearly two years he worked without pecuniary help from anybody, except the fees which he received from the people. Very recently the Government inspector of schools visited the school, and was so thoroughly satisfied that he recommended a small annual grant for the purchase of school materials, and for supplementing the teachers' salaries,—a grant of 50*l*. This is emphatically a Christian school. The American missionaries took great interest in it, and have given part of the old premises to the masters, the school being also held in their premises; they visit it, examine it, and discharge all the duties of Christian pastors to the boys. The boys regularly march to chapel on Sunday mornings; all heathen signs and symbols are discountenanced, and the American missionaries think the school is answering the ends of a Christian school in a more striking manner than any other of a similar kind. I think it a duty which I owe to the Ceylon Government to state that in the Government schools of Ceylon the Bible has been introduced from the first. (Cheers.) For nearly twenty years the Central School Commission has been carrying on school education, ramifying throughout the whole country, and one of the rules is that the first hour every day shall be devoted to the reading of the Bible. The attendance on that lesson on the part of the boys is optional; but I never heard of a single instance of a boy not coming to school during the first hour when the Bible was read. They know (for Hindoo boys are very sharp) that it is the most important lesson of the day, and it is never missed.

The Rev. F. TRESTRAIL having interposed a question as to the influence of caste,

The Rev. Mr. WALTON said,—I cannot illustrate the feelings of the boys better than by relating an instance which took place some years ago. There was a disruption of our principal educational establishment in Jaffna on the caste question. A boy of the fisher caste was introduced into a school composed chiefly of the cultivator caste. The boys of the first class, to which from his attainments he was entitled to be admitted, instantly rose, and said they would not sit with nor learn with him. After every measure had been exhausted on the part of their parents to induce the missionary to expel the fisher boy, the Brahmins and many of the Vellalas formed a caste school on rival principles. The master was a rigid heathen, but the parents insisted that in the school the Bible should be introduced. This idea thoroughly possesses the mind of the people of Ceylon that there can be no thorough education in English without the English Bible; the Bible was introduced into this school, and it held together for about twelve months.

The Rev. Dr. TIDMAN,—Are the teachers in these Government schools, who teach the Bible, heathens or Christians? *Are the teachers Christians?*

The Rev. Mr. WALTON,—In different parts of the island of Ceylon there are a number of sub-committees of Government schools, and it has ever been an admitted principle that all candidates who apply for the vacant places of teachers should be nominal Christians. It has been taken for granted in all sub-committees on which I ever sat, that a man who was a heathen could not conscientiously teach the Bible, and he was never appointed; but I believe that lately, within the last year or two, in some stations, heathens have been appointed to these Government schools. In these countries very much depends upon the circumstance whether there is a missionary or colonial chaplain in the neighbourhood, who is a member of the sub-committee, or whether the gentlemen connected with the civil service, who form it, are men of strong religious feeling. *Sometimes not: How?*

Dr. TIDMAN,—A second question I wish to ask is, whether in this process of English education, there are any school-books in English, or whether the Bible is merely the model of English instruction?

Mr. WALTON:—The schools are of two grades—elementary and central. The latter schools are of first-class character; in them education is conducted to its furthest limits; and the boys will compare with any boys you have in your English schools. Various school-books have been used, but for the most part, I believe they are the books of the Irish National Society. *School-books.*

H. CARRE TUCKER, Esq.—With reference to the Governments of Agra and the Punjaub, I beg to say that they lay the greatest possible stress upon their own officers, civil and military, learning the language as soon as possible; and their promotion is only obtained by passing a successful examination. With reference to village-schools, the Government has been raising a one-per-cent fund on the revenue from all the villages, and has been covering the whole country with village schools: my own Division of Benares is *H. C. TUCKER, Esq Village-schools in Agra.*

covered with village schools. It then became a question: if we could not supply these schools with Christian teachers, whether they would not be doing more harm than good. With the permission, therefore, of Mr. Colvin, the late Governor, I established at Benares a vernacular normal Training Institution, which was carried on upon strictly Christian principles. I selected the two best Christian masters I could find; one of them being the teacher in Mr. Leupolt's own school, who has since become a Christian missionary.

The Bible read. We had one hundred young men, and I told them I considered it necessary that they should read the Bible as the foundation of all that was good. At first, two or three Mahommedans objected; I told them, however, there was no compulsion; but all the Hindoos took to it; and these Mahommedans in a few weeks found it wise to swim with the tide, and agreed to read the Bible. The mother of one of these teachers told me that they made her quite ashamed of herself as a Christian woman, when she sat up-stairs and heard these young men read their Bibles. Mr. Colvin came down and presided at one of our meetings, where prizes were delivered to the most successful

Training-schools. students, the first prize-holder receiving a gold-watch. Government have established sixteen vernacular Training Institutions of their own; and it is deeply incumbent on all Missionary Societies, either directly or through this vernacular Training Society, to do their best to prepare a native Christian agency: otherwise we shall have

Native Christian teachers. a Government native agency. The best way in which missionaries in general can direct their efforts, is to prepare a Christianised agency, which can get admittance as teachers into Government schools, and thus throw a strong, a Christian element into the teaching of these schools. With reference to the Government neutrality, the Association in London has published a declaration of the rights of Christian servants of Government, a copy of which will be laid upon the table to-day, and any gentlemen who choose to sign it can do so. It declares that the right of a Christian man should not be forfeited by his becoming the servant of the Government. (Applause.)

Rev. J. L. Porter. The Rev. J. LESLIE PORTER, missionary of the Irish Presbyterian Church at Damascus :—For the sake of variety, I will say a few words about another mission-field. While India is a most important branch of mission work, there are other fields in the world quite as important, and there is at least one far more intensely interesting,—I refer to Palestine. Our programme alludes to vernacular literature, periodicals, tracts, and school-books: as well as to Christian education. I want to bear my testimony to the immense advantage which has accrued to Christian missions in Turkey, especially in Syria, from the translation of English books in Arabic, Turkish, and Armenian; the printing of these books in the mission presses, and their distribution by the missionaries. I believe if you had gone to Turkey thirty years ago, you would not have found a single treatise upon Christianity in any of the languages of the country, with the exception of one or two of the old books, copies of the Fathers, in some of the convents, covered with dust, and which nobody had ever read. If you go there at the present day, you will find in every large city throughout the Turkish Empire, immense numbers of Christian periodicals, Christian tracts and books, and especially Bibles and Testaments, issued at the mission presses, and distributed by the missionaries. To show the effects they are calculated to produce, I will just mention one case:—We have in Damascus a man of great influence, a native—his name may have been heard by some —I refer to Dr. Meshakah, one of the most learned natives of Syria, and one of the most acute reasoners in any country. He wields a powerful and ready pen, and has been for the last ten or twelve years employing all his influence and power and literary talents for the advancement of the cause of Christ; and yet this man has never received one single farthing from any Missionary Society. (Cheers.) How then was he brought to the knowledge of the truth? Fourteen years ago he was a member of the Greek Church; then he became connected with the Latin Church; then he became a professed infidel; and then, by chance and under the direction of the Spirit of God, he fell in with a copy of Keith's *Evidence of Prophecy*, translated long ago by the missionaries, and circulated in Syria. He then studied and read the Bible, and the Spirit of God impressed the Bible truths upon his heart. Another instance: I stated that he was a literary man, and that he has written some five or six large treatises which have been printed, as well as little tracts which have been printed also. Some three years ago, we heard in connexion with our mission at Damascus of a labouring man who lived in a distant part of Eastern Syria, a man who was most faithful in advancing the cause of God; he was a poor man, and his name is Khalil. When that man goes to plough, he teaches the Gospel to the man who drives the oxen, and to those who are engaged with him in that manual labour. When he returns in the evening to his village, instead of enjoying his pipe, like most other Orientals, or sitting down in his own house, he goes to the gate of the village, takes a copy of the Bible, sits down, and gathers round him all that he can; and there he reads and interprets Bible truths. How was that man, who never saw the face of a missionary until he had been engaged more than a year, brought to a knowledge of the truth? In this way:—A man, who would come to Damascus and visit the mission book-shop, had taken a little book published by Dr. Meshakah and a copy of the New Testament. These fell into Khalil's hands, and led to his conversion. I believe this man from his prayerful devotion and success may well be called the apostle of Bashan, for that is the district where he labours. We have opened a book-shop in Damascus in the street called "Straight." It contains books in ten different languages, and these books are not given away, but they are all sold. We find that the people come from the ends of the earth to buy books there. I found there one day a Nestorian from the mountains of Kurdistan: he introduced himself to me as a man from Kurdistan, and his story was this:—A friend of his had been on a pilgrimage to Jerusalem the year before, and in passing through Damascus he had been attracted to the book-shop, where he bought a Bible and two or three tracts; took them with him to Jerusalem, where he gave the tracts among a few friends, and carried the Bible home. That Bible was carried to the house from which that man from Kurdistan came; he was the oldest son of that house, and through the instrumentality of that Bible, he had been brought to the knowledge of the truth. (Applause.)

Book-shop.

Colonel LAVIE, late in the India Artillery, said:—On the question as to what part Missionary Societies should take in education, that it was clear to him "Teaching the Gospel" was only secondary to "Preaching the Gospel," and, if wisely conducted, was thoroughly missionary work; but he entirely disapproved of the employment in missionary schools of native teachers who have been instructed for ten and twelve years in Christianity, possessing a thorough head knowledge of its principles, even acknowledging its pureness as a religion, yet who are unwilling, by baptism, to declare to their countrymen they are Christians.

Col. Lavie.

Heathen teachers in Christian schools,

This subject had for many years been an anxiety to him, as, from what had come under his notice, not only in South India, but elsewhere, he has considered the employment of native heathen teachers a positive evil, and feels assured that where the practice exists, there must necessarily be a low standard of Christianity in the native Church. *an evil.*

If native Christian teachers are only partially procurable, missionaries, in his opinion, should confine the education given, to the children of converts only, till Christian teachers are raised up for them, when they may extend the privilege to the heathen children. So anxious had he long felt on this point, that nothing would rejoice him more than to hear that Missionary Societies had made it a rule that no heathen teacher should be employed in missionary schools; and he would go further, that no native teacher should be employed in missionary schools who had not given satisfactory evidence that he was himself a converted man, capable of teaching on Christian principles. Let this be done, and the result, under God's blessing, would surely be an improved tone of Christianity in the native Churches, and a stock of teachers of Christian character might be looked for, not only for the mission, but for Government and other schools. He expressed a wish that in our English system of education, parents, when placing their children in schools, would more generally require that not only their Head Master, but also the under teachers, should be converted men, when we might look for better results from schools among our own people at home. *They should employ only Christians; converted men, abroad; and in England.*

He would like to say a word in reply to the question put a short time back, "How is it that Heathen boys attend missionary schools, and schools where the Bible is taught?"

Pachapah's school at Madras has English-educated masters, receiving high salaries, men of ability capable of giving the best English education, but the Bible is a prohibited book; he has known many heathen boys to give up the advantages of their position in this school to enter a missionary or other school where Bible instruction was given; and on inquiring from them the reason, he has been told by those who could clearly express themselves, to the effect, that in their opinion boys instructed from the Scriptures were more clever and better than those taught in schools where there was no Bible; and his experience would lead him to say distinctly, that of the many hundred boys with whom he had conversed, all had expressed their wish for Bible instruction; and on speaking with their parents on the subject, the very general expression was, that they had not the smallest objection to their children being taught from the Bible; he had certainly met with a few exceptions, but they were very few. *Why heathen boys attend bible-taught schools.*

Rev. Dr. O'Meara.

English books not to be translated but adapted.

The Rev. Dr. O'MEARA said, it occurred to him that when they spoke of a vernacular literature, they did not mean merely certain English sounds, represented by certain vernacular sounds, but referred also to the style of thought. They did not go for vernacular English to a classical library, but to such books as Ryle's tracts, than which, he believed, there was nothing more excellent. He had translated tracts into the language of the North American Indians, but the author of those tracts would not know them if they were translated back again. He had translated the tract of *The Young Cottager*, but the description of the scenery of England and the Isle of Wight would have been lost to the Indian: so he was obliged to leave it out or considerably alter it, so as to bring it more nearly to the Indian style of thought. He thought that was a very important subject to be kept before the minds of their missionary brethren. About five years ago, he was very anxious to translate a book which would be generally useful to Indian missionaries in connexion with Indian congregations, and he obtained a very liberal list of one of the London Societies. He found a tract that had been prepared for the Indians in the colonies about a hundred years ago; and thought that was one he could make something of, but on the very first page there were two or three utterly untranslateable expressions, which would be incomprehensible by native minds. He thought the preparation of new tracts, adapted to the style of thought of the natives, would be much more advantageous than the literal translation of English tracts.

Rev. T. Gardiner.

Christian teachers not always to be had.

Why?

The Rev. THOMAS GARDINER, Free Church Missionary in Calcutta, said, that in their Institutions in Calcutta they had considerable difficulty in getting Christian young men to undertake the work of teaching. Every Christian youth had not a liking for it. Then they had another difficulty in the low salaries which only they were enabled to give. Young men said, "If we were to give ourselves to secular work, we could do very much better, and at the same time exercise a large amount of influence for good." A further difficulty was, that when some of the young men became Christians, the missionaries had a call at once made upon them to send them forth into the country districts to evangelise others. With regard to the general subject of Education, he rejoiced that there had not been a single sentence uttered against the great work of Christian Education as a means of evangelising the youth of India. That was the ground upon which their Missionary institutions had always been maintained, and upon which he was persuaded they would stand the test of every inquiry. But it must be admitted that their work, from its very nature, in providing this valuable English Education, raised up for them difficulties in the way of obtaining a native evangelistic agency. English Education had a high pecuniary value in the market, and all the young men in India, including their Christian young men, knew this; these latter saw how they could be useful as Christian magistrates, as Christian merchants, and in other capacities, with the knowledge they had acquired, and they did not see why they should neglect their own interests. He thought all missionaries engaged in Education should look these difficulties calmly in the face. If they did, they might be able to remove some of them, and get their young men to engage in the work. He believed also there was a danger of carrying secular education too far. They found that almost all young men in their schools, at some time or other, generally when they were in the higher school, or junior College classes, came under strong convictions, not merely of the truth of Christianity, but personal convictions, more or less, of their own sinfulness and of their need of a Saviour. If they passed that critical period without publicly professing their faith in Christ, they generally became indifferent, and there was less hope, humanly speaking, of their becoming Christians. He thought it might be an undue expenditure of missionary resources to carry on in advanced secular studies young men of that description, and that they should ever estimate their educational work according to its value and direct bearing upon the progress of the Redeemer's cause in the hearts of men. (Hear, hear.) He felt there might be a danger of spending unduly missionary resources, resources raised for the preaching of the gospel in that direction. (Hear, hear.) He would therefore give an education carried to the point of advancement at which it was in their junior College classes to such young men as came to them. He would carry them to that interesting period when they usually came under those religious convictions; and after that he would expend missionary resources in training specially those young men who might be willing to become helpers in the missionary work, instead of going on to teach the secular branches to those young men who presented, humanly speaking, but little hope of becoming Christians. There was another very important question. Several of their missionary schools in India had been affiliated with the Universities. They had agreed to take the lists of books and subjects prescribed for

Money value of education.

Secular education may go too far.

Point where it may stop.

L

University examinations by the Senates, which were very mixed bodies of men. He felt it was a grave question to be considered, whether, as missionaries, they were justified in putting themselves in the position of being bound to take lists of works which upon the whole might not be what they themselves would have chosen. And then there was another point connected with this subject, the general secularising influence possibly resulting from having in view the preparation of young men to pass examinations for degrees. Formerly they had simply laboured to evangelise; now there was an additional object in view, that their young men should be able to pass certain examinations. These subjects should be considered, being of the most grave and important kind. (Hear, hear.)

Influence of the new universities.

JAMES CUNNINGHAM, Esq., wished to throw out a suggestion. In the north, they had long felt the want of a good missionary map; constant reference was made to missionary fields, and they had no information as to their exact position. He believed such a map would require to be formed on a large scale; and he could not but think that in a commercial point of view it would be an advantageous undertaking to any one of our large publishing houses; greater completeness would be obtained than could be expected from any particular Missionary Society. However, they wanted two classes of maps; one on a large scale, for lecture and school-room purposes, and which would be useful in their families; and another, in which the friends of different denominations would indicate their own special mission localities. He was quite satisfied that such maps would be exceedingly useful to deputations, and enable the Christian public better to understand many of the missionary periodicals. The precise position of missionary stations is known only to a few, and the many do not take that interest in missionary labours which they otherwise would. If each Society would bring out maps of their own, with a few statistical remarks, they would form a most valuable volume of reference.

J. Cunningham, Esq.
A good missionary map.
Two kinds needed.

The CHAIRMAN intimated that the Church Missionary Society were preparing maps similar to those which Mr. Cunningham had indicated.

Being made.

The Rev. J. SUGDEN, formerly missionary at Bangalore, observed, that much of the value of the Conference would depend

Rev. J. Sugden.

on the substantial agreement of those who composed it. He be- *Agreement in moderate views.*
lieved that there was a thorough agreement as to the different
plans of missionary operation: the points on which they had differed being the relative positions which those various movements should occupy. He was exceedingly thankful to Mr. Gardiner, who had last spoken, for his remarks on education. There was a general misconception and prejudice amongst churches, abroad and at home, against English education in India. Their Free-Church brethren, and those who had taken an active part in English education in India, had, on the present occasion, expressed themselves in the most guarded and temperate terms possible; they had, he thought, only done simple justice to themselves, and not altogether done justice to the great subject they had in hand. During his missionary experience in India, he was most thoroughly interested in vernacular education. He would put ver- *All kinds of schools needed.*
nacular preaching and vernacular education in the first place;
but he thought that a great and glorious work was to be achieved in some spheres of labour, especially in India, through English teaching and English schools. He hoped that the field which had now been opened by the Vernacular Education Society would be entered upon by the friends of that institution, and that they would have the most cordial and ready co-operation of every Missionary Society, and every true friend to Christian missions, throughout the three kingdoms. In reference to education, they had, perhaps, been too prone to generalise from the requirements of their own particular position; forgetting that each country, and often each station, has its own special demands. With regard to the literature, if they had had to depend upon that prepared by native Christians, they would have been, at this day, without any Christian literature at all. He submitted that very little, if any, of the best native Christian literature now in existence had been prepared by native hands. Their dear Christian brother present, Behari Lal Singh, would be able to tell them what had been done in Bengalee by native Christians. If the present Christian *Christian literature prepared chiefly by missionaries.*
literature was available for any purpose in the conversion of souls
in India, he (Mr. Sugden) was sure it had been very much owing
to those dear and devoted European and American brethren, many of whom had now gone to heaven. They had entered into their rest, but generations to come would be blest by the fruit of their labours. They would remember well a dear Christian friend of his own, William Hoyles Drew, a great and godly man (hear, *Rev. W. H. Drew.*
hear, and cheers): who, though an Englishman, was such a per-

fect native scholar, that he could write in the Tamil language books which could be read, appreciated, and loved by the native population, both Christian and heathen. He gave much of his time, perhaps, as he had confessed, too large a proportion, to the study of heathen literature; and his example was a proof of the fact, that an Englishman might prepare books in the native language which were thoroughly idiomatic, and exceedingly acceptable, not only to the native population, but to the most talented of the native pundits. With regard to Mr. Leupolt's paper, he (Mr. Sugden) was not aware of one single point in which he differed from that gentleman. He believed that if the suggestion thrown out by Mr. Leupolt were acted upon with regard to native female missionaries, it would be attended with the most important benefits; for his (Mr. Sugden's) experience was, that there were many Christian Tamil women who would find a ready access to the homes of their own people, and who, by God's blessing, would be made the means of their salvation.

<small>Native female missionaries.</small>

<small>Dr. GUNDERT.</small>

<small>Can Chinese be written in Roman letters?</small>

The Rev. H. GUNDERT, Basle Mission, Malabar, was desirous of bringing forward a few suggestions with regard to teaching the Chinese language. He observed that the Chinese written language represented ideas by images, but that these images did not represent sounds; and that it required ten years to become familiar with the written language; whereas, if books in the Romanized character were prepared, somewhat after the plan of Dr. Lepsius of Berlin, persons might master the language in three or four months. He recommended, in order to reach the national mind, that more should be done in order to render available this system of writing. The dialect could be perfectly represented in Roman characters, and multitudes might thus be reached, who could not be gained by any other system.

<small>Rev. J. FORDYCE.</small>

The Rev. JOHN FORDYCE (Calcutta) said there was one point he wished to bring before the Conference, viz. the relation of the work of female education to the Missionary Societies. Hitherto it had been left very much to associations of ladies. It might be well that it should continue to be so; but he thought that all Missionary Societies should see that the work of female education was carried on by their agencies, or supplementary; and, if this were done, he was sure it would be far more effectually accomplished than it had hitherto been. There were two Societies in Scotland for this object in India, connected with the Free and

Established Churches. In London there had long been a Society for Female Education in the East; and more recently an association of Wesleyan ladies had been formed; and also a committee to aid female normal schools in India. The resources of these Societies were too limited. The London Society's income seldom reaches 4000*l*., though supported by all denominations, and having schools in Turkey, Africa, India, China, &c. Such incomes may do, if the great Societies share the responsibility; but if the enterprise is to be left, as hitherto, to ladies' societies, they should have larger means. The London Society, for example, with a sphere so vast, instead of an income of 4000*l*., should acquire an income of 50,000*l*. at least.

Female education.

The Rev. T. L. BADHAM, Joint Secretary of the Moravian Missionary Society, said that, while deeply interested in the discussions of the morning, he could not but think it seemed rather like a Committee on Indian affairs than anything else. India, no doubt, was a very important subject, but there were souls to be saved in America, in Africa, and in the Arctic seas; and it was from the west, the north, and the south, as well as from the east, that many would come and sit down in the kingdom of God. He would also point their attention to the large numbers of Indians in the North and South American continent, and to the poor degraded Esquimaux tribes on the shores of the great Polar basin. To all these the unsearchable riches of Christ were to be made known. He would make one remark in reference to vernacular literature. This was very much wanted, not only in the East, but in Greenland, among the Esquimaux, and throughout North and South America. It was also wanted among our English-speaking fellow-subjects of the West Indies, and South America. Very useful books and tracts, published by the Tract Society, were, after all, not suited, in many respects, to the variety of natives in the West Indies, and South America; the allusions, the imagery, and references to social and domestic life, being all calculated for English readers. This was a very important subject, and one well worthy of consideration.

Rev. T. L. BADHAM.

Books to be adapted.

The following MINUTE on the morning's discussion was unanimously adopted:—

MINUTE.

MINUTE ON MISSIONARY EDUCATION.

Schools quite proper. The Conference believe that Educational plans legitimately fall within the province of Christian missions; as affording means both for consolidating native churches, and promulgating the gospel among the heathen.

To be suited to each station. They consider that on this subject, more than on any other, attention should be paid to the great rule:— That, preserving their single aim of spreading the gospel, all missionary agencies should be most carefully adapted to the numerous varieties of places, people, and spheres of missionary labour; and that experience should be followed as the most valuable guide.

Vernacular. In all countries, as a general rule, VERNACULAR SCHOOLS, carried on in the language of the country, are the most natural and most important, both for the children of converts and for those of the heathen. The Conference believe that such schools should be increased in number, and be made as efficient as possible in the character of their teaching.

English. In some countries and localities where the natives earnestly desire to obtain a knowledge of the English language, ENGLISH MISSION SCHOOLS have been established on good grounds, have turned that desire to good account, and have been blest with a variety of valuable results. Their value has been proved partly in the conversion of souls; and chiefly in the extensive diffusion of a knowledge of the gospel, in spheres of usefulness which other plans of labour have not reached. Efforts, however, in this direction the Conference think should not be carried too far.

Orphan. In some countries, especially in India, where caste is so powerful, ORPHAN and BOARDING SCHOOLS, in which young people have been brought up, separated from heathen influences, have been found greatly useful in the conversion of their scholars, and in securing well-instructed native agents for the service of the mission.

Female education. Considering the position of women in the heathen world, the Conference think that great attention to FEMALE EDUCATION is not only desirable, but necessary in every mission; and that all opportunities for extending it and increasing its usefulness should be eagerly embraced, and thankfully employed.

They consider that, as the sphere of education widens, where teachers are demanded, and can be obtained, TRAINING INSTITUTIONS for teachers should be established and efficiently maintained. Training-schools.

They regard with much satisfaction the progress already made in raising up in various missions a VERNACULAR LITERATURE suitable both to Christian and heathen; and they think it a work of the greatest importance, that such a literature should be still greatly extended; especially in countries where the press is extensively employed by the heathen to circulate wrong views of religion and morality. Vernacular Christian literature.

For most valuable help in this important matter, this Conference recognise with pleasure the generous support given to all missionaries and Missionary Societies by the Bible and Tract Societies of England and America.

The Morning Session closed with singing the Doxology.

FOURTH SESSION.

WEDNESDAY AFTERNOON.

The members of Conference again dined together, and resumed their sitting at four o'clock.

MAJOR-GEN. ALEXANDER in the chair.

Programme. The following is the programme of subjects suggested for discussion :—

Subject: HOW THE MISSIONARY FEELING AT HOME SHOULD BE SO STIRRED UP AS LARGELY TO INCREASE THE PRESENT INCOME OF MISSIONARY SOCIETIES.

Paper, of ten minutes, by Rev. JAMES LEWIS, of Leith.

The great Expense of Religious Societies, from the necessity of constant begging, and the general neglect of St. Paul's advice (1 Cor. xvi. 2), to lay by periodically.

Private hospitality, and private carriage for Deputations.

How to avoid collectors' per-centage.

Paper. The Paper prepared was then presented to the Conference, as follows :—

THE BEST MEANS OF CALLING FORTH HOME LIBERALITY.

BY THE REV. JAMES LEWIS,

OF ST. JOHN'S FREE CHURCH, LEITH.

I feel the responsibility of being called to throw out even a few thoughts on a subject involving so deeply the practical success of missions, as the best means of awakening on their behalf the home church. That the Church, in all its sections, now confesses to her missionary obligation, let us gratefully acknowledge; but that our past deeds fall far short of our British capabilities, is broadly attested by the single fact, that the entire contribution for foreign missions does not exceed half a million, whilst the public revenue of Great Britain, to say nothing of the immense revenue of its individual members, is seventy millions annually. The question, therefore, is not uncalled-for: How may a larger portion of the wealth of Britain, the wealth that is in the hands of the professed members of its churches, be turned into missionary resources, and become the medium of bringing glory to God in the highest, and on earth peace? This is the problem for our solution. By many good men it is solved with great facility. Let but the religious life of our Christian community be quickened, and they are confident that there will be a consequent revival of missionary zeal, and a great outpouring of missionary liberality. It is not perceived that a revived Christian community possesses only a greater susceptibility for missionary action, a greater underlying power of being stirred to missionary self-sacrifice and work; that it is not necessarily and in itself more missionary. There have been revived seasons when the whole force of the quickened Christian mind has been turned in other directions; when missions have reaped no fruit amidst the in-gathering of a general spiritual harvest.

Small proportion of our wealth given to missions.

How to get more.

Increase of life does not necessarily secure larger liberality.

The fact is not sufficiently adverted to, that the expenditure of a Christian's income is, to a great extent, influenced by the reigning ideas of his time; the wave of thought along which he is borne determining that it shall flow in one channel, and leave another utterly dry. We must calculate and wield the subordinate forces that go to make up the wave of thought; or under a lively,

Influence of opinion.

spiritual state of the Church the mission treasury may still be empty.

Two points: Now, there are two elements that determine the state, at any time, of the Christian mind in relation to missions:—first, Their home organisations; second, their foreign operations.

Organisation to be enlisted. *First.*—The hold that missions have upon the Christian mind is largely dependent on the home organisation through which they are wrought. The products of our manufactures, in the curious perfection of their fabrics, are not more the result of the machinery by which they are woven, than the products of our missions are the results of their respective organizations. To perfect these, for the communication of missionary intelligence and the collection of missionary offerings, should be the great aim of the friends of missions. We offer the following hints as a contribution towards this end. Some of them may have been thrown out in the discussion of yesterday. Still we present them in the form and order in which they arose to our mind when called to the preparation of this paper:—

Children must be trained to sustain missions. 1. Let our missionary organization *meet at the first dawn of intelligence and responsibility the Christian child.* He has been baptized by a command that has wrapt in it the great missionary commission, "Go ye into all the world baptizing;" and he ought to know that in virtue of his reception of that baptism he is brought into connexion with that command. The fact of his Christian name should be bound up from his earliest years with the "Go into all the world;" and missions have the benefit of his freshest morning thoughts, those thoughts that never altogether die. Yet, after looking over not a few school collections, we do not recollect having found a missionary passage. With religious *School-books should refer to them.* extracts our school-books abound; but why do they strike no missionary note? The incidents of missions and of missionary travels, their scenes of strange lands and stranger races of men and children, are the very subjects to play around youthful imaginations, and by their rich, pictorial impressiveness, reach their hearts. Something, therefore, ought to be done by our Missionary Societies to secure that our subject should have its place in the preparation of our school-books. Let it have a fair start that it fall not behind in the race of thought, and be left to be taken up, with all the difficulties of a new subject, in after-life.

Sabbath-schools to be brought in more systematically. 2. I would suggest, as intimately connected with this first thought, that something ought to be done after a more regular plan for laying hold of the *immense juvenile influence that is associated with our Sabbath-school system.* Much has been done, by the circulation of juvenile missionary magazines and papers, for the spread of the more touching and telling incidents of missions. But to a great extent it has been done at random, and as teachers may have chanced to be imbued with the missionary spirit. Ought not the attempt to be made in a more systematic way to embrace the range of that great influence? Sabbath-school teachers, especially in all our larger towns, are bound together by Unions, which are the centres of conference and action. Through communication with these, by an agent from some authorised body, arrangements might be made for introducing as part of the weekly instruction of such schools, missionary intelligence; so that each school should have its missionary lesson, or its periodically recurring missionary night, with accompanying offerings. In a poor city district that came under our own observation, and from which we had gathered four hundred children in Sabbath-schools, the missionary contribution of the children for several successive years amounted annually to from 17*l.* to 22*l.*: a sum larger than was collected at the time from a congregation of upwards of four hundred members of all ranks and classes in the same district. But the pecuniary would be the least of the results. The Sabbath-school teachers, a great present moral force, and who are rising as the administrative men of the future to be a still greater, would be imbued with the missionary spirit, whilst the children under their charge would suck in missions with the first milk of the Word. Missionary lessons to be frequent. Result to both scholars and teachers.

It may appear a small matter to advert to, but it would be found fraught with great consequences if, in any arrangement that may be made for pervading the Sabbath-schools with the missionary element, pictures of the different races of men, black, red, olive, copper-coloured, curly, woolly, tufted, silken, or bristly-haired, with which our missions have been brought into contact, should be hung on the school walls. We should give our children the benefit of a personal introduction to the Hindoo, the Polynesian, the African, or the Chinese; and make them as familiar with the colour and contour of these races as with their own home faces. "No longer strangers and foreigners, but brought nigh," let them share in our early sympathies, partake of the interest of our familiar, and mingle with the warmth of our home thoughts, and there will be less difficulty in securing for them a large place in our British liberality. Pictures of the races on the walls.

3. And more important, I would suggest, in relation to

our adult community, as the most efficient means of sustaining its interest in missions, and drawing forth most largely its liberality, *the minute organisation of domiciliary visitation.*

<small>House-visitation</small>

The time is past when the friends of Missions should be satisfied with the results of the occasional impulsive movement of the pulpit and the platform, or be content that their cause should live upon the stimuli of periodic eloquent advocacy. Till they can live and thrive upon common fare, their health is precarious. No man, who has not had the subject experimentally brought before him, can conceive of the difference of results, of leaving a community to move to the missionary treasury, and of the missionary treasury moving systematically towards it. Organisation, on the principle of domiciliary visits, is a *sine quâ non* to a prosperous missionary treasury. Nothing can take the place of it, and where it is sustained in efficiency, it can dispense with much else. Dr. Chalmers was wont to say, that a house-going minister made a church-going people; as the people were sure to show the courtesy of returning the minister's week-day visits by their sabbath-day attendance. A house-going agency, we should, in like manner, say will be sure to make a thriving going mission.

<small>essential.</small>

But let us not be misunderstood. We think we estimate, at their proper value, the mission demonstrations that have been made over England and Scotland by such men as Williams, and Knill, and Duff, and Livingstone; and that are annually being made by the Deputations sent forth by our Missionary Societies. We have no objections to the provincial echoes of Exeter Hall, or to the occasional roar of a great African or Indian lion, as it starts across our ordinary, quiet-going, working-day life. But there are three conditions to which we would subject these spasmodic agencies; three conditions, at least, that are necessary to preserve the waste of their powers. (1) We would use them for extraordinary appeals, when a special fund has to be raised; or when an emergency has to be got over. Their quickening addresses admirably serve the temporary purpose of shaking out a contribution that is to be given once for all. (2) We would use them in preparation for setting-up a regular district mission agency. By all means let the angel descend and trouble the pool, around which have lain, in time past, the halt, the maimed, and the withered. Or (3) we would use their agency in reconstructing such organisations where they had fallen into disrepair. Experience shows, that from the languor that steals over all human arrangements, or from the shifting of the residence of agents, the most completely organised system of

<small>Deputations valuable,</small>

<small>but should be used for special appeals,</small>

<small>founding auxiliaries,</small>

<small>or reviving them.</small>

domiciliary visits gets out of full working trim in four or five years. A district loses its agent, or an agent becomes forgetful of his district. The machinery becomes shaky. I would therefore suggest, as a great advance upon the practical productive work of deputations, that, instead of simply delivering themselves of their speeches, they should be charged with an inquiry into the organisations of the districts to which they are commissioned, with setting-up new, or repairing old organisations. Their speeches would then be condensed, as a steam force, in the mission agencies they constructed anew or perfected, and would remain a working power long after the sound of their voices had died away.

4. Whilst we have named the School Book, the Sabbath School, the Domiciliary Agency, as means by which the Mission Spirit may be quickened and sustained, we name, lastly, the *Pulpit*. The regular pulpit to be more largely enlisted.

In speaking of the impulsive and therefore transient power of pulpit or platform demonstrations, unless linked with a permanent agency, we do not include *the pulpit in its ordinary ministrations*. We have no hesitation in placing amongst the foremost means of quickened missionary action the pulpit in its normal sabbath influence. Could our cause have but its full sustained representation from the pulpits of Britain it would need, I would not say no organisation, but no other vehicle for the diffusion of its information, or for its advocacy amongst the masses of our Christian people. Our faith is not great in the power of *printed* missionary intelligence. It is an important help, and we cannot dispense with it. But the lower we descend in the scale of mental culture, the influence of it is the less; with all, it is little compared to a word fitly and warmly spoken with the accompaniments of sacred time, and place, and the sympathy of numbers. Let the pulpit give its proper place to the subject that was the vision of prophets, the song of sacred poets, the consolation of the Redeemer, the labour of Apostles, the ingathering of the Gentiles; and missions would have a new standing in the church, a fresh development in the world. It is to us a mystery, the abstinence of good men from this divine theme, their reluctance to keep their people abreast of the good news of the spread of the kingdom. That there is such a reluctance is a fact; a reluctance, in many instances, passing into a strong aversion, that missions should be the subject of sabbath discourse. How the strong-hold of the pulpit is to be gained is a great question. If our time had permitted, I might have offered some suggestions on the best shape of presenting occasional missionary facts from the pulpit; or on the

Better than periodicals.

Reluctance to use it.

reasonableness of our churches recommending or ordering periodical missionary discourses; but I forbear entering upon subordinate points on this question. The difficulties that accompany it lie deeper than can be affected by minor ecclesiastical arrangements; they lie in the *existing education of our young divines.* I make no reflection on the training of our theological colleges, when I say they teach theology. They are not missionary. Missions do not form part of their intellectual and spiritual wealth. The subject does not bulk in the attention of their students, is not incorporated with their studies so as to become inwoven with the texture of their forming minds and hearts. Missions are consequently, through life, an exotic to the theological mind, and never have the kindly, luxuriant growth of an indigenous or thoroughly naturalized plant. Ministers are missionary, by starts and by external impulse, rather than through the resistless tendencies of an inward seed growth developing after its kind. Give to missions their place in the colleges of the rising ministry; let them become an essential element of early and studious thought; and they will live and grow throughout the student's life. Make him familiar with the home methods of missions, and with their foreign operations, with the races with which they have been brought into contact, their superstitions, their forms of heathenism, the philosophies inwoven with them, with their failures and their successes, and you will lay deep the groundwork for after continuous interested thought. You will put your mission seed into your future ministry at the spring-time, when all seeds are being sown that find a subsequent growth in the word of the pulpit and the organisations of the parish.

There is a chair in all our Universities, known as the Chair of Political Economy, and which has for its subject the causes that influence and determine our national prosperity. Why, in our Christian Universities, and in their more immediate theological departments, should there not be a chair, having for its corresponding subject, the Economy of the Kingdom, the ways and means through which its prosperity is to be advanced, until its destined extension be accomplished in the inheritance of the earth?

It may be long years before a Missionary Chair be erected in our Universities, and their fruits reaped in our British pulpits. But let a beginning be made — by the establishment of a Lectureship on missions — in connexion with one or more of our theological colleges; and we should witness the commencement of an influence destined to carry with it the pulpit as the great mission power. We cannot speak with confidence as to the way in which such a Lectureship might be most easily wrought into the arrangements of the English University system. That our English Universities are now practically moving in the direction of missions will make the introduction of such a lectureship, were provision obtained for its maintenance, a comparatively easy task. We have, in the Bampton, Hulsean, and Warburtonian lectures, examples of what might, in the first instance, be attempted in this department, and attempted in accordance with the usages of the English Universities. I feel certain that the heads of our Scottish colleges would hail the appointment of such a Lectureship. There would be difficulties in the way of the institution of a regular Missionary Professorship. It might be felt to interfere too violently with the present curriculum of study; but a Lectureship, with its limited course, annually or biennially recurring, under conditions in harmony with college arrangements, would meet with no opposition; and the Scottish churches, we are persuaded, would not be slow to recommend or require attendance upon it from theological students. The desiderata are the funds. For these we must look to the intelligent and wealthy members of the Church; and, if only a brief annual or biennial course were at first contemplated at the seats of our principal theological colleges, the draft on the liberality of the Christian community would not be excessive. Let the subject, and its importance, be kept steadily before the eye of the church, through our various missionary organs; or, better still, let a start be made by this Conference, or by parties connected with the localities of our several Universities, for the creation of a lectureship-fund, and the means will come. Missions are every day occupying a larger space in the attention of the Christian community, and a deeper place in its convictions; and a liberality which it would at one time have been extravagance to have anticipated, may now be calculated upon by the most cautious minds. It is time that missions should have the professed expositors of their principles, methods, and fields of operation.

Practicable:

difficulties in the way:

funds needed.

Let the Conference begin it.

We now pass to the second division of our subject. We stated at the commencement of our paper, that there were two elements that determined the state at any time of the Christian mind, in relation to missions. 1st. Their home organisations. 2d. Their foreign operations. We have offered our suggestions on the first of these. We now glance at the reflex influence of foreign operations on home mission liberality. A missionary income being an

Reflex influence of foreign operations.

income of opinion, depends for a response to its appeals on the felicity with which these strike the Christian mind or the different orders of Christian mind in a community. If a foreign war be popular with a nation, the war-tax is willingly paid; but if the telegram of battles and sieges has no echo in its heart, the impost is murmured against, and finally the supplies are cut off.

If approved, they will be well sustained.

Have our foreign mission operations been so planned as to call forth the largest amount of home liberality, self-sacrifice, and self-consecration to the missionary cause; or what has been wanting for that end? It may appear presumptuous to question the wisdom that has presided over the missionary enterprise of Britain; its piety, its fervour of holy zeal, have been so pre-eminent, its judgment so marked in carrying out the plans it has adopted, and in fitting them to the numerous and untried fields of operation. But has the enterprise been laid on a foundation so broad as to commend itself to all orders of Christian minds, and to draw from all their tribute of support? We think not.

Doubts.

1st. The limitation of its agency to one kind of labourers has excluded a wide range of talent and capacity that might have been embraced in its service, and ought to have been summoned to its side. The modern mission has been mainly formed on the idea of sending forth the man who could preach; and subsequent action has been revolution round this primary conception. Beyond a project for erecting additional missionary schools, or circulating more widely the Bible and Christian books, or commissioning another teaching agent into the field, our missionary thought has not extended. Missions have oscillated within the range of shifting the phase of the teaching man. The book and the tongue have been their recognised organs for the propagation of the gospel. Whilst we possess an embodied Christianity, a Christianity transfused into our civilisation, a presence everywhere discernible in our British social, industrial, domestic life, we have adhered to the idea of presenting it to the heathen through a teaching medium. We have not presented with sufficient breadth to the eye or feelings of the heathen that industrial, domestic life which is the product of Christianity, which is, more or less, radiant with its light, and attractive to its light, as the early miracles were attractive to the truths they symbolised. An occasional mechanic, as in the South Sea and African missions, has followed in the wake of the missionary; and Churches and Societies have been drawn out by circumstances into a freer allowance of this subsidiary agency than their principles originally contemplated; still

Ought missions to be confined to ordained men?

Subsidiary agencies only partially employed.

the rule of the modern mission has been to use but one kind of talent, the talent that could take the stamp of ordination, that could be commissioned to teach.

It may even be questioned whether the men of strong faith and noble daring, who first went forth into the heathen field, the tongue of the preacher their only instrument, and God their confidence, would have accepted the aid of other means. To have allied other agencies to the Word and Spirit of truth, in the hope of preparing their way or strengthening their influence, would have been regarded as the indications of a faltering faith. The fact was overlooked that there are ways and means of influencing the human heart established by Providence, and which, if placed within our reach, it were folly to neglect. Our Lord's miracles of healing, and deeds of compassion wrought to win human hearts to the Word, were his divine authorisation of those means that have been so sparingly introduced into the modern mission. He refused not to ascend through the lower in order to attract insensible minds to the higher spiritual benefits he dispensed. He opened hearts by the familiar key of human kindness and earthly good things, that they might open more readily to the grace of his kingdom, through the seen and temporal making way for the unseen and eternal. *Schemes of benevolence very useful.*

2d. This limitation in the conception of mission agency has necessarily limited mission action, and left the foreign field with comparatively little *visible* attractive fruit. Those who are acquainted with the history of the propagation of Christianity amongst the Saxon and Gothic nations during the sixth and seventh centuries, are aware of the effective place that was occupied in the conversion of these nations by the missionary monasteries or communities of the period. In later times monasteries became dormitories; monks, beggars; their prayer-book, the rosary; their worship, dead-men's bones; and their presence, an offence to an industrious society. When they went down under the shock of the Reformation, they had long outlived both their first necessity and use. Instead of the centres of aggressive missionary work, they had become the vanguard of the Popery which had matured into a new paganism. But the earlier monasteries were a mission power, in which all the members were not clergy in the modern sense of wielding the books or the tongue as the instrument of their mission; though all, according to the habit of the times, were ecclesiastical persons. There were in their ranks men more expert in handling the plough, the spade, the saw, or the hammer, *The early monasteries: handicrafts in them:*

than the word of doctrine or exhortation; who could do whilst others spoke; who made the desert disappear before them, and introduced amongst barbarous nations the arts and tillage which the church had preserved amidst the dissolution of the Empire. In this variety of their action lay the strength of these early mission institutions for bearing down upon a heathenism, the combined product of superstition, ignorance, and social degradation. While teaching the doctrines of the Christian faith, they presented to the heathen the accommodations and attractions of Christianised life; trained their new converts to the energy of self-support; enclosed them within the order; and threw around them the shield of regulated society; or taught them how to constitute such a society for themselves.

great good done by them.

Do we seek to rebuild these fallen institutions of a mediæval age? Certainly not. But we would translate the variety of their mission action into the methods of our own times. It is not necessary, in availing ourselves of their experience, to adopt their principle of community life. In harmony with our own habits of thought, the strictly-teaching missionary might still go forth as the accredited agent of the Church or the Missionary Society, whilst the Christian capitalist, planter, or factory proprietor, left to the bent of his own mind, could choose and organise his field of operation; yet so co-operate with the missionary teacher as that each should have the benefit of the services of the other, and the heathen the benefit of both. Why should not the arts, and agriculture, and mechanic skill of our British Protestants, be called to pay tribute to missions through their own characteristic channels, in rearing the foreign factory, cultivating the tea, indigo, rice, sugar, and cotton; and by prosperous industrial settlements exemplify to barbarous or half-civilised nations the arts of Christian social life?

Capitalists, planters, mechanics, should share mission-work now.

If a capitalist who has ten thousand at his command, and business skill to use it to advantage in a foreign field, be desirous of dedicating his skill and his capital to the gospel, why should he be compelled to turn himself into a preacher, and his capital into a fund for the support of preachers, before he can lay himself and his gifts on the altar? Let him go forth, and be encouraged to go forth, to the mission-work as he is; and gathering the heathen around his African or Indian settlement, he will prove more than a pioneer of the teaching missionary's work. He will be a choice fellow-worker, embodying to the eye the results of the word spoken to the ear, and more surely than by words training to those moral

They should continue laymen.

habits, without which Christianity amongst a rude or half-civilised people can have no permanence.

To establish missions of this more comprehensive nature in Africa, and widen thereby the circle of British sympathy in the mission enterprise, is the great work opening before our intrepid missionary traveller, Dr. Livingstone. Why should it be his alone? Other fields are ripe for the same operations. A large class of our practical working minds are becoming wearied with the oft-repeated tale of missionary preaching tours, bazaar-conversations, tract-distributions, and school-examinations; all necessary and invaluable means of sowing the good seed. But why these alone or exclusively? It is asked that other methods be incorporated with our missions, and other results presented than the reported pious lives of their converts. Let them be seen doing as we ourselves do; living in industrial, domestic, well-ordered communities; their new religion subjecting them to law and order, disciplining them to self-support, and binding them together in the spread of their own faith, to work with their own hands to give to them that need; and fresh strength would be brought to the mission cause, and convictions of its great work flashed upon many still doubting minds. It is from the higher measure in which the Polynesian missions have exhibited these results, that they have always commanded the liberal support and the warm sympathy of the British Christian mind. *People are tired of the old tales: let them see the converts natural Christian communities.*

3d. The limitation of mission agency and its consequent limitation of action have necessitated the dependence of the modern mission, its inability to rise to self-support. Dr. Livingstone has asked the question,—"Why the former mission stations, the early mission monasteries, were self-supporting, rich, and flourishing, as pioneers of civilisation and agriculture, from which we even now reap benefits; and modern mission stations are mere pauper establishments, without that permanence or ability to be self-supporting, which they possessed?" We need not go far to seek an answer to this question. Missions, from which has been eliminated every capacity but that which could preach or teach could not possibly be self-supporting. An action more varied, an organisation more complex, is demanded to reach this state. To attain it they must embrace in their conception, and ally to themselves all consecrated ability. *Self-supporting missions needed.*

And, because wanting in the element of self-support, or in the organisation from which it would grow, missions have failed to lay hold of the British Christian *mercantile* mind. The *The mercantile community approve of such.*

British thought is self-support, and help only to men to help themselves. If missions be permanently wrought in antagonism to this thought, our great mercantile community may contribute to missions, but its contribution will be as the dole that is extracted from the reluctant. It will be a contribution that will leave untouched the mass and magnitude of its wealth. Continued dependence is repugnant to the British mercantile mind. It suspects an enterprise that is wrought for long years in reliance on foreign aid and continual foreign drafts. It ceases to have faith in it. If we would draw from the mercantile community *Why?* according to the vastness of its resources, we must ask it to give in character, and work our missions in the line of its dominant idea. They must proceed on the principle that has made our nation the coloniser and merchant of the world. There must be inwrought into them the power of developing into self-support, of advancing on the strength of their organisation from enterprise to enterprise, till, like the colonies of our empire, they engirdle the earth. In a sense more literal than has yet been conceived, the merchandise of Tyre must become holiness to the Lord; the tea, the sugar, the indigo, the cotton, which are the materials of our traffic, must become the products of our foreign missions, the fruits of their Christian industry and their support.

Summary. Practically, then, under the second division of our subject, we would suggest,—

(1st.) That missions should give prominence in the advocacy of their interests to the fuller conception of mission work, that all gifts of Providence, as well as preaching and teaching gifts, have their missionary sphere.

(2d.) That they should summon by special appeal capitalists, planters, agriculturists, factory masters, to the work of missions, according as openings occur, for the beneficial employment of such agents in their respective fields of operation.

(3d.) That they should have an especial eye upon the movements now being made in every direction for the supply of the foreign products of our trade and manufactures.

There is no reason why Christian capitalists, with their business and administrative talents, should not be induced to enter into such fields as well as others. It were a great point gained were the truth established that, not preaching, but all other capabilities, might be consecrated to the direct service of missions.

Captain LAYARD observed, that the great question was; what

was best to be done, in order to prompt their fellow-Christians to this great work of helping forward the cause of the Lord. Deputation work was one involving a great deal of expense, though they could not say it was an unnecessary work. They had been attacked on all sides as to these expenses; and in reply to such attacks, he said:—"You object to the expense of Deputations; it is in your own hands; as soon as you will give the money more freely, we shall be happy to save the trouble and expense of deputations." One great want, in connexion with the support of missions, was that of pulpit ministrations. If every clergyman were to take up the question, and bring it forward on the strong ground of Christian duty and sympathy, depend upon it much of the expense which was complained of would be saved. The laity could only go forward with weak hands, unless they had the hearty concurrence of the clergy of their parish, or the minister of their congregation. (Hear, hear.) In his view, the missionary cause should be so closely identified with the church, that relaxing in the missionary spirit should be deemed an exhibition of indifference to the great objects of the gospel of Salvation.

Deputations expensive, but necessary.

The clergy can help greatly.

The Rev. CANON WOODROOFFE, of Alton, Hants, said:—I think we have very little to do, so far as the London collectors' poundage is concerned; that is a matter to be left to the judgment of the London Committee of each Society. Experience enables me to say that the expenses of the Church Missionary Society incurred in visiting the country Associations have been exceedingly moderate. Previous to the existence of railways I was in the habit of travelling about four thousand miles every year; and a considerable saving in the Society's expenditure was effected by the Christian hospitality of those friends, who not only received its representative at their houses, but forwarded him on his journey from place to place. I remember on one occasion, after going from London to Derby by the mail, I travelled through the county, preaching sermons and attending meetings every day, and scarcely a shilling was expended from the Society's funds, till I paid the fare for my return. The hospitality shown by friend after friend was in fact a large contribution to the Society's funds. I may say the same of the counties of York and Lancashire, and many others, where scarcely anything was expended, except for the cost of the direct journey from London and back. We are all concerned in diminishing this charge on the funds of

Rev Canon WOODROOFFE.

Hospitality lessens these expenses.

His own case.

each Society, as far as means admit; but it must be dealt with by the London Committee as any other item of needful expenditure. But a considerable saving has been affected to the Church Missionary Society, and, I doubt not, to others also, by the Christian liberality of provincial friends.

<small>Dr. Davis.</small>

Dr. DAVIS,—With respect to one part of the address, which refers to children, I am quite sure there can be no question upon any mind in this room, that it is most important that the children of our Christian households should be trained to understand and to sympathise with the missionary cause. But it would be necessary to look much higher for adequate contributions to the missionary cause. If children subscribed their pence, merchants must give their thousands. A friend had asked him that very day how it came to pass that the Anti-Corn-Law League could get its thousands, at any time, from the merchants of Liverpool, Manchester, or elsewhere, while you can only get your hundreds from Christian men, or your tens from Sunday-school children? It was obvious to reply that every one of those gentlemen believed he was going to get his ten thousand pounds. They knew perfectly well that anything they gave would be largely returned to them. Now does not God take advantage of this principle in human nature, and appeal to it in the Holy Scripture? While salvation is of grace through faith is it not equally true that there is a reward of grace? But is that great principle of Christianity brought out in our pulpits as it ought to be, and made a motive as it might be, to induce those who have large possessions to give largely to the cause of God? I ask, is there not to be a return for every sacrifice that is made for the sake of Christ? It is not a return of thousands here, in the enlargement of trade, or houses or lands, but it is one that is eternal. And I ask, is it not right to say to those who are saved only by grace, that the Lord is not unfaithful, and will not forget their services and their work of love, but will recompense them out of the princely riches of his own royal heart? If these great principles were brought more fully before our wealthy people, I ask, should we be thrown back for our chief support upon our Sabbath scholars and the poor of our churches? Would not the wealthy merchants, of whom there are so many in Liverpool, and London, and Manchester, instead of giving their annual donations of five or ten pounds, be prepared at any time to come forward, and in the name of the Lord give not to a Missionary Society, but to the Lord who gave himself for them, their thousands and tens of thousands? He could not help regarding it as rather disgraceful to the Church than otherwise, that there is scarcely a Missionary Society that is ready to enter the doors which the Lord has thrown open. He has thrown open doors in every land; but you want men, and you want means, and why should this be where Christians are living, surrounded with every comfort which skill can devise, or art and science can secure? Let us look to it. There is a reward of grace; let us teach that doctrine clearly, yet consistently with the doctrines of grace, in the pulpit; and we may hope that thousands, which are now locked up as useless possessions, will be cast ungrudgingly into the treasury of the Lord. (Applause.)

The Rev. R. G. CATHER, of Londonderry, though he rejoiced to hear the statements made on the previous day by Dr. Tidman respecting the success with which God had crowned the labours of the Christian Missionary Societies, had wondered, during the proceedings of the Conference thus far, not to hear a single expression of complaint, of humiliation, and of ardent and agonising desire, for a great increase in the number of missionaries, and a vast enlargement of the field of labour. He believed that the object of missions was, by preaching the Gospel in obedience to Christ's command, and in dependence upon his promise, to convert the whole world to the Church and faith of Christ. Now while Dr. Tidman had perfectly established the success of missionary labours, so far as they had gone in the past, and though there never could be failure where believing effort had been put forth, there had been failure, if the object of the fathers of the Church of Christ was to convert the whole world. It was a patent fact that the world was not converted to the faith of Christ; and in the view of that great fact there was abundant room for consideration, whether our views and the scale of our efforts were in harmony with the principles and spirit of our Divine Master. Mr. Cather then alluded to his connexion with the Systematic Beneficence Society, and observed that this formed his reason for speaking at the present point of the discussion. Missions, as he understood them, were an essential and integral claim, a part of the whole claim, of Christ upon his people. He never could distinguish between the claim of missions and of home churches. He believed the words, "Go ye into all the world and preach the Gospel," were inseparable. It was our duty, however, to provide for the heart, and then, as Dr. Chalmers had expressed it, the

Rev. R. G. CATHER.

More humiliation necessary.

Why?

Missions and home work one.

extremities would be invigorated. If our churches at home were pinched and struggling for support, if ministers were ill supported, if all the charities which the Church was bound to see fed, languished or were with difficulty maintained, how could we expect but that missions would share in these difficulties? There would constantly be found a reaction, and while the zeal and eloquence of deputations on behalf of Missions would stir up the hearts of the people, after a little time they would begin to say, "Ought we not to do more at home?" No doubt missionary liberality increased home liberality; and therefore he took the ground that this Missionary Conference had a common interest with the home churches and all the agencies of Christianity, in increasing upon principle the contributions offered to the cause of Christ. The individual Christians in this country have more than enough money for home purposes. With regard to the particular object of their present consultations, how the missionary feeling at home should be stirred up. He was satisfied with Mr. Lewis and Captain Layard, that the pulpit was really the responsible power; though he did not believe that the pulpit would ever work the Church on the principle referred to a moment ago; that they would ever overcome the reluctance of ministers to preach about missions, while there was the feeling in their minds that they were constantly telling the people to give—give—give. He had been told by ministers more faithful than himself, that they had preached for forty years, and had never used such texts as "Honour the Lord with thy substance;" "There is that scattereth and yet increaseth, and there is that withholdeth more than is meet and it tendeth to poverty." He held that these questions of Christian economics should be cheerfully and heartily entered into; for until ministers believed that they were unfaithful expositors of the word if they did not tell the covetous world and the covetous church the things which God commanded them to tell, they should never have the riches of the Gentiles laid at the feet of Christ.

They act on each other.

Liberality should be increased on principle.

The pulpit should do more in exciting it.

Rev. T. L. Badham

The Rev. T. L. BADHAM remarked, that the Church seemed to have forgotten that the work of missions was the *business* of the Church. It was looked at too much as a question apart, and the consequence was, that many considered themselves good Christians, and would wish to be thought so by others, who, after all, took very little interest in the spread of the knowledge of the truth as it is in Jesus. Some of the new churches formed from the heathen would put us to shame by and bye. There was a spirit of liberality in congregations of the Western hemisphere, which he thought, under God's blessing, would lead to very great results. Those congregations reasoned in this way; they said, "Our friends across the water have been doing much for us for a length of time. We have obtained great privileges through their instrumentality; we are now able to help ourselves; and it is our duty to support ourselves and help forward the Word of God in less favoured countries." That was the right principle on which the Church ought to go.

Some native churches an example to English ones.

The Rev. Dr. TIDMAN said,—Sir, I do not see that we have yet agreed on one practical conclusion (hear, hear), and our precious hours are passing away. My object is to bring the Conference to this point :—What is really to be done? What are the best means of increasing the missionary feeling at home? I think what we have to do, above all other things, is to imbue our *Ministers* with the missionary feeling. I find the young, and especially the poor, are forward to give to the missionary cause; there is a great deficiency in the higher classes of society; but I never found a minister who is in heart and soul a missionary man, who did not carry with him a missionary church, and a missionary congregation. (Hear, hear.) When you are told that many brethren in the ministry—and I believe it is perfectly true—do not from the beginning of January to the end of December preach a missionary sermon, you cannot wonder that the people are cold, heartless, and neglectful. (Hear, hear.) How can you blame the people if they do not systematically give, as my friend who has last spoken, would induce them to do? I hope it will go forth as an expression of our feeling in this cause, that we earnestly entreat our brethren in the ministry to cherish the missionary cause, and to instruct the people in this matter as one of the great branches of Christianity, and as one of the great means that God is now impressing on the Church with double force as its peculiar duty. I do not mean making missionary collections; people do not like to give money just because the sermon is about giving money. I do not like to hear the subject of Missions merely as an occasion of begging; but if my brethren would take a portion of the Scriptures once a-month, and employ the Sabbath morning in the serious, deliberate, and intelligent discussion of great missionary principles, I am convinced, Sir, that we should have a missionary spirit, and should not want ample funds. I believe the less we say about

Rev. Dr. TIDMAN.

Ministers should be more missionary.

A missionary pastor makes a missionary people.

Systematic teaching required from them.

money the better. We shall get the more money the less we talk about it. (Hear, hear.) It was once my happiness to be the pastor of a small congregation not exceeding six hundred persons, and I obtained a larger amount for Christian missions, home and foreign, than I received for salary; I induced the subscriber of one pound, to give five pounds; and the man of five pounds, to give ten pounds; and it is only in this way that you can carry on this great cause with efficiency. Now, Sir, I do hope that in the little time that remains we shall try to sum up our thoughts, and to put upon record our views as to how we may best promote the missionary spirit in our churches. (Hear, hear.) I again say—and I have some interest in the financial question—that I do not think we shall have any difficulty in getting funds when we have a good case to present. It is a good argument to tell our friends that within the last six months we have sent out six missionaries; if such be the case, they see that something is doing; that God has heard their prayers by raising up men, and that it is their duty to follow them with their sympathy and their support.

The Rev. Dr. TWEEDIE said he did not rise to weaken the force of what the last speaker had said by repeating it. His experience was not so extensive nor so deep as Dr. Tidman's, but as far as it had gone it was the re-echo of what he (Dr. Tidman) had said. He rose to try to deepen the effect of those remarks by suggesting a very practical measure. He found from the paper that their attention was to be drawn to the great expenses incurred by religious societies in gathering their funds, and to the difficulty of avoiding collectors' percentage. That expense, he knew, was often very heavy. Now these were two very practical points, and if they could dispose of them in a practical way, he thought they would have arrived at something to embody in their minutes to show that this Conference had conferred a benefit on all the churches. And in the section of the Church with which he was connected he thought they had arrived at a practical solution of every one of the difficulties; for he was not aware that in the course of a year they were at the expense of a single sovereign on these heads. They collected about 300,000*l.* a-year for all their purposes; their annual income was from 275,000*l.* to 325,000*l.*; at least, for the last eighteen years, their revenue had ranged between these sums, and upon the whole amount they had no collectors' commission to pay—not one farthing, he believed. They were charged, of course, the Queen's-head upon each letter sent, but they paid nothing more. The explanation was: they had from 10,000 to 12,000 voluntary agents and collectors spread over the Church; they had so many in each of their congregations; the elders, deacons, and collectors, in the churches went voluntarily, he believed in the great majority of cases most cordially, to collect the money contributed to the different objects home and foreign. They placed it in the hands of 1000 or 1200 local treasurers; they send it up monthly to the Edinburgh treasurer for distribution, and thus the object is gratuitously gained. Now he would like if the Conference could see their way to some practical measure of this kind; and would submit that suggestion as his contribution. He should be glad if they were able to say, as the result of their deliberations, We have succeeded practically in getting entirely quit of the collectors' percentage, or even have begun a plan tending to that result. Dr. Tidman said he believed that the people were far ahead of many ministers, and he (the speaker) entirely concurred in that sentiment, for he was convinced that many in their congregations were in a riper state for yielding the harvest of the Lord than some of those who occupied the pulpit. (Hear, hear.)

Their number.

The Rev. CHARLES RATTRAY, missionary of the London Missionary Society in Demarara, could not forbear mentioning a most important subject in connexion with the funds required for the support of missions, viz. the practice of using intoxicating drinks, and the amount of money expended in this way. Whether they would or not, this would very soon become the question of the Christian church. God would not bless their labours if they did not deny themselves in a matter of this kind. In the mission-field with which he was connected, if a new missionary were appointed who was not an abstainer he would be deemed to lack a most important qualification. They had just been hearing that half a million was expended by the whole church in the missionary cause; how much, Mr. Rattray asked, was expended by the whole church in the use of intoxicating drinks?

Rev. C. RATTRAY.

Total abstinence will increase funds.

The CHAIRMAN stated that the whole expenditure in Great Britain upon intoxicating drinks was fifty millions annually; and recommended Mr. Rattray to peruse Isa. iii. 16, as it contained a very full subject for exposition with regard to self-denial.

Fifty millions a-year spent in spirits, &c.

Rev. G. Scott.

Divine preparations for modern missionary work.

The Rev. Geo. Scott wished to throw out a single practical suggestion with regard to the money part of the question. He was convinced that God never sent his Church a warfare on her own charges. If, on the one hand, God had been opening up wide fields for action in foreign lands, He had on the other been providing the means at home for entering into and cultivating those fields. During the last twenty-five or thirty years many of God's children had been prospered, not for their own luxury or profit, but for the purpose of carrying on God's work more extensively. The question, then, was how to bring out the amount of liberality really required for the large amount of missionary work to be done. His suggestion was that some simultaneous use of the pulpit thoughout the whole country might be arranged, which would greatly help the object in view. They had lately had an invitation to prayer from a most interesting portion of the mission field; this had been responded to very generally throughout Christendom. Should they not send a practical response to their brethren labouring in these distant fields of missions, and arrange, *altogether separate from any collection,* to have a simultaneous presentation of the missionary subject from all the pulpits of the churches and chapels of the various Protestant communions throughout Christendom. (Hear, hear.)

Simultaneous sermon on missions.

Rev. J. L. Porter.

The Rev. J. L. Porter, of Damascus, mentioned the practice followed by the American Board of Commissioners for Foreign Missions, of having monthly missionary meetings on a certain evening. This practice was adopted wherever, throughout the world, they had a missionary settled or a missionary station. He had been present at such meetings in Constantinople, Smyrna, Malta, Beyrout, and Damascus; and he could hardly express how much the missionaries were stirred up and encouraged by such gatherings, when they knew that at that time in every part of the world a little body of truly Christian people were assembled together with the same purpose as themselves; to get information, and ask for God's blessing upon the work of missions. Could nothing be done like this generally?

Monthly missionary prayer-meetings.

Rev. J. B. Whiting.

The Rev. J. B. Whiting, in allusion to what had fallen from previous speakers, said:—Where are the ministers to derive the information to be given to the people? No doubt the existing periodicals were abundantly sufficient, but it is a fact that these are not regarded as a sufficiently simple means of obtaining information. A great impulse would be given to the cause, if short papers were drawn up and circulated by the various Committees. This would be of great assistance to ministers, and would greatly enlarge the number of those who were willing to go out as deputations. *Increased information.*

In vindication of the editors of the Church Missionary Society's publications, he said that no documents from the mission-field were overlooked, but, as far as possible, all intelligence was given to the public. The *Intelligencer* was especially designed to contain important communications from missionaries. The Church Missionary Society had published a beautiful Atlas of their missions, and there was some intention of publishing a large missionary map of the world. The friends of missions should relieve the Societies of the cost of such publications. *Pastors to be supplied with it.*

He thought "systematic giving" was a subject of very great importance. He knew that in a parish in Suffolk the clergyman had been enabled to induce his people to give thank-offerings for every blessing which they received. A farmer gave a thank-offering because his horse had fallen and had not broken its knees. It was not a matter to smile at, because the pastor had taught his people a thankful spirit, and they were accustomed when they received a blessing from Almighty God, as a matter of praise and as a sacrifice of gratitude, to offer an acknowledgment. (Hear, hear.) He said they ought to impress upon their people, not that they should give to this society or that, but that they should give to God according as He had blessed them, and at stated intervals. The weekly offerings recommended by St. Paul were of great importance. They wanted to teach the people to have a charity box; let them have a charity ledger, and with all the accuracy of a man of business put down what they gave to God. If we could get people to look back and see what they had given to God they would be ashamed. A gentleman had said to him that he would be glad to get out of his charitable payments for 10*l.* a-year; but when he got that gentleman to enumerate what he had given it was found only to amount to 2*l.* 17*s.* 6*d.* *Systematic giving. Thank-offerings. Weekly offerings. Charity-ledger.*

Mr. CUNNINGHAM asked if the map to be published by the Church Missionary Society would contain all missionary stations? *Missionary map.*

The Rev. Mr. WHITING replied that it would refer to the whole mission-field.

The Rev. HAMILTON MACGILL thought they were deeply indebted to Mr. Scott for the practical proposal he had made. He trusted that, throughout all their churches, that proposal would be adopted, and that they would have the benefit of universal sympathy on this subject through all their congregations on one Sabbath in the year. He was persuaded that what had been said in regard to the power of the pulpit in relation to missions was of very special importance. No minister could preach the Gospel intelligently and faithfully, without frequently bringing their duty with regard to missions before his hearers. This ought to be done, not, by any means, in a spirit of petulance and fault-finding, but in a spirit of faithfulness and love. It was, he held, impossible to preach aright without continually expounding what was the duty of the whole Church, and of all its members, in order that the great prayer for the coming of God's Kingdom, which they were ever offering, might really be answered.

He did not think they should gain their object, unless attention was secured in favour of *systematic contribution*. It was not required of the *rich* man merely that he should give of his abundance. He remembered the poor widow and her "two mites." He looked upon that small gift as being as important in the sight of God as thousands given by a man who was as able to spare his thousands as the widow was to spare her mites. Christian giving and personal exertion were intended for spiritual discipline in the Church. God had given them missionary work to do, that they might be prepared to serve him in other forms on earth; and at last and for ever to serve him in heaven. Contribution, like prayer, for the extension of the Redeemer's Kingdom, ought to be *frequent*, as well as universal, among Christians. What would they think of a *quarterly prayer?* It was the design of Christ to teach his people, by continued habit and discipline in this matter, to go not only to his throne of grace, but to his altar with their gifts, that with every sacred offering, great or small, there should be conjoined a separate exercise of Christian principle. Unless such views were carried into practice, they would would never gain the chief end for which Christian giving was intended. Systematic contribution was enjoined, not merely in order that missionary enterprises should be supported; not merely that the gospel might be preached unto all the world; but that the givers themselves might be made better men and better Christians. Their people might thus make to themselves "*friends* of the Mammon of unrighteousness," which, on the other hand, if abused, might prove their *foe*. What was the history of some of those nations which in ancient times grew rich and powerful? Their wealth, having found no benevolent outlet, corrupted them; and he trembled more for fear of the corruption that might come from such a quarter as this into the heart of our country, than on account of any foreign foe. If all their people should give systematically, on principle, and with frequency, he believed that thereby they should be offering to God what he would accept as a species of worship, as a service acceptable and well-pleasing in his sight. *[Nations corrupted by wealth. Liberality acceptable to God.]*

In the church with which he was more immediately connected, there was a Synodical recommendation, largely and increasingly acted on, that collectors should go through the families of each congregation, once a-month, to receive their missionary contributions. They had found that the disposition to give grew by exercise. It was like all other good Christian dispositions; it was strengthened by frequent repetition. He believed every Christian ought closely to connect working with giving; and if their pulpits were faithful in this matter; if ministers impressed upon their people the necessity of not only giving to the cause of God, but of personally working in that cause, the disposition to work and the disposition to give would mightily aid each other; and the result would be not only to strengthen the missionary spirit, but to invigorate all the great principles of the Christian life. *[Giving grows by exercise. Working also.]*

The Rev. P. H. CORNFORD,—I cannot but suppose that all the artillery directed against the pulpit has been directed by those who have never had the charge of young churches; of churches oppressed with debt, or in want of repair; but I am sorry to say I know from experience, that there are circumstances in which it is impossible to bring the churches immediately to do all that we feel desirous they should do, on behalf of the missionary work. Where increasing sabbath-schools want increased accommodation; where there is a large tract-distribution to attend to and provide for, and where there may be a large amount of interest to be raised upon a debt, you cannot, surely, lay all the blame upon a man who, perhaps, has not the heart to press his people for money for missionary purposes. I beg leave to plead not guilty to the charge. (Hear, hear.) In conclusion, Mr. Cornford said, that in his opinion the remedy for this want of missionary *[Rev. P. H. CORNFORD. Some churches are in difficulties.]*

liberality was to establish the habit of *systematic benevolence:* to cultivate the Christian habit of giving *week by week*.

Weekly offerings.

JOHN CROPPER, Esq., of Liverpool, said, that the practice of collection, which had prevailed in the place of worship with which he was connected, had worked wonderfully well in bringing in systematically by weekly contributions an amount quite equal to the amount ever previously raised by begging, by book or congregational collections, or by any other process. The plan adopted was to place a box at the entrance of the chapel, into which every one, on coming in, placed what they had laid by for the purpose during the week. The sums thus gathered have amounted to 650*l.* annually; while all the trouble and pain attendant upon the begging or ordinary collecting systems were saved, and are divided amongst religious institutions each half year.

J. CROPPER, Esq.

Success of the weekly-offering.

The Rev. J. MAKEPEACE, formerly of Agra, hoped that Mr. Cornford's case was an exceptional one. Great deference, Mr. Makepeace thought, should be paid to the excellent suggestion of Mr. Scott. One grand point should have the attention of the Conference fastened upon it; namely, that the pastors of churches should be more eminently imbued with the missionary spirit, and should more frequently avail themselves of the pulpit for the diffusion of missionary intelligence. As an instance of the result of pastoral zeal and earnestness in the mission work, Mr. Makepeace mentioned the case of a friend of his, a returned missionary, who undertook the pastorate of a church in England. When he settled first in the town, the missionary contributions of his own denomination did not exceed 35*l.* annually; whereas, before he left the town, after fifteen years' labour, his own church alone raised between 400*l.* and 500*l.* Not a sabbath passed over without his making a reference to, or offering up his prayers for, missionary enterprises; and this was the secret of his success. (Hear, hear.)

Rev. J. MAKEPEACE.

Pastoral zeal for missions.

Instance of its influence.

The Rev. DAVID THORBURN, of Leith, believed, that one great means of increasing the resources employed in propagating the gospel was the delivery of addresses from the pulpit to stir up the missionary spirit. He had not heard, however, any remarks made, indicating the views of the members of the Conference with regard to the nature and extent of the obligation imposed upon members of the Christian Church. So far as he had

Rev. D. THORBURN.

Extent of Christian obligation.

heard, it seemed to be understood that the obligation was one entirely of an indeterminate character: that though God had said every one should lay aside according as God has prospered him, yet the extent of the obligation was to be judged by the individual himself. Whether this were the case or not, it was not the case under the Patriarchal or Levitical dispensation. In the Patriarchal age, we found the nature and extent of the obligation indicated in the "first-fruits" and "tithes;" and passing to the Levitical, we found the obligation somewhat more definitely specified. The presumption was, that it would be stated more clearly in the dispensation under which it was our happiness to live. Such, however, was not the general impression. But there was a time in the history of the Christian Church when another opinion extensively prevailed, that the obligation to give, to a certain amount at least, was a determinate obligation. For many centuries such was the universal opinion throughout the Church. He (Mr. Thorburn) believed that our present views with regard to the obligation were defective, if not erroneous; and that, considering the vastly more important objects for which we were called upon now to give, it was surely reasonable to suppose that we should give more than was required under a former dispensation. In the New Testament, both by our Lord and his Apostles, the principles were very clearly laid down which should guide us in this matter. In the commendation given by the Saviour to the Pharisees for the scrupulousness with which they paid their tithes, he indicated that, to a certain extent, the duty was determinate as to the *minimum*, but indeterminate as to the *maximum*. Weekly gifts, also, were pointedly enforced by the Apostles.

Patriarchal and Jewish tithes.

Christians ought to give more.

The Rev. H. M. WADDELL:—I have observed that the words "missionary feeling" have occurred often in the course of the discussion. In my view this is not a matter of feeling, but of conscience. It is a duty; and a sense of duty is a surer foundation than any feeling. A man feels bound to pay his debts, his minister or his pew-rent, but he does not feel bound to give a missionary contribution. Why so? It has been a matter optional to them; not felt as obligatory. In looking for funds, when they fall short, whence are they to be obtained before we trench upon the necessities of individuals? There are luxuries in the Church that can be kept down. There is a tendency in the Church of the present day to run into a luxurious style of living, following the example of the world. As to wine-drinking, I will endorse all

Rev. H. M. WADDELL.

Conscience in giving.

Luxuries to be cut down.

what has been said by the friend from Demerara. I apprehend that the missionary supporters at home ought to be as self-denying as the missionaries abroad. This matter should be carefully looked into by brethren in this country, that they may not follow worldly fashions by increase of luxuries of the table and household furniture, and general style of living, but cut down such expenses to enrich the treasury for the spread of the Gospel over all the world. (Applause.)

Lieut.-Col. Edwardes.

Lieut-Col. EDWARDES,—I merely wish to throw out one practical suggestion which struck me as I was listening to Dr. Tidman. How would it answer for the various Missionary Societies to draw up once a quarter an interesting and popular account of the state of the mission-field in one separate quarter of the globe, and to issue that account to the pastor of every parish or church in connexion with their own Society, with an urgent request that that pastor would kindly consent either that himself, or one of his own fellow-labourers, should preach a sermon embodying that account, during the quarter? If that were done I think you would get Europe, Asia, Africa, and America, systematically put before each congregation in a popular way, and you would diffuse and excite an interest at a very easy rate. (Hear, hear.)

A suggestion.

MINUTE ON THE MEANS OF SECURING INCREASED LIBERALITY TO MISSIONARY WORK.

The Conference are of opinion that love to perishing souls, for the sake of Him who died for them, as the command of Christ and the essence of the Gospel, is the rule of genuine Christian liberality; and that this liberality stops short of its highest, yet legitimate exemplification, where it leads to no self-denial. They believe that giving to the support of schemes, which are maintained for speading the Gospel among the heathen, is itself a solemn duty, a part-fulfilment of the great commission; and that it is as much a duty to give as it is to labour or to pray.

The rule of liberality.

The proportion of income which should be given to this great object, in their view, rests with the conscience of every individual Christian. While in the Patriarchal and Jewish dispensations a stated proportion was laid down for all classes, they consider that under the Gospel the people of God are taught, that while all

Conscience the guide.

belongs to Him and must be accounted for as such, each of them should contribute according as God has prospered him. They consider that the exact amount such prosperity demands should be made a matter for prayerful, scriptural, and solemn deliberation: and that Christian benevolence should thus be based upon principle, and be exercised on system. *(Extent of giving. How determined. Systematic.)*

As the disposition to give grows by exercise, they consider that the result of such a mode of consecrating a due share of income to the Saviour's cause, would be a readiness to add to regular gifts, when new supplies were bestowed; and a hearty and prompt response to those special calls made upon the Church, when the providence of God opens, by special means, new and enlarged fields of usefulness in which the Gospel may be preached. *(Effect.)*

They think that in the cultivation of this benevolence, as a vigorous principle, a great deal rests upon all pastors of churches: experience showing that, where a pastor possesses an active missionary spirit, urges that spirit upon his people, strives to give them much information on mission-fields, and systematically presses their claims, his people become missionary likewise, and are prepared to give with a large heart to all worthy objects of Christian benevolence. *(Work for pastors. Result.)*

That such a spirit of increased consecration and of self-sacrificing liberality, may be poured out upon all the churches of Christ, is their earnest prayer; and that Christians may be able to abstain from copying the luxurious habits of the world, in order that they may overtake more efficiently the vast territories of heathenism yet lying unblest with divine truth.

The Doxology was then sung, and the Fourth Session closed.

SECOND MISSIONARY SOIRÉE.

WEDNESDAY EVENING.

A second missionary Soirée was held on Wednesday Evening, at the conclusion of the discussion above reported:—

JOHN CROPPER, Esq., presided.

Rev. B. L. Singh. After prayer had been offered by the Rev. J. M'KEE, the Rev. BEHARI LAL SINGH, licensed preacher of the Free Church of Scotland in Calcutta, delivered the following address:—

ADDRESS BY THE REV. B. L. SINGH.

The law of missions. Mr. Chairman, ladies and gentlemen, the great command and charter of missionary work is, "Go into all the world and preach the Gospel to every creature; go and teach all nations." Here is the warrant, here is the encouragement, here is the time, here is the place. "Lo, I am with you always, even unto the end of the world." "Why was the world created? For the manifestation of Jehovah's glory, for the habitation of man. And after man's fall why was it preserved?" Not for the gratification of man's selfishness, his pride, or for political intrigues; but for higher purposes, even for the manifestation of Jehovah's glory, for a state of preparation for God's elect in all righteousness, the nursery for the education of the children of God till the time of the restitution of all things should come; till all his gracious designs should be completed; which is and has been the cherished hope of his sons. Our Lord distinctly told his disciples that "other sheep I have which are not of this fold; them also I must bring and they shall hear my voice." To gather in these sheep is the work of missions.

Free Church Mission in Calcutta. Leaving other fields of labour, it is expected that I should say a few words respecting the Indian mission with which I have been connected for the last sixteen or seventeen years; they shall be very brief. There is no lack of knowledge among you respecting the means that are employed in India for bringing the truths of the gospel to bear upon the Hindoos and Mahommedans, by preaching in the English and vernacular languages, and circulating Christian books. But whether it be that some go throughout the length and breadth of the land, or those who go to preach the gospel in our large public towns, the teaching of all is drawn from the Bible. Whether it be those who are engaged in the work of teaching in the schools or colleges, they make the Bible a class-book, and a book of continual reference. Let me invite your attention, then, for a few moments to the divine power of the Bible, to what the Bible, through the blessing of the Spirit, has done for my poor and perishing countrymen. Let me bring to your notice that the Bible has been welcomed, received, and read; that the law of the Lord has been proved by the conversions that have been effected in my native land. In the year 1844 seven Jews and Jewesses were publicly baptised by Dr. Duff at Calcutta: the eldest was a venerable patriarch, who understood only Arabic; the second was a rabbi, and rather well versed in the Arabic and Hebrew scriptures; and there was a man of considerable attainments in the Hindostanee and Arabic. The Jews met in the house of a pious layman, and read the Bible in the Arabic and Hebrew languages, with a converted Jew who was employed as reader. They were put under my charge; I was the medium of communication between the Jews and the European missionaries. Some years afterwards some of them died, and whilst they were lying in their last illness in the Government hospital, they were severely tried by their countrymen who endeavoured to induce them to deny Jesus; but I, as well as many missionaries who witnessed their deaths, am glad to testify that they remained faithful unto death.

Its labours.

Success among Jews.

A venerable father in this Conference has asked me to give a short narrative of how I became connected with the Indian mission. (Hear, hear.) I do not assume, as a matter of course, that I am a converted man; the Lord alone knows my many imperfections and deficiencies. I feel rather diffident in speaking of the inward working of my heart; but I shall let you know a few facts connected with my external history: how I have been to this land, this highly favoured land; and how I came here privileged to speak a few words in such a meeting as this. I am sorry to say I belong to the rebel race of North-West India; still if you convert the rebels they will fight for you. (Hear, hear.) They will become your loyal subjects; they will defend your lives. (Applause.) I need not say much on this, as my friend, Mr. Leupolt, will bring many things to your knowledge respecting it. About forty years ago my father came down to Calcutta,

His personal history.

Birth.

	there being no missionary or school in the North-West Provinces.
Education.	My father was anxious that I should get a knowledge of the English language in order that I might obtain a Government appointment. He came down with myself and my brother in the year 1830. Dr. Duff, the first missionary of the Church of Scotland, opened his chool in Calcutta, and there I and my brother went to study the English language. Some years after, having finished his education, my brother got a Government appointment and returned to his native country; I remained some years longer in Dr. Duff''s institution. I read the Bible. I read the Bible just as I read any other common class-book. It was not reading the Bible in school that moved my heart; but it was the private ministrations of that great and good man, Dr. Duff,
Religious knowledge.	and of his excellent colleagues, Dr. Mackay and Dr. Ewart, that moved my heart to become almost a Christian. I had bright prospects before me; I was a favourite with a military officer, the late Major-General Macleod. I went from Dr. Duff's school to Medical College and learned the higher branches, natural philosophy and botany: then I passed an examination, got a Government appointment, and came in contact with a pious civil officer, who had defrayed the expense of my education in Dr. Duff's school, as well as in the Government Medical College. It was
Influence of Christian example.	the pious example of this gentleman, his integrity, his honesty, his disinterestedness, his active benevolence, that made me think that Christianity was something living; that there was a loving power in Christ. (Hear, hear.) Here is a man in the receipt of 2000 or 3000 rupees a-month, he spends little on himself, and gives away the surplus of his money for education, the temporal and spiritual welfare of my countrymen. This was the turning-point of my religious history, and led to my conversion. About that time, my brother, who was also in the Government service,
His brother a Christian.	had prepared his mind to embrace Christianity; but of his history I need not say anything, as my friend Mr. Leupolt knows him very well, and also my friend Mr. Tucker, who has been his great patron. He came to me and said, "I am ready to embrace Christianity, and I want to become a teacher. I must give up all, and you must support me." My father got a copy of the Persian Bible from Dr. Mackay, and the objection my father had to embracing Christianity was that the morality of the Bible was too high for man to follow. (Hear, hear.) We all made up our minds to embrace Christianity, and I am glad to say we did not suffer as much persecution as many of my brethren in Hindostan have suffered. My brother fell into the company of a very good and

pious missionary of the Church of England, by whom he was baptised, and he is now labouring in connexion with the Church Missionary Society. As I had received the truths of Christianity from Dr. Duff's instruction, I felt it my duty to go down to Calcutta to be baptised in connexion with the Free Church. In all my trials and difficulties as a Christian, and as a subordinate missionary to my countrymen, I have been strengthened and encouraged by the example of another officer and his lady, whose testimony for the Lord Jesus has been so remarkable, so simple-minded, and so consistent, as to lead my blinded countrymen to confess that he is after all their best friend. [Here the speaker turned his face to Major-Gen. Alexander and said,]—The officer, Sir, was the adjutant of the regiment of which you were the distinguished commander. Afterwards I laboured as a teacher in the Free Church institution, then as a teacher among the Jews, and then as a city missionary, and, last of all, a teacher among the Mahommedans of Calcutta. *Baptism, &c.*

Few of you, dear Christian friends, will rise from the hearing of the following affecting case without feelings of increased respect and veneration for the pure and gentle religion of Jesus, and feelings of hatred for the cruel spirit of Hindooism. Some of you may have seen the little narrative published by Dr. Sutton, of the General Baptist Missionary Society, of a Brahmin girl whose life was wonderfully preserved, and who was brought up by him and his lady in the nurture and admonition of the Lord. For the information of those of you who have not read the narrative, I beg to mention a few leading incidents connected with the wonderful preservation of this little girl. In 1829, among the pilgrims who travelled to the shrine of Juggernaut, there was a Brahmin family, consisting of husband, wife, and a little babe, about six months old, with one or two servants. On the arrival of the pilgrim party at Balasore, 150 miles distant from the temple, the wife of Punda-Narain, for that was the name of the husband, was seized with cholera. Narain was not to be found at this critical time. Whether he fell a victim on the way to this disease, or not, no one could say. The unfortunate woman found that everybody had forsaken her. Thus, a stranger seized by the ruthless cholera, with a feeble infant at her breast, she wandered to a neighbouring village, where she was informed medical aid could be obtained. Although, however, she reached the door of the doctor, who was a fat, wealthy Brahmin, she could get no assistance from him. How long she remained here is not certainly known. But it was so ordered that, in the good providence of God, Dr. Sutton went *History of a Hindoo girl. The Brahmin pilgrims. Cholera.*

one evening to preach in the village, and found the poor woman and child lying under the shade of a large tree. The shadows of the evening were closing apace. Not far from the spot were lying the bodies of many pilgrims who had fallen victims to this frightful malady, and where the jackals, the pariah dogs, and vultures, were tearing the flesh of the dead. Overhead, too, they were canopied with thick darkness, sadness, and gloom, as the great dense clouds were gathering from the west, and were threatening to burst upon them in a tempest of thunder, lightning, and rain.

Dr. Sutton's efforts. The missionary ascertained the nature of the disease and administered some medicine which he had with him. He went to the neighbouring village and pleaded long in vain for some food for the poor and starving infant. No one would give her any. At length an egg-cupful of milk was procured, and never was a more pitiful scene beheld than when the starving child crawled to the missionary, and, looking up to his face, seemed to say, "O sir, pity me, I have no friend in this wide world to care for my body and soul!" Dr. Sutton removed the helpless woman to a neighbouring shed, where he attended her for three days, but at the end of that time she expired. When the missionary perceived that the poor woman was fast expiring, he inquired of the Brahmin doctor, who was standing by, what was to be done with the child? to which the monster replied, "Oh! let it die also, what else?" The mother had some gold and silver ornaments about her, besides some money, and the possession of these was what the doctor sought to obtain. This he effected, and was unwilling to undergo any trouble respecting the child.

Orphan girl saved and educated. Seeing how matters were likely to go, the missionary determined to save the little girl, so he took with him an old female servant and intrusted the child to her protection. When the poor infant was brought to his house, some rice-pudding was placed on a plate on the floor before her, while a spoon was sent for; but no sooner did the child perceive that it was food, than she crawled towards the plate, and, helping herself with both hands with the utmost greediness, would not suffer herself to be removed until the whole was eaten up. As the missionary had no children, the little girl was soon adopted as a daughter.

Visit to America. She went with her foster-parents to America, where she was put to a boarding-school. She returned with them afterwards to her native land. After affording satisfactory evidence of her conversion, she was admitted into the Christian church by the sacred ordinance of baptism. She was for many years an assistant-teacher in the female schools of Orissa. It has been my privilege to have been united in marriage to this

Christian native lady. In India, when a man is married, it is [His wife.] not husband and wife that see each other and consult, it is the mothers and fathers or some distant relative, by whom the affair is settled. But such was not the case with us. I went down to Cuttack and shared the hospitality of the excellent Christian missionaries of the General Baptist Missionary Society. I stayed there for a long time, and then when both of us came to the conclusion that we should be a suitable match, then—we got married. (Laughter and applause.)

ON THE PESHAWUR MISSION.

By Lieut.-Col. Edwardes.

Lieutenant-Colonel HERBERT EDWARDES, who on rising met with a most hearty reception, then addressed the meeting as follows:—I have been asked to give you an account of the PESHAWUR MISSION, and I do so with pleasure, because the history of that English mission cannot but be an interesting and valuable narrative for all friends at home to hear. I suppose there can be no mission in any part of the world, which can reach a lengthened existence without exhibiting in its history some very interesting events. The Peshawur mission must necessarily have many instances of this. I will first tell you the position which that mission occupies. You will all suppose you have got a map of India at the end of this room and at the top, the very north-western outpost of your Indian empire, across the river Indus, there stands Peshawur. It is in fact the picket to British India. Peshawur, geographically speaking, is part of Afghanistan. The people who inhabit it are therefore Afghans. On the east is the river Indus, on the western side the Suliman range of mountains, in which stands the Khyber Pass. From that pass to the Indus is about fifty miles, and on the south side stands the Kohat Pass. The hills of Swât shut in the north. The valley lying between these ranges and the river Indus is most fertile, and produces crops and fruit in luxuriant abundance. For this valley the tribes have all contended for ages past, and the tribes that inhabit those mountain-ranges are the fiercest clans that can be found anywhere on the face of the globe. I do not think that finer specimens of physical human nature can be found. Nurtured on those hills with very little to support them, they have been reared in constant warfare. Each man is armed to the teeth, and he goes forth with his hand against every man, prepared to

[Lieut.-Col. Edwardes.]

[Position of the Peshawur valley.]

[Its tribes.]

meet every man's hand against him. Whatever truth or whatever falsehood there may be in the great Lord Macaulay's description of the mountain clans of our own north, I must say that if you were to take those pages, and apply them to the inhabitants of the Khyber Pass and the Afghan mountains, you would find it suit exactly. They possess every vice with which human nature is afflicted. But they have their virtues. They have the great virtue of manly courage, and they have the great virtue of hospitality. When the English soldier is brought in contact with them, it is a refreshment, after coming from the slavish plain, to meet a race able to struggle with him for empire. (Applause.) If you were to look over the map of Asia, certainly over the map of British India, and were to select the spot most ungenial for the establishment of a mission you would put your finger on Peshawur; but I am glad to be able to tell you that a mission has been planted there and flourishes at this time. (Applause.) The founder was a military officer, one of the best, and most consistent and earnest among our Indian Christians, Colonel MARTIN. (Applause.) He first conceived the design of having a mission there, and he and others united in prayers for this object. But they did not see their way clearly for a very long time. There were sundry hindrances in their path which are too painful for mention, and the persons who did hinder them were removed in the providence of God from off the scene. Permission was given ultimately by the authorities in the valley of Peshawur for the establishment of the mission. A great meeting of the civil and military officers was called to consider the question, and there was not one dissentient voice. (Applause.) I attended that meeting myself and I did not hear in the room where we were gathered one person who seemed to have any misgiving on the point of introducing a mission into such a place as that. When the subscription list went round there was, however, one name put down on that list,—I won't mention it as it is unnecessary,—and to it was sarcastically appended "one rupee." That is a thing which in India we fling about or give away just as we would a sixpence in England. The subscription of one rupee was intended to throw contempt upon the undertaking, and opposite the subscription was written, "To buy a revolver for the first missionary." Well it is a most extraordinary thing that that officer was one of the very first victims of the Indian mutiny, and it made a great impression on me afterwards when I came to look back on it. Here was a man who considered that in a frontier valley full of such a hostile race a Christian mission was unsafe, and who noted down one rupee to buy a revolver for the first missionary who should dare to enter that valley; he goes away to what he considers a safe cantonment in the very heart of our empire, and yet that man and his family in that safe place were among the first victims of the mutiny. I wonder if, when that sad hour came, any such thought flashed across his mind as that he had looked unharmed upon danger in dangerous places, and found it where he thought he was safe. How much better it would have been to have trusted his life and the lives of others in the hands of God. Well, the programme of the mission was put out, and it was responded to at once throughout India in a remarkable manner. There was something enterprising, something thoroughly missionary about the undertaking, which, like the sound of a clarion, seemed to awake the sympathies of every Christian in India; and the response to the call was immediate and loud. In a short time no less than 3000*l.* were subscribed: and from that day forward the mission has gone on prospering. (Applause.) We were blessed certainly with most admirable missionaries. The first, I think, the father of the missionaries, was Dr. Pfander, a most admirable man, who had spent forty years of his life in missionary labour. He was well constituted for the purpose. He used to go down into the streets of that city, which contained 60,000 inhabitants, and with the Bible in his hand would take his stand in the street. It was a service of danger to go into the streets of that city and preach the gospel of Christ; and when Dr. Pfander took up his stand in the street, opened his Bible, and preached Christ before the whole of those people, I consider that he performed an act of great Christian courage and great Christian faith. (Applause.) That man was admirably suited for the duty. His very face reflected all the Christian virtue of love to all men. It was impossible for the most thorough blackguard to take exception to such a man; and if there were any man who dared to interrupt him he would just stroke him down and pacify him; tell him that was not the time for discussion; but that if he wished he would accompany him to his house, or take him to his own, and there talk the matter over. The people at last got accustomed to the good man, and actually got fond of him. What I wish you to observe in this slight sketch of the Peshawur mission is, that it was founded in a very difficult place at a time when everybody looked gloomily upon it, but that God has honoured those who honour Him: for I believe that mission has brought a blessing to us in India in our

The mission a public blessing.

hour of need. Peshawur, as I told you, stood as an outpost to British India. Twelve miles from it frowned the Khyber Pass, beyond which was the immense country of Afghanistan. It will not matter now if I say that the war in which, twenty years ago, we engaged with the Afghans was an unrighteous war. I have expressed the same opinion to Government. We had no quarrel with them, and because we were afraid of Russia, that was no righteous cause for marching up with a poor refugee puppet prince like Shah Shoojah in our hands, and saying, "We will dethrone your king and put up this man in his place." That war ended, as all unrighteous wars should end, with disaster. Angry passions had thus been aroused between us and the Afghans, and though years rolled over, yet the angry passions remained. At length a

Change in Government policy.

change came over the policy of our Government, and I was, I am glad to say, instrumental in bringing that change about. (Applause.) In 1854, I recommended that "bygones should be bygones," and I was authorised by my Government to make efforts to bring about a more desirable state of affairs. I did make efforts, and in a very short time it was rumoured all over Central Asia that a

Treaty with the Afghans.

friendly treaty was made, and the quarrel was at an end. (Applause.) Again, on my recommendation, a still closer treaty of friendship was signed in the beginning of 1857. Three months had not passed over when the dreadful Indian mutiny broke out. If we had not been at peace with the Afghans, the old story of the Tartar incursions would probably have been repeated. The tribes of Afghanistan and the countries beyond would have rallied round the standard of their faith. They would have swept like a torrent

Its powerful influence.

through Peshawur over the whole Punjaub; Delhi would never have been taken, and the whole of the British possessions in India would have been wrested from our hands. But Peshawur, with its mission and the friends of that mission, the civil and military authorities, stood safely across the path of danger. Shall we attribute this result to this officer or to that officer: shall we say it was from the wisdom of this or that proposition? I trust no one in this room will do so. I say those thoughts were put into men's minds for good purposes, and I believe God himself inspired

Laus Deo.

us that we might reap the reward of having honoured God. (Applause.) I trust the safest policy may be pursued hereafter in India of honouring God in the government of that country. I am quite convinced that if we do we shall find Him the best sword and buckler, and that we may say with David, "MY GOD, IN HIM WILL I TRUST." (Applause.)

MISSIONS IN SOUTH AFRICA.

By the Rev. William Shaw.

The Rev. WILLIAM SHAW, of South Africa, said:—I regret that I should have been called upon at this late hour to address you, after the very interesting speeches you have heard; for I fear that the matter I have to bring before you will be found much less interesting. Had I time to address you at length, I might possibly have made a selection of facts to interest you; but it is exceedingly difficult, after listening to those thrilling details concerning the work in that most interesting part of the globe, British India, to take you away to an entirely different scene. I must, however, say a few words with regard to the missions in Southern Africa. This month it is forty years since I sailed to the Cape of Good Hope; and since that period I have spent there thirty-three years of my life. Without entering into details I may mention, that the chief scene of my labours has been in the extensive country bordering upon the eastern boundary of the Cape of Good Hope, and along the coast of Caffraria, which terminates as far up as Delagoa Bay. The missions in Southern Africa have a very extensive range; and I am happy to state that they are not prosecuted by one or two Societies, but by several of the more important Missionary Societies in this country and in Germany. Our excellent brethren the Moravians were first in the field; they were followed by the London Missionary Society, and these by the Wesleyan Missionary Society. These were followed again by others; there are now also missions there in connexion with the Free Church, and more recently with the Church of England. By the blessing of God great results have been derived from the labours of the brethren of the various Missionary Societies. Very recently a complete Kaffir version of the Holy Scriptures has gone forth from our press; so that with the Sechuana version of the indefatigable Moffat, the great tribes of Southern Africa now have the law of God which they can read in their own language. There are, I believe, at this time fifteen or eighteen thousand natives, regular accredited members of the various Churches, admitted to the communion of the Lord's table. (Applause.) There are at least 20,000 children who are in attendance at the various mission schools within and beyond the colonies. Taking together the attendance at the schools, the members of the church,

Native Christians.

and the still very much larger number of those who, although not recognised as members of the Christian congregations, and not admitted to the communion, are, nevertheless, more or less in the habit of regularly attending the administration of gospel ordinances, I estimate that at least 100,000 natives of the various classes may be considered as won over to Christianity. (Applause.) Very far indeed are we from thinking that all has been accomplished that we had hoped for when we went into the field; but, notwithstanding this, we may, I think, take courage, and hope to surpass what has hitherto been done. (Applause.)

The meeting concluded with singing and prayer, at nine o'clock.

PROCEEDINGS OF THE CONFERENCE.

THURSDAY, March 22nd.

THIRD GENERAL PRAYER MEETING.

THURSDAY MORNING.

The third general Prayer-meeting was held at Hope Hall, on Thursday morning, at 9·30 A.M. *Prayer-meeting.*

The Rev. PATRICK FORFAR, of the Church of Scotland, of Liverpool, presided.

The devotions of the meeting were led by the Rev. J. WALTON, Wesleyan missionary from Jaffna, in Ceylon; the Rev. CHRISTIAN HŒRNLE, Church missionary at Agra; the Rev. BEHARI LAL SINGH, of the Free Church Mission in Calcutta; and the Rev. Dr. TIDMAN.

FIFTH SESSION.

THURSDAY MORNING.

The members of Conference again assembled for business at 10·30 A.M., at the close of the Prayer-meeting, and held one of their most interesting and valuable meetings.

MAJOR-GENERAL ALEXANDER in the chair.

Before the proceedings commenced, the Rev. G. D. CULLEN announced that the Mayor of Liverpool, who took a deep interest in the proceedings of the Conference, had kindly invited all the members to breakfast with him in the Town Hall on Saturday morning, at nine o'clock. A letter, expressing great regret at his necessary absence from the Conference, was read from the Hon. A. KINNAIRD, M.P., who had joined with others in issuing the invitations by which the Conference was assembled. *Invitation from the Mayor.*

Rotterdam. Dr. STEANE intimated that a communication had been received from a new Missionary Society recently formed in the Netherlands. The communication comprised a letter, and the first Report of the society, both in the Dutch language. These documents had been confided to the Rev. Dr. Baylee for examination; Dr. Baylee had pronounced them to be of a most interesting character, and had prepared a fraternal reply.

On the motion of Dr. STEANE the reply was read, and having received the signatures of the Chairman and Secretaries, was transmitted as the answer of the Conference to the Society at Rotterdam.

SUBJECTS FOR DISCUSSION.

Programme. The business of the session then commenced, the following programme being read by the Chairman:—

Subject: NATIVE AGENCY.

    Paper, or Address, of ten minutes, by Rev. R. S. HARDY, formerly Wesleyan Missionary in Ceylon.

    Advantages of Native Agency.

    How should Native Agents be obtained? From among the most spiritually-minded and experienced adults of the Native congregations? Or from among the young? If the latter, should they be specially trained for their specific mission work among the masses of their fellow-countrymen, in Training Institutions, through the medium of their mother-tongue?

    How far should the English Language be employed in Missionary Education?

    Difficulties in the way of ordaining Natives as Evangelists and Pastors.

    How far should the Clerical principle be introduced into Native Churches?

    How far should each individual Christian be encouraged to strengthen his brethren, and propagate the Gospel among those still in darkness.

    On what principle should the stipends of Native Agents be regulated?

Chairman. The CHAIRMAN, in announcing that the subject for the day was that of NATIVE AGENCY, expressed a trust, that every one would consider the vast importance of this question with regard to all places where they had established, and hoped to establish Christian missions. He felt that they would need to keep their minds in the spirit of the prayers which had just been offered for the blessing of Almighty God upon their deliberations. They must maintain the principle of "speaking the truth in love;" and, on simple dependence upon God the Holy Spirit, seek his gracious and harmonising influences, that the "mind that was in Christ Jesus" might also be vouchsafed to all assembled here. He wished that there were more of their native brethren from other countries present, to express their sentiments, as he should call upon their Hindoo brother, Behari Lal Singh, to do his. They would, however, have the advantage of the experience of missionaries who had laboured in many lands, and been in actual contact with Asiatic and African minds, as well as with the untutored Indians of America; and thus this most important subject would be brought forward and illustrated with fulness in all its varieties. He adverted to what had already been before the Conference, as the record they had of the missionary agency and proceedings of the early Church; and turning to the 6th, 8th, 10th chapters of the Acts, and 16th of Romans, said it would be well to the purpose to consider the persons and positions in life of those who were then constituted or recognised as missionary agents and fellow-workers with the Apostles; that they were men and women of all classes, including the imperial household of Rome, the family of Herod, the hospitable Gaius, Phœbe the deaconess, Aquila and Priscilla, who each and all evangelised society around them, and spread Gospel light and truth among the idolatrous and unbelieving masses among whom they dwelt. In dealing with native agencies now, is it not well to look to what was done to raise up and extend it in apostolic times, at Jerusalem, at Antioch, at Corinth, at Philippi, and in Crete? They would also have to consider the weakness of some branches of the Christian church, the comparatively slow progress by means of existing agencies up to the present day, and the desirableness of devolving upon the natives of every country under heaven the obvious duty of evangelising the lands of their births, and the people of one blood with themselves. Considering the emergencies of the times, and the rapidity with which events are rushing towards that mysterious future, into which they could see no farther than the light of the Holy Spirit shining upon the revelation made by God in his Holy Word will permit,

Spirit of discussion.

Experience.

The earliest "native agents."

What to be considered.

surely no time should be lost in bringing native agencies into the fullest and most efficient operation, and committing them more to their own responsibilities, than it was his (the Chairman's) impression, they had hitherto been sufficiently permitted and encouraged to assume. He would but adduce one instance, taken from the sacred records, as strictly in point. A Gentile traveller picked up a wayfarer by the roadside. He read a book which he could not understand; a plain exposition of the word gave light; the result of a short intercourse, and the instruction given, while it lasted, were so blessed of God to the conversion of a soul, that the missionary effects of that day's journey are found in Ethiopia at the present time. Let them (he repeated) consider thoroughly the apostolic and early Christian ways of working; let them experience whether there is not as much facility now, as there was then, of making fellow-countrymen the fittest missionaries to each other, and how best to remove any impediments which prevent their being such; and may God, of his infinite goodness and mercy, guide the Conference to a wise deliberation, in accordance with his most holy will and word.

<small>Example in the Acts.</small>

The following paper on the subject was then read to the Conference by the author:—

ON NATIVE AGENCY IN FOREIGN MISSIONS.

By the Rev. R. S. Hardy, Ceylon.

The subject appointed for this morning's investigation and discussion is, NATIVE AGENCY. In this theme we have the culminating point of the Conference. All that is done at home is the mere mustering of forces; but where "the native" lies, is the battle. Are funds collected, or missionaries sent forth, or schools established, or the Scriptures translated, or books printed and circulated? It is the good of the native that is the first cause of all this preparation and sacrifice. Whatever is expended, whether in men, or money, or moments, that does not ultimately tend towards this issue, is so much power lost to the great cause of the world's salvation.

<small>Native agency the last point in missions.</small>

When we speak of Native Agency, we include the entire Church of the future; as it is evident that, if Christianity is permanently to live in the lands that are now the object of missionary care, it must be by means of Native Agency alone. Foreign agents

<small>Essential.</small>

<small>Why?</small>

could not be found in sufficient numbers. If sufficient numbers were forthcoming, the means of their support could not be provided; and if the men could be both provided, and provided for, this would be an inefficient instrumentality to accomplish the work to be done. The truth must be naturalised; it must cease to be regarded as an exotic, before it can thoroughly permeate and permanently regenerate any given nation. Its power can only be universally diffused by that which is alike native in its fount and its flowing: look, tone, word, imagery, idiom, all must be native. Every people, even the most degraded, has a nationality, and each tribe an idiosyncracy; sacred circles, that the stranger can never completely penetrate.

2. This position being established, we have then to ask: How is this Native Agency to be the most rapidly raised, the most highly gifted, and rendered the most powerfully procreative and germinant? Here we are in danger, lest, by looking at the subject from one single stand-point, we should seek to establish laws that, if universally carried out, would cramp the free play of the Church's action, and impede its intended course towards limitless conquest. As well might we try to grow all plants, from the lichen to the lotus, in one temperature and soil, as attempt to lay down rules that would be equally applicable to all nations. The mind of the contemplative Brahmin and that of the wild Bushman of Australia will not be influenced by the same process of instruction. We shall consider these classes as the two extremes, and therefore, in some sense, exceptional cases; and concede, that the circumstances of the one are best met through the medium of college tuition; and those of the other, through that of village localisation, the plough, and the alphabet. But we contend that, in other cases, the course that has been the most successfully pursued by the Church in the greatest number of instances, is the example we are called upon to follow now in the present position of the heathen world. *[marginal: How to be raised. Localities differ: modes also.]*

3. Guided by the light of the past, we say, then, that the truth has been propagated in all ages with the greatest efficiency by agents set apart for this one service, whether called preachers, evangelists, pastors, or ministers; with the schoolmaster, as a collateral, but most important auxiliary power. Those agents, again, have been the most efficient that have been "thrust forth" by the Lord, to use our Saviour's own expression (Matt. ix. 22), "as labourers into his harvest." They have been called from the plough, as Elisha; from the cattle-pen, as Amos; from the fisher- *[marginal: A special class required.]*

boat, as Peter; and from the school of the sage, as Saul of Tarsus.

Prayer for such. The prayer of the Church must therefore be, that God would raise up such men on all our mission-stations; and, secondly, that he would guide the responsible principals of all churches, in calling out and sending into the work of evangelisation the instruments that have been thus prepared by a divine call. The indications

Their qualifications. of the receiving of a divine commission will be a sincere and simple piety, an ardent zeal, a spirit of self-sacrifice, a right apprehension of the principal truths of revelation, and success resting upon the efforts already put forth to do good. Unless there be the presence of these qualifications, lay no hands upon the men, however else they may be gifted; and if these are possessed, however lowly and unpretending the men may be, reject them not, for by them will be made manifest the wisdom and the power of God.

How to be prepared. 4. The next question is: How are they to be prepared for the most efficient performance of their future labours? We would here make a distinction, that has already been acknowledged in

Distinction here. this Conference, between the course that is taken by the missionary for the general enlightenment of the native mind, and that which has reference exclusively to the formation of a native pastorate. To bring about the former issue, the vast importance of which we are ready to acknowledge, instruction in English literature is, in certain countries and under certain circumstances, indispensably requisite; to effect the latter, the same course now appears to be much less absolutely necessary, even in those same localities, than was once supposed by many good and great men. We have seen that in his homogeneity with the people, whom the teacher

Evils to be guarded against. seeks to influence, consists a considerable portion of his power; and, consequently, that whatever tends to deprive him of this, renders him, so far, less fitted for his work. This will be the result, more or less, of scholastic training, of temporary isolation from his usual modes of living; and, above all, of an increase of income greatly beyond the means of the people among whom he has to minister. These are evils to be guarded against in the training of native pastors; but they may be immensely overcome by the advantages gained from a course of regular and continued discipline; and in some instances they are evils to which it is necessary to expose ourselves, as much more direful consequences would result from an immature piety, a misguided zeal, or an imperfect theology.

5. But there is, we think, a more excellent way, as to those missions in which it can be accomplished; and that is, for the

missionary to superintend the studies of the native teacher whilst he is yet actively engaged in the work of evangelisation. This supposes that men, whose principles have been tested in private life, rather than untried youths, be called out; and that the instruction be in the vernacular alone. In rare instances a knowledge of other languages will still be gained, whilst the teacher is pursuing the duties he is required to attend to in the house, the bazaar, the school, or the church; as many ministers in England, who have not had the advantage of a college education, nevertheless, by self-culture, attain to literary distinction. From having had the opportunity of knowing the make and metal of his agents, when moving in inferior positions, the missionary will be better instructed whom to trust in places of greater responsibility and danger. *Instruction to be in the vernacular: practical work should go with it.*

6. This question of responsibility is another subject of great importance. The native pastors may be used as mere machines, every motion being regulated by a power exterior to themselves; or they may be sent abroad, as the unreined steed, which may have had a careful training, but yet cannot be left to run anywhere at its own will. Avoiding these extremes, the native pastor must be taught that, within the limit of certain fixed rules, he is responsible to another for the course he pursues; but that, in adapting himself to circumstances within that limit, he is to exercise his own judgment. He is to be a free and unfettered agent, within an appointed sphere of action. It will be better for him to be left, like the wild tree of the forest, which has room to wave in the wind, and put forth all its vigour and vitality, than to be tended and trellissed like the tree of the garden, and thus become sickly, stunted, and formal. Without the feeling of responsibility, there will be no putting forth of the entire strength of the mind or the full energy of the will. *The pastor responsible, but free.*

7. After an attentive study of the various organisations that have been tried upon the mission-field, none have appeared to me so perfect as the one carried out by the Rev. R. B. Lyth, in Fiji. He had to meet the wants of a large and wide-spread district of country, the native teachers being but babes in Christ; and to care for an extensive society of about 1400 church members, without order or discipline. The great principle by which he was enabled, under circumstances the most difficult, to reduce this chaos to comparative order, was " by training the natives *for* their work by training them *in* their work." " The entire circuit," he says, " was made a training institution with the mission-station *Rev. R. B. Lyth's system in Fiji.*

for the centre. The natives of these countries cannot endure the close confinement of an Institution; but give them plenty of work and exercise, and they will come to their studies with zest and pleasure, and what they learn they will digest and communicate; and what is quickly communicated is twice learnt."*

It will, perhaps, be said, that all this was among recent cannibals; but that the same rules will not apply to the more civilised portions of the world. We may pass, then, to Burmah. The following extract is from Doctor Mason, of the Toungoo mission. "When I stroll into the forest at evening, a long, peripatetic train, questions me at every step .... My school of theology is as wide as the province, and its pupils are as numerous as the students within its borders. Many, in this anomalous way, without pausing in their labours, learn more than those immured for years in brick-walls, who complete a curriculum under a dozen professors; and it is an undeniable fact, that when we need a man to go to a station, where there is real self-denial to be endured, it is not the man who has passed through a regular course of instruction who goes, but one of this irregular corps."

[margin: Dr. Mason's at Toungoo.]

When we come to India proper, we are not without proof that a similar course has been attended by the blessing of the Lord. It has been supposed that the illustrious missionaries of Serampore were never more successful in raising up an indigenous ministry, suited to the wants of the churches of Bengal, than at the commencement of their missionary career. They saw how necessary it was that their native agents should retain, as much as possible, the simplicity of their former habits; and that, by manifesting a holy walk and conversation, without, at the same time, losing their nationality of character, they would thereby present a more perfect example for the imitation of their converted countrymen.

[margin: In the early Serampore Mission.]

8. In conclusion. Whilst again acknowledging the unspeakable benefits derived from the establishing of high schools and collegiate institutions, and, in many instances, the necessity of their continuance; and whilst deprecating most strongly the employment of an untrained or uneducated pastorate, I would recommend:

[margin: Summary.]

1. That the native pastor, for the most part, and, as a general rule, be educated in the vernacular only.

[margin: Vernacular.]

2. That he be trained for the pastorate, by the simultaneous influence of personal instruction from an European missionary and active employment among his countrymen.

[margin: Teaching and work united.]

* Mr. Lyth's Paper on the subject will be found in the Appendix.

3. That no native be ordained for the ministry, until he has been well tried and found faithful. *Character.*

4. That, when ordained, he should be left in a great degree, but not absolutely, as a free agent, in the sphere of labour to which he is appointed. *Freedom.*

5. That the amount of his stipend be not more than a native church, of an average number of members and of average wealth, would be able to afford, upon the principles of the New Testament. *Stipend.*

6. That unpaid, though qualified, lay-agents, who work on the week-days at some secular employment, should be encouraged to act upon the sabbath as evangelists, under the direction of the chief pastor of the church. *Lay-agents.*

There are some of these recommendations that cannot at present be carried into effect; but something similar to them is a result at which, I think, we ought all to aim. They will, in some respects, be controverted by many of the wisest of the brethren who are around me; but they are put forth unhesitatingly as the product of long experience and a most careful study of the subject. And I would ever remind myself and others that these words are yet found upon the page of everlasting truth: "Not by might, nor by power, but by my Spirit, saith the Lord of Hosts." "God hath chosen the foolish things of the world to confound the wise; and God hath chosen the weak things of the world to confound the things which are mighty; and base things of the world, and things which are despised, hath God chosen, yea, and things which are not, to bring to nought things that are; that no flesh should glory in his presence." (Zech. iv. 6; 1 Cor. i. 27.)

The CHAIRMAN imagined there would be a wide difference of opinion amongst brethren present; but urged that their views should be freely and fully expressed, and received with cordiality, with sympathy, and the forbearance of Christian minds. This one point, amongst others, should receive grave consideration; Whether the native mind had not been too much kept in a state of tutelage; whether there was not existing an unwillingness to emancipate it from that state, and to throw it entirely on the grace of God and the supporting power of the gospel? *CHAIRMAN.*

The Rev. J. MULLENS expressed his satisfaction at the practical and concise manner in which Mr. Hardy had brought the question before them. He should, however, like to have had that *Rev. J. MULLENS.*

Two questions: gentleman's experience and opinion on one or two matters, which might be considered supplementary to the paper itself. One was the ordination of their native brethren. It was a very important

Ordination. question: Whether the ordinations, which were now beginning to take place in India and other mission fields, should be ordinations of native brethren to missionary service among the heathen, or ordinations of these brethren as pastors of native churches? The two things were entirely distinct; and some brethren who were present had had great experience on this point.

Salary of pastors. Again: Mr. Hardy had spoken of the ordained native brethren being appointed as pastors, and yet of a salary being given to them, in amount not greater than that which they would naturally and properly receive in their own sphere of life. Here arose a question of vital importance: If you ordain a man as pastor of a native church, who is to pay his salary; on what principle should a Foreign Society continue to pay the salary when a native agent is ordained over a church? He referred to the question, because their American brethren had been dealing with

Rule of the American Board. it in a clear and decided manner. When Dr. Anderson, the Foreign Secretary of the American Board, and his colleague, visited the Missions of the Board in Western and Southern India, they suggested, in regard to this matter; that whilst it was desirable to have their native brethren ordained as pastors of churches, and for those churches wholly to support them, the difficulty that arose, from a small church being unable to raise sufficient salary for a native ministry, should be met by the Society continuing to supplement any deficiency in the salary of the native pastor, year by year, until the church could take the entire duty upon itself. He believed that the Board in America unanimously approved of such an arrangement.

Rev. R. S. Hardy. Mr. HARDY, in reply, said;—That his paper was intended to be suggestive, rather than exhaustive. The manner of working the native ministry was different in the Wesleyan body, with which he was connected, from that pursued in other churches. It might, of course, be supposed that he most approved of their own mode.

Natives ordained over a circuit. The natives who were appointed to such a charge were appointed, not to one particular place, but to a circle of churches. There was generally a principal station under one native minister, with three or four chapels and flocks, and maybe three or four schools also; of all these he was supposed to have the care. According to their rule, he could not remain more than three years in one place. They did not, in their mission stations, absolutely insist upon this; but still he was liable to be removed at any time: and they ordained him, not as the pastor of any particular church, but as a pastor of the Church of Christ at large, liable to be sent to work anywhere where duty called.

Then, as to salaries, he (Mr. Hardy) agreed with the principle adopted in the American missions,— to supplement what the native teacher received from his congregation. Their own plan was to receive all that the native churches could give; and to supplement what was necessary. That necessity, he thought, had hitherto been supposed to be much greater than it really was. He believed they had acted in error in their own stations in South Ceylon, by giving so high a salary to their native assistants, that the churches alone could not continue it. The supplementary principle should be carried so far as it was applied in their churches at home, and no further. As to the amount of salary, he would make no distinction betwixt the remuneration given to a native pastor, whether he understood English or only the vernacular; unless he were appointed to some church in which English was used in the services he held; in which case his own congregation would be able to afford the extra remuneration.

Salaries are supplemented.

Colonel DAWES, Hon. East India Company's Service, and Lay Secretary of the Church Missionary Society, viewed the subject of native agency as one of the utmost importance. He did not wish to occupy any time in introducing himself, or by way of preamble, but he might mention that his opportunities had been frequent, whilst a resident in India, of becoming acquainted with missionaries of different denominations, and of witnessing the working of their various systems. The want of a good native agency had always appeared to him most pressing. He bore high testimony to the immense exertions and unwearied zeal of the European missionaries. It was above all praise. Nothing was assuredly wanting on their parts. But they had never been able to overtake the work, nor would they ever be able to do so, without a larger native agency. As to the description of agency best suited to the work, he preferred men brought up without a knowledge of the English language — men who were willing and able in their own tongue to declare "the unsearchable riches of Christ" to the heathen by whom they were surrounded. Another practical point which he would mention was the necessity that

Col. DAWES.

Native agency most necessary;

trained in their own tongue:

existed of native agents conforming, as far as was practicable, to the habits of the countries in which they laboured. They should endeavour to eschew the adoption of European customs, and even dress. And this he was happy to think was the practice adopted by the native agents, especially in South India. When a native visited a village station, the people should be induced to regard him as one of themselves, in appearance and general mode of life; whilst the great points of difference between him and them should be found, not in his dress and manners, but in his enlightened views and opinions respecting religious questions, especially this idol-worship. The Chairman had referred to the probable causes of "failure." He thought the word employed in the programme was unfortunate (hear, hear); and would himself rather be disposed to say, "partial success." The agency that had been used hitherto was in many instances inadequate, both as to quality and quantity. The native agent should be, as much as possible, like one of those amongst whom he labours; not coming amongst them as one having received education in a foreign language, and having adopted a dress and manners half English, half Indian, but as one, in these private matters, in all respects like themselves. It should at once be seen that the great difference between him and them lies in something beyond externals; in the views which he entertains of the blessed gospel which he has been led to embrace; and in the earnest compassion with which he invites them, one and all, to receive that message of reconciliation which has been proclaimed for the whole world. His impression, after several years' residence abroad was, that the European missionaries had far more work on their hands than they were able to attend to. In one place which he could instance there were three missionaries: the time of one was given wholly to the press; of another, to the work of translation; and of the third, to preaching; whilst if there had been an efficient native agency, the whole time of the three might have been devoted to the chief work, of proclaiming with their own lips the gospel of Christ. Since his return from India, he had read some hundreds of letters and journals from China, India, Africa, and New Zealand; these all united in confessing the great want at the present time to be—the extension of native agency.

The Rev. ISAAC STUBBINS, General Baptist Missionary at Cuttack, in India, said,—He had laboured for twenty-four years in the province of Orissa, where the great idol Juggernaut held his seat. Their work there was—from conscientious motives—carried on almost exclusively in the vernacular tongue. They both preached and taught in that tongue, so far as they had schools to teach; and they raised up native ministers to do the same to their fellow-countrymen. From all that he had seen of the use of the native language, he should most strongly urge that all missionaries,—especially missionaries going out to India, should acquire a clear, full, and comprehensive use of the native tongue. Unless they could or would do that, the sooner they returned the better. They had been taught by a wise Teacher that "the children of this world are wiser in their generation than the children of light." The Government makes it essential that their civilians learn the language of the people, and pass an examination in that language before they receive their full appointment to any sphere of labour; and he did think their missionary committees ought to require that all their agents should pass through a similar ordeal. Not only so, but their wives also learned the language of the natives—a most important thing to keep in view. In gathering around them native churches, there were native Christian females who required instructing in a variety of matters; and only the wife of the missionary could impart that instruction which they so imperatively needed. In their missionary tours, also, their wives frequently accompanied them; and while the missionaries attended the busy market, the festival, or the bazaar, their wives repaired to the villages to converse with the native heathen females. Such visits were always welcome, and had proved in many instances exceedingly useful. During these tours they did not pretend to sell their tracts or Scriptures, but endeavoured judiciously to distribute them; and in this way they parted with some fifty or sixty thousand tracts annually. . These had been conveyed into parts of the country which they themselves could never visit, and had been the means of drawing numbers out from heathenism; many of whom had afterwards died rejoicing in the faith of Christ Jesus, though they had never seen a missionary, or even a native minister. (Hear, hear.) God had blessed their labours in the vernacular tongue with great success. Between 500 and 600 native converts had been baptised during the last thirty-two years of their history, and their mission had been but small. Between twenty and thirty native preachers had been raised up, and some of these dear brethren had laboured with a zeal and an ardour scarcely equalled by any minister of our own land. They had exposed themselves to un-

Their zeal. numbered dangers; penetrated deadly jungles; slept under trees, in sheds, or in open verandahs; they had deprived themselves of everything but what was really necessary, to accomplish their great Master's work among their own countrymen; and he might *Their best men were once heathen.* remark, that the men who had, as a rule, specially devoted themselves, were those who had grown up in heathenism; had been converted in mature years; and had then given themselves to the preaching of the gospel. Out of twenty-three native ministers raised up in connexion with their mission, all of them, except eight, were converted and called to the ministry as adults. After a satisfactory period to prove their change of heart, they were baptised, and instructed, and commissioned to preach the gospel. *Their salary.* The stipend which had hitherto been allowed them was small, not exceeding ten rupees, or 1*l*. per month, in addition to something for travelling expenses, and something for the carriage of their books and clothing. The missionary, at whose station these native brethren may be placed, endeavours to make their instruction an important part of his duty. They are encouraged to come to him at all times for the reading and exposition of the Scriptures, and for general instruction; especially in relation to their all-important duties as ministers of the word of God.

Dr. Lockhart. Dr. LOCKHART said,—The mission churches could not do without native agency. The European missionaries must be the evangelists, but the great spread of the Gospel must be effected by *Native agents essential in China:* native agents; and in a great country like China, distinguished by the vastness of its territory and the difficulties of its language, it was incumbent on all systems of missions to raise up an extensive native agency. The London Missionary Society missionaries had all of them devoted themselves, from the time when they had acquired the language, to raising up a number of converts who *successful.* might go forth to preach. And to this was their great success in the north of China mainly attributable. Careless, apathetic, and indifferent, as the Chinese are in a heathen state, let them only come under the influence of Christianity, and the same change passes *Their zeal and eloquence.* over them as over Europeans: they become earnest, hearty, and steadfast in showing to their fellow-countrymen the way of salvation. To the eloquent declarations of gospel truth, made by some of them at Shanghai, he had listened with the greatest pleasure. They exhibited in their work as much carefulness as earnestness. They would carry on the work of the Gospel throughout China much more extensively and efficiently than any Europeans could. Dr. Lockhart then adverted to Mr. Stubbins' observations regarding the influence of females, which (he said) in China was imperatively demanded. Without it they could do little for the spiritual welfare of the women of that vast empire. Female converts must aid in the conversion of their countrywomen. Europeans had very little chance of access to them; but the wives, daughters, and sisters of native converts, could reach them. Female influence and agency were extensively and beneficially employed at Amoy and at Ningpo, rendering very great service to the cause of Christ. Miss Aldersey, whose useful labours are well known in Europe, went out on her own responsibility to establish and carry on a large school at Ningpo; and God had raised round her a number of females who had consecrated their time to the great work. In all the countries of the East, too great stress could not be laid on the agency of converted female natives. They visit the villages, and gather around them a number of women, to whom they declare Jesus and his salvation; and it was a cheering circumstance that even in China, which was generally supposed to be so unapproachable, and where women would come so little under missionary influence and teaching, the work was going on so heartily and well. He (Dr. Lockhart) then spoke on the subject of rendering into Roman orthography the signs of the Chinese language, briefly brought before the Conference on the previous day by Dr. Gundert. It might be to some extent desirable, that in a school small books and tracts should be printed in this particular orthography; but it could not be thus used extensively, because dialects in China differ so materially. A book written in the orthography of one place could not be understood in another place, thirty or forty miles distant. One produced at Shanghai would be perfectly useless at Ningpo. Every missionary has hitherto used his own discretion as to the sound of certain vowels and consonants. This produces endless confusion. No Roman orthography, however, can accurately render the sounds and tones of the Chinese characters so that it can be used in books for the natives. The Chinese language and character can be acquired by Europeans by industry and application, and they must use it if they would fully get to the minds of the natives. The native mind must be used to a large extent in the writing and translation of tracts; but of course natives should not translate the Scriptures unassisted. No European missionary ever idiomatically translated the Scriptures into any foreign language without a judicious employment of native teachers. The best-instructed native teachers, being obtained for the purpose, the translation of the meaning and spirit of the word of God from the original tongues must emanate from the mind of the missionary himself. It had been well put by Dr. Baylee, that he would not give his University Greek for all the vernacular Greek ever spoken.

<small>Rev. W. FAIRBROTHER.
Success of native agency.</small>

The Rev. WM. FAIRBROTHER, Secretary for Funds to the London Missionary Society, said,—that modern missions had a history to which they could now refer. In certain districts native agency had accomplished wonders. By it a great number of the South Sea Islands had been won to the church of the Redeemer; and the same might, under God, be said of Madagascar, and of the Karen church. Let them ask themselves,—Was it possible to apply the plans and measures which had been adopted in these parts, and which had been so honoured of God, to other parts of the mission-field?

<small>No rules universally applicable.</small>

<small>C. SWALLOW, Esq.</small>

CHARLES SWALLOW, Esq., Agent of the British and Foreign Bible Society, spoke of the tie which bound him to mission-work in a dear brother-in-law who had laboured and died at the Missionary Institution maintained by the Church Missionary Society at Cotta in Ceylon. He asked,—Could not the female native converts be more largely employed as evangelists, especially on the Sabbath, and among the unconverted heathen of their own sex? They might prove most useful and powerful auxiliaries. He thought that no more effectual plan could be adopted for increasing the liberality which the Sunday-schools of our land have bestowed upon Christian missions, than to show that something like a Sunday-school plan is prevailing in our missions. Children jump at conclusions without reasoning through the processes by which those conclusions are arrived at; and he believed that in the manufacturing districts especially, practical men also had a growing idea that by employing native agency in this way, missions would effect greater results.

<small>Native females should be evangelists.</small>

<small>Maj. DAVIDSON.</small>

Major DAVIDSON said,—I have very great diffidence in obtruding myself on this meeting; yet having resided for a long period in India, and having been brought very much in contact with the great body of the people; and having also had, when employed in the revision of the Land Revenue, to raise and educate a large native agency; I think I may be permitted to add my testimony to that of Colonel Dawes as to the great importance of having in missionary-work a native agency thoroughly suited to the work in which they are engaged. I believe there is a great deal of misapprehension with respect to the character of the people who are to be operated upon in India. I myself was ten years in India before I knew almost anything of the people of India. The reason was, that I was with my regiment going from station to station, and I came in contact only with those natives who are to be found at the large stations and in large cities. The last ten years of my residence in India were passed entirely among the native agricultural population. I pitched my tent by their villages and lived amongst them, altogether away from European society. For months I never spoke my own language. During that period I came in contact with what constitutes the great body of the people of India. Many people in this country view the natives of India as if they were all learned Brahmins. Now these said Brahmins constitute a mere fraction of the population. Are we, then, to educate our native agents as if they were to contend only with learned Brahmins; or are we to educate them so that they may be able to labour among the native population at large? I had, as I said, to raise a native agency for a special and a very difficult purpose, that of making a correct survey of the country; and also a careful estimate of the comparative productive powers of the soil, of each field, a work altogether new to them. I did not seek to make them qualified for anything more than the very work they had to perform. I selected them from the people amongst whom I was acting; they were mostly young men, whom I chose in a great measure from their intelligent appearance; I then educated them for their work, and for it alone. And this is, I think, the principle which we must observe in our efforts to evangelise India. I am far from considering a high education as thrown away. I do believe we ought to educate some of our native agents in the highest possible manner; but for the general agency by which we are to operate upon the people of India, I do not think so high a class of education is either necessary or desirable. We should seek to make native agents fit for the work they have to do. A great deal of time and labour have been wasted in attempting more than this. I fully agree also with Colonel Dawes as to the advisability of their not adopting our English dress and English habits. I think the native agent will have far greater influence when he goes amongst the people as one of themselves, differing from others only in having the love of Christ in his heart, and in seeking to impart

Character of the natives in India.

The peasantry.

Brahmins few.

Native agency in surveys:

how raised up:

so in mission work.

Native preachers to live like their countrymen.

that love to his fellow-countrymen. Having passed so many years in close intercourse with the rural population, I may be permitted to say that the impression left on my mind was in the highest degree favourable. There were two things that fixed themselves in my mind: the first, the almost inexhaustible resources of the soil in India, with the great extent to which it yet remains to be developed; and the other, the almost inexhaustible resources of the minds of the people of India. I was greatly struck with the fine heads and countenances of the rural population generally, and with the intelligence they displayed; these men had been brought up in the most primitive manner, and had scarcely ever come in contact with Europeans, yet they were ready to converse in an intelligent way on any ordinary subject. I was also much pleased with the great interest they take in theological discussions. I had not much time to devote to this great work; but on the Sabbath I was accustomed to invite them to my tent at the time when I was instructing my own servants, and to ask them to join in conversation on the subjects under notice. Large congregations would assemble on these occasions at my tent-door, and the conversations that took place were exceedingly interesting. I have felt most deeply, during the recent disturbances in India, that a very erroneous impression has gone abroad with respect to the natives of India. We take our opinion of them from the cases of atrocity that have come before us, and from the opinions of those who have come in contact only with the natives found at our military stations, who are the very worst specimens of the race. I myself have a great love for the people of India; and if I were to return to those districts where I laboured, I firmly believe that at every one of those villages I should be received with cordiality and friendship by those poor natives. It will, indeed, be a cause of rejoicing to my heart to find that something adequate is being done in order to communicate to them the "unsearchable riches of Christ."

Dr. MACGOWAN, American Medical Missionary from China and Japan, remarked, that he also might say things pleasant to the ear, suggesting encouraging prospects; but he thought their time would be more profitably employed in indicating the defects and difficulties attending the subject under their notice. If two hours were set apart to this end, for addresses of five minutes each, he felt assured there would be twenty-four speakers who could detail defects that had come under their own observation which would prove useful to us all. The great subject after all was: How fa have missions been successful? Considering the great outlay of money and labour that had been expended, there had been a want of success; the results had not been commensurate with the just expectations entertained. This subject they had not grappled with. He represented China, but his observations of the mission-field extended from Bengal to Japan; and, coming from that colossal country, he was bound to state that some mistakes of colossal proportions had been committed in his field. As regards the language, that man is an encumbrance who does not master it, whatever other qualifications he may possess. He must also strive to become intimate with the people, and grapple with the subject, not at arms'-length, but man to man, as it were. Their experience in China suggested that they should "make haste slowly," and that the employment of native agency had been, to some extent, detrimental to the healthful growth of missions in that empire. The results of the too early employment of native agents had been disastrous. Native agency was, indeed, all-important; but they had been pressed and impelled by friends at home to employ and trust to natives too soon; one of the results being, that they were filling their churches with hypocrites, because men were anxious for employment. The heathen outside saw this, and, as a consequence, became only too anxious to join us. He had suggested to his own Society that hereafter, in establishing new missions, they should rely for a time on native agency only so far as it was unpaid; that the natives, every man of them, should understand from the beginning that it is their business to propagate religion. It is safe, as a general rule, not to salary native assistants until their fellow-church members so far confide in them as to aid largely in their maintenance. It is by this slow process only that healthful churches can be established.

Our success not equal to our efforts.

Missionaries must know the language and the people.

Undue haste in employing natives.

Evil result:

its cure.

The Rev. THOMAS GARDINER, Free Church missionary in Calcutta, observed that he was known to be connected with a particular system; but the few words he should say expressed only his own individual views and sentiments. He fully agreed with Major Davidson, that there had been sometimes manifested a want of due consideration as to the fields of labour for which it was proposed to raise up these men. Missionaries in India laboured in very different localities. The Presidency cities were crowded with English educated young men, whilst in many of the rural districts scarcely an European idea or word had yet penetrated. It was thus perfectly clear that the trainings for these diverse

Rev. T. GARDINER.

Differences of locality require differences of training.

P

localities must be different; a uniform system was entirely out of the question. They of the Free Church mourned that they had not more native agency in connexion with their own mission. Perhaps they might have in some respects their own system to thank for it; and it behoved them to study to find out their weak points. No man had yet enunciated a perfect system; and he was a very hopeless man in many ways whom experience taught nothing. Now what was the training they gave to their men in Calcutta? They introduced them into the world of English thought and feeling, English science and literature; they felt its fascination and its charms; they lived therein for years, until they were brought through a college education, and had become to a very great extent anglicised and denationalised; and after all this, they sent them off into the country districts, where not a single English idea or sympathy was to be met with! Was it to be wondered at if such young men found themselves out of their element, and experienced a difficulty in settling down to the work of evangelising their countrymen? And were we to be surprised if a considerable amount of moral weakness continued to cling often to brethren who had been born, and brought up, and had lived for years under the influences of a system so unspeakably corrupting, perverting, and degrading, as Hindooism? If we are to raise up men to labour amongst their educated countrymen in a city like Calcutta, then English education is the thing required; but for men for the country at large it is manifest that, instead of this high English education, which has been made so much of, we should have a special training, very much in the vernacular tongue. Not that we should send forth any of them ignorant or uneducated, for there were works in theology and philosophy in which it was desirable they should all be instructed; but he did feel that great discrimination and judgment should be exercised in this matter. Mr. Gardiner further adverted to the difficulty attaching to the stipend of native agents. It was at present a standing difficulty with mission boards. He wished he could say, from his own experience, that even the high salaries they had given to their native brethren had satisfied them. They must, on these points, fight their way to the light, and endeavour to learn by experience, owning where the difficulties were of their own creation, and striving to get rid of them.

The Rev. P. LATROBE observed, that if there was any one subject on which, after forty years' connexion with missionary work, he still wished to learn something, it was that of native agency. The Society he represented had been a pretty long time in the missionary field, and God had blessed them with a large measure of success among certain tribes and nations of men; but he candidly confessed, that with regard to the training of native agents they felt themselves somewhat in the rear of their brethren, and would therefore be thankful for any suggestions which would enable them to do better in time to come. They had laboured amongst, perhaps, the most unfavourable races,—Greenlanders, Esquimaux, and the American Indians,—people who led a very peculiar kind of life; and amongst their poor sable fellow-subjects of the West Indies and Southern Africa—classes not to be compared for a moment with the intelligent races of British India, in the matter of intellectual advancement. Still he thought they ought to have been more successful in the North, West, and South, than they had been. In substance he agreed with the paper that had been read, as also with the excellent remarks that had fallen from Colonel Dawes and Major Davidson. He fully recognised the distinction drawn between native agents evidently called by God and those to a certain extent trained,—trained either by the missionaries in schools, or trained by God's providential dealings. In their own missions, they had some very striking examples of the power of the grace of God in preparing native agents. He would just name one: Samuel Kayarnak, the first Greenland convert, whose conversion taught a lesson not only to their own feeble and insignificant Church, but to the whole Christian Church throughout the world, in the circumstances that led to it,—the simple setting forth of the story of a Saviour's love. That man proved a marvellous evangelist among his countrymen. His life was short; but during the three years that followed his conversion, he made more converts—speaking after the manner of men—than the missionaries themselves. There were many others equally useful and energetic, although they possessed little of that knowledge deemed necessary for teachers—little of human wisdom or learning. He (Mr. Latrobe) doubted whether they were sufficiently attentive to the workings of God Himself, and particularly in times of gracious revival. Were they sufficiently careful to ascertain, who were fitted for the work in their hearts, although they might be deficient in those other requirements which were thought desirable? Our missionaries should be more attentive to this point, seeking amongst their flocks, especially the younger portion, for those who were trained by

God's Spirit, and by the workings of His Providence, to become useful among their fellows. Major Davidson's remark was of immense importance—that we should not fly too high, and should not employ men for work they are unfitted to perform. It was a remark peculiarly applicable to the natives of the West Indian islands. "To the poor the gospel is preached," and to the poor and ignorant they must have special reference in all their labours; praying for the outpouring of the grace of God upon them, and giving them such a measure of education as will fit them for the work of evangelists, before calling them into the service.

Don't look too high.

The Rev. Dr. O'MEARA stated. in reference to the North American Indians, amongst whom he had had considerable missionary experience,—that the rule so applicable to India did not apply to them. He had heard that in India it was desirable for the native agents to be as much as possible assimilated in habits and mode of life to their fellow-countrymen amongst whom they laboured. That was not the case among the North American Indians. It was strange that such a rule should be required amongst an educated and comparatively civilised people, and its very opposite amongst a barbarous nation. But he thought it arose from that very fact,—their being in a low state of social existence. The Indian looks upon himself as a being of an inferior race; and his desire is to rise as much as possible to the level of the white man. If a native goes amongst them to preach the gospel, but retains habits akin to their own, his word is regarded as of no moment whatever; for this reason it is desirable, nay, absolutely necessary, that a considerable degree of civilisation, and of the habits attaching to the white man, should be attained. It was not necessary that, in all cases, a very high degree of education should be imparted; but when that was possible, it would and did prove a most valuable adjunct to the native agent amongst the Indians of North America. He had found this to be the case with the one native missionary whom he had himself been enabled to prepare for the work, and who was now an ordained minister to the people of the fold which he himself had just quitted. This man had received a secular education under the care of Bishop Anderson, who gave him a letter of introduction to himself. Being at that time in want of an assistant, he employed him at first as a catechist. He resided at his house, and pursued his education under his own care. He found him very far advanced in classical and other knowledge; and he looked forward to making him an efficient

Rev. Dr. O'MEARA.

Difference of rules.

Indians look up.

Native agents should be like the English: civilized, yet zealous.

Instance.

agent in other portions of the work; and not in vain. After he had studied theology with him for two years, he went to present himself for ordination; and he (Dr. O'Meara) had the gratification of hearing that he stood second amongst a large number of candidates, the one above him being a Cambridge man. When he returned, and set to work, he did not show that his superior education had at all spoiled him for labour among his countrymen: he was just as ready to enter dirty wigwams as before for their sakes; and to sit down for the translation of the Scriptures when he was with himself. This man was at the present time engaged in preparing another native agent, a relative of his own, who would in due time come out in just the same way as his relative had done before him. Again he repeated, the North American Indians, as a people, were not only desirous to be raised from barbarism, but to raise themselves. Civilised men should go amongst them, men who would be looked up to by them. They viewed the white man as a being of superior race, and expected words of wisdom from his lips; and his cultivated and earnest native brother of whom he had been speaking was now just as much looked up to as was the European himself. *The Indian standard.*

The Rev. HOPE WADDELL claimed the interest of the Conference in favour of African missions. The question of native agency presented itself to him in regard to the African race in the West Indies, and in the African continent itself. He did not wonder at diversity of opinion on this subject. The mission-work was yet young: the Church was only now taking it in hand: but two generations had passed since its need had first been largely felt. They might have made mistakes, but they would learn from the experience of the past to correct the future. Missionaries everywhere felt the necessity of native agency, and were all desirous of employing it. But he feared that they frequently employed such agents too soon; urged by the greatness of the work, the opportunities pressing around them, the willingness of their young converts, and the pressure from home. The question had been raised whether young men prepared for service in the church would make the best agents, or those converted in middle life, and past the period for any considerable mental improvement. Perhaps a combination of both was the best. In the West Indies, middle-aged men, being the first converts, had been the first employed; and many true and valuable Christian men were amongst them, who would not by anything be turned aside from rendering service to the *Rev. H. M. WADDELL. Agents employed too soon. Older and younger men both required.*

Lord. But they had also found it advantageous to employ younger men, who had not been wedded to old things before they became converted, and had received some education under the care of the missionaries. He would, therefore, combine the two. As to the amount of education to be imparted, he would not aim too high. Latin and Greek, science and philosophy, were not essential to make a man a good minister of Jesus Christ. These our home ministry cannot well do without; but when a native Christian teacher entered upon his work, he would not be able to make use of them. There must, however, be a measure of comparison between the teacher and the taught. In this country, general education was prevalent, all minds were taught; and the ministry must not be below the ordinary level, but rather above it; and it must be so to some extent betwixt the native agent and those whom he is sent to instruct. Mr. Waddell then adverted to the idea which was at one time prevalent of making the West Indian coloured population a kind of native agency for the introduction of the gospel amongst the Negroes of Africa. It had not succeeded. Although the former were of the same race as the latter, they were no longer to be considered natives. He would not wish to undervalue their use for this purpose, but Missionary Societies had experienced too many disappointments to warrant him in saying that much dependence was to be placed upon this agency. In every country they must raise their native agencies on the spot. In Calabar all the missionaries learn the native tongue, and teach in it both in schools and from the pulpit: they deemed this a matter of the first importance. English, however, was taught in the schools, as it furnished a means of great improvement to the young people, who, as well as the chief inhabitants of the country, were quite ambitious of learning it. They may differ in their languages from each other; coast tribes may not be able to converse with each other; but they all know something of English. As to native teachers copying the dress and mode of living of the Europeans, in Africa, it was to some extent indispensable. It would be a great hardship to oblige them to conform to the heathen in these respects, for the dress of the latter, as they well knew, was almost *nil*. We did not insist upon their adopting all our dress, but something was necessary for decency's sake. As to the work of translating, when their native converts acquired a proper degree of education,— which in time they would assuredly do,—and gave proofs of true piety, then they might well be intrusted with this work. None are better than those who thoroughly understand the language into which the word is translated; for what sort of an English translation should we have, if it were made by foreigners.

The Rev. G. R. BIRCH, Secretary to the Turkish Missions' Aid Society, explained that the object of this Society was expressly that of raising funds for the rapid extension of native agency, in connexion with the American missions among the Turks. That mission presented this very remarkable feature; it was, to a great extent, a native-agency mission, and it was the aim of their American brethren to send their missionaries there simply as evangelists, not as pastors. They wished to raise up, as rapidly as possible, native pastors; educating young men for the ministry, and planting them over churches; but regarding their own work as wholly evangelistic, and willing to retire from the field so soon as native churches are supplied. The number of agents now employed was nearly 300. The missionaries announced openly, "We do not come here to be pastors in your churches; such is not our intention or desire: we come here to teach you the word of God, and to form churches which shall in due time govern and support themselves." He was incessantly receiving communications as to this work of native agency, which narrated wonderful results. Look at the wisdom of their system of education. In Constantinople, the capital seat, not only of the Turkish empire, but of their missions, they had established a college; and there, for 16*l.* a-year, they were educating a man for the native pastorate: this was the sum now charged to the Turkish Missions' Aid Society for the board and lodging of each student, during a five or six years' course of preparation for the native ministry. But some parties had said,— "How miserably these students are clad: why do not the Americans improve their condition?" "No," they say, "we want to keep these men precisely in the position we found them; we wish to educate them sufficiently for the work to which we send them: and it shall be for them a good thing to become the pastor of a native church, though that native church will never be able to give them salary sufficient to Europeanise them." Mr. Birch then animadverted upon the letter addressed by Rev. Dr. Wolff (whose peculiar missionary peregrinations were well known) to Professor Williams of Cambridge, to the effect that he had found one idea reigning among all the high dignitaries of the Greek and Oriental churches, that England should adopt the same principle as the Pope had adopted in Rome; viz. that of allowing colleges with professors and tutors of the Oriental churches: all that the Pope required being, that they should acknowledge him as head, and then they might teach whatever tenets they liked. Dr. Wolff urged, that since recent legislation had opened the doors of Cambridge University to Dissenters, it had also widely thrown open its doors for members of the Oriental churches; the plain proposition being that these men might not only enter as students, but might actually aspire to university degrees, without any interference, direct or indirect, with their peculiar tenets or usages. He (Mr. Birch) would only ask, if native agents were coming over here, what was to be done with them? In his office as secretary he was perpetually assailed by native agents, Nestorians, Turks, and others, dissatisfied with the salaries they got, and they never would be satisfied with an Europeanised education. This question had a very important pecuniary bearing, and was worthy of the deepest consideration of the members of the Conference.

[margin: to open the Universities to the Oriental churches.]

The Rev. BEHARI LAL SINGH being called upon, then addressed the meeting. He thanked Colonel Dawes and Major Davidson for the judicious remarks they had made. With the latter gentleman, however, he differed on one point. He had stated that the Brahmins composed a small portion of the native community. That was quite true; but they were, nevertheless, the lords of the Hindoos' consciences; they were worshipped as gods, and considered part of the Deity himself; and, moreover, these Brahmins were generally very learned men, distinguished for their metaphysical and theological acquirements; so that when the native brethren went to preach in villages and country places, they generally found that the mass of the people were most illiterate, and said, "We do not understand anything, we are just like the cows and bullocks; will you go and speak to our priest; if you can convince *him*, then *we* shall hear you." The people, in the presence of the colonel and major sahebs, did not speak out their internal sentiments. But when the people were found in the company of their own countrymen, then they were ready to disclose their hearts, and tell the missionaries what they thought of them and of the Christian religion. So that he perfectly agreed with Major Davidson, that when they went to preach amongst those rural people, not much learning was required; but when they had to encounter Brahmins and Moulvies, then it would be well for them to have such training. The speaker then narrated how, when he was labouring amongst the

[margin: Rev. B. L. Singh.]
[margin: Brahmins few but most powerful.]
[margin: Rural people simple, but rely on the Brahmins.]
[margin: Learning in the teacher required for the learned classes.]

Mahommedans, they confronted him with their Moulvie, who was well versed in the Hebrew and Arabic Scriptures; and the argument he brought against the truth of the Bible was, that it was perverted in the translation into Hindostanee. This, of course, he (the speaker) denied; when he was challenged by the Moulvie to read a chapter out of the Hebrew Bible. Having done so, the Moulvie said it was not translated by competent men. Having argued a little longer, he called upon him, in his turn, to read the same chapter out of the Hebrew Bible; and by that means thoroughly confuted him, by showing him that they both agreed in the main points. The Bible, the blessed gospel of God, was the only power that could convert the Brahmin or the Moulvie; but with different classes in India it required a different way of dealing with them. There was one way of attacking the Hindoo mind, and another of dealing with the Mahommedan; and it was requisite to understand this. He begged to differ on one point from another father of the Conference. The Scotch system of education was not too high; on the contrary, he thought that in one respect it was too low. The knowledge of Greek and Hebrew which Dr. Duff's College imparted to the students of divinity was a *mere smattering*, in consequence of which he learned these sacred languages with a converted Jew, and with the late Mr. Morgan, of the Doveton College. Nearly the whole list of subjects on their programme, concerning native agency, had been again and again discussed and considered in the Calcutta Missionary Conference; and the only difference that had arisen was respecting the salaries of the native agents. Perhaps his remarks might lead some to think that he received a very high salary, and that therefore he was not fitted to labour among the rural population. When he joined the Free Church mission as a teacher, for two years he had laboured five hours a-day, and got nothing. After that, he got the same pay with the convert pupils attending the Institution, viz. eight rupees a-month; then sixteen; then successively twenty, thirty, and forty; and, last of all, sixty and a house; and when last the subject of salaries was brought before the Calcutta Conference, he had said that if it would conduce to the welfare of the native churches, he was willing to surrender anything. (Cheers.) He had never stipulated for any amount of salary. But whilst they had been listening to the venerable fathers on his question, they must at the same time hear what the other parties had to say, in order to the formation of a correct judgment. The principle on which the salary of a native agent should be

Circum-stances that should determine their amount. regulated depended on various circumstances. The first, the real necessities of his position; secondly, the condition of the preacher prior to his baptism, and prior to his appointment as a preacher; thirdly, was he fed, and clothed, and educated, at the expense of the Missionary Society; or did he himself make considerable sacrifice in getting a theological education; also, as to the moral and physical qualifications of the agents themselves; and last of all, and certainly not the least important, the resources of the native churches; what they could pay? That question could only be finally decided when the native population should be elevated from their moral and physical degradation, and when their landed aristocracy should be evangelised, and become the nursing fathers of the churches. As to the amount of salary, the highest class of native preachers received betwixt 100 and 150 rupees per month,* which was much less than most of the English missionaries received, but nearly equal to what his friends of the General Baptist Society and American Free-will brethren got.

Actual pay given.

The CHAIRMAN here requested the speaker to tell the Conference, by way of comparison, what was received in Calcutta by the first class of Mahommedan native teachers.

Income of Moulvies, Brahmins, He replied, that he did not think the majority of the Moulvies and the Brahmins got more than from five to twenty rupees per month; but then, besides that, there were the annual feasts, when the grand idols or pirs were worshipped, and great numbers of persons assembled; and also the marriage festivals and funeral ceremonies of the Hindoos, at which they received various presents.

In answer to a further question, put by Colonel EDWARDES, as to what a principal pundit would get, Mr. BEHARI SINGH replied, that it altogether depended upon the different classes of *and pundits.* pundits, and the relation they bore to the wealthy heathen. For instance, only a few years ago, one man spent 50,000 rupees at a special celebration, and the Brahmins had their due share.

The second class of native Christian preachers received a salary of fifty to eighty rupees per month; the third class,

---

* Although his remarks are confined to the native agents of Evangelical Missionary Societies, yet he sees no harm in stating that some few of the native clergy of the Propagation Society receive higher pay than any of their brethren in connexion with other Missionary Societies.

between sixteen and thirty; and the fourth, between ten and twenty. The highest class was not always the most effective; and when he was asked how it was that so many of the second-class men got the lower salary, he answered, "Oh, greater would be their reward in heaven."

In answer to a question he had put to a highly-esteemed missionary as to the propriety of giving high pay to some native preachers, he received the following reply: "Oh, we have increased their salary because we have ordained them." Mr. S. remarked, that he could not appreciate the value of this answer, unless it could be shown that the native brethren had received calls from the native churches, whose members came forward to add to their salary. This the missionaries were never able to show.

The Rev. FREDERICK TRESTRAIL, Secretary to the Baptist Missionary Society, said,—That one of the main principles connected with the foundation of the mission with which he was associated, was this, that European missionaries should, as far as possible, be regarded as evangelists in the centre of some important district, and that they should direct thence as many native preachers as could be obtained. For a very long time that principle had been acted upon by the Serampore mission; but a change took place, and the Society at home somewhat departed to a great extent from that policy, very much to the regret of many of their friends. They were, however, at the present time, manifesting some degree of vigour, as returning to the practice of their fathers. In some parts of India they had four (if not more) native preachers for every European missionary. The mission at Delhi presented features of encouragement that were very remarkable. When the mission was resumed after the mutiny, they had only four native Christians remaining. Mr. Smith had since been joined there by two Europeans, for the purpose of helping him; and some twenty-four or twenty-five native Christians had been selected to take charge of certain small stations where there were schools set up, and preaching and praying going on constantly throughout the day. The consequence was, that additions had been made to that Christian community every month, so that they now numbered about 120. He was informed that sixteen were added during the month ending 20th February last. Whilst the presence of the missionaries in rural districts was esteemed to be requisite in order to certain operations, yet so far as the converts were brought in, it was mainly from the labours of the native agents. This result obtained at Chitoura, and other places in the North-West Provinces; where, too, both missionaries and native preachers had had to endure no inconsiderable amount of persecution. Then, as to Jamaica, the Calabar institution had been by some friends pronounced a failure. Though out of the twenty-four or twenty-five brethren who had passed through that institution, some after trial were found wanting in qualifications; yet they must remember that that sort of thing sometimes happened at home, and many were found attending our colleges and universities who ultimately were discovered to be unfit for the work they thought they were entitled to. His co-secretary, and the Rev. J. T. Brown, of Northampton, were in Jamaica now, and had been present at recent examinations held there; and he (Mr. Trestrail) was assured that, so far from being a failure, the examiners were perfectly astonished at the proficiency, intelligence, and aptitude of those young men, and expressed an opinion that the committee at home ought further to support that institution. Then, as to the great college at Serampore, they had a flourishing native class there, wholly trained in the vernacular; and when the confidence of the brethren in the country districts towards that institution became what they trusted it would be, they would soon find there the men suited for them. There was also a home aspect about this question. If they had not a native agency in England, what would become of religion? Take the Wesleyan body, for example, and ask, were they to lay aside all their local preachers, what would become of them? He himself was a kind of lay preacher for seven years before he became connected with the regular ministry. Where pastors would do their best to pour out from the churches themselves men to evangelise the surrounding districts, they would certainly have prosperous churches. These local preachers did not preach to the Brahmins of England, the churches had another and a different set of men to do that; but the Brahmins of England were few, and the Brahmins of India were few likewise. In conclusion, he trusted that from the flood of light now thrown on this great matter, they would most unquestionably return and adhere to the great principle that whilst the European is there for certain purposes, unless he is surrounded by an adequate staff of native agents, his efforts will be comparatively futile.

GEORGE F. BARBOUR, Esq., of Edinburgh, instanced the work

which had taken place at Amoy some six years ago. A very remarkable work of grace then commenced, and the agents in spreading it were mainly natives. It was the aim of the missionaries to gather together some of the more promising and hopeful young converts, for the purpose of training them as native evangelists; and, by means of this agency, the seeds of truth were rapidly disseminated from place to place, and an extraordinary outpouring of the Divine blessing attended the instrumentality of these native Christians. He understood that, at Shanghai and Singapore, the like agency had been blessed. As to the salary question, he knew that some of the native teachers were receiving less than they had previously received when following their several occupations. Five or six dollars a-month was the ordinary salary. He felt convinced the discussion that morning would establish, first, the desirability of native agencies being instituted; secondly, that the agents should be trained in the vernacular; and, thirdly, that according to the different fields of labour, a different agency was needed.

The Rev. G. PRITCHARD said, he had for thirty-three years laboured in a very important part of the mission-field, the South Seas; where, perhaps, more native agents might be found than anywhere else, and where God had most signally blessed their labours. The question, therefore, arose, How had they been trained? Some of them had been blessed with very little instruction. When the Tahitians first embraced the gospel, in a very short time willing and suitable persons were found, whom the missionaries sent to the neighbouring islands, selecting those whom they believed to be really changed characters, and who seemed to possess a talent for speaking their native tongue. Thus these pioneers went forth; and their numbers augmented, until now they had four or five colleges in the South Seas for training native agents, from which had proceeded a very considerable number of teachers well qualified for their work. He had listened to some of them, preaching to large congregations, with as much pleasure as ever he had heard a white brother speak to the people. Amongst the Feejees God had blessed the labours of the Wesleyan mission to such a degree, that they could not supply the native brethren fast enough. The people had got sufficient knowledge to lead them to refrain from breaking the sabbath, and were now waiting for teachers to come and preach the whole gospel to them; and in this case the missionaries were acting very wisely in sending the best men they could get. Wherever colleges for training these valuable agents could be established on the spot, by all means let them be founded. In those he had named, they had four years' hard study, but were supposed to have had a moderate education before they entered the colleges, like the youth in the High Schools of Edinburgh and Glasgow. Whilst there, they frequently acquired practice by preaching in the villages around. Chiefly by means of these native agents, directed by the European missionaries, the gospel had spread from Tahiti over all the groups in the Eastern Pacific, and a large portion of Central Oceania. Turning to the relation held by societies towards each other, Mr. Pritchard said, — It was not desirable to locate two native evangelists of different denominations in one small village. Where this has been done, many evils have arisen. Bad feelings have been excited; unnecessary expenses incurred; and much labour thrown away, which in other portions of the mission-field might have been productive of great good.

Extensive labours of those agents.

Different denominations.

The Rev. C. B. LEUPOLT, of Benares, said; he supposed it was quite unnecessary to say a single word as to the piety required to be possessed and manifested by their native agents. He was pleased to hear of their Hindoo brother who had addressed them, that he was of the same stamp as his brother at Azimghur. The latter had had his salary not long since raised; but he accepted the gift on the condition that if the mission fell short of money, they should not pay him the increase. This was unfortunately the case during the mutiny, and his salary was most cheerfully surrendered. As to the advantages possessed by their native brethren, they were not all exactly such as they might suppose. What Mr. Mullens had already stated he must repeat; that they did not generally receive a more attentive hearing in the bazaars than Europeans themselves received. The European missionaries were listened to in the bazaars quite as attentively, as their brother Behari had been listened to in an assembly of Englishmen that morning. There was another point which must not be overlooked. The more eloquent the native preacher was, and the higher his standing in society, the more abuse he got. The speaker instanced the cases of Mohan, Nehemiah Neel Kanth, and other native agents, who, for heavenly-mindedness and devotedness to their Master and His cause, could not be surpassed. He had at times been obliged to stand betwixt them and their congregations; though they spoke the language most eloquently, and their preach-

Rev. C. B. LEUPOLT.

Natives not better heard than Europeans.

Good preachers much opposed.

ing was quite of a superior order. Nor did he think that their native brethren were able to bear more fatigue than the missionaries. They could, perhaps, bear more of the sun, or of sleeping under trees, than we could; still as regards actual work, Europeans could stand quite as much as they. Nor did he think that the native Christians trusted them more than they trusted us. But notwithstanding all this, their advantages were immense. What we gained by the hard labour of years, they possess at once: the language they have. Very few natives understand the language well, who have had a purely European training. He had seen natives of first-class European training, who could not write a page of Hindostanee. The vernacular must form an important portion of the training that is given to them. Some Europeans could acquire the language as well as the natives themselves. Their brother Smith of Benares, for instance, and Mr. Lacroix in Calcutta, spoke the language equal to any native. Generally speaking, however, such excellence could only be acquired after twenty or five-and-twenty years' hard study. Another point was: the native agents understood the habits of the people much better than any body of Europeans did or ever could; and could thereby better effect an entrance into their hearts. Another advantage Behari had mentioned, namely, that they wanted less than Europeans did; in other words, they could do with less. For it was not asked with them as often it was with ourselves; How much can I get, and how little can I do? If they wanted to construct a large native agency, they must have men who would require smaller salaries than European missionaries. And this was generally the case with the native agents in India. Then, whence would they get these men? They must get most of them from amongst the adult population; for such had their own peculiar advantages. They knew all about their old religions; and in this respect they possessed an advantage, which the young man who had been trained in a college from his childhood did not possess. But the latter class had also advantages peculiar to themselves. By the knowledge which had been instilled into them, they were better able to meet and cope with the Brahmins, than those who were not converted until they were thirty or forty years of age. What he said, therefore, was: Get native agents wherever you can, whether from amongst the adults or from the orphan institutions. More men were wanted to be trained in the vernacular languages, to whom, also, science, philosophy, and everything else, likely to be useful, should be imparted, in such a way that they could

Can't bear more fatigue than they.

But possess great advantages.

Should be trained in the vernacular:

understand their countrymen better than we:

need less.

Old and young, all useful.

Higher and lower both needed.

again impart it in the native tongue. Let the native pastor or missionary be specially well trained, superior in mind to his native brethren; but, at the same time, in his habits simple as themselves.

Translation. As to the translation of the Scriptures, they would only get a good Hindostanee version when such was made by the natives themselves, on the soil; but before they could hope to come to that, they must have a Hebrew-and-Hindostanee dictionary, a Greek-and-Hindostanee dictionary, and an English-and-Hindostanee dictionary. The churches must be better established, they must have a full and settled native ministry; and then they might expect Luthers to rise up, who would set about translating the Word into Hindostanee for themselves. The native brethren would furnish the language, whilst our part would be to superintend the work.

Salaries. As regards the salaries of native agents, he had little to say. They must look to the native zemindars, for instance, partly in this matter. And as to female agency, it was required everywhere.

Native female missionaries. They wanted female missionaries, and also colleges for the proper training of females. He wished this matter had occupied the attention of the Conference to a greater extent. Pious native females might be of immense service in going from house to house; but they must be careful to select none but right persons for that work.

Rev. J. Walton. The Rev. J. WALTON, of Jaffna, followed:—The salary question, he said, had been felt to be one of great difficulty and much embarrassment in Ceylon. It had been inseparably connected

National customs not to be changed. with that denationalising process which attached to their present methods of training, and which, he held, emphatically unfitted their native brethren for mission work. Their mission to India was to carry the Gospel to the people: their national customs and habits, in so far as such were not heathenish, but simply national, they had nothing to do with. They had not to change their coats, but their hearts; they did not wish to destroy their national customs, but the enmity against God that was in their hearts. The

The position of the missionary temporary. present system of missions was purely temporary. They did not expect to have to send men and money for ever. India would not want them. It therefore now strongly behoved them to select native agents suited in every respect for the position they were to fill; and not to raise up in their churches a race of hybrids, dressing like Europeans, detached from their own countrymen, and needing an income which the native churches will, of themselves, be unable to furnish for a long time to come. If the right men are thus trained in the right way, when the time came for them to leave the churches to themselves, they might leave them free from customs foreign to their wellbeing.

Colonel TUDOR LAVIE, of the Church Missionary Society, stated his impression, as the result of a visitation of fourteen districts in India, from Delhi down to Southern India, that those native missionaries who had been invested with any kind of special responsibility, had been by far the most efficient and blessed in their labours. He had seen this exemplified with congregations numbering from 500 to 1200 persons.

Col. LAVIE.

Responsibility.

The Rev. Dr. TIDMAN, Foreign Secretary to the London Missionary Society, said that he had been both interested and instructed by what he had heard that morning. He felt deeply indebted to Mr. Hardy for his excellent paper, and also to their practical and devoted friend, Mr. Leupolt, whose observations were most valuable. As for himself, he was irresistibly drawn to this conclusion: that the largest amount of success which had been realised was, in the great majority of instances, attributable to native agency. He appealed to all missionaries present, to say whether they were not indebted for the greater number of their converts to the direct or indirect agency of Christian natives? With regard to the churches to which Mr. Pritchard had referred, they must permit him to say one word concerning the native pastors of Tahiti. Why did they become so? Just because our Europeans were sent adrift by French authority; they were thus called forth by the necessities of the situation. These native brethren were not ordained before; but as soon as they were called to the work in the providence of God, they proved quite equal to it. And after twenty years of French misrule; notwithstanding all the influences of Popery on the one hand, and of brandy and vice on the other; there were now living under the instruction and influence of these native pastors a greater number of church members than ever they had had aforetime. (Cheers.) Then as to another field in the South Pacific, the Samoan Islands. Almost at every village there was a native agent; in some instances, a pastor; and all these Christian teachers were supported by the natives themselves, and did not cost the Home Society a penny. With regard to Madagascar, twenty years ago or more, the European shepherds were all sent away; and a few poor timid lambs were left in the midst of wolves. And what had been the

Rev. Dr. TIDMAN.

Success largely attributable to native agency.

Native pastors in Tahiti.

In Samoa.

In Madagascar.

result? Why, men had been raised up by God to take the oversight; and instead of tens of Christians under the care of European pastors, there were now hundreds, nay thousands, under the teaching of these men. The conclusion he came to was this: that native agents had done the work in time past, and must do it for the time to come. As to gathering them into schools or colleges, that must be the work of discreet men on the spot; but they must be thorough *Christians*. They could afford to differ as to the mode of training; but there had been no discord in their discussion; though their respected Chairman had so carefully admonished them at the outset, as if he expected they were going to loggerheads! The great thing they had to aim at was, to fit the men for the particular work each had to perform. The man who would have to labour in Calcutta, must certainly have a different class of qualifications to the man whose sphere was confined to the Hindoo village. In his opinion, all the modes that had been named were extremely good; and it was a blessed thing that they had them all; they could thus borrow wisdom from each one. In conclusion, he trusted that their dear brethren in every part of the great mission-field would not look to them continually to send forth a great increase of white faces and European teachers; but rather consider themselves bishops in the best sense of the word, and labour, with God's blessing, to raise up suitable native agencies themselves.

<small>Their great value in the work.</small>

<small>To be fitted for their peculiar spheres.</small>

<small>Minute.</small>   In the following MINUTE are embodied the sentiments, which, with singular unanimity, found favour among the members of the Conference on the important subject of this discussion:—

MINUTE ON NATIVE AGENTS.

The members of this Conference recognise as of vital importance, in every healthy plan of Christian missions, the work of raising and employing, on the field itself, various classes of well-qualified native agents. The European or American missionary, who, in obedience to Christ's command, bears the gospel to some heathen country, is a stranger and a foreigner there : his work is temporary ; his position is exceptional ; and when Christianity becomes localised, his peculiar functions and duties come to an end. Christianity must be embodied in a living form in native churches; and the outward services it demands must be performed by native pastors and native missionaries of all grades. Apart from this circumstance, missionaries are few ; the work is large ; foreign climates are often unfavourable to their health ; it is difficult to acquire foreign languages and manners; the expense, moreover, of the voyages and maintenance of missionaries is heavy. In all these things native converts have the advantage ; they are at home ; the language they have learned in childhood ; the climate is their own ; the cost of maintaining them is comparatively small. These considerations show the maintenance of a native agency to be essential to the successful establishment of Christianity in a foreign land, and urge upon every missionary the duty of securing in his work as many well-qualified agents as, on careful inquiry, he is able to find. *[Native agency most important. Missionaries are foreigners, few and expensive: natives, at home.]*

They consider that, while among the converts, zealous lay-agents may be found, who, though supporting themselves, are willing systematically to fulfil the common Christian duty of urging, both on the heathen and Christian population around them, the faith which they have themselves received, it is still required that some of the converts shall devote all their time and all their powers to the service of the Lord ; and, in various spheres of duty, as pastors, evangelists, readers and teachers, endeavour heartily to promote his cause. In all such men personal piety, zeal for the work, and fitness to teach, they reckon essential to the right discharge of their important spiritual duties. *[Lay-agents. Native pastors and preachers. Their character.]*

Spheres differ:	The demands of numerous localities, states of society, and spheres of usefulness, differing greatly from each other, at once exhibit the necessity of securing a suitable variety in the native
also the men.	agents who are to occupy them. Some will be required to labour among a simple, rural population; others, among the people of great cities; some, among uncivilised tribes; others, among scholars, with minds perverted by false philosophy; some, among isolated communities, where a great deal is left to their own judgment; while others labour immediately under a missionary's eye.
All kinds are required.	They consider it a rule, of the first importance, that each native labourer should be placed, as far as practicable, in the sphere for which his various gifts render him suitable: and they believe that, in the present dearth of agents in the vast sphere open to their efforts, the services of all may be well employed,
Young men and old.	from the ablest to the most humble labourer. While young men, trained from their childhood amid Christian privileges, have proved most useful in leading a community to higher stages of Christian experience; older men also, converted from heathenism in riper years, have been found to bring their sober character and their knowledge of idol-systems to bear with great efficiency upon their still heathen neighbours.
The call of God:	The Conference consider it, therefore, the solemn duty of all missionaries to endeavour to secure for the Church of Christ the services of as many such agents as possible. They should watch well the call of God's Spirit, remembering that, in the exercise of his prerogative, he has taken his servants from all ranks, and has especially employed the lowly, making the weak things of the
inquiry:	world to confound the wise. They should seek out all agents that may appear to possess the right qualities of head and heart; and
prayer.	make it a matter of constant prayer that they may be chosen and called forth by the Lord of the harvest, whose fields they are required to reap.
Training.	The system of training adopted to render such agents, under God's blessing, competent and well-furnished teachers, should have direct and due regard to their intended spheres of labour.
Simpler and higher.	With the greater number an education, through the medium of their own tongue, will be found sufficient: with others, English

may be added to a certain extent; and with a few, an extensive knowledge of the English language and literature will be found a means of storing their minds with large knowledge, and furnishing them for those higher labours to which men of distinguished ability, in great heathen cities, are constantly called. In some cases, where native missionaries are pioneers of civilisation as well as of the Gospel, industrial pursuits have been found not only valuable but necessary.

The Conference, however, believe that in all cases the more directly theological portion of their education should be given in the native language; that in their own tongue they may become perfectly familiar with all the expressions, texts, technical terms and phrases, which are required in every hour of an active preacher's life: lessons on preaching, specimens of sermons, arguments and discussions, should all be given in the native tongue: and it would be well if, in their private reading, these native students used only their vernacular Bible. *Theological instruction in the vernacular.*

With this teaching of principles, should at the same time be associated direct practice in mission work; exercises in preaching and the like should be undertaken under the missionary's own eye; that the capacities of all may be thoroughly understood before they are appointed to positions of heavy responsibility. These studies also may most usefully be continued after native agents have been so placed: that as their experience increases, their knowledge also may grow, and they may be stirred up to seek higher attainments and greater ability for usefulness so long as they live. *Practice. Studies continued.*

The Conference would dread that any course of training should be so conducted as to injure their power to do good. A missionary should so guide, and teach, and train his converts, as not to injure their national character. While he should seek to improve that character in every way, to raise its tone, and to Christianise all its elements; when native customs are harmless, and are likely to continue among the community of his countrymen, the native teacher should seek to maintain them; he should, in his dress, food, manners, and style, continue to resemble his fellows; and show, that while he is a Christian indeed, differing from them in the possession of a purifying and ennobling *Native habits to be kept.*

faith, he is still one of themselves. By so doing, he will rather add to his influence with the heathen; on the opposite plan he may wreck it altogether.

Responsible, yet free. When the right men have been thus trained, and been duly qualified, the Conference consider that, in the various positions in which they may be placed, as pastors, evangelists, teachers or readers, of whatever grade, they should be placed under such responsibility as they are able to bear; should not be too closely tied down; but should enjoy that amount of freedom in action, which will both test their principle and stimulate their zeal: in this way the agents of the native Church may in due time grow out of pupilage, and be enabled to work perfectly alone.

Salaries. On the important question of native salaries, the Conference consider that no rules can be drawn from the artificial position occupied by the missionary himself. They think that it may most appropriately be settled in every case, by a careful consider-*Standard.* ation of the average incomes of natives moving in that rank to which the native agent belongs; and to evangelists, supported by Missionary Societies, they would apply the same rule as that of the foreign missionary; of securing an income that will supply real wants, give him ordinary comfort, and keep him free from all *Salary of a pastor.* anxiety. Where a native pastor has been appointed over a Christian congregation, they think that his support should come from them. It is neither natural nor just that his support should be derived from a foreign Society in a distant country; but where a church is poor or weak in numbers, a Society may well continue to supplement such salary as the church can give, by an annual grant, until it is able in due course to bear all the burden alone.

Native female agents. They believe that, in the extension of the gospel among the heathen, the power of female Christian influence should be employed as far as practicable; and that, where the state of society allows, and circumstances are favourable, Christian females should endeavour, not only as school teachers, but as visitors in heathen families, to lead them to an acquaintance with gospel truth and an acceptance of its claims.

Great success of native agents. The Conference rejoice that the native agents, in whose welfare they feel so deep an interest and for whose increase they so ardently long, have already, under the blessing of God, been made the instruments of great good. They rejoice and give thanks to God, that in many countries, in many spheres of missionary labour, converts, raised up from among the heathen, have been found faithful pastors, eloquent preachers, self-denying evangelists, and that in some cases they have joyfully laid down their lives for Christ's cause. They reckon this fact as one of the most gratifying proofs of the success of the gospel in modern days. They trust that this agency will be largely extended in every field of missionary labour; and they pray, that according to his own example, in answer to his own promise, and his people's intercessions, the Lord of the harvest will send forth more labourers to reap the harvest, to which the great field of the world is ripening.

After a few business announcements, the sitting was terminated by the singing of the Doxology.

SIXTH SESSION.

Thursday Afternoon.

After dining together as on the previous days, the members of Conference re-assembled at 4 p.m.

Major-General ALEXANDER in the chair.

The Friday session.

After prayer had been offered by the Rev. Dr. SOMERVILLE, the Rev. G. D. CULLEN proposed that the Friday morning's sitting, being the closing one, should be prolonged till three o'clock. The proposal was unanimously agreed to.

Committee on funds.

ROBERT A. MACFIE, ESQ., proposed the appointment of a COMMITTEE :— To inquire and report in such manner as they may deem most expedient, on the best means of obtaining increased income for religious Societies : and that the Committee consist of the following members ; viz.

Rev. W. ARTHUR, London ;
ROBERT BARBOUR, Esq., Manchester ;
Rev. R. G. CATHER, Londonderry ;
JAMES CUNNINGHAM, Esq., Edinburgh ;
Rev. W. FAIRBROTHER, London ;
Rev. H. M. MACGILL, Glasgow ;
Rev. JOHN ROSS, Hackney, London ;
AND
Rev. J. B. WHITING, London.

The proposal, being duly seconded by JOHN HENDERSON, Esq., was unanimously adopted ; and the above Committee were appointed, Mr. WHITING being Convener.

Programme.

The following is the programme proposed for the afternoon's discussion :—

SIXTH SESSION.

Subject: How may we best obtain and qualify Candidates of the right stamp for Mission Work?
Paper, or Address, of ten minutes, by Rev. Thomas Green, Principal of C.M.S. College, Islington.
Rev. E. H. Bickersteth's Letter for United Prayer in 1861.
How far it is possible, and advisable, to induce men and women of private fortune to devote themselves to missionary work?

The Paper named in the Programme was then presented and read to the Conference as follows:— *The paper.*

HOW MAY WE BEST OBTAIN AND QUALIFY CANDIDATES OF THE RIGHT STAMP FOR MISSION WORK?

By the Rev. Thomas Green,
Principal of the Church Missionary College, Islington.

It is obviously impossible within the few minutes allowed for our opening paper, to do justice to the important topic I have been requested to treat on this occasion. The utmost I can hope or shall attempt to accomplish, will be the suggestion of hints and outlines of thought; which may form a basis of discussion, and help to elicit the views and opinions of brethren, who feel interested, as every friend of Missions must necessarily feel, in the question; "How we may best obtain and qualify Candidates of the right Stamp for the Mission Work?" *An outline only.*

I need not occupy at any length the time of this Conference in the preliminary inquiry: Who are men of the right stamp? Mr. Mullens, in the valuable paper read by him on the first day of our sittings, described the qualifications we look for in the European missionary; enforced the necessity of a high standard; and fully exhibited the zeal, sound judgment, and decision of character, the gentleness, patience, and fidelity requisite for the arduous office. In this matter we are all agreed. Spiritual agents alone can rightly perform spiritual duties. The men we want are men of God, truly converted in heart, and holy in life; baptised with the Holy Ghost and with fire; taught by the Spirit; led by the Spirit; filled with the Spirit; men of one idea, one aim, one object; like the Great Apostle of the Gentiles, counting all things but loss for the excellency *Men of the right stamp defined.* *Spiritual men:*

of the knowledge of Christ; determined not to know anything save Jesus Christ and him crucified; loving Christ, living Christ, ready and willing, if need be, to die for Christ. Such men are born, not of blood, nor of the will of the flesh, nor of the will of man, but of God. They are God's workmanship. They are the special gift of the risen and ascended Saviour to the Church. So saith the apostle: "When he ascended up on high, he led captivity captive, and gave gifts unto men; some, apostles; some, prophets; some, evangelists; and some, pastors and teachers; for the perfecting of the saints; for the work of the ministry; for the edifying of the body of Christ." A live coal from the altar has touched their lips, and put away their iniquity. With Isaiah they have heard the voice of the Lord, saying, "Whom shall we send, and who will go for us?" and with the prophet, they are ready to reply, and have replied, "Here am I, send me."

devoted to Christ:
the gift of God;
sanctified by Him.

If the Church would obtain such men, she must not only remember the divine command; "*Go ye* into all the world, and preach the Gospel to every creature;" but, also, the no less imperative duty; "*Pray ye* the Lord of the harvest, that he will send forth labourers into his harvest." The Holy Ghost, now, as in the days of primitive missionary enterprise, separates men to the work, and fits them for it. It is *our* great business, to ascertain whom He thus calls; and to be humble fellow-workers with God, and instruments in the Spirit's hands, in preparing them for the glorious warfare.

We are to pray for them;
and seek them out.

Fully sensible of the necessity of divine agency to give us missionaries of the right stamp, and of the subordinate position which man occupies in obtaining and qualifying them for the office, I proceed to throw out some practical suggestions as to the best means of enlisting suitable labourers into the missionary ranks, and equipping them for the important duties in which they will be engaged.

Means of doing so suggested.

Connected, officially, as I am with an Institution in which there are, at the present time, not fewer than forty students preparing for missionary service, I have had opportunities of observing the various ways in which God is pleased, ordinarily, to direct the thoughts of his servants towards the work, and to bring them under the notice of those who may be instrumental in introducing them to the field of foreign labour. I will briefly refer to some of these various ways:

Experience.

1. Missionary Sermons. The value and importance of the pulpit as a means of enforcing missionary principles, eliciting missionary

By sermons.

sympathy, and exhibiting the results of missionary enterprise, have been fully acknowledged in the previous meetings of this Conference. The pulpit is, if possible, yet more valuable and important, as affording a means of influencing the hearts and minds of our pious youth in the direction of entire self-consecration to the missionary work. I am surrounded by brethren who have been engaged for many years in the foreign service: it would be interesting to ascertain in how many instances the first missionary thoughts and aspirations were awakened in connexion with appeals from the pulpit. Little as has been attempted in this direction, I find that one-tenth of our Islington students owe their earliest impressions to this source. *Example of their influence.*

In the United Kingdom there are probably not fewer than forty to fifty thousand pulpits, connected with the several Protestant denominations. What a powerful engine for good do we here possess! The press has been designated the fourth estate of the realm. What may not the pulpit become? Let the duty, the privilege, the trials, the success of the missionary work, have the place assigned them in the pulpits which their importance demands; and who shall predict the result? Might we not expect that our missionary force would, by this means alone, in the course of a few years, be increased many fold? *Much more can be done by them.*

2. A second instrumentality is the Missionary Meeting. The immediate object of the meeting is to communicate intelligence and report progress. Details, hitherto almost systematically excluded from the pulpit as though unsuitable, or beneath its solemn dignity, have been given in the annual, quarterly, or monthly meeting. And, mark the result! While one-tenth of the students in our Islington College trace back their missionary history to the pulpit, more than one-seventh acknowledge their debt of gratitude to the meeting. Need I suggest that at every such meeting one or more of the speakers should seize the opportunity of appealing to the conscience, the love, the sympathy of our younger Christian brethren; and of inculcating the obligation to honour that divine Saviour to whom the Father has promised the heathen for his inheritance, and the uttermost parts of the earth for his possession; and who gave as his last charge to the Church the command, "Go ye;" and as his last legacy the promise; "Lo, I am with you always, even to the end of the world." *Missionary meetings.* *Example of their influence.*

3. The next means to which I would allude, is the Sunday School. And here permit me to mention my own experience. I do so, believe me, in no spirit of egotism or boasting, but as a *Sunday-schools.*

brother amongst brethren, simply desirous of furthering the one great object we have in view, and of contributing any hint which may help to secure that object. Until recently I had charge of a parish in the West Riding of Yorkshire, containing about 2000 inhabitants, partly agricultural, partly manufacturing, and with few exceptions consisting of the operative class. When first appointed to the charge, about eleven years ago, there was no church, school or house, no parochial machinery or agency whatsoever in existence. It is hardly necessary to add there was no branch Association of Missionary or kindred Societies in connexion with the body to which I belong. Through the Christian munificence of a family resident in the neighbourhood, church, school, and house, were erected, and an endowment provided for the support of the minister. Before I had resided a month in the district, and whilst in possession of a mere temporary building which served the double purpose of Sunday School and place of worship, I endeavoured to interest in the work of missions the few young persons who at first constituted my Sunday School. The subject was novel: many had never even heard the name of a missionary; soon it became a familiar and household word; the feeling of interest deepened; God touched the heart of one and another of the teachers he had graciously raised up as my helpers; and, not to extend these remarks, or occupy too much the time of this Conference, as the result of these simple efforts, five devoted labourers have gone forth into the mission field. One, alas! is not. After a brief missionary life of fifteen months he succumbed to the pestilential climate of Africa: his remains lie in the churchyard of Aké in Abbeokuta. A second was compelled, after about the same period of service, to retire for a time to England; he will, with the divine blessing, shortly be ordained, again to go forth; the other three are all usefully employed in various parts of the field.

His own case.

Effect of the school.

Five missionaries.

Greatness of this field.

There are 300,000 Sunday-School teachers, and two and a half millions of Sunday scholars in England and Wales; add to these our youth in Scotland and Ireland. Is there not here an ample and inviting field for the cultivation of the missionary spirit, and the promise, with the divine blessing, of a rich harvest of missionary labourers?

I can only very cursorily touch upon other means of obtaining candidates for the work. We have now an important auxiliary in,

Young Men's Christian Associations.

4. Young Men's Christian Associations. Such Associations are of comparatively recent growth; but they are exercising in the metropolis and most of our provincial towns, an immense

influence over the class of persons for whose spiritual benefit they are specially designed.

It will afford some idea of the value such an agency may prove to our missionary operations, when I mention, that the metropolitan Associations alone have supplied us with no less than six of the forty students we have at present under training in our college. *Their effect.*

5. I would next speak of our Universities. In our first day's discussion some valuable remarks were made by Mr. Titcomb in reference to the various ways in which the missionary subject is brought before the notice of the undergraduates, and other members of his own University, Cambridge. Those observations proved that an agency, quiet and unobtrusive, yet most influential in its character and results, is at work in that seat of learning. *Universities.*

I may add, what was not stated by our friend, that during the last two years from fifteen to twenty zealous and devoted servants of Christ, connected with Cambridge, have offered themselves to the Church Missionary Society for her Indian and other spheres of operation. Of the 160 European ordained missionaries, labouring in connexion with the Church Missionary Society, forty, or one in four, are members of Oxford, Cambridge, or Dublin Universities. *Example of their influence.*

It must not be forgotten that Judson, and several of his honoured contemporaries in America, and Dr. Duff, Nisbet of Bombay, and others in our Scotch Universities, owed their first missionary impressions to influences brought to bear upon them during their College career. The universities, then, present a mine which may be worked with the greatest possible anticipations of eventual success. *Similar instances.*

6. Parental Influence must not be overlooked when speaking of the several means in our hands for obtaining a missionary supply. The Scudder family will occur to the recollection of many who listen to me. While the father is labouring in Madras, five sons are employed with a large measure of the divine blessing resting upon them at Arcot. Two of the students under my charge at this time have thus been led to offer themselves for the work. This is becoming from year to year a more decided and promising element of supply. Many proofs and illustrations occur to me. I will merely mention one. Twelve months ago, when attending the anniversary meetings in Dublin, a physician, a barrister, and a clergyman, quite independently of each other, spoke to me on the subject, stating that they had dedicated their sons to the work, and that it was the constant prayer of their hearts that the necessary missionary qualifications might be vouchsafed to them. *Parental influence. Instances.*

Individual effort.

7. Individual Effort has been greatly blessed of God to the promotion of the object we have in view. It may surprise some of the friends here present to be informed, that the large proportion of one-third of the students, to whom I have already so frequently alluded, trace their more direct and immediate call to missionary employment to the personal efforts and appeals of Christian friends *Examples.* interested in the cause. The clergyman or minister, the missionary, the student, the zealous private Christian, has employed the influence he possesses in directing attention to the subject, and enforcing the claims of the vast heathen world. May not the servants of the Lord Jesus do far more for their beloved Master than they have hitherto attempted in the way here indicated ? *I* may not be able to go forth *myself:* circumstances in which I am placed—social, family, relative ties—may oblige me to remain at home; but I am acquainted with one and another on whom no such debt of obligation rests; men who appear to have the right spirit, and the necessary qualifications; is it not my duty and privilege to present the matter to them, to commend it to their prayerful consideration, and bid them inquire whether they are not summoned to the help of the Lord, to the help of the Lord against the mighty ?

Special appeals.

8. Special Appeals by the Committees and Secretaries of our leading Societies have been found exceedingly valuable, and productive of large results. Only yesterday I was informed by one deeply interested in Moravian missions, that when, a short time since, an appeal was put forth amongst the Continental brethren *Example.* connected with that body, for volunteers to go forth to the untried fields of Thibet and Central Asia, though only two were wanted, not fewer than thirty responded to the invitation. In the early part of last year a special appeal of this nature was issued by the *Church Missionary Society.* Committee of the Church Missionary Society. Reference was made to the many open doors; to the loud cry for help from India, China, Japan, Turkey, Africa: to the exalted Saviour's inquiry, "Who will go for us ?" The response has been most gratifying. Amongst the many who have offered themselves, I will only allude to two: one, a Fellow of Peterhouse, Cambridge, who some time ago sailed for India, and may possibly by this time, have arrived at the scene of his future labours, Allahabad: The other, a Fellow of Emmanuel, Second Wrangler of his year, Tutor and Dean of his College, and Moderator in the public schools; both of them, men of devoted piety, singleness of purpose, and earnest missionary zeal.

Missionary literature.

9. I will simply add one word on the Missionary Publications

and Periodicals, as a further means placed in our hands of obtaining men of the right stamp for the work. It will be found on inquiry that these have largely contributed to the filling up of the missionary ranks; and it cannot be doubted that they are capable of yet more extensive usefulness in the same direction.

Let me impress upon my brethren one important consideration applicable alike to all these various instrumentalities. They involve no new agency or machinery; all we need is, fresh energy and life infused into existing instrumentalities. There is not a brother in the ministry present on this occasion,—there is not a brother amongst the thousands whom we represent, who has not, to a great extent, these several means of influence within his reach and under his control. Shall we, or shall we not, use the opportunities thus placed in our power? Shall we, or shall we not, put out to usury the one, the five, the ten talents intrusted to us by the Great Proprietor? Shall we determine, in the strength of our God, in humble, but firm, reliance upon his grace and promised blessing, that we will avail ourselves of the pulpit, the meeting, the Sabbath-school, aye, and day-school too,—the Young Men's Association, our parental influence, individual effort, special appeal, periodicals and publications, and all other agencies intrusted to us, for the promotion of this great object? If we thus resolve, should no other result or practical benefit follow from our Conference, we shall not have been called together in vain; and the very ends of the earth will, ere many years have passed, rejoice and call us blessed. *Summary.*

A concluding word on this topic. Let not the thought suggest itself that if we urge our pious youth to dedicate themselves to the foreign field of labour, we shall dry up our home resources, impair our strength, or deprive ourselves of adequate support in our more immediate spheres of duty. The contrary has invariably proved true. Here, as in the other exercises of Christian philanthropy, it will be found that it is more blessed to give than to receive, and that in what measure we mete, it shall be measured to us again. In lengthening our cords we shall at the same time strengthen our stakes; and, whilst watering others, shall be yet more abundantly watered in our own souls and within the denominations to which we belong. *Home work will not suffer.*

Time forbids me to dwell on the second branch of the subject suggested by our programme: the qualifying of the candidates who may have been obtained for the work. I would merely remark that the course of training, whether long or short, should *Studies of candidates.*

certainly include a systematic study of Holy Scriptures, if possible in the original languages; Dogmatic Theology, with a view to the clear apprehension and thorough grasp of the great distinctive doctrines of God's Word; the leading branches of Christian evidence; Church history, ancient and modern, including the more important efforts of Missionary Societies during the last hundred years; and, above all, the cherishing and maintaining throughout the entire course of study the true missionary spirit. I close these imperfect observations with the remark that the missionary spirit can only be cultivated by habits of simple dependence on God; by the practice of self-denial; and by active labours (in proportion to the limited opportunities leisure from study permits), in missionary work at home, in teaching and superintending schools, visiting the poor and the afflicted, holding cottage-meetings and Bible-classes, in open-air preaching, and, generally, in going to the highways and hedges, "compelling men to come in." "The harvest truly is plenteous, but the labourers are few; pray ye, therefore, the Lord of the harvest, that he will send forth labourers unto his harvest." (Matt. ix. 37, 38.)

[The missionary spirit.]

The Rev. Dr. BAYLEE, Principal of St. Aidan's College, Birkenhead, said; he rose to express himself strongly, but much less so than he felt, seeing that he presented himself under very peculiar feelings at this Conference. He could not call himself a "distinguished" missionary, for he was an *extinguished* missionary! It was to the missionary cause that he owed a large part of his present knowledge of God, of his present acquaintance with the Bible, and of his present earnestness for the salvation of souls. It had pleased God to bring him to a knowledge of his truth without any human means; he had not had one human teacher to instruct him; but under hedgerows when the Sundays were fine, and in his own bedroom when the days were wet, he studied his Bible for more than seven years of his earlier life. Unaided by any human help he had toiled through, and had overcome difficulties insuperable to every human eye, but not to faith and patience. Having at length attained the object of his toil and prayers, a degree at the University, eight-and-twenty years ago, he offered himself to the then existing committee of the Church Missionary Society; and it was the cold and official manner in which his application was received that created circumstances, which rendered it impossible for him to become a missionary. He had never ceased to regret it. It might be said that his was an individual and peculiar case; but he contended that it was not. One of the present most distinguished officers of the Church Missionary Society was also an extinguished missionary. It was true that in the providence of God he had been brought into the mission field at home, but he was lost to the foreign work. This was the case with many others; which only proved to him that, *Similar cases.* with the best intentions on the part of the Societies, their present arrangements were too often an extinguisher on missionary work. He was resolved to do his best to remove this for Christ's sake, and to speak and to labour until every needless hindrance was removed. Every word of Mr. Green's paper had gone home to his heart. But whilst listening thereto one passage of Scripture had forcibly recurred to his mind; "Betwixt us and you there is a great gulf fixed." In those strong observations he (Dr. Baylee) was not speaking in a merely critical spirit. He gave all honour to the men who had to originate missionary enterprise. It was one thing to create an institution; it was quite another to see its faults when created, and to endeavour to repair them. He (Dr. *Faults in* Baylee) had been permitted to found St. Aidan's College. That *systems.* institution necessarily partook of the faults of his own mind; and whenever it should please God to remove him (Dr. Baylee) from St. Aidan's College, those who succeeded him would find many of his weaknesses and mistakes, and would carry out many improvements which he had failed to perceive. He therefore did not speak in any spirit of fault-finding; but whilst there was on all sides a complaint of want of men, he would say that if he could *Offer to* get 3000*l.* a-year, he would guarantee to find and keep up a class *obtain men.* of a hundred young men, who would stand any test that might reasonably be required, that their hearts had been converted by the power of the Holy Ghost, and that they were desirous of devoting themselves, body and soul, to the service of the Redeemer. It was an easy experiment to try. Their Missionary Societies had generally (if he might use the expression) "begun at the end." A young man, truly earnest in mind and heart, but untried, *Difficulty of* uneducated, and unknown, presented himself to become a mis- *pronouncing on untried* sionary. Now he (the speaker) would like to know by what rules *men.* any one would be able to look through that young man and ascertain whether he had true missionary qualifications, or not. If he occupied the post of Mr. Green, he should be obliged to do what probably Mr. Green did, reject the majority of young men who presented themselves to his committee.

R

Mr. GREEN here explained that he was not the preliminary examiner of missionary candidates.

Dr. BAYLEE said that his remarks applied to any examiners.

Missionary classes in colleges. In conclusion, Dr. Baylee observed that he had been much struck on Wednesday with what Mr. Lewis had said, that they ought all to have missionary classes in all their theological schools. Here would be given an opportunity of trying young men; and instead of beginning at the end, beginning at the beginning. If they took the colonial as well as the heathen field, they would be able to find a niche in some part of the Lord's kingdom for all young men, of small talents it may be, but of devoted piety, who might offer themselves. He was not aiming at bringing "grist to the mill" of St. Aidan's College (if he might venture on the expression), but he should be happy if any body of people would *He will be glad to take students.* send him young men (if his various brethren could trust him with such), possessing no other qualification than satisfactory evidence of true conversion to God and devotedness to his cause, upon whom they might think it worth while to spend a few pounds annually, to see if they could not be fitted for the missionary work, either foreign or colonial. He had now in the *Several now with him.* College fifteen missionary candidates, one of them from near where Noah's ark rested in Armenia. He came to him with very little of the missionary feeling in a theological sense, and though only in his second term he was now full of it. Referring to the various conditions of life formerly occupied by his students, Dr. Baylee said he had one who had been in the Northampton workhouse; and that he would rather have such, with an earnest zeal for souls, than a hundred gentlemen without the love of God in them. When he (Dr. Baylee) ventured upon taking men of a lower social class, his prudent friends remonstrated with him. They feared *All classes of students welcome.* that gentlemen would not like to come and associate with men in a lower station in society. He replied, then let the gentlemen stay away. On their principle, if St. Peter were to present himself for admission to St. Aidan's College, he would be rejected. (Laughter and cheers.) If we want apostolic success let us have apostolic practice. It is Christian men that we want. Give him a class of earnest, pious men; let them mingle freely with gentlemen in their daily studies; let them unite in works of piety and love; and we shall soon see them become Christian gentlemen. There is even in the religious world a wisdom which is foolishness with God. But what has been the result? The number of gentlemen at the College has increased. He wished he could transfer Mr. Green and his forty students down to St. Aidan's College (where they would make him Professor of Missionary Theology); so that they might unite the whole ninety-five students in earnest preparation for the great work in contemplation. If candidates for instruction were unable even to spell, they were welcome to him. He put them into classes fit for them; and when they attained the necessary amount of knowledge, they entered the candidate class (translating the gospels in Greek, and *Examples.* a book in Latin). This tested them. And what had been the results? One did not know one letter in Greek from another at the beginning of the year, but at its close he beat his (the student's) master at the Greek Testament. Out of 500 or 600 theological questions he had correctly answered nine-tenths. There was another who would certainly not master Greek were he to study it for ten years; but he had the love of Christ in his heart, was able to carry a stout stick in his hand, and by his robustness and physical capacity could walk thirty miles a-day in Nova Scotia or some other colony. He had thrown out these hints that there might be as few as possible "extinguished missionaries" for the future, as the result of the present system and way of receiving youthful candidates. Further detailing the plan pursued with *Cost of their support.* regard to missionary students at St. Aidan's College, Dr. Baylee said they now received them for board and education for 30*l*. a college year; and if any brother knew of any pious young man who possessed the qualifications he had spoken of, and would prevail upon his friends to raise this amount annually, he would receive such with pleasure; or if any one would pay 30*l*. into his own hands he would undertake to find a pious and suitable young man for preparation for this great work. He was a constant poacher on their Wesleyan brethren, and on the raw material he found amongst them, to a very considerable extent, of earnest-minded and devoted young men fit for Church-of-England missionaries.

The CHAIRMAN explained that the other Societies did take up *Chairman.* these very young men, unprepared and uneducated, and had many of them brought under college instruction. Referring to a remark made by Dr. Baylee, he added that Mr. Green had not individually the power of rejection, that responsibility devolved on a committee.

Dr. Lockhart wished to impress upon the secretaries and officers of the different Societies the subject of the qualification of their medical missionaries. They should send them out as surgeons, and not as ordained missionaries. They would find by experience that the latter course did them injury in the field of labour; as it distracted them from their particular work. If a man tried to devote himself to two professions at once, he was sure to be perfect in neither. Some Societies were beginning to send out more medical missionaries than they had done previously. If medical missionaries were to do their work efficiently, they should be sent out as laymen; taking in hand the temporal welfare of the heathen, and endeavouring as much as possible to win their confidence and esteem, preaching and teaching the gospel as they had opportunity, if thereby they might win souls to Christ. If such were sent out as ordained missionaries, their minds became distracted from their special engagement; and the heathen, seeing them otherwise than perfect in their temporal work, would be apt to distrust them; and thus discredit was brought upon the heavenly message they had to deliver. A medical missionary might do as much spiritual work as any other missionary; but it was in all cases better that he should do it as a layman, and not as an ordained minister. A preaching missionary, who had a medicine chest and a good work on popular medicine, might be able to do much good in the relief of suffering, when other medical aid was not attainable; and this was often the case. But it was always better that one man should not profess himself to be qualified in the two professions, as this was likely to place him in situations of difficulty and responsibility, from which he was unable to extricate himself.

The Rev. G. D. Cullen expressed his obligations to Dr. Lockhart for calling attention to this subject; and further instanced efforts that were being made in Edinburgh, which were received with considerable favour, to draw the attention of the students in the Medical Schools there to mission work, both foreign and domestic. Medical missionaries were an exceedingly useful class, if qualified to teach "the truth as it is in Jesus," as well as to attend to the temporal well-being of their fellow-men. It was very desirable to ascertain that these brethren possessed both the missionary element and the requisite medical training. He suggested that they should be trained to medical missionary work in the lower parts of our own towns before they were sent out to foreign service.

The Rev. Dr. O'MEARA said that, in labouring amongst the North American Indians, having to travel great distances where there were no means for the natives to gain access to a medical man, he had himself obtained some little knowledge of medicine, and had accustomed himself to carry constantly about with him a few simple medicines. He thought it absolutely necessary for a missionary, placed in his circumstances, to have some knowledge of this nature; as frequently it proved a means of gaining access to the native heart, which they could not otherwise secure. This knowledge it was also exceedingly desirable for missionary students to acquire; thus combining in themselves the two qualifications referred to; the power of healing the body, and of applying the gospel antidote to the maladies of the soul.

Rev. Dr O'MEARA.

Value of medical knowledge to every missionary

The Rev. ROBERT C. KING, of the Colonial Church and School Society, Liverpool, remarked that one great opportunity for the evangelization of the heathen rested with their own people scattered among them. It had been a matter of regret to every one connected with direct missionary work, that there was so much practical negligence found among our own people who permeated the mass of the heathen. Missionaries bore testimony that there was a far greater difficulty in "making way" in the large towns than in the country districts. He held in his hand a communication from a Secretary of the Church Missionary Society, stating that the proportion of converts in the rural populations was far larger than in the towns; and the reason was obvious; for in towns there was a larger European element, and consequent immorality; so that when the missionaries pointed to the theory of Christianity, the heathen pointed to the practice of Christians; for the natives *would* look to see what kind of people Christianity makes, and what kind of a thing it was in its working-out. When, therefore, they talked of getting candidates of the right stamp for the missionary work, they should not ignore the fact of their own people going up and down amongst the heathen, as they might; and being a great element for good by their example and conduct. They were watched far more than they imagined. He was quite sure the Conference would agree that if their own people, moving amongst the heathen, were what they professed to be, it would work directly and to a great extent in

Rev. R. C. KING.

Evil influence of vicious Europeans on a native community.

furtherance of their missionary labours. He thought this matter was worthy of their most serious attention.

Rev. WILLIAM FAIRBROTHER said; that in his public services he frequently made appeals for young men, and was obliged to take the responsibility of saying, whether he would encourage or discourage them in making application to the Society he represented. But he was pained to say that many who had thus come forward did not present qualifications needful for missionary work; and in such cases he felt that if they were to present themselves before the committee, their offer of service would be declined. The number of young men from the middle ranks of life, offering themselves for this good work, was, he was happy to say, steadily increasing; and he hoped this would continue; but he wished to suggest what appeared to him a grave defect, attaching not only to the Churches with which he stood connected, but to others. He feared they did not sufficiently pray "the Lord of the harvest" to give them labourers. They had been using all sorts of means, by circulars and various appeals, to induce young men to come forward; but had in part forgotten the scriptural injunction, "Pray ye therefore the Lord of the harvest that he would send forth more labourers into his harvest." This was the chief thing. He had found in almost every instance, when speaking to such young men, that first thoughts of missionary consecration were entertained at a very early age. This fact gave an intense interest to those appeals which were made to their Juvenile Associations, showing that the Most High might influence even the little ones to offer themselves to God for missionary work. The young men in their Colleges had generally made up their minds beforehand whether they would labour in the home or foreign service; and his only hope had latterly been in appealing to devout young men engaged in commercial pursuits, but who had not yet made up their minds whether they would enter the ministry or no.

The Rev. J. B. WHITING said, they should all remember that a very great responsibility rested upon committees of Missionary Societies in the matter of accepting or rejecting those who came before them. It was possible that committees might sometimes, nay, often, reject those who afterwards became eminent clergymen in their own country, but who at the time of their candidature might not appear to possess all the qualifications necessary for work in the mission fields. Nay, the rejected candidate at one time might even again present himself after a year or two had elapsed, and be accepted. In no matter was there more caution requisite than in this. They had better (if the alternative were presented to them) reject a good man, than accept a bad one. He thought that missionaries would do well to correspond with boys in the schools with which they had been previously connected and associated at home. Suppose a missionary to have been at Rugby, Cheltenham, or any other public school in England; let him periodically send details from his distant location to the boys in such Schools, and he could not fail to stir up a missionary spirit there. He believed that the missionary spirit existed to a large degree in the academies and schools of the country. Ten years ago, some seventy men were in the habit of meeting in the rooms of Mr. Nicholson, Fellow of Emmanuel College, Cambridge, for the purpose of fostering their missionary spirit; the number has now increased to about 250; and the meetings are no longer held in private rooms. He thought that in general the missionary spirit was imbibed before men came up to the University. The happy circumstance to which he had alluded was rather an indication of the great spread of true religion throughout the country. There is an amount of family piety, and of religion in public schools, which delights the Christian heart; and this, he thought, was the source and origin of the great increase of religious feeling, and especially of the missionary spirit, at our Universities in the present day.

Missionaries to correspond with their old schools.

Increase of missionary spirit in young men.

The Rev. Dr. SOMERVILLE wished to present a point in order to elicit information. In the Church to which he belonged, there was no difference observed in the education required in a missionary from that required in a home minister. They both attended the same classes in the University, they underwent exactly the same amount of education, and stood in academic and theological training precisely on the same footing; nay, in reality, they were not accessible to the missionary committee until they had passed through their academic theological course. They, too, had experienced some difficulty in getting young men for the missionary field; and he was expecting that he should receive some hints from the brethren of other societies as to increased facilities by which their wants might be supplied. He should like to know, if the students attending those institutions over one of which, from the paper read, he should judge that their brother Green presided with admirable efficiency,—if such students had passed through the same

Rev. Dr. SOMERVILLE

Education of ministers and missionaries the same.

academical training ere they got into them, as the persons who were candidates for the ministry at home: in other words, was there any distinction observed between candidates for the home ministry and those destined for the foreign fields? He found that their American brethren had imbibed the idea, and had put it into print, that in England missionaries held an inferior place to home ministers; and one reason assigned for this was, that they were educated in a different and inferior manner from the home ministry. He mentioned that statement simply because he had seen it made; and he should like to know if there was any foundation for it. He thought they would never succeed in strengthening their mission staff, until they imbued the churches with this just idea; that, if a comparison must be made, the missionary occupied even a higher position than the home worker. His position was in the highest places of the field. Our Saviour's emphatic command was, "Go!" He knew comparisons were "odious;" but he did feel that a man going forth to preach among the Gentiles "the unsearchable riches of Christ," occupied the highest place that any one could fill upon earth. And for this lofty position the highest talents, learning, gifts, and graces, were needed. He was disposed to say that it required more talent and skill, and knowledge of human nature, to preach the Gospel to ignorant people, than it did to the preacher's own countrymen. He should also like to know, from brethren, whether persons, taken in because of their earnestness and piety, who had been practising some other vocation beforetime, but of no classical or academical knowledge, and who, after a course of training in these institutions, were ordained and sent abroad, whether such persons, when they returned, were deemed suitable to fill home churches, and were fully recognised as home ministers?

Idea as to the status of missionaries.

Their higher moral position.

The highest talents needed.

Are they eligible for home churches?

Rev. G. Scott.

The Rev. GEORGE SCOTT, formerly Wesleyan Missionary in Sweden, did not ask permission to speak, in order to state the mode in which they, as a denomination, found the men for their mission work. His purpose was to ask: How were they to obtain a larger supply of qualified mission agents? His impression was, that the tone of Christian feeling in this country generally needed to be elevated, and somewhat corrected, on the whole subject. Mr. Fairbrother had touched upon a point of vital importance; namely, that mission work was the ordinary work of the Church of the Lord Jesus Christ. They were too apt to regard it as something extraordinary, something extraneous, and rather wonderful; and because of this, there did not exist

Christian feeling to be improved.

that amount of deep and serious attention respecting it, throughout the body of the Church of Christ, that there ought to be. If he had read his Bible correctly, it was the ordinary and essential work of the Church of God to " go into all the world, and preach the Gospel to every creature." And he took the same ground as regarded those who might consider themselves called, by the Holy Spirit of God, to the great work of the Christian ministry. They all agreed in the necessity of such a divine vocation; and he could not make a distinction in the commission betwixt home-work and foreign work. He believed the providence of God would indicate special qualifications and reasons as to the sphere of a minister's calling. If Christ calls him to be a minister of his Gospel, he may send him wherever his providence may indicate. Then, further, they often met with parents who took an unworthy view of this matter; and, whilst not objecting to allow their son to go out to India in a civil or military capacity, they would think it a most marvellous sacrifice to permit him to go out there as a preacher of the Gospel of Christ. A case had occurred within his own knowledge. He would mention no names; but he happened to know a family in which the son felt he was called of God to preach the gospel. A way was opened for this through the Church Missionary Society, but the parents could not part with their son; they discouraged the attempt, and the consequence was, that the young man afterwards lost his relish for the work altogther, and at this moment was somewhere an outcast and a wanderer; where, the parents themselves did not know!

There were solemn lessons involved in this matter; and if that Conference should issue in the promotion of a healthier tone of feeling throughout Christian England on this question, he augured there would not be much difficulty in obtaining any number of candidates they needed. They, as Methodists, looked first of all at the conversion of young men to God; they then placed them under spiritual training in relation to their church-membership. They were thus enabled to discover, from those who had the oversight of them, whether there were necessary qualifications on the one hand, and a call by the Spirit of God on the other, to preach the gospel of Christ. They were then made to pass through various courts of examination before they were admitted into the Theological Institution; and they were asked, at every stage of their progress, whether they felt a special inclination to the home-work or the foreign; but when they came into the Institution there was no distinction whatever as to the training they received there. If they were destined for a foreign country, and the rudiments of the language had to be acquired, then peculiar assistance must of course be given; but as to the *status*, there was no distinction. He might be excused making a personal allusion. When he was first pressed in spirit to preach the gospel to his fellow-men, he could not decide whether it should be at home or abroad. He did not shrink from foreign work, because he wished to stay at home; but he felt that, of the two, the foreign work involved the heavier responsibility. It pleased God, however, to lead him to choose the foreign field; and, perhaps, the little experience he had had, even as a parent, showed that, as far as he could do so, he made no distinction in the commission. A son of his laboured in Africa; a daughter was now on her way to India, to commence a training establishment at Negapatam; and another son would shortly follow. (Hear, hear.)

The Rev. FREDERICK TRESTRAIL hoped that the observations which had fallen from Mr. Scott would be preserved and made known. Referring to a remark of Dr. Somerville's, he thought he might say that, in public esteem and sympathy, their missionary agents occupied a higher place than the home ministry. No persons were admitted into their five collegiate institutions who were not acknowledged members of their Christian churches, and who had not been recommended by the pastor of the church itself as the pre-requisite to their entering the college at all. Therefore, when any of their students offered themselves for the missionary work, it must be at the end of their term. In former times they educated them in colleges for the mission work; but it had been found that, whether from ill-health, or the absence of a facility for attaining languages, the plan did not answer. They required, first, some sort of evidence, both as to their preaching capacities and their power of acquiring languages; and, above all, satisfactory evidence that their hearts were in the mission work. Ofttimes some members of their churches, who had no training at all, but who were moved with an intense zeal, came and offered themselves; but when the question was asked, What education had they received, the answer frequently was, either none worth speaking of, or that given in a British school, with no knowledge of classical literature, not much preaching ability, and, indeed, very little of the ordinary furniture that any one would think requisite for a man to go forth successfully and prosecute this work. He agreed, therefore, with Dr. Somerville, that it required more ability to preach the gospel to ignorant people than to the cultivated and educated class. Just as it was with children. One of the most marvellous men at that kind of work who ever flourished was the celebrated John Foster. And the power that Samuel Drew exercised over the youthful mind, was extraordinary to a degree. When young men came of the stamp he had described, what was he to say? He could not do otherwise than candidly tell them; "If your pastor and church recommend you, and you wish it, you shall go before the committee; but you certainly present little aspect of suitability." And sometimes pastors, by thoughtlessly recommending candidates, placed the committees in a position of great responsibility and pain. (Hear, hear.) He thought that in this matter the pastor took the first responsibility, and ought to be specially careful what he is about. Sometimes they asked pastors, "Will *you* occupy this or that vacant post?" And so far as his experience had gone, they had never asked one to occupy a place which they thought him fitted for, to which he did not go, and admirably succeed. Then came the grave question of medical testimony. They went to some considerable expense in this matter, and threw the responsibility, as far as possible, on Christian men; getting, of course, a written certificate in respect to the constitutional fitness of candidates. After all this was done, and references had been obtained from parties who knew them, they determined whether or not the candidate should be received; and if they said, "Yes," he came before them for an interview of an hour, or half-an-hour, as the case might be; and if the general impression then was, that the man came up to the mark, he was affectionately received. Should he have already passed through the college course of instruction, he was sent out at once; but this was not always the case. They had also sent out former City-Mission agents; and capital missionaries they generally made. One was accepted last spring, who had been a British school-master, and whom they had placed for a short time in Regent's Park College, under the care of Dr. Angus. As a schoolmaster, he had been digging away at Hebrew, Greek, and Latin, insomuch that his own pastor said of him, "He has done about as much as I can help him on with." They had every guarantee that these men would turn out, under God's blessing, good and faithful missionaries. Then the question had been asked: When their brethren came back, whether they would occupy the same relative position

More difficult to preach to the ignorant than the wise: as with children.

Pastors sometimes send wrong men.

Sometimes pastors are invited to go abroad.

Medical examination.

Kinds of men sent out.

Examples.

Status at home.

in our churches as the ministers who had remained at home? To be sure they would. Two such were now present, filling the pastoral office in the same town, and had been greatly blessed there. If they could do their Master's work well in India, Africa, or the islands of the Pacific, they surely would not be deficient at home. William Knibb had received no great education, yet he had turned out to be a remarkable missionary. Another of their missionaries, Mr. Saker, had gone out as an engineer, and not only measured mountains, constructed, buildings, and taught the people how to make bricks and become carpenters, but had acquired the knowledge of two languages, and reduced one to a written form, in which he had sent home copies of his own translation of the four Evangelists and the Acts of the Apostles; whilst the last thing they heard from him was, that he had produced a volume of hymns in the Dualla language. Mr. Williams, again, had been taken out of the army to become a missionary. And their devoted brother, Mr. Gregson, who had been sent up to Cawnpore, by Mr. Carre Tucker, at his sole expense, as Sir H. Havelock's chaplain, had formerly been a country pastor, but was now at Agra, doing his work right well.

Dr. MACGOWAN thought, that while scholarship and scientific knowledge were desirable qualifications in a missionary, called as he is betimes to combat specious and Protean forms of error, yet these qualifications may often be dispensed with. When a man of the Harlan-Page type presents himself to the executive of a missionary body for foreign service, a man zealous in efforts for the conversion of those around him, let him not be cooped up within brick walls; but if he has had a good English education, and is possessed of sound common sense, send him out forthwith fresh and earnest. Young men, who are competent to conduct Sabbath-schools and Bible-classes, may be safely entrusted with the work of enlightening the heathen mind. They are not likely to prove dilettanti missionaries. They may not act the part of skilful engineers, sitting down to beleaguer the citadel according to prescribed forms, but, as leaders of a forlorn hope, they will make a dart at the ramparts and feel that it is theirs to go in and win.

The Rev. WILLIAM SWAN thought that if the pulpits throughout the country would echo the sentiments they had expressed, as to the kind of men that were wanted for the mission field, an excellent effect would be produced. It was unfortunate that an early prejudice on this subject still survived in certain quarters. It was, that men of an inferior standard were good enough to be sent out as missionaries. This idea was exploded in all intelligent circles; but it still lingered here and there; and ministers, if they were faithful and wise, would do their best to dissipate it, and that right early. Let them look at the spiritual state of the churches themselves; for from them came forth the young men to enter their colleges and training institutions; and if there was found a deep-toned piety pervading their churches, then assuredly a superior class of young men would offer themselves for the missionary service. And let all connected with the churches bear in mind the duty of encouraging such young men, speaking respectfully of the service to which they wished to devote themselves, and kindly help them onward in preparing to enter the institutions, where they would be instructed in needful branches of learning. He trusted both the press and the pulpit would be employed to disseminate the sentiments expressed by the brethren on this important subject.

Former idea about missionaries exploded.

Spiritual churches produce superior missionaries.

Young men to be encouraged.

Captain LAYARD said; that every Missionary Society was concerned in the matter now being discussed. He believed that the feeling described by the previous speaker, that the missionary service of the church was of an inferior grade to that of the ordinary ministry, was well-nigh exploded; one proof of which was found in the fact that graduates from the Universities were now so freely offering themselves to the work, from Cambridge more particularly. It was incumbent upon the churches to supply men to occupy the ground, as fast as the Lord opened up fields for them to labour in. If the church were alive to its duty, there would soon be a general and hearty response among its sons to the call to enrol themselves under the missionary standard; and he trusted that the result of that Conference would show, that God was doing, through them, a work far greater than they deserved, and that an "abundant entrance" into the now open doors would be granted unto them far more than they anticipated. The churches must supply the means, and God would not be slow with his opportunities. The difficulties attending the selection of proper persons had been increased by some of their friends bringing a pressure to bear upon the committees in favour of particular individuals, *protégés* of their own; and wherever a committee had allowed this external pressure to influence their selection, failure had resulted. Let every member of each committee remember

Capt. LAYARD.

Need of men.

Improper pressure on committees.

that he himself is responsible before God for the person that he selects to send forth to be " the observed of all observers" in the mission-field abroad, and the ambassador there of the Lord Most High.

<small>Rev. J. H. Titcomb.</small>

<small>Result of prayer-meetings:</small>

<small>of localising one's interest in missions.</small>

<small>In Sunday-schools, &c.</small>

<small>Candidates in the Church Missionary Society.</small>

<small>Their course in the Universities.</small>

<small>Examinations.</small>

The Rev. J. H. Titcomb spoke chiefly on the vast importance of prayer; and instanced the fact that the Cambridge Prayer-Union, one of the objects of which was expressly to supplicate God for an increase of missionaries, at the end of the first year of its existence, had been the means of raising up for the Church Missionary Society four University men. Faith led them to believe that this was attributable to that special exercise of prayer. He dwelt also upon the importance of the identification, in the minds of individuals, of some single spot in the wide mission-field, as a means of extension and increased support. The superintendent of one of his own Sunday-schools was led to embrace mission work, from the simple fact of his having selected a particular field, and identified the sympathies and interest of that school with it. He was sure he need only mention the honoured name of Paley to remind them of one who, though he enjoyed but a short career afterwards, was a true missionary and soldier of the cross. They would thus foster a more vitalising feeling in regard to the mission work. With respect to the qualifying of candidates, as a member of the Examining Clerical Sub-committee of the Church Missionary Society, he might perhaps be borne with if he said a few words. A question had been asked as to whether there were any distinctions made between the preparation of their missionaries and of their home preachers. In respect to missionary work, their candidates were drawn from two sources; from the Universities, on the one hand, and from the middle and lower classes of life on the other. In the Universities, no distinction of training could be made, because they were not, properly speaking, theological colleges. The ranks of the gentry, the professions of law, medicine, &c., were all recruited from these colleges; whilst only a comparatively small proportion, out of the large number of young men there trained, immediately entered the ministry. As to their University career, therefore, no distinction was made. The same might be said afterwards. When any young man presented himself to the Church Missionary Society, the first thing done was, for one of the secretaries to obtain three referees, all of them being subscribers to the Society, as a guarantee that his general principles were such as the Society would be likely to endorse. Then, if such testimony proved satisfactory, a printed set of papers was sent to the candidate, touching doctrine, and general theological opinion on points of church government, and on matters of faith and experience, but especially concerning vital piety; after filling up and returning which, the clerical sub-committee sat and considered the answers. Supposing these also satisfactory, the young man was then requested to make his appearance; and three out of the committee were appointed, privately, pointedly, and prayerfully, to have personal communion with him, as to the motives which prompted him; what elements of true missionary life there might be in him; what powers of mind he possessed; what his habits of life were, and had been; and particularly as to his love for the Lord Jesus Christ; and that his heart was thoroughly moved with zeal for the work. Some did not pass this last ordeal; but whenever it was otherwise, the next step was to report to the Corresponding Committee, and the question was then taken up, whether he should be admitted into the Islington Institution or not. This routine was universal. As to the social position and distinctions of the young men who came forward, these were curiously various; but whatever their different grades and positions in life previously, they were all placed on one footing as regards missionary work; and if at any time, after having been sent forth from England as ordained missionaries, they were to return to their own country, they would be in a fit position to occupy any pulpit in the land. *Papers, visits, &c.* *The classes: whence they come.*

The Rev. WILLIAM HARCUS, of Toxteth Chapel, Liverpool, said;—On this question I wish simply to refer to the mode adopted by a lately deceased minister and eminent missionary of the gospel of Jesus Christ; one who was, I believe, successful in introducing more young men into the work of the ministry, and into the mission field, than perhaps any other minister in this country. I refer to the Rev. Richard Knill. It was his custom, whenever he went forth on behalf of the missionary cause, to take some opportunity, either in public preaching, or during the addresses he delivered at missionary meetings, of making direct and personal appeals to the young men whom he saw collected together. I remember, some twenty years ago, being present at a meeting, which Mr. Knill was attending in the North; a very small gathering, in a very small village; and at the close of his address, after detailing both the encouragements and the discouragements of mission work, he looked down at a few young men, sitting in *Rev. W. HARCUS.* *Mode adopted by the Rev. R. Knill.* *Example.*

a pew just before the platform, and pointing his finger towards them, said, "Now, will none of you go forth to speak a word for Jesus Christ to the heathen?" And I know for a fact, that of the six or seven young men who were thus appealed to, no less than three devoted themselves to the work of the Lord, as the result, in a great measure, of the direct appeal made to them on that occasion by Mr. Knill. There are many young men, eminently qualified for this work, but who, from a distrust and diffidence of their own powers, or of the reality of their call to the work of the ministry, are kept aloof; when, perhaps, a few words kindly spoken to them by their minister or by Christian friends who know them, may be the means of deciding them for the Lord Jesus. It is a complaint in our churches, at the present time, that men of the right stamp cannot be found to go out and occupy the high field of Christian enterprise. I trust, therefore, that our friends, of the various deputations who go about from town to town, will remember how eminently successful was Mr. Knill, in inducing young men to take upon them this important charge; and will follow his example.

The result.

The Rev. Canon WOODROOFE said, that one means glanced at, but not largely considered, as a feeder for their missionary societies, were the Sabbath-schools. If properly worked, these would always be found to furnish a considerable number of candidates for mission employment. But to this end great pains and exertions were needed; the assembling of the teachers together, in order to instil into their minds those principles which it was desirable they should, by the Spirit of God, impart to others. He had a class of young men, who met statedly for reading and studying the Scriptures, and mutually asking questions and receiving information, and who never separated without prayer. There was, he had reason to believe, a work of grace now going on in their hearts; and they were asking, on different occasions, How can I employ myself usefully in the cause of Christ? Most of the brethren present had their Sabbath-schools; which, if rightly used, would constantly furnish suitable candidates for the mission-field.

Rev. Canon Woodroofe.

Sabbath-schools.

Bible-classes.

The Rev. HOPE M. WADDELL observed, that the conversation thus far had been very valuable and instructive; and the remarks made, on all hands, worthy of their best attention. Still, be it remembered, the case had been considered by the highest autho-

Rev. H. M. Waddell.

rity, and decided; and the proper means had been prescribed, which must precede or accompany all other means. "The harvest is plenteous; the labourers are few: *pray* ye therefore the Lord of the harvest to send forth labourers into his harvest." They had heard of the power of the pulpit as a means of inviting the contributions of congregations, and obtaining increased funds; and it should also be employed to augment the number of missionaries. But especially the prayers of the church, of families, and of individual Christians, should be bent upon this object more than heretofore; and a recommendation to this effect might properly emanate from this Conference.

The command to pray for men.

The Rev. THOMAS SMITH would only advert to the subject of *obtaining* missionaries; church organisations were so different from one another, and modified so much the modes of *training*, that he thought they could not do much in the way of discussing the latter question here. But the former was a matter of purely catholic interest; one in which they were all equally concerned. The first thing to be looked at, in order to get good and suitable candidates for the mission work, was to remove the obstacles that lay in the way. So far as his experience and observation had gone, that which prevailed as a hindrance, perhaps more than all all others put together, was the parental influence placed in the way of a young man consenting to be proposed, or offering himself as a candidate for the mission work. Now this parental influence could not be dealt with otherwise than by a tender and judicious hand. But it appeared to him that, so far as it originated in misconception, it was capable of being modified and influenced; and this was the point to which he wished more particularly to refer. In Scotland a very considerable portion of their clerical men belonged to the middle, or just above the middle, class of society. All of them were well educated for their station; but it did not follow that their mothers and sisters were; and he believed, generally, that there existed, in the minds of such, an idea that necessarily heathen lands were such as that the missionary must encounter a great deal more suffering than fell to his lot at home. He (Mr. Smith) would not say that there were not positions in the mission-field in which a European might have to encounter all that the most lively imagination could picture; but this was not ordinarily the case. Now, it would be of great consequence, if through the pulpit and the press, and in every way, the people's minds could be disabused of the idea that

Rev. T. SMITH.

Obstacles to be removed.

Misconceptions

about the perils which missionaries encounter.

there was necessarily, in mission-work, a kind of physical martyrdom. He believed they would find nineteen out of every twenty people in Great Britain (of the class to which he referred) who imagined that to go to India was necessarily to go to a land where their health was sure to be broken down, and probably their lives sacrificed in a very short space of time! But let them only look round that room, and they would see men who, in vigour and energy, were equal to any others of the same age who had remained all their lives at home. Well, next, something of the same kind of influence should be brought to bear upon the men themselves. He had, for a long time, admired the system referred to by Mr. Scott as appertaining to his body, that there should be a certain degree of despotic power exercised by the Church in sending men to places which they were best fitted to occupy. He always had a great veneration for (in some respects) that greatest man of his day, John Wesley; who always contended for the Church possessing the power of directing the location of all its ministers, and placing them in the posts in which they were likely to be most serviceable. It ought to be brought very strongly to the consciences of all candidates for the ministry everywhere, that they should consider themselves no longer their own, but " bought with a price;" should consecrate their energies and talents to that part of the great field in which they might be the most beneficially employed; and that all, who would eat the bread of the Church, should consider themselves bound to serve that Church in such a way as it thought the most advisable. He believed that it would be the best and truest course to refrain from so constantly putting before the students' minds, that in giving themselves up to this branch of the service, they were doing some mighty work; that it was a peculiar and extra honourable work they were aspiring towards; and that they were making great sacrifices in so acting; but rather to inculcate amongst their young men, that there were just two departments of the same work equally honourable, and equally requiring the best men; and that the one department which each was found to be most qualified for, was the one which he should choose, without reference to any supposed difference between them. A good deal of this would be effected, were the practice more common than it is, for men to embark in the missionary work, not immediately, but after they have made trial of their ministry in spheres at home. In many parts of the foreign mission field, as in Bengal and Caffreland, a moderate knowledge of the language might be acquired in a very short time. And thus it was not absolutely necessary that a man should be young in order to his learning the language. It would, in his view, have an excellent effect, both directly and indirectly, upon public opinion in regard to missions, if it were other than a rare or uncommon thing for men to relinquish their home churches and go abroad. Such a course, more extensively followed, would inevitably lead to the idea that it was not so great a sacrifice which men were making when they devoted themselves (as the phrase was) to the mission work, but would appear just like a transference or translation from one church to another. He thought that it would show a healthier state of things, when the missions abroad and the work at home were considered and deemed, both by ministers, the public, and the Church generally, as two distinct, indeed, but not very dissimilar, branches of one great work. *Effect of such a course.*

The Rev. JOHN SUGDEN said, he believed it would be a great thing for every man who sustained the office of a pastor at home, to have a few years' experience of mission work abroad. If any young man were to present himself to him as a candidate for the Christian ministry, and to consult him as to the particular department of the work in which he should engage, he should immediately ask him: Have you considered whether it is not your duty to exercise the ministry abroad rather than at home; and should point him to heathen lands as having the first claim to his attention and regard. Every minister of the gospel ought to do this. The field at home was limited, the foreign field was vast and almost limitless. He did not think that Missionary Societies would be doing other than their duty were they to go from church to church, select the most gifted men amongst the home ministry under forty years of age, or so, and ask them—leaving it to their consciences to settle— whether it was not their duty to go abroad? For whatever dignity a man occupied and enjoyed in the church at home, be he even an archbishop, it would add to his true dignity were he to consecrate himself to the work of foreign missions. It had been his happiness, since his return home, to introduce young men into the work of the ministry; and it was a great happiness to him to know that one young man belonging to his own congregation, one of the most gifted, who had taken high honours at the University of London, and withal of considerable social position, had, during the past year, devoted himself to the work of preaching the gospel of Christ to the heathen. Both he and others would gladly have *Rev. J. SUGDEN. Good for all pastors to spend some years abroad. Heathendom has the first claim. Societies might invite pastors to go out. His own experience.*

gone to the foreign field, had their physical health permitted. He (Mr. Sugden) felt like a man (to use the expression in a military sense) somewhat "degraded," having returned home from the foreign field of labour. He felt that the best part of his ministerial life had certainly been spent in the latter work.

Resolution on Mr. Bickersteth's Letter.

Rev. G. D. Cullen.

The Rev. Mr. CULLEN rejoiced that they had had so very lengthened and animated a conversation on this subject. The secretaries, however, now requested the Conference briefly to direct its attention to the next point in the programme; the Rev. E. H. Bickersteth's Letter for United Prayer in the year 1861. They must all, he thought, have felt sensible, during the proceedings of the Conference thus far, that a blessing had attended the united prayers offered from many pulpits and many meetings, that a spirit of wisdom and of love might be poured down upon them from on high; in the answer they were now receiving, manifested as it was in the large enjoyment they had had, the great unanimity exhibited, and (he trusted) in spiritual profit and benefit to their own souls. The prayer-meetings in the morning had been very gratifying; and he thought it would be a most becoming step that they should resolve, as a Conference, to sustain the proposal which had emanated from the excellent clergyman he had named; and that a certain week, early in 1861, should be devoted to prayer throughout the entire world: for it was evident that there was spread abroad at the present time amongst the nations an enlarged spirit of grace and of supplication. The proposal had first appeared in a letter from Mr. Bickersteth in the *Record* newspaper, copies of which letter had since been largely circulated, and was to the effect that the second week in 1861 should be set apart for this purpose.

Mr. Bickersteth's proposal.

Another week of prayer in 1861.

After considerable conversation on the subject, in which the members generally, while heartily concurring in Mr. Bickersteth's proposal, preferred the first week of January to the second,

It was unanimously RESOLVED:

Week of special prayer:

That the Members of this Conference cordially concur in the proposal made by Mr. Bickersteth, and will rejoice to see the whole Church of God throughout the world, again setting apart a WEEK FOR SPECIAL PRAYER on behalf of Missions, in January,

1861: they would prefer, however, that the first week of that month should be chosen for the purpose instead of the second: and they pray that a series of meetings may then be held, far exceeding, in their beneficial influence, the hallowed meetings of the present year. _{first week of Jan. 1861.}

They unanimously concur also in the proposal made by the Rev. G. Scott, that on the Sabbath-day following that week of prayer, the ministers of all the churches of Christ in every land be respectfully requested specially to bring the great subject of Christian Missions before the people of their charge. _{Univeral missionary sermons on the following Sabbath.}

The Rev. DAVID THORBURN, M.A., of Leith, in introducing the third subject specified in the Programme, namely, "How far is it possible and advisable to induce men and women of private fortune to devote themselves to missionary work?" said he had listened with great interest and admiration to the papers read by Mr. Green and others, and to the various remarks which they had educed; but it had occurred to him that the subject of missions was treated if not as extraneous to, still as the extraordinary work of the church. For his own part, he would go further than Mr. Scott, and say, that it is the one great object for the promotion of which every one of them, lay or clerical, had been called to become partakers of the grace that is in Christ Jesus. They had this grace imparted to them, not only that they themselves might be saved, but that they might become diffusers of that grace over all the world; and were thus all called upon to become missionaries, in one form or another. By prayer, by teaching in the Sabbath-school, by appeals from the pulpit, they might and would, of course, obtain missionary workers; but every believer in the Lord Jesus must view himself as a member of that aggressive army, and be ready, at his Master's call, to go forth. "The field is the world." Any one who had paid the slightest attention to the recent revival work in Wales, Ireland, and America, must have been impressed with the fact that it was attended by a sense of individual responsibility, which had never been observable to so large an extent before. That sense of individual responsibility, and an increased sense of the efficacy of prayer, constituted the grand secret of success in the matter of Christian missions. The whole church was divided into two great sections: those who were especially set apart, separated, for communicating the truth to their fellow-men; and those who in their various civil, military, or other walks of life, were called upon to help the work by contributing of their own substance, by inducing others to cast of their abundance into the treasury of the Lord, and in every other way in their power. He thought all their theological professors should be missionary professors. When Dr. Chalmers, who was one of the professors of theology to that section of the Church in Scotland to which he (Mr. Thorburn) belonged, was removed by death, he and many others of his brethren were of opinion that they should endeavour to get, as his successor, one imbued in the highest degree with the missionary spirit; and the brother to whom they looked was Dr. Duff: for they thought that, if they got him amongst them, he would stir up such a missionary spirit amongst the youth of Scotland, who aspired to the Christian ministry, as that they should not be contented to rest at home, but be fired with the ambition to make known to the heathen the unsearchable riches of Christ.

Theological professors to be missionary.

Invitation given to Dr. Duff:

Why:

The missionary service, in his opinion, bore the same relation to the work of the ministry at home, that that of the regular army, of which their Chairman (General Alexander) and other members of the Conference were so great an ornament, bore to that of the militia corps and of the corps of volunteers, which had recently been enrolled. However important the latter for the defence of their native land, the higher and more honourable service was that of those who were called upon, not only to protect their country from foreign aggression, but to carry its banners to the remotest ends of the earth.

Analogy between missions and military life.

The Rev. ROBERT G. CATHER, Wesleyan Minister, Londonderry, thought the spirit of sacrifice which led young men to offer themselves for mission work, was a very blessed manifestation of the operation of the Spirit of Christ in their hearts; and that the reason why there was not a more frequent consecration of this nature, even in regard to or in prospect of the most unwholesome climates and the most inhospitable parts of the field, was, that this spirit of sacrifice was not cultivated to a sufficient or scriptural extent amongst the home churches. A young man, desirous of becoming a missionary, was expected to bring out all the marks of refinement and education; and yet those who applauded him for his spirit and talent, too frequently did nothing besides towards the end he had in view. He thought that, if the habit prevailed amongst wealthy Christians of periodically devoting large sums from their worldly gains, without themselves being called to leave their business or other avocations, they would have better things to report very speedily. Not

Rev. R. G. CATHER.

Self-sacrifice to be cultivated:

among the wealthy.

only a consecration of zealous and pious men, but of men possessing means, was greatly to be desired.

The CHAIRMAN agreed with the last speaker, that it would be a great advantage were more men of wealth, talents, and pious energy, to throw themselves into the mission work. As to the personal dangers attending the work abroad, there was, as Mr. Smith had shown, a great deal of false sentiment floating through society on the subject. If a young man was going out to fill a post in the civil service, which is not without its occasional momentous and trying dangers ; or in the army, where danger is always objective, we might perhaps expect to hear parents and others considering the contingency ; but common observation shows us that such is not the case. We can never forget the perils to which missionaries have been exposed among the cannibals of the South Sea Islands, and the Dyaks of Borneo ; but, generally speaking, the missionary of the present day has no danger to apprehend that should weigh for one moment with him and his friends. He had seen missions abroad and at home, and had no hesitation in saying that missionaries to the Roman Catholics in Ireland had been exposed to more personal danger of life and limb, and subjected to grosser ill-treatment, than he had ever known, heard, or read of, elsewhere, except among savages in modern times. But, be this as it may, the thought of danger should never deter a soldier of Christ ; and he who shrunk from either the possibility or probability of joining the army of martyrs, ought never to offer himself as a candidate for the spiritual warfare of the mission field. He had a son, one of whom he might say with a father's pride, that he was a noble youth, who had just gone out to serve his Sovereign in her Indian army; and honourable as such an entrance into life is, it would have delighted both his mother's and father's heart, had the grace and providence of God led that son to become a standard-bearer in the missionary band. Still it is his prayerful hope that the young soldier will adorn the profession of arms with an uncompromising profession of the religion of Jesus Christ; and be among those who, in the true missionary spirit, without fear or shame, prove that they best serve their Queen and country, in proportion as they are faithful in allegiance to their Saviour and their God.

CHAIRMAN.

Personal danger in mission work now small.

Greater in Ireland than elsewhere.

Still we must not shrink.

His own case

The following MINUTE expresses the views generally entertained by the members of Conference on the subject of the present discussion :—

MINUTE.

MINUTE ON THE BEST MEANS OF OBTAINING WELL-QUALIFIED MISSIONARIES.

Missionaries appointed by the Spirit:

At the outset of this important question, the Conference are met by the consideration that to send forth messengers of divine truth is the peculiar prerogative of the Spirit of God; and by the command of their Lord, to make that appointment a matter of special prayer.

the Church to pray for them:

In the great need for missionaries, now pressing heavily upon the Church of Christ, they feel that such prayer is their first duty; and, that the more pressing the want becomes, the more earnest and importunate it should be. At the same time, they acknowledge it to be right on the part of the Church to search for men; and by the prayerful exercise of a sound judgment, endeavour to discover those who, by the possession of the requisite gifts, prove themselves called, by the Holy Spirit, to undertake the duties and responsibilities of missionary life.

and search them out.

Personal character.

On the personal character of missionary candidates they would lay great stress: the important spiritual position, which missionaries occupy, demanding from them deep piety, large faith, and hearty consecration to the work of saving souls.

Classes whence they have been drawn.

The Conference observe, in the past history of modern missions, that the larger proportion of missionaries have been drawn from the lower ranks of the middle classes, and the classes immediately below them: and they would wish to see the claim of missions on their personal service, admitted by the sons of the wealthy and the learned; that all classes in the Church may have a direct share in the work which the Church is carrying on.

Classes to be invited to offer their service.

Judging from experience they consider that these claims may be pressed, with success, upon Sabbath-school teachers; upon young men just entering on business; on students for the ministry; and on the younger pastors of churches. The majority of these will require to enter upon a course of study to fit them for their work: but a young pastor, of four or five years' experience, and not too old to learn a foreign language, is already prepared to offer a service of peculiar value.

The Conference consider that several methods may be most properly adopted, in order to draw, from these and other classes, those whom the Lord has fitted for his work; and in employing them, they would follow the teachings of experience. All means that convey correct information about missions; that exhort to duty; and stir up a hearty missionary spirit, they deem useful for this end. Sermons from the pulpit, pressing the claims of missions; addresses and appeals at missionary meetings; the instructions of the Bible-class and Sabbath-school; the opportunities furnished by Young Men's Associations, now so numerous and influential; missionary classes and prayer-meetings in Colleges and Universities; the extensive circulation of missionary works and periodicals; the special appeals of Societies; and the personal efforts of individuals;—should, in their opinion, all be employed, with the direct purpose of reaching the hearts of the young, and inducing many of them personally to devote themselves to missionary life. *Methods of pressing the claims of missions.*

In the missionary information given in public addresses or by the press, they think that special attention should be given to the removal of obstacles that stand in the way of their consecration. Right views of the real position of a missionary abroad; of the people, climate, exterior life and circumstances, by which he is surrounded; right views of the work itself, as one with the work of the ministry at home; and of the position which a missionary occupies in the estimation of the church, will also contribute to make the way clear. *Obstacles to be removed.*

Into the mode of qualifying missionary candidates for their work they would not enter: beyond expressing their opinion, that keeping in view the great purpose of fitting a missionary to be a faithful preacher of the gospel in other lands, that training in its various elements should have distinct regard to the capacities of the man and the wants of his sphere of labour. *How to qualify them.*

While conscious that these plans are not new, the Conference trust that, in the advanced position which missions have recently attained, a greater vigour, and more earnest spirit of prayer, may accompany their employment for the end in view; and they pray that, through the Lord's blessing on such means employed for his cause and in dependence on his aid, an abundance of labourers may be speedily sent forth to reap his harvest. *New life in old plans.*

The Conference concluded with prayer.

THIRD MISSIONARY SOIRÉE.

Thursday Evening.

Soirée.

At half-past seven P.M., this evening, a third Missionary Soirée took place in Hope Hall, which was most numerously attended, the Hall being closely crowded.

Edward Dawson, Esq., of Aldcliffe Hall, Lancaster, occupied the Chair.

Prayer having been offered by the Rev. J. L. Aikman of Glasgow,

Chairman.

The Chairman observed, that in presiding on the present occasion, he rejoiced to testify his long-continued attachment to the great cause of Christian missions among the heathen. He trusted that the Conference was destined to exercise a very decided influence upon the prosperity and advancement of Christian missions in every part of the world.

INDIAN CONVERTS IN THE MUTINY.

BY THE REV. C. B. LEUPOLT, OF BENARES.

Rev. C. B. Leupolt.

Rev. C. B. Leupolt, missionary of the Church Missionary Society in Benares, who was received with hearty cheering, addressed the meeting as follows:—I have been requested to say something respecting the conduct of our Christians in India during the mutiny, and I do so with very great pleasure. Before doing so, however, I will just say a word about my friend and brother, Behari Lal Singh. He told us yesterday, that a gentleman had supported him, but he did not tell us his name. As he has not prohibited me from doing so, I will mention that that gentleman is Mr. Donald Macleod: (Cheers)—a very curious man, who always likes to lay out his money where he can get

Mr. D. F. Macleod.

cent per cent interest. (Laughter and cheers.) He invests it all in a Bank, where he is sure it is safe; "where rust will not corrupt, nor thieves break through and steal." Doubtless there are many others at this meeting who act upon the same excellent principle.

With regard to our Christians during the mutiny, their conduct was everywhere nearly the same. About a year and a half before it broke out, I received a long letter from a dear friend of mine, Colonel Wheeler (loud applause); who wrote and said,— "I have recently had a conversation with a friend respecting the native Christians; and we came to the conclusion that, if any persecution should arise, it was doubtful whether many would remain firm." I wrote back in reply,— "My dear friend, it is evident that persons in India can be friends of missions, and yet not know the native Christians in whom they take a deep interest." (Hear, hear.) There were indications of the approaching mutiny before it actually broke out; but we scarcely believed them, or understood their real import. It was on the 17th May, 1857, that our friend Mr. Tucker, then Commissioner of the Benares District, came to our mission station at Sigra in the city, to tell us what had transpired at Meerut; how the sepoys had burned the cantonment, killed several officers, had gone off to Delhi, and there murdered all the Europeans. He likewise informed me that we had in Benares about 1300 native soldiers, whom we could not trust, and only thirty-five Europeans to protect us. It was not, however, in human means alone that we trusted. We took our measures; and it was agreed that, if anything should happen, the residents were to rendezvous at the Mint. This was on Sabbath day, the 17th of May. I believe that the time of evening service was the hour fixed by the rebellious troops for the murder of the Europeans in Benares; but there was One who reigned above, and who at the time sent a terror among the native soldiers, so that they deferred their purpose. They delayed; they wanted more help; and the other regiments did not come to help them. I believe the time they next fixed was the 4th of June. But the Lord again interfered on our behalf. At two o'clock that afternoon the gallant Colonel Neill arrived in Benares with a body of 120 European soldiers; who joined about eighty others, who had reached us a few days before from Dinapore. At five that afternoon it was resolved that the native soldiers should be disarmed. They were drawn out on parade, and refused to pile their arms. The fight then commenced, and, though our defenders numbered only 250 men, in one hour the native soldiery were scattered before the wind. The Lord again gave us the victory. (Loud cheers.) He was with us, and our enemies could not prevail against us.

When the mutiny broke out in Benares it was, of course, as was the case all over India, ascribed to the missionaries; and I think my friend Mr. Tucker got his full share of the blame. It was said,—"There he is, and there he has his school"—a Government school—where there were about 200 young men, who read the Bible with great pleasure: it was therefore partly ascribed to him that the mutiny broke out. At the beginning of the mutiny we were quiet; but this did not last long; and we soon saw that all the great towns round Benares had fallen. Azimgurh, Jaunpore, Allahabad,—all had fallen; while Benares, with its 300,000 inhabitants and 1300 mutinous soldiers, still stood. The Lord protected us; all was owing to the prayers and faithfulness of his servants. (Cheers.) When the mutiny broke out, I did not think much about myself. That I might be murdered, never entered into my head; but I thought a great deal about the native Christians at Agra and other stations; and wondered whether, when they saw the sword of the enemy over their heads, they would continue faithful to their Saviour, or become Mohammedans to save their lives. But the first thing that happened, when the fight took place at Benares, convinced me that our Christians would prove stronger than I expected. I went among them and spoke to them separately. They were quite calm; but perfectly resolved, come what might, to stand firm to the faith which they professed. We soon afterwards heard of the fall of the various towns, where the Europeans and native Christians had been murdered. There was a time, also, at Benares, when I requested our native Christians to leave that city and go to other places for safety. But their language was always the same; the language of all the native Christians throughout India was the same. (Cheers.) From the beginning of the mutiny they cast in their lot with us, and said: "Where thou goest I will go, where thou diest I will die; thy people shall be my people, and thy God my God." (Loud applause.) And the Lord owned his native children. (Renewed applause.) You have heard how many of them perished; how they were blown from guns; how they were cut down by the sword; how they died of starvation in their wanderings. Yet when we came to collect, after the mutiny, and compare notes, so far as we could discover, we found that, among all the native Christians whom we knew, only two had consented to become Mohammedans through fear. All the rest proved faithful. (Loud and enthusiastic cheers.)

Soon after the commencement of the mutiny, a great many Christians came gradually to Benares, from the various stations which had been destroyed;—from Lucknow, from Cawnpore, from Futtehguhr, Futtehpore, and Allahabad; and we had our Christian village of Sigra filled with fugitive Christians. At one time we sent two boat-loads of Christians down the Ganges to Calcutta. Nehemiah Nil Kanth, one of our native preachers, had saved seventy rupees; and when we wanted money to help the fugitives, he gave us the whole sum towards the payment of a boat. (Hear, hear.) And not he alone, but all the Christians gave freely, and at all times, of that which the Lord had given them, towards the support of the Christian fugitives who came into our settlement. We had a missionary at Goruckpore; and when the Europeans all left, he was obliged to leave also. I wrote to him, advising him not to stay any longer, lest his life should be uselessly sacrificed. He left for Benares; but the Christians remained, determined to see through the storm. The enemy came and took possession of Goruckpore; the Christians were then summoned before the native judge, who told them quietly that they must make their choice between becoming Mahommedans or being put to death. Three days were given them for consideration, and they received those three days thankfully. As soon as they came home, Pathras, the senior catechist, a young man who had been educated in our Orphan Institution, stood up in the assembly and said: "You have heard what the native judge has told us, that we have the choice either of dying or of becoming Mohammedans. One thing I am sure of, none of us will become Mohammedans." Looking at his wife and children, he said: "I should not like to die; but remembering our Lord's words, 'If they persecute you in one city, flee into another,' my advice to you is, that we quietly break up into small parties, meet afterwards in the jungle, and then go off towards the Ganges." Before they had time to act upon this advice a friendly Mussulman came to their station, and requested the native Christians to flee as soon as they could; for, said he, "you will be all killed if you stay." They left the place the same night; and after remaining unmolested in the jungle upwards of a week, they made their way towards Chaprah, without money, food, or clothes. As they emerged from the jungle they saw a band of European soldiers. "This was a joyful sight to us," Pathras wrote; "and the Europeans were delighted when they heard that we were Christians. But," continued Pathras, "they were not soldiers such as we had seen before; they were curious-looking men, all very broad and sunburnt; and, instead of having soldiers' red coats, they were all dressed in blue, and had with them guns so large that we might have put our heads into the mouth." They were, in fact, the blue-jackets of Peel's Naval Brigade, with their huge 68-pounders. (Loud cheers.) When one of these generous men saw that our poor Christians had no food and no money, he took off his cap, went round among his comrades, and collected sixty rupees for them on the spot. (Loud cheers.) They were afterwards also provided for in other ways. Throughout the mutiny, indeed, the Lord has been very gracious to our native Christians, and has acted just as a mother acts to her children in this world. The strong son of eighteen is allowed to go forth and push his fortune in the world; but the tender child she takes in her arms, and leads by the hand. Thus did the Lord act to our native Christians of tender faith; so that they were enabled by his grace and power to make a faithful confession of the name of Jesus amid unusual perils. At Goruckpore, the scene of this trial, a new village has been erected since the mutiny; and a large number of persons have been baptized. (Loud cheers.)

ON MISSIONS IN TURKEY.

BY THE REV. J. R. TUCKER.

Rev. JOSEPH R. TUCKER, Clerical Secretary of the Turkish Missions' Aid Society, observed that the society was established to aid the work of their American brethren, which had been progressing in Turkey for above thirty years. In the first instance, two missionaries were sent to Constantinople. They laboured amid great difficulty and opposition, established schools, and distributed Christian literature. But very few converts were gained in many years. During the last few years, however, they had been permitted to gather the fruit of their zeal in a great number of flourishing churches, now established in various provinces of Turkey. The Bible Societies had introduced the Holy Scriptures into Turkey in the Armenian, Turkish, and Bulgarian languages, and the missionaries had distributed them widely among the people.

They also introduced their printing-press, and had worked it most *Their press:* actively; printing publications of their own composition, and translating others into the languages spoken by the races in Turkey. By these means they had largely distributed Christian literature throughout the land. The printing-press was established in 1833, and down to the year 1854 there had been issued from it more than one million volumes, printed in the various languages spoken in Turkey, comprising one hundred and twenty million pages, and *its issues.* including forty different works. At present they were able to report upwards of one million and a quarter of books and tracts, including some two hundred millions of pages; and they had now no less than one hundred and fifty different works in the Greek, Turkish, Armenian, or Armeno-Turkish languages; as well as in the Syriac and Arabic tongues.

Another feature was the establishment of schools. When the *Schools.* missionaries went to Turkey there were no schools throughout the country. There was great opposition to their introducing schools; but they had been enabled, in connexion with their mission stations, to establish 154 schools, the scholars in which were calculated at 4500. (Applause.) They had also seven schools, in which a higher education was given; and where they had 156 males and females. They had, in fact, given such an impulse to the spread of education that the Armenian church, long so dead, had taken up the matter; now there were schools established in connexion with all the Armenian churches, and also among the Greeks. One of the *Female* most striking features of this scheme in Turkey was seen in the *schools.* female schools, which had been generally established. There was great opposition to these at first, and for many years the missionaries were not able to collect more than twenty or thirty girls. This opposition had ceased, and in their own schools they had *Schools* 900 hundred girls. The Armenian and Greek churches had taken *among Armenians* this subject up, and in Constantinople there was a large committee *and Greeks* of ladies, who had established in that city thirteen schools for girls, some of which contained more than 200 children. These Greek ladies collected among themselves 800*l.*, which had been spent in this way. The Government had also taken up the subject, and had established a system of education in Turkey which very much resembled that which prevailed in our own country. There were 396 free-schools in Constantinople alone, with more than 22,700 *Government* children in them. Referring for a moment to churches which had *schools.* been established by these missionaries, Mr. Tucker said that *Native* there were 45 such churches established in the midst of large *churches.*

populations, varying from 10,000 to 30,000, which were centres of influence whence the light of truth might radiate around. In these churches were collected from the Armenians nearly 2000 members, and there were 7000 persons who, though not converted, professed their conversion from superstition and erroneous forms of Christianity to pure Protestantism; and were legally recognised by the Government as a Protestant community. The speaker mentioned, as a specimen of these churches, and of a model missionary church, showing forcibly the power of the reproductive principle, and the self-supporting character of a well-conducted native agency, that some fourteen years ago a converted Armenian, with a native of the country, went into a place thirty miles from Aleppo, and was stoned away from it when endeavouring to propagate the truth. They returned again, and ten years ago they were able to report eight persons of whom they could speak hopefully as the nucleus of a Christian church. During ten years that little company grew on and on, until now there were more than 1000 nominal Protestants; including 233 church members, who, under the conduct of a native pastor, were devoting their influence and time to the extension of the work in the districts all around them. (Applause.) They had four flourishing day-schools, self-maintained, and upwards of 600 bible students; and the missionaries mentioned as a remarkable fact, that no less than 300 women of the congregation there had learnt to read. Five native pastors had been sent out from this place; one of whom was labouring at Tarsus, another at Antioch, and two or three on the banks of the Tigris. A Christian Young Men's Association had been established there, in which fifteen young men devoted half their time to missionary work, and the other half to work, in order to maintain themselves.

Example of their growth.

Progress of one church.

Native pastors.

Influence on Mohammedans.

He should mention, also, the wonderful influence of this Armenian movement upon the Mohammedan mind. The toleration now given to Christianity, and the Firman of the Sultan, which gave permission to Mohammedans to renounce the Koran and embrace Christianity, had paralysed Mohammedanism. Mohammedanism had been extended by the sword; its dictum had been—Submit to the Koran, or die. Once having submitted, no man could depart from it but with his life. The Mohammedans were availing themselves of this permission. (Loud cheers.) A few years ago, the first convert from among the Mohammedans in Constantinople was in danger of losing his life. He was to be summoned before the Padishah; and missionaries hurried him out of the city on board an

English vessel, with his wife, and sister, and children, and they sailed to Malta, where they remained a considerable time. When this firman, however, was made known, he returned to Constantinople, and was the first ordained Mohammedan who was introduced as a preacher of the gospel. He had now a place of worship, where he ministered without let or hindrance. Numbers of Mahommedans listened to him continually, and a letter recently received, stated that the Turks who came to him for private conversation were thronging his house morning, noon, and night. In fact, he counted nearly 400 visits in one month. The private Secretary of the Sultan had been attending Selim Effendi's ministry, had embraced Protestantism, and had given up his office. (Cheers.) Another instance of the result of this firman was that of a colonel from the frontiers of the empire, close to the borders of Persia, who had come to Constantinople to associate himself with this work. Some religious books had fallen into his hands; he had afterwards read the New Testament, and having determined to renounce Mohammedanism and embrace Christianity, he had come to Constantinople in order to communicate with the American missionaries, and to secure the intervention of the British ambassador, should any persecutions arise. He asked for no maintenance; he had rank and influence; and he had determined to devote himself to the spreading of the gospel of Christ. The Turkish Mission Aid Society had been established in England for the purpose of promoting this great work, and by the money which it contributed, more than sixty native agents were employed throughout Asiatic Turkey. (Loud applause.)

FEMALE EDUCATION IN THE EAST.

BY THE REV. J. FORDYCE.

The Rev. JOHN FORDYCE, formerly missionary of the Free Church in Calcutta, having been requested to give some information upon the subject of Female Education in the East, with which he had been specially connected, observed, that the first effort on a considerable scale was originated by the appeal made by a Baptist missionary from China, many years ago, which led to the formation of the London Ladies' Society for Female Education in the East. This was altogether a catholic Society, assisting Episcopalians, Baptists, Independents, and Methodists alike. There were other Societies of a smaller kind in England, the Wesleyan Methodists having recently formed a Ladies' Committee for carrying out this work. Again, there was a special Society, having a great work in hand, in which the Hon. Mr. Kinnaird, and his friends in London, took a very active part, for the promotion of Normal Schools to train teachers for entering into the zenanas of the rich in India, and teaching also the schools for the poor. Besides these in England, there were two Societies in Scotland, one connected with the Established, and the other with the Free Church. Hitherto, missionary efforts on behalf of women had not been carried forward on that large scale of liberality which was desirable; the London Ladies' Society, for instance, only having an income of from 3000*l.* to 4000*l.* He was most anxious that their fathers and brethren, with the religious community generally, should be impressed with the immense importance of making greater efforts in this direction. If such efforts were to be made exclusively by Female Societies, they should have an income of 50,000*l.* to 100,000*l.* annually. With regard to the state of woman in India at present, he would remind the audience of a single sentence which described it pretty clearly and fully: "She was unwelcomed at her birth, untaught in her childhood, enslaved when married, accursed as a widow, and often unlamented at her death." She was not only like her brethren, the sons of India, spiritually benighted; but, unlike them, she was socially enslaved and degraded. Nay more, a large class of females in India, especially in Bengal, were positively imprisoned; tens of thousands were incarcerated for no crime except that of being women. Under these circumstances, Mr. Fordyce urged that an earnest appeal should be presented to the mothers and daughters of England; an appeal which should reach the ears of our beloved Queen, and prompt efforts to redress the wrongs of the suffering sisterhood. (Loud applause.) Though he acknowledged the great liberality and sympathy which many English ladies in India, including Lady Canning, had manifested on this question, Mr. Fordyce said that hitherto it had been very much trifled with; observing that, if a large and enlightened view were taken of the state of women in India, an effort worthy the country and the cause would be doubtless put forth; and that a host of Florence Nightingales would arise, and go forth to save millions, not from the diseases of the body merely, but from the more destructive maladies of the soul.

ON MEDICAL MISSIONS IN CHINA AND JAPAN.

BY DR. MACGOWAN.

Dr. MACGOWAN, American Medical Missionary to China and Japan, observed, that the medical or lay element imparted to the work of missions was a most important agency. Medical men were needed more in some countries than in others. Among a people, low in civilisation, it was not necessary to have a fully educated physician; for there the clergyman or missionary might very usefully blend the duties of a physician with his ministrations. But when the missions were amongst a people far advanced in civilisation, possessing an extensive literature and medical systems of their own, it was desirable to send among them men who had received the best advantages of the most favoured of our medical schools. You must not, Dr. Macgowan continued, in sending missionaries to China and Japan, attempt to unite the two professions. That to which I belong is in itself sufficient to fill an angel's mind; and if you attempt to engraft it upon the higher and nobler profession of divinity, you will, at the same time, spoil a divine, and make a quack. The need of medical missionaries must be admitted by all. And here I would pay a tribute of respect to the members of my noble and ennobling profession connected with the Honourable East India Company and her Majesty's naval and military services. I take pleasure, as an American especially, in acknowledging their gratuitous services to my missionary countrymen and to missionaries generally. The medical men of the army and navy of both services have been to a very large extent, assistant medical missionaries; and the Christian public have not sufficiently recognised their indebtedness to those members of the medical profession. The duties of a medical missionary are, in the first and least important place, to prescribe for the sick; then to devote himself to imparting instruction in the teaching of the healing art and its collateral sciences to the native practitioners. But the highest calling of the medical missionary is, like that of the missionary proper, to labour for the conversion of souls and the strengthening and edification of the infant churches. With regard to their utility, medical missions are required for the care of missionaries and their families; and are necessary to conciliate the people, particularly those of China and Japan; and to counteract the evil influences exercised by our Godless fellow-countrymen in those lands. The medical missions are a corrective to the wrongs we are inflicting upon those peoples. Where now you hear of a riot in China, you would, but for medical missions, hear of an extermination or of a general massacre; and for one expedition that you now send out you would have to send out two. In Eastern countries they associate with religion the idea of doing good; and a system of religion that does not exhibit benevolence they think is wanting, at least, in the "grace of congruity." We are brought into contact with a vast mass of misery in those lands; a millionth part of which it is not possible to relieve. Here is an economical way of doing some good, and of showing that our religion enjoins benevolence. We can best show the benevolence of our religion by healing the sick; and thus give the evidence for which they are continually asking —mere preaching of the gospel is not convincing evidence as to the character of our holy religion. Secular labour is needed in the mission work; first, in the founding of missions; and again, when the churches are planted, laymen are useful as deacons and as general assistants to the pastor in his various duties. As the time to which I have been limited has expired, I shall conclude by stating, that in the most recently opened of all lands, Japan, nothing else can be done, for some time to come, but some form of secular labour; this being the only kind acceptable to the Government. Did time afford it, I could give you strong reasons why we should send out aid like this at once, in order to diminish the hostility of the Japanese.

How they work.

Only these practicable in Japan.

The Doxology was then sung, and the Rev. W. HARCUS, of Liverpool, closed the meeting with prayer.

PROCEEDINGS OF THE CONFERENCE.

FRIDAY, March 23d.

FOURTH GENERAL PRAYER-MEETING.

FRIDAY MORNING.

THE fourth General Prayer-Meeting was held at Hope Hall, on Friday morning, at 9.30 A.M. A larger number of ladies and gentlemen, than on any previous day, united with the members of Conference in their supplications. *[margin: Prayer-meeting.]*

The Rev. WILLIAM M'CLURE of Londonderry, of the Irish Presbyterian Church, presided.

The devotions of the meeting were led by the Rev. GEORGE OSBORN, Secretary to the Wesleyan Missionary Society; the Rev. ISAAC STUBBINS, of the General Baptist Missionary Society in Orissa, India; and Major-Gen. ALEXANDER.

SEVENTH SESSION.

FRIDAY MORNING.

After the prayer-meeting, the members of Conference gathered together at 10.30 A.M., and commenced their seventh and last session.

Major-General ALEXANDER in the chair.

The following is the programme of the subjects proposed for consideration:— *[margin: Programme.]*

Subject: NATIVE CHURCHES.

> Paper, or Address, of ten minutes, by Rev. F. TRESTRAIL, Secretary of the Baptist Missionary Society.
>
> Village Congregations.
>
> Organisation of such Congregations for Self-support, Self-government, and the Propagation of the Gospel to the regions beyond.
>
> Building of Churches and School-houses.
>
> The formation of separate Christian villages.
>
> How can the character and social influence of Native Christians be raised?
>
> How far should the European Missionary interfere in the affairs of Native Congregations?
>
> The evils resulting from constant dependence upon the Missionary, and from involving him in secular business.

CHAIRMAN.

The CHAIRMAN said that the two words "Native Churches," would suggest a vast scope for thought and discussion, for which on this, the last day of the Conference, he feared they would hardly have sufficient time. Referring to their accepted manual and guide, he directed attention to the xith and xvth chapters of the Acts of the Apostles, which had a bearing on the subject, in the references to the churches at Jerusalem and Antioch; the mistakes that were made; the corrections that followed; the conclusions opposed to the spread of the gospel that were arrived at by many home-formed minds at Jerusalem; and the disposition of unaccommodating ecclesiasticism to impose a heavy yoke on the necks of the young Christians. In considering native churches, they would bear in mind that it is a question how far we should impose our ecclesiastical machinery upon the natives of other countries, with entirely different habits and thoughts, produced by widely different circumstances; and how far it was necessary, as it were, to compress them into moulds of forms and rules which every day is showing us are no longer considered to be altogether suitable to our own churches at home. Why not introduce to the converts plain, simple, unambiguous modes of worship, which should obviate the conscientious differences, from which he believed that few or none of our Protestant churches are now quite free? Experience will provide for this.

The first churches.

English church systems: how far suitable to other countries.

Simpler forms desirable.

He then called upon the author of the following Paper to present it to the Conference:—

ON NATIVE CHURCHES.

By the Rev. F. Trestrail.

Some time ago, at the monthly meeting of the Secretaries of various Missionary Societies whose offices are in London, this question was proposed for discussion: "What form of government is best for mission churches in heathen lands; Episcopalian, Presbyterian, or Congregational?" *[Important question.]*

In one thing all present were agreed, that Christian Churches in heathen lands should not be established by law; and they were pretty well agreed in another, that while the ecclesiastical form and polity of a Christian Church is of great importance, it is not so vital as the right of a Church to choose its own officers, and maintain its own discipline. *[The right of a church more important than its form.]*

1. There is no exact *definition* of a Christian Church in the Scriptures. The one which is found in the Articles of the Church of England — "a congregation of faithful men" — would doubtless be accepted by all here. But the Scriptures speak much about the CHURCH OF CHRIST, and of the individual churches which compose that grand whole. From these sayings we get the notion that a Christian Church is a congregation of believers in the Lord Jesus Christ, meeting in one place for the worship of Almighty God, and the observance of Christ's institutions; having its appointed officers of elders or pastors, and deacons. *[Definition of a church.]*

2. Be it observed that these views are not incompatible with the adoption of any order of Church government existing among evangelical Christians; since the Scriptures, while laying down general laws, permit the exercise of a large discretion in working out details. *[Many forms of order allowable.]*

3. At the outset of the Christian dispensation, the first churches were evidently called into existence by the labours of the Apostles and Evangelists. They were *sent* forth to preach the gospel. Missionaries in these days are sent out to heathen lands to do precisely the same work. Very seldom are they natives of the lands in which they labour. Divest the Apostles of miraculous power, and the gift of inspiration, though perhaps not all even of them were thus endowed; and you have the *modern missionary*, a true successor of the Apostles. *[Missionaries like the Apostles.]*

4. When, by his labours in any given district, he gathers souls to Christ, it is for him to organise them; to teach them their duty

They found churches, start, and advise them.

to one another and to the world; to aid them to select those best suited to be office-bearers; and then to interfere as little as possible in their affairs. To visit them as often as practicable; to advise, to strengthen, correct; to set in order what may need rectification; appear to be some of the duties arising out of the relation which the missionary sustains to native churches.

They are not pastors, but overseers.

5. Hence it follows that the missionary should not become a *pastor*. His position, habits of thought, education, his belonging, in many parts of the world, to the dominant race, place him too far apart from the mass of the people for him to exercise the pastoral function with success. His sphere is larger. He is, *or ought to be*, emphatically an overseer of others; his taking a pastorate should only be allowed on the ground of urgent necessity; and his continuance in that office should terminate, when the necessity which led to his taking it has ceased.

Suitable men as pastors, few:

6. The pastorate is a grand difficulty in regard to Churches in heathen lands. Suitable men for this office are not abundant. This, indeed, can hardly be expected. Christianity and its institutions are new things, brought from afar, and by another race.

why:

But with great deference it is submitted that the want of men suitable for the pastoral office, which is so generally felt, may have

there has been too much dependence;

arisen — first, from the too dependent state in which the Churches have been kept on the missionary, who has, therefore, almost inevitably united in himself the functions of every kind of office; and, secondly, from the want of sufficient confidence in the natives. The best use, with all the defects attached to it, is not made of

freedom will give strength.

the material at hand. Self-reliance, independence in thought and action, and administrative ability, cannot be developed and flourish in the face of this depressing influence. Perhaps we have not only expected too much from native Christians, but have too rigidly insisted on things being done according to the home type and formula.

Native pastor officially settled;

7. The *status* of these pastors should be a real official one in the churches, and only fraternally, as far as practicable, with the Society at home. If pecuniary support be needed, it should be

salary paid by the church;

given, only as a supplement to what the church over which he presides gives; and that on the principle of the strong helping the weak. All sorts of difficulties arise when they are appointed

supplemented, if need be.

and paid by a Society. This system widely prevails. Wherever practicable it should be abolished; or vigorous, active, self-supporting churches can never grow and multiply.

8. The *titles* given to these pastors should harmonise with the

customs, habits of thought and expression, regarding official persons, prevailing in their own country. To transfer to these regions our titles, and the style of behaviour and address connected with them, seems worse than absurd. Titles to be natural.

9. As far as possible, they should be kept from the English tongue. Much has been said about the advantages of English literature, especially biblical. In some few cases, confined mostly to Training-Schools, and perhaps rarely permitted even there, it may be of use. Besides the obvious remark that this literature is filled with strange idioms and illustrations—and its whole structure and style, are very different from the languages of the East, especially—it is not to be denied that the main body of native preachers are not prepared either to appreciate or use it. Let them have English, and they get English notions on all questions, and by so much are unfitted for their proper work. These observations are intended mainly to apply to India, and to those countries in which English influence largely prevails. Where our own language is in somewhat general use, a different course of observation would have to be taken; but this is a case which need hardly occupy the attention of this Conference. Not to know English. No use generally: It spoils them.

10. The relation of Native Churches to Home Societies naturally comes within the scope of these remarks. The policy of keeping churches that can support their own pastors associated with the home institution is most questionable. Societies don't like to diminish the number of churches in connexion with them, and churches deprecate a separation, as involving a loss of *status* and powerful influence. But if now and then the fact could be announced, that a few churches had taken all their responsibilities on themselves, some work would seem to have been done and completed; and in all future time such churches would supply a stronger motive for fresh exertion, and be a standing proof of success. Self-supporting churches to be made independent. Effect.

11. The practice of forming what are called Christian villages is open to serious objections. It withdraws native Christians from the mass of the people. It seems to be the design of our Divine Master that his people should be like leaven. *I pray not that thou shouldest take them out of the world, but keep them from the evil that is in it*, are words which bear this construction. This practice moreover creates a new caste, and raises up a secluded community, instead of a body of people who, in the world, fight the great battle of the Christian life, and exhibit the virtues of the Christian character. Separate Christian villages objectionable.

Native churches, not Societies, must evangelise heathen lands.

12. Until the state of things here sketched out be brought to pass, native churches cannot be of much use in diffusing the gospel in the regions round about them. Injury has been inflicted on the great cause of Evangelisation, by the currency given to the idea that Missionary Societies are to enlighten the whole world. The men whom they send out are too often regarded as almost the sole instruments to accomplish this work. As a consequence, native churches in heathen lands have not been fully taught their duty in this respect; and it needs enforcement as much now as ever. Missionaries cannot be had in sufficient numbers to work out present plans; and if they could, the resources of the Societies do not advance with sufficient rapidity. It may be questioned whether some of these Societies are not now too large, and getting unwieldy, and expanding beyond the natural limits of such institutions.

Property of Societies.

13. The state of dependency in which native churches mostly are, greatly affects the question of the property belonging to Missionary Societies. Chapels, school-houses, and residences, have been called "*the property of the Society.*" Hence the cumbrous machinery of trustees at home and abroad. In British colonies great difficulty has arisen from this practice; for when churches become independent, an extraneous control over property still exists, and it is difficult to get rid of it. In India matters are more simple; but even there the practice obtains. Doubtless there would be much risk in the contrary practice; but the risk would be amply compensated by the earlier freedom and stronger growth of native churches.

Buildings often too expensive.

Moreover, as naturally connected with this subject, it may be questioned whether the style of building sometimes adopted is not too expensive and costly. As much as possible, edifices connected with missionary institutions should be conformed to the native idea of size, cost, and general structure. Large sums have been uselessly expended in many parts of the mission field, for want of a due regard to these principles.

Money wasted.

Poverty an obstacle to independence:

14. The poverty of the people is unquestionably a great obstacle to the freedom and growth here contended for; severe persecution, and heavy loss of property, are often the consequence of a profession of Christianity. It is natural that the weak and feeble should fly for shelter to the missionary. But the history of our mission in Jamaica, with all the drawbacks that exist, shows that his presence and protection are not essential to the stability and growth of native churches. Recent intelligence in regard to the

churches attaining it.

Sandwich Islands, and the present state of the native churches in Madagascar, afford still more striking examples; while over nearly all the isles of the Pacific, and the West Indies, the great majority of the churches is fast becoming self-supporting.

15. It would seem, therefore, but fair to conclude, that in the same measure as the principles here advocated are enforced and acted upon, the results so intensely longed for will be realised.

16. Finally, the question may be asked: Are these native churches as often remembered in prayer before God as they ought to be? The members composing them have been called out of a deplorable state of sin and degradation. They are exposed to terrible temptations. They are often tried and weak. Let us affectionately remember them at a throne of grace. It will quicken our own sympathies to do so. It will give greater breadth and power to our own views and feelings. Intercessory prayer has ever been honoured by God. May more earnest mutual prayer for each other ascend together from churches in heathendom and Christendom, to the throne of the heavenly grace. *Do we pray enough for these churches?*

The Rev. J. MULLENS said: I venture, Sir, immediately to follow Mr. Trestrail on this important question; perhaps the most important in the range of topics which have come under our consideration, and certainly second only to that of the Native Agencies we examined yesterday. As missionaries and Missionary Societies, we aim to establish in heathen lands a Christianity which shall not only be healthy and self-supporting, but which shall also commence in its own sphere a new course of missionary labour in "the regions beyond." Under the Spirit's blessing our work has already effected something: of late years native churches have increased in number, been growing in size, and been advancing in knowledge and in character. It becomes, therefore, increasingly important that mistakes be avoided; that the churches be constituted on sound principles, and started in a right direction. *Rev. J. MULLENS. Important subject. Churches increasing.*

We all seem to consider it a settled thing, that in the mission-field a European or American missionary is a stranger; that his position is exceptional and temporary; that he is the founder, instructor, and adviser of the native churches. We all want to see Christianity localised in heathen lands; we want to see it transplanted, take vigorous root, and become naturalised in the new soil. If a missionary, then, be rendered the means of founding a native *Missionary not a pastor:*

except for a time: church, though he may be its pastor during its infancy and early growth, as soon as circumstances allow, as soon as he finds sufficient numbers, a right spirit, and a fit man, he should lay down his pastorate, and let the church be instructed and governed by a well-qualified native Christian like themselves. Perhaps we have been backward in this matter, and kept the churches in tutelage too long: but stirred up as we have been of late years, it would be well if missionaries would make it a rule, that when a church attains a certain point in numbers, spirit and means, it should be encouraged to start for itself in a course of Christian

Preparations to be made for self-government. progress and usefulness. Preparations should be made for this result from its very foundation: from the first, the members should be taught to aim at self-government, the maintenance of gospel ordinances among themselves, and earnest missionary work among their neighbours: giving grows by exercise; self-control grows by exercise; pastoral duty and responsibility are better fulfilled by practice: from the first, therefore, let us start on right principles, and the transition from pupilage to independent action will be natural and safe.

Churches to be natural. We all agree that, in their dress, manners, and style, native pastors and missionaries should continue to live like their countrymen: our aim being not to make them hybrids, but to Christianize their own native life. Ought not the same rule to apply to Native Churches? I am sorry, however, that in some cases mistakes have been made on this point. Look, for instance, to

Style of their buildings. the style in which many of the churches, intended solely for native congregations, have been built. Ought they not to be so built, that hereafter other congregations may erect similar ones from their own means, and of their own means maintain them

Mistakes on this point. and keep them in repair? I have seen, however, in Tinnevelly, and in other districts and stations in India, churches to which such a principle could not apply. Among the simple Shanars, with their limited means, our brethren have erected some grand and capacious Gothic churches, of a much more expensive character than the locality seemed to demand. For instance, there has been built at Megnanapuram a Gothic church of freestone, spacious, handsome, with elegant windows, one of the prettiest churches in all India. The only fault I would find with it is, that, in my judgment, it is out of place: it is much too good for a Shanar people, good Christians though they be. I think that such proceedings are a mistake, and should receive the most careful consideration on the part of all our brethren in every part of the world. May I add, that my own practice has been in accordance with these views. Five years ago, when I was able to secure a separate building for the worship of my native church, we erected a simple, neat, and inexpensive chapel; to which the people contributed a good sum: since we entered it the native congregation have paid all the expenses of their worship, have kept the building in repair; have not received a halfpenny from our Society; but have taken off our hands the expenses of a bazaar chapel for the heathen, in which many of the members themselves preach. *His own case.*

There is another point of a higher character, which I am anxious to lay before the members of this Conference for their opinion. In our great missionary fields, we have learned the benefits of union and of hearty co-operation: we work together cordially; we help each other with facts, experience, and mutual counsel: from which all learn and all derive benefit. An illustration of this union we see in the monthly Conferences held by missionaries of all Societies in the three Presidency cities of India. *Another point:*

I wish that we should go a step farther than this; and look at some things in our own systems, of which, it seems to me, we ought to keep clear, when we carry the gospel and transplant it in another land, amongst another people. We profess to carry the very gospel of Christ to heathen lands, its full doctrine, its active life. We have done so largely; but have we done nothing more? Let me mention a case in illustration of my meaning. *English elements in our church systems.*

I was present some few years ago, when, in Calcutta, three excellent native converts were ordained as missionaries of the Free Church of Scotland. After the usual questions had been put relating to their personal piety, their consecration to the ministry, and their doctrinal views, they were asked, if I remember rightly, whether they assented to the principles contained in the Deed of Demission of 1843, by which the original ministers and elders of the Free Church severed their connexion with the Established Church of Scotland. I thought at the time: What have these young men *directly* to do with that document? Indirectly, of course, they are concerned with it. They have been instructed, converted, received into membership, and now ordained in connexion with that branch of Christ's Church. Nothing can be more right than to take proper guarantees that they possess the spirituality of character, the purity of doctrine, and personal consecration, that should rule every minister of Christ in every country; that they should possess those elements of spiritual Christianity which are *Ordination in Calcutta: question asked:*

essential in every climate and nation; but why should young Bengali Christians commit themselves to certain transactions which have occurred in the history of Scottish Christianity?

Ordination in Tinnevelly:

Again: when in Tinnevelly, in February, 1853, I saw the four native brethren who had just been ordained by the Bishop of Madras as clergymen of the Church of England; the first of that valuable band, who have since been appointed pastors of the churches both in Tinnevelly and among the Syrian districts of Travancore. I understood that in preparing them for their work, their valued instructor, Mr. Sargent, had carried them through a course of instruction similar to that which clergymen usually follow in England; had given them lectures in Tamil, embodying *Pearson on the Creed, Burnet on the Thirty-nine Articles,* and

Articles subscribed.

the like; and that beyond this, on their ordination, though judicious alterations were allowed in their standards of knowledge, they had been required to affix their signatures to the same Articles of Subscription as those signed by clergymen in England. Here then are native converts ordained, not simply into Christianity as such, but into the English forms of that Christianity. Is this necessary for the missionary purpose we have in view? It is because I think it unnecessary and unwise that I bring the matter before you.

English systems formed by controversy.

Sir, Dr. Baylee told us the other day, that our English forms of Christianity are, to a large extent, the products of controversy; controversy that has sprung out of great events in our history. You, sir, have spoken to the same effect. Ought we not then carefully to modify them before we settle them in other lands? Can we not, each in his own sphere, endeavour to look through these

To be modified in other countries.

systems, get away from their mere technicalities, their historical elements, their local peculiarities; and in planting Christian churches in heathen countries, transfer only those elements which are essential to the spiritual progress of all churches wherever they are maintained? The question concerns us all; we are all liable to the same mistake; all should adopt the same great principle. We

To be modified by those who hold them.

ought to carry Christianity as such, not English Christianity. At the same time all needed modifications in our systems should be made by ourselves; no interference is required on the part of others. Adopting the principle for which I argue, the members of each Church, of each Society, should look into the matter for themselves, and strive to make such corrections and modifications as they may themselves consider necessary.

They have hindered us at home.

Have we not all been hampered by these things at home? Have we not been hindered in our brotherly union, our co-operation? In God's great grace, during this missionary age, we have been learning better things: we have all been getting away from our loneliness, and drawing nearer to each other. We have been fighting our way back from those isolated positions in which our controversies left us, and reaching a better and a purer field of action. In all our churches have we not allowed many elements of exclusiveness to become obsolete, and sought to attain a broader, more brotherly Christianity than our fathers saw? Our controversies are pretty well-nigh dead; our union is growing daily; our respect for each other, our mutual affection, are increasing; all things are leading us to a peace and prosperity which the Church has never enjoyed till now. *We have been growing out of their exclusiveness.*

I want, sir, that our Mission Churches should BEGIN from this state of things; that they should be taught this spirit from the outset; that outward elements of discord should never be introduced among them; that in the form of their life and government we should look at essentials, and not at our own denominational views; and that elements of exclusiveness still remaining among us should not be reproduced among them. And it may be, as the result of such a course, that higher forms of excellence, a nobler exhibition of the oneness of Christ's Church, may be witnessed on the fields of heathenism than Christendom has yet attained. *Native churches to begin free from it.*

The Rev. G. F. FOX, of Durham, sympathised with some of the remarks of the last speaker, especially in reference to the introduction of technicalities into native churches. But, in defence of Mr. Sargent, he would like to say, that a book like *Pearson on the Creed* could hardly be classed among the technical: for he doubted whether, if you wished to instruct a young man in Christianity generally, you could well give him a more desirable text-book to study; a book entirely independent of technicalities, and one which he was sure Mr. Mullens would appreciate as much as any one in the room. He admitted that technicalities ought to be avoided, whilst every church may naturally exercise its own judgment as to the mode in which Christianity ought to be taught. *Rev. G. F. Fox. Defends Pearson on the Creed. Technicalities to be avoided.*

The Rev. J. WALLACE said, that in the early stage of missions in India the establishment of Christian villages was a matter of much importance. Connected with the mission station of Boroud in the district of Mahi Kanta, in Guzerat, there was a *Rev. J. Wallace.*

Christian village which had been most prosperous. For a number of years it enjoyed the fostering care of the London Missionary Society, from which it had been recently transferred to the Irish Presbyterian Church. He first visited it soon after its establishment, eleven years ago, by the Rev. W. Clarkson; there were then only four families in the village, which he believed now contained between 100 and 200 professing Christians. Before it was founded, there were in various villages scattered converts to Christianity, who were in positions of much difficulty as to earning their own support, and in being surrounded by heathen influences; it was thought advisable on these grounds to help them to earn a livelihood; and in order that they might mutually strengthen one another, to have them brought together. Mr. Clarkson and Mr. Taylor got them cottages erected, rented land from the Government, and persuaded some people to go and settle, and support themselves by their own industry. Others, by and bye, were induced to join them; and so far from their influence being lost, he believed it became much stronger than that which scattered individuals could have exercised. Frequently he had heard this village spoken of at other villages one hundred miles distant. He conceived, that in an early stage, when Christians were few, among masses of heathens, it would be very unadvisable to have them scattered and kept isolated in villages distant from one another. In a more advanced stage it would be advisable, where there were even a few, to locate a native catechist amongst them as teacher; so that by and bye a little Christian congregation might be established. In early stages, especially in a country like India, where there was a difficulty in earning support, and where there were many adverse influences by which isolated Christians must be surrounded, Christian villages, he conceived, ought to be established. At a later period, when the Christians become more numerous, and public opinion is more in their favour, they may well be allowed to mingle more with the heathen population, and not only by their words, but by their example, influence them in favour of the gospel.

The Rev. P. LATROBE admitted that Moravians were not free from the imputation of having occasionally made Moravianism a little too prominent in their missionary operations; it was important that this should be avoided. He was struck with the pertinence of the remarks made by Mr. Mullens, as applicable even to the question of doctrine; sufficient consideration had not been given to the question, whether missionaries did not err in some respects, in rendering their teaching a little too systematic, especially at the outset. This was strongly impressed upon his mind, during the discussion of the qualifications of missionaries. He felt rather jealous of the great preference given to missionaries educated at schools and colleges, however valuable and needful these were. Evangelists ought to go forth, specially called of God, like the apostles and disciples of Christ. About a century ago, as was well known, a small community, consisting of no more than 600 members, had established five successful missions, in five consecutive years; and by the help of men who were trained, not in schools and colleges, but in fastnesses and wildernesses. Native converts, in his opinion, required to be fed with the milk of the gospel; they were hardly prepared at once to receive our systems, which, to some extent, were the growth of years.

Technical modes of teaching.

Colleges not always necessary.

The Rev. W. SHAW accepted most cordially the principle so well laid down, that it would be a most unwise thing to plague and distress the minds of native Christians in foreign countries with the mere technicalities of our different kinds of church organisation; but he did so with some qualification and reserve; because each of us had adopted some idea concerning church organisation, which he conscientiously believed to be that which, whatever its form or defects, will, on the whole, tend most to the advancement of religion in the world. He accepted the principle so far as it concerned mere technicalities; but he could not go the length of saying that a missionary, honoured of God to be the means of forming a Christian church, ought not to feel that he might give to that church that form, and complexion, and general order, which he himself believed to be most for the edification of the believer and the honour of Christ. He did not think it was intended; but the principle that had been laid down would, in point of fact, lead to the adoption of Congregationalism, if taken broadly, and without qualification; because nothing could then be borrowed from Presbyterianism, Methodism, or any other denomination, the peculiarities of each being regarded by others as "technicalities." The various Missionary Societies are sustained by particular sections of the church; what would be said by those supporters of a missionary if he adopted a system of church organisation which was not in accordance with the general views they had of what was best? If it was only meant that mission-

Rev. W. SHAW.

Mere technicalities should be avoided.

Missionaries will teach the systems they prefer.

Societies require it.

aries were not to press their church technicalities on a people, so as to hinder and impede rather than assist their growth in grace, then he thought the principle an important one. He should think that he was acting most absurdly, and with a want of Christian consideration, if, as a Wesleyan, he were to perplex and plague a people just emerging from barbarism with opinions as to the ecclesiastical powers of the Wesleyan Conference; but if he had formed a religious society, and taught them that missionaries were under the supervision of the Societies which sent them out, and thus inculcated ideas of general responsibility and church order, he did not think that this would be technicality, but that it was rather calculated to promote the spread of the gospel in the world.

Converts not to be hindered or troubled.

Dr. G. H. DAVIS, in a conference with one of the Secretaries of the Church Missionary Society, had been asked, "Are we to reproduce in India all the divisions of English Christianity?" This naturally raised the question, "How is it possible to do otherwise?" The last speaker had put this matter fairly. Missionaries went forward connected with certain Societies and ecclesiastical organisations: in the very nature of the case, a missionary attached a convert to himself and thus to his own ecclesiastical organisation. It was scarcely possible to do otherwise. A gentleman highly honoured in the Conference had put into his hand these words, "Surely it is possible and practicable for Christianity to be divested of the merely superficial dress of ecclesiasticism, and of all merely national and historical circumstances. New churches must eventually be left to form ecclesiastical systems to suit their own notions, climate, and circumstances." Now though we might agree in this last statement, surely the time had not come when the native churches were ready to be cast upon themselves to construct ecclesiastical systems and organisations. Therefore, at present, all that missionaries could do was to reproduce the various ecclesiastical systems with which they were connected. But the Missionary Societies need not tread upon one another in the same localities; there was no necessity for every Society to exist in the same place; attempt the same work for the same people; and draw comparatively few converts, each into its own separate organisation. If committees in this country could only take and divide the world, and decide that those who were settled in one place should have it to themselves, whilst others should go forward and endeavour to spread the truth where it had not been received, then comparatively little

Dr. G. H. Davis.

Missionaries naturally teach their own views.

A suggestion: Local forms and dress may be thrown off.

Reply.

We must reproduce the old systems.

Division of localities:

and co-operation.

evil would arise from diversity. In the meantime, it was evident that the doctrine of Christian love must be taught abroad as well as at home. This had brought them here, where they knew nothing of each other except as Christians; and this would enable the several churches abroad to walk in the unity of the spirit, and the bond of peace.

The Rev. Dr. TWEEDIE rose to say; that Mr. Shaw appeared to him to have put this matter in exactly the right position; and he had little to add to what was said so well. Our brother, Mr. Mullens, had not added dignity to the principles distinctive of the Free Church, by ranking them among technicalities or external things. That church regarded them as vital things; and could not easily leave them out of sight. At the same time, the mode of ordination referred to by Mr. Mullens was appointed by the General Assembly; and the Presbytery of Calcutta had, consequently, no power to alter the forms. Their power was merely executive. If those who were ordained had conscientious scruples on the subject, that would modify the case: but, judging from his correspondence with at least some of those who had been ordained, the distinctive tenets set forth in the documents named by our brother were held by them as firmly as by our Free Church ministers at home. Rev. Dr. TWEEDIE.
The principles of the Free Church not technicalities.
Converts attached to them.

The Rev. T. GARDINER said, their native brethren in India were ordained, not as pastors for separate native churches, but simply in connexion with the ecclesiastical community of the Free Church, as part of which their native church was as yet retained. These brethren (said he) were to sit with us in the Presbytery, and have the oversight of congregations, European as well as native, along with ourselves. He quite agreed with what Mr. Mullens said as to the undesirableness of introducing technicalities, and such historical references as were connected with the churches in this country, into the native church when instituted entirely *per se*. But at present, in India, the native church, in their mission, was ecclesiastically one with the general Free Church community; and that was the reason why it was that these native brethren, in being associated with it, passed through much the same course, and had the same questions put to them, as ministers ordained in this country. Rev. T. GARDINER.
Native missionaries ordained into the Free Church generally.

But there were *two* points which he desired now to advert to, in the hope that the experienced missionary fathers present might favour the Conference with their views upon them. The first Advantages and evils of Christian villages.

was: How far it was desirable to separate their native churches into village communities, apart from the heathen community around them? There were, no doubt, advantages resulting from this, in their being saved from continual contact with the pollutions of heathenism, and from persecution which would almost certainly be directed against them; and in their being gathered together for the worship and service of God, and for Christian communion and intercourse, that so they might be strengthened and exercise a mightier influence for good upon the heathen around.

Disadvantages. But were there not disadvantages also resulting from such arrangements, in the hothouse-plant character they were apt thus to give their converts; from their faith and love being thus much less tried, and many opportunities being thus denied them of boldly and manfully witnessing for Christ unto their countrymen? The second point was this: How far it was desirable, in the opinion of experienced missionary fathers present, that missionaries should

How long should missionaries watch over self-supporting churches. retain authoritative control over native congregations of which native brethren had been made pastors? There were, doubtless, many difficulties, varied and complicated, likely to arise in the management of such congregations, from the peculiar weakness and inconsistencies of those lately brought out of heathenism; difficulties with which the native pastors, excellent men as they might be, might be little able to grapple. Should the missionary, in such circumstances, content himself simply with giving counsel; or should he go farther, and seek to exercise authoritative direction and control? The interests of truth, and the peace and prosperity of the church, might be in danger of suffering without the latter; and yet would not such action tend to keep the native churches in that state of pupilage and dependence, from which they all felt that it was so desirable they should be extricated?

Rev. B. L. Singh. The Rev. BEHARI LAL SINGH said that native Christians had met at his house three or four times a-month for ten years, in connexion with the Temporal Aid Society. There were Episco-

Native converts not much attached to mere denominations. palians, Presbyterians, Baptists, and Independents; but they never talked of the peculiarities of any church. When a Bengali Christian went from one denomination to another, he did not do so because he always attached importance to the peculiarities of the denomination he joined; but because he thought he might be more useful.

Importance of the native pastorate. The appointment of a native ministry over a native congregation is a subject which is growing in importance every day. I believe that there are upwards of 15,000 native Christians in

Bengal alone. Many of them are good Christians, and some, according to the published testimony of the Rev. Missionaries themselves, will stand comparison in intellectual and moral gifts and graces with their more favoured brethren in Europe and America. Why are not such distinguished men appointed pastors over native churches? Without pretending to solve this important question, which has not been satisfactorily solved by those who are most competent to do so, I shall point out to you briefly the various causes which have tended to retard the development of the self-sustaining character of our churches in Bengal. If we take the Christian population of Bengal to be 15,000, we may safely say that 13,000 are Christian ryots, or peasants, who rely for their subsistence upon the produce of the land. The monthly income of each ryot does not exceed eight or ten shillings a-month. If inundation or murrain occur, he is reduced well-nigh to starvation. If he be a tenant of the heathen zemindars, which is generally the case, he is over-taxed. To resist such oppression would ruin him. How upright soever the judge may be, the ryot is sure to go to the wall. Witnesses to disprove his statements would always be in attendance, and one suit, even if he were successful, would ruin his farm. Should he succeed in defraying the expense, he would probably be in the hands of the police in a short time, under a fictitious charge of assault or felony. This alone is sufficient to account for the wretched condition of the majority of our Christian population. Of the remaining 2000, many are employed as servants in Christian families. Not a few young men are in various situations of usefulness and respectability. Two or three of them are employed in the medical service, and others of them are clerks in merchant offices and in the service of Government. One gentleman is an opulent landowner, and two or three are merchants of some property. It is from this class principally that pecuniary assistance is anticipated for the support of the native ministry. But whether from their having been hitherto provided with religious ordinances without cost, or from their not having had the subject sufficiently impressed upon them, the fact is, that there is not a single self-supporting church in Bengal.

Among the external causes which have retarded the development of the self-supporting character of our churches, I may mention the false position in which a European missionary is placed by continually retaining the pastorship over the native church. To say nothing of the difference of the elements of which the church is composed, and the interference with other important kinds of duties which the missionary is expected to perform, and the little interest which congregations take in church matters, because most of the ecclesiastical power and discipline are retained in the pastor's hands, what a cringing disposition this state of things tends to nurse and foster, if not to create, in the native flocks! If the union was formed solely for the purpose of training up the congregations to self-reliance and self-exertion, and if the missionaries gave themselves entirely to the ministry of the word and prayer, no one would object to such an union. But, however pure and exalted may be the motives and intentions of the European pastor, he is driven by his position as a gentleman of comparatively larger income, and as an accredited agent of the Missionary Society's funds, to be constantly beset with applications for pecuniary aid. If he complies with the request, he satisfies the craving appetite only for a time; if he withholds relief, he raises an obstacle to the success of his ministry by creating heart-burning jealousy. Does not this impede the growth of a manly and independent Christianity among the Asiatic churches? Another hindrance is the adoption of the high scale of expenditure in the erection of our churches, school-houses, and dwellings for our native Ministers. If the Missionary Societies were to withdraw pecuniary gifts, and ask us to lay the foundation of God's temple, many of us who have seen the magnificence and sumptuousness of your churches would, like the Levites and fathers of old, lament at the vast disproportion.

Would we, then, altogether despair of raising a self-supporting church? By no means. While wisdom demands that we should fairly meet the difficulties, faith and fortitude forbid our being repelled by the shout, "a lion in the way," till the experiment be fairly tried. But has this been done in the right way? No. To assist our churches to become self-supporting, I would propose the formation of a Christian landholders' society, for the protection of the Christian ryots from the oppression of the heathen zemindars, and for elevating their physical and intellectual condition. I know of one Christian zemindar (Mr. Hugh Fraser of St. Andrews), who has protected the Christian ryots by freely inviting them to settle down on his estate. If others would follow his example, it would be a blessing. 2d. I would propose the establishment of Christian vernacular schools, which will elevate the Christian ryots to a higher intellectual and moral *status*. 3d. I would propose as pastors the appointment of the more spiritually-minded, experienced, and intelligent of the native Christians, who form the village congregations.

Mr. MACFIE heard with gratification the remarks of Mr. Mullens, and of the preceding speaker particularly, as to the necessity for caution with regard to the expenditure on churches in India. He was especially gratified with the indications of hearty response he heard given to their remarks by the Conference. There could be no greater hindrance to the multiplication of churches than needlessly augmented cost. Even in this country, a great deal might be saved, without impairing comfort and convenience. In his belief, the more simple and economical, the more Christian,—a rule, by the way, of most extensive application,—it being applicable to other matters besides church-building. He traced the root of the evil among Nonconformists— (for it is with regard to them only he spoke; he would not say a word as to the Church of England: and in what he did say, he represented his own sentiments only; he did not commit the Conference, nor any person but himself;)—to deviation from the habits of their forefathers, in whose days their place of Christian assembly was called the *meeting-house*, the name indicating that there brethren met with one another. Nowadays, in hymn-books and elsewhere, it often is called the *house of God*. The moment it is thought of as such, and not as a meeting-place of brethren, people *will* decorate and embellish. A word to his Scotch friends: there is danger in having dropt the fine old word "kirk" for the modern "*church*." The former, resembling the word κυριακη, suggested "the Lord's," the Son of man's; and reminded us of Him, who laid aside his glories to tabernacle in human flesh, and who dwelt in the same humble tenements as the plain men with whom he associated, and whose nature he took. If these principles were borne more in recollection, we should be simpler in our tastes, and better able to multiply churches, beneficially for India; where (might he add), as he had heard (he hoped wrongly), a new order of modern canonised *saints* had been introduced; a church in —— having been called after the name of one departed labourer, for whom in life he, the speaker, entertained most justly the highest esteem and regard. The report to which he had alluded, is credible; for at home the same tendency had developed itself; and churches now bear the honoured names of Knox, Willison, Chalmers, McCrie. He hoped these frank observations would be taken in good part.

Captain LAYARD, speaking to the question, "How can the character and social influence of native Christians be raised?"

Converts to be elevated by the missionary's self-denial.

said that the late Mr. Daniell, of the Baptist Missionary Society in Ceylon, brought his influence to bear upon the hearts of the natives, by "condescending" to them, by bringing his own mind and his own habits down as much as possible to the level of the native mind and habits; in order, by God's blessing, to raise them from the position they occupied. He was eminently useful in his labours; as those might be who followed him in the manner in which he pursued his heavenly calling. His association with the natives was of a truly apostolic character, fulfilling to the letter what the apostle meant when he said, "being all things to all men."

Example of Mr. Daniell in Ceylon.

He went without scrip or purse; God gave him a heart full of love to his brethren. He was out in all weathers, going from village to village, lying down on a mat on a mud-floor, and so associating himself with the habits, thoughts, and feelings of the people. Thus was he able gradually to bring them up to higher habits and thoughts. If one had fallen into a well, it was not by another standing at the top and saying, "Come up here," that he could be saved; but the latter must obtain a rope and, perhaps, himself descend. In proportion as we brought these principles to bear on a heathen population, we should succeed in elevating them to our level.

Rev. C. B. Leupolt.

The Rev. C. B. LEUPOLT said; that in Benares, where he had been placed over a congregation more than twenty years, having also the superintendence of three or four others, different denominations adhered, as it was natural they should, to their own forms; but the missionaries never spoke about the distinctions between them. In every mission establishment, one missionary must give his time to secular affairs, or the management of his mission; he could not help it: but that missionary would not allow secular duties to interfere with his duties as a missionary. The only respect in which he was a loser was a personal one; he remained stationary, whilst others could devote leisure to self-improvement. When he himself returned home, he found he was fifteen years behind his brethren; but, in heaven, that would not matter. With regard to congregations, he had advocated from the beginning, and still advocated, where it was possible, the aggregation of converts in villages. Unless truly converted, firm, and men of experience, they would, if scattered among the heathen, be carried along with the stream. As soon as they had a catechist who could stand alone, they placed him in the village in an independent sphere; and to him, as at Sigra, native brethren would send their children dis-

Indian missions Catholic.

Secular affairs.

Christian villages advisable:

tances of two hundred miles to be educated, and pay for their education. There were difficulties with regard to the association of congregations with pastorships; but those difficulties might be obviated. At Sigra they had three different departments. The first was the judicial; for at the beginning they had to be magistrates, and to inflict punishment. Then a system of two juries was introduced to settle the affairs of the village; and if the people were not satisfied with the decision of a jury, there were the missionaries to appeal to. Every Christian who wished to belong to the community must subscribe to its laws. So, for the last few years, native brethren had managed their own affairs without any difficulty; the missionary had little to do with them; and the more they were thrown back upon themselves, the better it would be. There were poor, and there was a poor-fund; there was a box to receive what the people could spare every Sunday; and there was usually sufficient to relieve distress. There was also established a widows'-fund, to which every one belonging to the community subscribed. There was also a missionary-fund; and all subscribed a certain amount to the mission. A pastoral-fund was wanted, and he hoped that now it would soon be established. As pastor, he had only to do with the spiritual department, and occasionally to look after temporal affairs; and when a jury sat he had to sign the papers. He had an assistant who was the senior-catechist, and who helped him in going from house to house, to speak and pray with the people. Besides him, there were five other assistants. They divided the village, and selected several pious men, each of whom had a certain number of Christians under him, to endeavour to see that all the people attended a place of worship. In this way they were able to superintend the village with the greatest ease. Church discipline was exercised; and perhaps the greatest punishment that could be inflicted was expulsion from the Christian village, in which no one was permitted to live except his walk and conversation were in accordance with the gospel. Thus they were able thankfully to say; "If you want to see Christians, come into our village." As to edifices, he would say erect good, substantial brick buildings: wood was too expensive to be used. There was a difficulty in raising Christians to respectability; but all was done that could be done to help them on. At Sigra, every man must earn his own bread; those who did not, could not belong to the community. Every young man, before marrying, must prove that he is able to maintain a wife, and the girls had their own choice. He might almost thank God for the

marginalia: a Christian municipality: juries: appeal to the missionary. Poor-fund: widows'-fund: mission-fund. House-visitors. Discipline. Buildings. Converts should support themselves:

mutiny, which had helped them on, so that Christians could maintain themselves better now than before. They still remained members of the congregations; and as they were able to obtain larger salaries, they had been enabled gradually to maintain their own pastors. At Sigra, they never had a press which required a European superintendent; but they had a carpet manufactory which was carried on by his wife (Mrs. Leupolt), and a native superintendent. Now there were in the Benares Mission two native churches with native pastors, maintained by the people; and three more churches required native pastors.

and maintain their pastor.

The Rev. R. SPENCE HARDY said:—I always felt a degree of jealousy as to the formation of villages of the kind referred to by one or two brethren. It was thus at the commencement of monachism. The thought was a good and pure one, that, by isolating those who wished to serve God from the evil around them, they might be preserved in their integrity, and glorify God; but I think the whole history of the Church shows it was entirely a mistake, and has worked great evil. I look upon all isolation that can be avoided, as carrying out the same principle I have seen to be evil. The isolation of individuals from the persons around them, and of communities from other communities around them, I think is so much power lost to the general good. It may be for the benefit of the individuals, and for the benefit of the persons connected with these village communities. That I will grant to a certain extent; and then there, I think, we must pause. Some of these individuals would perhaps be overborne by the evil influences to which they would be exposed from the want of a power within them; but as to the greater masses, if they had to battle and fight, and had those persecutions to brave that we read of in the institution of Christianity in all countries, these men would have come out much more prominently than they possibly can do now. Their example would have been more prominent than it can be now; and consequently the influence they would have exercised upon their country at large would have been much more than it possibly can be under the circumstances in which they are now placed. Some of the prejudices I had against the system have passed away since I listened to the details. If in each station there is something like a model village that can afterwards be imitated by natives, as there is no doubt it will be, I say so far the system may be allowed, but no further; except in such cases as are presented by South Africa, where the people are

Rev. R. S. Hardy.

Villages monastic; and a mistake.

Power lost in isolation.

Weak converts benefit;

but communities lose; in strength; and in influence.

A model village useful.

nomads, and must be located before Christianity can be brought before them in its power.

With respect to the teaching of technicalities, it has been said that it cannot be avoided; but let us take into all our intercourse with each other abroad the same principle so beautifully manifested by the present Conference. The echo of the present Conference I should wish to be heard by the world; and it would be, "Behold how good and pleasant a thing it is for brethren to dwell together in unity!" By all means let us have this principle always and everywhere before us, and we shall have God's blessing. There is, however, confessedly, a difficulty with which the missionaries have to contend, arising from the necessity, under the present constitution of the Societies to which they belong, to transfer the church forms of Britain, in their utmost rigidity, to the churches established among the heathen. In all that concerns doctrine, and in much that relates to discipline, there must be uniformity of faith and practice between the several sections of the same church, or confusion and collision will ensue. But there are instances that will recur to the mind of every one, in which the course now referred to has acted as a hindrance to the spread of the truth; and in all cases in which it is impossible for the native mind rightly to comprehend the origin or purpose of our home requirements and regulations, or in which their adoption would be attended by no advantage to the converts from heathenism, and only tend to perplex and puzzle them, it would be a great boon to our native churches to allow of their being disregarded.

Technicalities to be avoided.

In the transfer of English Church forms;

essentials must be retained;

but a rigid adherence to details will hinder and perplex the native Churches.

The Rev. J. H. TITCOMB said:—Mr. Mullens had made one or two remarks in regard to the building of churches by Missionary Societies, which the natives could not keep in repair. So far as the Church Missionary Society was concerned, he believed, it was no longer in the habit of building churches. The churches for native converts were now built out of their own funds, aided by the subscriptions of benevolent individuals in their respective countries. With regard to the more general question of the ecclesiastical constitution of native churches, it appeared to him that it was in the very nature of circumstances that the organisation of the old churches ought to be, and must be, reproduced. Truth must necessarily be encased in some outward form; and if that outward form be of any value at home, it must be worth reproducing abroad. At the same time, there should be a large amount of elasticity, a great amount of latitude, allowed to it. We should

Rev. J. H. Titcomb.

Churches in the Church Missionary Society built by private funds.

Old systems will be reproduced:

elasticity and latitude should be allowed:

in the standards of instruction; and the like.

not cling to every principle we endorse at home in an old country with settled institutions. There may be principles which we fight for here, which it would not be wise to contend for under other circumstances. Suppose a bishop, ordaining native converts, uniformly required of them a knowledge of Latin and Greek literature, he apprehended that would be an instance in which, whilst maintaining the right theory abstractedly, there would be too strict an adherence to it in particular.

Between different Societies, non-interference and co-operation.

It appeared to him that the remarks of Dr. Davis were perfectly just. In cultivating Christianity among the heathen, no missionaries could be expected to abandon their own forms of church government for the sake of external unity. Nevertheless, they ought to abstain from all interference with one another, and from every attempt to gain an advantage for themselves at the expense of the brethren near to them. But might he not go further than this, and say, that it would be well if we

Native churches should be catholic and unsectarian.

could begin the organisation of our native churches, apart from that narrow sectarianism, and those selfish jealousies, of which we have all been so guilty in this country? Ought we not to learn wisdom from an experience of the unprofitableness of all our past divisions and dissensions? Why should these be reproduced in other countries? If we seek liberation from them here, surely we should guard against them there. Surely it

All missionaries the same.

would be well if, while retaining our own views of ecclesiastical arrangements, we could carry them out in a spirit of Christian brotherhood before the heathen; devoid of that bigoted attachment to every minute particular, and that intense feeling of separation, which has too often marked our churches at home. He would impress upon every missionary that, as they were labouring in a common cause, they should do all things for God's glory, and seek to have no emulation amongst each other, except in their love for Christ, and their success in the salvation of souls.

Col. LAVIE.

Native pastors not to be interfered with.

Colonel LAVIE said, as regards the native evangelists and pastors, the less they were interfered with by the European missionaries the better; the period of their probation should be the time for ascertaining their gifts and graces; the greatest care should be taken in recommending native Christians for ordination; but once ordained, let them, according to their qualifications, be placed in more or less responsible positions to develope those gifts and graces. The character of the native is such, that so long as he can rest on the European, he will do so, and not rise; it is far better he should stumble than remain the best part of his life dependent. As regards the native church, it has been hitherto placed under great disadvantages, having so few of its members men of independent character and independent means. The consequence is, that the European missionary has much of his valuable time occupied in investigating acts of injustice, often amounting to great cruelty, perpetrated by Government officials and others against the native members of the congregations. It is impossible for them to remain passive when persecutions arise; and the interference in secular concerns is deprecated by most Societies. Few European missionaries can look on with indifference when they see members of their congregation subjected to gross injustice; and that often for no other reason than that they profess Christianity. This evil may be remedied when India is blessed with European settlers; men living on their own estates, and conducting their own factories. As regards denominational church systems, he was happy to say, in India, so far as he had seen of it, Christians were so few they could not afford to split on non-essentials. Their only inquiry is, does a man preach and teach salvation by faith; and is his life such as to exalt the blessed Saviour? These being decisive, he has found he could work well with any Christian, to whatever denomination he belonged.

Poverty and weakness of the native church hitherto.

Missionaries must help their converts.

Dependence; how to be cured.

Catholicity in India.

The Rev. J. MULLENS said: May I be allowed a word or two of explanation. I must have spoken very indistinctly, if it be thought that I wish to make my brethren Congregationalists, or to lay down, for their adoption, principles which would have the effect of landing them in Congregationalism. Such a thing never entered my head; and such principles of Christian union never came from my heart. I wish to see our systems applied in the most elastic way: and their essentials separated from their local, technical, and historical elements. My friend, Dr. Tweedie, does me a little injustice in thinking I class the principles of the Deed of Demission among the technicalities of the Free Church. Not at all: the principles are very grave ones; but the circumstances of the case form part of that history of Scotch Christianity, which has made the Church what it is. The native brethren, when ordained, may justly be committed to the result, without being asked to commit themselves to the process by which that result was produced.

Rev. J. MULLENS does not wish to lead brethren to one system.

Principles of the Free Church not technicalities.

Co-operation does exist already.

I think, sir, that the position advocated by Dr. Davis is excellent: that there should be division of spheres, division of labour, no interference, a kindly spirit, and hearty loving co-operation. Such co-operation is a great step in the practical union of the Church. But it is nothing new with missionaries abroad. We have attained it already; and have had it long. The point I urge goes far beyond this; though it deals with us not together, but in our separate capacities, as Churches and Societies. I wish that we should be willing to examine into our own deficiencies; to put them aside; and not lay upon our native brethren a burden which we have begun to find too heavy for ourselves.

Adaptation of plans of labour in India.

In respect to our plans of labour, much has been done in this very way already? Look at the position of missionaries in India. They belong to many Societies, many Churches, many denominations. Yet when they have come conscientiously to adapt their plans to their position, to the demands of the people and of their sphere of labour, they have really come to adopt very much the same plans, and to act in the same way. In many of our Indian provinces, if you walk from one mission into another, you can scarcely tell the difference between them.

The same required in churches.

I want the same wise adaptation in respect to the forms of the churches, their organisation, their mode of worship, and their bonds of union.

Must the old denominations be reproduced?

It is said these denominational peculiarities must be reproduced. I should be sorry if it were true. We are beginning to file down their most prominent angles; why should we reproduce them as they are? It is natural that we should start from the platform on which we ourselves stand; but if we reproduce these systems entirely we do the native church a wrong. We ought to do so in such a general way, that if we think it right to retain them at all, we may at the utmost preserve their essential features, and adapt them to local wants.

Rule of the American Board.

The American Board of Missions on this point in clear terms have laid down the principle that their missionaries may adopt those forms of organisation which they prefer, and which they find most suitable.

The essentials which we do require.

Our missions, in all Societies, have been well instructed, are thoroughly scriptural, and well taught in the word. What we want is pure doctrine, a holy life, an earnest zealous ministry, active Christian and missionary churches, growing in liberality, united to each other, sound in discipline, pure in fellowship. May not these essentials coexist with many outward forms? Let us look more to the spirit in our mission churches, and they may attain a way far better than our own.

The Rev. J. SUGDEN said:—I should be happy if the Conference adopted some Address to the native churches throughout the world. Such an address should have a direct reference to our Christian affection and sympathy for them all; and should state in few words the views of the Conference with regard to the subject of self-support; impressing this matter upon them, and referring also to some other questions of vital moment. I would suggest a subject mentioned the other day, that of Temperance; and also that the address should have special reference to churches which are at the present time self-supporting. I believe it would have an important and happy bearing upon churches at home and abroad, if a considerable number of churches could be pointed to as self-supporting and evangelizing. With regard to the teaching of missionaries, I believe that very little attention has been given to matters affecting Church government; and I believe that the great concern of missionary brethren has been to preach the unsearchable riches of Christ. I hope that those who venture, in the exercise of their ministry, to introduce questions affecting principles and modes of Church government, will be just as conscientious in dealing with the several weaknesses of their denominational systems, as in setting forth their excellencies and virtues. With regard to descending to the level of the natives, a man may descend too low; and there have been instances of missionaries who desired, by the adoption of native habits, to increase their influence; but who in the long run have not only diminished their power to do good, but even lost their self-respect, and injured the cause of the gospel. Christian condescension does not involve any sanction, much less any adoption, of doubtful habits, customs, and institutions.

Rev. J. SUGDEN.
Address to native churches from the Conference.
Topics it might contain.
Teaching about Church government:
defects in our systems, to be pointed out, as well as their excellencies.
Missionaries not to go too low.

D. F. MACLEOD, Esq., Financial Commissioner in the Punjaub, observed that, after thirty-two years' experience in India, he had come to the fixed conclusion, that in our administration of that country we had committed no error fraught with more serious results, than that of practically excluding the bulk of the people from all share in the management of their own affairs; and he believed that the difficulty which the missionary brethren found with regard to the establishing of self-government in native churches, was precisely analogous to the difficulty which public officers had

D. F. MACLEOD, Esq.
Difficulty in self-government, the same in missions as in government.

experienced in connexion with the affairs of the Government itself. Though for a century India had been under British rule, up to the present time the whole nation had been kept in a state of pupilage. Now, under the native rulers, there was a most admirable municipal form of government: in point of fact, the only government of India which then existed was one of self-government by the body of the people themselves, under a municipal system, a system which maintained its vitality in the most remarkable manner.

<small>The old municipal system.</small>

We had, unfortunately, virtually put an end to that system; not intentionally, but unconsciously, and through ignorance of the ultimate result of our laws. We had established in the place of the public opinion of the people the authority of our courts, which are now the arbiters of everything; and even where we professed to allow the people any voice, we found that, in practice, our officials prevented their exercise of it, though quite contrary to our wishes.

<small>Our rule has destroyed it.</small>

A very remarkable instance of the effects of our Rule, might be adduced in the fact; that whereas, the "Panchâyet" (a kind of jury) was a most favourite and effective mode of adjudication under native rule, it has become wholly inoperative under ours; and all our efforts to incorporate it with our procedure, by legislative enactment, have hitherto utterly failed; owing, without doubt, to the fact, that we insist on maintaining our right of supervision and control; and so widely are our races apart in sentiment, enlightenment, and power, that this circumstance at once puts an end to all independent action.

<small>Our Courts and appeals override it.</small>

The conclusion he (Mr. Macleod) had come to was, that the chief reason for this state of things is that we insist upon too great perfection, and are not prepared to bear with something of defectiveness in native modes of management. He had himself, in past times, as a public officer, urged that the heads of villages should be invested with authority, to a certain extent, in the suppression of crime and the punishment of slight offences; and that ten or twelve perhaps of the principal or most reliable of these heads of villages should be occasionally collected together for the holding of courts of a superior character, to dispose of complaints of a more serious nature; but his views were always regarded as Utopian, and were not acceded to. His own impression, however, was, that until we did something of this kind, we should never create vitality amongst the people; who would remain, as now, totally estranged in their feelings and distinct in their interests. The

<small>We have looked too high.</small>

<small>His own efforts to restore self-government.</small>

very same thing applied, he conceived, to the Church: the same analogy held good. We expected too much from the natives, and were unwilling to give over everything to them, taking our chance of imperfections. Mr. Leupolt had described a state of things approaching towards self-government; but even in that system there seemed to him to be too much of reservation. We laid down the laws or rules of guidance; we selected men to rule over the communities of converts; and when juries were to be appointed, if we did not actually nominate them, we exercised our influence and control over them. But why not leave them entirely to themselves? Let them select the men they think best, and allow them to make their own laws. These laws and arrangements might be very imperfect; but unless we consented to them, we should never have a robust constitution, either in social or in missionary government. He would strongly advise that we should consent to leave the natives more to themselves in matters of this kind; and from the tenor of Behari's remarks, he gathered that his opinions were shared by that excellent native minister. Observations had been made upon the churches formed in the West Indies, in the Pacific, and in other places, as exhibiting somewhat of self-government; but he called attention to the fact, that we had, in immediate contact with our older provinces in India, a Church which, though perhaps the youngest of all, seemed to have arisen to maturity in advance of all the rest. He referred to the church amongst the Karens. It was marvellous that people, just emerged from barbarism, should all at once have arisen in the most extraordinary manner to a degree of energy, self-government, and Christian enthusiasm, which was seen nowhere else. They selected and appointed their own counsellors, pastors, and teachers; supported them; built churches and schools; and, in fact, managed the affairs of their own communities, which amounted to several hundred. Everywhere amongst them was manifested an indigenous native vigour. An investigation into this subject might elicit much practical and valuable information; and any one who could explain the causes of this great difference between their rate and mode of progress, and that exhibited in other parts of India, would confer a great benefit on the cause of missions. The people of Hindostan had not the simplicity of the Karens; but still human nature was everywhere essentially the same; and if those people were once left to themselves, we should find them exhibiting more or less of the vigour of apostolic times. From the impossibility of our correctly estimating character and

The same principle applies to the Church.

Defect in Mr. Leupolt's plan:

why have any appeal to a missionary.

Let us leave the converts to rule themselves.

Maturity of the Karen churches.

How shown.

What are its causes.

x

Natives will choose the most suitable men.

qualifications, when dealing with a race to whom we are strangers and foreigners, the selections made by the native communities would probably be very different from ours; but he was much mistaken if, in the end, these native selections would not be found by far the best. (Cheers.) Let us, therefore, consider well this subject, and agree, if possible, upon some mode of throwing the natives more upon themselves, not hesitating to allow imperfections. They might at first, perhaps, abuse this authority; but its exercise would create the cure and remedy for such abuse in a thousand ways. (Applause.)

Mistakes will cure themselves.

Rev. H. M. Waddell.

The Rev. H. M. WADDELL said: It should be the desire of Missionary Societies at home that, so soon as missionary churches abroad were prepared to assume all responsibility, they should be left to themselves; and he did not suppose the churches at home would attempt to form organisations for them. He had had something to do with the building up of new congregations, one on each side of the Atlantic; and for himself and brethren he might say, it had always been their desire to promote self-government in a congregation as much as possible: in doing which, they had succeeded as well as any others. He was not sure that the withdrawal of the benefit of their experience from their mission congregations would lead to improved forms of church government. The natives might strike out new and strange, not better, forms for themselves. It was quite a legitimate thing for missionaries to carry out, in a reasonable and moderate way among Christian converts, and in native churches, the systems of the denominations with which they were connected; their own feelings and judgments, and, it might be, their own prejudices, would lead them to it. At the same time, all this might be done in perfect harmony, and that harmony might be promoted, as it was here, by forgetting the historical associations of the different churches. Our native churches had no need to know anything of them; and he was happy to say that, for the most part, the missionary churches harmonised exceedingly well. Discussion might arise, but it might be conducted in a Christian way; and for the most part he thought congregations did not seem disposed to go into anything that would mar their accord.

Mission churches to be left to themselves.

Perhaps improved forms of government will arise.

Historical elements of old systems to be left out.

Rev. S. Hislop.

The Rev. S. HISLOP said, that, while he would rejoice to see native Christians in India gradually accustomed to independent action, yet in considering this question some allowance should be made for the difference of national character. Near his station there were two classes of people very distinct: Hindoos in the plains, Aborigines on the hills. He had come in contact with both; and whatever the Hindoos might become after they had surmounted the evil effects of systems, under which they had been crushed for centuries, there could be no question that, at present, they are a dependent, feeble, and deceitful race, while the hill tribes are manly, energetic, and truthful. Even in Burmah, to which Mr. Macleod had referred, the experience of their American Baptist brethren had by no means been uniform. Among the Karens they had found a people, as it were, prepared of the Lord. Not only were these mountaineers, by their traditions and freedom from priestly institutions, placed in circumstances favourable for the reception of the truth, but, after they had embraced it, by the remarkable energy of their character, directed by God's grace, they were fitted for communicating it far and wide over their native hills. But among the Burmese, in the plains, it was well known there had been no such general willingness to receive the gospel—no such exemplary zeal in diffusing it; and if this had been the case with Buddhists, who were unfettered by caste, was it wonderful that it should have been so with Hindoos, whose individuality and independence had been well-nigh annihilated by the working of that iniquitous system? *In India. The hill tribes independent and truthful. The Karens quite unlike the Burmans.*

Lieut. S. FLOOD PAGE said; that it was with very great deference that he ventured to address the Conference. His apology for doing so was, that several members of Conference were anxious to know something of the work going on amongst the Karens; and that a recent speaker had expressed the greatest desire to know how it was that the Karen churches were, to so great an extent, self-supporting; and how they were able to govern themselves. He had been stationed in Burmah for eighteen months; sixteen months of that time at Toughoo, the chief station of the Karen mission in Eastern Burmah. During that time he knew the American Baptist Missionary, and some native Karen catechists. One main reason that the work had progressed more in the Toughoo district than in almost any other place, he thought, was owing to the fact, that there the Karens, though part of the Burmese empire, never acknowledged more than a very slight allegiance to the Burmese government. Each village governed itself by means of a headman. Doubtless, this system of local government had enabled them to govern themselves in ecclesiastical matters. With reference to the Karen churches being self-supporting, for years there had *Lieut. S. F. PAGE. The Karens. Independence of the Karens of Toughoo.*

been a tradition among them that a white man would come with a book; and whenever they saw a white man with a book, they were anxious and ready to listen to him. The Rev. Mr. Whittaker was quite unable to provide as many catechists as the different villages were desirous of supporting. The Karens build the huts for the catechists to live in, and furnish them with clothes and food; and this is all the pay the catechists get. From May until December it was absolutely necessary that the Karen churches should govern themselves; for, owing to the rains, the jungles could not be penetrated by Europeans. The system followed by the American Baptist Missionaries was to train catechists, and send these catechists as pioneers before them. The Rev. Mr. Whittaker, on one occasion, came to a village where a white face had never been seen, and out of the 300 inhabitants found 130 candidates for baptism: after examination, he baptized only a small number; the remainder, headed by the chief man of the village, followed him for fifteen miles, begging that they might be baptized. The Assistant-Commissioner of the district was, at one time, anxious that a man who valued the English system of government should go amongst the Karens, and prove to them the advantage of attaching themselves warmly to the English. The Commissioner sent for their teacher, by name Sau Quala, known as the "Karen Apostle," and offered him a salary equal to 300*l*. a-year to undertake the office. Sau Quala was not receiving one penny in the way of pay; he had no home of his own, no income, and knew not in the morning where he would sleep, or how he would live; yet he declined the offer, saying, "Suppose I accept it, what will my countrymen say? Will they think I preach the gospel for the sake of Jesus Christ, or because of the salary I get from government? But if you like I will, when in the district, look out for three good, steady men: you can give them the salary; I will not touch it." This, he believed, had since been acted upon.

The wonderful success in this mission was, doubtless, to be very greatly ascribed to the fact, that the Karens were without any religion, and were waiting for one; to their power of governing themselves; and to the system of making the natives pioneers of the Europeans: but it must be especially ascribed to this fact, that it had pleased our Father in heaven that it should be so. And it was what we might have looked for, when we remember the work and labour of love of God's devoted servants, Dr. and Mrs. Judson, and their able successors; when we recall the Karen martyrs hanging on the cross, refusing to deny the Lord that had died for them, and to the last preaching from the cross to the multitudes around them. Dr. Davis had alluded to the fact, that there was room in the mission-field for all to work without interfering with one another; he (Mr. Page) had asked the Rev. Mr. Hazledine, the devoted chaplain of Tounghoo, whether it was his intention to persuade the Church Missionary Society to send a missionary to labour amongst the Karens? He replied, No; God is pleased so to bless the labours of the American Baptists, that I should not think it right to try and take the work from them. Another speaker had alluded to the necessity of union and love between fellow-workers for Christ. The Rev. Mr. Hazledine was ordered to England on medical certificate; there was no clergyman ready to take his place. Captain Bond, Commander of the Madras Artillery at Tounghoo, said to the Rev. Mr. Whittaker, the Baptist, "Will you object to preach to my men? I myself must read the Church of England service; will you come and preach the sermon?" Mr. Whittaker replied, "I am here to preach the gospel of Christ to every man that is willing to listen;" and Sunday after Sunday did this good man preach the gospel to those English soldiers in the building used for the Church-of-England service. The Karen mission is second to none in the world in interest; and in no portion of the world has God's Holy Spirit been more manifestly working with, and blessing the efforts of his devoted servants. *Non-interference: example. Union and co-operation: example.*

In the following MINUTE are embodied the views entertained by the Conference generally, on the subject discussed during the final session:— *Minute.*

MINUTE ON NATIVE CHURCHES.

The subject of native Churches is, in the opinion of the Conference, equally important with that of native agencies already brought before them. Native Churches are the germs of those Christian communities, of those Christianised nations, which, according to the sure word of prophecy, will at length occupy every country of the world. It is therefore of the greatest importance that they should be based and built up, from the commencement, on perfectly sound principles. *Their importance.*

Such Churches should, in their view, be formed of those "faithful men" who make a public profession of their belief in *Members.*

MINUTE ON NATIVE CHURCHES.

Christ, and of their consecration to his service; and who desire together to maintain gospel ordinances for their own spiritual benefit, and as a means of usefulness to others. Guided by the teachings of the New Testament, they should in every land aim to maintain pure doctrine, holy life, and active zeal amongst their members; preserve purity of fellowship by the exercise of proper discipline; and fully support Church ordinances among themselves, as administered by duly appointed officers. From the first, these essential principles should be pressed upon their infant Churches by the missionaries who found them; and from the outset such measures should be adopted as will steadily tend to accomplish the object in view. Depending, not upon distant and foreign Churches, but upon their own exertions and their own spiritual graces; and possessed of those essential elements which underlie the spiritual prosperity of all Christian communities, these Churches may, in the opinion of the Conference, very naturally adopt various modes of worship, various systems of Church order, and different principles of fraternal association.

Aim of their fellowship.

Self-support.

Systems of order various.

The missionary their adviser, not their pastor.

The European missionary is the founder, instructor, and adviser of native Churches; and, except in their mere infancy, ought not to be their pastor. The higher Christian civilization from which he has come; his position as a messenger of foreign Churches, as a man of superior social rank, and as one of a dominant race, render him unfit to be merely their pastor; while they fall in with his influence as an adviser and friend. It is feared that, from the dependence generated by the continued pastorate of a European missionary, many Churches have been kept back from that healthy and vigorous growth which leads to self-support and self-control. Self-reliance grows only by exercise, and learns the most valuable lessons from the experience of mistakes and errors.

National character and customs.

The Conference are of opinion that, in cultivating that self-reliance, and leading it to higher degrees of vigour and of usefulness, missionaries should take advantage of such national customs, notions, and tendencies as will help to foster and render it efficient. The national independence of the Bghai-Karens, and the village municipal system of Northern India, illustrate the importance of this step.

Desiring to see increased the number of native pastors, who are merely superintended by a missionary, they judge that in the management of their various churches these pastors should be freed from all needless control, and encouraged to settle all difficult questions by the prayerful exercise of their own judgment. Until they are entirely supported by their people, such income as the churches can give may well be supplemented to a proper amount, by a grant from the Society which was the means of founding them. But the Conference think that, from the outset, it should be kept in view that, whatever forms of union be adopted by the native churches, in every mission-field, dependence for instruction, ordinances, or discipline upon the mother churches is, in due time, to cease; as it does in the case of colonial churches that have sprung up amongst our countrymen in the different colonies of the British Empire. *[Native pastors to be left free. Salary supplemented for a time. Dependence on Societies to cease.]*

In thus starting forward these new communities of converts on the race of personal and social progress, the Conference consider that everything unsuitable to their national life should be rigidly guarded against. In the salaries given to native teachers and preachers, or sanctioned and supplemented for native pastors and missionaries to the heathen; in the size, style, and cost of church buildings, native parsonages, and dwellings of teachers, due regard should be paid to the customs of the native brethren; and the same scale be adopted from the first as will probably prevail among them when Christianity becomes naturalized. *[Their national customs to be preserved. Salaries, dress, buildings, and the like.]*

In regard to the formation of separate Christian villages in the midst of a heathen population, the Conference are generally of opinion that Christian converts should not be separated from the heathen community; and they believe that the practice in most missions throughout the world has been to keep them mingled with the heathen. Such a practice they deem beneficial to the converts, in testing their principles, making them watchful, increasing their usefulness, and preventing a great deal of evil; it is beneficial also to the heathen by keeping constantly before their view the practical fruits of the new and pure faith which their Christian countrymen have adopted. They allow, however, that in a country like India, where a small, weak church, may be overshadowed by the *[Separate Christian villages, unadvisable. Benefits of living among the heathen.]*

great, powerful, and wealthy system of Hindooism, and where its members are, by the laws of caste, cut off from the ordinary social intercourse still admissible in other lands, such Christian villages may be found useful in securing converts from social disabilities and from very severe trials of principle, in the infancy of their community. But they would urge that this be allowed only for a time; and that as soon as converts grow more numerous and influential, they should be encouraged to dwell among the heathen, in order to leaven them with gospel truth.

<small>Advantage of separation to a little community.</small>

The Conference think that, though not their pastor, and though directly interfering but little in their concerns, a missionary should make the general elevation of the Christian communities an object of continual care; he should watch over their growth in knowledge, their improvement in piety, their purification from heathen vices and deficiencies, and in every way strive to raise the tone of their personal, social, and public character.

<small>General elevation of the Christian communities.</small>

On one important topic laid before them, the transfer of European systems of Church organization to foreign countries, several members of Conference gave it as their opinion, that while a missionary, in commencing the organization of a church, will naturally begin with the system which he and his supporters conscientiously follow, still he should apply it to the new country and the new people with considerable latitude: he should endeavour to retain only its essential features; to rid it of mere technicalities, and of those historical elements which all systems, political and religious, absorb into their constitution in the course of years. It was suggested that, in respect to the ordination of native pastors and missionaries, while the Scriptural tests of character enjoined by the Apostle should be retained in full, the standards of knowledge should have reference to the circumstances of the churches, and of their own training; and that in general all these systems should be judiciously adapted to the communities, climates, and people among whom they are introduced.

<small>European systems of church order; essentials to be retained; technicalities avoided; the systems to be adapted.</small>

The Conference rejoice to learn that in some fields of labour the work of missions has so far been accomplished, that native churches, growing in numbers, knowledge, and resources, are supporting their own pastors; fully maintaining the ordinances

<small>Great progress made by some churches and communities.</small>

of the gospel, supplying seminaries with students for the ministry, and commencing missionary work for themselves. They rejoice to learn that in some places, tried by severe and long-continued persecution, grace has been given according to their day, and the converts, remaining steadfast in their faith, have increased in number daily; and they offer their earnest prayer to the Lord of the whole Church that, while missionaries may be wise to win souls, and wise to guide the churches into which they are gathered, these churches may be greatly increased in number, may be enlarged by the Holy Spirit, and filled abundantly with the fruits of his salvation; and that more largely than ever they may themselves go forth among their heathen countrymen to spread that gospel which has blessed themselves. *Prayer for their increase.*

CONCLUSION OF THE PROCEEDINGS OF THE CONFERENCE.

The Report on the Missionary Lectureship was brought up, and adopted. It was announced that three subscriptions had already been presented towards the establishment of the Lecture Fund, viz.: JOHN HENDERSON, Esq., had promised 250*l.*; R. A. MACFIE, Esq., 100*l.*; and JAMES CUNNINGHAM, Esq., 100*l.* *Lectureship on missions.*

The following Resolution was then moved by the Rev. F. Trestrail, seconded by the Rev. Dr. O'MEARA, and unanimously adopted :—THAT the thanks of the members of this Conference be presented to the numerous Christian friends in Liverpool who have so kindly extended to them their hospitality, and given them such a warm welcome. *Thanks of the Conference to their hosts.*

It was next moved by the Rev. T. SMITH, seconded by the Rev. G. F. Fox of Durham, and unanimously resolved :—THAT the thanks of this Conference be presented to the several Stewards of the Conference for the kind attention paid to their comfort, and the arrangements so successfully made to secure it. *Thanks to the Stewards;*

It was moved by Dr. DAVIS, seconded by the Rev. I. STUBBINS, and carried by acclamation :—THAT the Conference hereby express their grateful thanks to Major-General ALEXANDER for his kindness in taking the chair of the Conference at their request ; *to the Chairman:*

and for the ability and courtesy with which, throughout its sittings, he has presided over their deliberations.

Major-General ALEXANDER briefly responded.

to the Secretaries. The Rev. GEORGE OSBORN said that the Conference, with a grateful recollection of the valuable services of the Secretaries, and without anticipating the duties they would have to discharge when the Conference had broken up, duties that would be of no trivial character, would cheerfully assent to the following Resolution:—
THAT the thanks of the Conference be presented also to the SECRETARIES, who have so admirably arranged the important business of the various sittings; and the other services in which they have been engaged.

Dr. LOCKHART seconded the motion, which was carried unanimously.

Rev. G. D. CULLEN's reply. The Rev. G. D. CULLEN, speaking for all the Secretaries, said:— I express the feelings of those acting with me in these important services when I say, that the kindness and forbearance we have received, during the protracted proceedings, have greatly tended to sustain and encourage us in doing all we possibly could to arrange business, save time, observe order, and secure freedom of expression in these remarkable deliberations. I suppose there has never been such a gathering of brethren from all parts of the world, or from so many different countries and Societies, enjoying such a free interchange of thought and opinion, without any jarring word or painful feeling of regret. The fruit of the Spirit is love, joy, and peace; and we have experienced the blessedness of His presence with us. We esteem highly the expression of your confidence in us, and are happy to have contributed in any way to the success of this Conference.

Resolution on parting. These Resolutions closed the business proceedings of the Conference. The following Resolution was then proposed by the Rev. Dr. SOMERVILLE, and seconded by the Rev. G. OSBORN:—

RESOLUTION ON PARTING.

Privilege in meeting: At the conclusion of the proceedings, the members of this Conference desire to record their devout thanks to their Lord and Master, for his great goodness in bringing them together, and giving them so largely his presence and blessing during their pleasant meetings. They acknowledge with gratitude the great encourage- *benefit from their discussions:* ment in their work, which by their mutual consultations they have been able both to give and to receive : and trust that the information and suggestions that have been laid before the Conference, will tend to increase their fitness, consecration, and zeal in the important work in which they are all engaged. In bidding each *affectionate farewell.* other farewell, the members of the Conference commit each other, with all affection, to the tender mercies of their common Lord ; and would assure each other that they part with increased affection and esteem, rejoicing that they are fellow-workers in advancing the Kingdom of the Redeemer among the heathen.

The Rev. Dr. SOMERVILLE, in moving its adoption, said :—In *Rev. Dr. SOMERVILLE.* proposing this Resolution, I wish that I had had leisure to select terms sufficiently expressive of the feelings which exist in my own mind. But, Sir, this is unnecessary. I believe the sentiments *Feelings inspired by the meetings.* expressed in that Resolution exist in every heart in this Conference. I felt when I came here on Monday evening, and saw the brethren assembled, that we were like the disciples when they met in an upper room, with one accord lifting up their hearts in expectation of the fulfilment of the promise of the exalted Saviour. I do think *Presence and fruit of the Spirit.* that, though we have not seen an external manifestation of the Spirit, we have felt that the Divine Spirit has been in the midst of us, in his gracious influence, giving us wisdom, directing our feelings, and uniting us together in the bonds of brotherly love. I regard the information collected as being of the most important and *Value of the information given.* practical character. It has been drawn from a wide surface, and it has been given in a candid and obviously honest manner. It embodies the results of the experience of many good and practical men. I do not say that we have evolved or settled great principles ; but I think the information which has been supplied is fitted to correct our rules of action where they may have been wrong, or to confirm them where they are right. The substance of that information going abroad cannot fail to have a very useful and beneficial effect. I have been specially delighted with the obvious unanimity *Unanimity on great principles.* existing among us in regard to great and sacred truths ; I have not seen the least difference with respect to the great doctrines of the Gospel of Christ, which, when communicated to unenlightened and perishing men, awaken those feelings, which, nursed from above, mature themselves into the image of God and meetness for the heavenly world. I have seen no essential difference: I have not heard a doctrinal statement to which I have not assented. There

Some differences: are amongst us no doubt differences of external organization which are held conscientiously; but these have not been obtruded in a way that can have offended the feelings of the most sensitive and delicate mind. I have been delighted exceedingly. Some of my friends from Edinburgh know I came hither with no very fervid anticipations: but my best expectations have been more than realised; they have been vastly exceeded, and I am grateful to God that I came. I feel that my heart has been enlarged, and that the Church of Christ

but substantial unity. is after all one church, and that all here acknowledge one Head, one Way, one Service, one Gospel, and one Divine Spirit. We have no hope but in the creating, renewing, sanctifying energy of that one Spirit. Every brother has spoken in language that recognised the

All servants fact that, whatever we do, we do but as servants, as mere instruments; the success is of God. And as, in the first creation, the Spirit brooded on the dark waters, and evolved those beautiful elements, which constitute our material world; so now that same

The Spirit preparing the new creation. Spirit is going abroad, over all our world, diffusing those influences which are to bring forth that new creation which, unlike the other, will never wax old, but be transferred to the eternal state, the admiration and the joy of all pure and happy intelligences. And I have felt here—I cannot sufficiently express it—extreme delight in listening to brother after brother bringing forward statements upon this subject. I feel in parting with these brethren

The prospects before us. that they are brothers in Christ. I have looked back; I have also looked forward: I have thought of that one assembly, standing on the sea of glass, with palms in their hands and crowns on their heads; all human imperfections done away; all bearing the one Divine image; all hearts thrilling with love, perfect love; all beating in unison; and all uniting in giving glory and praise unto Him that sits upon the Throne and unto the Lamb. I trust we are all in the way to that blessed place; and when we reach it, I do not think that any of us, looking back to earth, will regret that we were here. We will feel that on this occasion, during the four days' Conference, we received an impulse that helped us forward on our journey, and that we were encouraged and stimulated in the great and blessed work of the Divine Master, the glories of which we shall then see around us, and in some degree appreciate and understand. But, Sir, in parting with these beloved brethren, let me say, as a United Presbyterian, I am prepared to take every one by the hand and cordially to exclaim: Go on, Brothers, in the work of the Lord, depending upon Him that guides us, and praising God for all His mercies.

The Rev. GEORGE OSBORN, in seconding the Resolution, said:—I wish to say "Ditto" to my eloquent friend who has just sat down. I adopt the sentiments of the mover as well as of the Resolution, and am glad to find that much of what it would have been in my heart to say upon the general subject has been already said. You will permit me to add a word or two, more particularly as I have not troubled you since the Conference commenced. I understood, partly from the terms of the invitation, and partly from some other expressions employed, that it was not considered desirable that those of us who filled official positions at home should take any very prominent or active part in the deliberations of the Conference; but that what was said should be said mainly by our friends and brethren who had been personally occupied as labourers in the foreign field. I trust that the proceedings and deliberations of this Conference will be found to have exercised an important influence in preparing for that great and blessed outpouring of the Holy Spirit, to which all the Churches of Christ have lately had their attention so strongly directed, and upon which, whatever denominational differences there may be, we are all agreed that the whole success of Christian Missions must depend. I trust that the influence, which the harmonious and prayerful spirit of this Conference will exert, will not be confined to this country, but will be felt, not merely through Christendom, but throughout the world. Wherever felt, I rejoice to believe it will be an influence for good; and will have the effect of encouraging our brethren in the labour which God's providence has assigned to them, and of giving them full assurance that they are remembered in the prayers of Christians at home; and that the sympathies of the Christians of this country go fully, strongly, and continuously in favour of all who labour for the spread of Christ's kingdom, by whatever name they may be distinguished amongst men.

Rev. G. OSBORN

Agrees.

The Conference will aid in preparing for the great outpouring of the Spirit.

Its harmony felt through the world:

a great encouragement to missionaries.

The Resolution was unanimously adopted.

Prayer having been offered by the Rev. EDMUND PRUST, of Northampton, the Doxology was sung; the Rev. CANON STOWELL pronounced the benediction; and the Conference separated.

GENERAL PUBLIC MEETING.

FRIDAY EVENING, May 23d.

Public meeting.
At half-past six o'clock a great Public Meeting of the friends and supporters of the Missionary cause took place, in connexion with the Conference proceedings, at the PHILHARMONIC HALL. It was one of the largest Missionary meetings ever held in Liverpool, the Hall being densely crowded in every part. Upon the lofty platform were seated the various members of Conference, and a great gathering of both clergy and laity.

CHAIRMAN.
On the proposal of the Rev. Dr. RAFFLES, made in brief terms, and carried by acclamation,

The Earl of SHAFTESBURY took the chair.

The Rev. G. D. CULLEN then gave out Bishop Heber's Missionary hymn, "From Greenland's icy mountains," which was sung by the audience, the organ accompanying.

The Rev. GEORGE SCOTT, formerly Wesleyan Missionary in Sweden, having offered up prayer,

Major-Gen. ALEXANDER.
Major-General ALEXANDER was called upon to describe, in brief terms, the proceedings of the Conference during their several sittings. He said the members of the Conference had been pleased to elect him as Chairman over the very interesting meetings which had been held during the past week; and he had been requested
Brief statement of the Conference proceedings.
to complete the duty that had devolved upon him, by bringing briefly before that meeting a general statement of the manner in which the Conference had been conducted, and the results to which they trusted it would lead. In the first place, it had pleased
Object in view.
God to put it into the hearts of some of his servants to meet and take counsel together, regarding the best way of giving a new

impetus, if possible, to the work of carrying out their Saviour's command to carry the everlasting gospel to every creature under heaven. All had joined heartily in the task they had set before them. He mentioned no names, not even one that all present would hail, because he felt that he might offend Christian delicacy by a well-meant, but perhaps blundering, compliment, if the inadequacy of his expression should unhappily fall short of the ardent sincerity of his feelings on the subject. The first and great object set before them was the grand commission to make known the glorious gospel of the Lord Jesus Christ, which had been issued for eighteen long centuries; yet hundreds of millions were still living and dying in ignorance and error. This was the deep and solemn thought impressed by those Christian minds which had convened this Conference. Among the objects of their discussion they had considered, first, European missionaries abroad —how to seek for them, how to select them; and having sent them forth, how best to guide them in their several spheres of labour. They had taken into consideration their use of the vernacular languages of the peoples to whom they were sent, the necessity of their acquainting themselves with the customs, manners, thoughts, and religious observances of the different nations to whom they were despatched. In connexion with that topic, they had also deeply and anxiously considered the reflex character of the missionary work abroad upon the Church at home, and on that catholicity in the Church, which they were all most anxious to promote. The next subject considered was, How best to stir up, direct, and work the missionary feeling at home. He would not attempt to describe at length, that which would be published hereafter. The result of their deliberations had not been drawn up in authoritative resolutions, but had been embodied simply in the form of Minutes; for from the beginning it was felt to be essentially necessary not to lay down anything in a dictatorial and dogmatic manner, but rather to give those engaged in missionary matters the practical experience, the Christian knowledge, the wisdom that had been gathered in the different fields of labour throughout the world. Then came the subject of education. That, of course, referred principally to education abroad,—to education, not as a primary object of missions, but as a necessary and indispensable adjunct of missionary work. They had considered the important subject of vernacular literature, as well as English periodicals, tracts, and school-books; also native agency; and how best to obtain and qualify candidates of the right stamp for their

[Marginal notes: The great aim of missions. The missionary and his work abroad. Reflex influence of missionary work. How to stir up missionary feeling. Minutes. Education. Literature. Men.]

own mission work. And that morning they had concluded the whole by considering the organisation of the native churches, and how far it was wise and expedient to impose upon them, in all their rigidities, the ecclesiastical systems which had arisen in our own country. He thought he need not enter into details on these subjects. He might say, that when they assembled, he believed there was a deep conviction in the mind of every member of the Conference, not only of the solemnity, but of the difficulty of what was before them. Men of all the great evangelical missions and from every clime had been present, and had freely expressed themselves, without yet exhausting the subject. Indeed, he might almost say, that they had but so far gone into the past, as to lay a better foundation for the greater efficiency of future missionary effort, and that another Conference may hereafter be deemed desirable. They had had no differences in doctrines. A wonderful unanimity, a sanctified and Catholic spirit had been vouchsafed throughout all their proceedings; a spirit which, he hoped and trusted, would be borne by the various members of the Conference into the several branches of the Church universal, and permeate through the hearts of all the congregations in our land. Were the doctrines and evangelical principles, in which God had, by the presence and power of his Holy Spirit, united the hearts and minds of his servants on this occasion, to be carried forward and through, in preachings from our pulpits, and teaching in our schools and families, the missionary cause would become the cause of all. Protestant Britain would be in the midst of the world as a fountain sending forth the pure streams of the water of life to every kingdom and people under heaven. The purpose for which God has exalted us above all nations, and given us a dominion to the very ends of the earth, would be fulfilled. We should be honoured in carrying peace to mankind, and proclaiming salvation from the rising of the sun to the going down of the same; instead of, as we now are, spreading bloodshed and devastation, in a warfare caused by forcing a soul and body-destroying opium traffic, upon one-third of the human race in China, while in our two viceroyalties we nationally foster Popery in the West, and impede the free course of the word of God, in that which is providentially established for the spiritual and eternal, as well as for the temporal welfare, of the hundred and eighty million inhabitants of our God-given empire in the East.

The CHAIRMAN, who was greeted with loud and prolonged

cheering, then said:—Ladies and gentlemen of Liverpool, when any one is called to preside over such a meeting as this, he is bound as Chairman to consider whether he should say much or little. In my judgment, the present occasion calls upon me to say but little; and for this reason: I can give you no personal experience of my own of the information acquired, or the feelings excited, during the meetings of this Conference, not having been able to attend them. I cannot enter into those important details that have been just sketched out for you by Major-Gen. Alexander; I can only deal in general principles; and it might be sufficient— and I think it ought to be sufficient—that the Chairman, having indicated what is to come, should be allowed to sit down and not weary the assembly by any oration of his own. (Cheers.) But it is the custom, and I must conform to the custom, that the Chairman should say something; and I confess that, when I look at this vast assembly, and when I consider the purpose for which it is brought together, I am moved to call you to feelings of congratulation, and to thank Almighty God that He has put it into the hearts of so many to be warmed by the desire, which all here manifest, to spread abroad his holy name, and bring millions now sitting in darkness to the light and liberty of the gospel. (Applause.) You are here to-day, as it were, a National Synod; you are here to-day collected, the representatives of all branches of the Christian Church,—Baptists, Moravians, Wesleyans, Independents, members of the Church of England, members of the Church of Scotland; branches of all those denominations that love the Lord Jesus Christ in sincerity. That is your symbol; that is your connecting link; that is the principle that guides you; that is the object you have in view. (Applause.) I must say that it appears to me something like an Œcumenical Council of the dominions of Her Majesty Queen Victoria (hear, hear), and I trust that it will be quite as pure in spirit, wiser in conduct, and happier in issue, than most of the Œcumenical Councils that have been held in other times (laughter); and that it will be a great precedent and example to all the habitable parts of the globe to meet together as we have done, every one in his own nation, and see what he can do to spread abroad the glad tidings of salvation from one extremity of the earth unto another. (Applause.) Now, the business of this Conference, so far as I gather it, has been this: to inquire and to conclude in what way the missionary spirit could be best stirred up in this country; in what way the means for bringing that spirit into action could be best raised; and then to see in what manner both could be best directed to the object you have in view abroad. This will be set before you by gentlemen of great personal experience; by those who speak to what they know, and can tell you what they have seen; and I am convinced that their rhetoric and their exhortations will command your sympathies, and will guide your judgment.

<small>Present position of the world.</small>

But, my good friends, do, for one moment, consider the present position of the world. Do consider, that at this moment the numbers of those who do not believe in the name of our Lord are ten, twenty, perhaps thirtyfold, those to whom the knowledge of salvation has been administered. Recollect, that though the state of things be so, the world has been for eighteen centuries in this condition; and, during the latter part of these centuries, it has been in the power of those who hold the truth, having means enough, having knowledge enough, and having opportunity enough, to evangelise the globe fifty times over. And yet they have done nothing of the kind; and now, after eighteen centuries of saving

<small>Only a fraction of its people Christians.</small>

knowledge, we find there is but a small fraction of God's creatures who have any knowledge of his word; and a still smaller fraction who have any desire to make it known. But I hope, when we lay seriously to heart our responsibility; when we consider how much has been given to this nation; and particularly when we consider its energy of heart; when we consider its extent of intellect; when we consider the peculiar character of our people; when we consider the enterprise of England's sons; when we consider the enormous wealth we enjoy; when we con-

<small>Arguments for tenfold vigour in Christ's work.</small>

sider that we have been professors,—ay, and free professors of the Protestant faith for some three centuries; when we consider that we have an open Bible, no man forbidding us (loud cheering); and when we consider that we have means and resources such as never yet fell to the lot of any nation; when we consider that our dominions extend from one end of the earth to the other, that one hand of the Queen rests upon the East and the other hand rests upon the West; when we consider that every enterprise of the kind we have now undertaken has been blessed by God with signal success;—how can we sit still and not tremble under the weight of responsibility that devolves upon us, if we delay for one moment, from the hour at which I am now addressing you, to come forward with tenfold vigour, tenfold resolution, tenfold amount of prayer, praying that God would be pleased to put into our hearts these great designs, and enable us by his grace to bring them to good effect? (Applause.) This responsibility is indeed terrible; this responsibility is more than fearful. Our neglect of it, therefore, would seem to be unpardonable. Nevertheless, in God's mercy, there are indications of a better spirit; and if we could from this day go forth, like John the Baptist, and announce that there was a dawn beyond; that there was something coming that would bring light, and liberty, and shining light to the nations sitting in darkness and the shadow of death; then, indeed, we might have hope; then, indeed, we might have confidence; then, indeed, we might retire to our rest this night, in the full and assured belief that a great, a long, and a glorious period of usefulness and joy was reserved in the service of Almighty God to this great, blessed, and ancient Protestant Kingdom of Great Britain. (Loud applause.) *Our national responsibility. Signs of a better spirit.*

But now, my good friends, while every heathen and benighted soul ought to be to us an object of solicitude and prayer, ought we not to consider, whether God has not given to us a peculiar field for our operations, and whether our principal efforts ought not to be made in that land where lies our principal responsibility? For what purpose, think you, were two hundred millions of heathens consigned to our care in her Majesty's dominions in the East? For what purpose has India been placed under the sceptre of Queen Victoria? Is it that it may add to our idle state? Is it merely for the extension of commerce? Is it merely that India may take our goods, and we receive hers in exchange? Is it not for some greater, mightier, holier purpose than that? Most unquestionably it is. Most undoubtedly that is our duty. (Loud applause.) Ay, and the nation at one time, almost to a man, recognised that great and sacred obligation. Well do I remember the time when the mutiny in India had carried terror to every man's heart. Well do I recollect that many men who cared no more for Christianity than they did for the ground they walked upon; many such men said to me,—"Clear it is, that nothing is left for the saving of that empire but that the people should be Christianised: we must introduce the Christian religion among them; that will be the true conservative principle, and will bind the people of India to the throne of Queen Victoria." (Loud applause.) Ay, they said that; many said it in sincerity and with deep devotion; many said it in mere policy, and as a temporary expedient. The mutiny subsided, and so subsided their convictions, and a greater deadness ensued after the mutiny than existed before it; and soon,—ay, and rapidly soon, shall we lapse into that nondescript, that inconceivable, that wild condition called Government Neu- *One special sphere: India. Why given to England. Obligation felt during the mutiny. Convictions have grown dull.*

trality. (Hear, hear.) Recollect, my friends, that Government neutrality will shortly become national neutrality (hear, hear); that Government indifference will shortly become national indifference; ay, and that Government sin will shortly become national sin. (Hear, hear.) After all, what is this neutrality? Neutrality is a word you may read in the dictionary; and neutrality is a thing you may find in the grammar. But neutrality in the moral life of man is a thing that cannot have existence. (Applause.) Politicians talk of neutrality, because they delight in mutual mystification. (Laughter.) But neutrality in religion is impossible. (Applause.) A man must either believe or disbelieve. If he disbelieves, he is an infidel; and that is an end of the matter. If he believes, he is bound, by every consideration of heaven or of earth, with all his soul, with all his heart, with all his mind, with all that he possesses, with all that he covets, with all that he can lay his hand upon, by every energy of body and soul, he is bound to do all that in him lies, in a legitimate way, to labour that the Word of the Lord may have free course and be glorified. (Applause.) This union of all evangelical and orthodox denominations is a great sign of the times. (Hear, hear.) It shows that there is a mighty effort directed to one single view, and that, the holiest and the purest that can enter into the mind of man. Setting aside all externals that are non-essential, and looking to the internal that is indispensable, these churches set before them the one single object of preaching Christ crucified to every ignorant soul on the surface of God's earth. It is a great discovery to have made, that we can have a common feeling; that we can have a common heart; that we can have a common action; that we can have a common sympathy; and this, because we know that we have one common Master; and therefore we can have a common affection and a common labour towards the attainment of this great and mighty end. This great union is one mighty protest against idolatry, against indifference, against sluggishness in all matters of religion. Nay, it is more than a protest against them; it is a great combination; it is one great aggression against the strongholds of Satan. The time is past when we should stand in an attitude of resistance. The time is come when we should go forward, and show that the Kingdom of Heaven may suffer violence, and that the violent may take it by force. (Hear, hear.) The attitude of resistance sometimes is necessary, but it is always more or less the attitude of weakness. I remember well the great Duke of Wellington saying to me one day, when discussing the question of the frontier between our provinces and those of the Burman Empire: "I advise the Government to take that point; because, take my word for it, no point is ever good for defence unless it is equally good for attack." And if that be true in military matters, it is still more true in religious matters. Let us no longer stand in this attitude of resistance; in this quiet attitude of waiting what may come; but let us go forth boldly and courageously to attack all that is before us; and there is no doubt that the whole thing will fall,—ay, and more speedily than we are aware of, before the united efforts of this combined attack. (Applause.) But if you go forward, there must be no shrinking; there must be no hesitating; there must be no looking back; no falling off to the right or to the left; and no pause in the great work when begun. Why should you pause? I ask you whether, in the history of the world, there was ever a time, whether it be in the old country or in the new, whether among nominal Christians or those sitting in heathen darkness; was there ever a time when men's minds seemed more ready to receive good impressions? Was there ever a time when men were more inclined to listen to the truth; when there was a greater opportunity offered; when a wider sphere was opened for the efforts of the missionary? Never, I believe, was there a time more favourable. All things are far more advanced than they were. It hath pleased God to remove many obstacles and to give many facilities. All spiritual things are as good as they were; the prospects of the future are as powerful as before; but all secular things, and the condition of the world itself, open ten thousand means, present ten thousand advantages in the present day, that we never enjoyed in any antecedent period. Ah! but you must turn your minds very seriously to the state of things in the world around us. It deeply concerns your temporal peace. It deeply concerns the security and enjoyment of yourselves and your children. Can any be blind to the stirring events taking place in every nation under heaven; can any one be indifferent to the perils that surround us; can any one feel secure under those mysterious movements that are taking place, and that leave us in doubt from day to day whether we shall be to-morrow in a state of peace or in a state of war? Can anybody hesitate to believe that some great conflict—(who can decide the form and pressure of it?)—can any one hesitate to believe that some great conflict of the nations is at hand? Can any one hesitate to believe that some great judgment is impending upon all peoples? It may fall lighter upon some and heavier upon others. It will fall lightest upon those (though all, perhaps, will feel the scourge) who in the day of trial will be found watching, engaged,—if not all, at least ten out of the city,— engaged in watching, and in their Master's service. (Applause.) I do implore you to put your shoulders to the wheel. I do implore you to be more earnest and active in your endeavours. I implore you to be more intense, and earnest, and devoted in your prayers. I implore you to have more constantly, more unceasingly, more vigorously before you, the great work that has been opened to you this evening. It is for temporal, as well as for eternal things, the one great object of our existence. It will give you security; it will give you peace; it will save you in the great trial and danger that is coming on; and if at that hour when the judgment shall arrive, you be found busily engaged in the work of the Master, then, after a period of suffering and purification, you will, by the blessing of the Almighty God, be found to be an acceptable—aye, and an accepted people. (The noble Chairman resumed his seat amidst rapturous applause.)

Major DAVIDSON, formerly of Bombay;—It has been hinted during the deliberations of this memorable Conference, that India has, perhaps, been too strongly represented; especially as we profess to deal with missionary work in all parts of the world. But I would bring to the recollection of this meeting, as your lordship has already done, that while "the field is the world," India is that portion of the field for the culture of which England is peculiarly responsible. Is not India a part of the British empire; and have not the heathen millions of India, as our fellow-subjects, a peculiar claim upon our sympathy? I will not apologise, then, for speaking of India. On the contrary, I cannot find words to express our deep responsibility with respect to that great country; and if ever there was a period when our position with respect to India was more than usually interesting, it is the present. God has, in his wondrous mercy, restored that land to us. God has once more put us on our trial, and it will be an awful thing for England, if she fail to render a better account of her stewardship in the future than she has done in the past. (Hear, hear.)

My Lord, I have spent the best years of my life in India. Half of that period I was engaged in the prosecution of a work, which had for its object the relief and improvement of the agricultural population. Although the prosecution of this work required me to give up the society of my countrymen, and to live in comparative solitude, without the amenities of social and civilised life, yet I look back on those days as among the happiest of my life; and on the gratitude and affection of that simple people, as a precious and unlooked-for reward. (Applause.)

My Lord, I love and respect the rural population of India. I see in them the elements of a great people; and I could wish that my countrymen were better acquainted with this portion of their fellow-subjects; but the fact is, that while the agricultural classes form the great body of the people, and contribute the bulk of our revenue, they are the class who, of all others, have been least known and most sadly neglected. (Hear, hear.) For example, I would ask, what has been done to educate these people, and so to elevate them in the scale of moral and intellectual worth? Some slight efforts have been made by Government in the way of education; but these efforts have been almost entirely in favour of a class who, for ages, have sucked the life-blood out of these simple villagers. In other lands the tax for education has been chiefly a tax upon the rich for the education of the poor; but in India it has been exactly reversed, and the poor and industrious cultivator has been taxed for the education of the indolent and supercilious Brahmin. (Hear, hear.) The result of this system is, that the Government native agency is composed almost entirely of Brahmins; and so great is the influence of these men, that the cultivators, among themselves, speak of our Government as the Brahmin *raj*, or Brahmin reign.
Character of its rural population:
they have been greatly neglected:
oppressed by the Brahmins:
and for their gain.

Let the Church be careful to avoid the same error; and let me urge that redoubled efforts be made more effectually to reach this interesting portion of the people. They are living in the most primitive condition, reminding one of the patriarchal ages; and who can venture to say they are not in a favourable condition for the reception of the gospel? The Bible is to them the most attractive of all our books. Its histories and illustrations have the clearest light thrown upon them by the customs and incidents of their every-day life. Indeed, in many respects they can understand the Bible better than we can. (Hear, hear.) This fact was brought strikingly before me by an occurrence which came to my notice when I was living among them. An officer, engaged in the same work with myself, had occasion to take a long ride through a part of the country that had been rarely visited by Europeans. He halted at a village in order to escape the hottest hours of the day; and sitting down in the usual resting-place for travellers, the village temple, he entered into conversation with some of the villagers who happened to be there. The news soon spread that a *gora sahib*, or white gentleman, who spoke Mara-
Their condition.
The Bible most suitable to them.
Illustration
Visit of an officer.

thee like a native, was sitting in the temple; and in a few minutes the whole village, men, women, and children, flocked to see and hear this wonder.

His talk with them.

To their surprise, he not only conversed freely with them, but he could talk about all their processes of husbandry, knew the nature and peculiarities of the soil they cultivated, the tenures by which they held it, and, in short, was familiar with all the outs and ins of their village life. In the course of this conversation one of the natives asked him if he knew anything about Yoosuph, which is the native name for Joseph. This surprised him; and the more so, when on further conversation he found that many of them were quite familiar with the history of that patriarch. On asking how they had got this information, he found that one of their number, when on a visit to a distant European station, had

The History of Joseph:

got possession of a tract entitled *The History of Joseph*. It was, in fact, a simple extract of the Bible narrative translated into Marathee. Unable to read himself, he got the *koolkurnee*, or

very popular with them:

village clerk, to read it for him; and it was liked so much, that he and his fellow-ryots used to assemble in the evening by the village well, while the koolkurnee read and read again the inspired story of Joseph and his brethren. (Cheers.) To them it was peculiarly interesting. They knew too well from their

its case, their own.

own sad experience what famines were. Within the precincts of their village were the *pekows*, or underground granaries, for storing grain against such emergencies; and they had, in the place of Pharaoh, the hard-hearted village corn-dealers, to dole out to them, at famine prices, just grain enough to keep them alive and to furnish seed for their fields. In spirit, the picture drawn by the inspired penman was one for which they might themselves have sat; and it is an interesting fact, that some of them stated their conviction that the God of Joseph was the only true God. (Cheers.)

They should have the Bible.

Now, My Lord, I trust I have shown that the Bible is peculiarly suited to the natives of India. How important is it, then, that they should be taught to read, and that the Bible should be put into their hands. Let us do this; let the people of England insist that education be made available to their fellow-subjects in the East; and then may we look for the Holy Spirit to do his blessed work, and to write the words of that book on the hearts of the people.

Hope for India.

My Lord, I have great hope with respect to the future of India. It is part of the inheritance which God has given to his Son, and his Son will assuredly claim it. Much prayer has been put up for India, especially of late; and I am a humble believer in the irresistible power of prayer. (Applause.) The blood of native Christian martyrs has been freely shed in India, and will shortly prove the seed of a glorious church, gathered from among the heathen, to Jesus. (Cheers.)

Often, My Lord, in my solitary rides over the vast plains of India, I have watched the first streak of light that indicated the approach of day. Methinks I now see in that dark horizon a streak of light, which, though faint and feeble, is the harbinger of a glorious dawn! Yes, the Sun of Righteousness will soon arise on India, with healing in his wings, and will dissipate the thick darkness that so long has brooded over that deeply interesting land! (Applause.) *The dawn coming.*

The Rev. JOSEPH MULLENS, of Calcutta, next addressed the assembly as follows:—My lord, ladies, and gentlemen, I stand upon this platform as the representative of my missionary brethren. At this meeting wise and experienced officers of our various missionary Committees, as well as clergy connected with our home churches, will plead before you the obligations of that great and glorious work in which we are engaged; but I stand here to speak a word in the name of those numerous brethren, whom the providence of God has brought together at this time, from their various fields of missionary labour in many and distant lands. At least six times have I begged to be excused from occupying a position so difficult before this immense audience; but the work has been pressed upon me, and however unworthy, I cannot refuse to say one word in respect to the features which our glorious work is of late years beginning to assume: though an Indian missionary, however, I shall to-night leave my own sphere of labour, to deal with our missionary work at large. During this most memorable Conference, there have been gathered in Liverpool no less than thirty-seven missionaries from various parts of the world. One of our brethren has come from among the Red Indians, in the snowy settlements of Upper Canada. Another has told us of his experience in the Islands of the South Seas; the only representative of that great band, of whose lowly labours and marvellous success we have now been accustomed to hear great things during a long course of years. Two brethren have laboured amidst the tropic heat of the West Indies and the swamps of the Gulf of Guinea; another has spent years of solitary toil among the Buriats of Siberia. Two have visited us from *Rev. J. MULLENS.* *Speaks in the name of the missionaries.* *Thirty-seven present.* *Where from.*

Caffreland; and one from the city of Damascus. Two of our honoured brethren, distinguished as Medical missionaries, who have laboured long on the coast of China, represent the eighty missionaries of all Societies at present living on the seaboard of that thickly-peopled empire; and more than twenty of us have resided in the various provinces of India. I find that, without exception, we have enjoyed intensely the delightful meetings of this Conference; that we have all benefited greatly by those solemn and searching discussions, which we have held with each other, with the valuable and experienced Secretaries of our many Societies, and with other brethren who have shared in these deliberations; and I believe that in us all the result has been, only to lodge more completely, at the very bottom of our hearts, the solemn conviction, that there is nothing in this world so great and glorious as the work of the missionary; and that, by the grace of God, if our brethren at home continue their confidence in our character, our purposes, and our plans, we will go forth with fresh energy and fresh consecration, with a deeper earnestness and a heartier love, to become once more the messengers of the churches, and the servants of the Lord Jesus Christ. (Applause.)

Impressions received by them:

Their resolves.

The union prevalent:

My lord, it needs not that much should be said about that delightful union which has been exhibited in such practical forms during the proceedings of this Conference. Very little was said about that union there: the thing itself was so obvious: we made very few professions of affection and good feeling towards each other. We stood on higher ground; and from the first, recognising ourselves as a single body, though representing many churches and many agencies, we sought to bring all the materials and the results of our experience to bear upon that work of salvation, which we felt to be the object of our highest admiration and of our most devoted love. Our union has been of the closest and most practical kind. We have gone over all our plans; we have discussed the suitability of our various agencies to the many spheres of labour in which we are engaged; we have endeavoured to count our gains; to see where the obstacles to our work lie, and what is the blessing of the Spirit that has been poured upon our efforts. The practical union that has been thus exhibited in our deliberations is, I am happy, as a missionary, to say, nothing new among the servants of God in foreign lands. (Applause.) Many here are aware that it prevails extensively in India and in China, where numerous missionaries of several Societies are found labouring together. For instance, the missionaries of all Societies residing in

its practical character:

not new in missionary fields.

the three great cities of India, Bombay, Madras, and Calcutta, are accustomed to meet each other month by month, for homely discussions of the very kind which we have been carrying on in Liverpool. In our various labours we strive to co-operate on system. It is a RULE with us that we should work together. Because, my lord, we all feel, that if there be any place in the world where the disciples of Christ, whilst respecting to the fullest degree each other's conscientious convictions, should yet endeavour to show, that there is to those disciples but one Lord, one faith, one baptism, one God and Father of all, one aim and purpose in their Christian life, and above all, one love to the perishing souls around them; it is when we stand face to face with those gigantic systems of heathenism, by which the devil has enslaved the minds of millions during a long course of ages. Before those giant systems of error, our differences of organisation grow small. If we are separated by varying judgments on the externals of the gospel, we are all one in relation to its great heart. In the awful darkness of heathenism,—darkness that may be felt,—'tis only the "children of Israel" who have light in their dwellings. That golden light streams on us from the Cross; and, therefore, "the children of light" cling more closely to each other, and to the Great Master, whose compassion to lost souls is their own ruling motive in that fearful gloom. Stirred up, therefore, by the exhortations of the Word of God, and feeling that the peculiarities of our position draw us much nearer to each other, I believe that throughout the world at this time it is not only the solemn conviction, but the standing practice of all missionaries, not only that they shall love each other as brethren, but, as far as ever they can, that they shall work together for the same grand and glorious end,— the salvation of the dying world around them. (Applause.)

Instances in India.

Co-operation is the rule.

Why:

in the presence of idolatry they feel ONE:

cling to each other:

and do one work.

In prosecuting that work of compassion, my Lord, how numerous are our encouragements. What a glorious position do we now occupy compared with that in which the fathers and founders of our Missionary Societies stood when they commenced it only a few years ago! Our modern missions are only sixty years old, and already we see the face of the wide world rapidly changing under their mighty influence. I doubt, my lord, if through those labours a single convert had been made before the year 1800. Dr. Carey had gone to India; his few brethren had joined him, and they had settled at Serampore as the centre of their labours. A few of our brethren had sailed for the South Sea Islands. There were one or two in Africa, one or two in the West Indies, and the rest of

Position of modern missions.

Contrast in 1800

the dark world was an awful blank. But now we look abroad upon the earth, and, without reckoning the work carried on in our English colonies, we see at this moment 1600 foreign missionaries from Europe and America labouring in heathen countries and in many languages; the hand of the Lord has opened their way. As one result of our work, we have already gathered 200,000 communicants, in many thousands of native churches. Including them, more than a million of converts, young and old, who otherwise would have lived in heathenism and died in despair, are now sitting beneath the banner of the gospel, rejoicing in Sabbath ordinances, and all the blessed privileges that cluster round the gospel of Christ. (Applause.) Our work began, my lord, amidst the apathy of friends, and the loudest obloquy on the part of our enemies. Society in England was thoroughly devoted to worldliness, and steeped in the most shameless wickedness and vice. Beau Brummel and his crew ruled in the world of fashion. French infidelity, the great product of the Revolution, was all the rage among the so-called thinkers of the day; an infidelity which found its way to our colonies, and to the English settlements in India; and which there, as elsewhere, brought forth its bitter fruit. But just when the enemy had come in like a flood, the Spirit of the Lord lifted up a standard against him (applause); and now, thanks be to God, that glorious standard has been lifted high; and all branches of the Christian Church, throwing aside their doubts and casting away their apathy, are delighted to enlist in its service and to go forth under the Great Captain of our Salvation, conquering and to conquer idolaters in his name. (Cheers.)

How great the work which has already been accomplished! We go to one part of the earth, where the missionaries followed the track of Captain Cook. Island after island, tribe after tribe, have cast away their idols; and all the children are growing up, like our own, entirely ignorant of the idols, the temples, and the cruel systems that were honoured by their fathers. (Cheers.) More than two hundred thousand Christians are now gathered into the Church of Christ in those many islands, by the four great Societies that have laboured to convert them to God. These new converts, young in the faith but active in zeal, are drawing on towards that position at which we all aim; their native churches are striving to provide for their own native ministers; and they are constantly sending men, drawn from their own number, to be missionaries in the islands far to the west, that still lie in the darkness of cannibalism and heathenism. (Applause.) Amongst other things stated during the Conference, the delightful fact was mentioned, that our brethren of the American Board, who have laboured with so much success in the Sandwich Islands, have for some time been planning to reduce considerably, in those islands, their staff of American missionaries. Eighty thousand people in the Sandwich Islands, the entire native population of the group, now profess Christianity like ourselves. They gather together in churches like ourselves; every place is provided with its own schools; numbers of native pastors preside over the worship and discipline of those churches; the Sabbath is kept better than in London; the Bible is the standard of public and social law; and now our brethren have received fair warning, that only a small number will for the future be maintained in those islands; to train a native ministry, to expound difficulties in the Scriptures, and to act as advisers, guides, and overseers of the weak faith and imperfect knowledge of the native churches, until their services are no longer needed. (Applause.) *[Sandwich Islanders all Christians. Missionaries will soon leave them.]*

We go to Africa; and where, at the beginning of this century, the Hottentot, and Fingoe, and Kaffir, were shot down without mercy, there we find a people, 100,000 in number, saved from destruction, brought to Christ, and adorning the doctrine of the Saviour whom their fathers never knew. (Cheers.) We go to the Negro settlements in the West Indies. How many thousands there have become Christians; redeemed not only from the slavery of earth, but from the slavery of sin. They who only thirty years ago were sold in the open market, have proved the most liberal supporters of gospel schemes that the modern Church has known, and were the first converts to maintain ministers of their own. Only seventeen years ago the various ports of China were open to gospel teaching for the first time; and now we see in those ports no less than eighty Protestant missionaries of many churches working for Christ. Already, in the course of those seventeen years, they have been permitted to gather into their churches some 1400 communicants, and 3000 Chinese Christians. We pass on to Burmah; and there we find rejoicing in the light and liberty of the truth, 100,000 Karens; every one of whom, thirty years ago, was entirely ignorant of its very existence. There they are, meeting like ourselves on the Sabbath; working like ourselves for their ignorant brethren; supporting their pastors with the most active and self-denying zeal; contemplating the destitution of their heathen countrymen with compassion; and sending forth one and another of their brethren, with their lives *[Success in Africa: in the West Indies: in China: in Burmah:]*

in their hands, to preach Christ among the barbarous tribes, still living in the mountains and the dense jungles of their own wild land. (Applause.) We pass on to India; and again we see, in several provinces of that great empire, churches and Christians gathered, and the foundations of a large and great work in the future, laid by the hand of missionaries who have been working there for many years. Obstacles to our entrance, to our permanent residence, to our safety in the country, have all passed away; and, blessed be God, after the appalling history of the recent mutiny, we rejoice to know that India has found, not only order and peace, not only the services of faithful missionaries within her own borders, but has at last found a place, deep and firmly fixed, in the hearts of our brethren at home; and we feel sure that, when the claims of that mighty continent are faithfully pressed upon them, our voice will be heard and a hearty response given to our appeal. (Applause.) And let us not forget the successful toil of our brethren in Turkey, to revive the decayed churches, and to grapple with Mahommedan error at its very heart. (Applause.)

Further: Not only may we rejoice in these great successes; but, with all my missionary brethren here present, I cheerfully acknowledge, that in securing them, we have been largely indebted to our native brethren, working side by side with us, in these fields of labour. We were told in very affecting terms by Dr. Tidman, the other day, to look at the poor island of Madagascar. More than twenty years ago the English missionaries were driven from that island by the unrighteous queen, and scarcely fifty native Christians were left behind. They possessed but very small portions of the Word of God, some little tracts, and a few hymns. They have been bitterly and unrelentingly persecuted with Satanic cunning and Satanic hate. They have been fined, imprisoned, degraded, and made slaves; they have been poisoned by the tangena-water; they have been speared to death; they have been cast over lofty precipices; they have been burned at the stake, while the glorious rainbow arched the heavens and inspired them with more than mortal joy; they have given more than a hundred martyrs to the Church of Christ: but, far from being rooted out of the land, while, twenty years ago, when the persecution began, there were not fifty Christians on the island, it is believed that there are now at least 5000: all of whom have been raised up by the special blessing of the divine Spirit upon the teachings of native agents and the secret study of God's holy

Word. (Repeated applause.) We pass away to the island of Tahiti; and there we see that, whilst French Popery has endeavoured to exert its influence, and to present its blandishments, to those who were despised as the poor and ignorant natives of the country, they have adhered most faithfully to their Protestant religion. We find that when the missionaries were compelled to leave the country, their own native pastors came forward; received from heaven all the grace ever promised to Christ's children in the time of need; and at this hour, in spite of French Popery, and in spite of French brandy, the members of the Tahitian churches are more numerous than when the missionaries were compelled to leave them. (Applause.)

in Tahiti also:

success of the native pastors.

Lessons taught us by success.

I might allude to other facts of a similar kind; but these will suffice. I merely seek, in the name of the missionary brethren around me, to direct your thoughts to a few of those great results with which the Spirit of God has been pleased to bless our labours. In looking at these things; and finding, in our discussions, not only how important, how efficient, our plans have been rendered, but how well calculated they are to secure the great end for which missionary agency has been appointed, we have no desire to boast. If we have learned anything during the discussions of this week, we have learned that all boasting is utterly excluded: we have rather learned, from our successes, and from the marvellous grace poured upon our fields of labour, notwithstanding all our short-comings, to lie more low than ever before the footstool of that Redeemer, who condescends to accept our poor and imperfect service in his cause. Whilst, therefore, my Lord, I speak of the changes that have passed over missionary fields; whilst I allude to one great fact and another, here and there, that exhibits the substantial progress of the gospel, I desire not to be lifted up, but to feel more deeply than ever,—"Not unto us, O Lord, not unto us; but unto thy name give glory." Henceforth, I trust, on the part of missionaries, on the part of our committees, of our ministers at home; on your part, Christian brethren, and on the part of all churches of Christ throughout this favoured kingdom, there will be but one feeling and one purpose: that because of these things, we will give ourselves with fresh humility, with purer motives, with more complete consecration, with more earnest prayers to the work of Christ; and that, like the Apostles, the model missionaries of ancient times, we will go forth, more than we have ever done, to spend strength, time, experience, wealth,

Not boasting, but humility:

praise to God:

and more complete consecration.

completely and without reserve, in the service of our Divine Master. (Applause.)

If that be our resolve; if, in looking back to the past we only learn to derive greater strength, greater faith, greater humility for the future, what a glorious day must be secured in answer to our petitions, and in accordance with the promise of God himself: "All nations which thou hast made shall come and worship before thee, and shall glorify thy name." Not only the uncivilized tribes; not only the barbarous and scattered populations of the earth; but the great races and the mighty people, that fill the provinces of empires like India and China, shall all come to Him. The learning, thought, and skill of China shall all be sanctified to the Lord. Even India itself, poor erring India, after her long wandering, her fearful systems of superstition, her slavery of opinions, her multitude of vices, her awful ignorance and degradation, shall be brought safe home to Christ. From the lofty range of the Himalaya, crowned with the stainless snow, and clothed with redundant forests of the soft, feathery pines; from the towering crags, where the pure, crystal air, wafted from icy caverns, breathes life and vigour into the weary invalid; across the heated plains, where for ages the hand of violence has stained the earth with blood; over countless fields, tilled by a teeming population of precious souls, whose willing hand shall cover the smiling soil with richest harvests of waving corn; over mighty cities filled with the beautiful products of ingenious skill; over cities now marked by the lofty towers of Hindoo temples, the gilded pagodas of Gaudama, the marble mosques and jewelled palaces of Mahommedan kings; down to the very verge of the land, where the dark Ghauts, clad in dense jungle, yet lightened by silver waterfalls, o'ershadow the sand-fields of Christianized Tinnevelly and the green slopes of Travancore, with their glorious forests of waving palms;—over all these noble provinces, rich in material wealth, but richer far in their priceless heritage of immortal souls, the Redeemer shall extend his mighty march of love. Joy, righteousness, and peace, shall spring where'er he treads. Gorgeous in its tropic beauty, but lovelier far in the rich adornments of his jewellery of grace, the land shall pass under his perfect sway; all wrongs redressed; all sins forgiven; saved from destructive errors, the multitude of its immortal nations, with hymns of jubilee shall bend before his feet; the crowns of every city, every province, shall be clustered on the Saviour's brow; and, in spite of the crimes of ages, his children brought home at last, the Redeemer shall behold the work of his bleeding cross accomplished: "He shall see of the travail of his soul, and SHALL BE SATISFIED." (Loud and protracted applause.)

Lieutenant-Colonel HERBERT EDWARDES was next called on to address the meeting, and was received with tremendous and repeated cheers. He proceeded to speak as follows:—My Lord, and ladies and gentlemen of Liverpool, our noble Chairman has given good advice to all the speakers at this meeting, that they shall speak what they do know; and, having myself recently come from the scene of the Indian Mutiny, and believing, as I do, that that great mutiny throws a bright, though indeed a lurid, light upon the great object for which this Conference is assembled, I think that I cannot do better than direct the few remarks, with which I shall trouble you, to the lessons which I think England may learn from that great war. (Hear, hear.) Friends and fellow-countrymen, you know as well as I do the history of India's past. You know that it is now somewhat more than a century ago since God gave the empire of India to us on the battle-field of Plassy. Within that century you know well what changes have come over that empire. It is told in all our histories, and in all our schools; it is learned how we found a shivered empire; how we bound that empire up; how we absorbed its rebel governors; how we introduced justice where we found violence and crime; how we have abolished some of those cruel and bloody rites which debased the land; how the perfidious crime of Thuggee; how the bloody custom of infanticide, by which the chiefs of tribes, from the mere pride of lineage, murdered their infant daughters by thousands, in order to prevent the possibility of their contracting inferior marriages, have, under English rule, been thoroughly abolished. With all these things you are familiar. And far be it from me to undervalue those great triumphs of our country's labour. They are, indeed, noble triumphs of English civilisation. They witness to a true heart of humanity; they witness, in spite of ourselves, to a true feeling of Christianity, which we cannot repress, although we try to do so; they tell that the Englishman, wherever he bears rule, will carry with him some of that Christianity which he has drunk in with his mother's milk. Still, in spite of these efforts, we must all know, —if we are honest men, and will dare to look the matter in the face we must all know, that there are duties which we have not

Lieut.-Col. EDWARDES.

Missions illustrated by the mutiny.

Growth of our Indian Empire.

England's moral triumphs:

Effect of our Christianity.

Our duty to India.

z

performed towards that country. (Hear, hear.) I take it, fellow-countrymen, that that country was not given to us,—one hundred and eighty millions of our fellow-creatures were not handed over to our charge, purely for our own benefit. It was not merely that we should enrich our land with commerce; it was not merely that we should provide for our sons and daughters; it was not to gratify the lust of conquest and the pride of our own nation; nor was it that we should abolish those crimes and hideous customs, and cover the country with roads and telegraphs: these were not the objects for which God gave empire to us in India. I do believe, in the bottom of my heart, that that empire was given to England because we were the country of the open Bible. (Hear, hear, and applause.) If you look in the page of history, you will see that other foreign nations preceded us to that land, and yet they have not now got a footing in it. We have succeeded to the charge; and why? I conceive it is because we have sternly, and after bloody contests, held fast our Protestantism and our Bible. We have had it open, and insisted on having it open; and fought for it that our children should hold it; and I conceive God looks down on this people and says,—"Here is a people that values the open Bible, and I will give the charge of that great empire to them."

But have we fulfilled this charge; have we met our responsibilities? I tell you, with the Chairman, that it has been, from the very first, our English policy in India to conceal this Bible, and, if possible, hide its light. We have taken up at the very beginning, with that devil-fearing, God-dishonouring policy of neutrality in religion. Our Government has endeavoured, if possible, to keep the very name of Christianity from the natives. Shiploads of missionaries went out, and shiploads were driven back again. The great Judson went out with his brave countrymen; and does it not call a blush on every face, when I say, that Judson was not sent out from these shores, but from our cousins in America, who have not one acre of land on those shores, but who feel what we have been so slow to feel, the responsibility of Christians and Protestants? Our Government repelled those missionaries. Judson was driven from the shore of India, and where did he go? He landed upon heathen soil, where a heathen king sat on the throne, the shore of Burmah; and there he was received, and founded that mission which has now reaped the rich harvest of which you may have heard. A hundred thousand Karens are now the fruits of the labours of the great Judson and his colleagues; and they are now holding prayer-meetings, and praying for the outpouring of the Holy Spirit on their brethren, just like ourselves. These are the fruits which we might have had in India, if we had dared to follow a brave and a Christian policy. In every shape we have carried out that policy of neutrality. We have held partnership even with Juggernaut. We have collected revenues from that great idol temple. We have taken into our charge and management the revenues of other temples: we have made our civil officers administer to them. Is that or is it not a shame to Christian England? (Hear, hear.) And when Government has attempted to educate the people, has it founded that education upon the only root which education can ever take? Has it struck the roots of education into the Holy Word of God? No; it has declared that the Koran may be in the schools, the Shastre may be in the schools; but the Holy Bible may not be in the schools. (Hear, hear.) *[margin: Our connection with idol-temples. Education without the Bible.]*

Now I must do justice to our country, and say, that in following this policy they have not been actuated altogether by those base and ignoble principles which might appear upon the surface. They have, at all events, thought they were acting upon some broad principles of justice. They did at least think they were giving fair play, as they called it, to the heathen. But has this been understood by the native? The native has never from the beginning been able to comprehend this policy of our government. The native is constituted altogether differently from us: his mind is of a totally different construction. Whether he is a Hindoo or a Mahommedan, religion is to the Asiatic the very beginning and the end, the Alpha and the Omega, of his existence. Its fibres run through every act of his life. There is no feast, no fast, no event of happiness or sorrow in that man's family: he never eats or drinks, but in whatever he does, he does it to the glory of his god. Can a people whose heart is thus fixed in its religion,— can it understand how the English people can go, as conquerors, perfectly free and unbound; free to follow their own convictions, and do as they choose in the management of India? Can they understand how that noble Saxon people can begin their government by abnegating God? And when they see such a phenomenon as that, they argue upon it; and the conclusion to which the people of India has come is, not that England is just and fair, and wants to let the light of truth force its own way among them, but the conclusion, that the English are a tricky *[margin: Liberalism in this policy. The native did not comprehend this: He is a very religious being. He ascribes bad motives to it.]*

people; that they dare not go straight to the object they have in view, but are approaching it by some sly contrivance of their own. The consequence has been, that throughout the length and breadth of India suspicion has gone abroad; and the whole Indian people are always in doubt, always suspecting their government and rulers, and wondering what next is coming.

Suspicion wide-spread.

Whatever measure of civilisation we introduced, we might tell them anything we chose; explain its science, philosophy, and object, as we liked, they would look on and think, "Beneath this there is some contrivance to take our religion from us." I have hundreds of times heard natives tell me that, some of these days, when the telegraph wires were spread all over India, the Governor General would pull a string, and those wires would convert the whole of the natives to Christianity. (Laughter.) Take another instance: Along the great line of road from Calcutta to Peshawur our Government has established little hostelries for the traveller to rest in at night. Formerly, under the native rulers, there were strong forts along the roads, for the protection of the people from highway robbers; but the roads now are perfectly safe, and mere lodging-places are required. A few years ago, when these hostelries or caravansaries were being built on the main line of road, the people asked; "What can possibly be the object of building all these along that road?" The native, you must know, is a very avaricious creature, and cannot understand how any one could lay out money, unless it is to bring him in money in return. Reflecting, then, upon these caravansaries, the natives speculated: What can be the object in building these places? At length some wise man knocked out this idea: That he should not be at all surprised if some fine night, when all the travellers at the season of some great pilgrimage, in passing along the road, had lodged within these hostelries, all on a sudden the Governor-General gave orders that the doors should be shut, and that all of them should be made Christians. (Laughter.)

Illustrations:

The electric telegraph.

The native hostelries:

Why made.

I will give you another instance: We never take a new country in India,—and when I say we never take a new country, it seems as if we were in the constant habit of taking new countries. However, after all the talk about annexations, having studied the history of past annexations, and having had an unworthy share in some other annexations (Applause), I can truly say that I believe, with a very few exceptions, which I should not wish to conceal or blur over, that the annexations of our country in India have been forced upon us by the native

Another case.

rulers. (Applause.) But I was saying that we never have taken a new country without the report being immediately spread abroad that all the little babies were being kidnapped by the English; what do you suppose for? They say we are going to make *moomeai* of them. This, with them, is an ointment, a mysterious ointment, which possesses most extraordinary properties, with which, if anybody is rubbed, he becomes a very *Rustum* in the field, the strongest of heroes. But this mysterious ointment can only be extracted with the most extraordinary incantations; and these poor little babies must be got, and hung over a very slow fire, that their poor little innocent fat may be drawn out of them! And, actually, there is scarcely a population in any province of India that does not, first of all, hail our advent, by expecting that we are going to boil their babies! These are the suspicions which are entertained in consequence of our indirect proceedings in the matter of religion. Another instance just occurs to me. There is scarcely a half-year passes over India but what you hear the report that all the flour which is in the market has been adulterated with bone-dust by order of the Government; and that certain rascals, native confederates of our Government, are going about underselling the really wholesome, sound, good flour, selling it 2 lbs. or 3 lbs. cheaper than the real flour, in order that the poor people should buy the flour adulterated by bone-dust, go and make their cakes with it, eat it, and every one of them be turned into Christians! *Suspicion about boiling down their infants: Another: flour mixed with bone-dust: why:*

Now, fellow-countrymen, I have mentioned these facts, because they speak more in reality than a thousand figures of rhetoric. They tell the real truth. There you get into the very heart of the people; you understand their idiosyncrasies; and you see at once what a fanciful, imaginative, suspicious people the Asiatics are. Now, if you had come forward and told these Indian people that you were Christians; that you came to them in the name of God and of his Son; and that, without violence, without persecution, yet with consistency, you desired in all your heart and soul to give them the best thing that you could confer upon them, the most bountiful and best possession God has given to you;—if you had told them that, and encouraged them, by all the legitimate means in your power, to read the Bible and become Christians, and explained to them how only they could become Christians; they would then have honoured you, have respected you, and have loved you, and would never have feared or suspected you. (Applause.) What, then, have *The people very suspicious. Open dealing about the Bible absolutely necessary.*

been the consequences of this neutral policy which we have pursued? Thank God, we have had at home hundreds and thousands of earnest Christian hearts, taking a different view of that great question. They have, at their own charges, sent out missionaries to the East; and these missionaries have reaped a harvest which, though small in comparison with the field, is not small in comparison with the means you have employed; for out of 180,000,000 of heathens and Mohammedans, they have, within the period related to you by the previous speakers, made 120,000 Protestant native Christians. (Cheering.) True, that is only one Christian in 1500 heathens and Mohammedans; but still it is a great reward for their labours, and a great encouragement to you all to send out more labourers into that harvest. But while these have been the rewards of the missionaries, you see what the fearful balance of the heathen and Mohammedan population is. The balance of nearly 180,000,000 stares us in the face, still unconverted at this day; still not only unconverted, but looking upon their rulers with suspicion.

Now, let me explain to you, in a few words, what has been the basis upon which our power in India has been sustained. Of course, one great element of our strength in India (thank God!) has been our moral power. I thank God that there has gone abroad widely in India an impression that, at all events in secular matters, we do desire to do justice betwixt man and man; and that has certainly been a great moral strength to us. But that moral power could never for a moment enable a handful of Englishmen to hold that vast continent in an imperial way. It would be impossible for a small band of thirty or forty thousand Englishmen to hold two hundred millions in their hands, and bid them do their will. What, then, has been the contrivance? We have called unto our aid a native army. As we, bit by bit and step by step, advanced in our career of empire, we have added regiment to regiment, brigade to brigade, division to division, army to army; till at last, in the year 1857, there stood three hundred thousand native soldiers under English arms. That army was divided between the three Presidencies; the army of Bengal, the army of Bombay, and the army of Madras. Now, I do not know to what I am to attribute that, in the Madras presidency, from the very beginning, there has reigned, for some reason or other, a more Christian spirit than has prevailed in the other two Presidencies. I suppose it has been attributable, originally, to some band of real earnest, devoted, and praying Christians, who from the very beginning have prayed to God for the Presidency to which they belonged; but certainly, bit by bit, there have crept into the Madras army numbers of native Christians who have not been expelled from that army; there has been no ban put upon them; and they have been wholly regarded merely in their physical capacity. The consequence is, that the Madras army is largely leavened with the element of native Christianity. In the Bombay army this state of things has not been obtained. But there has been a transition state there. They, too, have been wise in their generation; they have seen the great evil and the great tyranny of caste, and have from the very beginning ignored it, and declared that they will have no caste in the Bombay army. You see the Sudra and the outcast stand side by side with the proud Brahmin; and here is a lesson. Does the Brahmin refuse to stand by the side of the outcast in the ranks of the Bombay army? No! There is such a sight as this: a Soubadar or native Captain, of low caste, commanding a body of one hundred men of mixed races, in which the Brahmin shall be largely seen. If that can be done in one army, why not in all? Pass to the Bengal army, and there you will find the very temple of heathenism, there you will find the real refuge and stronghold of caste. From the very beginning this policy was taken up, the respecting of castes of native soldiers. From the very beginning, the Government has enjoined upon the officers on no account to do one single thing, which shall in any way offend the caste of any one of his sepoys. And the consequence has been, that bit by bit the native army of this part of India has become more distinguished, for its rigid and strict observance of caste, than any other portion of the population of Bengal. Now, fellow-countrymen, *a priori*, do you consider that a wise or sound policy to pursue? I suppose there is not one man in this room who would not be able, in his own wisdom, without any experience of India, to foretell that no good could come of a policy like that. (Hear, hear.) The results were soon to be seen. An army thus constituted was like a sheet of gunpowder spread over the land; one single spark of offence might any day set fire to that army. And our Government knew it well. Our Government gradually, as that army grew, and as province was added to province, and new regiments were obliged to be formed, looked with alarm upon that great army growing under its hands. It was like the old story of Frankenstein: this great monster we had created, and we now viewed it with the utmost horror and alarm. We lived in the greatest dread lest some day this monster should turn upon us and tear us. Consequently, our Government enjoined upon our officers never to offend the natives in this Bengal army; and the native soldier, a very quick-witted, intelligent fellow, soon saw how things lay; and soon saw that he was not the servant, but the master of the Government. He began, a very few years ago, to dictate as well as serve. He began to tell our Government that he could march *here*, but that he could not march *there*. He began to tell our Government that there were certain rivers which it was against his caste to cross; and that he could not go into boats; and go down upon certain wars, because he would have to cross the sea. He began, I say, to tell these stories to our Government; and our Government, unable to dispense with him, and lacking the courage to grapple with the difficulty, coaxed the sepoy; begged him to go on board the boats; and even promised him a little money;—begged him to go to Affghanistan; and pampered him till the monster grew a hundred times the monster that he was. At last the year 1857 came round. We, in our desire to complete the organisation of our Indian army, and in our extraordinary infatuation, perhaps, planned to put that magnificent weapon, the Enfield rifle, into its hands. The Enfield rifle, you all know, is of no use without the Enfield cartridge; and this cartridge is anointed with grease. I suppose a more ingenious device was never laid hold of by the devil himself, than to throw out the idea that the Enfield cartridge-grease was made of pig's-fat and beef-fat; because that hit at once the prejudices of both the Hindoo and the Mahommedan soldiery.

The Hindoo religion is a religion of externals; and it is not with him as with the Christians; he is not taught that the defilement comes from within; he is not taught that to "eat with unwashed hands" defileth *not* a man; he is taught, rather, that contact with inferior caste defiles; that he may be defiled by accident; that if by accident he touches his own conqueror, his own master, the Englishman, he is a defiled being from that moment. It is no uncommon thing for a Mohammedan missionary;—for even they (and let us take example by it;—let us take example where we can)—even the Mohammedan, in his zeal, unable as he is now under the English rule to propagate his religion by the sword, is obliged to sheathe his sword, but he has the courage to open his Koran,—it is no uncommon thing for such a one to find it easier to shut the Koran, and take the Hindoo by a trick. He dresses himself as a Hindoo, associates with Hindoos, invites them to sit along with him, and eat a jolly good dinner. And after they have freely partaken of dishes which they thought orthodoxly cooked, the host turns round and informs them that he is a good Mahommedan, not a Hindoo, and consequently that every one of them has lost his caste! That is a common thing, and tells you at once that this is a people which believe that they can have their religion taken away from them involuntarily, without their heart entering into the matter at all; that they can be converted from Hindooism against their will. But why do the Mahommedans enter into that view? They ought to have a true idea of the one living and present God;—they ought to have an idea of the religion of the heart (and very many of them have); but they have been conquered by the very customs of the people whom they have conquered themselves. The Hindoos have Hindooized the Mahommedans in India; and the Mahommedans in India are now half Hindoos, and largely subject to this accursed caste. When, therefore, they were told that these cartridges were mixed with beef and pig's fat, there was no Hindoo in our army but believed that if he once bit off the end of the cartridge (which he was obliged to do before he put it into the barrel), that by that act he would be un-Hindooized; and there was no Mahommedan but believed that by that act he would be turned into a Christian. Now, my fellow-countrymen, you who have not travelled in the East, will find it difficult fully to enter into this; but, whatever the value of the opinions of old Indians may be on other points, and I know they are very much questioned, at all events they ought to know something of the people among whom their lives had been passed; but do take the experience of an old Indian when I tell you, that there never was a more unfounded or absurd witticism invented, than that one pronounced in the House of Commons by one of our most brilliant speakers, when he said that "Revolutions were not made with grease!" The greatest revolution, perhaps, this world had ever seen,—the Indian mutiny of 1857,—if anything in this world was made with material elements, was made with grease. (Cheering.)

Mahommedans influenced by Hindoo ideas.

Strong feeling of all about the cartridges.

The mutiny sprang from it.

Having explained that to you, I turn round upon this meeting, and ask you if this misconception could ever have taken place, if we had not systematically kept the people of India ignorant of our Christianity? (Applause.) Had you from the very beginning opened your Bible, put the Bible into your Government schools, and made your schoolmasters explain the beautiful doctrines of the Christian religion, it would have gone forth over the land, among your people and among your armies, that the religion of Christ

By full and honest teaching, misconception would have been removed.

was a religion which could only be made in the heart and not in the stomach. There would have been no misconception upon that great cardinal point; there would have been perfect safety to us in dealing out that cartridge; you would never have had one man suspecting you had, at all events, a mind to convert your armies to your religion by a material device like that.

The mutiny took place.

But you did not do it, and you reap the harvest. One hundred thousand sepoys, with your bright arms in their hands, with your discipline and drill, handed down through one hundred years of military exercise, rose like one man against you to drive you out of India.

Number and strength of the mutineers.

When they rose, they took us certainly at a fearful disadvantage. They were in possession of all our forts, of all our magazines, of all our arms, of two-thirds of our artillery, and they stood sentry over all our houses. Well might they suppose that it would be an easy thing to drive these English out of the country. They rose, indeed, and took us at a disadvantage; but they little counted that, many as they were against us, there were more with us than were with them. (Applause.) Thank God, our countrymen then recognised the crisis which was at hand. They saw that this was a war of extermination; that it was race against race, religion against religion, Hindooism and Mahommedanism against Christianity, and that we must look up and trust in our God for safety. (Applause.)

Heroism of Englishmen;

I trust it was in a Christian spirit that our Englishmen displayed the heroism of which you have read, and which you have applauded whenever it was read. And not only our Englishmen, but let me bear testimony to the

and Englishwomen.

heroism of our Englishwomen. (Applause.) Then, indeed, in that hour of danger, you saw what it was to have a Christian woman put face to face with danger. You had not got the poor girl who from her infancy had been a slave; you had not got the poor creature, whose heart had been stunted by tyranny, by idolatry, and by slavery; you had not got the creature whose finest feelings as a wife had been repressed and almost extinguished in her breast; but you found a girl who had come from a country, where she had been taught from her earliest infancy to be a Christian wife. (Applause.) She saw the danger that her husband was in, and she rose like a Christian woman, hand in

Their noble deeds.

hand, to share it with him. (Loud applause.) And whenever the history of that great war shall come to be written, I do believe that no brighter page, no more affecting passage, will be found in it, than that which tells how our Englishwomen bore those extraordinary dangers; how they faced the foe; how they helped their husbands; how they attended the sick; how they disregarded cannon-balls; how they went through all things; and how, with a woman's wish to do honour to the dead soldier to the last, they wound him in his winding-sheet with their own delicate hands, while the roar of a siege was going on. (Applause.) I say, fellow-countrymen and countrywomen, that that indeed is a spectacle which you may all look on with a hallowed pride. I don't say with an unsanctified pride, but with a hallowed pride; for it is, indeed, the fruit and savour of Christianity alone. (Applause.) Well, this heroism, as it came from God, so also indeed it was blessed by God. We had our noble soldiers there. We had our Henry Lawrences. (Loud cheers.) We had our Henry Havelocks. (Renewed cheers.) We had our John Nicholsons. (Cheers.) I perceive that you do not applaud enough the name of Nicholson. (Renewed and louder cheers.) Let me tell you, that though he fell young—he fell at the age of thirty-five—in no army, not only in your own, but in no army that stands a-foot in Europe, lived there a soldier in whom the greatest gifts of the warrior were more skilfully, and happily, and nobly combined with the highest order of humanity, than were welded together in the noble heart and form of John Nicholson, who fell at Delhi. (Immense applause.) We had, too, our Neils: do justice to *that* name. (Loud cheering.) We had, too, our William Peels. (Renewed cheers.) We had, too, our last sacrifice, our Adrian Hope. (Reiterated applause.) And these heroes did not fall in vain. They with their blood won for us a brilliant victory; and, in two short years, this mighty army of 100,000 soldiers has been subdued, and once more England is master of the British Indian empire.

The great soldiers:

Nicholson.

But, fellow-countrymen, in winning back your empire, you have had fearful chastisements from the hand of God. Our Queen has lost these noble spirits, these noble generals, whom, indeed, she will find it most difficult to replace in the hour of danger. There is scarcely a village in our land which does not mourn fathers, brothers, sisters, wives, and children. This awful chastisement must, indeed, fall like a deep shadow upon our hearts; and I would counsel you, as one who has come from those scenes; I would counsel you, fellow-countrymen, not to wish to get from out that shadow, not to wish to emerge from it, and get within the glare of your old levity, and frivolity, and carelessness, and indifference about India; but walk, all the rest of your lives, within the deep shadow of these judgments. I tell you that they

Great chastisements:

their many serious lessons.

come from the hand of the same God that gave you India. They come laden with fatherly advice; they come to tell you that you have neglected the great responsibility that was put upon you; that you have forgotten that 180 millions of your fellow-creatures were put into your hands for holy, and not merely for commercial and selfish, purposes (Cheers); they come to teach you lessons which, I trust, you will all carry away with you to-night, if you have not read them for yourselves.

Lessons of mercy.

There are *lessons of mercy* which I will first recount. I tell you that if ever in any war,—if ever in the history of any nation,

The hand of God aided us

—the hand of God was seen coming forth out of the cloud, to interfere on behalf of any people,—the hand of God was seen fighting for us in British India during this war. (Applause.) I will recount to you some instances of it, for they are fresh in my recollection. There were both war and peace on your side. You had made a war with Persia; you had a large division of your army

by peace:

absent there, both natives and Europeans. With that army you had two of your best generals, Sir James Outram and Henry Havelock. (Loud cheering.) That war, for no reason that I can see, was brought to a close; and peace was made precisely in time to enable that army to return to India, with Outram and Havelock, to fight against the Indian mutineers. That was peace. Now I will tell you what war did. You made a war with China:

by war:

you had a great difference of opinion as to whether you should make war with China; but you made war with China. You sent out your armies, and they arrived at the threshold of India just as we were in our extremity, and wanted them. Lord Canning put out his hand, and drew that Chinese division into India; and they were the first reinforcements which enabled us to hold our own in that country. This I conceive to have been an interposition of Almighty God in our behalf. A third was this; that just before this mutiny broke out, the system of

by the electric telegraph.

electric telegraphs had been completed over the surface of British India. There was a poor little boy employed in the electric telegraph-office at Delhi, who, when the mutineers came over from Meerut, and were cutting the throats of the Europeans in every part of the cantonment, had that sense of duty, in those tender years, to manipulate a message all the way from Delhi to Lahore, to tell Mr. Montgomery that the mutineers of Meerut

Message from Delhi to Lahore.

had arrived, had killed this civilian, and that officer; and wound up his message with the significant words, "We're off!" That was the end of the message. Just look at the courage and sense of duty which made that little boy, with shots and cannon all around him, manipulate that message; which, I do not hesitate to say, was the means of the salvation of the Punjaub. (Loud cheering.) When that message reached Lahore, it enabled Sir Robert Montgomery to disarm the native troops before they had received one word of intelligence on the subject. The same message was flashed from Lahore to Peshawur; and we took our measures there in the same way. And just before any of the mutineers or Hindoostanee regiments had the opportunity of laying their plans, we had taken all ours, and were able to defeat them when the hour of difficulty arose. *which saved the Punjaub.*

Another interposition I consider to have been, that the chiefs of India, as a body, sided with the English. Now, fellow-countrymen, if there is one class of Indian people from whom we should have least expected assistance, surely that class was the Indian aristocracy. It was the very necessity of the case that English rule should crush the aristocracy. We could not help it. It would have been a happier and a kindlier thing, if, in our career of empire, we could have welded the aristocracy into our system; but they would not let us. They were the people we found in power; they were the very people we were obliged to depose; and the whole of our system, from beginning to end, has operated to reduce the aristocracy, and to elevate the people. Thus, in the hour of danger, the class from whom we should least have expected assistance, were the native chiefs of India. But what has been the result? This very class has stood firm and loyal to the English. (Loud applause.) Another blessing to us was, that the King of Cashmere, that great country which is above the Punjaub, stood firm. Had he chosen to revolt, had he chosen to call upon the Sikhs, his late comrades in the Punjaub, to rise against us, no doubt they would have risen at his command, and we should have been unable to hold that province. But he remained firm from beginning to end; and I consider this, among others, to have been an interposition of Providence in our behalf. *The native princes on our side.*

The Raja of Cashmere also.

Another, perhaps still more remarkable, was this: that the Affghan people never once moved from their fastnesses to come down upon us as enemies. You all know the history of the Affghan war, and I will not repeat it. You all know it was a most unhallowed, unrighteous, causeless war; and that we reaped in due time the reward which those deserve who enter upon and carry on such unrighteous wars. We lost a whole army of *The Affghans.*

The former wicked war.

12,000 men amongst the fastnesses of Cabul; and from that time forward there had reigned in both the hearts of Affghans and English a mutual enmity and hostility. But it pleased God, foreseeing these events, to put into the hearts of your rulers to make peace beforehand with these Affghans; to review the events of the past; to feel ashamed of the Affghan war, and to stretch out across the border the right hand of fellowship; and in our hour of security and power, before one speck of danger had appeared in the horizon, when we could do it with dignity and honour, we came forward in the hour of the danger of Affghanistan, stretched out to them our hand, and gave them a subsidy of a lac of rupees a-month, to enable them to defend their frontier against the encroachments of Persia. That treaty was made with Dost Mahommed in January 1857. Scarcely had he returned to his own capital when the Indian war broke out. What would have been our position had we not made that treaty; and if that great, wily chief had raised the standard of his faith, bound the green turban of the Prophet around his brows, and called upon his hordes of barbarians to rise in a crescentade against the infidel and the Christian? We should have been unable to maintain our position at Peshawur; and, swept away by that great avalanche, we should have been carried through the Punjaub down to Delhi; Delhi would never have been taken; and the English would have been driven helpless to the sea. (Loud cheers.)

Recent reconciliation,

and assistance.

Probable result of an opposite course.

Another interposition was this: Not only did the chiefs of India side with us, but, in general, the people of India sided with us too. I announce that fact without the slightest hesitation. Let party men for their own party purposes, let men with peculiar crotchets and peculiar views of their own, try to disseminate this view throughout England, that this was a rebellion of the Indian people, and not a mutiny of the Indian army; but I tell you, on the honour and the word of an English soldier, that this was not the case; and say that, however sad are the consequences of that war for England, however melancholy a page that will be in our history hereafter, I do say that it will be a bright speck, a bright spot in it, to find that the Indian people as a mass, over whom we had ruled for a century, stood aloof from this great contest, and showed at least that *they* did not think we had been tyrants and oppressors. (Loud applause.) Had they not been satisfied that our rule was at least beneficent; had they not thought that, at all events, the English conquerors were animated by a sentiment of humanity and justice; would

The people also with us.

They did not think us tyrants.

they not, when they saw the heroes and leaders of their country, the armed soldiers, rising to fight the national battle, would they not have joined them, with their agricultural implements in their hands? Of course they would: they would have risen like one man; and with a handful of thirty, or forty, or fifty thousand English standing in the midst of two hundred millions of heathen and Mohammedans, what possible hope could we have had, except in a miracle itself? Then I say, this is a proud thing for England to look back to, as it shows that our countrymen have done justice in India. But it should also be a humbling thing, a cause of humble gratitude to Almighty God, that He has enabled us, at all events, with all our shortcomings, to sow these seeds of gratitude in the hearts of that great people.

A further interposition was this: that no leader, no able native leader, arose in that great army of mutineers. Is it not a most astounding and extraordinary thing that 100,000 native soldiers, drilled and disciplined, with magnificent arms, all our own, and with a knowledge of war, should turn upon us, burning with hatred, and every desire of nationality in their hearts, desiring to win their own country back and expel us from their land; and yet that from out their ranks not one single man should come forward to lead them on to victory? Not one man appeared from out those rebel ranks whose military talents were in the least above mediocrity. Had there come forth a Tippoo Saib, had there come forth a Hyder Ali, I say there would have been no hope for the English, except, indeed, it was in God. But it was our God's pleasure that it should not be so; and this infatuated army fought without management, without wisdom, without advice of any kind, and so came on like sheep to the slaughter. We won the victory by this confounding of the counsels of our enemies. (Cheers.) *No able leaders among the mutineers.* *Their counsels confounded.*

Once more; was it not strange, that the Punjaub province, the last province which we had acquired in India, the last in our series of annexations, instead of being (as you might suppose) raw and galled under the new yoke of conquest, should stand up and be, under God, the main means of our salvation in British India. It was from that province that we drew our new army to fight against the mutineers; it was from these heroes that that very man, whose name I call upon you to receive with the honour it should always meet from every Englishman;—it was from that province that Sir JOHN LAWRENCE (immense and repeated cheering)—I thank you on behalf of my master and my friend (re- *The PUNJAUB on our side.* *Sir J. Lawrence and the Sikh force.*

newed applause)—it was from that province that Sir John Lawrence drew the noble army which, under the command of that noble soldier, John Nicholson, went down and carried the breach of Delhi. It was that army which went down to supplement the exertions of our own noble English soldiers. A handful of English soldiers alone could never have done the work; but, supplemented by that brave Punjaub army, 8000 soldiers, led by John Nicholson, dared to enter into a breach which was defended by 25,000 of the rebel mutineers. (Enthusiastic cheering.)

Lessons.

And now, fellow-countrymen, when these have been the interpositions of our God in our behalf, what are the lessons which we, as Englishmen, are to learn from this great page of history? I

The giver of empires is God.

say that, first, we are to learn, and take it much to heart, that the giver of empires is our God. Let us no longer go on with the godless, heartless, senseless theory, that you can have a nation without a national feeling of religion. (Loud cheers.) I say that if you allow this cold, demoralising, denationalising principle to take root amongst you, you will have no national actors in future in your history; and you will find that some day—you who choose to act without your God,—you will find that you *shall* act without your God, and that you will be deserted in your hour of need.

India given that it may be blessed by us nationally

(Applause.) Learn, secondly, that that God has given India into your charge, in order that you may confer upon it the benefits that He has conferred upon you. Learn, thirdly, that you must in that empire begin your labours by honouring the God who gave it you. (Cheering.) I counsel you, fellow-countrymen, if you look forward to any future in India; if you hope, indeed, to attach that great country to your own; if you hope, indeed, to weld it into this empire, and to proclaim your good and great Queen Victoria as the Empress of Hindostan (loud applause); if you have that in

with the BIBLE.

your hearts, as Englishmen, I counsel you to lay your foundations in the Holy Bible. (Renewed applause.) I counsel you to begin as a nation, not as individuals; I counsel you, as a nation, to begin to declare that in the schools for which you pay, and to which you attach your name as an English government, the very first book, always the first book that is put into the hands of the native scholar, shall be the best book that you can put into them. (Cheer-

The native religions not to be despised and neglected.

ing.) Fourthly, let us all learn that Hindooism and Mahommedanism are not things which can be neglected. Let us learn that these are not names; let us learn that they are principles. Let us learn, too, that Christianity is a principle; let us learn that these great things lead on to great ends. Let us look to what Hindooism has shown itself to be in that great land. I do not wish to dwell upon painful details; I do not wish to mar the effect of the kind and Christian words which have been addressed to you by that great and good English soldier, Major Davidson; I fully share with him those feelings of kindliness towards the natives of India, and add my testimony to his that some of the happiest days of my life have been passed amongst that people; and that if God has been pleased to put honour upon me to render any measure of usefulness to my countrymen in that land (cheers), it has solely been through the instrumentality of those good, kind, and noble men, the natives of British India. (Loud applause.) I say that they are a people who will respond to our kindness; I say, their humanity is a great humanity; I say that they have warm hearts, and can return gratitude for kindness; and that they are impressible to every kind act you like to bestow upon them. But still, in spite of this, which I feel and am ready to admit, I tell you that beneath all this goodness and amiability, beneath all this charming exterior, there lies a substratum in their hearts of Hindooism and Mahommedanism. And when the hour of trouble comes, and you reach that substratum, and stir it with a feeling which appeals to the deepest thought they have within them, you will find that people will leave you in your extremity; and you will find no man to stand by you when your real hour of distress comes, except the native Christian, who shares with you the faith of the Redeemer. (Loud cheers.) *The natives good in many ways; but still are swayed by those religions.*

And now, lastly, fellow-countrymen, let me tell you, if these things be true, what we can all of us do. I have told you what we can do nationally. Now let each individual resolve at least to do something for himself. I tell you as individuals, that every one of you here can come forth with a resolve this night that, by the help of God, you will assist missions for the future. Those who have got means—(and where in England shall I speak to men— where shall I find an audience, who are more possessed of means, than this audience I address to-night: where shall I find an audience which has been more blessed in the labour of their hands by God, than you men of Liverpool?)—I counsel those of you who have means; I beg of you, as a friend, a brother, and a fellow-countryman, to consecrate your riches by giving a large portion of them to the missionary labours of your countrymen. I also ask you to bid your brothers, your friends, and your sons, whom you send out to India; and I take the same advice to myself, for I am not preaching to others what I do not wish to practise myself; *What shall we do as individuals. Christian liberality to missions.*

A A

(applause;) I say, bid each man, who has a sphere of labour in India endeavour, by God's help in the future, in the new era which we are opening in India, and bid all, endeavour to lead more Christian lives than we have done. (Hear, hear.) Let us endeavour, if we have been kind before, to be kinder still; if we have been Christians before, to be more Christian; and if not Christian before, let us endeavour to be Christians now, in order to set before the heathen and the Mahommedan a life and an epistle which can be read and known of all men. (Great cheering.)

Christian example to the natives:

I ask you, also, fellow-countrymen, to remember that in that country you have not only got the souls of the heathen and Mahommedans to care for, but the souls of your own fellow-countrymen, the British soldiery, to look after. (Hear.) I tell you that in India the machinery for Christianising the British army is a weak, inefficient, and inadequate machinery; and I counsel you each, to the extent of your power, to send out Christian readers to your regiments; in order that these men may carry into the heart of the regiment, into the hospital and barrack, that Bible which alone will teach them the plan of salvation, and make them true soldiers of their country. (Loud applause.)

care for the English soldier in India.

Yet once more: I ask you, as individuals, to perform one of the most sacred rites which you as Englishmen can perform. We have talked to-night somewhat of the blame which attaches to our country as a nation, and the blame which attaches to our Government as a government; but I tell you that you cannot blame your government, you must blame yourselves. You, as Englishmen, live under a representative system. (Hear, hear.) You are not Frenchmen, living under a despot (cheers); you are not Russian serfs (renewed cheers); you are not Austrians, living under a worse tyranny still (reiterated applause); but (thank God!) you are Englishmen; living under a representative system, and under an accessible, a condescending, and a gracious Queen. (Cheering.) Your Government is not your master; your Government is the climax of yourselves. Your Government, men of Liverpool, is just what you choose to make it. If Government has not acted a Christian part in India, you men of Liverpool have not acted a Christian part in India. I told a story the other day in Manchester, which seemed to please them very much; and I will also tell it to you. It is now ten years ago since I was crossing over your ferry to Birkenhead. In a corner of the steamer there were two gentlemen who were very loud and noisy in debate; and I could not help overhearing their conversation. They laid it down; they hit the

Act also through and on the Government.

Our system representative.

What the Government do, we do.

Illustration.

deck; they hit the side; they hit the bulwarks; they seized each other by the arm; and at last one said, "I tell you, sir, the ministers DAREN'T do it!" "Why not?" said the other, shaking his fist in the face of his companion; for he was evidently on the other side of the question. "Why not?" said he. "Why not!" replied the other, "*because Lancashire won't let 'em!*" (Great cheering and laughter.) If there is any force in that story, any truth in that saying; if, indeed, that is your strong self-dependence; if, indeed, you have got that pluck in you which justifies that saying; then I call upon you, men of Lancashire, to look to it at the hustings in the autumn. (Cheering.) After an earnest appeal to the female portion of the audience, "the witches of Lancashire," whose co-operation and favour he solicited on behalf of India, the gallant speaker withdrew amidst loud and protracted applause.

"Lancashire won't let 'em!"

The Rev. CANON STOWELL, who was greeted with loud applause, next rose and said:—My Lord and my Christian friends, it seems to me that our hearts and heads are so full that it would be better to let what is full alone, than, by endeavouring to make it overflow, diminish the effect. If, however, my Christian friends in Liverpool will bear with me for a few moments (hear, hear), I will endeavour to bring before them as briefly as possible, and as pointedly as I can, a few of the great moral lessons that have been enforced upon us by these solemn assemblies. This solemn assembly is but the climax of those assemblies of a smaller kind, but not of a less efficient nature, which have been held throughout the week in this town; and though I have had the privilege to be present but on this one day, I can truly say I carry away a refreshing influence on my spirit, such as I scarcely remember to have carried away from any former assembly. And I will tell you why. It is because the scene realised that spirit of apostolic brotherhood, devotion, and simplicity of purpose, which is needed more than anything besides in order to unite the disunited members of the church of Christ; for though there were representatives of many distinct sections of the church, they rose to their glorious enterprise with one heart and with one mind. We have met, my lord, in a most auspicious place, the Philharmonic Hall, for this Philharmonic meeting (hear, hear); for surely there is no way of uniting the servants of the cross so effectually as uniting them in common action in a common cause. (Hear, hear.) It is not enough

Rev. CANON STOWELL.

Lessons.

Brotherhood of the Conference.

Christ's servants do one common work.

to meet and reciprocate words of kindness, and talk of brotherhood and love; but the great means of concentration is, to gird themselves to the common work of their common Master, and become so absorbed in that work as to be comparatively dead to all besides. The question then will not be: What is your particular sect? but, How true are you to your Master, and how earnest in his service? My lord, when St. Paul came up to communicate his gospel at Jerusalem, he did it first privately, lest by any means he should have run in vain. Now it appears to me that our missionary brethren, from the east, the west, the north, and the south, have thus come together in this town, in order that they might confer together, and compare the common gospel that they were preaching in heathen lands. And it is delightful to find that, however varied the instruments; some, the flute; some, the trumpet; and some, the harp; yet they have all had one concert pitch and one divine key-note. The pitch has been love to God and man; and the key-note glory to God in the highest; on earth, peace, good will towards men. (Applause.) Now, my lord, what is to be the practical issue of this Conference at home and abroad? I believe it will be the giving to the churches wiser, and broader, and juster views of the purposes and plans of missionary labour. The deduction especially as to the Indian missions is that we must not neglect native agency; but foster and cherish it by every possible means; we must not keep down the native population, and, because our skin is white, look upon them as of an inferior race. (Hear, hear.) Look upon a people as degraded, and you make them degraded; keep them down, and how can you elevate their minds? I fear there is too much tendency in the missionary, and in missionary agency in general, to keep the native converts in a state of pupilage, and not to let them walk independently and alone. Now if you keep the Christian child too long in the go-cart, the Christian child will become rickety and unsteady in his gait. It is true you may endeavour to keep him from falling; but it would be better to let him have a fall or two, than that he should be rickety all his life. (Hear, hear.) Why I am told of Europeans that would not bear to be under a black Bishop; but for my part I should rejoice to be under a black Bishop. I fear that we must have a little of the taint of our former slave-trading and slave-holding still amongst us; and whilst we point the finger of just reprobation at our transatlantic brethren, they may to a certain extent retort the charge, if we would not

The Conference gathered from many spheres.

All in harmony.

Practical result:

native agency to be enlarged:

pupilage cramps.

Colour not to be despised.

consent to be under the superintendence of a black Pastor or Bishop, just as soon as we would be under one whose skin is as fair as our own. (Hear, hear, and applause.)

I come to two or three lessons that we at home ought to learn. I conceive that we have entered upon a new epoch in the history of the means and condition of the church in the world. I consider that it is an epoch emphatically of enlargement. God is enlarging the borders of Japhet and making him dwell more and more in the tents of Shem. He has given to the people of this country a grasp of a large proportion of the human race. How enlarged are our openings! The time is not far gone by, when we scarcely knew what fields were open to us, —whither the missionary could go. Now, however, the difficulty is to find labourers. China with her hundreds of millions is open to us; Japan is open to us; the uttermost ends of Africa are open to us, with all the boundless interior; and Livingstone, the noble Livingstone—(cheers)—is carrying commerce thither, that commerce may be the harbinger and the herald of salvation. And then we have all the outlying countries opening; the very Bedouins of the desert, the wild Arabs, that were neglected and forgotten, are asking for the gospel; a missionary to the Jews has been preaching the gospel amongst the Arabs under the guidance of our Consul in Syria, who is so beloved by them, that they have chosen him as Prince of the Arabs of the desert. Now if God is so throwing open proportionately the world to receive the gospel, are we preparing for the glorious work? Are we prepared to be enlarged in our liberality? Merchants of Liverpool, will you give the challenge to Manchester—(hear, hear)—to adopt a nobler scale of consecrating to the Lord. (Hear, hear, and applause.) Why you know some twenty or thirty years ago, when Manchester and Liverpool had a far smaller revenue, not perhaps a third of what they have now, they gave a considerable amount. The style of giving was 1*l*. 1*s*., 1*l*. 1*s*.; and 2*l*. 2*s*., 2*l*. 2*s*.; and what is the style of giving now? It is very much the same; but there is no proportion here. Manchester, they say, is getting its half a million a-week; but take it at half that amount: what then ought to be the effect? Oh, let the men of Liverpool and the men of Manchester resolve, that in proportion as God has increased their income, they will increase the consecration of the first-fruits to him. (Hear, hear.) Let them resolve, by the help of God, to give in a new proportion. Why should not every Christian man say, I will give five per cent upon the increase of my traffic to God's work. (Hear, hear.) Now if all had done so, I venture to say that Manchester would have had to give this year very nearly her million; and Liverpool would have had to give very little less, if not perhaps something more. (Hear, hear.) And do you think that that would not have been more satisfactory and more noble than to have been building finer houses, setting up grander equipages, living in greater luxury and pampering every desire? Oh, that we knew the luxury of self-denial for our Saviour's sake! (Hear, hear.) Oh, that the style and measure of giving came up more to the Apostolic times, when they sold all they had and dealt out to every man as he had need.

The luxury of self-denial.

There is another point in which we need enlargement. We need enlargement in the devotion of our young men to this noble service of the Captain of their salvation. Our young men have come forward nobly in their country's defence; and whatever some may think of the volunteer movement (applause), it is in my opinion a glorious movement (applause), a righteous movement, a movement for peace, not for war (hear, hear); for defence, not for offence. (Hear, hear.) May we never wish to draw the sword again in aggressive war (hear, hear); may we never, if possible, embark in war at all (hear, hear); but if it should ever be necessary, let it be only to guard our own shores, or to defend the oppressed against the oppressor; the freeman against him that would make him a slave. (Hear, hear, and applause.) Now that volunteer movement is a noble one. Tens of thousands of young men, accustomed to peaceful pursuits, have put on uniform, and girded themselves with swords. But where are the volunteers for this far nobler service, this far more glorious enterprise? (Applause.) Here is an enterprise not of earth, but of Heaven; here is an enterprise under the Captain of our salvation, the King of kings, and the Lord of lords; here is an enterprise in which every soldier, from the commonest to the highest, shall have his recompense of reward; here is a glorious enterprise, in which the laurels never drip with blood, and victory is never stained with cruelty; here is an enterprise not to destroy, but to save; not to desolate the earth, but to bless it and glorify Heaven. My Christian friends, are we prepared, above all, to do all this readily, promptly, and effectually, with all devotedness and delight?

Enlargement in devoting young men.

The volunteer movement good:

but the mission cause is higher.

Signs of the end.

The signs of the times are expressive; there are indications that we are not so far from some grand revolution in the state of the civilised world. The fact we have this day so often reiterated and insisted upon is, that the gospel is being preached in every nation for a witness, and He that uttered that prediction said, "Then the end cometh." Is not the gospel being preached *Preaching.* in every nation? Where is the country under Heaven, where it is not sounded: what, the language in which it is not heard: where the people, to whom it has not gone forth? If then it is being preached to all nations for a witness, lo! "the end cometh." And are there not other signs? The world is arming. Look at *Alarms of war.* Italy. Hear the tocsin of terror sounding in the affrighted ears of the boasted successor of Peter, the Antichrist of Rome. See the noble bearing of the oppressed and scattered nationalities; see what scenes there are everywhere; all are arming for the battle. Is not all Europe resounding with the din of arms? Is not every country resounding with the anvil, beating the sword-blade, and forming the musket? Do we not find every nation in a state of uncertainty and disquietude? Are we not every day seeing *Distress of nations.* strange and eventful circumstances? And what is the voice that God is addressing to us, but 'Blessed is he that watcheth, and blessed is he that worketh:' 'Blessed is the servant that his King when He cometh shall find so doing;' diligent, not disturbed, courageous, not disquieted.

Let others fear; what have His people to fear? Let them fear Him, and they shall have nothing else to fear. Oh, Christian *All Christians should* men and women of Liverpool, let us give ourselves to the Lord's *work at once, and* work; let us do it more heartily; as the season is shorter, let us *with zeal:* give double diligence to be found as His children; and let us thank God that we have such noble encouragements in the agents which He has raised up. We talk of ministers and clergy as the great instruments for evangelising the world; and so in their measure they are: but thank God that we have such men as the *not the clergy alone.* noble officer that has addressed us to-night (hear, hear, and cheers); and, praised be God, we have many such noble warriors, some who, whilst wearing the uniform of their Queen, are true to the uniform of their Captain in Heaven (hear, hear); and who, while the boldest in battle and the most prudent in council, are the most bold to confess their Master, are not ashamed to own Him amidst scoffing and sneering, whether at home or in India. (Cheers.) Whilst we have such men, if the ministers of religion were to be wanting in their duty, and should not take up the blessed work, why our very soldiers will take it out of our hands, and God will raise up missionaries from the ranks of our army. (Cheers.) Let us, above all, be enlarged in the spirit of prayer, *Prayer to be* of faith and Christian zeal. Oh for more prayer! (Cheers.) We *increased.*

want the Spirit to be poured down upon our little plantations in the wilderness of heathenism; we want our missionary stations to become centres from which the Spirit may flow forth. We have Him descending in Ireland, in Wales, in Sweden; and in some measure, as we trust, in England. And shall we not pray that He may descend more abundantly on our missions? Thank God there are indications that the Spirit is at work in our own land. I look upon the fact that thousands of the outcasts of our population, almost as low as the heathen, to whom we are sending missionaries, are flocking to the theatre, to the open-air assembly, or to wherever the minister of the gospel or lay minister of the church lifts up his voice,—I look upon this stir and movement and inquiry as the precursor of the coming of the Spirit of God; and therefore, my friends, ask more; expect more; plead more; intercede more; meet for prayer; pray in private; pray in secret; and then you will be in the right attitude. "Fear not, believe only." You will be prepared for every emergency. Living in Christ, labouring in Christ, you will be saved in Christ, and die in Christ. I believe that the glorious consummation of Christ's promise is coming, when His knowledge shall cover the earth, as the waters cover the sea.

"Faith, mighty Faith, the promise sees,
And looks to that alone,
Smiles at impossibilities,
And cries, 'It shall be done.'"

Amen. Amen. (The rev. gentleman resumed his seat amidst loud applause.)

The Rev. G. D. CULLEN :—I have a pleasant duty to discharge. In the name of the Conference, I have to express here, what has been expressed at Hope Hall in a formal Resolution, the hearty thanks of the members of the Conference to the friends in Liverpool, for the very great hospitality shown on this occasion. We are deeply sensible of the kindness which has been expressed in many ways during the Conference. To the esteemed chief magistrate of this town, whose kindness we have experienced; to those who have received our friends, and in any other way have manifested an interest in our object, we are laid under a deep obligation. We cherish the hope that this visit will not be without a blessing on their households; and that as Joppa, the seaport of Jerusalem, was the scene of the vision that proved the prelude to the calling of the Gentiles, so the vision we have had this week, in this great seaport, will be the prelude to a great increase, advancement, and prosperity of the cause of God, in all Christian missions both at home and abroad. We have encouragement to hope, that if we are patient and persevering, the blessing of God will rest upon our labours. I understand there is a United Prayer-Meeting to be maintained in Hope Hall; and I can testify to the great benefit accruing to all ministers and congregations, from sustaining such a meeting of the people of God, having this one object, the outpouring of the Holy Spirit. In the name of the Conference I return to our friends our hearty thanks for the kind reception with which we have met. (Applause.) *Benefit of United Prayer-Meetings.*

The Rev. J. B. LOWE: I, too, have a debt to perform. The duty has devolved upon me, as a Liverpool clergyman, to express on our behalf, how deeply thankful we are to our Christian friends, who have come among us from all parts of the country, I may say, from all parts of the world. Deeply interesting indeed have been these Conference meetings, as I can bear testimony; not merely for the catholic spirit which has pervaded them; not merely from the prominence which Christian laymen have taken in the meetings; but that our missionary brethren should have made us feel how great a privilege it is to combine in the worship of our common God. May his blessing rest upon all that they have said amongst us; and through the mighty influence of God's Holy Spirit, which I pray may rest on all our efforts, when the great day of judgment shall come, may we then find that our meeting has not been in vain. *Rev. J. B. LOWE.*

The MAYOR, who was received with loud applause, which was several times renewed, said his duty that evening was a very pleasing, as well as a very simple one. He had to propose that their grateful thanks be presented to their noble Chairman for the honour he had done them by coming among them on that occasion; for having taken part in the proceedings of the evening, and for having presided over that large meeting. (Applause.) He begged to assure his Lordship that whether he came down to Liverpool as the advocate of Social Science, the promoter of sanitary or other measures, which had been the means of improving so materially the social and moral condition of the people of this country; whether he came down to plead the cause in which he took so deep an interest, the cause of Ragged Schools; whether he appeared as President *The MAYOR proposes a vote of thanks to the Chairman.*

of that noble society, the Bible Society (applause) ; or whether he came down, as on that evening, to stimulate them by his presence and by his counsel to renewed missionary exertions, not only at home but abroad ; he hoped Lord Shaftesbury would believe, that they fully appreciated the honour of his presence among them, and that Liverpool would always give him a most cordial welcome. (Loud applause.) He was sure they would wish him on their behalf to tender his lordship their warmest thanks for having come down amidst so many pressing engagements to preside on that occasion.

R. A. MACFIE, Esq., seconds it.

R. A. MACFIE, Esq., who was received with cheers, said: At this late hour, whatever in other circumstances I might be disposed to do, I will not detain you by many words in seconding the motion so properly, and so deservedly, proposed by the Mayor, that most excellent Mayor who presides over this town. I wish to join in testifying our gratitude, not only for the speech which this favoured audience has heard, to-night, from the Right Honourable Earl, worthy of being reproduced in letters of gold, and which, I hope, will be extensively read by friends absent, but for his Lordship's great kindness in responding to the call of the promoters of the Conference, to come to Liverpool. This, indeed, is but an instance of the favour shown them from so many sides. Let me also express concurrence with Mr. Cullen. He has thanked you in the name of those esteemed visitors who have enjoyed the hospitality you have exercised ; I thank you, in the name of the Stewards who asked that hospitality, for the reception you have given them. I beg leave to second the vote of thanks to the noble Chairman. (Loud cheers.)

The Resolution was put to the meeting by the Mayor, and heartily adopted.

The CHAIRMAN.

Lord SHAFTESBURY : Ladies and gentlemen, when I was last in Liverpool, I warned you not to give me so good a reception : " because," I said, " depend upon it if you do, I shall be induced to come again." (Cheers.) It is possible you may have too much of a good thing (laughter and applause) ; but, however, I thank you very deeply for this mark of your kindness. I can say that I do cherish a deep sentiment of affection for the people of Liverpool (cheers), and it will always give me the greatest pleasure to come down and meet them ; but more especially when we come to join together for so great, so glorious, so blessed, so holy a purpose as that which has called us together on this evening. (Cheers.)

A Hymn was then sung ; the Rev. J. B. LOWE pronounced the blessing, and the proceedings of the meeting closed.

ON SATURDAY MORNING a large number of the members of the Conference, and a few well-known ministers and other inhabitants of Liverpool, breakfasted, at the Town Hall, with his worship the MAYOR, who gave them a hearty reception. The meeting broke up about noon, and the members finally bade each other farewell.

<small>Saturday morning.</small>

APPENDIX.

I.

PREVIOUS CONFERENCES ON MISSIONS.

By the Rev. Joseph Mullens.

DURING the last few years several important Conferences have been held respecting the best modes of furthering the great work of Christian missions in heathen lands. The growing union of all branches of the Church of Christ in England and America, on several occasions led to suggestions respecting a gathering of the chief managers of missions, lay and clerical, that they might combine their sympathies and their efforts, more openly and more completely, in extending the Saviour's kingdom. For a considerable time, however, the carrying out of such a plan was hindered by the fear, expressed in many quarters, lest some Utopian scheme should be broached for confounding combined action with unity of association; and substituting, for the affectionate co-operation of independent Churches and Societies, the action of some single Missionary Society, to be formed by the union of the whole. At length meetings of the kind were successfully commenced; and common discussions on missionary principles and plans of labour were permitted to take place. *[Desire for these Conferences. Early difficulties.]*

The first Conference of the kind actually inaugurated was the UNION MISSIONARY CONVENTION, which met in NEW YORK, on May 4th, 1854; and was occasioned by the visit to America of the Rev. Dr. DUFF. Stirred up by his fervent appeals, and anxious to take advantage of the presence and experience of one in whose labours all branches of the Church felt a deep and sympathising interest, various brethren in Philadelphia and New York joined in inviting the officers and supporters of all Missionary Societies to hold such an assembly; " to illustrate the practical unity of the *[NEW YORK CONVENTION.]*

Its object:
Church; to excite an increased interest in her holy work; and to combine and judiciously direct her efforts, for the salvation of the millions of our race, perishing for lack of knowledge." All idea of merging existing agencies in some Utopian centralized missionary organization was repudiated; and the hope was expressed that, while each branch of the Christian Church endeavoured to render more efficient its own share in the great cause, such an assembly of men, aiming at one common object, might collect and concentrate

Its plan:
scattered fragments of foreign experience; might inquire into the best method of raising funds; might discuss the relative advantages of the several modes adopted in evangelizing the heathen; and arrange for a freer interchange of information among existing Missionary Societies. On the day appointed a hundred and fifty

Its members:
members of the Convention met in the lecture-room of Dr. Alexander's Church in New York: including eleven missionaries and eighteen officers of various Missionary Societies and Boards. They sat, however, for only a day and a half, and the range of topics discussed was necessarily limited. But the harmony, the

Its spirit.
practical union of affection, the earnest desire to maintain a cordial co-operation in the Saviour's work, manifested on every side, were most delightful; and in this respect the success of the Convention was complete.

Its three chief topics.
Besides the consideration of general scripture principles, on which the work of missions is based, three practical questions were taken up by the Convention, of which two related to foreign work, and one to the raising of missionaries at home: on each of these a distinct opinion was pronounced.

1. Central stations with itineracies.
(*a.*) On the subject of concentrating or scattering labourers in a foreign field, the Convention resolved: that while approving the plan of diffusing the gospel by means of judicious itinerancies; it was equally proper and desirable to seize on commanding stations, especially in countries possessing ancient systems of error; and to concentrate a powerful agency there; which by harmonious co-operation in different departments of missionary labour, may both largely influence the heathen, and perpetuate the gospel in pure Churches to succeeding generations.

2. Societies not to interfere with each other.
(*b.*) On the expediency of different Boards planting stations on the same ground: the Convention expressed their thankfulness that Societies have interfered so little with each other, decided; and resolved; that, considering the vast domain of heathenism yet untaught, it was very desirable that an efficient pre-occupancy of any portion of the field by one Evangelical

(c.) On the important question of multiplying and preparing qualified labourers; the Convention considered that much depended on a deeper missionary spirit in pastors of Churches; leading them to constant efforts, in their pulpits, Bible-classes, and Sabbath-schools, to impress parents, teachers, and the young, with the duty and glory of personal dedication to the work of the Lord. On these topics the conclusions reached are similar to those adopted by the recent Conference at Liverpool.*   *3. How to find and prepare Missionaries.*

The next Conference on missions was gathered in LONDON, in the autumn of the same year; and sat for two days, October 12th and 13th, 1854. Like that at New York, it was limited in the range of its discussions; and dwelt rather more on general principles. Members of all the principal Societies were present; but many of the Secretaries were unable to attend.   *Conference in LONDON.*

The Conference was deficient, therefore, to a large extent in practical elements: but the kindly feeling and harmony prevailing among the members of the different Churches present, evinced an earnest desire heartily to co-operate in the great work of preaching the gospel to the heathen. Three long and able papers were read to the Conference; of which the second only dealt with the plans of missionary life; having discussed the increase of native agents and the extension of itinerating operations. No resolutions were adopted on this or other questions: the object being to make the expression of opinion free and unrestrained. This first gathering in England of brethren deeply interested and engaged in missionary work tended greatly to prepare the way for the more practical assembly which has recently taken place.†   *Its spirit and character. Topics discussed. Its effect.*

To these gatherings among the home friends of missions succeeded several more PRIVATE CONFERENCES on the actual fields of labour: all of a much more complete, searching, and practical character. The earliest took place among the AMERICAN MISSIONS in India and Syria. At the close of 1854, the Rev. Dr. Anderson, Foreign Secretary of the American Board, and the Rev. A. C. Thompson proceeded to India as a Deputation from the Board; and spent the following year in visiting the entire range of their missions in those countries. In each case they examined   *Conferences in the MISSION-FIELD. American Conferences in India.*

---

* "Proceedings of the Union Missionary Convention held in New York, May 4th and 5th, 1854." New York: Taylor and Hogg. 1854.

† "The Missionary Conference in London: Evangelical Christendom." Dec. 1854.

the stations occupied by the Board in all their detail; and gathering the missionaries together for consultation, went over with them all the questions involved in every plan existing in operation in their peculiar circle of missions. The following extract from their Report exhibits a specimen of the topics discussed in each of their circles: it is the list of questions suggested for discussion in the Jaffna Mission in Ceylon:

Their plan.

Their topics.

Object of missions.

"1. *The governing object in missions to the heathen.* Should it be the conversion of sinners, the gathering of those converts into churches, and the ordaining of native pastors over those churches?

Preaching.

"2. *Preaching.* Its connexion with schools; difficulty of obtaining stated congregations from those not in the schools or supported by mission funds; permanent congregations; preaching at the stations and in the villages; comparative disposition of the heathen to attend at the churches and at school bungalows; preaching by the missionaries; amount and value of native preaching.

Native churches and pastors.

"3. *Native Churches and Pastors.* Evidence of piety to be required for church-membership; organization and discipline of the native churches; is the church covenant sufficiently explicit; names given to children; in what circumstances churches should be formed, and have native pastors; whether native preachers should be ordained, except as pastors; licensure as catechists and preachers; the proper relations of native churches and pastors to the mission; relation which missionaries and the mission should bear to them; why no native pastors hitherto; power of the mission, as such, to organise native churches, ordain native pastors, and to superintend the same; advantages arising from this being done by the mission, as such, rather than by a separate body organised for the purpose by missionaries in their simple character of ministers of the gospel; whether all native pastors should be educated alike, and what education should be afforded them; where it is desirable that churches should now be organised, and native pastors ordained; whether native pastors are desirable at any of the station churches.

Caste and polygamy.

"4. *Caste and Polygamy.* How far caste exists among church-members; how far there are specific actions in church-members, bearing a relation to caste, which ought to be discountenanced in native preachers and catechists, and how far such actions are observable in the social life of church-members; what should be done to eradicate such causes of disunion and dishonour from the native churches; whether there is any actual regard paid to caste-distinctions anywhere in the distribution of the cup in the Lord's Supper; whether any one should be ordained as a pastor, or licensed as a preacher, who, on being directly questioned on the subject in his examination for licensure or ordination, refuses to declare himself willing to eat any kind of food with a Christian on the ground of its being prepared by a low-caste person; how far caste is regarded in admissions to the Seminary, and the Female Boarding-school; how far *Polygamy* exists here; whether found at all in the church; how it is regarded and treated.

"5. *Station Schools.* (1.) *English Schools.* Number of these and their relation to the Batticotta Seminary; why called *English* schools; their effect to cultivate a taste for English studies in the villages; missionary value of these schools; their effect on the village female schools; effect of their discontinuance. English schools.

"(2.) *Girls' Schools.* Prejudice against female education; means employed to bring girls to the schools; whether the donations of clothes, &c., ought to be continued; effects of these on Christian parents and their children; condition and prosperity of village-schools for females. Girls' schools.

"(3.) *The Free Schools.* Their rise; comparative prevalence, in periods of five years; employment of heathen masters; how far the mission took schools that were actually existing into pay; what was taught; number taught in these schools; estimated average time of continuance in the schools; preaching to them; were there conversions in these schools; what is known of the pupils since leaving the schools; what of their heathen masters; how far parents were drawn to hear preaching, and the effect of this; estimated cost of these schools on the whole; how far they now exist; native books used in the schools; whether these schools have answered expectation in promoting the grand object of the mission; on sustaining the free schools mainly for children of Christians. Free schools: their plan, cost, &c.

"6. *Oodooville Female Boarding-school.* Historical facts; statistical views; results; difficulties that were to be overcome; how far this has been effected; changes now to be made; exclusion of English studies; shortening the period of residence in the school; reduction of the number of pupils; preparations to be required in Tamil studies. Female boarding-school.

"7. *Batticotta Seminary.* Rise and progress of the institution; what was its design at the outset, and what it has been since; what has been the number of pupils, and what they have done since leaving the institution; the education given; the number of English studies attended to compared with those in Tamil; why the native mind is so intent on English studies; feelings of native teachers in the Seminary towards Tamil text-books, as compared with English; effect of the English studies on the several Principals, retarding their acquisition of Tamil; effect of introducing pay-scholars upon the character of the Seminary, and upon its relations to the Female Boarding-school; has there been a decline of piety among the students; contemplated changes; in the studies required for admission; in the number of pupils; in the manner of support; in the time of residence; in the *curriculum* of studies; class of advanced students in Theology; instruction in English to a selected body of students after the academic course. Batticotta seminary: its working and results.

"8. *Native Helpers.* Their number; origin; education; employment; salaries; training and supervision; whether too many at any of the Native helpers.

stations; whether employed and paid after they are superannuated; whether they should pay their rent.

Changes required. " 9. *Modifications in the Stations.* Ooodooville and Manepy, &c.; number of missionaries required for the mission; peculiarities of the Jaffna field.

Letters. " 10. *Restrictions on Correspondence.* Rule of the mission; reasons for its discontinuance.

Press. " 11. *Printing Establishment.* Extent of it; work done; whether this establishment and the one at Madras are both needed; is the English department needed; expediency of continuing to print a part of the *Morning Star* in English; how far the mission is responsible for the contents of that paper; how far, for the printing done in the office; publishing committee; statement concerning the depository; what ought to be done with the unsaleable books, and sheets, and stationery on hand; has the existence of the press here been an advantage to the mission.

Widows. " 12. *Provision for Widows, Children, and Invalid Missionaries.* Is it desirable that any additional provision should be made.

Bibles, &c. " 13. *Grants of the American Bible and Tract Societies.*

Furlough. " 14. *Visits to the United States.* Is any further legislation needed; how far to be provided for from the mission treasury; rules for preventing unnecessary cost in returning home; health stations connected with the mission; the overland passage.

Salaries. " 15. *Salaries of Missionaries.*

Medical mission. " 16. *Medical Establishment.* Where should the head-quarters of the mission physician be; what are his duties; medical practice out of the mission; presents; medical class; should their instruction be in the vernacular; general results.

Mission property. " 17. *Mission Property.* Property in lands; in dwelling-houses, &c.; in churches; how far the government have a right in the property; tenure on which the property is held; what is being done to improve the tenure; real value of the Dutch churches and parsonages to the mission; buildings at Varany; land near Manepy.

Grants in aid. " 18. *Government Grants.* Grants received, and how applied; whole amount received; implied condition of the grants; school commission at the seat of government; school commissioner and his visits; views of the Prudential Committee with respect to government grants for schools.

Expenditure. " 19. *Estimates, Appropriations, and Expenditures.* What the estimates should contain; intent of the appropriations; whether the expenditures should be restricted to the specific objects; whether balances should be used for other objects; whether money received by the treasurer from every source should not be credited in his accounts with the treasurer of the Board; new estimate for 1856.

Mission houses. " 20. *Houses.* Plan and cost of a house for missionary residence; station and rural churches; houses for native helpers; expediency of reducing the space in the present station-churches.

"21. *Temporal Aid for Missionary Funds to indigent Native Christ-* Aid to poor converts.
ians. Ought this ever to be given."

The American Board has three great spheres of missionary American Board in the East. operations in India; in the Deccan, North Ceylon, and Madura; with two smaller missions in Madras and Arcot; and has two chief centres of missions in Western Turkey, at Beirut and Constantinople. In all these missions, this or a similar range of Conference in all their missions. searching topics was discussed in full by the missionaries and the Deputation; the views of the brethren were interchanged, and the results of their experience on heathen ground were freely detailed. The deductions of this experience appear in the form of PAPERS Record: drawn up by the missionaries (similar to the MINUTES of the recent Conference), and of LETTERS, commenting upon them, by the Deputation. They are contained in a volume of 600 pages, printed its contents and character. privately for the use of the Board and its friends; and it is not too much to say that no volume of equal size, published during the era of our modern missions, contains so much valuable information on all the details of missionary experience on several most important fields of labour, as that volume of missionary papers. It might be published with great advantage to the friends of all Missionary Societies; and deserves the careful study of all missionaries, and the managers of all missionary agencies, especially in the countries and provinces of Asia.*

About the same period E. B. UNDERHILL, Esq., the able and Conferences in the Baptist Missions in India. accomplished Secretary of the Baptist Missionary Society, visited all the missions of that Society in India and Ceylon, as a Deputation from the London Committee, and acting on a plan similar to that of the American deputation, gathered the missionaries of the Society in four separate Conferences, for a similar examination of every element in their local plans. A range of topics was dis- Plan, results, record. cussed similar to that of the American brethren; and the result, as in their case, was embodied in reports by the missionaries and letters by the deputation. They are also equally valuable.† To the missionary in India no works will give a more complete insight into the worth and working of all sorts of plans, than the nine sets of Papers and Letters contained in these volumes of the two Societies.

* "REPORTS and LETTERS connected with Special Meetings of the India and Syria Missions of the American Board in 1855." Printed for the use of the Prudential Committee. Boston.

† "Minutes and Reports of Conferences of the Baptist Missionaries in Bengal; the North-West Provinces; Behar; and Ceylon, in 1855-6." Printed for the use of the Committee and the Missionaries.

372 PREVIOUS CONFERENCES ON MISSIONS.

Three General Conferences in India.

Three other Conferences, of a more general character, also on Indian ground, accompanied, or have since followed the meetings of the American and Baptist missionaries. They had to consider not merely general principles, but the minute details of each circle of missions. The GENERAL CONFERENCES which followed, included missionaries from many Societies, were confined to the principal plans of labour adopted by Indian missionaries, but illustrated them by experience, drawn from a wide surface and contributed by the most able men, who had been engaged in carrying those plans into effect.

Bengal Missionary Conference:

The BENGAL MISSIONARY CONFERENCE met in Calcutta in September, 1855; it consisted of nearly fifty missionaries; sat four consecutive days; held eight sessions, with meetings for devotion; enjoyed the most delightful harmony in its meetings; and its members were greatly cheered by their mutual counsels.

its topics.

The topics discussed were as follows:

The progress made by missions in Bengal:
The peculiar difficulties encountered in them:
Preaching the gospel in the native tongue:
English missionary education:
Influence of the Indigo and Zemindary systems on the progress of the gospel in rural districts:
Vernacular Christian literature:
Vernacular schools: and
Native female education.

Plan adopted.

Each subject was introduced by a brief paper; the discussions were conversational, pointed, and searching; and the opinions of the brethren were embodied in the form of Resolutions, which were submitted to them and approved. The papers, brief notes of the discussions, and the resolutions passed, were also published in a thin volume, of great value to missionaries and the officers of their Societies.*

Record.

Benares Missionary Conference.

A second GENERAL CONFERENCE was held by the missionaries of the NORTH-WEST PROVINCES, at Benares, in January, 1857, three months before the mutiny. Thirty missionaries were present belonging to seven Churches and Societies, and, as in Calcutta, were greatly encouraged and instructed by the relation of their common experience. The plan followed and the topics discussed were very similar to those adopted in the Bengal Con-

---

* "Proceedings of a General Conference of Bengal Protestant Missionaries, held in Calcutta, Sept. 1855." London: Dalton, Cockspur Street. Price 4s.

ference; and the opinions of the members were embodied in the form of Resolutions. These Resolutions, and a few brief notes from a private pen, are all the account now remaining of this instructive Conference; the whole of the MSS. and printed proofs having been destroyed when the Allahabad Mission Press was burnt by the mutineers in the following June.* *Record destroyed.*

The last CONFERENCE held in India, a gathering of the SOUTH INDIA MISSIONARIES, took place at Ootacamund, in the Nilgherry Hills, in April, 1858. It differed from the previous general Conferences in the wide range of topics brought forward, and in the length of time devoted to their examination. Thirty-two missionaries met on the occasion, and having retired from the heat of the plains, were able to spend a quiet fortnight in the cool air of the Hills, in a full and satisfactory examination of all the plans adopted in their different fields of labour. The results are published in a large volume, and are of very great value to all who would know the character and progress of Christian missions in the Madras Presidency.† *South India Conference.* *Its record.*

The volume opens with a series of twenty-seven narrative papers, descriptive of the growth of the chief missions of the Presidency, in the several provinces speaking four great languages. These narratives contain a great deal of valuable information, from which a general view of that growth may be easily derived. They are followed by papers read on no less than twenty-one subjects connected with missionary life and plans. The papers are thirty in number, written by men most competent to produce them, and are followed by Resolutions, in which the common views of the Conference are embodied. The subjects include not only the prime topics of native agency, missionary education, vernacular preaching, village congregations, and the like, but more special topics, as industrial institutions, caste, public morals and the Government, Government education, and others. A number of statistical tables close the work; recent, and of the best authority. The book is a great storehouse of information on all that concerns the missions of South India, and deserves most careful study. *Narratives.* *Subjects discussed:* *Statistics.*

The records of these various missionary gatherings, both general and special, embody, to a far greater extent than any works previously written, the tested experience of missions in *Value of all these records.*

---

* "Outline of the Benares Missionary Conference." *Calcutta Christian Observer*, March 1857.

† "Proceedings of the South India Missionary Conference, held at Ootacamund, April 1858." London: Missionary Societies.

various localities as to the worth of existing plans; and they are calculated to confer great service on all who wish to learn from that experience the most efficient methods of carrying out the great commission to preach the gospel, which underlies them all.

Work yet needed to combine the results of all. A work might yet be written which shall gather up, in relation to the whole, the principles, facts, and teachings thus presented respecting the various sections of our wide-spread Indian missions: a work which shall seize on general features of locality, work, and results; discriminate between them and local peculiarities; and fairly deduce the results taught by the entire field to the missionaries and managers of all Protestant Societies. The writer of this notice has, for some time, planned the preparation of such a volume, but want of opportunity has compelled him for the present to lay it aside.

Relation of the Conference in Liverpool to these its predecessors. From these brief notices, the reader will at once see how far the recent CONFERENCE ON MISSIONS, held in LIVERPOOL, has differed from its predecessors. Embracing in its details the experience of missionaries and Societies in all parts of the world, it has examined a wider range of field than the Conferences in India, though it has not, like them, descended to a great variety of minute details. Dealing less with general principles, and going more deeply into plans, its discussions were of far greater value than those of its predecessors in London and New York. It is with confidence, therefore, that its records are commended to the managers of all Societies, in the belief that all may derive help from the facts and principles they present in such a complete form; and that by their means all may improve the agencies they employ in many spheres of Christian toil, for the one common end of saving immortal souls.

II.

SUGGESTIONS.

By James Douglas, Esq., of Cavers.

I beg to offer the Missionary Conference at Liverpool a few hints, upon subjects which have not yet been sufficiently attended to, which may be either used or not as circumstances may seem to point out. *Suggestions.*

That is a noble undertaking which seeks to co-operate with Dr. Livingstone in Central Africa. The African tribes, however, are more easy to deal with than other branches of human society, who are more advanced in civilization and more confirmed in various errors. The African tribes give indications of having had a religious system formerly, but now retain only dark, and, in some instances, almost diabolical fragments of the past. Civilization, whenever it takes hold of them, by giving them a new life and new modes of thinking, will sweep these into the abyss of former days. *The University Mission to Africa.*

With regard to the Moslem, who are the neighbours in Africa of the rude tribes, and who stretch far into the recesses of Asia, the case is very different. They have a system, simple, compact, definitely determined, and armed at all points. *The Moslem system.*

We understand that Dr. Pfander's books reach many of the vital points of the system, but it is not easy to procure English copies. Perhaps the missionary Conference, or some member of it, might make the English copies more accessible in Britain. *Dr. Pfander's works.*

We can speak conscientiously in high praise of Mr. Wm. Muir's work upon Mahomet, who has written partly at Dr. Pfander's suggestion. If the documents were well arranged for the purpose, they would surely produce a great effect upon the Moslem mind. *Mr. W. Muir's Life of Mahomet:*

The *Life of Mahomet* is divided into two distinct periods; the first, when he was only a preacher of the Divine Unity; the second, when he became a pretended prophet. *Its two periods:*

In an account of the first division of Mahomet's life, we and the Moslem might sympathise together; an advantageous commencement of a discussion which must ultimately end in controversy. Had Mahomet died when he was young or middle- *character of Mahomet's early life.*

aged, there need have been but one opinion formed about him. All might agree that he excelled many nominal Christians; a modest, meritorious, talented young man, who lived strictly, and with scarce an exception apparently, according to his own views of morality, which might be considered high for the time and the country.

His later life:

But the office of prophet was in some measure forced upon him; and he, an awful lesson of human instability, was forced down the precipitous descent of imposture; at first with many an

inward struggles:

inward struggle and great agony of mind, which produced their traces even in his outward appearance. Pointing to his beard, he said, "These are the grey hairs of the prophet Houd;" a mysterious but significant sentence. In plain language, "You have reproached me for preaching without being a prophet or invested with authority, like Houd. I have assumed the office with inward torture, and have prayed to Allah to be delivered

All should be laid before his followers.

from all error and delusions." We think that if a true picture of what was passing in Mahomet's mind, according to his own confession, or at least intimations, could be placed before his disciples, it would not fail in several instances of a beneficial effect.

Buddhism:

The same may be said of the last of the Buddhas. Words, which evidently proceeded from his own lips, for he had no disciples capable of inventing them, and they speak from heart to

its great defects:

heart, deeply represent the misery and the inefficacy of the Buddhist system, and afford a large opening for the introduction of Christianity, as the only repose of the soul and its escape from all finite evil. Such a work might be written also in a conciliatory spirit. The last of the Buddhas, Sakya-Muni (and that name

Buddha's spirit.

reveals some historic mysteries), was a person of great feeling and of high principles, according to his own mistaken system.

Brahminical writings:

The writings of the Brahmins also contain the refutation of Brahminism. The first Veda shows that the Asian race were originally without caste. What an immense gulf between the *Rig-Veda* and the *Institutes of Menu!* The *Institutes*, far from establishing caste, are occupied in counteracting the aberrations

their character.

of a system which had been long established. Everything in the Hindoo writings indicates change and instability. New creeds and new deities throw the old Indian objects of worship into the shade, and indicate the not-distant time when they also shall pass away.

III.

ON THE TRAINING OF NATIVE AGENTS.

By the Rev. B. Lyth of Fiji.

As the plan of working the Lakemba circuit was one into which I was led, by providential circumstances, in order to meet the wants of a large, wide-spread, and increasing circuit, having then 1400 Church members (now increased to about 5000) to care for, the teachers themselves but babes in Christ, and the societies without order or discipline, my remarks must be directed to this one point; viz. to show some of the steps by which the teachers were raised to comparative efficiency, the several infant churches reduced to order, pastoral and educational machinery set in effective operation, means for the support of a native agency provided, and new agents of all classes called forth for the sustentation of the work. *[Lakemba circuit in Fiji: its wants: work required and done.]*

My predecessor, feeling the great need of a better-instructed native agency, had conceived the plan of a large training institution for the qualifying of young men for the work. His scheme appeared to my mind, under the then-existing state and circumstances of the mission, to be an impracticable one. It was premature: and then it left the present pressing wants of the circuit unprovided for; for the important fact looked me in the face that God had already given us a number of men, whom He had graciously raised up, with small churches under their pastoral care. These men were of various ages and abilities, some humble enough, but they were *converted men*. I was therefore fully convinced, that it was my duty to abandon the beautiful scheme of a formal institution for mere candidates, (and where were they?) for the more laborious one of attempting the cultivation of the entire field, and the endeavour, by God's help, to qualify the men God had given us by training them *for* their work, by training them *in* it. The entire circuit was made our training institution, with the mission station for its centre. *[Training institution unsuitable: why: Men to be trained in their work.]*

The circuit was divided into seven branches; native assistant-missionaries, consisting of the best-qualified men we could command, were entrusted with their pastoral oversight and management, under the general superintendency of the missionary. These *[Circuit divided.]*

native assistant-missionaries had catechists, (Fijian travelling preachers,) occupying smaller spheres of labour under their general supervision. Thus was the whole machinery put in motion.

Men employed.

The duties of the missionary were threefold:—

Duties of the missionary.

1. To superintend the entire work of the circuit.
2. To set the example to the native assistant-missionary class of agents, in his mode of superintending the branch of the circuit under his more immediate charge.
3. To set the example to the catechist class, in his mode of working a still smaller section of labour, answering to a catechist's station.

So much for the general machinery of the circuit.

The training of native agents in scriptural theology was as follows:—

Plan of training.

1. The first step up the ladder was to have their views quite clear on the subject of their personal salvation. You will understand what this means, and the importance of it in the class of persons under consideration.

First step:

2. The second step was to instruct them from a large chart, embracing the grand outline of the plan of salvation; describing repentance, faith, justification, regeneration, the Holy Spirit's office in conversion, the first-fruits of the Spirit, and the duties of Christianity.

charts on chief points:

All these were presented to them under the various terms and aspects, in which they are severally presented in Scripture. The charts, indeed, were three in number:—

    a. Man's fallen estate.
    b. The plan of salvation.
    c. Christian duties and privileges.

These supplied the teachers with a key wherewith to open the Scriptures, and their own experience enabled them to use it.

3. The third step was to conduct them through a course of systematic theology; including the evidences, doctrines, duties, and institutions of Christianity.

Theology.

4. The fourth was to train them in sermonizing. A text furnished by one of the class was written on a black board. Then the arrangement would be discussed, or rather elicited by questions. Then the first division, the second, &c., were written by a native on the board. The discussion of the text, in which all took a part, brought out much material, the exercise was made as practical as possible, and was thus rendered, by God's blessing, a useful and delightful means of grace. There was both bread for

Sermonizing:

how taught.

the eater, and seed for the sower. Afterwards a short outline, with Scripture references, was written out for them, which the preachers copied into their sermon-books.

The theological class consisted of the various native agents residing on the island; including one or more native assistant-missionaries, catechists, local preachers, and promising young men anxious for instruction, from all parts of the island, and frequently some from other islands. *Scholars.*

The adoption of the system of itinerancy in the stationing of our native agents, and the principle of *unity of action;* or, in other words, the rule, that what was done in the way of instruction by the missionary must be done by the native assistant-missionary and catechist in their several spheres, imparted a diffusiveness to the entire scheme, the results of which were most gratifying, and satisfactorily proved to us that we had been led in the right way. The seal of the Divine approval was put upon the means used in the spiritual prosperity of the entire circuit. *Itinerancy. Information different among the agents.*

It would be tedious to you, and, indeed, it is unnecessary that I should enter particularly upon the other branches of training included in our plan of instruction; but simply to add, that it embraced practical training and instruction in pastoral duties, church discipline, and school routine. The teachers were, moreover, instructed in reading, writing, arithmetic, geography, singing, &c., for everything was new to them. My colleagues were most excellent fellow-helpers, and by working harmoniously and systematically in our several departments, the agents improved rapidly; new life was infused into their souls and labours; they found themselves endued with new power, and entrusted with a most responsible trust; and they devoted themselves to the service of the Redeemer with renewed zeal. *Other elements in their training. Working of the plan.*

The most intelligent of the teachers felt themselves relieved of a heavy burden, the burden of duties they had not known how to discharge; but now, being instructed *in* their work, and the *manner* of its performance, their duties, although increased, were rendered a pleasant burden, and attended to under a new inspiration. *Effect of it.*

The instituting of a simultaneous meeting for prayer, to be held throughout the circuit every Friday morning, was a special means of promoting the prosperity of the work and the success of all the means. It was a meeting of the few in each place who felt the deepest interest in the promotion of the Redeemer's kingdom. *Simultaneous prayer.*

Among other evidences of the Divine blessing, was the arising up of young men of promise. These were carefully looked after by *Young men offer.*

Salaries:

the teachers; and the result was a constant flow from every part of the circuit of these candidates for various spheres of usefulness.

One word respecting the support of paid agents. Catechists receive a certain allowance quarterly from the Church members under their charge, according to a scale fixed upon from year to year. As there was no currency in the group, the allowance con-

how paid:

sisted of native clothing made and contributed by the female members of the Church, and of various articles of produce by the men.

The men-attendants on public worship do not contribute to this collection, but assist in a variety of other ways to the material maintenance of the cause.

Native assistant-missionaries receive, in addition to the contributions of the members of the Church, a small supplement in the form of clothing or articles of barter from the mission store.

Experience.

My observations upon this very important subject may fall very far short of the work, and have but a very limited bearing upon the whole question, but they are what I could furnish; and the principles and practice they advocate are the result of experience, and have been tested by experiment; and, I may add, the success with which they were crowned exceeded our most sanguine expectations.

Training institutions not suitable.

Training Institutions for resident students on stations, similar to those of Fiji and Tonga, have not, so far as my observation has extended, answered the expectations of their promoters. They are more beautiful in theory, but less successful in their results.

Why.

The natives of such countries cannot endure the close study and confinement of such institutions; but give them plenty of work and exercise, and they will come to their studies with zest and pleasure; and what they learn they will digest and communicate, and what is quickly communicated is twice learnt.

IV.

MODERN WORKS ON CHRISTIAN MISSIONS.

1. GENERAL WORKS.

AIKMAN, Rev. J. A.: Cyclopædia of Christian Missions. Glasgow, Griffin and Co. 1860. 6s.
This excellent little work gives a summary view of the labours of all the Protestant Missionary Societies. Modern Works on Christian Missions.

BARTH and BLUMHARDT, Rev. Drs.: Christian Missions. Religious Tract Society. 2s. each.
    Africa, Vol. I. Heathen Asia and America, Vol. II.

BROWN, Rev. Dr.: History of Protestant Missions to the Heathen. 3 vols. Blackwood, 1854. 1l. 11s. 6d.

CAMPBELL, Rev. Dr.: The Martyr of Erromanga; the Philosophy of Missions, illustrated in the Rev. J. Williams. Snow, 1842. 6s.

CAMPBELL, Rev. Dr.: Maritime Discovery and Christian Missions. Snow, 1840. 12s.

CLARKSON, Rev. W.: Christ and Missions. Snow, 1858. 6s.

GRANT, Ven. Archdeacon: Bampton Lectures on Missions to the Heathen. Rivingtons, 1845.

HAMILTON, Rev. Dr. R. WINTER: Prize Essay; Missions, their Authority, Aim, and Encouragement. 2s. 6d.

HARDWICKE, Archdeacon: Christ and other Masters: the Heathen Systems of Religion compared with Christianity. 4 parts; each 7s. 6d.

HARRIS, Rev. Dr.: Prize Essay; The Great Commission. Ward, 1842.

KINGSMILL, Rev. J.: Missions and Missionaries. London.

MACFARLANE, Rev. Dr.: Prize Essay; The Jubilee of the World.

MISSIONARY BOOK FOR THE YOUNG: A first Book on Missions; Religious Tract Society, 1859. 1s.

MISSIONS, on Christian: Encyclopædia Britannica; by JAMES DOUGLAS, Esq.

MOORE, E. D.: Life Scenes from Mission Fields. A Popular Book of Facts. New York, 1857. 6s. Trubner; London.

NEWCOMBE, Rev. H.: Cyclopædia of Missions, &c. New York, 1855. 1l. Trubner, London.
This valuable compendium of Missionary information is a Gazetteer; it gives in alphabetical order the different Missionary stations throughout the world, and describes the work done in each place.

NOEL, Hon. and Rev. BAPTIST: Essay on Christian Missions. Nisbet, 1842.

RAMSDEN, R., Esq.: Missions: a Word for the Heathen: Facts and Anecdotes from the Journals and Letters of Missionaries. Nisbet, 1859. 6s.

SWAN, Rev. W.: Letters on Missions.

THE YEAR-BOOK OF MISSIONS, by the Rev. Dr. Hoole: A General Sketch of Missionary Stations and Operations throughout the World. Longmans, 1847. 10s.

THE MISSIONARY GUIDE-BOOK: a Survey of Missionary Operations in various Countries of the World. Seeleys, 1846.

2. HISTORY OF SOCIETIES.

AMERICAN BAPTIST UNION MISSIONS: Gammell's History. Boston, 1850. Trubner. 5s.

AMERICAN BOARD OF COMMISSIONERS FOR FOREIGN MISSIONS: Tracy's History of the. New York, 1842. Trubner. 5s.

AMERICAN METHODIST EPISCOPAL CHURCH MISSION: History of, by Barge and Strickland.

AMERICAN MISSIONS TO THE HEATHEN: History of, by the Rev. S. Worcester. 1840.

AMERICAN PRESBYTERIAN MISSIONS: Green's Historical Sketch.

AMERICAN PRESBYTERIAN MISSIONS: Manual of the, by the Rev. J. Lowrie. New York, 1854. Trubner. 5s.

BAPTIST MISSIONARY SOCIETY: its History, by the Rev. Dr. Cox. 2 vols. Ward and Co. 1842.

BASLE MISSIONARY SOCIETY: Manual of the, by Rev. Dr. Blumhardt.

BIBLE SOCIETY, British and Foreign: History of, by the Rev. G. Brown.

BOHEMIAN AND MORAVIAN BRETHREN: Bost's History.

CHURCH MISSIONARY ATLAS: C.M.S., 1859. 2s. 6d.

CHURCH MISSIONARY SOCIETY: Jubilee Memorial.

CRANTZ's History of the Brethren.

FATHERS AND FOUNDERS OF THE L.M.S., by the Rev. Dr. Morison.

LONDON MISSIONARY SOCIETY: History of the, by the Rev. W. Ellis. Vol. I. Snow. Vol. II. in preparation.

LONDON MISSIONARY SOCIETY: Jubilee Memorial. Snow.

RELIGIOUS TRACT SOCIETY: Jubilee Memorial, 1850. 7s.

UNITED BRETHREN: Holmes's History of the. 97 Hatton Garden, London.

UNITED BRETHREN: Holmes's Historical Sketches of their Missions.

WESLEYAN MISSIONS, by the Rev. Dr. Alder; their Objects stated, and their Claims enforced.

WESLEYAN METHODISM: Centenary Volume, by the Rev. T. Jackson. 1840.

3. WEST INDIAN MISSIONS.

BERNAU, Rev. J. H.: Missionary Labours among the Aboriginal Indians of Guiana. C.M.S., 1847. 7s.

BLEBY, Rev. H.: Scenes in the Carribean.

BRETT, Rev. W. H.: Indian Missions in Guiana. Bell and Daldy. 1851. 5s.

BURCHELL, Rev. T.: Life of, by the Rev. F. W. Burchell. 1849.

COKE, Rev. Dr.: History of the West Indies.

DUNCAN's Narrative of Wesleyan Missions in Jamaica. 1849.

HORSFORD, Rev. John: A Voice from the West Indies.
KNIBB, Rev. W.: Memoirs of the, by Rev. J. H. Hinton. 1847.
MOISTER, Rev. W.: Memorials of Missionary Labour in the West Indies and Western Africa.
PHILLIPPO, Rev. J. M.: Jamaica; its Past and Present State. Snow. 1843.
SAMUEL, Rev. P.: Wesleyan Missions in Jamaica and Honduras. 1850.
SMITH, Rev. J. of Guiana: Memoirs of, by the Rev. E. A. Walbridge.
UNITED BRETHREN, Missions of: to the Danish West India Islands.
UNITED BRETHREN, Retrospect of their Jamaica Mission. 6d.
UNITED BRETHREN, Retrospect of their Mission in Antigua. 6d.

4. MISSIONS IN SOUTH AFRICA, ETC.

AFRICA'S MOUNTAIN VALLEY, by the Author of "Ministering Children." Seeleys, 1856.
ARBOUSSET, Rev. C.: Narrative of a Tour to North East of the Cape.
BOYCE, Rev. W.: Notes on South Africa.
BROADBENT, Rev. S.: Memoirs, by Threlfall.
CALDERWOOD, Rev. H.: Caffres and Caffre Missions. Nisbet. 4s. 6d.
COLENSO, Bishop: Ten Weeks in Natal. MacMillan and Co. 1856.
ELLIS, Rev. W.: History of Madagascar. 2 vols.
ELLIS, Rev. W.: Three Visits to Madagascar. 1859. 16s.
FREEMAN, Rev. J. J. and Rev. D. Johns: Persecutions in Madagascar. 6s.
FREEMAN, Rev. J. J.: A Tour in South Africa. Snow. 7s.
HATFIELD, Rev. E. F.: Missionary Life of the Rev. J. M. Bertram in St. Helena and the Cape. New York, 1852. 4s.
ISENBERG and KRAPF, Messrs., Church Missionary Society: Journals of Travels in Abyssinia. 1851. 12s.
LIVINGSTONE, Dr.: Missionary Researches and Travels in South Africa. 1858. 21s.
LATROBE, Rev. C. I.: Journal of a Visit to South Africa.
MOFFAT, Rev. R.: Missionary Labours and Scenes in South Africa. 1842. 12s. and 3s.
SHAW, Rev. B.: Memorials of South Africa.
SHAW, Rev. W.: Narrative of Missionary Labours in South Africa.
SMITH, Rev. THORNELY: South Africa delineated.
SOUTHERN AFRICA: A Geographical, Ethnological, and Natural History of the Country and the Condition of its Inhabitants, by the Rev. F. P. FLEMING. Hall, Virtue, and Co. 10s.
The Kaffir, the Hottentot, and the Frontier Farmer: Passages of Missionary Life, by Archdeacon MERRIMAN. Bell and Daldy. 3s. 6d.

384 MODERN WORKS ON CHRISTIAN MISSIONS.

Modern Works on Christian Missions.

5. MISSIONS IN WEST AFRICA.

BEECHAM's Ashantee and the Gold Coast. Mason. 1841.
BOWEN, Rev. T. J.: Adventures and Missionary Labours in Central Africa. Charleston, 1857. 6s. Trubner.
EAST, Rev. D. J.: Western Africa and the Baptist Mission. 1844.
FREEMAN, Rev. T. B.: Two Visits to Ashanti. Mason. 1843.
FOX, Rev. W.: Wesleyan Missions in Western Africa. 1851.
JOHNSON, Rev. W.: Church Missionary in Sierra Leone, Memoir of. 1853. 10s.
OTHIELLE; OR, VILLAGE LIFE IN THE YORUBA COUNTRY, by M. A. S. Barber. Nisbet and Co.
TUCKER, Miss: Abbeokuta; Outline of the History of the Yoruba Mission. Church Miss. Soc. Nisbet, 1853. 3s. 6d.
WALKER, Rev. S. A.: The Church Mission at Sierra Leone. Seeleys, 1851. 12s.
WEST, Rev. Daniel: Memoirs, by the Rev. T. West.
WESTERN AFRICA, its History, Condition, and Prospects; by the Rev. J. L. Wilson, eighteen years a Missionary. Sampson Low and Co. 8s. 6d.

6. MISSIONS IN THE PACIFIC.

BAMBY, Rev. J.: Memoirs, by the Rev. A. Barrett.
BINGHAM's History of the Sandwich Island Mission.
BISHOP OF NEW ZEALAND: his Views of the Church Mission. 1843. Seeleys, 6d.
BROWN's NEW ZEALAND AND ITS ABORIGINES. 1845.
CROSS, Rev. J., of Fiji: Memoirs, by the Rev. J. Hunt.
DIBBLE, Rev. S.: History of the Sandwich Island Mission. New York, 1839. 12mo.
ELLIS's Polynesian Researches. 4 vols. 12mo. 24s.
FARMER, SARAH S.: Tonga and the Friendly Isles. 1855.
FIJI AND THE FIJIANS: by the Rev. Messrs. Williams and Calvert. 2 vols. 1859. Heylin, London. 12s.
GARDINER, Capt. Allen, of Patagonia: Memoir, by the Rev. J. W. Marsh. Nisbet, 5s.
GILL, Rev. W.: Gems from the Coral Islands; an Account of Recent Missionary Success in the New Hebrides. 2 vols.
HUNT, Rev. J., of Fiji: Memoir, by the Rev. G. S. Rowe. 1859.
HUNT's Past and Present of the Sandwich Islands.
LAWRY, Rev W.: Missions in Tonga and Fiji. 2 vols. 1852. 5s.
LEIGH, Rev. S., Missionary to New Zealand and Australia: Memoir, by Strachan. 1855. 6s.
MARSDEN, Rev. S. of Parramatta: Memoir of, by his Son.
MISSIONARY RECORDS OF THE SANDWICH ISLANDS: Religious Tract Society. 2s.
NICHOLAS's Voyage to New Zealand.
PROUT, Rev. E.: Memoirs of Rev. J. Williams. Snow. 12s. and 3s.
TUCKER, Miss: the Southern Cross and the Southern Crown; or the Gospel in New Zealand. Nisbet. 3s. 6d.

VA-TA-AII: the Fijian Princess, by the Rev. J. Waterhouse. *Modern Works on Christian Missions.*
WILLIAMS's Missionary Enterprises in the South Sea Islands. Snow. 2s. 6d. and 8s.
WILLIAMS, Richard, of Patagonia: Life of, by the Rev. Dr. James Hamilton. Nisbet. 3s. 6d.
YATES's Account of New Zealand.

7. MISSIONS IN CHINA.

ABEEL, Rev. D.: Journal of a Residence in China.
DEAN, Rev. Dr.: The China Mission. A History of the Missions of all Denominations among the Chinese, and Biographical Sketches of deceased Missionaries. New York, 1859.
DYER, Rev. S.: Memoir of, by the Rev. E. Davies. Snow. 4s. 6d.
EDKINS, Rev. J.: The Religious Condition of the Chinese. 1859. Routledge. 2s. 6d.
GILLESPIE, Rev. W.: The Land of Sinim. 1854.
GLANCES AT MISSIONARY WORK IN CHINA. Nisbet and Co.
GUTZLAFF, Rev. C.: Three Voyages along the Coast of China.
LOWRIE, Rev. Walter: Memoir of, by his Father. Philadelphia, 1854. 5s.
MEDHURST, Rev. Dr.: China, its State and Prospects. Snow. 12s.
MILNE, Rev. W.: Life in China.
MISSIONARY RECORDS: China and Burmah. Religious Tract Society. 2s.
MORRISON, Rev. Dr.: Memoirs of, by his Widow. 2 vols. Snow. 24s.
MACKEAN, Rev. T. S., of Tahiti: Memoir. 1847.
SMITH, Bishop: An Exploratory Visit to China. 1844-46. Seeleys, 14s.

8. MISSIONS IN BURMAH.

BAILLIE, Rev. J.: Rivers in the Desert; Incidents of Missions among the Karens.
BOARDMAN, Rev. C.: Memoir of, by King.
JUDSON, Mrs. Ann Hazeltine, Memoir of, by Knowles.
JUDSON, Mrs. SARAH: Memoir of, by Mrs. Emily Judson. New York, 1850. 5s.
MALCOM, Rev. Dr. HOWARD: Missionary Travels in South Eastern Asia. 1839.
MASON, Rev. Dr.: The Karen Apostle.
WAYLAND, Rev. Dr.: Memoirs of Rev. Dr. Judson. 2 vols. Boston, 1853.
WYLIE, Mrs.: The Gospel in Burmah. Dalton, London, 1859. Third thousand. 5s.

9. MISSIONS IN INDIA.
a. *North India.*

BACHELOR, Rev. O. R., American: Hindooism and Christianity in Orissa.

BALLANTYNE, James, Esq., LL.D.: Christianity contrasted with Hindoo Philosophy. Madden, 1859. 9s.

BENGAL CONFERENCE OF PROTESTANT MISSIONARIES: Proceedings of. Dalton, London, 1855. 4s.

BIBLICAL TRANSLATIONS IN INDIA: Contributions towards a History of. Dalton, 1855. 2s.

BUYERS, Rev. W.: L.M.S.; Recollections of Northern India. London. 10s. 6d.

BUYERS'S LETTERS ON INDIAN MISSIONS. Snow. 5s.

CALCUTTA, BOMBAY, AND COLOMBO: An Account of the Missions of the S.P.G. Pall Mall. 2s.

CAMPBELL, Rev. J. R., of Saharunpore: Missions in Upper India. 1856.

CAREY, Rev. EUSTACE: Memoir, by his Widow. 5s.

DUFF, Rev. Dr.: India and India Missions. 1840. 12s.

DUFF, Rev. Dr.: Missions the Chief End of the Christian Church. 2s. 6d.

DUFF, Rev. Dr.: Missionary Addresses. Johnston & Hunter. 1850.

FUTTEHGURR: The Martyrs of, by the Rev. J. J. Walsh. Nisbet. 10s. 6d.

KAYE, J. H., Esq.: Christianity in India. Smith, Elder, and Co., 1859. 12s.

LEUPOLT, Rev. C. B.: Recollections of an Indian Missionary. Seeleys. 2s.

LONG, Rev. J.: Handbook of the Church of England Missions in North India. Shaw, 1848. 9s.

LOWRIE, Rev. J. C.: Two Years in North India.

LOWRIE, Rev. J. C.: Manual of the Missions of the Presbyterian Church. New York, 1854. 5s.

MACDONALD, Rev. J., of Calcutta: Memoir of, by the Rev. Dr. Tweedie. Johnston. Edinburgh, 1849.

MACKAY, Rev. J., of Delhi: Memoir of, by the Rev. J. Culross.

MARSHMAN, J. C., Esq.: Memoirs of Carey, Marshman, and Ward, their Life and Times. 2 vols. Longmans, 1859. 24s.

MARTYN, Rev. Henry: Journals and Letters of. 2 vols.

MULLENS, Rev. J.: Results of Missionary Labour in India. 1852. Dalton. Third Edition. 1s.

MULLENS, Rev. J.: The Religious Aspects of Hindoo Philosophy. 1860. Smith, Elder, and Co. 9s.

MULLENS, Mrs.: The Missionary on the Ganges: or What is Christianity. Dalton, London. 1s.

NOYES, Rev. E., American: Christian Missions in Orissa.

ORISSA: Missions in, by the Rev. J. Peggs. 1846.

SHERRING, Rev. M. A.: The Indian Church during the Rebellion. Nisbet, 1859. 5s.

STORROW, Rev. E.: India and Christian Missions. Snow, 1859. 1s. 6d.

STORROW, Rev. E.: The Eastern Lily gathered: A Memoir of Bala Soondari Tagore. Snow. 1s. 6d.

SUTTON, Rev. Dr.: Orissa and its Evangelisation. 1850.
WARD, Rev. W., of Serampore: Farewell Letters on Hindoo Worship and Superstition. 1821.
WARD, Rev. W.: The History, Literature, and Religion of the Hindoos. 2 vols. 4to. 1817. 3 vols. 8vo. 1822.
WARREN, Rev. Dr.: Fifteen Years of Missionary Life in North India. Philadelphia, 1856.
WEITBRECHT, Rev. J. J.: Lectures on Protestant Missions in Bengal. Shaw, 1844. 5s.
WEITBRECHT, Rev. J. J., Memoir of the, by his Widow. Nisbet. 7s. 6d.
WEITBRECHT, Mrs.: Missionary Sketches in Northern India. Nisbet, 1858. 5s.
WILKINSON, Rev. M.: Christianity in North India. Seeleys, 1844. 6s.
WILSON, Bishop: The Life of, by the Rev. J. Bateman. 2 vols. Murray, 1860.
WYLIE, MACLEOD, Esq.: Bengal as a Field of Missions. Dalton. London, 1854. 10s.
WYLIE, MACLEOD, Esq.: The Urgent Claims of India. Dalton. 1s.
YATES, Rev. Dr.: Memoirs of, by the Rev. Dr. Hoby. 1847.

Modern Works on Christian Missions.

b. South India.

ARTHUR, Rev. W.: Mission in the Mysore. 1849. 6s.
BUCHANAN, Rev. Dr. C.: Christian Researches in India. 2 vols.
BUCHANAN, Rev. Dr. C.: Memoir of, by the Rev. Dean Pearson. 6s.
CAMPBELL, Rev. W.: L.M.S., Bangalore: British India. 12s.
CALDWELL, Rev. Dr.: Lectures on the Tinnevelly Missions. London, Bell and Daldy, 1857. 3s. 6d.
FOX, Rev. H. W.: Chapters on South India Missions. Seeleys, 1848. 3s. 6d.
FOX, Rev. H. W.: Memoirs of, by the Rev. G. Fox. 5s.
GROVES, Mr. Anthony: Memoir of, by his Widow. Nisbet. 4s. 6d.
HOOLE, Rev. Dr.: Madras, Mysore, and South India. 1844. Longman and Co.
HOUGH, Rev. J.: History of Christianity in India. 5 vols. Nisbet.
  The Syrian Church and Romish Missions to 1800. Vols. I. and II. 24s.
  Modern Protestant Missions from 1706–1816. Vols. III. and IV. 24s.
  The same, 1816–1832. Vol. V. 10s. 6d.
JŒNICKE: Life of, by Fellowes. 1833.
MADRAS AND CUDDALORE IN THE LAST CENTURY: Journals of the S.P.C.K. Missionaries. Longman and Co.
MADRAS: Account of the S.P.G. Missions in the Diocese of Madras, by the Rev. A. R. Symonds. Pall Mall. 2s. 6d.
MULLENS, Rev. J.: Missions in South India, Lectures on. 1850. Dalton. 4s.
PETTITT, Rev. C.: The Tinnevelly Mission of the C.M.S. Seeleys. 1851. 5s.
REID, Rev. J., of Bellary: Memoir of, by the Rev. Dr. Wardlaw.

RHENIUS, Rev. C. T. E.: Memoir of, by his Son. Nisbet, 1841. 10s.

SOUTH INDIA MISSIONARY CONFERENCE: Report of. Madras, 1858.

SWARTZ, Rev. C. F.: Memoirs of, by the Rev. Dean Pearson. 2 vols.

THE LAND OF THE VEDA: India briefly described, in various Aspects, by the Rev. P. Percival. Bell and Daldy. 10s. 6d.

TREVOR, Rev. G.: India; its Natives and Missions. Religious Tract Society. 3s.

TUCKER, Miss: South Indian Missionary Sketches. Nisbet. 6s.

WARD, Rev. F. de W., of Madras: American Board: India and the Hindoos: Christian Missions among them. Hartford, 1854. 8s.

c. Bombay.

ALLEN, Rev. Dr., American Board: Missions in India.

CLARKSON, Rev. W.: L.M.S., Guzerat: India and the Gospel. Snow. 6s.

CLARKSON, Rev. W.: Missionary Encouragements. Snow. 1s. 6d.

HALL, Rev. Gordon: Memoirs of.

NESBIT, Rev. R., of Bombay: Memoirs of, by the Rev. Dr. Mitchell. Nisbet. 6s.

NEWELL, Mrs., Memoirs of.

WILSON, Rev. Dr.: Free Church, Bombay: Addresses on the Evangelisation of India. Whyte. Edinburgh, 1849.

WILSON, Rev. Dr.: Exposures of the Hindoo Religion.

WILSON, Mrs. Margaret: Memoirs of, by the Rev. Dr. Wilson.

d. Ceylon.

BUDDHISM IN CEYLON, by the Rev. R. Spence Hardy. 7s. 6d.

EASTERN MONACHISM: by the Rev. R. S. Hardy. Williams and Norgate. 7s. 6d.

ECKARD, Rev. J. R.: Residence in Ceylon and Hindostan. Philadelphia, 1844.

HARVARD, Rev. W. M.: The Wesleyan Mission in Ceylon.

SELKIRK, Rev. J.: Operations of the C. M. S. in Ceylon. 1844, Hatchard. 12s.

TENNENT, Sir J. E.: History of Christianity in Ceylon. Murray, 1850.

10. MISSIONS IN TURKEY AND PERSIA.

DWIGHT, Rev. Dr.: Christianity in Turkey; the Armenian Race and Church. Nisbet. 5s.

FISK, Rev. Pliny: Memoirs of.

FLAD, F. M.: the Journal of; Missionary in Abyssinia, by the Rev. W. D. Veitch of Jerusalem. Nisbet. 2s. 6d.

GOBAT, Bishop: Three Years in Abyssinia. Seeleys, London, 1850. 7s. 6d.

GRANT, Dr. A.: The Nestorians, or Lost Tribes. New York, 1841. 6s.

GRANT, Rev. Dr. Asahel: Memoir of, by the Rev. C. Lakross. New York. 3s. *Modern Works on Christian Missions.*
HAMLIN, Mrs. H.: Missionary in Turkey, Memorials of. Boston, 1853. 6s.
HARTLEY'S, Rev. J.: Researches in Greece and Asia Minor.
ISENBERG AND KRAPF, Messrs.: Journals of Travels in Shoa and Abyssinia. 1839–42. Seeleys. 12s.
JOWETT, Rev. C.: Christian Researches in the Mediterranean, and in the Holy Land. 2 vols.
Nestorians of Persia: History of the People, and Progress of Missions among them. Philadelphia. 1s. 6d.
PARSONS, Rev. Eli: Memoir of.
PERKINS, Mrs.: Memoir of. Boston, 1854. 3s. 6d.
PERKINS, Rev. Justin, D.D.: Residence in Persia among the Nestorians. Andover, 1843. 12s.
SMITH and DWIGHT: Missionary Researches in Armenia.
SMITH, Mrs. S. L.: Memoirs of. Religious Tract Society. 1s.
STERN, Rev. H. A.: Journal of a Missionary Journey to the Jews in Arabia Felix.
STODDARD, Rev. D. T.: Memoir of; and of Dr. Lobdell, by the Rev. Dr. Thompson. New York. Sheldon.
TEMPLE, Rev. D., Missionary in Western Asia; Life and Letters. Boston. 7s. 6d.

11. NORTH AMERICA.

BRAINERD, Rev. David: Life of, by President Edwards.
CRANTZ's History of the Moravian Missions in Greenland.
EGEDE, Hans: the Moravian; Life of.
ELIOT, John, Missionary to the Indians; Memoir of.
FINLEY, Rev. T. B.: History of the Wyandott Mission at Upper Sandusky, Ohio. New York. 4s. 6d.
LOSKIEL's History of the United Brethren's Mission in North America.
MISSIONARY RECORDS OF NORTH AMERICA: Religious Tract Society. 1s. 6d.
MISSIONARY RECORDS OF NORTHERN COUNTRIES. 2s.
MORAVIAN MISSION AMONG THE NORTH AMERICAN INDIANS: 97 Hatton Garden. London. 2s. 6d.
MORAVIANS, The: in Greenland, and in Labrador.
SLIGHT, Rev. BENJ.: Researches among the North American Indians.
TUCKER, Miss: The Rainbow in the North; Account of the Church Mission in Rupert's Land. Nisbet. 3s. 6d.

12. ADDITIONAL BIOGRAPHIES.

COKE, Rev. Dr.: Memoirs, by the Rev. Dr. Etheridge. 1860.
EDDY's Heroines of the Missionary Enterprise: Sketches of Prominent Female Missionaries. Boston, 1850. 5s. Trubner.
HODGSON, Rev. T. L.: Memoirs, by the Rev. Thornely Smith.

KNILL, Rev. Richard: Life of, by the Rev. C. Birrell. Nisbet, 1859. 4s. 6d.
PATERSON, Rev. Dr.: The Book for Every Land; Memoirs of. Snow. 1857.
ZINZENDORF, Count: Life of.

13. MISSIONARY PERIODICALS.

American Board: Missionary Herald.
Amer. Bapt. Union: The Missionary Magazine. Boston, Mass.
Baptist Missionary Society: The Missionary Herald, 1d.; and Juvenile Herald, a halfpenny.
London Society for promoting Christianity among the Jews: Jewish Intelligencer.
Archives du Christianisme. Paris.
Evangelical Christendom. 6d.
News of the Churches and Journal of Missions. 6d.
Periodical Accounts of the Moravian Missions.
Lond. Miss. Soc.: The Missionary Magazine, 1d.; and Juvenile Missionary Magazine.
Church Missionary Intelligencer. 6d. Church Miss. Record, and Church Miss. Juvenile Instructor.
Free Church: Home and Foreign Missionary Record.
Estab. Church of Scotland: Home and Foreign Miss. Record.
United Presb. Church: Missionary Record.
Wesleyan Miss. Soc.: Monthly Notices, and Monthly Juvenile Offering.

** *Friends who may wish to supply Mission Stations with Books of reference and consultation, which are much wanted, will oblige by sending contributions, in money or works of a* SUPERIOR CLASS, *to the Publishers of this volume, who will forward them to the gentlemen who acted as Stewards of the recent Conference.*

Readers of this Volume who may desire to offer the results of experience in suggestions or information, calculated to promote " the Work of the Lord," in connexion with the testifying the truth " to all nations," are invited to address these in short memorandums to the Editors and Stewards of the Conference before January next.

Attention is respectfully called to the Resolution of the Conference at page 260, and the Suggestions on page 261.

INDEX.

*** In this Index the initial words are printed according to the following plan: names of members of Conference who spoke, thus, *LEUPOLT;* names of persons not in Conference, but spoken of, thus, *Henderson;* names of places and stations, thus, CHINA; ordinary topics, thus, Afghan War; important general topics, thus, **Bible.**

ACTS of the Apostles is a missionary record, and forms one-eighth of the New Testament, *Green*, 76.

Afghan War, its unrighteous character; effect of pacification on missionary work shown in the late mutiny (see *ED-WARDES*).

AFRICA, missionary experiences in, *Shaw*, 29; *Waddell*, 39; *Tidman*, 55. Extent and success of different missions; translations of Scripture; number of native Christians, *Whiting*, 51; *Shaw*, 189; *Mullens*, 333. Native agents, their proper training, education, costume, &c.; West Indian negroes not successful teachers in Africa, *Waddell*, 213, 214.

Age of missionaries, should not exceed twenty-five before getting into their work, *Shaw*, 31; *Leupolt*, 32.

Agency of native converts in the missionary cause (see Native agents).

ALEXANDER, Major-General, appointed Chairman of the Conference, 10. His addresses, on introducing Resolution of welcome, 12; on opening the business of First Session, 15. The late Rev. John Anderson; his successful efforts in India, despite his ignorance of the native tongues, 35. Misconduct of Englishmen abroad a cause of failure, 45. The effect of European ecclesiastical systems, ib. Missionary periodicals, 71. Spirituality of giving for mission purposes, 88. Native agency: vast importance of the question; difference of opinions; necessity for calm discussion; valuable experience of many members of the Conference; of Rev. B. Lal Singh, as a native agent; reference to the "native agents" of the Primitive Church (the fellowworkers with the Apostles); their example to be considered, 192, 194, 199. Native churches: the example of the Primitive Churches of Jerusalem and Antioch to be studied in discussion; English church systems not always suitable to other countries; simple forms desirable, 278. Vote of thanks to him as Chairman, 313. His address to the Public Meeting at the close of the Conference, describing its proceedings and their results, 318.

AMERICA, missionary experience among the Red Indians, *O'Meara*, 33; in Patagonia, *Stirling*, 40; in Jamaica, *Cornford*, 43; in Polynesia, *Tidman*, 53. Effect of the conduct of Europeans on the Ojibbeway Indians when in England, *O'Meara*, 49, 50. Translations for the Indians by *O'Meara*, 144. Great want of books suited to the country; modes of life and thought, *Badham*, 149. Jamaica, *Trestrail*, 220. Views of the Indian tribes, *O'Meara*, 212.

American Medical Missions to China (see Medical Missions).

American Mission Board makes supplementary additions to the insufficient stipends of native pastors abroad, *Mullens*, 200; one of its rulers, 302. Their success in the Sandwich Islands, *Mullens*, 333.

American Missionary Conferences in India; called by the Rev. Dr. Anderson and the Rev. A. C. Thomson; their plan; their topics; specimen of the range taken in their discussions; the valuable record of these proceedings, 367–371.

American Missions in Turkey (see TURKEY).

Anderson, the late Rev. *John*, of Madras, his ignorance of the native tongue no impediment to his missionary influence, *Hislop, Alexander*, 35.

Anderson, Rev. Dr., of Boston, Sec. to the American Board; his visit, as their Deputation, to India and Syria leads to several Missionary Conferences in those missions, 200, 367.

ANDERSON, Rev. J., of Calcutta, all gifts should come from spiritual men, 83.

Anecdotes, *Walton*, 36; *O'Meara*, 34, 49, 50; *Hughes*, 46; *Macgill*, 81; *Campbell*, 136; *B. L. Singh*, 183; *Davidson*, 328.

Arctic Missions, their results, *Latrobe*, 37, 211.

Associations, quarterly meetings for prayer and collections advocated, *Hislop*, 79.

Association meetings desirable, *Latrobe*, 83. Should be devotional, and much information should be given, *Whiting*, 63; their fruits, *Green*, 77.

Associations, Juvenile (see Juvenile Associations).

Athanasian Creed and Articles of Church of England, 66.

BADHAM, Rev. J. L., vernacular literature wanted in Greenland for the Esquimaux, and in North and South America; should be adapted to their styles of thought, 149. Missions the business of the church; liberality in the Western hemisphere an example to us, 169.

"Baptist Magazine," defended from the general censure of the missionary press by the Rev. T. Smith, *Trestrail*, 73.

Baptist Missionary Conferences in India; called by E. B. Underhill, Esq.; their plan, their topics; record of their discussions; its title and its value, 371.

Barbarous and civilized nations; their respective difficulties to the missionary; success in modern missions greatest among the former, *Wallace*, 67; *Latrobe*, 211.

BARBOUR, G. F., Esq., the church backward in gifts, prayer, and faith, 99. Remarkable success of native agency at Amoy, Shanghai, and Singapore; salaries of some Chinese teachers only five or six dollars per month, 221.

BARODA, heathen festival at, *M'Kee*, 131.

BAYLEE, Rev. Dr., proposed Quarterly Review; our ecclesiastical systems shaped by controversy; study of human nature required in a missionary; Mr. Hardy's work on Buddhism, 66, 67. Missionary professorship; annual lectures to the public, in large towns, preferable to lectures in the Universities; theological professors cannot teach everything, and should be aided by special missionary lectures; the lectures should be given in London, repeated in large towns, and published, 93. Committee appointed to consider his suggestion for lectures; their report, 94, 95. Biblical translation; its principles, illustrated by the history of the Irish version; English scholars better qualified than natives; value of University training; real knowledge of language, 132, 133. His early wish to be a missionary rejected by the Church Missionary Society; other similar cases; his work in the mission-field at home; faults in systems; difficulty of pronouncing on untried candidates; St. Aidan's College, Birkenhead, founded by him; if 3000*l*. a-year provided, will keep a class of one hundred students, if they can be got, at 30*l.* a-year; has now fifteen missionary students; all classes received, whatever their attainments; examples of the results of his system, 240–243.

BENARES (see INDIA).

Benares Missionary Conference; description of its proceedings, 372, 373.

Bengal Missionary Conference; date, topics discussed, plan adopted, record of its proceedings, 372.

Beschi's anecdote in illustration of the difficulty of the Tamil language (India), *Walton*, 36.

Bible, English version superior to all others, *Baylee*, 134. Read in all Government schools in Ceylon, *Walton*, 138, 139. Introduced in Training institutions at Benares; adopted by Hindoos, and afterwards by Mahommedans, *Tucker*, 140 (see INDIA). Not in Government schools in India, *Edwardes*, 339. Adapted to the natives of India, *Davidson*, 327.

Bible-classes and Sunday-schools (see Sunday-schools).

Bible translations: value of native translators, *Singh*, 26, 129. Translators not always the most successful spiritual labourers, *Latrobe*, 37. Translations in modern times made into a hundred languages, *Whiting*, 51. Competency of English translators, *Candy*, 131. Principles of translation: experiment in Ireland; necessity of varied learning; English scholars more competent than natives, *Baylee*, 132. In Palestine; their effects, *Porter*, 140 : in African languages, *Shaw*, 189: in India, prepared by missionaries, *Sugden*, 147: in China, necessity of the union of European and native learning for its accomplishment, *Lockhart*, 205. Well-trained natives the best translators, *Waddell*, 213, 214. For India, many dictionaries required ; when these are prepared, the natives will be the best translators, *Leupolt*, 223, 224.

BICKERSTETH, Rev. —, his proposal to devote a week, in 1861, for special prayer throughout the world in behalf of missions, discussed and adopted by the Conference, 260.

BIRCH, Rev. *G. R.*, " Turkish Missions' Aid Society," established to extend native agency in connexion with American missions; 300 agents employed; missionaries only act as evangelists; natives as pastors; natives boarded and educated in college, at Constantinople, for 16*l.* a-year; Dr. Wolff's proposal to open the Universities to the Oriental churches, 215, 216.

Black Bishops and Pastors. *Stowell*, 357.

BLACKHEATH, subscriptions of children there influenced by reading the "Juvenile Instructor," *Lavie*, 79.

Bond, Capt., Page, 309.

Book Clubs recommended for the circulation of missionary periodicals, *Whiting*, 61.

Brahmins, their learning, influence, and salaries, *Singh*, 219.

Brown, Rev. J. T., of Northampton, *Trestrail*, 220.

Bruce, Rev. R. (North India), his communication on the importance of a knowledge of the native languages, 29.

Buddhism, Rev. R. S. Hardy's work on, 67 ; observations on, *Douglas*, 376.

Buildings (see Church buildings).

BURMAH, missionary operations in, 51 (see Native churches and Karens).

Burton, Dr., medical missionary in China, 106.

CALABAR, missions in, *Waddell*, 39, 214.

"Calcutta Review," an example for imitation at home, *Cullen*, 69.

Cambridge University (see Universities).

CAMPBELL, *Rev. W.*, importance in India of knowing the native tongue; illustrative anecdote; effects of the attention to this matter in Madras and Bombay, as compared with the neglect of it in Bengal, 135. Value of missionary deputations ; *facts* should be disseminated from pulpit as well as platform, 88.

"CANDIDATES FOR MISSION WORK."
Paper by the Rev. Thomas Green:
"How may we best obtain and qualify Candidates of the right stamp for Mission Work," 233-240. Men required must be spiritual men, devoted to Christ; they are the gift of God, and are to be prayed for and sought, 233, 234.

Influences used to bring them forward:
1. Missionary sermons; importance of pulpit appeals, as shown by their results.
2. Missionary meetings; their importance illustrated.
3. Sunday-schools; example of their influence; five missionaries sent out by the exertions of the author in one parish in Yorkshire.
4. Young Men's Christian Associations; their value; six of their members students in the Church Missionary College, Islington.
5. Universities; numerous missionaries have proceeded from them; and their agency is actively at work.
6. Parental influence; instances of its operation.
7. Individual effort; mode in which it is and may be exercised.
8. Special appeals for particular mission-fields; examples of their powerful effect.
9. Missionary publications and periodicals. All these means available to all, requiring only fresh energy; what the studies of candidates should comprise, 233-240.

Discussion on this Paper:
Difficulty of judging an untried man; Dr. Baylee's early wish to be a missionary rejected; other similar cases; faults in systems; St. Aidan's College, Birkenhead, open to 100 students, at 30*l.* a-year; all classes received, whatever their attainments; results of the system, *Baylee*, 240-243. Medical missionaries should not be ordained; attention to two professions diminishes their influence, *Lockhart*, 244. Union of spiritual and scientific qualifications; attention to this in the medical schools in Edinburgh; desirable to train them first at home, *Cullen*, 244. Value of medical knowledge to missionaries; should be acquired by students, *O'Meara*, 245. Evil influence of vicious Europeans on a heathen community, *King*, 245. Applications of young men, willing, but not qualified; necessity of rejecting them; need of prayer for labourers in the harvest; early impressions the ground of such applications; importance of appeals to Juvenile Associations and young men in business, *Fairbrother*, 246.

Caution necessary in accepting candidates; better to reject a good than to accept a bad man; missionaries should correspond with boys in their old schools at home; strong missionary spirit in Universities and public schools, which should be fostered, *Whiting*, 246, 247. Education of the minister and the missionary; American idea that in England the latter is thought inferior in status; moral position of the missionary higher than that of the home-worker; men, without academical knowledge, but trained in missionary colleges and ordained, are they eligible on return as home ministers? *Somerville*, 247, 248. Missions, part of the ordinary work of the Church; no distinction between home and foreign work; erroneous ideas on these points; disastrous results of parents' objections to a Divine call in children; Wesleyan examinations and admission to Theological Institution; education there the same for home as foreign work, except languages, &c., *Scott*, 249, 250.

In the Baptist Missionary Society, the status of missionaries is higher than that of home ministers; mode of selecting them; special difficulties in getting the best men; medical examination; home ministry open to returned missionaries; some of their best missionaries taken from secular occupations, *Trestrail*, 251, 252. Freshness of zeal often more valuable than scholarship; young men, leaders of Sabbath-schools and Bible-classes, very desirable, *Macgowan*, 252. Press and pulpit should aid the cause; a high religious standard should be maintained, *Swan*, 252. Missionary service as elevated as the ordinary ministry; more men needed; inferior candidates urged on Committees, as *protégés* of friends; this pressure to be resisted, *Layard*, 253. Importance of prayer; result of prayer-meetings at Cambridge; effect of individual interest in a special mission-field; course of examination in the Church Missionary Society described; returned missionaries eligible as pastors, *Titcomb*, 254, 255. Success of the Rev. R. Knill in enlisting candidates; his direct personal appeals to young men; the willing, but diffident, should be encouraged, *Harcus*, 255, 256. Christ's command to *pray* for labourers, *Waddell*, 256. Importance of Sunday-schools and Bible-classes, *Woodrooffe*, 256.

Parental influence, how to be dealt with; misconception of the missionary's dangers; distaste for special fields should be discouraged; men should feel bound to serve anywhere; not as making sacrifices, but as working in their proper sphere; previous home-experience beneficial; pastors might quit home for mission service, *Smith*, 257–259. Paramount claims of mission work; young pastors should be invited to go out; an ex-missionary, in a military sense, is "degraded" to home service, *Sugden*, 259. Laymen also should work for missions; individual responsibility; theological professors should be missionary in their spirit and instructions; invitation to Dr. Duff; analogy between military and missionary life, *Thorburn*, 261, 262. Self-sacrifice to be cultivated among the wealthy, *Cather*, 262. Personal danger in mission-work not great now abroad; greater in Ireland, *Chairman*, 262.

MINUTE of Conference on the above: duty of special prayer; candidates to be actively sought for; their personal religious character to be of a high standard; important to enlist persons of a higher social rank; susceptibility of particular classes; methods of appealing to them; erroneous views to be removed; training to have regard to individual capacity and sphere of action; general vigour to be infused into old plans, 264, 265.

CANDY, Rev. G., impracticability of fixed rules for all kinds of work in all kinds of spheres; influence and necessity of missions to Europeans in India; evils of former European example, and improved state of affairs, 44. Vernacular Indian tracts not to be prepared entirely by natives, 131. Their dissemination increased by sale, instead of giving them away, 132.

Carnegie, Dr., medical missionary at Amoy in China, 105.

Carpet manufacture under *Mrs. Leupolt*, 298.

Catechists in Indian villages, *Leupolt*, 33.

CATHER, Rev. R. G., failures not sufficiently brought forward; more humiliation necessary; identity of missionary and home work; their action on each other; liberality at home should be increased on principle; want of pulpit aid in calling it forth, 168. Self-sacrifice to be cultivated among the wealthy, 262.

Causes of failure (see Failure of missions).

CEYLON. Plan of the Wesleyan missions; itinerancies; house to house visits; work of native agents and classes, *Hardy*, 42, 43. English schools in Jaffna, by American and English missionaries; their success; changes in the system, *Walton*, 137, 138. The Bible read in the Ceylon Government Schools; teachers, caste, and books, *Walton*, 139. Native pastors in Ceylon; how supported; their circuits, *Hardy*, 200. .

Chairman of Conference appointed (see ALEXANDER, *Major-General*), 10. Vote of thanks to him, 313.

Chalmers, Rev. Dr., sayings of his, *Lewis*, 156; *Cather*, 167; his professorship, *Thorburn*, 262.

Children; interest in missions excited in them (see Education, Schools, Contributions, Juvenile Associations).

CHINA, necessity of Medical Missions and of learned missionaries to refute the learned heathen, *Mullens*, 22, 24. Missionary experiences in China; itinerancies and settled stations; native churches the result, and native agents, *Lockhart*, 38. Medical Missions in; address by *Dr. Lockhart*, 100–107. Medical Missions in China and Japan; address by *Dr. Macgowan*, 275. Possibility of reducing the language to a Romanized character to facilitate teaching, *Gundert*, 148. Objections to the plan; necessity of learning the native character, *Lockhart*, 205. Native agents employed with undue haste; hypocrites anxious for employment engaged; natives should not be paid till tried, *Macgowan*, 208. Success of native agency at Amoy and Shanghai; also at Singapore, *Barbour*, 221. Recent success of missions in China. *Mullens*, 333.

Christian Advocate at Cambridge, his office and operations, *Titcomb*, 93.

Christian Vernacular Education Society (India); testimony to its expected value, *Titcomb*, 126; *Hislop*, 134.

Church, definition of, 279.

Church buildings abroad too costly, *Trestrail*, 282; *Mullens*, 284; *Singh*, 294; *Macfie*, 295.

" Church Missionary Intelligencer," its merit as a missionary organ, *Smith*, 70 (see Press); *Green*, 77.

" Church Missionary Juvenile Instructor" (see " Juvenile Instructor").

" Church Missionary Record," its circulation and merits, *Green*, 77.

Civilized and barbarous tribes; their respective difficulties to the missionary; success among the latter, *Wallace*, 67; *Latrobe*, 211.

Clarkson, Rev. W., Wallace, 288.

Coldstream, Dr., his lectures on ethnology and ethnography; their utility to missionaries, *Cullen*, 92.

Collections (see Contributions).

Collectors' poundage (see Contributions).

Colledge, Mr., of China, *Lockhart*, 105.

Colleges (see Theological Institutions, Universities, and Professorships).

Collins, Mr., medical missionary in China, 106.

Commerce, its spread in North America injurious to the missionary cause, *O'Meara*, 50. Its promotion available for mission purposes; Dr. Livingstone's example, *Lewis*, 163.

Committee appointed " to inquire and report on the best means of obtaining increased funds for religious Societies," 232.

CONFERENCE, summary of; its origin, objects, and plan; invitations issued; course of proceedings; their success, and value of the discussions; its record; *Introduction*, 1–3, 285, 319, 355.

CONFERENCES, PREVIOUS MISSIONARY. Desire for such Conferences; difficulties in the way; New York Convention, 365, 366; Conference in London, 367; American Conferences in India, 367–371; Baptist Missionary Conferences in India, 371; Bengal Missionary Conference, 372; Benares Missionary Conference, ib.; South India Conference, 373; relation of these gatherings to the Conference at Liverpool, 374.

CONSTANTINOPLE, American mission at, *Birch*, 215, 216; *Tucker*, 270–273.

" CONTRIBUTIONS, LIBERALITY IN," to the mission cause.

Paper by the Rev. J. Lewis: Small proportion of British wealth given to missions; how to get more; revivals do not always aid missions; influence of current opinion on religious expenditure, 153.

I. Home organization should commence with training children by school-books full of incidents and scenes; Sabbath-schools to be systematically brought in, 154; by regular and frequent lessons and collections, 155; by pictures of heathen races in schools, ib. House visitations a *sine quâ non*; deputations to be employed chiefly for appeals for special funds, and for founding or reviving auxiliaries, 156. Pulpit influence better than printed intelligence; reluctance to use it, 157. Causes thereof; want of due education in colleges by professors and lectures; remedy practicable but difficult, 158.

II. Foreign operations of missions as affecting home contributions; missionaries should not be limited to preaching and teaching, 160. Works of benevolence wrought by missions very useful; illustrations; the early monasteries were mission-houses, by spreading arts and civilisation, 161. Capitalists, planters, mechanics, and other laymen should share mission work, 162. Dr. Livingstone's example; also Polynesian missions; missions not self-supporting, and therefore not attractive to the mercantile mind, 163.

Discussion on Mr. Lewis's Paper:

Contributions to the missionary cause should be regarded as devotional; increased by information respecting missions; gross subscriptions of Christendom, for foreign missions, amount annually to 600,000*l.*, *MacGill*, 81, 82. All gifts should come from spiritual men, *Anderson*, 83. Necessity and duty of asking for contributions; apostolical precedent for it, neglected by laymen, *Leach*, 87. Contributions should be spiritual, *Alexander*, 88. The Church backward in liberality, *Barbour*, 99.

Expense of deputations; want of pulpit aid, *Layard*, 165. Collectors' poundage a question for London Committees; expenses saved by hospitality of friends, *Woodrooffe*, 165. Apathy of the wealthy; necessity of stimulating them, *Davis*, 166. Reciprocity of mission and home work not sufficiently recognised; home liberality should be increased on principle; the pulpit must do more to call it forth, *Cather*, 168. Our ministers should be more missionary; a missionary pastor makes a missionary people; pastors should be entreated themselves to cherish the missionary cause; systematic teaching on the subject is needed; illustration in his own case; frequent pulpit teaching *without collections* necessary; a good cause brings money, *Tidman*, 169. In the Free Church, no percentage paid for collecting; 12,000 voluntary collectors, *Tweedie*, 170. Total abstinence; its tendency to increase funds, *Rattray*, 171. Preparation in the Church for enlarged labours; simultaneous pulpit appeal throughout Christendom *without collections* urged, *Scott*, 172.

Encouraging effect of simultaneous monthly prayer-meetings throughout the world, *Porter*, 172. Necessity for abundant information; effect of systematic giving; thank-offerings; weekly offerings, *Whiting*, 172. Contributions of the poor as acceptable as those of the rich; pulpit appeals desirable, but systematic and frequent giving essential; nations grow corrupt through wealth; liberality acceptable to God; monthly collections in U. P. Church, *MacGill*, 174, 175. Special claims on some churches impede pastoral efforts; systematic benevolence required; weekly offerings, *Cornford*, 175. Weekly contributions to boxes in places of worship successful, the expense of collection being saved, *Cropper*, 176. More pastoral zeal required; successful efforts of a returned missionary as a pastor at home, *Makepeace*, 176. Extent of Christian obligation less defined than under the patriarchal and Jewish dispensations; Christians should give more; the tithe a minimum, *Thorburn*, 176. Contribution a duty, not a matter of feeling; luxuries to be cut down, *Waddell*, 177. A quarterly report of one quarter of the globe, if prepared by each Society, and sent to all churches connected with it, would form the basis of a sermon, *Edwardes*, 178.

MINUTE of Conference on the above: the ground of liberality; as much a duty to give as to work and pray; conscience, under the influence of prayerful deliberation, must guide the amount; gifts, if systematic, would be increasing; a more active missionary spirit desired in pastors, and abstinence from luxury in all, 178, 179.

Controversial character of ecclesiastical systems, *Chairman*, 16; *Baylee*, 67.

Converts (Indian and Tahitian) neglected on their arrival in England, *Hughes*, 46. Should be used to aid missionaries in raising native churches, *Titcomb*, 48. Immensely increased number in modern times, *Whiting*, 51; *Tidman*, 53; *Mullens*, 331–335.

CORNFORD, *Rev. P. H.*, the necessity of addressing the lowest classes; the temporal action and medical influence of missionaries, 43. Other claims on churches prevent their support of missions; weekly offerings desirable, 175.

CROPPER, JOHN, *Esq.*, appointed on Executive Committee, 10. Success of weekly offerings; a box at the entrance of his chapel saving the expense and trouble of ordinary systems of collecting, 176. Chairman of Preliminary Meeting, 10. Chairman of Second Soirée, 180.

CULLEN, *Rev. G. D.*, his assistance in preparatory arrangements, 2; on Executive Committee, 10; appointed as Joint-Secretary and Editor, 11. Proposed Quarterly Review, 69. Lectures by Dr. Coldstream on ethnology and ethnography; their utility to missionaries, 92. Home training of medical missionaries desirable; spiritual and scientific qualifications essential to them; attention to this in the medical schools of Edinburgh, 244. Rev. Mr. Bickersteth's proposal for united prayer-meetings and missionary sermons in January, 1861, 261. At Public Meeting, returns thanks for hospitality shown to the Conference, 360.

Cumming, Dr., medical missionary in China, 105.

CUNNINGHAM, JAMES, *Esq.*, suggests special and general maps, showing all missionary stations, 146.

DAMASCUS, mission at, its successful operations, *Porter*, 140.

Dangers of foreign missions exaggerated by parents of missionary candidates, *Smith*, 257. Actual dangers encountered in many cases abroad not greater than those incurred by missionaries to Roman Catholics in Ireland; the thought of danger should never deter a soldier of Christ, *Alexander*, 263.

Daniel, the late Rev. J., of Ceylon; his great devotedness and eminent usefulness among the natives, *Layard*, 296.

DAVIDSON, *Major*, value of missionary efforts among our own countrymen in India, 47. His employment of native agency in the revision of the land revenue of India; mode of proceeding; application of it to missionary purposes; native preachers should not live or dress as Europeans; learned Brahmins very few; not necessary to educate native agents to encounter these; general character of the natives far better than is generally supposed; their intelligence and aptitude for religious instruction, 206–208.

Address at Public Meeting; our responsibility in India; his own life among the rural population; their condition and wants; the Bible most suitable to them; illustration of their interest in its stories; hope for India, 326–329.

DAVIS, Dr. G. H., on the vernacular literature issued from the native presses of India; number and character of these works; must be met by large issues of a Christian character, 127. Apathy of the wealthy; necessity for stimulating them, 166. The reproduction abroad of all the divisions of English Christianity is at present unavoidable; new churches must eventually form systems suitable to their own circumstances; different Societies need not occupy the same ground; they may divide the work between them, and co-operate for the general good, 290.

DAWES, Colonel, native agents most necessary; should be trained in their own tongue, retain native habits and dress, differing from the heathen only in religion; missionaries generally overworked, and in need of native help, 201, 202.

DEPTFORD, subscriptions of children there influenced by reading the "Juvenile Instructor," *Lavie*, 79.

Deputations, missionary : best mode of conducting them; should be directed to villages as well as to large towns, *Fordyce*, 85. Information to be given by deputations should consist of *facts* and individual cases, whether of success or failure, *Mullens*, 85, 86. Suggestions for pulpit as well as platform addresses, *Campbell*, 88. Eloquent speakers not always the best friends of missions, *Alexander*, 89. Should convey full and clear information, MINUTE, 95. Their great value; best mode of their application for increasing funds, *Lewis*, 156. Their necessary expense, *Layard*, 165.

Diffusion or concentration of missionary effort, *Mullens*, 21. Settled stations valuable, as the starting-point of itinerancies, *Lockhart*, 39; *Waddell*, 40; *Hardy*, 42; *Minute*, 56; *New York Convention*, 366.

Dissolving views of missionary incidents recommended for meetings, *Whiting*, 63

Douglas, James, Esq., of Cavers, his suggestions, 375.

Dress of native converts and preachers, *Waddell*, 214; *Walton*, 224.

Drew, Rev. W. Hoyles, his familiarity with the Tamil language, 147.

Duff, Rev. Dr., baptises seven Jews in Calcutta; his labours in the English Institution of the Free-Church Mission, 181–183; received impressions at college, 237; invited to succeed Dr. Chalmers, 262; his visit to New York, in 1854, leads to the New York Convention on Missions, 365.

Ecclesiastical systems of Europe, a cause of hindrance to missionary efforts, *Chairman*, 16, 278; the products of controversies, *Baylee*, 66; to be adapted to new localities, when transferred to other countries, *Mullens*, 285, 302; *Hardy*, 299; *Titcomb*, ib.; mere technicalities to be avoided, *Shaw*, 289; *Fox*, 287; *Latrobe*, 288; must be reproduced in foreign lands, *Davis*, 290; *Titcomb*, 299 (see Native churches).

"Edinburgh Review," its improved tone on missions, *Hardy*, 90.

Editors of the proceedings of the Conference; their appointment, 11.

Education, home, how to be made available for mission funds, *Lewis*, 154. Missionary (see Missionary education).

EDWARDES, Lieut.-Colonel, each Society might prepare a summary quarterly of the state of missions in one quarter of the globe, as the basis of a sermon in every church connected with such Society, 178. Address "On the Peshawur Mission:" description of the valley, and its warlike tribes; most unpromising spot for the mission; founded by Colonel Martin; its struggles; meeting of officers; scornful donation by one of "a rupee, for a revolver for the first missionary;" that officer and his family among the first victims of the late mutiny; success of the mission; Dr. Pfander's exertions under personal danger; pacification of Afghanistan after the unrighteous war; change of policy through Lieut.-Colonel Edwardes's influence; this change, aided by the mission, kept the Afghans loyal during the late mutiny; " Laus Deo," 185–188.

His speech at the Public Meeting, 337–355.

Missions illustrated by the mutiny; growth of our Indian empire; England's moral triumphs there, over Thuggee and the like; our duty to India; why was it given to us? because we have the open Bible, 338. Former opposition to missionaries in India; Judson and others expelled; temples patronised; education given without the Bible; justice intended in this, 339.

The natives very religious; very suspicious of English policy; illustrations; suspicions about the electric telegraph, roasting their children, flour and bone-dust, 340, 341. Open dealing about the Bible necessary; great success of missions, 342.

The native army, its growth; caste in the Bengal army; its influence, extent, and power; Hindooism a religion of externals; Mahommedans sometimes proselyte them by stealth; strong feeling about the cartridges, 345. The mutiny; strength of the mutineers; our heroes, English men and women; their noble deeds; the great soldiers, 346, 347.

Lessons of the mutiny; its chastisements; proofs of Divine aid; the telegraph; the native princes; the Afghans at peace; the people on our side; no leaders among the mutineers; the Punjab with us, 347–352. India to be blessed with the Bible; with Christian missions; with Christian government, 355.

Eloquence of the Hindoos, *Walton*, 36.

Eloquent speakers not always the best friends of missions, *Alexander*, 89.

Elphinstone, —, Bombay, *Campbell*, 136.

Employment, secular, of missionaries (see Secular employment).

Esquimaux missions, *Latrobe*, 211.

Ethnology and ethnography, lectures on, by Dr. Coldstream, *Cullen*, 92.

Europeans abroad; necessity of missions to them, *Hebert*, 42; *King*, 245. Effect of missions on them, *Candy*, 44; *Davidson*, 47. Effect of their conversion on natives, *Candy*, 45.

European compared with native preaching (see Preaching).

"EUROPEAN MISSIONARIES ABROAD." *Paper by the Rev. Joseph Mullens:*

Importance of the missionary; peculiarity of his position; he is a representative man; his personal character; questions respecting his qualifications; purpose he has in view; he should study his health, should know the people well amongst whom he ministers, and should learn their language; which is best begun at home, as the process is slow at first; he should also master thoroughly a brief manual of the customs, &c., of the country to which he is going; he will best learn the language of the people among themselves; to preach in the vernacular should be his principal aim, as it best suits native customs and modes of thought; he should establish itinerancies; Societies should secure men competent to preach in the vernacular; importance of Medical Missions; their establishment in China and India; varieties of acquirements in missionary work; also in its spheres of labour; the missionary should be adapted to the place he occupies; tendency in modern missions to make missionaries superintendents and advisers; instances of it; disappearance of it when churches attain their maturity; kind of men now needed for superintendents; also for dealings with native scholars; study of the learned languages requisite; daily efforts of the missionary should be devoted to make himself " wise to win souls," 17–24.

" Evangelical Christendom " to be sent to all mission stations, *Steane*, 89; its usefulness, *Hardy*, 90.

Ewart, Rev. Dr., Calcutta, Singh, 183.
Executive Committee of the Conference; their appointment, 10.

Facts of more importance in missionary narratives and addresses than general views, Mullens, 85, 86; O'Meara, 86.
Failure of missions; its causes, Alexander, 16; misconduct of Europeans abroad, Candy, 45. Failure denied, Whiting, 51; Tidman, 53.
Failures in individual cases tend to excite sympathy; their injudicious suppression by the press, Fordyce, 84; Mullens, 86.
FAIRBROTHER, Rev. W., success of native agency in the South Sea Islands, Madagascar, and the Karen mission, 206. Applications of young men, willing, but not qualified; necessity of rejecting them; need of prayer for labourers in the harvest; early impressions the ground of such applications; importance of appeals to Juvenile Associations and young men in business, 246.
FALKLAND ISLANDS, Stirling, 41.
"Female Education in the East." The unregarded, uneducated, and enslaved condition of women in India; history of the Societies formed for the education of native females; their limited nature; small funds available for this object; necessity for their extension by an appeal to the mothers and daughters of England, Fordyce, 273, 274. Its great importance in all missions, Leupolt, 112, 113; Titcomb, 127; Minute, 150.
Female missionaries (see Native female missionaries).
Fifth Session of Conference, 191.
Fiji mission; its success, Pritchard, 221. Native agency there; how formed; how carried out; its great success, Hardy, 197; Lyth, 377.
First-fruits and tithes, Thorburn, 177.
First General Prayer-meeting, 11.
First Missionary Soirée, 99.
First Session of Conference, 12.

FORDYCE, Rev. J., the missionary press; a new paper not desirable; better to improve those existing; discretion of editors; failures of missionaries too often suppressed to the injury of the cause, 84. Deputations should extend to villages as well as towns; illustration from Indian experience; importance of juvenile support, 85. Female education in India left too much to Ladies' Societies; their means inadequate, 148. Address on "Female Education in the East;" history of the few efforts already made for the education of native females; various Societies formed; their limited resources; necessity for their extension; uneducated and enslaved condition of women in India; an appeal necessary to the mothers and daughters of England, 273, 274.
Fourth General Prayer-meeting, 277.
Fourth Session of Conference, 152.
Fraser, Mr. Hugh, Singh, 294.
Free Church Mission, Calcutta; its success among the Jews, 181; exertions of Dr. Duff and his colleagues, Singh, 182; its educational system described, Smith, 118–122; difficulties in the way of the system, Gardiner, 144, 145; moderate views approved, Sugden, 147. Native missionaries ordained in it; principles of that measure examined, Mullens, 285; Tweedie, 291; Gardiner, ib.
Free Church periodical publications defended; their circulation, Tweedie, 75. Large funds raised without paid collectors, Tweedie, 170.
Fox, Rev. G., opinion of "Pearson on the Creed;" technicalities of English church systems not to be introduced in native churches, 287.

GABB, Rev. J., his suggestions for the establishment of a penny Missionary Newspaper and a first-class Quarterly Review, 64.
"Gardiner, Allen," vessel so named employed in Patagonian mission, 41.
GARDINER, Rev. T., on limiting

itinerancies to small localities, to sustain the effect of novelty, 38. Difficulty of getting Christian teachers in India; their English education leads them to better-paid work; secular education should not be extended too far to doubtful scholars; effect of the new University examinations, 145, 146. Training of native agents in India; difference of localities; for the Presidency cities, English education necessary; for rural districts, a vernacular training; natives highly trained in Calcutta unfitted for rural work; high salaries, given by the Free Church, have not satisfied the natives; difficulty of the question of salaries, 209, 210. Native missionaries are ordained into the Free Church generally, as in Scotland, but historical and local peculiarities should be avoided in the native church, *per se;* advantages and disadvantages of the "separate Christian village" system; should missionaries control, or only advise, self-supporting native churches? 291, 292.

General Prayer-meetings (see Prayer-meetings).

General Public Meeting (see Public Meeting).

Government education in India; countenance given to heathenism (see INDIA).

Government support to colonial missionaries, *Hebert*, 42.

Gratuitous distribution of tracts in India less effective than their sale (see INDIA).

Greek Church in Turkey (see TURKEY).

GREEN, *Rev. T.*, his address on the opening Resolution of welcome, 14; on a knowledge of native languages, 29. The pulpit not sufficiently used for missionary purposes; "Acts of the Apostles" a missionary record; one-eighth of the New Testament; his own pulpit efforts, and their results; periodical publications; reply to strictures of the Rev. Thos. Smith; value of the "Juvenile Instructor" and "Church Missionary Record," 76. *Paper:* "How may we best obtain and qualify Candidates of the right stamp for Mission Work," 233-240 (see Candidates for mission work).

GREENLAND, want of vernacular books, *Badham*, 149; Moravian missions in; its distinguished native agents, *Latrobe*, 37, 211; and (see Arctic Missions).

GREENWICH, subscriptions of children there influenced by reading the "Juvenile Instructor," *Lavie*, 79.

Gregson, Rev. —, of Cawnpore, *Trestrail*, 252.

GUNDERT, *Rev. H.*, time necessary to teach the Chinese language; possibility of writing it in a Romanized character, 148.

HARCUS, *Rev. W.*, success of Rev. R. Knill in enlisting missionaries; his direct personal appeals to young men; the diffident should be encouraged, 255, 256.

HARDY, *Rev. R. S.*, European as compared with native preaching, 25; the missionary work in Ceylon, 42; his work on Buddhism, 67. The missionary and general press; value of the "Evangelical Christendom" and "News of the Churches;" improvement in "Edinburgh and Quarterly Reviews," "Times," and other newspapers, 90. *Paper:* "On Native Agency in Foreign Missions," 194-199 (see Native agency). Wesleyan native agents ordained over a circuit, and limited to three years in one place; insufficient stipends of native agents should be supplemented from home; but stipends should not be too high, 200, 201. On Christian villages; advantages and disadvantages of isolation of religious communities must be regulated by circumstances; generally an evil, as shown by the history of monachism; weak converts benefit by seclusion, but the communities lose strength and influence; a model village, to be imitated by natives, may be allowed; teaching of technicalities can be avoided; the *essentials* of different churches may and should be trans-

ferred, but *details* only hinder and perplex, 298, 299.
Havelock, General, *Edwardes*, 347, 348.
Hazledine, Rev. Mr., chaplain of Tounghoo, *Page*, 309.
Health of the missionary; its importance, *Mullens*, 19; mistakes about it, *Smith*, 258.
Heathen teachers in Christian schools an evil; heathen boys in Bible-schools, *Lavie*, 143.
HEBERT, Rev. C., on the necessity of missions to Europeans abroad, 42. Missionary prayer-meetings not sufficiently employed; example of their results, 78.
Henderson, Dr., medical missionary in China, 106.
Hepburn, Dr., medical missionary in China, 105.
Hirschberg, Dr., medical missionary in China, 105.
HISLOP, Rev. S., importance of associations for quarterly meetings for prayer and collections; example of their results, 79. Government countenance of heathenism in India; sale of tracts by colporteurs more effective than gratuitous distribution; importance of the "Vernacular Education Society;" gross ignorance in Nagpore, 134. Independence of native churches desirable, but allowance to be made for national character; the Hindoos dependent, feeble, and deceitful; the hill tribes, energetic and truthful; the Karens, energetic and prepared by the Lord; the Burmese of the plains far less willing and zealous; influence of caste adds to the weakness of the Hindoos, 306, 307.
Hobson, Dr., medical missionary in China, 105.
Hodgson, Rev. C., his suggestion of a penny missionary newspaper, and a Missionary Review, 64.
HŒRNLE, Rev. C. T., infants and children in Indian mission schools; mixed schools of heathens and children; success of schools in India, 116.

HOLLAND, new Missionary Society in, 192.
"HOME LIBERALITY: BEST MEANS OF CALLING IT FORTH." Paper by the Rev. James Lewis, 153-165 (see Contributions to the mission cause).
Home piety, its connexion with missionary success abroad, *Somerville*, 52; *Tidman*, 54.
Hospital and dispensaries of Medical Missions, *Lockhart*, 101-105.
Hospitality to the members of Conference, by friends in Liverpool; vote of thanks for it, 313, *Cullen*, 360.
House-to-house visiting, *Mullens*, 21; in Ceylon, *Hardy*, 43; in India, *Davidson*, 48; to excite a missionary spirit at home, *Lewis*, 156.
HOWELL, JAMES, Esq., appointed on Executive Committee, 10.
HUGHES, *Lieut.-Colonel*, extent and usefulness of Juvenile Associations, 79. Large circulation of the "Juvenile Instructor" and the "Gleaner," 80. £20,000 annually subscribed to the Church Missionary Society by the poor, 80. Misconduct of Europeans a cause of failure, 45. Neglect of Indian converts and other foreigners in England, with illustrative anecdotes, 46. Want of interest in the cause on the part of clergy and ministers, 88.
Humility taught to missionaries and the Church at large, as the great lesson of success, *Mullens*, 335.
Huron, Lake (see *O'MEARA*).

Income, 82.
INDIA: Missionary experiences in, *Mullens*, 20-24; preaching to children in Ceylon, *Hardy*, 25; *M'Kee*, ib.; *Singh*, 26; *Smith*, 27; *Bruce*, 29; *Leupolt*, 31; *Hislop*, 34; *Walton*, 35; *Lavie*, 36; *Gardiner*, 38; *Hebert*, 42; *Candy*, 44; *Alexander*, 45; *Hughes*, 45; *Davidson*, 47; *Titcomb*, 48; *Whiting*, 50; *Tidman*, 53, 54; *Wallace*, 67; *Fordyce*, 85; *Mullens*, 85, 86. Medical Missions, *Lockhart*, 100. Sugges-

tions for education of heathen and Christian natives, infants and children (orphans especially), boys and girls, and training institutions for native teachers and evangelists; female missionaries; teaching English as a *language;* all *knowledge* to be conveyed in the vernacular, *Leupolt,* 111–116. Successful working of schools at Agra, *Hœrnlé,* 116. School education in India, its principles, practice, and results; education of females and converts, *Smith,* 118–123. Missionary education; English and vernacular schools; want of native masters for training-classes, *Titcomb,* 123. Statistics of the native literature; not sufficiently Christian in its character, *Davis,* 127. Bible translations best executed by natives, *Singh,* 129. Professed neutrality of Government in religion not real; consequent discouragement to Christianity, *M'Kee,* 130. Englishmen competent to write native tracts; their dissemination greater when *sold* than when *given, Candy,* 131, 132. English scholars best qualified for Biblical translation, *Baylee,* 132. Government countenance of heathenism; ignorance in Nagpore; sale better than gifts of tracts, *Hislop,* 134. Importance to missionaries of a knowledge of the vernacular; cultivated in Madras and Bombay more than in Bengal; result, *Campbell,* 135. Success of English schools in Ceylon, and especially of one opened by a native Christian; Government schools there; Bible read in all; teachers not always Christians; school-books used; caste ignored in mission schools, *Walton,* 137–139. Spread of Government village-schools; Bible read in Training Institution, Benares; Government training institutions established, *Tucker,* 140.

Difficulty of getting a good supply of Christian teachers; secular education may go too far with doubtful scholars; Indian universities; effect of their examinations, *Gardiner,* 145. Best literature produced by Europeans; Tamil writings by the Rev. W. Drew, *Sugden,* 147, 148. Free Church mission in Calcutta; its success among Jews, 180, 181. Personal history of Rev. B. Lal Singh; affecting history of a Hindoo girl (now his wife); her mother's death; her own education, and missionary efforts, *Singh,* 183. "THE PESHAWUR MISSION;" its influence on the loyalty of the Afghans during the late mutiny; its foundation by Col. Martin; Dr. Pfander's exertions and dangers, *Edwardes,* 185–188. Misconceptions as to danger from the climate an obstacle to raising candidates, *Smith,* 258. "INDIAN CONVERTS IN THE MUTINY;" rising at Benares; extreme danger of the position; firmness of faith in the converts; only two in India became Mahommedans through fear; refugee converts protected in Benares; Goruckpore; converts offered the choice of death or recantation; their consultation and flight; danger in the jungle; meeting with Peel's Naval Brigade; kindness of the sailors, *Leupolt,* 266–270. Female education in (see " Female Education in the East"). Native agency in (see Native agency).

Individual effort, its influence in raising candidates for mission work, *Green,* 235 (see Candidates).

Industrial schools at missions essential; affording employment to converts, *M'Kee,* 26; *Leupolt,* 114.

Interpreters employed by missionaries in North America; difficulty of the native language, *O'Meara,* 33; sometimes also in West Africa, *Waddell,* 40.

Irish Bible, its revision attempted by Rev. Dr. Baylee and two brethren of varied knowledge; the result, 132; (see Bible translations).

Islington Church Missionary College, notice of its operations, *Green,* 234, 235; its course of examination and education, *Titcomb,* 254.

Itinerancies compared with fixed local preaching, *Mullens,* 21; to be made very carefully in India, *Leupolt*, 32; their great success in China; should be conducted systematically and repeated, *Lockhart*, 39; in West Africa; advantage of fixed centres and frequent local visits, *Waddell*, 40; in Ceylon, *Hardy*, 42; in Orissa, very systematic, and greatly successful, *Stubbins*, 203; *Minute* of Conference on the above, 56, 57.

JAMAICA (see AMERICA).
Jews, converted by Rev. Dr. Baylee, 133; baptised in Calcutta, *Singh*, 181.
Josenhans, —, *Leupolt*, 112.
Joseph, history of, Indians' interest in, *Davidson*, 328.
Judson, Dr., *Wallace*, 67; *Green*, 237.
Juvenile Associations, their importance and organisation, *Whiting*, 63; extent and usefulness; example at St. John's Wood, *Hughes*, 79; their immediate and prospective value, *Fordyce*, 85; importance of their extension, *Minute*, 94; their importance in raising candidates for mission work, *Fairbrother*, 246.
"Juvenile Instructor," its circulation and influence, *Green*, 77; *Woodrooffe*, 78; its effect on children of Blackheath and neighbourhood; their subscriptions, *Lavie*, 79; its circulation and influence, *Hughes*, 80.

KARENS, missionary work among the, *Mullens*, 23; Dr. Judson's observation, *Wallace*, 67; education of native agents among them, *Hardy*, 198; success of native agency, *Fairbrother*, 206; maturity of their churches, shown in their self-support and missionary zeal; its causes, *Macleod*, 305; full account of the Karens of Tounghoo; their independent habits; their liberality; their teachers; causes of success among them, *Cornford*, 43; *Page*, 307, 308; number of converts among them, *Mullens*, 333.
Kayarnak, Samuel, the first Greenland convert, *Latrobe*, 211.

Keith's "Evidence of Prophecy," its effects, *Porter*, 141.
Kerr, Dr., medical missionary in China, 105.
KING, *Rev. R. C.*, evil influence of vicious Europeans on a native community; should be counteracted by missionaries, 245.
Knibb, Rev. William, *Trestrail*, 252.
Knill, Rev. Richard, *Harcus*, 255.

LABRADOR (see Arctic Missions).
Lacroix, Rev. —, Calcutta, *Leupolt*, 223.
Ladies' working-parties; their utility and management, *Whiting*, 63.
Languages of native heathens; necessity for a missionary to thoroughly master them; mode of acquiring such knowledge; "colloquial" compared with "sacred;" vernacular preaching; importance of a manual of native languages, *Mullens*, 15-21. Communication from the Rev. R. Bruce, North India, 29. Every missionary should learn the vernacular, *Leupolt*, 32; difficulties of learning, and modes of acquiring them, *Shaw*, 30; of the Red Indians of North America; its extraordinary difficulty surmounted, *O'Meara*, 33. The late Rev. John Anderson an exception to the rule of the necessity of knowing the native tongue, *Hislop*, 34; *Alexander*, 35. Differences between the written and spoken Tamil languages (India); illustrative anecdote, *Walton*, 35. Experience of the Arctic missions, *Latrobe*, 37. India should be learnt in villages rather than in large towns, *Lavie*, 36. "Colloquial" essential to the itinerating minister; research and learning for his translating colleagues, *Swan*, 37. Of China; its importance, *Lockhart*, 38. Occasional value of interpreters in West Africa, and of teaching English, *Waddell*, 40. Unwritten Patagonian; its obstacles to missionary exertion, *Stirling*, 40. Importance of the vernacular tongue to missionaries and their wives, *Stubbins*, 203; they

should know the language and the people, *Macgowan*, 209. *Minute* of Conference on the above, 56. Necessity of philosophical and critical knowledge for biblical translation, *Baylee*, 133. Chinese; proposal to Romanize its characters, *Gundert*, 148. Difficulty of doing so; better to acquire the language and signs by application and industry, *Lockhart*, 205 (see Palestine, Native agency, Missionary education).

LATROBE, *Rev. P.*, importance of cheap periodicals, but a high-class Review desirable; also extended pulpit exertions; Association meetings and prayer-meetings, 82. On vernacular acquirements, preaching and research for translation, compared with success in spiritual labour, 37. Experience of the Moravian missions among the Greenlanders, Esquimaux, and American Indians, and in the West Indies and South Africa; difficulty of training native agents; importance of those called by God without training; Samuel Kayarnak of Greenland an example; others to be watched for among the younger converts; high education to be carefully applied, 210–212. Neither technical modes of teaching in native churches, nor technicalities of English systems, should be allowed; the Moravians have occasionally erred in this respect; untrained missionaries have been as successful as those educated in colleges, 288, 289.

LAVIE, *Colonel*, importance of studying Indian languages among the natives rather than with the Europeans in large towns, 36. Missionary periodical press; large subscription by children of Blackheath and neighbourhood influenced by the "Juvenile Instructor," 79. Heathen teachers in Christian schools an evil; heathen boys in Bible-schools, 143. Natives in India with special responsibilities have been found by large and long experience more efficient than Europeans, 225. Native evangelists and pastors too prone to lean on mission-

aries; best to teach them self-dependence by not interfering with them; poverty of native churches throws secular work on missionaries; they must protect converts in cases of oppression; little interest felt in India in denominational differences, 300, 301.

LAYARD, *Captain*, utility of the "News of the Churches," 90. Expense of deputations; its necessity; want of pulpit and clerical aid, 164, 165. Missionary service as important as ordinary ministry; more candidates urgently required; inferior men selected as *protégés* of friends; Committee should resist this pressure, 253. Influence of Mr. Daniell on native Christians in Ceylon, from associating familiarly with them, 296.

Laymen, their power of collecting funds, *Leach*, 87.

LEACH, *W., Esq.*, work for laymen in collecting funds; its great importance; necessity of asking for contributions; apostolical precedent for it; his own efforts, trials, and success, 87.

Learning of native heathens; the necessity for some missionaries who can refute it, *Mullens*, 24. But such missionaries often disqualified for translation or teaching, *Singh*, 27.

Learning and systems of heathenism, *Wallace*, 67.

Lectures, their facilities for advancing the missionary cause, *Whiting*, 63; by Dr. Coldstream on ethnology and ethnography; their utility to missionaries, *Cullen*, 92. Annual lectures in large towns by able missionaries, on the subject of their special knowledge, desirable; in aid of theological professors, *Baylee*, 93. Committee to consider Dr. Baylee's suggestion, 96. Their "Report:" that an annual lecture be given in some large town by a lecturer of superior attainments, on the higher relations of missionary subjects; lecture to be afterwards published; a fund to be raised for the purpose; Committee formed to appoint a lecturer, 97, 98. Importance of such a lectureship, *Lewis*, 158.

Lectureship, Missionary; Report of Committee adopted, and subscriptions announced, 97, 313.

LEUPOLT, *Rev. C. B.*, appointed on Executive Committee, 10. On native languages, 32. Paper " On Missionary Education " (see Missionary education), 111–116. Comparative advantages of European and native preachers in India; the former as attentively heard, and as capable of actual work and fatigue, as the latter; natives, however, have the language without years of study, and know the habits of the people; they require smaller salaries than Europeans; men converted in mature age the best agents; converts trained in colleges from youth possess acquired habits, and less of native knowledge, though they are better able to contend with the Brahmins; natives the best translators, when proper dictionaries are produced; female agency and female colleges much needed, 223, 224.

Address on "Indian Converts in the Mutiny." Liberality of Mr. Donald Macleod, the patron of Rev. B. L. Singh; account of the mutiny at Benares; fears about the converts' firmness; extreme danger of Europeans and native Christians; blame of the rising ascribed to missionaries; firmness of converts proved; only two became Mohammedans; refugees protected by converts in Benares. Converts at Goruckpore offered the choice of death or recantation; their consultation and flight; their danger in the jungle; their meeting with Peel's Naval Brigade; kindness of the sailors, 266–270. Christian villages advisable; account of that at Sigra (Benares) under his management; municipal arrangement; juries; funds for missions, poor, and widows; house visiting; church discipline; buildings; press; carpet manufactory, &c.; no denominational differences, 296–298.

LEWIS, *Rev. J.*, Paper on "The best Means of calling forth Home Liberality," 153–165 (see Contributions).

Liberality, Christian, misconceptions as to, *Whiting*, 63; defective, *Barbour*, 99; ought to be very large, *Lewis*, 153; *MacGill*, 175; *Stowell*, 357. Ought to be systematic and frequent, *MacGill*, 174; based on hearty principle, *Cather*, 168; its amount greater than the Jewish tithe, *Thorburn*, 177; its root, its amount, carried out on system, *Minute*, 178, 179; exemplified by natives of India, 269.

List of Members of the Conference, 4.

Literature, ancient and Oriental; its knowledge most useful to the missionary, *Mullens*, 24 (see Bible translations.)

Literature, Christian vernacular, in mission-fields; statistics of native literature in India; its objectionable character and great activity, *Davis*, 127. Translations of Christian books best executed by natives, *Singh*, 129. In Damascus, its success, *Porter*, 140. English books should be altered in translation to suit the native style of thought; illustrations, *O'Meara*, 144. Best literature produced by Europeans; writings in Tamil by the Rev. W. H. Drew, *Sugden*, 147, 148. Books wanted in Greenland for the Esquimaux, and in North and South America; should be adapted to modes of life and styles of thought, *Badham*, 149.

Livingston, of China, *Lockhart*, 105.

Livingstone, *Rev. Dr.*, *Stowell*, 357.

LOCKHART, *Dr.*, on native languages; on itinerating; its success in China, 38, 39. Address "On Medical Missions in China," 100. (For abstract, see Medical Missions.) Native agents essential in China; success, zeal, and eloquence of those already trained; female agents employed at Amoy and Ningpo, under the charge of Miss Aldersey; their operations and success. The Chinese language; impracticability of rendering it into Roman orthography; difference of local dialects; the language and character can be learned by application; importance of acquiring it; natives could not without help translate the Scriptures. Translation: tracts might be left to natives; but the union of missionaries and natives necessary in translating Scripture, 204-206. Medical missionaries should only exercise their spiritual influence as laymen; if ordained, they lose power by attending at once to two professions, 244. Seconds vote of thanks to Secretaries, 314.

Long, *Rev. J.*, his report on the vernacular press of Calcutta, 128.

Lowe, *Rev. J. B.*, at Public Meeting, presents thanks for the assembling of the Conference at Liverpool, 361.

Lyth, *Rev. B.*, his paper on native agency in Fiji, 377; his systems, 197.

M'Cartee, *Dr.*, medical missionary in China, 106.

MACFIE, *R. A., Esq.*, appointed on Executive Committee, 10. Best use of periodical publications, to provide ministers with information for pulpit use; this plan should be extended by printing special papers for the purpose, 74. Expensive church buildings a great drawback, and at home also; the forefathers of Nonconformists had their "meeting-house;" it was now called "the house of God," thus leading to decoration; "kirk" more expressive than "church;" modern "saints;" a church in India, and others in Britain, named after individuals, 295. At Public Meeting, seconds vote of thanks to Chairman, 362.

MACGILL, *Rev. H. M.*, effect of cheap periodicals on missionary funds; a high-class Review desirable; large circulation of papers in the United Presbyterian Church, 80. Necessity of active missionary work by pastors, 81. Giving contributions to be regarded as devotional; the style of giving expressive of current ideas. ib. Gross annual missionary subscriptions in Christendom, 600,000*l.*; more life required in the Church, 82. A simultaneous pulpit appeal desirable; but systematic, regular, and frequent giving most essential; in United Presbyterian Church, collectors visit monthly, 174, 175.

Macgowan, *Dr.*, of Jerusalem, his valuable labours and recent death, 107.

MACGOWAN, *Dr.*, of Ningpo, medical missionary in China, 106, 107. Success of missions unequal to the efforts that have been made; great mistakes have been committed; in China, native agency was employed too soon, and therefore to some extent detrimental; hypocrites anxious for employment; natives should not be paid till tried, pay being an inducement to the unqualified; a knowledge of the language of the people indispensable, 208. Scholarship in many cases unnecessary in the missionary; freshness of zeal most valuable; Sabbath schoolmasters and Bible-class teachers very eligible, 252. Address "ON MEDICAL MISSIONS IN CHINA AND JAPAN."

In civilised countries the missionary and the physician should act separately; dangerous to unite the two professions; duties of the medical missionary, both in his science and religion; his utility to missionary families, and in conciliating the natives by benevolence, as part of religion; in Japan, at present, secular missionary labour alone available; services of army and navy surgeons to missionaries, 275.

Mackay, *Rev. Dr.*, Calcutta, *Singh*, 182.

M'Kee, *Rev. J.*, secular employment of missionaries, in part necessary, 25. Government education in India; its professed neutrality not real; official encouragement of idolatry, 130.

MACLEOD, *D., Esq.*, his liberality to the mission cause; Rev. B. L. Singh supported by him, *Leupolt*, 266. Errors of Government in India, a chief cause of their depriving the people of self-government; the same principle applies to the Church; the converts should be left to rule themselves; mistakes would cure themselves, and the native selections of officers would be better than our own; illustration of self-government in the success of the Karen mission, 303-306.

MADAGASCAR, success of native agency, *Fairbrother*, 206. Increase of converts after the expulsion of European missionaries a proof of the value of native agency, *Tidman*, 225. Remarkable triumphs of the gospel, *Mullens*, 334.

Mahomet, two periods in his life, *Douglas*, 375.

MAKEPEACE, *Rev. J.*, importance of more pastoral zeal and pulpit appeals; successful exertions of a returned missionary as a pastor in England, 176.

Manuals of heathen tongues, customs, and ideas; their desirability for missionaries, *Mullens*, 20.

Maps of mission stations suggested, *Cunningham*, 146. Some in preparation by Church Missionary Society, *Alexander*, ib. These will embrace the whole mission-field, *Whiting*, 173. *Martin, Colonel, Edwardes*, 186.

Mason, Rev. Dr., of Tounghoo Mission, *Hardy*, 198.

Mayor of Liverpool, at Public Meeting, proposes thanks to Chairman, 361.

Medical Missions, their importance, in China, *Mullens*, 22; in India also, 22; *Smith*, 27; *Cornford*, 44; in Africa, *Smith*, 27. Minute on, 56.

MEDICAL MISSIONS IN CHINA. Address by *Dr. Lockhart*.

Their adaptation to that country, and to India; his own exertions at Macao, in Batavia, Chusan, and Shanghai, 100, 101. Mode of operation; no native surgery in China; fears of the natives overcome; preaching added to healing; success and extent of results, 102. Special cases; vaccination, its introduction and growing popularity in China, 103, 104. Cure of ophthalmia; surgical operations on Chinese wounded in several battles, 104. Dispensaries and hospitals, 104, 105. History of the movement in China; exertions of other medical men, ib. Necessity for further efforts, 106. Depravity of sailors in foreign seaport towns a great obstacle to missions; instances in China and Japan, 107.

Double qualifications of medical missionaries; efforts to enlist them in the medical schools at Edinburgh; should be first trained at home, *Cullen*, 244. Should not be ordained, but act as laymen; attention to two professions diminishes their influence, *Lockhart*, ib. Medical knowledge; its value to all non-professional missionaries; should be acquired by students, *O'Meara*, 245.

MEDICAL MISSIONS IN CHINA AND JAPAN. Address by *Dr. Macgowan*.

Danger in civilised countries of uniting the missionary and the medical man; duties of the latter in his own profession, and as a lay-missionary; his utility to missionary families, and to conciliate, by presenting benevolence with religion; in Japan, secular labour only available at present; valuable assistance of army and navy surgeons, *Macgowan*, 275.

Medhurst, Rev. Dr., associated with Dr. Lockhart's medical mission in China, 39, 101.

Meeting, Public, at the close of the Conference; report of speeches, 318-363.

Meetings, missionary, their importance, if well conducted; necessity of eliciting *facts* rather than making orations; dull speaking objectionable; presence of "great men" unnecessary; should be more devotional; suggestions for the management of quarterly and monthly meetings, *Whiting*, 62.

Meetings of associations and for prayer desirable, *Latrobe*, 83.

Meetings, their power to raise candidates for mission work, *Green*, 235 (see Candidates for mission work).
Meetings (see Prayer-meetings).
MEMBERS OF THE CONFERENCE, List of, 4.
Meshakah, Dr., Porter, 141.
MESOPOTAMIA, *Whiting*, 51.
MINUTES, embodying the opinions expressed at each Conference, ordered to be prepared, 11.
MINUTE *on Missionaries abroad:*
The missionary's character; his attention to native languages; adaptation of his plans to circumstances; his aims; preaching, stations, itinerancies, medical missions; efforts among Englishmen abroad; general results of modern missions, 56, 57.
MINUTE *on the Missionary Spirit:*
Information essential to create a missionary feeling at home; of what kind; pulpit ministrations and the systematic efforts of pastors. Prayer-meetings, deputations, the press, and missionary periodicals; the latter to be of a higher class; efforts to be made to enlist the young; and missions to form part of a theological course of study, 95, 96.
MINUTE *on Missionary Education:*
School education a legitimate province of missions; should be suited to each station; vernacular schools most important; English schools in some countries most successful and desirable, but should not be carried too far; orphan and boarding-schools valuable in some countries; female education, its great importance; training schools desirable where possible; vernacular literature, its progress satisfactory, extension desirable, 150, 151.
MINUTE *on Christian Liberality:*
As much a duty to give as to work and pray, 178. Conscience, regulated by prayerful deliberation, must guide the amount, 178. Giving should be systematic, and, if so, would lead to increased liberality; a more active missionary spirit desired in pastors, and abstinence from luxurious habits in all Christians, 179.
MINUTE *on Native Agents:*
Exceptional position of missionaries abroad; their office temporary and costly; climates unhealthy; languages difficult; contrasted circumstances of natives to whom the work must hereafter be left; lay native agents, but some converts must become pastors and preachers; their special qualifications must vary with circumstances; men of all qualifications, young and old, required; those called of God to be sought by prayer; education also varies with circumstances; theological instruction to be given in all cases in the vernacular; the degree of English to be properly modified; under teaching, the agent should combine practice with study; all harmless native habits to be strictly preserved; agents to be placed under due responsibility, with proper freedom; their salaries suited to their social native position; pastors to be paid by native churches, supplemented from home where necessary; females as teachers and visitors to be sought and trained; thanks to God for past success, and prayers for its continuance, 227–231.
MINUTE *on Missionary Candidates:*
The Church to seek out and pray for missionaries appointed by the Spirit; what should be their personal character; classes who have furnished men, and those to be invited to offer themselves; methods of pressing the claims of missions : sermons, missionary meetings, Young Men's Associations, missionary classes and prayer-meetings in Universities, circulation of missionary works and periodicals, appeals of Societies, and individual effort; all obstacles should be removed from the path of those who are willing to consecrate themselves to the work; how to qualify them; new life to be infused into old plans by vigour and prayer, 264, 265.

MINUTE *on Native Churches:*
Standard of membership in native churches; aim of their fellowship; importance of self-dependence, notwithstanding various systems of order; the missionary the adviser of native churches, and, except in their infancy, should not act as pastor; continued European pastorate has been injurious; native pastors to be left free; their income supplemented, if necessary, for a time, on the understanding that dependence must in due time cease; national customs to be preserved; salaries, cost of buildings, &c., to be suited to native wants; separate Christian villages unadvisable, save in exceptional cases; missionaries to seek to elevate new churches; Church systems; their essentials to be retained, but technicalities avoided, and the systems to be adapted to circumstances, 309-313.

Misconduct of Europeans abroad a cause of failure, *Hughes, Candy*, 45.

Missionary, the, his importance, peculiar position, personal character, qualifications, purpose, health, necessity for knowledge of native languages, *Mullens*, 17-24 (see also MINUTE on First Session), 56.

Missionary Conference in London, in 1854; its spirit and character; topics discussed; its effect, 367.

"MISSIONARY EDUCATION."
Paper by the Rev. C. B. Leupolt:
Chiefly on the best mode of carrying it out in India: by schools, in which the young and females can be reached, 111. English and vernacular schools; their respective advantages and mode of operation; scholars should pay for instruction; village-schools, their great importance; female schools essential; female missionaries, their power for good, 112. Separate schools for *Christian* infants and for children and orphan schools; English to be taught only as a *language;* all religious and secular *knowledge* to be given in the vernacular, 113. Training institutions for native teachers and evangelists; several already; these need not be confined to Christians, 114. Caste should be ignored entirely. Results of schools; their effect on the native religions; missionaries and laymen both suitable for the work of education, 115. Schools of a district to form a circle under an inspector, 116.

"MISSIONARY EDUCATION."
Paper by the Rev. Thomas Smith:
The missionary may give secular instruction; importance of female education in India; aim of English school-teachers not conversion, as in India; education applicable to particular localities; preaching not to be neglected for it; success of education in India; in securing converts and preachers; difficulty of getting them with proper qualifications; more attention to vernacular education needed, 118-123.

"MISSIONARY EDUCATION."
Paper by the Rev. J. H. Titcomb:
I. *Introductory stage:* Schools for heathens, in which English language must be taught, 123.
II. *Permanent stage:* Vernacular education of native agents, 124.
III. *Reproductive stage:* Boarding and industrial schools, to facilitate education of converts; want of native masters for training classes; value of the Vernacular Education Society; girls' schools; literature for converts, 125-127.

Missionary Lectureship (see Lectures).

"MISSIONARY SPIRIT AT HOME: HOW BEST TO EXCITE AND MAINTAIN IT."
Paper by the Rev. J. B. Whiting:
This spirit defined; how to excite and extend it; means for doing it; subjects of the true missionary spirit only converted hearts; its manifestations; missionary spirit to be fostered; its increase; it must be exalted to its

true position; it must be kept alive in our pastors and theological students, also in laymen. Information on missions should be sought by all; missions should be worked in a Catholic spirit; danger from its absence; efficacy of prayer in producing missionary ardour; the pulpit should be frequently used to spread correct knowledge on missions, and not merely to beget a transient enthusiasm; society generally should be used to diffuse information on missions; newspapers also a powerful medium for conveying such intelligence, as they are seen by all; missionary periodicals should be abundantly circulated; nature of such publications described; missionary scenes and narratives should be introduced into school reading-books; correct missionary prints on cottage walls, and well-executed pictures on drawing-room tables. Missionary meetings : their characteristics; what kind of information is to be given at them; facts and incidents from the best sources should be culled, well arranged, condensed, and cleverly related, to be effective. Danger of relying on "great men" to push the cause of missions, and not upon its own greatness and intrinsic merit; monthly meetings in aid of missions recommended; programme for such meetings; the information given at them to be systematic, aided occasionally by dissolving views; lecturers to literary societies, ladies' missionary working-parties, and juvenile societies, should be enlisted in the cause of missions; every missionary association should be thoroughly organised; youths should be trained suitable for mission work; Christian liberality considered; every pastor should frequently urge his people to contribute to missions; only an increase of God's people can enlarge the true missionary spirit, 58-64.

Missionary Soirées (see Soirées).

Missionary students, 243.

Mitchell, Rev. Dr. Murray, Davis, 128.

Modern "saints;" churches named after individuals, *Macfie*, 295.

Modern Works on Christian Missions, list of, 381.

Moffat, Rev. Robert, his missionary work in Africa, *Tidman*, 55.

Monasteries, their missionary influence by spreading art and civilisation; similar influence needed, *Lewis*, 161; most objectionable, *Hardy*, 298.

Moravian missions in Greenland, North America, South Africa, &c., *Latrobe*, 210-212.

Morrison, Rev. Dr., of China, *Lockhart*, 105.

Moulvies in India, their learning, influence, and salaries, *Singh*, 218 (see Native agency).

MULLENS, *Rev. J.*, appointed on Executive Committee, and as Joint-Secretary and Editor, 10, 11. Paper on "EUROPEAN MISSIONARIES ABROAD," 17-24. Secular employment of missionaries, 25. Native and European preaching, 25. His "South Indian Missions" quoted. *Whiting*, 61. Points necessary in missionary letters and addresses; facts and individual cases more desirable than general advocacy of missionary effort; cases of failure instructive, and tending to excite sympathy; interesting personal stories in New Testament; Cornelius, Lydia, the gaoler; Indian experiences, 85, 86. *Native agency:* should natives be ordained to service among the heathens, or as native pastors? How should the stipends be met, if a native church has insufficient means : practice of the American Board, 200.

Native churches; missionary may at first be pastor of a church, but no longer than necessary; the church should be prepared from the beginning for independence; church buildings should be in harmony with the country and with native means of imitation; examples of costly Gothic churches out of place; his own practice; the peculiarly English elements in our church systems not to be introduced in native churches; case at Calcutta; converts, on ordination, asked to assent to Deed of Demission of Free Church; in Tinnevelly, to sign standards of the Church of England; these peculiar elements formed by controversy, and injurious at home, should be modified abroad; exclusiveness decreasing here; native churches should *begin* free from it, 283–287. Disclaims seeking for *congregationalism;* systems should be applied in the most elastic way; ordained natives may be committed to the *result*, without reference to the *process* by which it was produced; urges division of spheres, non-interference, and co-operation; in missionary labour this is done, and the same is required in churches; if the old denominations must be reproduced, it should be in the most general way, 301, 302.

Address at the Public Meeting: missionaries attending the Conference; thirty-seven present from all parts of the world; the favourable impressions they received, and their resolves for future work; unanimity in the Conference; the same unanimity strikingly shown at mission stations; where, in the presence of idolatry, all feel as *one*. Progress of missions since 1800; change in English society in that period; work accomplished in the Southern Seas, in Africa, in the West Indies, in China, in Burmah, in India, in Turkey; work of native preachers under extreme difficulties in Madagascar, in Tahiti; lessons taught by success, humility, and more complete consecration; promises for the future; all nations shall be Christians, 329–336.

His paper on Previous Conferences on Missions, 365.

Munro, *Sir Thomas, Campbell,* 136.

Murdoch, *Mr.*, his active exertions in Ceylon, 129.

Mutiny in India, conduct of native Christians (see " INDIAN CONVERTS IN THE MUTINY"): its causes, progress, and suppression; also its many solemn lessons, *Edwardes*, 343–355.

Natives of heathen lands, the necessity to a missionary of a full knowledge of them, their languages, &c., *Mullens*, 19, 24; *Shaw*, 30; *Leupolt*, 32; *Lavie*, 36; *Lockhart*, 38.

Native agents, greatly increased number in recent times, *Whiting*, 51.

"NATIVE AGENCY IN FOREIGN MISSIONS." Vast importance of the question; necessity for calm discussion; the "native agents" of the Primitive Church fellow-workers with the Apostles; their example to be studied, *Alexander*, 192–194, 199.

Paper by the Rev. S. Hardy:

Its importance greater than home efforts; the life of the future church in all lands dependent on it, 194. Each people has a nationality of its own; no general law applicable; a special class required, 195; their qualifications, piety, zeal, self-sacrifice; homogeneity with the people essential, 196; their instruction should be in the vernacular alone; their studies, while in actual work, should be superintended by the missionary; their responsibility to missionaries, and its necessary limitation. In Fiji, Rev. R. B. Lyth trained the natives whilst at their daily work, 197. The same plan successful in more civilized places, as in Burmah, under Dr. Mason, and in the early Serampore mission, 198. Stipend to be moderate; lay agents to assist, 199. How should agents be ordained, as missionaries or pastors? how stipends to be met, if funds of native churches inadequate, *Mullens*, 200. Stipends of Wesleyan agents, supplemented from home salaries, should not be too high; their agents ordained to circuits, and limited to three years in one place, *Hardy*. Necessity of agents identifying themselves with their countrymen in secular habits, dress, &c.; should differ from them in religion only; missionaries generally overworked, and in need of native help, *Dawes*, 201, 202; *Walton*, 224. In Orissa (seat of the idol Juggernaut), success of the mission there, and its native agents; the best of them converted in mature age; their stipend 1*l*. per month, *Stubbins*, 202–204.

In CHINA, success, zeal, and eloquence of those already trained; female agents at Amoy and Ningpo under the charge of Miss Aldersey; their operations and success, *Lockhart*, 204, 205. Success of natives in the South Sea Islands, Madagascar, and among the Karens, *Fairbrother*, 206. Importance of female agency, *Swallow*, 206. Natives employed in the revision of the land revenue of India; mode of proceeding; its application to missionary purposes; native preachers should not live or dress as Europeans; Brahmins but few, therefore high education unnecessary; natives of India, their intelligence and aptitude for religious instruction, *Davidson*, 206–208.

In INDIA, Europeans as attentively heard, and as capable of fatigue, as natives; but natives have the language, and know the habits, of the people; they require smaller salaries; converts of mature age make the best agents; boys trained in colleges possess acquired rather than native habits, but are better able to contend with Brahmins; when proper dictionaries are produced, natives will be the best translators; female schools and agency much needed, *Leupolt*, 223, 224. Employed too soon in China. Natives should be proved before they are paid, salary being an inducement to the unqualified, *Macgowan*, 208.

In INDIA, difference of localities; English education necessary for labour in cities, vernacular for rural districts; natives highly trained in Calcutta unfit for rural work; the high salaries paid by Free Church have not satisfied the natives, *Gardiner*, 209, 210.

Moravian missions, Greenland, Esquimaux, South Africa, North America; difficulty of training natives; importance of the untrained when called by God; an example; others to be watched for; high education to be applied with care, *Latrobe*, 210–212.

In NORTH AMERICA, agents there should assume the habits of Europeans, who are looked up to by the Indians; high education not essential; remarkable instance of an ordained native; his high education combined with aptitude for the work, *O'Meara*, 212.

In AFRICA AND WEST INDIES, employed prematurely; comparative advantages of younger and older agents; both necessary; education; teacher should be superior to the taught; negroes from West Indies fail as teachers in Africa; agents must be trained where they are to act; vernacular essential; English useful; African native agent must be clothed at least partially; well-trained natives the best translators, *Waddell*, 213, 214.

In TURKEY, 300 agents employed by Turkish Missions' Aid Society (American mission); these act as pastors, missionaries as evangelists only; college at Constantinople; agents educated and boarded for 16*l*. a-year, *Birch*, 215, 216.

In INDIA, learning necessary to refute Brahmins and Moulvies, who, though few, are influential; different modes of dealing with Hindoos and Mahommedans; classical education too low in the Scotch system; salaries of native agents; Moulvies, Brahmins, and principal Pundits; circumstances on which salaries must depend; one being what the native churches can pay, *Singh*, 216–218.

Missionaries should be evangelists, not pastors; success of Serampore mission; recovery of Delhi since the mutiny; rural converts chiefly made by native agents; Jamaica Institution successful, though some few agents have been found wanting; Wesleyan local preachers the "native agents" of England, *Trestrail*, 219, 220. Extensively and successfully employed in SOUTH SEA MISSIONS (*Tahiti, Fiji, &c.*); agents have little instruction beyond the native dialects; training colleges established; agents of different denominations should not work in the same place, *Pritchard*, 221, 222.

In INDIA, present mode of training agents destroys their nationality; they should retain their native habits; the missionary will not be always needed; therefore the country must be left to well-trained native teachers, *Walton*, 224.

In INDIA, extensive experience shows that native agents with special responsibility have been most effective, *Lavie*, 225. Its success at *Amoy, Shanghai, and Singapore*; salaries of some Chinese teachers only five or six dollars per month, *Barbour*, 221. Success of native agency in Tahiti and Madagascar, where, under native pastors, the converts remained faithful when, from political causes, English missionaries were expelled; native teachers in the Samoan Islands, South Pacific; the great object of training is to fit each man for his particular work, *Tidman*, 225, 226.

MINUTE of Conference on the above: Exceptional position of missionaries abroad; their office temporary and costly; climates unhealthy; languages difficult; contrasted circumstances of natives to whom the work must hereafter be left; lay native agents, but some converts must become pastors and preachers; their special qualifications must vary with circumstances; men of all qualifications, young and old, required; those called of God to be sought by prayer; education also varies with circumstances; theological instruction to be given in all cases in the vernacular; the degree of English to be properly modified; under teaching, the agent should combine practice with study; all harmless native habits to be strictly preserved; agents to be placed under due responsibility, with proper freedom; their salaries suited to their social native position; pastors to be paid by native churches, supplemented from home where necessary; females as teachers and visitors to be sought and trained; thanks to God for past success, and prayers for its continuance, 227-231 (see also Preaching, native and European compared, and Bible translations).

"NATIVE CHURCHES:" how forming in China, *Lockhart*, 39; discussion should be governed by a consideration of the history of the churches of Jerusalem and Antioch; how far should English church systems be employed? simpler forms desirable, *Alexander*, 278. *Paper by the Rev. F. Trestrail:*

The *right* of a church to its officers and discipline more important than its *form*; definition of a church; many forms of order allowable; missionaries to found and aid churches; not being pastors, but overseers; churches have been kept too dependent on missionaries; difficulty of getting suitable pastors; their proper status and titles; should as far as possible be kept from the English language; self-supporting churches should be made independent of Societies; separate Christian villages objectionable; these churches, not the Societies, must evangelise heathen lands; difficulty from church property being vested in Societies at home; poverty an obstacle to independence, but has been overcome in Jamaica, &c.; necessity of prayer for the native churches, 279-283.

Discussion on this subject:

Great increase of native churches; missionaries should cease to be their pastors as soon as possible; they should be trained for independence; church buildings should be suited to the country, and such as the natives can imitate; examples of costly Gothic stone churches; peculiar English elements not to be introduced; converts in India asked to sign Articles of Church of England; others to assent to Deed of Demission of Free Church; such elements should be modified abroad, and the churches *begin* free from all exclusiveness, *Mullens*, 283–287. Technicalities of English systems objectionable, *Fox*, 287. Christian villages found useful; a few converts scattered among heathen are persecuted, and lose their livelihood; together they strengthen one another; example; in districts where converts are more numerous they should mix with the people generally, *Wallace*, 287. Church technicalities, and technical modes of teaching, objectionable; colleges not always necessary; successes of untrained men, *Latrobe*, 288, 289. Converts not to be hindered or troubled by mere technicalities, but missionaries should teach the systems of the respective churches they represent, *Shaw*, 289, 290. Reproduction of all the English systems at present unavoidable; natives must eventually form systems adapted to their circumstances; Societies need not all occupy the same ground; they may apportion the world between them, and co-operate for the general good, *Davis*, 290.

Form of ordination in Free Church settled by General Assembly; Calcutta Presbytery could not alter it; the ordained converts firmly held the principles of the church, which were not technicalities, *Tweedie*, 291. Ordination in the Free Church is *general*, and according to English form; English peculiarities avoided in the native church *per se*; separate village system; its advantages and disadvantages; should missionaries control or only advise self-supporting churches? *Gardiner*, 291, 292. Converts not interested in denominations often pass to another church, if they can be more useful; Bengal churches not self-supporting; converts nearly all peasants of the poorest kind; much oppressed by landholders; vernacular schools would elevate them, and a Society might protect them from oppression; evils of the missionary pastor system; expense of church buildings, *Singh*, 294. Expensive buildings highly objectionable; early Nonconformists had their "*meeting-house*," now termed the "house of God," thus leading to costly decoration; "kirk" a more expressive word than "church;" a modern "saint," a church in India named after an individual, *Macfie*, 295. "How can the Character and Social Influence of native Christians be raised?" Influence of Mr. Daniell by familiar intercourse with the natives, *Layard*, 296. Christian villages advisable; account of that at Sigra (Benares), under Rev. C. B. Leupolt; municipal arrangements; juries; funds for missions; poor; and widows; house visiting; church discipline; buildings; press; carpet manufactory; no denominational jealousies in Benares, 296–298.

Advantages and disadvantages of village system; religious isolation generally an evil, as shown in monachism; weak converts gain, but the community loses strength; a model village, to be imitated by natives, may be allowed; nomads of South Africa exceptional. Teaching of technicalities can be avoided; the essentials of the different churches must be retained, but *details* hinder and perplex the native, *Hardy*, 298, 299. Church Missionary Society build all churches by private funds; English systems must be reproduced, but adapted to local circumstances; Societies working together should study non-interference and co-operation; all missionaries labour in the common cause, and it would be well if native churches could be made Catholic and Unsectarian, *Titcomb*, 299, 300.

Tendency of native pastors to rest

on missionaries; should be taught self-dependence by not interfering with them unnecessarily; secular work of missionaries in protecting converts from oppression; Catholicity of feeling in India, *Lavie*, 300, 301. Deed of Demission fundamental in the Free Church, but ordained natives might be committed to the *results*, without reference to the *process;* division of spheres, non-interference, and co-operation all-essential; if the old denominations must be reproduced, it should be in the most general and elastic manner, *Mullens*, 301, 302.

Desirableness of an address to native churches on self-support and other subjects, 303. Converts should be left to rule themselves; mistakes would soon be cured, and better officers chosen, than the missionaries could select; illustration of the results of self-government in the Karen mission, *Macleod*, 303–306. Self-supporting churches should be left to themselves; historical elements of old systems should be left out, *Waddell*, 306. Their independence desirable; an obstacle in the weakness of the Hindoo character; increased by caste distinctions; contrasted with the energy of the hill tribes; effect of such a contrast in Burmah; the Karens of the mountains energetic and prepared of the Lord; warmly receive and spread the Word; the Burmese of the plains far less willing and zealous, 306, 307. American Baptist mission to the Karens (Eastern Burmah) under the Rev. Mr. Whittaker at Tounghoo; its wonderful success and its causes; character of the people; their system of self-government; its influence enables them to make their churches self-supporting; mode of operation described; harmony, co-operation, and non-interference exemplified in the case of Mr. Whittaker and the Rev. Mr. Hazeldine, army chaplain at Tounghoo, *Page*, 307.

MINUTE of Conference on the above subject: standard of membership in native churches; aim of their fellowship; importance of self-dependence; notwithstanding various systems of order; the missionary the adviser of native churches, and, except in their infancy, should not act as pastor; continued European pastorate has been injurious; native pastors to be left free; their income supplemented, if necessary, for a time, on the understanding that dependence must in due time cease; national customs to be preserved; salaries, cost of buildings, &c., to be suited to native wants; separate Christian villages unadvisable, save in exceptional cases; missionaries to seek to elevate new churches; Church systems; their essentials to be retained, but technicalities avoided, and the systems adapted to circumstances, 309–313.

Native agency in Turkey (see TURKEY).

Native female missionaries desirable, *Leupolt*, 112; great benefit to be expected from them, *Sugden*, 148; required in China, openings for them, *Lockhart*, 205; may be of great use, *Leupolt*, 224; also *Minute*, 230.

Native languages (see Languages).

Native preaching compared with European (see Preaching).

NEGOMBO, CEYLON (see CEYLON).

Negroes of West Indies unsuccessful as teachers in Africa, *Waddell*, 214.

Neill, General, Leupolt, 267; *Edwardes*, 347.

" News of the Churches and Journal of Missions;" its utility, *Fordyce*, 84; *Hardy*, 90; *Layard*, ib.

Newspapers; their facilities for advancing the missionary cause, *Whiting*, 61. Penny missionary paper proposed, *Gabb*, 64 (and see Press).

New York Convention; its occasion; object; plan; members; spirit; chief topics; record, 366, 367; recommends missionary instruction in seminaries, *Somerville*, 92.

NEW ZEALAND, missionary efforts in, *Whiting*, 51.

Nicholson, General, Edwardes, 347.

E E

Nil Kanth, Nehemiah, native preacher in India, *Leupolt,* 269.
Nisbet, late *Rev. Dr.,* of Bombay, *Green,* 237.
North American Indian Mission (see AMERICA).

O'MEARA, *Rev. Dr.,* on Native Languages, 33; his remarkable success in acquiring the difficult language of the Red Indians of North America, 34. Prejudices of the Ojibbeway Indians and other North Americans; their disgust at European irreverence and intemperance; trade and commerce in North America injurious to the missionary cause, 50. Importance of *facts* in missionary addresses, 86. English books should be altered in translation to suit the native style of thought; illustrations, 144. In North America, native agents should not, as in India, preserve their native manners, but adopt those of Europeans, who are looked up to by the American Indians; a high degree of education not essential; instance of an ordained native; his high education, combined with aptitude for the work, 212; his experience of the value of some medical knowledge to all missionaries; should be acquired by students, 245.
Ophthalmia in China, 103 (see Medical Missions).
Ordination of native agents as pastors (see Native agency).
OSBORN, *Rev. G.,* proposes thanks of the Conference to the Secretaries, 314; seconds parting resolution, 317.
Oxford University (see Universities).

PAGE, *Lieut. S. F.,* account of the American Baptist mission to the Karens of Tounghoo, under the Rev. Mr. Whittaker. The Karens almost independent of the Burmese government; their general system of local self-government; its influence in enabling them to render their churches self-supporting. Mr. Whittaker's procedure, by sending native catechists as pioneers; extraordinary success; its causes; harmony, co-operation, and non-interference, between Mr. Whittaker and the Rev. Mr. Hazledine, the army chaplain at Tounghoo, 307.
PALESTINE, missions in; translations into the native languages; extensive circulation; their effect in conversion; illustration, *Porter,* 140.
Parental influence; its power in raising candidates for mission work, *Green,* 235 (and see Candidates for mission work). Exaggeration of missionary dangers, *Smith,* 257; *Alexander,* 263.
Parker, Dr. Peter, medical missionary in China, 105.
Parker, Dr. W., of China, *Lockhart,* 106.
Parting Resolution of the Conference, 314.
Pastors at home, should be more thoroughly missionary; a missionary pastor makes a missionary people; illustration, *Tidman,* 169, 170; *Green,* 77. Ought to use their pulpits systematically to instruct their people in the principles and facts of missions, *Macfie,* 74; *Green,* 76; *Lewis,* 157; reluctance to use it, *Lewis,* ib. Help of the clergy much wanted, *Layard,* 165; *Cather,* 168; *MacGill,* 174. Results of pastoral earnestness, *Green,* 77; *Tidman,* 170; *Makepeace,* 176.
Pastoral work, local and itinerary, compared, *Mullens,* 21; should not fall into the hands of missionaries, except for a time, *Trestrail,* 280; ought to be done by natives, ib.; *Mullens,* 283; the missionary not suitable for it, *Singh,* 293. Reasons for all this, *Minute,* 310.
PATAGONIA, the mission described, with its peculiar features, its modes of operation, and its progress, *Stirling,* 40, 41.
Pathras, native catechist, *Leupolt,* 269.
Paul, St., his probable imperfection in pronouncing the Greek tongue an encouragement to missionaries in vernacular preaching, *Shaw,* 31.
Pearson, Alexander, of China, *Lockhart,* 104.
PEGU (see Karens).

Periodicals, Missionary; their great importance; suggestions for their style, character, and circulation, *Whiting*, 61 (see Press).

Personal character of the missionary; its importance, *Mullens*, 17.

Personal intercourse with natives essential to acquiring their language (see Languages).

PESHAWUR: the Church Mission there; its position; the valley; its noble tribes; establishment of the mission; its founder; its missionaries; its progress and influence, *Edwardes*, 185-188.

Pfander, Dr., an English outline of his works about to be published by the Church Missionary Society, 69; very desirable, *Douglas*, 375; his position, courage, and labours at Peshawur, *Edwardes*, 187.

Pictures, prints, and picture-cards, recommended for schools, cottages, and drawing-rooms, *Whiting*, 61.

Pictures of mission scenes available for aiding funds. *Lewis*, 154, 155.

Political action of missionaries occasionally unavoidable, *Cornford*, 44.

POLYNESIA (see S. S. ISLANDS).

Poorer classes, necessity to address missionary efforts to them, *Cornford*, 43.

PORTER, Rev. J. L., missions in Palestine; tracts in Arabic, Turkish, and Armenian; effect of translations in making converts; examples, 140. American missions hold simultaneous monthly prayer-meetings throughout the world; their effect very encouraging, 172.

Prayer-meetings, on each morning of the Conference, 11, 109, 191, 277. Not sufficiently employed for missionary purposes, *Whiting*, 63; *Hebert*, 78; *Woodrooffe*, 78; *Latrobe*, 83. Minute on Second Session of Conference, 95; of American missions held simultaneously monthly throughout the world, *Porter*, 172; their importance in raising mission candidates; results at Cambridge, *Titcomb*, 254.

Christ's command to *pray* for labourers, *Waddell*, 256. Prayer-meetings and missionary sermons determined to be held throughout the world in behalf of missions in January, 1861, 260.

Preaching, native and European compared, *Whittemore*, 24; *Mullens*, 25; why the latter is better remembered by children, *Hardy*, ib.; *Singh*, 26; *Smith*, 27. The missionary listened to as attentively as the native, *Leupolt*, 222.

Preaching, *Minute* on, 56.

Preliminary meeting of the Conference, 10.

Press, The; its opportunities for advancing the missionary cause, *Whiting*, 61. Penny missionary newspaper and a Quarterly Review proposed, *Gabb*, 64; *Waddell*, 65; *Baylee*, 66; *Cullen*, 68; *Smith*, 69. Missionary periodicals, their importance; their inferior character; "Church Missionary Intelligencer" an exception; desirability of the proposed Quarterly Review, *Smith*, 69. Rev. T. Smith's censure objected to as too sweeping, *Somerville*, 71; *Tidman*, 72; *Trestrail*, 73. Value of penny periodicals; expense and difficulty of producing a Quarterly Review, *Tidman*, 72. "Missionary Herald" described and defended; its circulation, *Trestrail*, 73. Information should be read from the pulpit on the Sabbath; special papers should be printed to carry this out, *Macfie*, 74. Objections to Rev. T. Smith's strictures; defence of Free Church publications; their circulation; proposed Quarterly advisable, if practicable, *Tweedie*, 75. Proposed Quarterly Review secondary to smaller publications, *Smith*, 76. Further objections to the Rev. T. Smith's strictures, *Green*, 77. Value of the "Juvenile Instructor" and the "Church Missionary Record," *Green*, 77; *Woodrooffe*, 78. Influence of "Juvenile Instructor," *Lavie*, 79; *Hughes*, 80. Effect of cheap papers on missionary funds; their large circulation in the United Presbyterian Church, *MacGill*,

80. Importance of cheap papers, and also a high-class Review, *Latrobe*, 82. A good weekly paper better than a monthly or a magnificent quarterly, *Towers*, 83. Best course to improve existing papers; discretion of editors; their omission to report the trials of missionaries detrimental to the cause, *Fordyce*, 84. Kind of information most acceptable from missionaries; facts and individual cases of success and failure most desirable, *Mullens*, 85, 86. The "Evangelical Christendom" to be sent to all mission stations; quarterlies losing influence compared with good weeklies, *Steane*, 89, 90. Value of the cheaper special periodicals, but desirability of a general high-class mission periodical (*Minute on Second Session*), 93, 94; in Turkey, 271.

Press, The Native, in India, statistics of, *Davis*, 127. Press in Palestine; its activity, successful results, illustrative anecdotes, *Porter*, 140. Vernacular Christian literature, 151. Its influence in raising candidates for mission work, *Smith*, 238. Should aid in raising mission candidates of a high religious standard, *Swan*, 252.

Prints, picture-cards, and pictures, recommended for distribution, *Whiting*, 61.

PRITCHARD, *Rev. G.*, native agency in the South Sea Missions; its extensive and successful employment; some agents had little instruction besides the native tongue; several colleges established; in Tahiti and Fiji success equally great; native evangelists of different denominations should not work on the same spot, 221-222.

Private prayer essential to foster a missionary spirit, *Whiting*, 60.

Professorships, missionary, essential in theological institutions, *Tweedie*, 90; *Somerville*, 92. Theological professors cannot teach everything, and should be aided by the most able missionaries to lecture on their special departments, *Baylee*, 93. Their importance in aid of the pulpit, *Lewis*, 158.

PROGRAMMES OF SESSIONAL MEETINGS OF CONFERENCE, first, 15; second, 58; third, 109; fourth, 152; fifth, 191; sixth, 232; seventh, 278.

PUBLIC MEETING at the close of the CONFERENCE, 2. Report of speeches, 318-363.

Public schools, strong missionary spirit existing in them; necessity for fostering it, *Whiting*, 247.

Pulpit, The, its powerful influence on the missionary cause, *Whiting*, 61. Not sufficiently used for missionary purposes, *Macfie*, 74; *Green*, 76; *Woodrooffe*, 78; *Latrobe*, 83. Facts from, as well as from platform, *Campbell*, 88. *Minute* on Second Session, 95. How best to render it available by improved education of pastors, *Lewis*, 158; *Layard*, 165; *Cather*, 166; *Tidman*, 169; *Tweedie*, 171; *Scott*, 172; *MacGill*, 174; *Thorburn*, 176; *Edwardes*, 178. Other claims sometimes impede pastoral efforts, *Cornford*, 175. Its power to raise candidates for mission work, *Green*, 234. Should aid in raising mission candidates of a high religious standard, *Swan*, 252 (see also Candidates for mission work).

Qualifications of the missionary, *Mullens*, 18-22.

"Quarterly Review," its improved tone on missions, *Hardy*, 90. Proposed Missionary Review (see Review).

RATTRAY, *Rev. C.*, effect of total abstinence in increasing mission funds; in his own field all new missionaries abstainers, 171.

Reading-books, picture-cards, &c., for schools on missionary subjects recommended, *Whiting*, 61.

Red Indian language, its difficulty, 33. Remarkable success of the Rev. Dr. O'Meara in acquiring it, *O'Meara*, 34.

"Religion," literal meaning of the word, *Baylee*, 133.

Resolution of welcome on opening the Conference, 12.

Review, Missionary Quarterly, suggested to be of first-class character, *Gabb*, 65; *Cullen*, 68; *Smith*, 69; *Waddell*, 65; *Baylee*, 66; formerly proposed by Mr. Isaac Taylor, *Smith*, 70; expense and difficulty of producing it, *Tidman*, 72; can only be for the few, *Trestrail*, 74; advisable, if practicable, *Tweedie*, 75; secondary to smaller publications, *Smith*, 76; secondary to cheap papers, *Hughes*, 80; *Latrobe*, 82. Proposed Review desirable, and should treat of all Christian missions in a high-class manner. *Minute*, 96.

Reviews, improved tone of the "Edinburgh" and "Quarterly," *Hardy*, 90. Quarterlies losing influence; weeklies have more effect, *Steane*, 90.

Revival, the recent, *Thorburn*, 260.

Sailors, their vicious conduct in foreign seaports an obstacle to missions, *Lockhart*, 106. *Macgowan*, 275.

"Saints" (see Modern "saints").

Saker, Mr., missionary, *Trestrail*, 252.

Salaries of native agents: those of native pastors to be paid by their churches, *Trestrail*, 280; may be supplemented by a Society for a time, till the church is strong, *Mullens*, 200; practice in the Wesleyan missions in Ceylon, *Hardy*, 201; in Orissa, of native preachers, 1*l*. a month, *Stubbins*, 204; principle that regulates the amount, *Minute*, 230. Salaries of native agents, Brahmins, Moulvies, and Pundits, *Singh*, 218. In Amoy, *Barbour*, 221.

Sale of tracts more effective in some parts of India than gratuitous distribution (see INDIA).

SANDWICH ISLANDS; remarkable success of missions there; all the population are Christians; the missionaries are preparing to quit them altogether, *Mullens*, 333.

Sargent, Mr., Mullens, 286; *Fox*, 287.

Sau Quala, the Karen Apostle, *Page*, 308.

Schools, at home, their facilities for advancing the missionary cause; mode of rendering them available, *Whiting*, 61. Converts supported by them; this movement commenced in Scotland, *Alexander*, 89, 247. Masters of Sunday-schools, and teachers of Bible-classes, fresh in their youthful zeal, desirable as missionaries, *Macgowan*, 252. In India (see INDIA, and Candidates for mission work).

School-books and pictures to be made available for mission funds, *Lewis*, 154.

SCOTT, Rev. G., suggests a simultaneous pulpit appeal throughout Christendom, without collections, 172. Missionary work not extraneous, but the ordinary work of the church; error on this point the cause of its neglect; no distinction between home and foreign work; objections of parents to a Divine call in children; disastrous results; Wesleyan mode of proceeding with youth; their examinations and admission to Theological Institution; education there the same for home as for foreign work, except as to language, &c.; his personal experience; his sons and a daughter devoted to foreign missions, 249, 250.

Scudder, Rev. J., on vernacular preaching, 48.

Scudder family, *Green*, 237.

Secretaries to the Conference, their appointment, 10; vote of thanks to them; reply by Rev. G. D. Cullen, 314.

Second General Prayer-meeting, 109.

Second Missionary Soirée, 181.

Second Session of Conference, 58.

Secular employment of missionaries, *Whittemore*, 24; *Mullens*, ib.; *M'Kee*, 25; *Leupolt*, 298.

Serampore mission (see INDIA).

Sermons on behalf of Missions to be preached throughout the world in January, 1861, 146 (see Pulpit appeals).

Seventh Session of Conference, 277.

SHAFTESBURY, Earl of, Chairman of Public Meeting terminating the Conference; his Lordship's opening address; congratulations on the present national synod of all branches of the Christian church, 321. Present position of the world; only a fraction of its people Christians; our national responsibility, 322. Union now existing among all branches of the church; neutrality in religion impossible, 324. India a peculiar field for missionary operations; it must be Christianised; attack of error as necessary as defence; favourable openings to the world generally; conflicts in progress; judgments impending; necessity for exertion to procure acceptance, 325, 326. At Public Meeting, returns thanks, 362.

SHAW, Rev. W., similarity of missionary experience in India and Africa; importance of a knowledge of native languages; the difficulty of its acquirement, and modes of attaining it, 29. Address on "Missions in South Africa." Range of missions very extensive; prosecuted by various Societies; successful results; translations of the Scriptures; 18,000 communicants, 20,000 school-children, and, in all, 100,000 native Christians, 189. Converts ought not to be hindered or troubled by mere technicalities, but missionaries should teach the systems they prefer; if not, it would lead to congregationalism; missionaries responsible to the churches they represent, 289, 290.

SIBERIA, missionary experiences in, *Swan*, 37.

Similarity of missionary experience in different climes, *Shaw*, 29.

SINGH, Rev. B. L., native agency compared with European, 26; native translations of the Bible, ib.; best executed by trained natives; character of vernacular literature, 129. Account of the Free Church Mission in Calcutta; its success among Jews, 180, 181. His personal history, his education, acquirement of religious knowledge; influence of Mr. Donald Macleod's example; embraces Christianity; missionary exertions. Affecting history of a Hindoo girl; her mother's death by cholera; the child saved by Dr. Sutton; the Christian education and teaching in female schools; her marriage to the Rev. B. L. Singh, 183. Brahmins and Moulvies, in India, though few, most learned and influential; relied upon by the people; much learning not required to preach to the rural people, but very necessary to contend with the learned heathen; example; different mode of dealing with Hindoos and Mahommedans; Scotch system of Hebrew and Greek education in India too low. Salaries of native agents; his own, 60 rupees per month and a house; circumstances on which salaries should depend; one important point is, what the native churches can pay; highest class of preachers receive from 100 to 150 rupees per month; second class, 50 to 80; third class, 16 to 30; fourth class, 10 to 20; Moulvies and Brahmins get from 5 to 20 rupees, with many additions at feasts and ceremonials; salaries of principal pundits depend on their classes and relation to wealthy heathen, 216–219. Supported by Mr. Donald Macleod, *Leupolt*, 266. Converts not much interested in denominations; they pass from one church to another, only to be more useful; no church in Bengal self-supporting; converts nearly all ryots or peasants, very poor, oppressed by landowners, and unable to aid the church; vernacular schools would elevate their status; a Society should be formed to protect them from oppression; missionaries should not be pastors; evils of the system; church buildings too expensive, 294.

Sixth Session of Conference, 232.

SMITH, Rev. T., native compared with European agency; Medical Missions, 27. Inferior character of missionary periodicals; the "Church Missionary Intelligencer" an exception; a Quarterly Review desirable, 69. Quarterly Review secondary to smaller publications, 76. *Paper on* "MISSIONARY

EDUCATION," 118-123 (see Missionary education). Obstacles to obtaining candidates for mission work; parental influence; how to be dealt with; it often arises from a misconception of perils to be encountered, from climate and other causes; distaste for special fields in missionaries themselves; men should feel bound to serve anywhere; should not feel as making sacrifices, but as selecting the departments they are best fitted for; preparatory home experience desirable; pastors becoming missionaries would have a good effect, 257–259.

Smith, Rev. —, Benares, *Leupolt*, 223.

Social intercourse, its opportunities for advancing the missionary cause, *Whiting*, 61.

Soirées, missionary, proceedings at, first, 99; second, 181; third, 266.

SOMERVILLE, Rev. Dr., missionary success the work of the Spirit; dependent on piety at home; revivals at home bring revivals abroad, 52. Objects to the Rev. Thos. Smith's censure of the missionary press, 71. United Presbyterian Church has ordered missionary instruction to be given by theological professors, 91. New York Missionary Conference advised the same course, 92. Importance of missionary professorships, 92. Academic and theological education of the minister and the missionary is the same; an idea exists in America that, in England, the latter is inferior in status to the former; moral position of the missionary higher than that of the home worker; men without academical knowledge, but trained in missionary colleges and ordained, are they eligible on return as home ministers? 247, 248. Moves parting Resolution. Feelings inspired by the meetings; presence and fruit of the Spirit; unanimity on great principles; the prospects before us, 315, 316.

South India Missionary Conference; its proceedings; its record; narratives of the various missions; subjects discussed; statistical tables; value of this record, 373.

SOUTH SEA ISLANDS, missionary operations in, *Mullens*, 23. Character of the people, *Wallace*, 68; of the missions, *Whiting*, 51; extent and examples of their success, *Tidman*, 54; summary of it, in the four chief Societies, *Mullens*, 332, 333. Success of native agency, *Fairbrother*, 206; *Pritchard*, 221; in Samoa and Fiji, *Pritchard*, ib.; native agency in Tahiti, *Tidman*, 225; in Samoa, ib.

Special appeals for particular missions; their influence in raising candidates for mission work, *Green*, 235 (see Candidates for mission work).

St. Aidan's College, Birkenhead, founded by the Rev. Dr. Baylee (see *BAYLEE, Rev. Dr.*).

St. John's Wood Juvenile Association; its extent and usefulness, *Hughes*, 79.

STEANE, Rev. Dr., appointed on Executive Committee, 10; and as Joint-Secretary and Editor, 11. Information should be sent to missionaries; the "Evangelical Christendom" to be sent to all mission stations, 89. Quarterly Reviews losing influence; such a periodical as the "Saturday Review" preferable, 90.

Stewards of Conference, vote of thanks to them for services, 313.

STIRLING, Rev. W. H., special circumstances of the Patagonian mission, with particular reference to their unwritten language, 40, 41.

Stories at Missionary Meetings useful, *Mullens*, 86.

STOWELL, Rev. Canon, his Address at Public Meeting; congratulations on harmony and unanimity; native agency to be enlarged; further opening of the mission-field; liberality should be extended in proportion; appeal to the wealth of Liverpool and Manchester; enlargement in devoting missionaries; necessity of preaching and prayer, that revival may come at home and abroad, 355–360.

STUBBINS, Rev. ISAAC, his experience

of twenty-four years in Orissa, the seat of the idol Juggernaut; the mission small, but very successful; zealous native preachers trained; the best of them converted in mature age; their stipend 1*l.* per month; their operations tended by the local missionaries; importance of vernacular tongue to missionaries and their wives; its knowledge enforced on civilians by Government, 202–204.

Subscriptions for foreign missions; gross amount annually, 600,000*l.*, *MacGill*, 82.

Subscriptions (see Contributions for mission work).

Successes of modern missions, *Whiting*, 50; *Tidman*, 53, 225; *Mullens*, 332, 333; among Englishmen abroad, *Candy*, 44; *Davidson*, 47.

SUGDEN, *Rev. J.*, the relative importance of vernacular and English schools in India; best Christian literature prepared by Europeans and Americans; the Rev. W. H. Drew, his familiarity with the Tamil language; value of native female missionaries, 147, 148. Paramount claims of mission service; desirable that all home pastors should have foreign experience; felt himself, in a military sense, "degraded" from mission to home work; Societies might invite young pastors to go out, 259. Suggests an address to all native churches, on self-support, temperance, &c. In teaching missionaries on points of church government, the *defects* of systems should be pointed out as well as their *merits;* too much familiarity with natives deprecated, 303.

Sunday-schools, their large contributions for missionary purposes, *Hughes*, 80. Converts supported by them; the movement commenced in Scotland, *Alexander*, 89. How to be made available for mission funds, *Lewis*, 154. Desirable at mission stations, *Swallow*, 206. Their power to raise candidates for mission work, *Green*, 235; number of teachers and scholars, 236 (see also Candidates for mission work).

Sunday-schools and Bible-classes; their importance in raising mission candidates, *Woodrooffe*, 256.

Superintendents and advisers of native teachers; modern missionaries as examples, *Mullens*, 23.

Surgery in China, 101 (see Medical Missions).

Sutton, the late *Rev. Dr.*, 182 (see SINGH).

SWALLOW, *C.,Esq.*, employment of native females as evangelists; introduction of the Sunday-school system in missions desirable, 206.

SWAN, *Rev. W.*, on the study of native languages; its importance to itinerating missionaries; requirements of others for translating, &c., 37. Press and pulpit should aid in raising spiritual missionaries; a high religious standard of qualification should be maintained, 252.

Systems of heathenism compared with barbarism; their respective difficulties to the missionary, *Wallace*, 67.

Systematic giving (see Liberality).

TAHITI mission, its success, *Pritchard*, 221. Increase of converts after the expulsion of English missionaries; a proof of the importance of native agents, *Tidman*, 225.

Tahitian converts, neglected in England, *Hughes*, 46.

Tamil language, written and spoken; their differences; difficulty of the latter; illustrative anecdote, *Walton*, 36.

Taylor, Mr. Isaac, his proposal for a Quarterly Review; plan abandoned; its proposed revival, *Smith*, 70; *Tidman*, 72.

Theological institutions, want of missionary professorships at, *Tweedie*, 90. Christian missions should be brought systematically before students. *Minute* on Second Session, 94. Wesleyan: education of candidates for mission work, *Scott*, 249, 250. Church Missionary College at Islington: course of examination and education, *Titcomb*, 254 (see Papers and remarks by *Green*, *Baylee*, *Somerville*; see also Candidates for mission work; and see Colleges).

Third General Prayer-meeting, 191.

Third Missionary Soirée, 266.

Third Session of Conference, 109.

THORBURN, *Rev. D.*, necessity of pulpit appeals; *extent* of Christian obligations with regard to contributions not so exactly defined as under Patriarchal and Jewish dispensations; Christians ought to give more than was then given; weekly gifts enforced by the Apostles, 176, 177. "How far is it possible and advisable to induce men and women of private fortune to devote themselves to missionary work?" Missions should not be treated as the Church's extra work only, but a positive duty of all classes; individual responsibility the grand secret of success; all theological should be also missionary professors; analogy between missionary and military life, 261, 262.

TIDMAN, *Rev. Dr.*, his addresses to the Conference: in proposing opening Resolution of mutual welcome, 12; denies the failure of missions, 53; their success in India, Polynesia, and Africa, 53–55; admits the neglect of the home church, 54. Missionary periodicals; value of penny publications; expense and difficulty of starting a Quarterly Review, 72. Ministers should be more missionary, by frequent pulpit teaching, without collections; a good cause brings money, 169. The increase of converts in Tahiti and Madagascar, when the European missionaries were expelled, a proof of the importance of native agency, 225, 226.

TIERRA DEL FUEGO, *Stirling*, 41.

"Times" and other newspapers, their improved tone on missionary subjects, *Hardy*, 90.

TINNEVELLY, missionary work in, *Mullens*, 23; churches in, 284; natives ordained, 286.

TITCOMB, *Rev. J. H.*, importance of prayer-meetings in raising mission candidates; result at Cambridge; effect of local interest in a particular mission-field; course of examination of candidates in the Church Missionary Society described, 254, 255. In the Church Missionary Society all churches are built by private funds. English Church systems must be reproduced abroad, with due elasticity and latitude to suit them to circumstances. Different Societies, working together, should act on the principles of non-interference and co-operation; all missionaries labour in a common cause; and it would be well if native churches could be made Catholic and unsectarian, 299, 300. Vernacular and itinerating preaching in India; reflex influence of Europeans there; employment of converts in aid of missions, 48. Missionary teaching not wanting in Cambridge University; sermons on missions; annual work by the Christian Advocate; lectures by Divinity professor; exertions of students in the cause; attendance at meetings of a Secretary of the Church Missionary Society; missionary reading-room; University Prayer-union; missionary professorship neither possible nor necessary, 93, 94. His Paper on "Missionary Education," 123–127 (see Missionary education).

Tithes, *Thorburn*, 177.

Tongues, the gift of, as exercised by the Apostles, *Shaw*, 31.

TOWERS, *Rev. J.*, a good weekly newspaper preferable to a monthly or quarterly missionary organ, 83.

Tracts, their sale in parts of India more effective than gratuitous distribution (see INDIA and Press).

Trade, its spread in North America injurious to the missionary cause, *O'Meara*, 50.

Training schools in India (see INDIA).

Translation (see Bible and Languages).

TRESTRAIL, *Rev. F.*, on missionary periodicals; objects to Rev. T. Smith's strictures on them; defends the Baptist Missionary Magazine; its large circulation, 73. Missionaries should be evangelists, not pastors; the Serampore mission acted on this principle, also that at Delhi; the latter has recovered since the mutiny, and is prosperous; converts in rural districts made chiefly by natives. Jamaica Institution is not, as stated, a failure; though some agents have proved wanting in qualifications; Wesleyan local preachers the "native agents" of England, 219, 220. Baptist missionaries occupy a higher status than their own ministers; process for their admission to colleges, and tests for their selection to missionary work; many zealous but untrained applicants rejected; more difficult to preach to children or to the ignorant than to the wise; doubtful candidates are referred to their pastor, who sometimes errs in his recommendation; pastors themselves sometimes invited to mission work, and generally successful; importance of candidate's health; City missionaries and British schoolmasters good candidates; their returned missionaries fully eligible as pastors at home; examples, 251, 252. His Paper "On Native Churches" (see Native churches), 279–283.

Trials and failures (see Failures).

TUCKER, *H. C., Esq.*, conductor of preparatory arrangements, 2; appointed on Executive Committee, 10; and as Joint-Secretary and Editor, 11. Spread of Government education by village-schools in India; necessity of introducing the Christian elements into them; his training institution at Benares; successful introduction of Bible reading; Government training institutions, 139, 140; at Sigra, *Leupolt*, 267.

TUCKER, *Rev. J. R.*, Address "On Missions in Turkey." American Mission established thirty years; Turkish Missions' Aid Society formed to support it; slow but steady progress; perseverance and its reward; extensive operations of the mission press; numerous works original and translations into Turkish, Armenian, Bulgarian, Greek, Syriac, and Arabic; schools, male and female; native agency and native churches; the reproductive principle; slow progress and ultimate prosperity of one church under a converted Armenian; Mahommedan Government and Greek and Armenian Churches stimulated by Christian efforts; firman of the Sultan permitting conversion to Christianity; its extraordinary effects; the Society has sixty native agents, 270–273.

TURKEY, the Christian press, its activity and successful results, *Porter*, 140, 271. American missions in, *Birch*, 215, 216. Missions in; American missions and Turkish Missions' Aid Society (see TUCKER).

TWEEDIE, *Rev. Dr.*, on missionary periodical publications; objections to Rev. T. Smith's strictures on them; defence of Free Church periodicals; proposed Quarterly advisable, if practicable, 75. Missionary professorships needed in universities, colleges, and other theological institutions; missionary subjects essential to the student's education, 90. Principles of the Free Church not technicalities, in the mode of ordination of converts objected to by Mr. Mullens (see Native churches), the Presbytery of Calcutta acted on the authority of the General Assembly, and could not alter the form; the ordained converts were attached to the principles of the Church, 297.

Universities of Cambridge, Oxford, and Dublin, *Titcomb*, 93; their power to raise candidates for mission work, *Green*, 235 (see Candidates for mission work). Strong missionary spirit existing in them, which should be fostered, *Whiting*, 247. Many missionaries have lately proceeded from them, *Layard*, 253; *Titcomb*, 254.

Vaccination in China, 103 (see Medical Missions).

Vedas, *Douglas*, 376.
Vernacular Education Society for India, *Titcomb*, 126.
Vernacular native idioms; importance of a familiar knowledge of them (see Language).
Vernacular preaching (see Preaching), *Mullens*, 20, 21 (see Languages).
Visiting from house to house, *Mullens*, 21; *Hardy*, 43.
Village-schools in India (see INDIA).

WADDELL, *Rev. H. M.*, on languages and itinerating; no general rule applicable; value of central stations and frequent local visits; occasional value of interpreters, and of teaching English, 39. Missionary periodicals, 65. Contribution a duty, not a mere feeling; necessity for cutting down luxuries to aid the cause, 177. African and West Indian missions; native agency often employed too soon; comparative advantages of younger and older agents; both necessary according to circumstances; high education not necessary, but, as at home, the teacher should be superior to the taught; negroes trained in West Indies unsuccessful in Africa; agents should be trained where they are to act; vernacular knowledge essential, but English useful; native teachers in Africa must clothe partially, if only for decency; well-trained natives the best translators of the Word, 213, 214. Christ's command to *pray* for labourers, 256. Mission churches, when self-supporting, should be left entirely to themselves; has always endeavoured to promote self-government; English systems should be carried out without reference to their historical elements, 306.
WALLACE, *Rev. J.*, the respective difficulties presented by organized systems of heathenism, and by comparative barbarism; success greater with the latter; illustrations from India, Ceylon, and the Karens, 67. Separate Christian villages, where a few converts are scattered among many heathen; they are protected and protect each other in villages; but where converts are more numerous, they should mix with the people generally, 287.
WALTON, *Rev. J.*, interpreters and native languages, 35. English schools in Ceylon; their success in training native Christians; the American Mission School abandoned, but reopened with great success by a convert; the Bible read in all Government schools in Ceylon; the teachers not always Christians; nature of school-books; effects of caste exclusiveness, 137–139. Present method of training native agents in India destroys their nationality; they should retain their native habits; the missionary will not be always needed, therefore the country must be left to well-trained native teachers, 224.
Wealthy persons to be induced to devote themselves to missionary work; their duty as common members of the Church, *Thorburn*, 261.
Welcome, Resolution of, at the opening of the Conference, 12.
Welton, Dr., medical missionary in China, 105.
Wesley, Rev. John, a principle of his, *Smith*, 258.
Wesleyan examinations of candidates; education in Theological Institution, *Scott*, 249, 250 (see Candidates for mission work).
Wesleyan local preachers analogous to the "native agents" of foreign missions, *Trestrail*, 220.
WEST INDIES, Success of missions in, *Cornford*, 43; the Christian negroes in, *Whiting*, 51; *Mullens*, 333.
Westminster Confession and Catechisms, *Baylee*, 66.
Wheeler, Colonel, Leupolt, 267.
WHITING, *Rev. J. B.*, on the number of Bible translations and of converted heathens in modern times; the success of missions equal to that of the Apostles; increase of native agents, 50: his Paper "On the Best Means

of exciting and maintaining a Missionary Spirit," 58–64. Want of information for pulpit ministry beyond existing publications; maps issued and preparing by Church Missionary Society to include the whole mission-field; systematic giving, weekly offerings, thank-offerings, 173. Great caution necessary in accepting or rejecting candidates; some rejected who have since become eminent at home; others accepted on second application; better to reject a good than accept a bad man; missionaries should correspond with boys in their old schools at home; strong missionary spirit in Universities and public schools, which should be fostered, 246, 247.

Whittaker, Rev. *Mr.*, of Burmah, *Page*, 308.

WHITTEMORE, Rev. *W. M.*, secular employment of missionaries; native compared with European preaching, 24, 25.

Williams, late Rev. *John*, *Hughes*, 47; *Trestrail*, 252.

Wolff, *Dr.*, his proposal to open the Universities to the Oriental churches, 215, 216.

Wong-fun, *Dr.*, medical missionary in China, 105.

WOODFALL, HENRY, *Esq.*, appointed on Executive Committee, 10.

WOODROOFFE, Rev. *Canon*, importance of periodical devotional meetings; success of the "Juvenile Instructor" and other cheap periodicals, 78. Collectors' poundage a question for London committees; expenses saved by hospitality of friends, 165. Importance of Sunday-schools and Bible-classes in raising mission candidates, 256.

Working-parties (see Ladies' working-parties).

Written and spoken languages in India; their differences, *Walton*, 35.

"Young Cottager," Richmond's, *O'Meara*, 144.

Young Men's Christian Associations; their power to raise candidates for mission work, *Green*, 235; an Association formed on the banks of the Tigris, *J. R. Tucker*, 272 (see Candidates for mission work).

Young missionaries advised to work under older ones, *Leupolt*, 32.

Youths; their availability for mission work, *Whiting*, 63.

The following document has been translated from the German or English originals into most of the European languages, as French, Italian, Spanish, Portuguese, Turkish, Armenian, Dutch, Danish, Swedish, Hungarian, Russian, &c.; as well as into various dialects of India, China, and other languages of Asia and Africa. Copies may be had at various Missionary Stations and Tract Depôts. Any reader who may with affectionate interest recollect a friend so situated that these words of kindness and counsel are adapted to his case, will do well to obtain or transcribe a copy and send it to the brother thus addressed.

ADDRESS TO THE BRETHREN SCATTERED ABROAD.

From the Conference of Christians of various Nations held at Berlin, September, 1857 (English Version).

"The Christians from Germany, Great Britain, the United States of America, France, Spain, Denmark, Holland, Sweden, Switzerland, and other countries, assembled for conference in the city of Berlin, in the month of September, 1857.

"To their brethren in Jesus Christ, who are scattered abroad in various parts of the globe, send affectionate salutation.

"BRETHREN beloved in the Lord,—While enjoying the happiness of united worship, and of communication on the affairs of the kingdom of our common Lord, our hearts have been directed in brotherly regard to you, who in lands of darkness have been visited with the 'dayspring from on high.' (Luke, i. 78.)

"With you who are restrained from the utterance of your religious convictions we deeply sympathise, and we offer our fervent prayer that there may be granted to you, speedily, times of freedom and enlargement. We would urge you, meanwhile, to 'hold fast the beginning of your confidence steadfast unto the end' (Heb. x. 35), and to persevere in a watchful, charitable, and holy life, such as your 'adversaries will not be able to gainsay nor resist.' (Luke, xxi. 15.)

"Those of you who are under no such restrictions, but who are yet isolated and imperfectly known to each other, we would earnestly recommend not to neglect 'the assembling of yourselves together' (Heb. x. 25), but to meet for Christian fellowship and worship every Lord's day; or, when that is impracticable, at the most frequent possible intervals, encouraged by that promise of our Lord, 'Wheresoever two or three are met together in* my name, there am I in the midst of them.' (Matt. xviii. 20.) Where it is possible to open communication with evangelical congregations, either near or distant, it will be most desirable to do so: where it is not, the most blessed results may, nevertheless, be anticipated from gathering together, simply 'to search the Scriptures' (John, v. 39), 'which are able to make us wise unto salvation through faith that is in Christ Jesus.' (2 Tim. iii. 15.)

"We, though attached in our several countries to various forms of church government, and holding divers opinions in harmony with our common love to God, have found it so good to 'dwell together in unity' (Ps. cxxxiii. 1), that we have the greater confidence in offering to you this counsel. We entreat you to receive it as a proof of our affection, and of our readiness to obtain from you any communication which you may desire to make to us, as well as an assurance of our earnest prayers for your prosperity and final acceptance 'at the coming of our Lord Jesus Christ.' (2 Cor. v. 9, 10.)"

(Signed) E. KUNTZE, *Chairman.*

* (Memorandum for translators:) Εἰς: unto, towards, in order to, upon. R. A. M.

From a paper, which it is proposed to circulate widely, the following subjects are extracted as those which, it is hoped, will profitably occupy a special place in thought, prayer, and exhortation, on Sunday, January 6, and following days:—

The promise of the Holy Spirit.

An especial blessing on all the services of this week, and the promotion of brotherly kindness among all those who love the Lord Jesus Christ in sincerity.

The attainment of a higher standard of holiness by the children of God.

A large increase of true conversions, especially in the families of believers.

The free circulation of the Holy Scriptures, and a blessing upon Christian literature.

A large outpouring of the Holy Spirit upon every Gospel Missionary among Jews or Gentiles, upon the converts of his station, and upon his field of labour.

The speedy overthrow of all false religions, and the full accomplishment of the Prayer, "Thy Kingdom come."

Thanksgiving for past revival; and the enforcement of the solemn responsibility resting on every Christian to spend and be spent in making known the name of the Lord Jesus at home and abroad.

The Missionary Conference in its Sixth Session "unanimously concurred in the proposal made by the Rev. George Scott, that on the Sabbath-day following that week of prayer"—viz. the 13th January, the last of the days contemplated in the foregoing programme—"the ministers of all the churches of Christ in every land be respectfully requested specially to bring the great subject of Christian Missions before the people of their charge." On page 172 of this volume Mr. Scott states his proposal thus:—"The question was how to bring out the amount of liberality really required for the large amount of missionary work to be done. His suggestion was that some simultaneous use of the pulpit throughout the whole country might be arranged, which would greatly help the object in view. They had lately had an invitation to prayer from a most interesting portion of the mission field; this had been responded to very generally throughout Christendom. Should they not send a practical response to their brethren labouring in these distant fields of missions, and arrange, *altogether separate from any collection*, to have a simultaneous presentation of the missionary subject from all the pulpits of the churches and chapels of the various Protestant communions throughout Christendom."

OPINIONS OF THE PRESS.

"The parties entrusted with the management of this Conference have done well to secure so fitting a memorial of it as this handsome octavo supplies. The volume is an extensive one, extending to above four hundred pages of beautiful letterpress, and containing a very careful report of the various sederunts, as well as the names of members. *There is no such collection of opinions of mission work extant.* The book is more than a record of facts; it contains suggestions and principles which, when carried into full effect, will issue in the millennium. The Conference was a great event in the history of Christianity, and it was beseeming to preserve a suitable memorial of it, as it will prove a stimulant to Christians of the present and coming generations. Nothing could be more complete than the getting up of this volume, and the friends of missions cannot better aid them than by furthering the circulation of a book so well fitted to inform and excite. We should like to see it in the hands of every Christian man."—*Glasgow Examiner.*

"The present volume comprises a full account of the several meetings of the Conference, with the papers read, the addresses delivered, and the conclusions arrived at respecting the principal plans of missionary operations. It is a book containing a large amount of important information relating to missions, and will stimulate the churches in their efforts to promote the spread of Christianity among mankind."—*Watchman.*

"The volume altogether is, undoubtedly, the most important contribution to the literature of missions which has ever been published, and we sincerely trust that those who have undertaken to give it to the world will be provided with the means, not only of sending it, as was proposed, to every mission station on the globe, but of placing it in every village library and on the study table of every minister in this land."—*British and Foreign Evangelical Review.*

"It is a production which we have examined with the most satisfactory result to our own minds. Nowhere did we ever find in the same compass so much to inform and to guide our judgment in reference to missionary affairs. The deliberations were most intelligent, calm, and judicious. Discouragements were impartially estimated, and success measured in the same spirit. The leading speeches were admirable, and we find no traces of lost time in irrelevant discussion and feeble prosy remarks. The volume is carefully edited, beautifully printed, and though containing 431 pages, will be sold for half-a-crown. Every Christian household should have a copy."—*Evangelical Magazine.*

"This volume contains a vast amount of missionary facts and thoughts from all the ends of the earth, and from nearly all the churches. Our own peculiar mission was not overlooked, and its great importance was heartily acknowledged. Let our readers get the book, and see and hear this 'cloud of witnesses' for missions."—*Eastern Female's Friend.*

"We have longed for the appearance of this volume, and now it is before us. . . . It is the most original publication of the day,—a vast storehouse of valuable thought, touching the spread of the everlasting gospel. These seven sessions brought forward an amount of thought and suggestion on the question of missionary labour never before comprised in a single volume. The mere Appendix is a matter of superior value."—*Christian Witness.*

"A detailed report which, after attentive perusal, we can cordially commend as edited with great care and ability. There are excellent marginal references to each of the papers and speeches, which greatly assist the reader in taking a connected view of the subject. The Minutes have also been drawn up with much skill and accuracy, and must, we think, give satisfaction to all who were present."—*News of the Churches.*

"We have already called attention to the missionary Conference held in this town during the present week. It may be stated, in explanation, that the Conference has been organised under the auspices of the principal Missionary Societies and committees of the three kingdoms."—*Liverpool Chronicle.*

"The most important parts of the work are the Minutes which record the united convictions of the Conference on various important points. All who actively co-operate in mission work should assist their judgment by the valuable suggestions and advice contained in this volume."—*Brighton Gazette.*

OPINIONS OF THE PRESS.

"Of the great evangelical series of meetings which this important work fully and faithfully records, the Christian public had previously learned just enough from the current and condensed newspaper reports to excite a desire to know more about it — its nature, origin, objects, and general proceedings. We can assure them that no more ample or trustworthy information upon all these and other correlative subjects could be supplied than that furnished by this carefully got-up volume, which is edited by the Secretaries to the Conference."— *Banner of Ulster.*

"The convention which honoured our town with its presence in March last is worthy of some prominent memorial in our annals of religious progress. The ordinary public meetings assembled on behalf of Missionary Societies have been regarded by many cordial friends as somewhat vague and unpractical in their character, the result of them being obviously more dependent on the eloquence of the speakers than upon the merits of the cause committed to their advocacy. The members of the Conference, both in their consultations and in the public meeting, evinced that they not only sympathised with missionary work, but that they thoroughly understood it, both in its relations to the churches at home and to the heathen abroad. We presume that this volume will find its way into the hands of almost every Protestant missionary throughout the world, and we may anticipate, with cordial pleasure, that the heart of many a devoted evangelist will be cheered, and his energies revived, in the midst of discouragement and opposition, by the proof afforded in these records that he is not forgotten in the prayers and the purposes of his brethren in a distant land. . . . This volume is no less unique in its character than interesting in its contents."— *Liverpool Courier.*

"The reverend Secretaries have discharged their editorial duties most industriously and faithfully. . . . The conclusions arrived at by the Conference respecting the principles and plans of missionary labour and economy were embodied at the time in expressive Minutes, which were submitted to and approved by the members; and to these Minutes, as containing opinions of importance and value with respect to future operations, the editors invite the special attention of all interested in the success of missionary efforts."—

"To those who feel interested in the progress of missionary enterprise, this work will prove a most valuable handbook. . . . The statements by returned missionaries will be found worthy of special notice. The volume is a perfect mine of information relating to missions, and it has been published at a price that will enable the friends of gospel diffusion to give it a wide circulation."—

"Considerable regret was experienced that the meetings of the important Conference on Missions which took place in this town in March last were not open to the public; but this regret has been satisfactorily obviated by the publication, under the direction of the promoters of the Conference, of a copious and authentic report of the proceedings at all the meetings. . . . The value of the work is much enhanced by accounts of the previous missionary conferences in New York and London; and also by the various indices."—

"The Conference was more than an assembly for deliberation or discussion. It was a gathering of the representatives of the great actors in the mission field, of men ripe in the experience acquired by the conflict of long years with unnumbered forms of heathenism. It might have been seen in the countenance of a large portion of the members that they had looked upon the sun in its Indian and African fervours. . . . In this assemblage of the actual workers of the mission field the opportunity was given, and it was the characteristic feature of the Conference, for the rehearsing and the comparison of those experiences out of which the happiest mission consequences may yet flow. At the missionary meetings of individual churches or Societies the experience has been often detailed that falls within their own limited and sectional operations. For the first time the Conference brought into play what we may call the catholic experience of missions. The results of long years of observation in all fields and by all classes and denominations of missionaries were thrown into a common stock, and the materials furnished out of which there may be drawn, if not a new theory of missions, new and wiser methods of mission operations. We know not a more valuable contribution towards the formation of a science of missions than the volume that records these meetings. It has not only added largely to the experience that has been accumulating for half a century,— it has concentrated it. And now it but awaits a mind of reverence and power to digest it into principles that shall save the mission enterprises of the future, as far as human wisdom can save them, from the dreariness and disappointment of unproductive labour, and turn them into the channels of proved greatest results. . . . It is a mission mine that has been opened to them at great expense, which, if searched, will enrich their minds with fresh thoughts, stimulate their endeavours, and furnish them with inexhaustible store of varied and interesting material for their public enforcement of the great New Testament commission ' to preach the gospel to every creature.' "— *Witness.*

MISSIONARY WORKS published by WILLIAM OLIPHANT & Co.

NARRATIVE OF A MISSION OF INQUIRY TO THE JEWS FROM THE CHURCH OF SCOTLAND.
By Messrs. BONAR and M'CHEYNE.
Twenty-fourth Thousand. Post 8vo. 5s.

MISSIONARY LIFE IN SAMOA,
As exhibited in the Journals of the late GEORGE ARCHIBALD LUNDIE (Brother of Mary Lundie Duncan).
Foolscap 8vo. 3s. 6d.

THE TENT AND THE KHAN:
A JOURNEY TO SINAI AND PALESTINE.
By the Rev. ROBERT WALTER STEWART, D.D., of Leghorn.
Containing Notices of Missionary Labour in the East.
With Map and Illustrations. 8vo. 10s. 6d.

THE MORAVIANS IN GREENLAND:
An Account of the Missions of the United Brethren. Third Edition. 18mo. 2s. 6d.

THE MORAVIANS IN LABRADOR.
Second Edition. 18mo. 2s. 6d.

MEMOIR AND REMAINS OF THE REV. C. C. LEITCH,
Missionary in the East Indies.
By the Rev. DAVID SMITH, D.D., Biggar. With Portrait. Fcap. 3s.

Edinburgh: WILLIAM OLIPHANT & CO.   London: HAMILTON & CO.

WORKS ON HOME MISSIONS.

THE MISSING LINK; OR, BIBLE WOMEN IN THE HOMES OF THE LONDON POOR.
By L. N. R., Author of "The Book and its Story."
Twentieth Thousand. Small crown 8vo. 3s. 6d. cloth.

HASTE TO THE RESCUE; OR, WORK WHILE IT IS DAY.
By Mrs. CHARLES WIGHTMAN.
With a Preface by the Author of "English Hearts and English Hands."
Fifteenth Thousand. Small crown 8vo. 3s. 6d. cloth.

RAGGED HOMES AND HOW TO MEND THEM.
By Mrs. BAYLY. Tenth Thousand. Small crown 8vo. 3s. 6d. cloth.

OUR HOMELESS POOR, AND WHAT WE CAN DO TO HELP THEM.
By the Author of "Helen Lyndsay." Second Edition. Crown 8vo. 3s. 6d. cloth.

ENGLISH HEARTS AND ENGLISH HANDS; OR, THE RAILWAY AND THE TRENCHES.
By the Author of "Memorials of Captain HEDLEY VICARS."
Forty-third Thousand. Small crown 8vo. 5s. cloth.
Also a Cheaper Edition, 2s. cloth limp.

MENDIP ANNALS; OR, A JOURNAL OF THE CHARITABLE LABOURS OF HANNAH AND MARTHA MORE.
Edited by ARTHUR ROBERTS, M.A., Rector of Woodrising, Norfolk.
Third Edition. Crown 8vo. 4s. 6d. cloth.

London: JAMES NISBET & CO., Berners Street.

RECENT WORKS.

I.
NEW ZEALAND;
PAST AND PRESENT—SAVAGE AND CIVILIZED.
By ARTHUR S. THOMSON, M.D., Surgeon-Major 58th Regiment.

Second Edition. Maps and Illustrations. 2 vols. Post 8vo. 24*s.*

"Dr. Thomson's narrative is clear, concise, and comprehensive, and conveys a very complete and exact idea of the country, the climate, the natural history, the people, the language, &c. It is rare indeed to get so intelligent and satisfactory an account of any land."—*Quarterly Review.*

II.
MADAGASCAR;
DURING THREE VISITS:
Including a Journey to the Capital, with Notices of the Natural History, and of the present Civilization of the People.

By REV. W. ELLIS.

Fifth Thousand. With Portrait and Illustrations. 8vo. 16*s.*

"The friends of the London Missionary Society may be fairly congratulated on the wonderful popularity of Dr. Livingstone's work. It has conveyed ideas of our work amidst the heathen—of its civilizing results, and its spiritual successes—into quarters where the achievements of Evangelical enterprise had before been little known. That another work, by another of our missionaries, should issue from the press, within little more than twelvemonths afterwards, bidding fair to rival its predecessor in celebrity, is matter for even greater surprise, and still more grateful congratulation. Mr. Ellis is a brave, adventurous man."—*Evangelical Magazine.*

III.
SOUTH AFRICA;
MISSIONARY TRAVELS AND RESEARCHES:
Including a Sketch of Sixteen Years' Residence in the Interior, and a Journey from the Cape to Loanda, &c.

By REV. DAVID LIVINGSTONE.

Thirtieth Thousand. Portrait and Illustrations. 8vo. 21*s.*

"Geographical discoveries are with Dr. Livingstone the prelude to missionary exertions."—*Christian Observer.*

"Dr. Livingstone is an invaluable pioneer, both to civilisation and Christianity."—*Christian Remembrancer.*

IV.
DANIEL WILSON, LATE BISHOP OF CALCUTTA;
HIS LIFE, LETTERS, AND JOURNALS.
By his Son-in-law, REV. JOSIAH BATEMAN, M.A.

Third Thousand. Portrait and Illustrations. 2 vols. 8vo. 28*s.*

"Bishop Wilson could not pass from the stage of life without a strong desire being awakened, not merely to see the very last of him, but to trace out the course of his life, and, if possible, to detect the mainsprings by which the whole man was set in action, impelled, and controlled.

"This constitutes the real value of these volumes, and we are bold to say they will disappoint none of their readers."—*Christian Observer.*

JOHN MURRAY, Albemarle Street.

Just published. Price 3s. 6d. cloth.

THE LIFE OF THE REV. JOHN HUNT,

Missionary to the Cannibals.

By REV. GEORGE STRINGER ROWE.

"This is a good book, teeming with facts of an interesting character."—*Christian Witness.*
"John Hunt, dying at the early age of thirty-six, of whom can it be said, even among our most devoted Missionaries, that they have endured and achieved so much?"—*Critic.*
"The volume will impart much information and instruction to all readers."—*Wesleyan Times.*

Price 5s. cloth.

THE LIFE AND JOURNALS
OF THE
REV. DANIEL WEST,

Wesleyan Minister, and Deputation to the Wesleyan Mission Stations on the Gold Coast of Western Africa.

By THE REV. THOMAS WEST.

"There is much interesting matter in this volume, to the progress of the Gospel in West Africa."—*Church of England relating Magazine.*
"Written with loving fervour."—*Athenæum.*
"A valuable contribution to the Missionary literature of Africa."—*British Standard.*

London: HAMILTON, ADAMS, & CO.

CHRISTIAN MISSIONS.

MEMOIR OF AN INDIAN CHAPLAIN,

The Rev. CHARLES CHURCH, M.A., of the Madras Establishment of the East India Company.

By the REV. JAMES HOUGH, A.M.

Fcap. 8vo. 2s. Cloth boards.

MEMOIRS OF THE REV. SAMUEL MARSDEN,
OF PARAMATTA.

Edited by the REV. J. B. MARSDEN, M.A.

With Portrait. Royal 18mo. 3s. boards; 3s. 6d. extra boards.

MISSIONARY BOOK FOR THE YOUNG.

A First Book on Missions. 18mo. 1s. cloth; 1s. 6d. extra boards, gilt.

MISSIONARY IN SYRIA;
OR, THE LIFE OF MRS. S. L. SMITH,

Late of the American Mission in Syria. 18mo. 1s. boards; 1s. 6d. half-bound.

MISSIONARY RECORDS.

CHINA, BURMAH, CEYLON, &c. 18mo. 2s. cloth boards.
NORTH AMERICA. 1s. 6d. cloth boards.
NORTHERN COUNTRIES. 2s. cloth boards.
SANDWICH ISLANDS. 2s. cloth boards.

The Religious Tract Society, 56 Paternoster Row, and 164 Piccadilly.
Sold by all Booksellers.

WORKS ON MISSIONS.

I.

THE RELIGIONS OF SYRIA: including Notices of the Maronites and the Druses. By JOHN WORTABET, M.D., Beyrout, Missionary at Aleppo of the United Presbyterian Church. Demy 8vo. 7s. 6d. cloth.

II.

NOTES FROM THE JOURNALS OF F. M. FLAD, one of Bishop Gobat's Missionaries in Abyssinia. Edited, with a brief Sketch of the Abyssinian Church, by the Rev. W. DOUGLAS VEITCH. Small crown 8vo. 2s. 6d.

III.

ENGLAND AND INDIA. An Essay on the Duty of Englishmen towards the Hindoos. By BAPTIST WRIOTHESLEY NOEL, M.A. 8vo. 12s. cloth.

IV.

MISSIONARY SKETCHES IN NORTHERN INDIA, with some References to Recent Events. By Mrs. WEITBRECHT. Crown 8vo. 5s. cloth.

V.

A MEMOIR OF THE LIFE AND LABOURS OF THE REV. A. JUDSON, D.D. By FRANCIS WAYLAND. D.D. Two vols. 8vo. 12s. cloth.

VI.

NOTES OF A TOUR IN SWEDEN IN THE SUMMER OF 1858. By EDWARD STEANE, D.D., and JOHN HOWARD HINTON, M.A. Crown 8vo. 3s. 6d. cloth.

VII.

CAFFRES AND CAFFRE MISSIONS; with a Preliminary Chapter on the Cape Colony as a Field for Emigration, and Basis of Missionary Operations. By the Rev. H. CALDERWOOD. Plates. Crown 8vo. 4s. 6d. cloth.

VIII.

CHRISTIANITY IN TURKEY; being a Brief Historical Sketch of the Armenian Race and Church. With some Account of their Doctrines, Rites, &c. By the Rev. H. D. O. DWIGHT, Constantinople. Crown 8vo. 5s. cloth.

IX.

A MEMOIR OF THE REV. J. J. WEITBRECHT, late Missionary of the Church Missionary Society. By his WIDOW. With a Preface by the Rev. H. VENN, M.A. Crown 8vo. 7s. 6d. cloth.

X.

A MEMOIR OF THE LATE ROBERT NESBIT, Missionary of the Free Church of Scotland, Bombay. By the Rev. J. MURRAY MITCHELL. Crown 8vo. 6s. cloth.

XI.

MEMOIR OF ANTHONY GROVES, Missionary to India, containing Extracts from his Letters and Journals. Compiled by his Widow. Crown 8vo. 4s. 6d. cloth.

XII.

THE RAINBOW IN THE NORTH. A Short Account of the First Establishment of Christianity in Rupert's Land, by the Church Missionary Society. By Miss TUCKER. Fcap. 8vo. 3s. 6d. cloth.

XIII.

THE SOUTHERN CROSS AND THE SOUTHERN CROWN; or, the Gospel in New Zealand. By the same Author. Fcap. 8vo. 3s. 6d. cloth.

XIV.

ABBEOKUTA; or, Sunrise within the Tropics. An Outline of the Origin and Progress of the Yoruba Mission. By the same Author. Fcap. 8vo. 3s. 6d. cloth.

XV.

THE LIFE OF THE REV. RICHARD KNILL, of St. Petersburgh; being Selections from his Reminiscences, Journals, and Correspondence, with a Review of his Character by the late Rev. John Angell James. By CHARLES M. BIRRELL. Fifth Edition, with Portrait. Crown 8vo. 4s. 6d. cloth.

XVI.

THE INDIAN CHURCH DURING THE GREAT REBELLION. An Authentic Narrative of the Disasters that befel it, its Sufferings, and Faithfulness unto Death of many of its European and Native Members. By the Rev. M. A. SHERRING, M.A., formerly Missionary at Benares. Crown 8vo. 5s. cloth.

LONDON: JAMES NISBET & CO., 21 BERNERS STREET.

www.ingramcontent.com/pod-product-compliance
Lightning Source LLC
Chambersburg PA
CBHW020524300426
44111CB00008B/539